M.O.D
AIR FORCE

UNITS

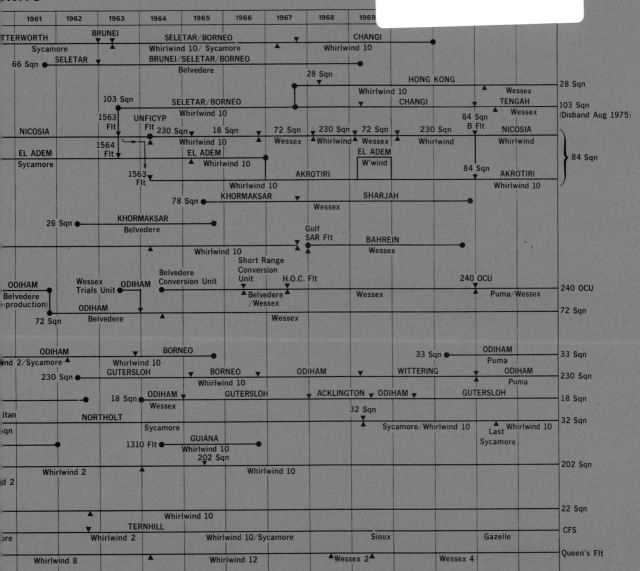

RAF Helicopters

The three Belvedere pilots who formed the crew for the Placing of the 'spire' and sculpture on Coventry Cathedral in April 1962—left to right:
Flt Lt J H Martin (crewman), the author (captain), Flt Lt R Salt (co-pilot).

MINISTRY OF DEFENCE
AIR HISTORICAL BRANCH (RAF)

RAF Helicopters

The First Twenty Years

London: HMSO

© Crown copyright 1992
Applications for reproduction should be made to HMSO
First published 1992

ISBN 0 11 772725 3

CONTENTS

ILLUSTRATIONS

Chapter 2

The Far East Air Force Casualty Evacuation Flight, Changi, 1951. Officers from left to right: Flt Lt J R Dowling, Flt Lt K Fry (Flt Cdr), Fg Off A J Lee, Flt Lt Partridge (Engineer Officer).

Initial handling trials in Malaya, 1950. The Dragonfly HC2 has a starboard external pannier fitted. The condensation in the tip vortex shows the high level of humidity.

Initial handling trials in Malaya in 1950—the external pannier for the Dragonfly HC2 with a practice casualty.

The Dragonfly basket stretcher, which replaced the external pannier, being used to load a casualty in North Malaya in 1952.

A casualty receiving medical attention in transit in the Dragonfly basket stretcher—Malaya 1950.

Re-fuelling a Dragonfly in the rain from an air dropped 'flimsy' petrol can in Malaya. The fuel had to be poured through a special filter.

Dragonfly servicing at Changi (1950–53); an Auster Mk 5 of No 656 AOP Squadron is seen in the background.

A typical clearing cut in Malaya in 1952, used in this case for the evacuation of a complete patrol of the Cameronians—see text.

A supply drop parachute is used as a marker and the platform from which the passenger embarked while the aircraft hovered can be seen just above it.

Chapter 3

Operational trials with the Sycamore Mk 10 in Ulu Langat clearing near Kuala Lumpur in 1953.

The Mk 14 sycamore could carry 2 stretchers athwartships (but rarely used the upper stowage). A stretcher was sometimes not available and had to be manufactured 'on the spot'. The passenger doors enlarged in the Mk 14 to facilitate stretcher carriage are clearly shown.

Malay troops deplaning by rope from a Whirlwind Mk 4 of No 155 Squadron in Malaya in 1957.

Deplaning from a landed Mk 4 Whirlwind.

A Whirlwind Mk 4 of No 155 Squadron in a training clearing in Malaya.

Troops deplaning by rope from a Sycamore Mk 14 of No 194 Squadron in Malaya in 1956.

Whirlwinds Mk 4 of No 155 Squadron near Kuala Lumpur in 1956.

A Sycamore Mk 14 of No 110 Squadron paying a regular visit to a jungle fort in North Malaya in the closing days of the 'Emergency'. (Pilot Flt Lt B Cann).

Prototype of the Bristol 173 (1954)—developed from the Sycamore and with Sycamore rotor blades (front rotor blades reversed) and powered by two Leonides piston engines, it was the forerunner of the Bristol 191 and 192 (the Belvedere).

The Bristol 192 pre-production version of the Belvedere with two Napier Gazelle turbine engines and four bladed rotors, but still with wooden Sycamore blades and fully manual controls: used for service trials. (In the background: Ampleforth Abbey.)

Chapter 5

Sycamore in transit in North West Cyprus.

Sycamore troop lift from Nicosia—Cyprus. Baggage and cabin doors have been removed. Note extra passenger carried by rotating the co-pilot's seat to face aft.

Troop training in Cyprus—deployment by knotted rope which is jettisoned by the pilot in the absence of a crewman.

Cyprus rescue of the crew of the trawler Suyeznik near Famegusta in January 1960.

Sycamore in typical troop deployment position—Cyprus.

As above.

Chapter 6

Mk 11 Sycamore of 1906 Air Observation Post Flight on exercise in Germany (1952/4)—Major B Repton and Captain J Spittal—the only two pilots.

Mk 11 Sycamore of 1906 Air Observation Post flight landing on HMS Implacable for transit to Guyana—October 1953.

Whirlwind Mk 2, Sycamore Mk 14, Dragonfly Mk 4 of the CFS Helicopter Unit at South Cerney—late 1950s.

Skeeter on trial at CFS—1955.

Sycamore Mk 13 showing the duplicated collective lever which was replaced by a single central collective lever in the Mk 14 production aircraft.

vii

The Queen Mother alighting from the CFS Dragonfly borrowed later and absorbed into the Queen's flight—1956/7.

The entire CFS Helicopter Wing in transit from South Cerney to its new home at Ternhill in 1962. 9 Sycamores, 1 Skeeter, 3 Whirlwinds, one Dragonfly.

Chapter 7

Winch fitted to Sycamore Mk 14.

Double lift development.

Double lift training.

'Sproule' Net.

Trawling for survivors with 'Sproule' net.

Helicopter crewman preparing casualty for helicopter lift while the rescue helicopter stands off out of danger from pitching superstructure.

Bringing a casualty aboard in the Neil Robertson stretcher.

SAR training by the CFS Flight at Valley.

SAR cliff rescue training by the CFS Flight at Valley.

SAR training with Mk 10 Whirlwind with crew of three.

Chapter 8

The three wooden-bladed pre-production Belvederes leaving Weston-super-Mare on delivery to Odiham by the Belvedere Trials Unit—October 1960.

Pre-production Belvedere of the BTU near Odiham. Note the small wheels and large tail stabilisers—both modified in the later production aircraft.

Last flight of the wooden-bladed full manual controlled pre-production Belvedere, just prior to the crash while rehearsing for the 1961 SBAC show at Farnborough. The Sycamore type rotor blades are clearly shown.

The result of loss of a nut retaining part of the Belvedere control linkage—Aden.

Avpin starter explosion—Aden.

Avpin starter explosion and fire—Singapore.

Machine gun mounting in rear hatch of Belvedere in Aden.

Belvedere positioning 105 mm guns North of Aden.

'One ton containers' ready for re-supply in forward area. Dust problem very evident in the prolonged hover required.

Belvedere landing near a Beverley at Beihan.

Belvedere at Thumair attempting to land ahead of its dust cloud.

Belvedere refuelling at Thumier using 44 gallon drums and a mechanical pump. Note the proximity of the front engine jet pipers.

Belvedere re-supply at Obad—6000 ft above sea level and 15 miles West of Beihan. The tail stabiliser constituted a considerable problem amongst the rocks.

Re-supply in the Radfan 2 miles East of Thumier. Note the front wheels 'castored' to prevent movement down the slope.

Belvedere in the Radfan 4 miles East of Thumier.

Engine change at Beihan (XG474 is the RAF Museum Belvedere).

Arab village used as an army defensive position with the Wadi Taym in the background.

One of the key positions overlooking the Wadi Taym—named 'Cap Badge' (also known as 'November One').

Defensive position South of Wadi Taym (Foxtrot 3) showing the typically limited space for re-supply operations.

78 Squadron crew in Aden showing the 0.76 mm GP Machine Gun mounted in a Wessex. The crew are wearing Flak Vests and a 'Mae West' fitted with a Sarbe beacon.

78 Squadron Wessex operating near Sharjah in 1971.

78 Squadron Wessex operating near Sharjah in 1971.

Chapter 12

Unlike the Whirlwind, the Sycamore could be loaded into the Beverley without the need to interfere with the rotor hub and blades. This method of deployment was used as part of the immediate response to the Brunei revolt.

The first Belvederes in Malaya were shipped to the Singapore Naval Base and towed by road to Sembawang overnight for re-assembly.

Helicopters requiring redeployment between Singapore and Borneo were usually carried as deck cargo either on RN Aircraft carriers when available, or on civilian ships.

Manoeuvring a Belvedere on a supply ship deck prior to being lifted off by crane.

It was possible to fly single Belvederes directly on to the supply ship deck.

Four Belvederes and one Scout as deck cargo on the Maxwell Brander.

Twelve Whirlwinds of 230 Squadron on HMS Bulwark in Singapore Naval base estimate from UK to Borneo early in 1965.

Preparing to re-deploy a 105 mm gun near the Indonesian border.

Re-fuelling the front tank of a Belvedere at a forward base in Borneo. Note the proximity of the front engine jet pipes to the re-fuelling airman, and the fuel dipstick which passes through the rotor disc.

Belvedere re-fuelling at a typical semi permanent Army base near the Indonesian border.

Forward semi-permanent army post near the Indonesian border, with 105 mm positioned by helicopter in its emplacement centre left of the picture. Note also the extensive use of corrugated iron, all of which had to be delivered by air.

105 mm gun placed by helicopter in its firing position near the Indonesian border.

The height which the troops had to jump from the Belvedere was rather too high for comfort wearing full kit, but to use the ladder was even more difficult and slow.

Semi permanent Belvedere LZ in Borneo.

Semi permanent Belvedere LZ in Borneo.

Recovering a forced landed RN Whirlwind Mk 7 from Brunei to HMS Albion in January 1963.

Belvedere preparing to deploy 'Green Archer' radar near the Indonesian border.

Deploying Bloodhound anti aircraft missile to Kuching from the ship in which it was sent from Singapore.

Whirlwinds Mk 10 over Singapore.

The Whirlwind Mk 10 could deliver the 105 mm gun and ammunition, but the gun had to be stripped to allow the load to be spread over several sorties.

The Belvedere had a permanent LZ built for it on the top of Penang Hill in North Malaya, where the aircraft was used extensively to deliver components for the Ground Radars station being built there.

The permanent helicopter base at Nanga Gaat had sites for five helicopters, one large enough for a Belvedere.

Nanga Gaat from ground level in its usual state of brisk activity.

The first operational use of the SHNAP was made at this site in a rubber estate in central Malaya when several re-supply sorties were carried out in total darkness by a Whirlwind of 103 Squadron as part of an Army/RAF exercise. The three poles for the red lights (see Appendix 4) have been enhanced on the photographic print.

A Belvedere of 66 Squadron positioning the cross on the steeple of the Hakka Methodist Church in Evelyn Road Singapore in December 1966. The technique was the same as that for placing the sculpture in the flèche in the Coventry Cathedral operation. The ground handling party can be seen at the base of the steeple.

66 Squadron near the end of its life in early 1969, flying all eleven Belvederes in formations round Singapore.

66 Squadron air and ground crews on the day of disbandment in March 1969 with the eight aircraft used for the final ceremonial demonstration at Seletar.

As an innovation in the world of flight, the helicopter has perhaps had less attention than it deserves. However, recent events in the Gulf and in Northern Iraq have served to highlight the growing capability of the helicopter in a variety of military applications from search and rescue to logistic support and from ambulance to an effective gun ship.

The use of the helicopter was pioneered by the military and it is for this reason that the history narrated by this book has a significance far beyond the confines of its title. Although the book deals with the first 20 years of helicopter operations in the Royal Air Force, the story it tells can be taken to apply to the history of the helicopter itself. Indeed it is only latterly that the helicopter has acquired some exclusively military roles as a combat vehicle. Most of its earlier military applications had direct equivalents in civil use as indeed they do today.

I have a close personal interest in this story for during the 1960s I commanded a Royal Air Force helicopter squadron, then equipped with the Wessex, which operated both in Germany and in this country. I am therefore very conscious of developments in the helicopter world, and one can only be struck by the vast increase in the capability of this machine, even during such a short period. For example, in the first three weeks of the recent relief operations on the Turkish/Iraqi border, three Royal Air Force Chinooks flew over 650 hours, carried 1300 tons of relief stores and moved over 500 refugees, many of them requiring considerable medical assistance. The aircraft were flown over mountains in excess of 13000 feet and in temperatures as high as 50°C. On several occasions the Chinooks were able to lift as many as 120 refugees in one flight. All this was achieved after the aircraft had been flown from the UK to Turkey in under three days. By comparison, the earlier Whirlwind Mk2 could carry only four people with enough fuel to go about 50 miles, but those modest beginnings laid the foundations of helicopter operating techniques and paved the way for all of today's multifarious and indispensable uses.

John Dowling's credentials for writing this book could not be bettered. Not only is he an historian and an author, but he is a pilot whose military career was primarily associated with helicopters in the Royal Air Force almost from their inception. In his researches, he had unrestricted access to official sources and in its original form the book was written for official purposes only. I am delighted that it can now be made available to a wider public. It will be of value not only to those concerned with rotary wing operations but to everyone who has an interest in the origins and development of this most versatile of aircraft.

WING COMMANDER JOHN DOWLING MBE DFC* AFC AMRAeS
RAF (RETD)

Wing Commander Dowling was educated at Ampleforth College. He joined the RAF in 1941, and after pilot training in Arizona, flew an operational tour on Lancasters in 1944/45, followed by a period flying Spitfires and Hurricanes with a bomber defence training flight. After the war he was with the Middle East Communications Squadron and then flew Yorks of Transport Command on the Singapore route. He flew in the Berlin Air Lift and then joined the Transport Command Development Unit where he flew his first helicopter in 1949. From that time onwards he specialised in helicopters.

He went to the Far East with the first RAF operational helicopter unit (1950–53) and on return to the UK became the first unit commander of the Central Flying School Helicopter Unit constructing the pilot and instructor training syllabi and visiting all overseas helicopter units. After a staff tour in Air Ministry he commanded the Belvedere Trials Unit at Odiham (1960) and formed successively the three Belvedere Squadrons before returning briefly to staff duties at No 38 Group (1963). In 1964 he was back in Singapore in command of the Helicopter Wing at Seletar consisting of one Belvedere and two Whirlwind squadrons operating mainly in Borneo. After staff duties in Air Support and Strike Commands he began writing the RAF helicopter history in a supernumerary post in the Air Historical Branch (1973/4). Interrupted by a final staff appointment in Ministry of Defence in Ops (Search and Rescue) he retired from the RAF in 1978 and completed the helicopter history in a Civil Service post in 1986.

INTRODUCTION

The history of helicopters in the Royal Air Force starts at the point when they were first employed operationally in 1950 in Malaya. The earlier period, when autogiros gave way to helicopters with no real operational capability, is outlined in the Prologue.

Thereafter the history is divided into four phases, the first (1950–52) dealing mainly with the Casualty Evacuation Flight in the Far East, which proved the readiness of the helicopter to enter the field of military operations and laid the foundation for the subsequent expansion.

In the second phase (1953–60) an enthusiastic growth of the helicopter forces was nevertheless restricted by financial constraints and also by the limited operational capability of the available aircraft, many desirable roles for the helicopter being excluded simply because they were beyond the scope of the aircraft then in service. Even so, their contribution to the campaigns in Malaya and Cyprus was crucial.

At the end of this second phase however there came a significant breakthrough with the arrival of turbine engines with their great advantage in power/weight ratio. The third phase (1960–70) thus belongs to the Whirlwinds Mk 10, the Belvederes and later the Wessex, with the Borneo and South Arabian operations occupying the centre of the stage. Phase 3 is extended into 1972 in the Far East in order to complete the withdrawal of the last RAF helicopters in Malaysia.

The fourth phase (1971 onwards) is only introduced here and will in due course cover the formation and operations of the Puma/Wessex/Chinook squadrons as a tactical helicopter army support force in the NATO context, with the Northern Ireland operations as the main example of various other activities undertaken after 1970, eg detachments in Oman, Belize and the Falklands.

Running continuously from 1953 and in parallel with operational aircraft type developments is the Search and Rescue helicopter force in the UK maritime environment, and also, after 1954, the Central Flying School Helicopter Unit. Both of these appear in each phase after the first, as do the communications helicopters of The Queen's Flight and the Metropolitan Communications Squadron.

In each phase an outline is given of the policy considerations at Ministry level which affected the choice and procurement of helicopters, and incidentally dictated the scope of role development, and so ultimately the rate of helicopter type development.

The background to the RAF's responsibility for the procurement of helicopters for army tasks but not for the Royal Navy is explained in Chapter 1.

The Royal Air Force came into existence in 1918, that is near the point when the dream of early helicopter inventors of achieving vertical take-off and landing was in sight of realisation, but before any truly useful solution had been proved. The side by side contra rotating rotor arrangement with two forward facing propellers designed by Sir George Cayley in the early 1800s was the earliest effort of any practical significance in this field, significant also because that side by side twin rotor idea was later chosen by Focke to produce the first practical helicopter, and also forms the latest configuration for tilt rotor/wing VTOL aircraft. In 1842 a single rotor helicopter model weighing 44 lb designed by W H Phillips is reported to have 'crossed two fields' with a tip jet driven rotor powered by gas produced from the combustion of a mixture of charcoal, nitre and gypsum, and in 1859 the first British patent was granted to Henry Bright for a scheme comprising contra rotating co-axial rotors. In 1893 Sir Charles Parsons experimented with a rotor driven by a steam engine and in 1905 a comparatively large machine was built by Denny having six 25 ft diameter lifting screws and is reported to have left the ground briefly. In 1908 Breguet finally succeeded in matching with a helicopter the Wright brothers' success with the fixed wing aeroplane.

The mechanical difficulties with rotating wings led to a comparatively rapid advance in fixed wing development and in the 1920s and 1930s the rotary wing field had come to be regarded as an eccentric sideline in aeronautical development and even tended to generate ridicule.

In later years (after 1950) the RAF was to suffer a good deal of uninformed criticism by new enthusiasts for having apparently failed to grasp the potential of the helicopter with adequate enthusiasm, but the true perspective derived from the facts leads to a different conclusion. Even inside the RAF itself during the helicopter renaissance of the mid 1950s there was inevitable frustration due to the inability of the technical and commercial system as a whole to meet the sudden urgent demand for useful helicopters and the Air Ministry inevitably came in for a large share of the criticism. In fact the Air Ministry had already itself experienced some thirty years earlier the frustrations being felt by its later critics. In 1923 when even the continued existence of the five-year-old independent Air Force required strenuous defence in Parliament, the Air Ministry announced a prize of £50000 for the successful completion of certain flight tests of 'a helicopter or equivalent flying machine'. This attracted a censorious comment by the Council of the Royal Aeronautical Society that such an offer 'gave a wrong view of the relative values of serious work on well established lines (ie fixed wing aircraft) and such highly speculative constructions as the helicopter'.

In this environment Louis Brennan built and tested a helicopter at the Royal Aircraft Establishment (RAE), Farnborough in 1925. It had a 60 ft diameter rotor driven by two propellers mounted at the blade tips and connected to a centrally mounted rotary engine. A crash in 1926 brought this work to an end. In 1928 Vittorio Isacco, who had been experimenting on the Continent for some years, came to England and built a helicopter to a contract from the Air Ministry, but it never flew.

Just as fixed wing development leapt ahead of rotary wing development for technical reasons, autogyros started to occupy the centre of the stage for rotary wing aircraft because they were technically simpler to design and build than helicopters. Juan de la Cierva, having experimented with a number of unsuccessful models, achieved in 1923 his first autogyro flight. In 1925 he demonstrated his C6 Autogiro* at the RAE, Farnborough and the Air Ministry was sufficiently enthusiastic to order a number of them. As a result, the Cierva Autogiro Company was formed to handle the patent rights etc, the construction work being done by A V Roe Ltd.

One consequence of this purchase of Cierva autogiros by the Air Ministry was that the RAE became involved and a good deal of investigatory work into the theory and mechanism of the flapping rotor was generated. The autogiro became quite popular and demand for it grew. Series production was set up not only in the United Kingdom but also abroad, under licence, especially in the United States and France. Flying demonstrations were given in many parts of the world, one notable one being by R A C Brie (later as a Wing Commander in the RAF to generate the first helicopter procurement in quantity for British forces)** who, in the mid 1930s, demonstrated the capability of the autogiro to land and take off from a ship—the Italian cruiser Fiume—in the Mediterranean. In 1932 the Cierva Flying School was created and operated at Hanworth under H A (Alan) Marsh as Chief Instructor until the outbreak of war in 1939.*** In this period nearly 10000 hours were flown and 368 people qualified as autogiro pilots.

---

*'Autogiro' was the registered trade mark for the autogyros produced under the licence of the Cierva Autogiro Company.

**Brie flew as an observer in the First World War with the Royal Flying Corps, afterwards becoming a pilot in the RAF. He was on the RAF Reserve of Officers from 1922 and test pilot for Cierva from 1930.

***Alan Marsh was originally a flight sergeant pilot in the RAF between the wars. He was commissioned on rejoining the RAF in 1939 and, after about two years in the RAE at Farnborough, took command of No 1448 Rota Autogiro Flight in place of Wing Commander Brie, who had been sent to the United States for autogiro deck landing trials.

Also in 1932 the first successful direct control autogiro was flown in which attitude control was achieved by direct tilting of the rotor hub and thus rotor thrust, rather than by elevators and ailerons as in previous machines. This advance produced the C30 autogiro, six of which were purchased by the Air Ministry in 1934 for the RAF School of Army Co-operation at Old Sarum. Other orders followed and the ultimate development of the Cierva autogiro followed soon after: the C40 with jump take-off ability.* The Air Ministry obtained 5 C40s in 1939.**

---

*The jump take-off was achieved by applying engine power to spin the rotor at low blade pitch angle in excess of auto rotation speed before take off, and causing the blades to revert to their normal pitch angle when the engine torque was directed to the traction propeller instead of to the rotor shaft. This caused the machine to jump off the ground where rotor speed could be maintained by the acquisition of forward speed by means of the propeller. The blade pitch change was achieved automatically by tilting the blade hinges so that application of torque through the rotor shaft caused the blades to reduce pitch temporarily while the rotor was being accelerated by engine power. The pilot had no means of increasing blade angles for landing.

**Closely associated with the Cierva Company was G & J Weir Ltd which, under licence, built a number of small autogiros, W1, W2, W3 and W4. The last had a direct take-off capability and was demonstrated in 1936 at Hounslow Heath together with the Cierva C40 autogiro. In 1937 Weir turned its attention to the helicopter and built the W5 and W6 which were side by side configurations. Both flew successfully, but the outbreak of war put an end to them. At about the same time Raoul Hafner, who had built two experimental helicopters in Austria and then come to England in 1933, formed AR III Construction (Hafner Gyroplane) Company and built an autogiro which first flew in 1935. It differed from the Cierva machines mainly in its rotor control and blade suspension which were like those in modern helicopters. Thus, instead of tilting the rotor hub, it achieved tilt of the rotor disc by cyclic feathering; it also had collective pitch under the pilot's control. As a result, not only could it perform more controllable jump take-offs, but the degree of control for zero speed landings was greatly increased. Weir in postwar years gave birth, through the Cierva Autogiro Company which it then controlled, to the Air Horse and Skeeter helicopters, while Raoul Hafner, after designing the Rota-chute rotary wing glider during the war, went on to design the Sycamore and Belvedere helicopters.

3

Wartime Developments

At the start of the Second World War the Air Ministry sent two of the C40 autogiros with RAF pilots to France for Army Co-operation duties, but the aircraft did not return after the evacuation from Dunkirk. All the remaining autogiros, including civil C30s and C40s which had been promptly requisitioned, about 16 in all, were collected at RAF Duxford, given the RAF title of Rota and formed into No 1448 Rota Calibration Flight under Squadron Leader Brie. Its task was to provide facilities for the calibration of radar sites, work hitherto attempted cumbersomely by barrage balloons which proved of very limited use. The autogiros could not hover (except in very strong winds) but they could orbit at the required spots and heights while performing a turn of sufficiently small radius to achieve the desired effect for the radar operations. The technique was successful. No 1448 Flight was re-formed in 1943 at Halton as No 529 Autogiro Squadron under Alan Marsh then a squadron leader.

For radar calibration work the individual Rotas operated as independent units with a pilot, engine fitter and a rigger. These 'units' moved around the coastal radar stations in much the same way as operational helicopters were to do later with their crewmen. After navigating to the required points, usually over the sea, a sea marker was dropped and the Rota then performed a very tight orbit over the marker at various heights as required to enable the ground radar station to calibrate its equipment. During the war, No 529 Squadron carried out almost all the ground radar calibration in the country and in five years over 9000 hours were flown. It moved to Upper Culham Farm at Henley on Thames in 1944 and was not disbanded until October 1945.

Shortly after handing over No 1448 Flight to Squadron Leader Marsh in 1941, Wing Commander Brie (as he had then become) was loaned to the Admiralty which had now become interested in the possibility of employing the autogiro for anti-submarine convoy protection. Brie, who had demonstrated the Cierva autogiro on the cruiser Fiume in the 1930s, joined the British Air Commission in the United States and achieved the first landing of an autogiro on a small platform mounted on a merchant ship (the Empire Mersey) in Chesapeake Bay. This was done in a PA 39 of the Autogiro Company of America—an American version of the C40 and one of seven ordered by the Air Ministry for radar calibration purposes. Igor Sikorsky witnessed these trials and Brie received an invitation to see his experimental single seat helicopter, the VS-300, in early 1942. He was much impressed, and later sought and obtained an opportunity to fly its production successor—the YR-4 (later known in England as the Hoverfly 1).

Brie was the first British pilot to fly this helicopter and from that moment the autogiro had had its day. Brie went straight to the head of the British Air Commission in Washington, Air Marshal Sir Roderic Hill, and explained that a helicopter had at last appeared which effectively eliminated the only serious disability of the autogiro—the inability to hover. Its lifting capability was scarcely an issue; it was the principle which mattered. Action was swift and from then on only the helicopter was given further consideration. An order for YR-4s was placed on behalf of the Admiralty and this marked the beginning of the Naval involvement in helicopters for anti-submarine and, later, SAR duties.

To obtain pilots trained to fly these helicopters a training school was set up in conjunction with the US Coastguard Service at Floyd Bennett Field near New York (the US Navy was unenthusiastic about this diversion of the war effort) and because the Royal Navy had no rotary wing pilots on whom to draw, RAF assistance was requested. Brie obtained British instructional staff from No 529 Autogiro Squadron, starting with Flight Lieutenant 'Jeep' Cable* and later Squadron Leader Basil Arkell. Deck landing trials on a merchant ship, the Daghestan, continued with the first two R-4 helicopters delivered, both in Long Island Sound and during an Atlantic convoy crossing in 1943.

The larger R-5 helicopter followed the R-4 and had sufficient power to carry a pilot and observer and some sort of weapon weighing about 200 lb in addition. An order for R-5s was placed on behalf of the Admiralty and construction commenced but in late 1944, with the submarine menace being brought under control, the Royal Navy decided to reduce its main helicopter commitment and cancelled the order for R-5s.

Arkell and Brie persuaded Sikorsky to modify the R-5 to enable the pilot to sit in the perspex domed nose instead of the observer, as was originally planned, and then recommended that this aircraft (which became known as the S-51 and later the Dragonfly, and could now accommodate a winch operator behind the pilot) should be ordered on behalf of the RAF for SAR duties.

This urgent effort by Brie and Arkell to persuade the RAF to take up the cancelled Naval order failed because of what was to become a familiar refrain in the next few years—there was no demonstrable specific need for the aircraft. The US Army was by now becoming interested and enthusiastically absorbed the surplus production thus created. When the R-4s already purchased eventually started to arrive in England, a so-called training school (really a demonstration flight) was set up under Squadron Leader Cable at Hanworth—the site of Cierva's old autogiro training school. This was the first use of helicopters in the United Kingdom. The RAF had also purchased R-6s—Sikorsky's modified version of the R-4 for Army Co-operation duties. It had a more powerful engine than the R-4 but was still

---

*Marsh and Cable were both killed in the crash of the Air Horse in 1950.

dangerously underpowered for most conditions and in addition was extremely unreliable because there seemed to be no way of preventing oil leaking from the engine into the magneto.

Postwar Developments

In the last months of the war nine R-4s, including the flight from Hanworth, were formed into the RAF Helicopter Training School at Andover under Squadron Leader Arkell with the object of training Army AOP pilots to fly helicopters. First, however, 12 autogiro pilots of No 529 Squadron were converted and one R-4 was added to that unit for trials in the radar calibration role. Cable, with some of the RAF pilots, took the first two R-4s to the Airborne Forces Experimental Establishment (AFEE) at Sherburn in Elmet and later to Beaulieu, where an experimental rotary wing flight was formed. Later some Army pilots joined this unit. The Army AOP squadrons would fly into Andover from Germany in their Austers for a five-week 30-hour helicopter conversion course, afterwards returning in their Austers. Twenty-nine Army pilots were trained in this way but they never obtained operational helicopters. RAF Andover also operated a Maintenance School and provided instructional courses for helicopter ground crews.

During 1947, with No 529 autogiro Squadron disbanded, an RAF pilot (Flight Lieutenant K Fry) carried out a variety of trials concerned with radar development based at Defford, hovering in an R-4 at heights of up to 6000 feet with a 2 ft diameter metal ball of known radar response suspended from a 1400 ft length of wire. This helicopter was also used for simulating the flight of a balloon for radio sonde trials, drifting slowly upwards with gradually increasing forward speed. Trials of an Airfield Surface Movement Indicator were also carried out, as was a brief evaluation of the R-4 in the SAR role by the Air/Sea Warfare Development Unit at St Mawgan.

By the end of 1947 the RAF considered that they had exhausted the development possibilities of the R-4 and R-6 and reluctantly concluded that they could not be used operationally. There were no replacement aircraft and these helicopters were maintained only by using the few still crated as they had arrived from the United States to supply spare parts. It was a rapidly wasting force. Two R-4s were borrowed, one each from Brize Norton and Hanworth, for the King's Flight in 1947 and again in 1948 for mail deliveries from Aberdeen to Balmoral when the King was in residence there. They were flown by Flying Officer A J Lee and Flight Lieutenant E B Trubshaw (later Concorde Test Pilot). The operation was not repeated subsequently. A few were maintained by the Royal navy for SAR development and training until the Dragonfly appeared in 1950, and the remaining R-6s were allotted to the Army for AOP development work—No 1901 Flight of No 657 AOP Squadron formed for the purpose at Andover in May 1947 (Captains N Gow,

Mr Raoul Hafner flying (tethered) his R-2 helicopter—being the second experimental machine he designed and built in Vienna, and the one he brought back with him when he came to England in 1933—Heston airport.

C-30 Autogiro, the RAF's first rotary wing aircraft—1935—named 'Rota', it was used during the second World War for ground radar calibration.

Cierva W9 (1947), one of the series of experimental helicopters by Weir.

The Cierva W11 or Airhorse (1948).

Scale model of the Fairey Mk 1 Gyrodyne—selected in 1950 for use in the Malayan operations but superseded by the more readily available Dragonfly.

The Mk 2 Gyrodyne having two forward facing propellers. It was used experimentally only.

Sikorsky R-4—the first helicopter to enter RAF Service as the Hoverfly 1 (1944).

The first helicopter pilot training course in the UK, held at RAF Andover in 1945. The instructors are seated with the unit commander, Sqn Ldr Basil Arkell, in the centre.

Cierva Skeeter prototype—1950. Much development work was needed to bring it into service in the mid 1950s.

Bristol 171 prototype (1947) which entered RAF
service in 1962 as the Sycamore.

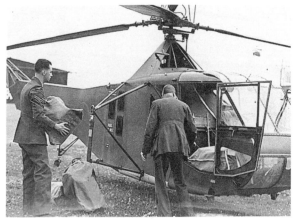

Sikorsky R-4 (Hoverfly Mk 1) carrying mail for
Balmoral while on loan to the King's flight—1947/48.

The Sikorsky R-6, which entered RAF service in 1945
as the Hoverfly II: here bring flown by Major N Gow
of No 1906 AOP Flight. Note the central collective
lever; the pilot must sit on the opposite side from the
stretcher which has to be on the starboard side
because of cyclic control limitations.

P Wilson and R Smith). This RAF unit with Army pilots did a considerable amount of demonstration and AOP trial work and managed to prolong its life as No 1906 Flight to within a few months of receiving Sycamores as replacements in September 1951, so maintaining a substantially continuous existence until the formation of the separate Army Aviation organisation in 1957.*

---

*Although its early life belongs in this Prologue and extends in diminishing strength through Phase 1 (1950–52), the main operational life of No 1906 AOP Helicopter Flight is part of Phase 2.

References to Prologue

1. The sources for this prologue are:

   Journal of the Royal Aeronautical Society, Jan 1966, Raoul Hafner, 'Record of British Rotorcraft'.

   Aeroplane, Mar 1960, 'Rotary Wings in the RAF'.

   No 657 Sqn ORB.

   Tape recorded interviews with Sqn Ldr B Arkell (RAF retd) and Wg Cdr R A C Brie (RAF retd).

   Personal reminiscences from Mr D T D Hosegood (RN retd) and Lt Col J Spittal (RA retd).

PHASE 1

1950-52

RAF RESPONSIBILITY FOR THE PROVISION OF
HELICOPTER SUPPORT

In the later chapters of this study instances continually occur of the problems posed by inter-Service rivalry in the field of aircraft procurement. In order to explain the responsibility of the RAF for the provision of adequate helicopters for Army support, as well as the competition between the Navy and the Air Force for the limited supplies of Dragonfly and Whirlwind helicopters available during the Malayan Emergency, the relationship between the Services in this respect needs clarification—a relationship which goes back to the formation of the RAF itself, the allocation of responsibilities at that time and the changes which were negotiated subsequently. What happened then bears a striking resemblance to later developments in the helicopter world and the relevance of recounting the salient features of these events here will become readily apparent.

It is usual to regard the history of the RAF as beginning with the amalgamation of the Royal Flying Corps (RFC) and the Royal Naval Air Service (RNAS) in 1918, but in fact the original flying service established in 1912 was one body—the RFC—comprising a Naval and a Military Wing maintained at the expense of and administered by the Admiralty and the War Office respectively. There was also established a single Royal Aircraft Factory, common to both Services, and a Central Flying School. From the very first there was a tendency for the two Wings to drift apart and by the start of the First World War the Naval Wing of the RFC had already changed its title to the Royal Naval Air Service. With the outbreak of hostilities the separation of the two Wings was virtually complete. For the first two and a half years of the war the two branches of the Air Service developed independently, both in organisation and supply, the RFC all in France, and the RNAS consequently charged by Lord Kitchener with responsibility for home defence. Each Service placed orders for aircraft, equipment and engines with the Royal Aircraft Factory, or with civilian firms as seemed expedient at the moment. The result was described in 1922 by the Lord Privy Seal (Austen Chamberlain) as a 'fierce inter-departmental competition in a market having inadequate resources, a haphazard, accidental and therefore dangerous arrangement involving overlapping and waste of effort, one Department bidding against another in the distribution and application of available resources, not according to a considered view of the Country's needs, but to relative skill in securing departmental advantage'.

Many detailed examples of this confusion are described elsewhere, for example by Hilary St George Saunders in his account of the rise of British air power in Per Ardua. He includes a reference to problems arising from French aircraft industry involvement—yet another echo from the past of subsequent events in the helicopter world. In the context of the First World War, however, he described French shortages of materials which resulted in manufacturers being induced to fulfil orders only 'by a process of bargaining in which it is hard not to detect the essential features of blackmail and bribery', and gives examples. The point was that in Britain not only were there two quite separate policies for the choice and employment of aircraft, but no policy at all for the coordination of supply.

The first attempt at setting up a coordinating body—the Joint War Air Committee— lasted less than two months, its chairman, Lord Derby resigning on the grounds that the committee, having no executive powers, had no authority either. Later in the same year—1916—it was succeeded by an Air Board under the chairmanship of Lord Curzon, charged with recommending to the two Services the types of aircraft they should order and coordinating the supply of material to prevent competition between them. Such was the antagonism of the Admiralty, however, to any interference with its plans, that the Air Board's power merely to 'recommend' a course of action was quite inadequate to achieve effective coordination. When in late 1916 the Admiralty obtained Treasury sanction to spend some £3000000 on aircraft and engines without reference to the Air Board, a formal protest was met merely by a formal denial of the Board's right to protest.

In November 1916 Asquith was replaced by Lloyd George. The new government widened the powers of the Air Board and transferred responsibility for the design and supply of aircraft from the Admiralty and War Office to the Ministry of Munitions. The new Board under Lord Cowdray was thus an embryonic Air Ministry and the Aeronautical Department of the Ministry of Munitions became in effect a Ministry of Aircraft Supply, although the actual power of the Air Board to direct policy had to await the report by General Smuts in August 1917 recommending the formation of an Air Ministry. The Air Council was established on 21 December 1917 and the Royal Air Force on 1 April 1918 under Sir Hugh Trenchard.

The formation of the RAF was thus no easy option, but one stage in a series of attempts to coordinate the air arms of the Army and the Navy and to foster the development of air power in its own right. The opposition was intense and while the arguments for an independent Air Force may have been convincing to many, it was the pressure of events, including the bombing of London, which forced the government to act and resolve the dispute. No sooner was the war over however than the Admiralty set to work to reverse the decision and, supported by the War Office, mounted a political campaign to separate the Fleet Air Arm from the RAF. An essential element in all the arguments for and against was the question: who was to be responsible for the selection of aircraft and equipment, and it was this question which turned out in later years to be at the root of the matter, particularly in the case of helicopters. In the House of Commons debate on the Navy Estimates of 1922 Austen Chamberlain, now Leader of the House, resisted the proposal to dismantle the RAF in the course of a long speech in which he reviewed all the stages which had been gone through in order to achieve the formation of the Air Ministry, adding: 'It will be seen that it was war experience which led to the creation of the Air Ministry, and to the constitution of a homogeneous Air Force. It was not theory derived from speculation in the past, but it was practical experience, after trying a great many other experiments, and the deficiencies which they left, that proved to the Government in the pressure of the War, and for the successful conduct of the War, the necessity of creating the system now in force ... However elaborate the machinery for coordination, whatever the goodwill and the desire to cooperate between the different Departments, it was found during the War supremely difficult to achieve full efficiency in the Air Services as long as those Services remained divided—part under the War Office and part under the Admiralty. As long as the supply of machines and engines remained under the two Departments, there resulted only a disastrous and wasteful competition.'

At a later point in the debate the Prime Minister was careful to point out that he was describing a solution which would hold good for the foreseeable future, adding: 'If the Air Services were required only as an adjunct to the Naval and Military Services, there would be much to be said for their reabsorption, though I do not think that even then the case would be conclusive, for there would remain the necessity for preventing the kind of competition which took place with such unhappy results during the War.' The Admiralty, however, maintained unrelenting pressure for many years and nearly twenty years after the end of the First World War, in 1937, the Fleet Air Arm was divorced from the RAF and placed wholly under Admiralty control, along with the responsibility for the choice of aircraft and equipment. Another twenty years or so later, in 1957, the Army followed suit and an independent Army Air Corps came into existence. It did not, however, assume responsibility for all army support aviation since this was clearly impossible, including as it must all transport as well as ground attack aircraft. The line was drawn at aircraft with an all-up-weight of 4000 lb, the Corps' roles being restricted to AOP and light liaison. The RAF was therefore left with the responsibility of providing the Army with cargo and troop lift and a casualty evacuation service.

The appearance of the helicopter can now be seen to have recreated, in principle at least, all the problems which the Air Force had been designed to solve, but with three contestants where before there had been only two. Without it the Fleet Air Arm would have ceased to exist, the last Naval fixed wing pilots' course having been completed in 1968—and without helicopters the Army Air Corps could scarcely have gained a separate existence.

The restriction of 4000 lb all-up-weight for Army aircraft prevented the Army Air Corps from entering into direct competition with the Navy and the Air Force for the supply of helicopters, at least until after 1960 by which time the Fairey, Saunders Roe and Bristol Aeroplane Company helicopter divisions had been absorbed by Westland, and the suppressed—but in time inevitably successful—ambitions of the new Corps had succeeded in eroding the all-up-weight limitation. Apart from orders for comparatively large numbers of small helicopters, it was not until the fourth phase of RAF helicopter development (the Wessex and Puma) in the early 1970s that Army orders for the Lynx emerged as a potential challenge to the RAF position.

In the three main conflicts involving British helicopters between the end of the Second World War and 1966—Malaya, Suez and Borneo—it proved necessary to bring in Naval helicopters to supplement those of the RAF in the task of army support. At Suez the RAF contribution was provided through the short-lived Army/RAF Joint Experimental Helicopter Unit. In Malaya the diversion to the RAF of helicopters ordered by the Navy was most reluctantly agreed and came about only as the result of an overriding decision by the Chiefs of Staff in response to the demands of General Templer. Experience has shown therefore that in time of peace the ambitions of the Air branches of the Army and the Navy have led to the disintegration of the system of centralised control of resources, and in war it has been necessary to bring in an external authority to impose whatever degree of unity of effort could be achieved in the time available.

To sum up, the RAF has played no part in the choice of Naval aircraft since 1937, but has been wholly responsible for selecting the helicopters used by and for the Army (except for the AOP and light liaison roles where the choice has been the responsibility of the Army since 1957). These facts explain why the Air Ministry found itself the target of Army criticism in the areas of both development and supply (the shortage of helicopters being always acute), while at the same time being obliged to compete with the Navy for limited production facilities—once Treasury approval had been obtained to buy helicopters to support the Army.

The procedure for ordering aircraft consisted of constructing a formal operational requirement (OR) which the Ministry of Supply, controlling research and development, would attempt to match with a suitable aircraft type. It was normal procedure to consult with the Ministry of Supply to see what might be available, so avoiding the risk of constructing a totally impracticable requirement. This was, in fact, the fate of the first helicopter OR, drawn up to meet troop and cargo lifting tasks; failure in this case was inevitable because there were no helicopters in production at the time from which to assess with reasonable accuracy what could be achieved. Thus OR 280 prepared in 1949 had to be withdrawn and reconstructed as two separate ORs in 1954 matching current technological developments.

Such was the background against which Air Ministry policy evolved and decisions were taken during the helicopter renaissance in the 1950s, a renaissance which sprang from the need to evacuate battle casualties from the jungles of Malaya. The response to this emergency requirement was the provision of three Dragonfly HC Mk 2 helicopters based in Singapore from 1950; and it was their activities in the following two years which provided the 'launching pad' for all subsequent RAF helicopter development (with the exception of that of the SAR units, whose origins were quite separate). To understand the problems and tensions which arose in the course of this development, it is essential to distinguish between two quite different attitudes held by helicopter proponents. Without this understanding many of the decisions taken and much of what resulted will seem strangely inappropriate.

In the 1930s and 1940s RAF leadership in this new field of aeronautics was accepted as natural; radar calibration, field trials, army cooperation were all obvious outlets. The idea of wings whirling above the aircraft to achieve take-off and landing may not then have seemed so outrageous an alternative to rushing along the ground out of control and with inadequate brakes as it did a short time later when fixed wing aircraft had acquired a relatively conventional image. The question was rather what could be achieved in terms of vertical take-off and landing (VTOL) performance than what purposes could be served thereby. To question the rationale or even the economics of encouraging rotary wing development would have seemed absurd and irrelevant. The advantages would have been obvious and it was not until several years later that the epithet conventional came to be used when comparing fixed wing aircraft with helicopters.

It was however the failure of early autogiros and helicopters to achieve a performance which had any true military relevance which came to determine the different attitudes of the three Services towards rotary wing development. A serious intention to proceed with the helicopter in a hard unfriendly financial climate could be based on one or other of two assessments: that there would inevitably be an infinite variety of tasks arising in the future merely by reason of the helicopter's existence (the doctrine of inherent flexibility), or that the tasks for which it was needed were solely helicopter tasks and unsuited to fixed wing aircraft.

An example in this second case would be the Naval need to move and hover over the sea, while the ambition to airlift practically everything an army uses is characteristic of land forces worldwide. The RAF therefore was left without an identifiable single Service use for the helicopter and in 1948 had to withdraw except for a residual and theoretical interest in maritime applications and a 'toe hold' in the AOP role—No 1906 AOP Flight was maintained by the RAF ostensibly for this purpose at the insistence of the Army. The result was that the Royal Navy demanded sea hovering for anti-submarine work and sea rescue from the very earliest days—and thirty years later was making exactly the same case, having added only such specialised applications as anti-surface ship weapon launching and troop carrying roles as they were developed elsewhere. The Army meanwhile had

19

conceived a virtually unlimited number of roles for helicopters to match its constantly developing pattern of operations and equipment.

The RAF shared the Navy's interest in anti-submarine and SAR work, but not as an exclusive helicopter role, and the Army's enthusiasm for the inherent flexibility of rotary wing aircraft, but not to the exclusion of other and more important aspects of air power. It felt however that it had nearly had its fingers badly burned by a premature venture into the helicopter field and was determined to be more careful in the future.

The RAF's helicopter policy thus became in 1948 one of waiting for tasks to arise, and has remained so ever since in the face of the ever increasing pressures of financial stringency. Bids had therefore to be not only exclusively appropriate to helicopters but also to have a clear priority over other air operational demands. The case had to be made and the resulting conflict of priorities resolved before the first steps could be taken to fulfil any task with helicopters.

For more than half of the twenty years of maximum helicopter expansion after 1950, therefore, events must be seen against the background of a clear, consistent but highly specialised Naval requirement which virtually monopolised Britain's limited helicopter manufacturing capacity. At the same time the RAF was obliged to meet a succession of emergencies worldwide without having had the opportunity to respond by other than theoretical contingency planning in the helicopter field.

Meanwhile the Army was applying increasing pressure to develop the range of helicopter tasks, but found itself compelled to formulate its demands within the restraints imposed by the currently accepted definition of the roles appropriate to Army Aviation and the RAF policy of establishing in advance that the proposed task was not only essential but also exclusive to the helicopter. Thus discussion centred on AOP, then AOP and light liaison, followed by light liaison and reconnaissance, although the true demand was for an adequate supply of helicopters with which to develop all the helicopter support roles which were found to be fully established by 1970.

Although the roles of tactical troop movement and logistic resupply by helicopter remained at least officially an RAF responsibility, the formation of an independent Army Air Corps in 1957 went a long way towards relieving the psychological frustrations inherent in the situation. The twin constraints of financial stringency and limited industrial capacity remained however, although the shortage of suitable helicopters was now no longer blamed automatically on the RAF alone.

A further element was that while in the fixed wing field it was large-scale military demand which engendered rapid development with consequent benefit to the civil market, financial limitations made the reverse true of the helicopter, at least in Britain. All the early development was aimed at the civil market, with the RAF buying in emergency whatever was immediately available. Thus the great range of promising developments by Short (Air Horse), Bristol (large tandem rotor helicopters), Percival (low pressure tip driven rotor), Fairey (Rotodyne), Westland (larger developments of Sikorsky helicopters) and others all withered away and eventually disappeared completely, leaving the field to helicopter manufacturers in the United States, where huge purchases of crude and barely satisfactory helicopters by the armed forces were of great benefit to the aircraft indusry—with consequent long term advantages for helicopter development—but also in the short term vitiated the drive towards radical research and innovation.

Into this partial vacuum the French aircraft industry was able to insert the whole range of Sud Aviation helicopter developments and by 1965 the RAF was committed to a mixture of these and American designs made under licence by the only manufacturer remaining in Britain—Westland Aircraft Ltd. In the meantime the postponement of the large (medium lift) helicopter for yet another year on the grounds of economy had become an annual event.

References to Chapter 1

1. The sources for this chapter are:

    Hilary St G Saunders, Per Ardua, The Rise of British Air Power, 1911–39, 1944.

    Parliamentary Debates (Hansard).

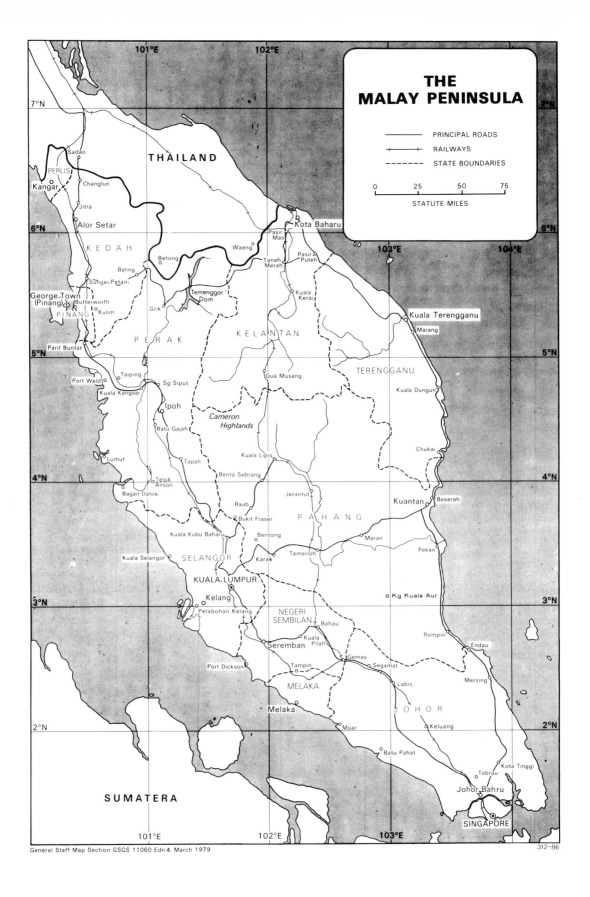

THE
MALAY PENINSULA

PRINCIPAL ROADS
RAILWAYS
STATE BOUNDARIES

0   25   50   75
STATUTE MILES

THAILAND

PERLIS
Sadao
Kangar
Changlun
Jitra
Alor Setar

KEDAH
Betong
Waeng
Pasir Mas
Kota Baharu
Tanah Merah
Pasir Puteh
Baling
Sungei Petani
Temenggor Dam
Kuala Kerai

George Town (Pinang)
Butterworth
Kulim
Grik
PINANG
Parit Buntar
PERAK
KELANTAN
Kuala Terengganu
Marang

Taiping
Sg Siput
Gua Musang
TERENGGANU
Port Weld
Kuala Kangsar
Ipoh
Kuala Dungun
Batu Gajah
Cameron Highlands
Lumut
Tapah
Kuala Lipis
Chukai
Benta Sebrang
Telok Anson
Bagan Datok
Jerantut
Kuantan
Beserah
Raub
Bukit Fraser
PAHANG
Kuala Kubu Baharu
Bentong
Maran
Kuala Selangor
SELANGOR
Karak
Temerloh
Pekan
KUALA LUMPUR
Kelang
Kg Kuala Aur
Pelabohan Kelang
NEGERI SEMBILAN
Bahau
Rompin
Endau
Kuala Pilah
Seremban
Gemas
Segamat
Mersing
Port Dickson
Tampin
Labis
MELAKA
JOHOR
Melaka
Muar
Keluang
Batu Pahat
Kota Tinggi
Tebrau
Johor Bahru
SINGAPORE

SUMATERA

General Staff Map Section GSGS 11060 Edn 4 March 1979

312-86

CHAPTER 2

THE MALAYAN EMERGENCY I

The call, when it came, for the RAF to start actual helicopter operations was clear and urgent. It originated in the Far East and was addressed to the Chiefs of Staff in London on 8 March 1949.(1) Operations against 'bandit gangs'*, the signal stated, were likely to intensify in the coming year in the more remote jungle areas of Malaya. They were being hindered or even cancelled because of the need to carry wounded men for long distances through the jungle. The remedy was to use helicopters whose presence would also have a considerable effect on the morale of the troops. The signal specified no particular type of helicopter or required performance, but referred to 'production models of a British helicopter likely to be available in the autumn'. Three were requested for casualty evacuation trials.(2)

In the Air Ministry it was remembered that the possibility of using helicopters for casualty evacuation had been mooted in the latter part of 1948, but that in the absence of a firm Air Staff requirement and an agreed establishment, no unit could be formed.(3) But to meet such a need was described as a long term policy and the Ministry of Supply had been asked to investigate the possibilities. As a result of their studies, the aircraft they had in mind were the Fairey Gyrodyne and the Bristol 171 (Sycamore), but neither was expected to be in production before 1951. The Admiralty, however, already had in production at Westland the British version of the American S-51, and if speed of response was the most important criterion, this rather less satisfactory type would probably meet the Malayan casualty evacuation requirement. The Admiralty were reluctantly prepared to release three aircraft from the production line after their first six had been completed.

Note was duly taken of the urgency of the Malayan requirement and the threat to a successful outcome to the military operations there, and the Commanders-in-Chief, Far East were told that the best solution was being sought. Ministerial pressure was also evident and a question in the House of Commons by Sir Anthony Eden (later Lord Avon) elicited a response from the Minister of Defence (Mr Shinwell) that helicopters would be sent. The War Office, while deeply concerned, was content to leave the choice of aircraft and the manning of the unit to the RAF. There was no argument about those aspects.

The choice of aircraft, however, had a dramatic effect on later helicopter development and provides an insight into the level of understanding current at the time. The Gyrodyne, Sycamore (Bristol 171) and Dragonfly (S-51) were compared in terms of

---

*Later known officially as communist terrorists.

performance, suitability, availability (by far the most important element in these discussions) and cost; a significant difference was expected between the three main contenders and they were accordingly graded in terms of effectiveness in the order listed above.

Information, however, on performance was inadequate and proved to be optimistic. The Skeeter, for example, which was also considered briefly, was thought to be able to lift a casualty but was disqualified because it would not have been able to carry a nursing attendant as well to look after him. In fact, the Skeeter would not have been able to carry a pilot under Malayan conditions, and the performance of the Dragonfly too was similarly over-estimated (see below p 31).

An element of confusion had been introduced by the Ministry of Supply advice given at an Air Ministry meeting which suggested that even if the Dragonfly was chosen because the better candidate, the Gyrodyne, was not available, there need be little concern over the lack of tropical trials for the Dragonfly so long as it was to operate only in Malaya—because the atmospheric conditions there were believed not to be tropical and the reduction in performance compared with that in an English summer would be only slight.(4)

This extraordinary misconception seems to have been accepted without comment. Indeed, the chairman of the meeting noted that even if tropical trials were not needed for the Dragonfly when destined for Malaya, they would eventually be needed for the aircraft finally chosen because it would have to be able to operate anywhere, that is by implication in more difficult climates!

The Sycamore did not show up very well in the course of these comparisons mainly because there seemed little chance of it being ready in time. There was also adverse comment from the Far East about the alleged inadequate height of its main rotor above ground obstacles. Three years later it was to prove so vastly superior in performance to the Dragonfly that it replaced it and for twenty years was operated successfully in all theatres where helicopters were used.

As the Gyrodyne never went to Malaya there is no evidence about it under those conditions. However, its projected performance was greatly superior to that of both the Sycamore and the Dragonfly and it was also preferred by the medical staffs because the casualties were carried internally, unlike in the Dragonfly, and lengthwise, unlike the athwartships arrangement in the Sycamore which they disliked. At no time was the radically different aero-dynamic principle of the Gyrodyne a factor in the discussion, except that its mechanical simplicity was commented on favourably by the Ministry of Supply. Nevertheless, the Gyrodyne was preferred by the Air Staff and although the need for haste eventually dictated the decision to send three Dragonflys to the Far East initially 'for experimental purposes', that is with strong misgivings, the Air Staff intention originally was to replace them as soon as possible by enough Gyrodynes to form a complete unit with 100 per cent backing. Shortly afterwards, however, one of the two prototype Gyrodynes crashed, killing the test crew, and the type was not proceeded with in that form. By the time it reappeared some years later with a tip propulsion rotor, both the RAF and the Navy were committed to pure helicopter types.

There remained the problem of crews for the new unit and it was decided that 25 ground crew would be trained at the manufacturers (Westland) and that they, together with a technical representative of the firm, would be enough. Thus the RAF was now entering the helicopter field with actual operations in prospect and with only three operational aircraft which were, practically speaking, irreplaceable. As for pilots, expertise in this field had not been husbanded, the time scale was short and training facilities were uncertain—although it was assumed that Westland could oblige. In the event, they were unable to provide the training for the four pilots needed immediately.

Personnel records showed four pilots still in the Service who had helicopter experience. One however was due to leave shortly (Brian Trubshaw); the other three were given a mere 15-hour familiarisation course on the Dragonfly at AFEE and sent to the Far East where it was discovered that one of them had a hearing defect which made it impossible for him to use headphones—a disability which did not prevent him from being sent on initially to Malaya, but made it essential to replace him as soon as possible.* Two vacancies thus remained and were filled by volunteers who still needed the basic helicopter training which Westland were unable to provide.

In this situation the only option was to call on the Admiralty for help, although it was later realised that as the first Dragonfly had only just been delivered to the squadron selected (No 705) the Navy was scarcely in a position to offer normal training facilities, a conclusion which was borne out by the stark facts on the day the two RAF pilots arrived in Gosport. The first Dragonfly was laying on its side outside the flight office, a tangled mass of twisted rotor blades. The embarrassed squadron commander (Lieutenant Commander J Suthers) explained that further machines were being assembled and everyone would soon get the hang of them. Meanwhile, some of the old R-4s from the 1945–48 era were still available and although on no account were they to be trusted at heights above six feet they could still be used for initial hovering practice.

---

*He was a test pilot at AFEE where apparently it was usual for some of the helicopter pilots to fly bare headed, the reason given being that this enabled them to detect more easily by ear any significant changes in rotor speed! Whether this practice had caused the hearing defect or merely allowed it to go unnoticed is not known.

Thus the Far East Air Force Casualty Evacuation Flight came into being in May 1950 with three Dragonfly helicopters whose performance in the tropics was unknown, two pilots with some limited Hoverfly experience and a brief Dragonfly conversion course at AFEE, and two more whose experience consisted only of a period of mutual pioneering with the Navy at Gosport—none had any helicopter experience overseas.* The unit however was a resounding success from the very beginning and operated throughout Malaya for 20 months before losing its first aircraft to the far from neutral jungle. It grew in time into a fully fledged squadron and practically every type of task and technique was developed as a matter of necessity with the sole exception of winch operations for which the aircraft performance was inadequate. The true significance of these events was that they demonstrated that the provision of a tactical troop carrying helicopter squadron was now a necessity.

OPERATIONAL CONDITIONS (5)

The arrival of the helicopter in the Far East almost coincided with the appointment of Sir Harold Briggs as Director of Operations to coordinate the efforts of military and civilian authorities in anti-terrorist operations. The first outburst of communist activity had slackened off, but in late 1949 a second and more organised offensive began. The 'Briggs Plan' consisted in essence of concentrating the scattered and mainly Chinese 'squatter' farmers into defensible 'new villages', so forcing the terrorists to operate in the jungle fringes, and enabling the military authorities to withdraw their long range jungle patrols except for specialised units. The plan took some two years to implement—although it had the effect of reducing the terrorists to near starvation almost at once—and patrolling continued on a substantial scale throughout that period together with a number of larger coordinated operations.

The expression 'jungle fringes' should not be thought of in terms of European woodland. Almost every area not under cultivation in Malaya consists of either primary or secondary jungle, the former made up of continuous forest with an average tree height of 180 feet (roughly the height of Nelson's Column in Trafalgar Square, London), and the latter of extremely dense and often almost impenetrable undergrowth up to 60 feet deep. A patrol's rate of travel on foot varied greatly, depending on the nature of the surface and the general topography, but was generally found to be about three miles a day in primary jungle and 500–1000

---

*Flight Lieutenant K Fry, Flying Officer A Lee, Flight Lieutenant J R Dowling, with Flight Lieutenant A J Clarke in reserve with the Far East Communications Squadron.

yards a day in secondary jungle, rates which might be reduced if there were casualties to be carried. For the RAF the restriction of operations to jungle fringes merely altered the distances to be flown. The problems of operating helicopters remained because, although the existence of roads near the scene of operations made it possible for the final operating base to be close by and fuel loads to be satisfactorily low, it in no way reduced the reliance placed by ground troops on helicopters if there were casualties to be removed. Nor did it reduce the problems faced by the ground forces in finding or making clearings large enough to allow helicopters of extremely limited power to descend or climb away among such tall obstructions.

Weather

The weather in Malaya is conditioned by the north-east monsoon in 'winter' months and the south-west monsoon in 'summer' months. Except on the east coast, which experiences strong on-shore winds during the north-east monsoon, there is little difference in seasonal weather or temperature throughout the year at the low levels used by helicopters. Winds have a generally small value at transit cruising heights of 2000–3000 feet and only very local and extremely variable effects at tree-top height. There was no wind at all where helicopters were confronted by their main problems, that is, at the bottom of clearings, although great care had to be taken to face into any slight wind there might be while entering or emerging from a clearing.

The main problems were low cloud, heavy rain and turbulence. There seemed to be no reliable pattern of weather, although low stratus, impenetrable because it mingled with the tree tops, could be expected for about three hours after dawn and also after the passage of heavy rain. Thunderstorms could be expected anywhere and nearly always over the hills, especially after midday, and turbulence was then at its worst. Heavy rain had to be avoided because of its effect on the rotor blades and because it restricted visibility; the Dragonfly was particularly bad in this respect because of its curved perspex surfaces and the impracticability of fitting them with wipers.

Turbulence produced control problems for the early helicopter pilot rather than the bumps characteristic of fixed wing flight and was particularly unpleasant because of the limited control margins of the Dragonfly coupled with the often impractical provision for obtaining a satisfactory centre of gravity position. This is described below, as is also the reason why an aircraft on its way to lift a casualty normally had its C of G on the aft limits (see p 34). In this situation, in order to obtain a reasonable cruising speed of 60 knots, the stick was often held hard against its forward stops for up to 20 minutes at a time. As the effect of up currents is to increase both rotor and air speed, the nose up pitching and rapid throttle and pitch adjustments needed to regain control were particularly tiresome in turbulence. No-

29

one on the unit was knowledgeable or experienced enough to realise the potentially dangerous effects of flying for such long periods on the limits of cyclic control, but it is difficult in retrospect to see what the alternative was. Disposable ballast in the cabin would have greatly increased the risk of vortex ring during the steepest descents, which were already often being done beyond the limits of control in terms of power.*

Temperature and humidity conditions significant for helicopters were encountered at the bottom of jungle clearings and it was not necessary to measure them scientifically to realise that both were usually at higher values than those measured by the meteorological instruments at the nearest airfield. Attempts to do so showed that they were extremely variable in the jungle, but values of 100 degrees Fahrenheit and 100 per cent humidity had to be expected, that is 10–20 per cent higher than open space measurements. It is likely that this was one of the main reasons for the extraordinary underestimation of aircraft performance in preliminary calculations. Blade distortion due to damp and tropical rain had a variable effect which had been foreseen, at least in principle.

---

*Vortex ring is a phenomenon which may be experienced when the helicopter flight direction is at right angles to the plane of the rotor disc when the relative airflow is from below—for example, during a powered vertical descent in still air. If the downward flow of air produced by the rotor (induced flow) is balanced by the upward flow resulting from the rate of descent (relative flow), the result is reduced mass flow through the rotor disc and a vortex at its periphery. The effect is a very greatly increased rate of descent for a given engine power, coupled with a marked instability in aircraft attitude and therefore direction. The recovery consists of re-establishing air flow through the rotor disc. This may be either upwards air flow by reducing power and blade pitch (involving loss of height of several hundred feet) or by increasing the downward flow by a large increase in engine power or by establishing forward flight or by a combination of these two. So, if vortex ring is allowed to develop when a helicopter is in a confined space and already with maximum engine power applied, the resulting loss of control is not recoverable. When the descending helicopter gets close enough to the ground to experience ground cushion effect (below 50 feet) the vortex ring phenomenon disappears, but the ground effect may take some seconds to be established. An element of luck thus appears in whether or not the rate of descent is too great to allow the ground effect to decelerate the helicopter sufficiently to avoid damage before it makes contact. A further element of luck is involved in whether this point of inadvertent touchdown is suitable to allow the aircraft to remain upright.

Distribution of Bases

The main RAF bases in the Far East were all in Singapore Island; during the emergency in Malaya however Kuala Lumpur was the main centre of flying operations. In the later stages Butterworth assumed progressively more importance in the support role, but there were no other purely RAF flying bases in the Federation. The Dragonfly helicopters, based at Changi, had a cruising speed of 60–65 knots and an endurance of about three hours with a full fuel load. On transit flights it was prudent not to stray too far from recognised communication features— roads, railways or rivers—not only because a failure of the single engine would almost certainly be fatal if there was no space into which to attempt an engine off landing, but also for the more important reason that the irrecoverable loss of a virtually irreplaceable helicopter would have had a crippling effect on the ability of the unit to maintain a continuous standby to meet emergency calls, an essential feature of its usefulness and credibility in the eyes of the troops in the jungle. The helicopters were regarded as so valuable that until the expansion in 1953 flights across large areas of jungle were accompanied whenever possible by a fixed wing escort—usually an AOP Flight Auster.

In addition, the Dragonflys had no instrument flying capability, could not fly at night in this area, and had to avoid flying in heavy rain because of the risk of damage to the wooden-ribbed fabric-covered rotor blades. They carried only VHF radio and used 100 octane fuel. As a result of all this, operations more than 30 miles from Singapore had much of the character of an 'ad hoc' safari. All first line servicing equipment had to travel with the aircraft, including grease guns, engine oil, hydraulic fluid and an extremely bulky fuel filter, as well as sten guns and ammunition, and jungle survival kit. Refuelling had to be arranged by air drop (in four gallon disposable tins) wherever the helicopter found itself obliged to stop, the pilot using either Army or police radio or, if fortunately available, the civil telephone to make the demand. For most of the time these were the only channels for reporting progress or receiving new tasking.

In these circumstances the presence of the Auster flights of No 656 Air OP Squadron (RAF) on airstrips at Johore Bahru, Seremban, Taiping and Termerloh was of very great assistance. They did not store the 100 octane fuel needed by the helicopters and had no hangars or permanent servicing facilities, but they did have RAF ground crews and static, if not permanent, domestic accommodation. More important, they had Army pilots who were thoroughly trained as professional aviators and had an absolutely expert knowledge of their local area and what was going on within it. Best of all, they had the ground stations of the AOP M/F radio 'net' through which voice communication was possible between all the flights as well as with any Auster, whether airborne or not, throughout the Federation. They could also talk to the troops on the ground, which the helicopter could not do except when directly overhead using a walkie-talkie (Type 88) set.

There were additional ground stations on the AOP 'net' at Kuala Lumpur, where the AOP squadron headquarters and HQ Flight were based, and also at RAF Changi. The result was that if the helicopter pilot could get to an Auster flight or even to a strip which had an Auster on it at the time, he could speak both to his base at Changi and to his tasking authority at Kuala Lumpur, as required. This facility had important operational implications as will be readily apparent.

Tasking and Control

The helicopters belonging to the Fast East Air Force were placed under the operational control of Air Headquarters Malaya based at Changi. By the time they arrived, however, operational control of air activity in the Federation was being exercised by the Advanced Air Headquarters established at Kuala Lumpur along-side the Army Headquarters, Malaya District, which directed all military operations connected with the emergency. Unfortunately, with the helicopters based at Changi on Singapore Island and therefore under the direct control of the main AHQ until they crossed the Johore Straits and entered the area controlled by the Advanced AHQ, the main AHQ represented a further link in the tasking chain and one which was not only superior to the Advanced AHQ operations staff who were processing tasks, but also completely divorced from the military staffs at Kuala Lumpur who were submitting bids.

This arrangement sometimes caused needless delays in warning the Casualty Evacuation Flight to prepare for action, the difficulty being that the steps to be taken varied greatly, depending on the distance involved, the numbers and types of casualty (walking, sitting, lying), whether immediate life or death considerations applied, enemy tactics, and especially what type of clearing existed or was in the course of preparation. As there was no way of de-fuelling the Dragonfly short of dismantling part of the fuel system, the regular standby fuel load permitted one hour of flight only—this was necessary to enable tasks to be undertaken within 30 miles of Singapore.

Not only was tasking often delayed for these reasons, but also in the early months there was nearly always a shortage of detailed information of the kind described above, and no easy way in which the helicopter pilot could obtain by question and answer the facts which were vital to him but which often seemed of doubtful relevance to some or all of the links in the chain. Thus a very elementary problem in communication and tasking appeared in a highly critical form at the outset and it was purely fortuitous that the AOP radio 'net' had a terminal at Changi and that the set was located in the same building as the helicopter flight. It was discovered that all the detailed information the helicopter pilots needed could be obtained by an AOP Auster wherever the incident had occurred. It could then be passed directly to the pilot on stand-by at Changi who would also have the opportunity to finalise any further details connected with the transit arrangements and timings. In this way the pilots usually received prior warnings of tasks and frequently knew far more about the essential details than the tasking authorities themselves.

Later it became possible to feed this information directly into the tasking chain and Advanced AHQ Malaya learned to use AOP Austers as a vital reconnaissance element before accepting a helicopter task. The Auster pilots quickly became expert at assessing whether or not a clearing would prove acceptable to a helicopter pilot. If not, they could either advise the ground troops on what was needed to bring the clearing up to standard or instruct them how to move to a better position near by. The Auster pilot's judgement in these matters was entirely reliable and came to be trusted implicitly. During the time of the Casualty Evacuation Flight all the casualties whose lives depended on minimum delay in obtaining treatment were saved because of the preparations made by the Auster pilots while the helicopter was beating its laborious way to the scene. Once there, the helicopter pilot's task was further simplified because not only were the ground troops properly organised to receive the helicopter, but also the Auster was able to escort it to the site in an area often strange to the helicopter pilot but quite familiar to the Auster pilot. In this way vital time was saved and a waste of valuable helicopter hours avoided. As a communication link with the outside world the Auster was invaluable.

Operating Techniques

In Malayan jungle conditions of temperature, humidity and a total absence of wind, it was found that the Dragonfly could not be expected to hover outside ground effect with more than 30 minutes' fuel (at cruising consumption rate) and a payload of 200 lb, that is one passenger, and even then hovering could not be relied upon. For take-off in a jungle clearing with no approach or climb out path it would be necessary to climb vertically about 180 feet. Sometimes the Dragonfly would just manage this, but often it would not. Very small variations in temperature or humidity could occur and make all the difference between success and failure in a delicately balanced manoeuvre, but a more significant and even more unpredictable variable was distortion of the rotor blades due to heat, damp, weather and wear. Tropical rain on the rotor blades even when stationary was liable to accelerate a tendency for the fabric to lift away from the rib formers, and if this happened the blades were ruined; even a slight degree of distortion, too small to be detected visually, could have a very marked effect on rotor performance.

The troops themselves varied considerably in weight: the lightest Malay or Gurkha might be no more than half the weight of some of the others, the King's African Rifles or Fijians for example, and the average British soldier would be somewhere in between. It was also usual for a soldier being evacuated by helicopter to have his kit thrown in after him, but after one or two experiences in which the kitbag appeared to have been filled with pig iron, it became standard practice to refuse to carry any kit out of deep clearings—a procedure which the troops found very difficult to understand. Again, because of the risk of the engine not restarting from the aircraft's internal accumulator, it was never shut down in a clearing unless some special circumstance made this absolutely essential. The pilot was therefore unable to let go of the controls and still less to judge the weight of what was being loaded into the helicopter, other than by watching carefully the amount of physical effort which seemed to be employed in carrying it.*

Control range was so limited that the aircraft's centre of gravity had to be adjusted for all significant weight changes in the cabin. Six $17\frac{1}{2}$ lb lead weights were provided for this inconvenient procedure and stowages for them were constructed in the nose of the aircraft behind the instrument panel and near the base of the tail cone externally on either side. Two weights were to be moved from the front to the rear stowage for each passenger carried in the cabin, but to transfer these weights in a clearing with no crewman and the pilot unable to let go of the controls was usually out of the question. In any case to carry all six weights would have left inadequate aircraft performance with a heavy passenger; the practice therefore was to carry two weights in the forward stowage, two on the floor under the stretcher carrier at the back of the cabin and none in the rear stowage, and so fly into the clearing with the C of G on the aft permissible limit. The aircraft then embarked one passenger and flew out with the C of G nearer to the forward permissible limit. On at least one occasion when the ground surface did not permit landing and loading was being carried out at the low hover—fortunately in a large and comparatively open area—a second soldier unexpectedly climbed into the hovering helicopter which immediately dashed off into forward flight. The pilot just succeeded in translating this inadvertent manoeuvre into a continuous steep turn while shouting for the baffled man to jump out.

As it was not the practice at that time to fit either torquemeters or blade pitch indicators, there was no accurate way of measuring engine performance without tying the aircraft to the ground, applying full take-off power and pitch, and observing the rotor speed achieved. This manoeuvre required a comparatively elaborate fixed facility which existed only at Changi. As the test did not reveal

---

*On one occasion when the pilot became suspicious of the weight of a sack which the troops were proposing to load, because of the way they were handling it, he insisted on inspecting the contents. He was shocked to find that it contained five or six severed heads—high priority freight for bandit identification, as it was impractical at that time to carry the bodies out complete.

any loss of climbing power which might be due to blade deterioration, diagnosis of the cause of a vertical climb performance which seemed even worse than usual was often difficult.

To measure vertical climb performance an arbitrary standard of 200 feet per minute was decided upon for a payload of 200 lb and 30 minutes' fuel load—seemingly quite fast but in fact involving motion which is scarcely discernible except when near to fixed objects for comparison: it would, for example, take between 50 seconds and one minute to reach treetop height. It was also very important to detect any diminution in the rate of vertical climb out of clearings, because if the climb stopped before the aircraft could transfer to forward flight, there would be insufficient power to hover and the aircraft would start to sink. The circumstances would then be ideal for the onset of vortex ring and a very hard landing.*

As for practical purposes it had to be assumed that there would be insufficient power to hover outside ground effect, provision was needed for transition to forward flight at about 100 feet after acceleration to this height from within ground effect. It was also desirable—for reasons of visibility as well as performance and the avoidance of vortex ring—to be able to keep moving forward during the descent for landing until about 50 feet from the ground. Both these requirements could be met if there was a gap in the trees on one side of the clearing, and consequently the minimum requirement first put forward was a clearance area with surrounding obstructions forming a 45 degree slope in at least one direction, with a 30 degree

---

*An emergency procedure was developed for the Dragonfly for use if the aircraft climbing vertically was almost clear of the trees but showed signs of stopping the climb too soon to allow transition to forward flight. The collective pitch lever was raised slightly and the extra power to prevent consequent over-pitching obtained by reducing the tail rotor pitch to zero by application of half right rudder. This resulted in a small if temporary surge of lift which raised the aircraft about 20 feet while in an accelerating turn on the spot to the right. On reaching treetop height the aircraft was flung into forward flight in whatever direction it happened to be facing. This dangerous procedure had to be used in severe conditions when the ground troops were still unaware of the helicopter's limitations in vertical perform-ance and the need for inclined approach and take-off paths. There was considerable argument subsequently as to the theoretical efficacy of this manoeuvre, but what was often not appreciated was that extra power was made available to the main rotor by thus unloading the tail rotor, and although this diminished in proportion with the rate of turn and consequent reduction in blade true air speed, an advantage, albeit diminishing, was obtained so long as the rate of turn was increasing. The early Dragonfly pilots were very conscious of this brief advantage on the occasions when the procedure had to be used.

slope preferred. When helicopters with better power margins become available, this requirement was retained to give added safety and better visibility during the descent. The ground clearance requirement consisted of a circle 30 yards in diameter cleared to ground level, with a further 10 yards all round with obstacles no higher than two feet. These requirements were rarely met in Malaya, but they became the standard criteria demanded for tactical helicopers for the next 25 years or more. The space required on the ground could be reduced if the angle of descent was more shallow, but there was no way of devising a formula for this which would be simple enough for ground troops to use to make their own adjustments. They had to do their best to meet the standard criteria and the helicopter pilot had then to assess the results and decide whether the task was acceptable or not.

The size of the clearing demanded was in fact a compromise between aircraft safety requirements and the difficulties involved in clearing areas of jungle. The ground troops would often find the requirements impossible to achieve and the pilot had always to guard against asking for too much. On the other hand, to accept a clearing which was too dangerous was to risk losing the aircraft and with it the chance of helping an unknown number of future casualties. Each new clearing had to be reassessed, and with special care when the casualty was dying. These considerations, together with the strain of flying a manually controlled, single-engined helicopter over many miles of primary jungle imposed a high degree of stress on the helicopter pilots of this period.

OPERATIONS (5)

The FEAF Casualty Evacuation Flight formed officially on 1 May 1950 at Kuala Lumpur, although it was not to reside there for another two years. In addition to its three officers (pilots), it had thirteen airmen, with three NCOs from an Air Ministry Aircraft Servicing Development Party attached to assist with the assembly of the three crated Dragonfly HC 2s which had arrived by sea during April and also with the training of the servicing crews.

The aircraft were assembled and test flown at Seletar during April and May, the first helicopter flight in the colony of Singapore taking place on 22 April. The flight moved to its permanent base at Changi on 22 May and began operational trials immediately. It was not however thought practical to move the technical support away from Singapore at this early stage.

These operational trials lasted two months and were followed by the submission of reports and recommendations (though casualty operations did in fact start at

The Far East Air Force Casualty Evacuation Flight, Changi, 1951. Officers from left to right: Flt Lt J R Dowling, Flt Lt K Fry (Flt Cdr), Fg Off A J Lee, Flt Lt Partridge (Engineer Officer).

Initial handling trials in Malaya, 1950. The Dragonfly HC2 has a starboard external pannier fitted. The condensation in the tip vortex shows the high level of humidity.

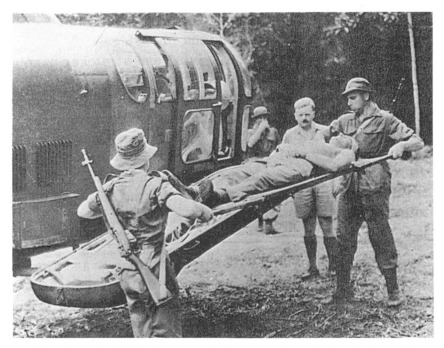

Initial handling trials in Malaya in 1950—the external pannier for the Dragonfly HC2 with a practice casualty.

The Dragonfly basket stretcher, which replaced the external pannier, being used to load a casualty in North Malaya in 1952.

once). After winching trials* and stretcher pannier demonstrations in the breezy atmosphere of Changi a jungle clearing was made available by the Far East Land Forces (FARELF) Jungle School in south Johore and on 12 June a helicopter landed in a clearing for the first time. It became apparent immediately however that there was no possibility of carrying a stretcher pannier if the aircraft was to have a reasonable chance of negotiating jungle clearings in the operational areas. This conclusion was confirmed by one of the helicopter pilots who had gone up to Kuala Lumpur to carry out helicopter trials at 4000 feet at Fraser's Hill, and had then made a brief experimental sortie over the central mountain range to the AOP Auster strip at Temerloh.**

There were in any case objections too from the medical authorities, who had at one stage practically ruled out the Dragonfly on account of its external stowage. Flying in the stretcher panniers was a terrifying experience: the patient was completely enclosed in a metal coffin-like structure, his vision restricted—through small perspex panels at the head—to the whirling rotor hub. There was also considerable vibration.

Consequently, one of the first tasks of the engineering officer who joined the unit in June 1950 was to help in the design of a stretcher and stretcher carrier which could be stowed internally without modifying the aircraft. This was quickly done and consisted of a lightweight platform (canvas on a metal frame) fitted to the cabin floor and door sill, projecting diagonally forward out of the door far enough to accommodate the foot of the stretcher. The latter was a coffin-shaped basket about 12 inches deep and able to accommodate virtually any combination of ad

---

*The hydraulic hoists provided with the first three Dragonflys were installed in the ordinary course of assembling the aircraft, and successful trials were carried out at Changi. The performance of the Dragonfly in jungle conditions, however, precluded their use while hovering outside ground effect, and the occasions on which the hoist would have been useful when the aircraft was able to get within ground effect for hovering were soon judged to be so rare that the equipment had no practical role. Moreover, the weight penalty (110 lb) was found to be wholly unacceptable for jungle operations and the time taken to fit and remove the hoist precluded its use on an occasional basis. After a few weeks the Dragonfly hoist was discarded and never refitted.

**The specification had asked for a helicopter to lift two casualties and a nursing attendant and fly for over an hour at 75 knots. In practice, the Dragonfly in Malaya, though designed to carry two patients in external panniers, could not carry even one with both panniers fitted, and flying with only one pannier produced control problems. With both panniers removed and the casualty carried as the sole passenger inside, it could only lift vertically from a jungle clearing with enough fuel for 30 minutes' flight at 60 knots.

hoc splints and bandages. It was fixed to the platform with four quick-release spring-loaded pegs and cost an insignificant sum of money having been custom built by a basket furniture maker in Changi village. After approval in July 1950 this admirable arrangement was the only stretcher used in the Dragonfly throughout its service in the Far East.*

In the first weeks the helicopter unit was engaged in discovering the capabilities of its aircraft, and also enjoying a formidable number of visits from important personages, civil and military. It was however only half way through the month of June when the first casualty evacuation call was received. On 14 June 1950 a British soldier, shot in the foot during one of the frequent ambushes of the night train from Singapore to Kuala Lumpur, was brought to Changi by helicopter from the Auster strip at Segamat, which was waterlogged at the time, so inaugurating RAF helicopter operations a few weeks before the first American operational helicopter sorties in Korea. Five days later a Gurkha soldier with glandular fever became the first casualty to be lifted from a jungle clearing, and on 28 June 1950 a Malay constable with gunshot wounds in the thigh became the first casualty whose life can be said to have been saved by the helicopter when he was lifted from a village compound in south Johore direct to the British Military Hospital at Johore Bahru. At the end of June a fourth pilot arrived to replace the non-effective member of the trio.

This splendid start to helicopter operations in Malaya went some way towards convincing the very large number of sceptical observers that the helicopter might have to be taken seriously after all. It also had the effect of translating some of the existing enthusiasm into euphoria, particularly among the ground troops.

The distances covered in these operations were very short and the heights above sea level were negligible. Most important of all, no very small or very deep jungle clearing had yet been negotiated and no communications problems had occurred. In sum, anyone who believed that true VTOL flight in deep jungle was now well established had a great deal to learn in the following months.

In fact, there were three significant failures in the course of the very next month and no successes (apart from the stream of demonstrations given to important onlookers and the formal acceptance of the locally designed stretcher basket and

---

*The disadvantage was that the casualties were not wholly inside the aircraft, but this had to be accepted. On many occasions too, when the helicopter was unable to land because of the wetness or unevenness of the ground, the stretcher could not be loaded and the casualty had to be bundled in by any means. Even with severely injured patients this was clearly preferable to inevitable death in the jungle.

platform). Of the three attempted casualty evacuations, the first could not be carried out because the clearing was far too small; the second involved a flight of over 350 miles only to find that the task involved operating on a cliff face and well outside the capabilities of the helicopter; and the third required a flight of nearly 400 miles before it was discovered that the call was a false alarm brought about by a misunderstanding due to communication difficulties. So many wasted flying hours could not be tolerated; the solution lay in the coordination of operations through and with the Auster Flights of No 656 AOP Squadron.

In the following month a single long-range casualty evacuation marked a turning point in three respects. The patient was a Malay soldier with serious gunshot wounds received during a river ambush in Kelantan state (corresponding in Malaya to the geographical position of Northumberland in England).* A Dakota escort was provided for that part of the flight which lay east and north of Kuala Lumpur (corresponding to Birmingham). This was the last occasion on which such elaborate assistance was given, and in the event the Dakota pilot erroneously declared the landing site to be inadequate for the helicopter.

The new basket stretcher was now used for the first time and its value was immediately apparent. The patient's wounds had been very bulkily dressed and he was in great pain when moved; the basket however provided very satisfactory restraint. He was also apparently in extremis, resigned to death and with good reason as without the helicopter his situation would have been hopeless. Tended and encouraged by a second pilot in the aircraft he showed a dramatic recovery in spirits when the open rice fields and coconut trees near Kota Bharu (corresponding to Newcastle) came into view. Had he travelled in the external litter it is more than likely that he would have died from shock.

This was the last occasion on which two pilots were carried; the intention had been to provide both training and experience in unfamiliar territory, and also to relieve the strain of long hours of flying. The Mk II Dragonfly had manual controls and required an awkward hunched forward sitting position to operate them, always in the atmosphere of a tropical greenhouse. In addition, the pilot was busily engaged throughout the flight maintaining continuous control of the rotor RPM with the manual throttle. He had also another problem to face: the Dragonfly was provided with elastic cords in parallel with the control cables to counter steady control forces in one direction, and electric motors controlled by a switch on the cyclic stick (trimmer) to alter their tension as flight conditions varied the feedback loads. Unfortunately, the randomly varying control forces were of a magnitude which,

---

*To enable the relative positions of the places mentioned to be more easily appreciated they are compared with roughly corresponding places in England, where for example the Isle of Wight corresponds to Singapore, and the Scottish border to the Malay/Thai border.

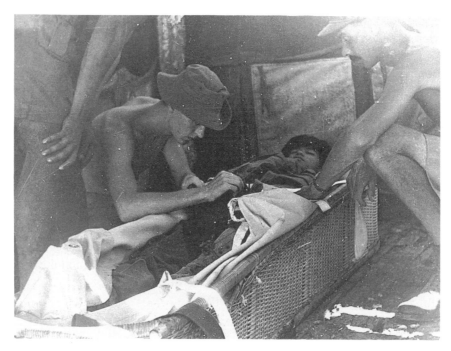

A casualty receiving medical attention in transit in the Dragonfly basket stretcher—Malaya 1950.

Re-fuelling a Dragonfly in the rain from an air dropped 'flimsy' petrol can in Malaya. The fuel had to be poured through a special filter.

when coupled with the vibration, made it difficult for any but quite experienced pilots to detect whether these electric motors were giving assistance or not.

As experience was gained, the pilots found that they began to match the three-hour endurance of the helicopter, but that it was usually necessary to lie down in the shade for 20 minutes afterwards. There were however other tasks to be carried out—refuelling the helicopter from four-gallon cans, greasing 20 or so points on the rotor hubs and transmission (after each five hours' flying), and removing or replacing all the gear which had to be carried but was taken out before setting off on the actual jungle lift. More urgent was the need to rectify, or at least diagnose, each technical defect as it became evident. For these tasks a qualified technician was needed, and so was born the helicopter crewman, a technician first and a pilot's assistant second. In place of a relief pilot, therefore, senior NCO aircraft fitters were carried, able to deal with both engine and airframe faults. Later, experienced corporal engine or airframe fitters were employed, who had learned enough of the others' duties to carry them out satisfactorily. This practice had yet to receive the formal approval of the engineering staffs, but it was dictated by common sense and operational necessity, and worked well.

There was no shortage of enthusiastic volunteers for the work—enthusiasm being an essential prerequisite—but although these men accepted most of the risks which were part of the aircrew task and all the discomforts of these particular duties, it proved impossible to find any way within Service regulations of providing an appropriate financial reward. Twenty years later the problem of obtaining a fully satisfactory helicopter crewman policy still remained, made worse by economic pressures.*

---

*When purely search and rescue units (as opposed to transport support) were formed for operations in the coastal areas of the United Kingdom, the helicopter crewman task became so highly specialised that it clearly called for a full time aircrew category, and later when crewmen began to operate from the lower end of the winch cable they earned many flying awards for bravery. But in point of fact the first two helicopter crewmen awards were to technicians employed as support helicopter crewmen, Sergeant Bowman and Flight Sergeant Moss, the senior NCOs successively in charge of the Casualty Evacuation Flight servicing groundcrew. They were not formally described as crewmen as the role had no official existence until later and they had no official aircrew status. Both however did so much operational flying with the Casualty Evacuation Flight Dragonflys that they received the distinction as aircraft fitters of being awarded the AFM and DFM respectively at the end of their tours. The citations refer to them as 'crewmen technicians' and record the comparatively large amount of flying they carried out and the numerous operations in which they took part; stress is also laid on their courage and resourcefulness and on the fact that 'the risks were always apparent'.

The Later Months of 1950

By the end of 1950 the unit was exceeding its planned flying task as a matter of course, so many and so varied were the demands upon it. In the course of a few days in December, for example, a single helicopter rescued a Chinese woman from near the Thai border; flew the AOC Malaya to Kallang (the Singapore civil airport), where it carried out a rescue demonstration, with its winch fitted for the occasion; and then was back near the Thai border again on the following day to evacuate a Malay soldier.

It was however the case of the Chinese woman which was most instructive. She had been found, one of a party of four bandits, suffering from malignant malaria and semi-starvation, and with ulcers and maggots between her toes. All four terrorists were naked, one was wounded but escaped, and two died of starvation; in all, a dramatic illustration of the effects of the food denial policy contained in the Briggs Plan, and of the contrast between life as usual in the controlled areas and the dire conditions outside them. It was also a contrast which the helicopter crews experienced at close quarters and in rapid succession.

The year 1950 closed with the Maria Hertogh riots in Singapore when hysterical and disorganised Muslim mobs roamed the streets. The city was rapidly placed under curfew and a helicopter loaded with tear gas grenades provided for police use. None of the grenades were in fact used because whenever the helicopter appeared all activity ceased and everyone stood still to stare up at it. Apart from this the helicopter's reconnaissance capability was of the utmost value; the only occasion on which a helicopter had appeared previously in this role was when a Hoverfly of No 1906 AOP Flight had been similarly employed in May of the same year during Communist rioting in Berlin.

By the end of the year, after six months of operations, the Casualty Evacuation Flight had evacuated 29 casualties, established new operational techniques, and enabled Air Headquarters to issue an operation order embodying the lessons learned so far in what amounted to standard operating procedures. Included was an official statement of the role of the AOP Flight Austers in reconnaissance and escort duties for the helicopters.

A gradual shift in role however was already becoming apparent. Casualty evacuation remained the primary function of the unit and had first priority throughout, but the enormous tactical potential of the helicopter was too obvious to be ignored. The Chinese woman terrorist mentioned above was certainly a casualty, but her evacuation by helicopter would have been required in any case for intelligence purposes. Again, when the helicopter pilot arrived at the starting point for an evacuation he would quite commonly find a soldier waiting to be carried in to replace the one due to be brought out. In the light of subsequent developments, this can be seen as an embryonic form of tactical troop movement, while the spare batteries and radio replacements which were often carried on the outward flight were elementary resupply.

Flying the High Commissioner (Mr Malcolm Macdonald) between his residence in south Johore (Bukit Serene) and his office in Phoenix Park, Singapore was becoming a frequent task and anticipated the wide use of the helicopter by General Templer in Kuala Lumpur, General Harding in Cyprus and many others elsewhere, for reasons partly of speed but more especially of security. Again, in January 1951 the helicopter was called upon to assist a government sponsored party carrying out a survey for a possible road route between Kota Bharu (corresponding to Newcastle) and Grik (corresponding to Windermere) to be built out of American aid funds (Operation Noel).

The party had crossed the wild and mountainous, bandit-infested jungle which lay across the northern part of the country and emerged at the remote hamlet of Grik. It had failed however to complete the vital contour plotting owing to the failure of the party's barometer. To repair the omission on foot would have taken several months and considerable military support; the helicopter completed the task in an hour and a half by hovering at various points on the Perak river. In those circumstances it was hardly necessary to argue the propriety of using a casualty evacuation flight in such a role, and it also seemed sheer common sense for the crewman to spray the surrounding jungle with sten gun fire before the aircraft settled into the hover. The principle was thus established of arming the support helicopters with removable crewman-operated machine guns for prophylactic defensive fire—a tactic often used thereafter and reaffirmed, after much discussion, twenty years later for the Wessex and Puma force.

Grik was the scene of another incident one late afternoon a few weeks later when a policeman reported that he had just escaped being ambushed by four terrorists at a spot only three miles away on the road to Kroh. Ambushes late in the day were one of the bandits' favourite ploys as they were well aware of the comparatively long time which the security forces took to respond by surface travel and could usually count on no action being taken until the following morning. On this occasion however, although the helicopter pilot had completed his task for the day and was preparing to night stop, the opportunity was too good to miss. A soldier was seated in the doorway of the helicopter armed with a Bren gun and not more than ten minutes later the patch of secondary jungle where the terrorists were hiding was thoroughly sprayed at close range with two magazines of Bren. This incident must be classed as a rapid reaction air strike, and although the follow up next day did not discover direct evidence of terrorist casualties, the speedy and aggressive response must have caused some urgent reappraisal of tactics. Such activity was not, however, accepted as an established role for the helicopter.

The Next Two Years

In the following six months the Casualty Evacuation Flight, still with only three Dragonflys, continued to maintain its daily standby successfully and evacuated a further 42 casualties from positions throughout Malaya. It also added further roles to its repertoire: search and rescue in the case of a Brigand pilot who baled out after an air strike (he was unfortunately found dead) and crop spraying. A small area of grass (15 acres) specially maintained by Singapore Cold Storage for the only herd of dairy cows in the country had become infested by some type of insect, so threatening the city's only source of fresh milk. Rapid action was therefore required: a spray rig was locally designed, built and fitted, and the helicopter completed the task in under three hours.

By the middle of 1951 resettlement under the Briggs Plan was largely complete and regular troop activity could be restricted to the jungle fringes, deeper penetration being limited to special forays by the Malayan Scouts, a commando type force under Colonel Calvert which was later to become part of the Special Air Service Regiment (SAS). It was therefore the Malayan Scouts who began to absorb an increasing proportion of the helicopter effort, and after a brief lull for reorganisation in August activity rose once again to its previous level and then began to exceed it. There were special reasons too for this close association with the Malayan Scouts: they had a higher sickness rate because their patrols tended to last for several weeks; they suffered a number of accidental self-inflicted injuries because their techniques involved a great deal of work with explosives; and most important of all, they were now the troops most likely to meet the enemy in comparatively large numbers, as his jungle fringe activities tended to be conducted by very small parties.

Helicopter tasks however were now expanding beyond the capability of the three aircraft available. The Dragonflys were also becoming more difficult to maintain: not only were the rotor blades and electrical components in repeated conflict with the damp conditions, but the general spares provisioning also was inadequate. This last fault was due at least in part to the unit's origins. It had been described as experimental with no expectation that it would have to last for more than a year, and there were some who believed that its life span would be even shorter. Additionally, the sole reason for acquiring the Dragonflys in the first place was to meet the needs of the Malayan Emergency and by late 1949 there was some hope that it would be over before the helicopters needed replacing.

In the Far East, however, it had become clear within six months of the unit's arrival that three helicopters would not be enough and in January 1951 Far East Air Force asked for two more. The Air Ministry agreed and duly raised the unit establishment—an action which unfortunately had no immediate result because the situation at home was, if anything, more difficult than before.

Then, in October 1951, after sixteen months without a major accident, the Casualty Evacuation Flight lost its first aircraft. The cause was almost certainly some sort of technical failure of engine or airframe, but this could not be established from the evidence because the aircraft fell back into the deep jungle clearing from which it was attempting to climb with a Gurkha casualty in the basket and was completely wrecked. Both pilot and passenger suffered only superficial injuries—a remarkable testimony to the basket stretcher design—and each was individually evacuated next day by another Dragonfly. It proved operationally impracticable to put an investigating team into the jungle at this point in the remote hope of determining the cause of the accident. Meanwhile the helicopter flight was reduced to two aircraft.

Simultaneously it began to suffer severely from a shortage of spares and the next three months were very lean. There followed however a sustained burst of activity in February and March 1952 during which the two remaining helicopters broke all previous records in flying hours and in the number of casualty evacuations, mainly in the course of two notable large-scale operations, one a planned support operation and the other the emergency rescue of a complete jungle patrol. Both attracted widespread interest and helped to crystallise the view that larger helicopters were needed to function in a tactical role. Some account of these operations from the helicopter pilot's viewpoint will serve to illustrate what took place in the course of many other similar operations at about that time.

The objective of Operation Helsby in February 1952 was the evacuation of the entire population of the remote Belum valley in the far north of Malaya. Lying very close to the Thai border, it is a wild and mountainous part of the country where the main ridges run north and south, and the only inhabitants are a handful of aborigines. The valley itself lies in the centre of this region and is in contrast to it, running east and west and possessing a flat floor. This was cultivated by a group of some 200 Patani Malays, who were almost totally cut off from the rest of the country, being visited by the District Officer in Grik only every six months or so (his mode of travel on the two weeks journey being at one time an elephant). Because of their remoteness and their position astride the bandit routes to and from the Thai border they were wholly under the domination of the terrorists and were obliged to grow rice for them—a further consequence of the food denial aspect of the Briggs Plan. That they were doing so was clear from photographic reconnaissance. Resettlement was therefore desirable and with it the destruction of existing crops.

The operation marked the first use of parachute troops (SAS) in Malaya, who were to mop up any terrorists caught in the valley and provide organisation and protection while the move was being supervised. It was not however a drop into primary jungle, a technique which was developed more fully later, although a few of the parachute troops ended up in the trees. For the helicopters it was ideal country because although the landing sites on the generally wet surface of the valley were small, vertical performance was scarcely needed; flight time from Grik was 45 minutes.

Between 8 February and 9 March 1952, 21 SAS casualties were evacuated to Grik and also 15 Patani Malays who for one reason or another were unable to join the difficult trek out of the valley on foot, shepherded by the SAS. Passengers in and out also included the District Officer and his assistant, a medical officer, the colonel of the SAS and the GOC Malaya District. Obviously however the whole operation could have been carried out in the space of a few days with a smaller number of troops and no casualties if troop carrying helicopters had been available.

As it was, with only two Dragonflys in Malaya—the replacement for the one which had crashed in October had arrived but was not yet operational—neither aircraft could be allotted exclusively to Operation Helsby. Both had to dash to and fro to deal with other casualties elsewhere in Malaya and then return to Grik to run the shuttle service to the Belum valley carrying one or two passengers on each sortie.

At the same time as Operation Helsby another helicopter operation of equal significance was taking place. This however was unplanned. At the beginning of February a patrol of the Cameronians—seventeen men in all, including a civilian reporter, an Iban tracker and a terrorist who had surrendered, with a tracker dog—entered an area of primary jungle, mostly swamp, near Sungei Tinggi (corresponding to Stafford) not far from Kuala Lumpur. The patrol was expected to last for about three or four days. On 7 February they requested their first casualty evacuation, but the terrain was so appalling that their first attempt at making a suitable clearing was unsuccessful. On the following day after much effort the helicopter managed with great difficulty to evacuate the casualty and rejoined the other aircraft at Grik for Operation Helsby. Three weeks later and still manoeuvring laboriously through the jungle swamp in pursuit of a party of terrorists, the patrol had two further casualties. On this occasion two unsuccessful attempts were made to reach them before the clearing was made adequate and the evacuation completed. The aircraft then returned once again to Grik.

At the beginning of March the patrol was still in the jungle and in dire straits because of the proximity of the enemy, and their own exhaustion and sickness. The swamp level too was rising. After careful consultation with the helicopter pilot the decision was taken to evacuate the whole party by helicopter, in spite of the awkward implications of having to do so one man at a time, and with only one helicopter and no reserve. It was also stipulated by the Army that if the operation took more than one day, not less than six men had to be left overnight.

As usual, the work of the reconnaissance Auster pilot had been excellent and when the helicopter joined him on the Auster strip at Sungei Tinggi the patrol had made

Dragonfly servicing at Changi (1950–53); an Auster
Mk 5 of No 656 AOP Squadron is seen in the
background.

A typical clearing cut in Malaya in 1952, used in this
case for the evacuation of a complete patrol of the
Cameronians—see text.

A supply drop parachute is used as a marker and the
platform from which the passenger embarked while
the aircraft hovered can be seen just above it.

a very deep and narrow, but satisfactorily elongated, clearing (about 70 yards long) with a platform at the deep end from which the soldiers could jump into the hovering helicopter, landing being out of the question on the surfaces available. The distance from the Auster strip was estimated at a three or four day march and a ten minute flight by Dragonfly. The Auster pilot had arranged tins of 100 octane fuel, enabling the helicopter to be refuelled after each 20 minute sortie, and also a supply of batteries in case the frequent engine starts which would be necessary proved too much for the aircraft's internal accumulator.

The helicopter was able to start the evacuation on the afternoon of 2 March and after successfully extracting six of the soldiers retired at last light to Kuala Lumpur. Early next morning, the usual low stratus cleared well, the helicopter remained serviceable and the lift was continued—a nerve wrecking experience for all concerned as the patrol was progressively reduced below a viable size. The dog handler obviously had to travel with his dog, but as he was the only one who could pick the animal up he had to throw it into the hovering helicopter before he could climb in himself. The last man in the clearing—the patrol commander, Lieutenant Cameron—stood on the platform with his radio strapped on his back, gun cocked in one hand and a grenade in the other, waiting hopefully for the helicopter to return. The task was completed by midday on 3 March and the helicopter then set off to Kampong Kuala Aur (corresponding to East Anglia) where a police casualty was evacuated that afternoon.

Operation Helsby and the Cameronian patrol evacuation took place shortly before the three Commanders-in-Chief in Singapore formulated and submitted their bids in mid 1952 for more helicopters, and for a larger type of aircraft able to carry troops for tactical deployments. Indeed, by the time that a trickle of new Dragonflys and pilots started to arrive in the later part of 1952, the pre-planned attendance of helicopters at the scene of major operations had become standard procedure.

Examples of the great development in helicopter activity are provided by the events of July and August 1952, when three major ground operations—Habitual, Pilchard and Hive—attracted pre-planned helicopter attendance and required a total of 40 casualty evacuations. Reconnaissance sorties were flown in searches for a crashed Dakota and a Hornet, mis-aimed bombs were plotted, an eye kept on enemy movements after air strikes, and area patrols mounted for Army commanders. It was also becoming possible to establish detachments specifically for these purposes, instead of operating the helicopters exclusively from Changi, and during this period temporary detachments were mounted at Kuantan (corresponding to Boston), Kuala Lumpur, Seremban (corresponding to Warwick) and Grik.

It was at about this time that preparations were being made for the next major development in the anti-terrorist campaign, the establishment of jungle forts. By now the terrorists had been effectively denied food and support from the populated areas and were relying more and more on the jungle dwelling aborigines, the Sakai. The plan therefore was to create permanent centres in the remote jungle areas where the Sakai could be persuaded to settle and where administrative and medical services could be provided; these centres could also act as bases from which military and eventually police authority could be extended over each area and its aborigine population. Helicopters were later to play a vital role in the establishment and maintenance of these jungle forts (it was only later that they acquired airstrips); in the meantime the Casualty Evacuation Flight contributed by providing (in mid 1952) transport and support for the reconnaissance parties responsible for siting the first of these vital new centres.

It was in November 1952 while engaged in this task that a helicopter crew first found itself under active attack on the ground. Senior Army and police officers had been flown into the site of the first fort (Fort Legap, corresponding to Huddersfield) for a tour of inspection when it was attacked by a sizeable force of terrorists. Pilot and passengers had to join the SAS troops in defensive positions to beat off the attack. The helicopter happily escaped damage and the take-off was made behind a hail of covering fire without waiting for the Auster escort which was due to arrive later.

In the previous month the first aircraft loss due to pilot error had occurred. One of the newly arrived pilots landed in a clearing where the troops had failed to prepare the landing point adequately. Being inexperienced the pilot placed too much reliance on their efforts and committed himself to a full landing. The ground collapsed under one wheel, the helicopter fell over and although no-one was badly hurt the aircraft was wrecked.

One further pointer to future activities was an experiment carried out by scientists in December 1952 employing the Dragonfly spray rig which had previously come to the rescue of Singapore's dairy pastures. The aim of the experiment was to test the feasibility of destroying the small hidden areas of cultivation on which the terrorists were becoming increasingly dependent in their attempts to obtain food supplies in the remote jungle areas. The results were very promising.

The last two months of 1952 and the first month of 1953 saw the beginning of the build up of the Casualty Evacuation Flight into No 194 (Helicopter) Squadron. Two Dragonfly Mk 4s were received, with metal blades and hydraulically assisted controls, and three new pilots appeared. A permanent detachment at Kuala Lumpur was established. But in the very last month of operation as a Flight (January 1953) the first fatality occurred when one of the new aircraft flown by one of the new pilots, with a senior policeman and an Army officer on board, lost a rotor blade at 3000 feet owing to a fracture in the rotor head. The aircraft fell to the ground disintegrating on the way; all aboard were killed.

The Casualty Evacuation Flight had been in existence for two years and four months, had evacuated 265 casualties, pioneered operational helicopter techniques in support of ground forces in the most difficult conditions of climate and terrain in the world, with grossly underpowered aircraft, and had experienced only one major accident due to pilot error—inexperience. The foundations for No 194 and later helicopter squadrons were thus well and truly laid.

DEVELOPMENTS IN WHITEHALL (6)

In June 1950 the helicopter proponents in the Royal Air Force had listed its military roles as casualty evacuation, AOP and seaward defence, but their arguments had been opposed on the grounds that its usefulness had not been demonstrated. A proposal to provide a VIP helicopter link between Northolt and the Air Ministry roof was also first put forward at about this time, but received no support partly because of the expense and partly because examination revealed that the Air Ministry roof could not easily be strengthened.

However, in August 1950 (that is, two months after helicopter operations had begun in Malaya) the Air Staff issued the first helicopter operational requirement—OR 280—which foresaw the need for an air transportable helicopter with four seats (including that of the pilot), a speed of about 75 knots, a range of about 400 nautical miles, and the ability to hover at 5000 feet outside ground effect. Its roles were to be primarily ambulance, with easy conversion to passenger and freight carrying, signal line laying and rescue duties. Three months later in November the Air Ministry pointed out to the Ministry of Supply that it was not enough merely to wait for civil developments in the helicopter field in the hope that something useful or easily adaptable to Service needs would appear, and strongly urged that research and development in this field be accelerated.

By the end of 1950 the two RAF helicopter units in the United Kingdom equipped with R-4s—No 1906 AOP Flight and the Air/Sea Warfare Development Unit (ASWDU) in Coastal Command—were arguing strongly for re-equipment with the Sycamore helicopter; the War Office however in its Land/Air Warfare Policy Statement No 9 concluded that two types were needed, one for AOP and one for light communications. The former requirement was aimed at the Sycamore, the latter at the Saunders Roe Skeeter. The Air Staff was not convinced by the arguments in favour of two types for these roles, but the replacement in due course of the Hoverflys in No 1906 AOP Flight and ASWDU by Sycamores was agreed, and ASWDU with its four Sycamores was seen as developing eventually into a SAR unit with 16 helicopters.

However FEAF's bid in early 1951 for two more helicopters for service in Malaya was to be met by Dragonflys and not Sycamores partly because of the technical difficulties of adding a second type to the hard pressed unit in Singapore and partly because the Sycamore was still not ready for operational use.(7) The problem was, also, that only Westland were producing Dragonflys and all were reserved for an Admiralty order which would take up to two years to complete at the expected rate of production of four a month; and what was obvious to the Air Ministry— that there was no alternative to the FEAF bid being met out of this Admiralty order—was by no means obvious to the Admiralty. Explanations therefore took most of 1951 and it was not until October that the Admiralty announced that the very earliest date for releasing the two Dragonflys from their programme would be April 1952.(8)

As October 1951 was also the month in which the FEAF Casualty Evacuation Flight lost its first aircraft, a stream of very urgent signals reached the Air Ministry from Singapore stressing the importance of an early delivery of the two Dragonflys approved at the beginning of the year and at the same time arguing the case for a third aircraft which would bring the unit's establishment to six. In December the Admiralty agreed to release one Dragonfly and to explore the possibility of finding a second; their existing plans however were on no account to be interfered with.(9)

The promised Naval Dragonfly was transferred to FEAF by February 1952, thus restoring the Casualty Evacuation Flight to its original strength of three aircraft exactly one year after an establishment increase of two had been agreed. By now, however, FEAF's demands were becoming very insistent and in February 1952 a claim was put forward for straight priority over the Navy. Reference was made to that earlier occasion on which access to materials in short supply had been gained exclusively by one Service and to the conclusion of the ensuing Smuts Committee in 1917 that the formation of a unified air service was more economically efficient than separate air arms in the Army and the Royal Navy. FEAF argued that while the Navy was interested in establishing (inter alia) a rescue service for their carrier aircraft, lives were actually at stake in Malaya where there was demonstrably no alternative means of rescue.(10) The Air Ministry replied that FEAF's position was appreciated and that in addition to the three Dragonflys already in Singaore a fourth aircraft might be expected in March, a fifth in August and a sixth in September, with a seventh in March 1953 which would ultimately have to be returned to the Navy.(11)

Helicopters however had made their mark in Malaya and there was no going back. The Air Ministry's piecemeal approach was brushed aside and in May 1952 the Commanders-in-Chief in the Far East submitted a bid for a squadron of 12 helicopters immediately and for its establishment to rise to 18 in 1953 with six larger helicopters for tactical troop movements in addition. General Sir Gerald

Templer, the newly appointed Governor of Malaya, added a footnote: the bid was undoubtedly justified but further examination was needed and the true requirement was likely to be of the order of 50 larger aircraft.*

A reappraisal of the situation revealed that apart from comparatively large Naval holdings the available stock of Dragonflys could be counted in twos and threes. Westland production had turned out to be slightly higher than had been expected (five a month instead of four), but this increase was compensated for by the somewhat embarrassing fact that sales had been arranged in small quantities to France, Belgium, Egypt and Yugoslavia and an Iraqi bid was receiving favourable consideration.(12) Any interference with these sales was generally opposed by the Foreign Office; however, in most cases the aircraft were either powered by American Pratt and Whitney engines or prepared to a standard which made them unsuitable for Malaya. The fundamental problems with the Dragonfly remained the slow production rate and the fact that to increase it would require capital investment out of the defence budget—a quite unacceptable proposal at that time. The Chiefs of Staff therefore decided that Naval priorities would have to be adjusted so as to release the required number of Dragonflys for Malaya.

This was however by no means the end of the helicopter problem. All the first Whirlwinds had been ordered for the Navy programme and even if they were diverted to the RAF there was no hope of their being ready in time to meet the Malayan requirement in 1952–53. Further, the only source of larger helicopters was the United States and attempts to obtain the American S-55 under the provisions of the US Aid Programme became bogged down in legal difficulties (for example, the status of Malaya as a colonial dependency). The alternative was to start the Naval build up with a squadron of American S-55s supplied as part of the NATO defence forces and—in response to pressure from General Templer for the provision of tactical trooplift helicopters in Malaya—to divert this squadron temporarily to the Far East until it could be replaced by Whirlwinds diverted to the RAF. American agreement was obtained in October.**(13)

The stage was thus prepared in the middle of 1952 for a steady build up of Dragonflys to a planned squadron strength of 12 by the end of the year and 18 in 1953, and for the addition of a squadron of Naval S-55s in 1953, to be replaced in due course by RAF Whirlwinds.

---

*He had succeeded Sir Henry Gurney, who had been murdered in a terrorist ambush on the road from Kuala Lumpur to Fraser's Hill, and had assumed the dual role of Governor and Director of Operations.

**As the squadron was officially part of the NATO anti-submarine force it was considered necessary for the Navy to operate the S-55s while they were in Malaya.

While Malayan requirements were being met, the broader issues were not neglected. In March 1951 the Army made the first of many bids for a helicopter lift of 10000 lb payload and requested the formation of a development unit of three Bristol 173s. By itself, this expensive proposal found little favour, but when a few months later the Naval and Air Staffs jointly put forward a bid for a helicopter in the maritime role with much the same performance as the Bristol 173, the idea seemed more attractive. There was also a British European Airways requirement for a 30/40 seat helicopter with a 10000 lb payload and a radius of action of 150 nautical miles.

Towards the end of 1951 the general feeling in the Air Staff was that helicopters had reached the same stage as fixed wing aircraft in 1910: there were definite uses for them, but insufficient experience to determine precise roles and therefore to define proper operational requirements. It was considered, however, that the achievements of the Casualty Evacuation Flight in Malaya, together with Naval experience in the sea rescue role, justified in principle proceeding with the projected SAR unit for Coastal Command.

The belief that the helicopter had a role to play was confirmed by American experience in Korea and in 1951 an official American report stated that the versatility of the helicopter as an instrument of war had received formal recognition in the United States. Indeed in 1950, before Korea, the United States had 105 helicopters on order; by the end of 1951 this figure had risen to 2085.(14)

In January 1952 British Service bids for helicopters included, in addition to Malayan requirements, 16 Whirlwinds or Sycamores for SAR (including a bid by Fighter Command); 4 Dragonflys and 4 Whirlwinds for No 1903 AOP Flight in Korea; 3 Sycamores, 3 Skeeters and 3 Whirlwinds for a flying training squadron; 4 Sycamores and 2 Whirlwinds for Transport Command; 3 Whirlwinds for technical spares delivery; and 4 Bristol 173s for the maritime/army heavy lift requirements. There was also a bid for 20 helicopters for civil defence in time of war.(15) These extravagant and consequently (with the exception of the SAR role) unsuccessful proposals serve to indicate the swing of opinion in the first 18 months after the Casualty Evacuation Flight was established.

In June 1952 the Air Council approved a general transport squadron with an establishment of 18 S-51s and 6 S-55s for use in Malaya while the emergency lasted, and also approved in principle SAR flights for Fighter and Coastal Commands with 4 S-51s and 4 S-55s respectively, and 3 Bristol 173 twin rotor, twin engined helicopters for evaluation. Further orders were to await the results of the expected defence review.(16)

References to Chapter 2

1   SEACOS 883 in PRO Air 8/1562.

2   Ibid.

3   AHB ID/53/1/265/Pt 1, Mar 1949.

4   Ibid: Meeting on 23 Aug 1949 chaired by ACAS(TR).

5   Unless otherwise stated, the sources for this section are the ORBs of the Casualty Evacuation Flight and AHQ Malaya or eyewitness evidence.

6   Unless otherwise stated, the source for this section is AHB ID6/463/Pt 2.

7   AHB ID/53/1/265/Pt 1.

8   Ibid, Pt 2.

9   Ibid.

10 HQ FEAF signal A682, 15 Feb in AHB ID/53/1/60/Pt 1.

11 Air Ministry signal A2578, 25 Feb in AHB ID/53/1/60/Pt 1.

12 Ibid; AHB ID9/H54; AHB ID/53/1/265/Pt 2.

13 AHB ID9/H54.

14 Report of the air attaché in Washington in AHB ID9/94/10/Pt 1.

15 Air Council paper in AHB ID/53/1/60/Pt 1.

16 AHB IBD9/94/10/Pt 5.

PHASE 2

1953–60

INTRODUCTION

The second phase of RAF helicopter development stretches from 1953 to 1960, but excludes the turbine engined helicopter units which were introduced shortly before the end of the period. They belong to the start of Phase 3.

It was during this second phase that the helicopter became a useful aircraft in widespread demand and several operational helicopter units were born in various parts of the world. The period begins with the formation of helicopter squadrons in Malaya immediately after Phase 1 and in the Malayan context continues until the end of the emergency there. Overseas Units were formed in the Mediterranean and Aden areas as well as Christmas Island under the Far East Air Force. In Europe helicopter units were formed at Sylt and in Northern Ireland, while elsewhere in the United Kingdom Search and Rescue squadrons, the Central Flying School helicopter unit and the Joint Experimental Helicopter Unit came into being in the course of this second phase. Helicopter sections were introduced into The Queen's Flight and the Metropolitan Communications Squadron. The helicopter types involved during this period were the Sycamore Mk 14, the Skeeter and the Whirlwind Mks 2 and 4.

CHAPTER 3

THE MALAYAN EMERGENCY II

The turning point in the development of the tactical helicopter had been reached in principle in 1952 in Malaya, coincidentally with the much more ambitious American operations in Korea. The impetus in the British case came from the High Commissioner and Director of Operations in Malaya, Sir Gerald Templer, and the beginning of 1953 saw this initiative coming to fruition.

The Mk 2 Dragonflys were now being rapidly replaced by the metal bladed Mk 4s with hydraulic power assisted controls. Payload was not increased because the aircraft was now heavier, but the overall performance and consequently the safety margins were improved and, more important, were more accurately predictable. The power assisted controls allowed a much greater degree of precision in control movements and so of efficiency, and reduced the physical strain involved.

The three original Casualty Evacuation Flight pilots (Flight Lieutenants K Fry, A J Lee and J R Dowling) were tour expired at the end of 1952, but Flight Lieutenant Dowling was retained for a further nine months (partly to carry out operational trials on the Sycamore) and he, together with the three newcomers who had joined the unit during 1952 (Flight Lieutenants A J Clarke and G L Jacques, and Master Pilot Cox), continued to meet the operational tasks by means of a detachment at Kuala Lumpur, and provided training for the new No 194 Squadron forming at Sembawang in Singapore under the command of Squadron Leader D R G Henderson. At the outset the squadron had six Dragonflys against an establishment of twelve, but by the end of April 1953 its strength had risen to 11.(1)

In the meantime No 848 Squadron (Royal Navy) with ten American built S-55s had arrived at Sembawang in HMS PERSEUS on 8 January 1953 under the command of Lieutenant Commander Suthers, who had provided the training facilities for two of the Casualty Evacuation Flight pilots in 1950, a coincidence which made the introduction of the Naval squadron to helicopter operations in Malaya comparatively easy. Nos 848 and 194 Squadrons jointly formed the operational strength of No 303 Wing (Wing Commander W R Williams), which was established at Sembawang on 2 February 1953 with operational control of both squadrons, and administrative and training control of No 194 Squadron. Administrative services for the RAF squadron were provided during this period by RAF Tengah, and for the Naval squadron by RNAS Sembawang.(2)

The policy directive for No 194 Squadron listed its roles as follows:

    a.   the tactical movement of troops, including the reinforcement of outposts;

b. tactical reconnaissance;

c. casualty evacuation from forward areas;

d. search and rescue.

The relegation of the casualty evacuation role to third place did not represent a diminution of its importance: on the contrary, it was now possible to keep two aircraft at one hour readiness for this task instead of only one. What it did mean was that the tactical roles were now formally stated instead of being a departure from standard behaviour requiring special authorisation.

The new pilots on No 194 Squadron needed a considerable amount of training because the arrangements for their conversion and training at home had been less than satisfactory.* With insufficient knowledge of helicopters and the pilot training required, the Air Ministry had been obliged to accept a pilot conversion course at Westland which specified little more than that it should include 50 hours flying (the generally accepted figure at that time). The pressure on the one and only test pilot originally entrusted with the training task at Westland had resulted in a very variable product. All the pilots arriving in Singapore had 50 hours training recorded, but in fact some had only six or seven hours dual instruction and one only just over four.(3)

The Naval squadron however was in the happy position of arriving as a fully manned unit in full flying practice (it had even had the opportunity to make a number of training flights from the carrier while on passage from the United Kingdom) and with a full complement of serviceable aircraft. All it needed was theatre conversion training, which would give it an introduction to the geography of the country and the manner in which operations were conducted. As with the RAF pilots this theatre familiarisation was carried out mainly by means of individual attachments lasting one or two weeks with the ubiquitous and ever helpful Auster flights of No 656 AOP Squadron. Performance trials were carried out immediately and established that the S-55s could carry five fully armed troops to large cleared spaces. They could also operate to small clearings, prepared to the same standards as for the Dragonfly, with four armed troops, but their cruising speed was no better than the Dragonfly's (about 60–65 knots). For casualty evacuation the S-55 could carry three stretcher cases and two walking patients; the aircraft was fitted with a winch and had a cargo hook underneath which was able to carry netted loads of up to 800 lb.(4)

---

*See below p 108.

For tactical troop deployments as opposed to casualty evacuation, it was clearly necessary to deplane troops from the hover in places where there was no one to prepare a landing site, a practice later known as 'roping'. True to tradition the Navy experimented with scrambling nets for this purpose, but these were swiftly abandoned—a soldier equipped for landing in an operational environment consists almost entirely of protuberances, some blunt and some extremely sharp. Contact with the scrambling net therefore produced a series of hopeless entanglements and the alternative of providing a thick rope knotted at intervals became standard practice.

In the event, the S-55s of No 848 Squadron had already carried out a triple casualty evacuation at Kuala Pilah (5) a week before the formation of No 303 Wing, and then in February were able to proceed immediately with transport operations, including 17 casualty evacuations and two tactical trooplifts, the second one of which was significant enough to be described in some detail.(6)

A Dragonfly pilot from the No 194 Squadron detachment at Kuala Lumpur had been briefed on 15 February to carry out a reconnaissance near Port Swettenham in the delta of the Klang river, an area of low lying wet land with much mangrove swamp. Near the seaward end of a long spit of cultivated ground surrounded on three sides by water or mangrove swamp was a small hut believed to be the home of Siew Hoong, the terrorist district committee chairman for the Pun district of West Selangor. All previous attempts to raid this hut had been abortive, because news of the entry of security forces at the landward end of the peninsula was easily transmitted to the terrorists at the other end. On this occasion however the intention was to approach overnight by Sampan along the river and the purpose of the reconnaissance was to identify at surface level the entrance of the particular creek running from the river through the mangrove to the edge of the cultivated area near the hut. It was hoped that a dawn assault by boat from the end of this creek would achieve the necessary surprise.

The Dragonfly pilot however thought this a desperate plan and recognised the situation as one ideally suited to a troop assault using the S-55s. With his helicopter he called personally that same day at his own headquarters and that of the Army unit concerned to obtain agreement to this novel procedure. As further reconnaissance might mean the loss of surprise it was decided that the Dragonfly, flown by the same pilot, would lead three S-55s each with four soldiers.

They would fly at very low level down the river and along the creek to surround the hut at first light and within 30 seconds of the aircraft becoming audible to the inhabitants. The Dragonfly, with an armed soldier in the doorway, would be able to prevent anyone leaving the hut while the troops were deplaning for the assault. The operation was codenamed Wellington II.

The troops employed on this operation were mostly national servicemen, none of whom had ever been in a helicopter before. However, half an hour's troop training was carried out with the S-55s together with a brief practice formation sortie with the Dragonfly. It was found that the maximum speed which allowed the S-55s to keep up with their leader while manoeuvring was 50 knots. The operation was to be mounted at dawn on 16 February 1953.

The intention was to take off as soon as the horizon became visible (just before dawn), but at the moment of take-off it was discovered that the cockpit lighting had been removed from the Dragonfly concerned and not replaced—Dragonflys were not used for night flying in the Far East theatre. Consequently, the pilot could not see the all important rotor rev counter and an anxious 15 minutes passed before he had enough light to do so. After that however the operation went exactly as planned. Contact was made on VHF with the ground liaison officer (GLO) who had positioned his vehicle at Port Swettenham, and height was reduced to just above ground level (20 feet). Landmarks were followed without much difficulty, the formation being half way between line astern (to allow the Dragonfly to make rapid turns) and echelon (to avoid flying in one another's slipstream, all being at the same height). At the final landmark before the last straight run into the target, the S-55s were brought to line abreast and the order to break was given a moment later as the target came into sight. The four aircraft reached their hovering positions without difficulty and the troops were all disembarked within 30 seconds of the target coming into view. The S-55s then withdrew and landed alongside the GLO at Port Swettenham, where reinforcements were waiting in case they were needed.

The Dragonfly meanwhile was in a commanding position next to the target, hovering above the ground troops' field of fire with its gun trained on the doorway of the hut at a range of about 30 yards. As soon as the troops entered the hut, the Dragonfly landed and disembarked its armed passenger who now acted as liaison officer with the ground forces. The solitary occupant of the hut was captured without a shot being fired (not however Siew Hoong, as had been hoped), the S-55s were recalled to embark the troops and their prisoner, and everyone was back at their bases in time for breakfast.(7)

For the aircrews there were two lessons: it was unwise to discard cockpit lighting (or any other role equipment) merely because there was no formal intention to employ the aircraft in the role for which that equipment had been provided; and in the case of the S-55 the pilot needed a better method of signalling the troops to deplane than stamping his foot on the floor! The paratroop light signalling system subsequently adopted was an obvious requirement. It was also clear that troops could be taught to use the helicopter with only a very short period of training.(8) Further, the employment of a pathfinder helicopter with a fire capability had anticipated by some 20 years the procedure which the American forces developed independently and used in a more advanced form in Vietnam.

Indeed, Wellington II had a profound effect on operational planners and ground troops alike. Although it was appreciated that the target was altogether exceptional in the Malayan theatre, the scenes of most operations being able to accommodate only one helicopter at a time, the tactical troop movements which the S-55 made possible had been dramatically demonstrated within a few weeks of the unit's arrival. This new capability was accordingly exploited without further delay and by the end of 1953 the S-55s had carried 12000 troops.(9) Paratroop trials using dummies were also initiated with the S-55s during February; the results were encouraging and the trials were satisfactorily completed by July.(10)

Troop carrying operations by the S-55s immediately revealed that there were certain basic considerations to be taken into account. First, the number of aircraft which could be employed was found to be limited by the size of both the delivery point and the departure area. Operation Commodore in May 1953, for example, was a maximum effort and eight S-55s were used, with the result that not only did the aircraft completely fill the Auster strip which was being used as the loading area, but flying hours were wasted in queueing at the delivery end of the shuttle because there was room for only one aircraft to land at a time. The conclusion was that it would have been more efficient to have used half the number of aircraft with a relief pilot in each.(11)

Second, where more than one landing site was being used a locally based controller was needed to direct each element of the lift to its correct destination. The first answer was to use a Dragonfly as an airborne command post or air coordinator, but as a ground controller was also needed with a VHF radio and direct contact with the unit being lifted, the air coordinator was later dispensed with and the despatch of a ground based operations controller from RAF Kuala Lumpur became standard practice.(12) From these control teams and the parallel units developed to support airborne operations by fixed wing aircraft sprang the Mobile Air Operations Teams (MAOTS) which were later established in all three Services.

The third consideration was the training of the troops involved. In Malaya rehearsals with troops and helicopters were at first carried out automatically, but the very severe competition for helicopter flying hours led to this practice being questioned and may have unduly influenced the decision that, although no crewmen were carried in the aircraft and a very high proportion of the troops concerned were quite unused to any form of flying and many spoke no English, rehearsals were unnecessary, although desirable, and that a comprehensive briefing would be adequate.(13)

Problems of low level navigation and the identification of the correct landing zone (LZ) without the appropriate navigation equipment would be solved, so it was hoped, by using coloured smoke marking and fluorescent identification panels. The use of both did in fact become a standard procedure, but the practice of relying on a Dragonfly to provide a pathfinder and initial prophylactic strike service had to be abandoned after a few operations as far too wasteful and often impossible to arrange. Austers provided any smoke marking required and Brigands, and later Hornets, carried out precautionary air strikes when appropriate.(14)

Meanwhile, during the build up period in early 1953 No 194 Squadron was facing two major problems: a heavy pilot training commitment, as explained above, and an acute shortage of aircraft. After the fatal rotor head failure in January 1953 all the Dragonflys had been grounded and were released only after Magnaflux crack detection of the rotor hubs, a time consuming procedure which had to be repeated after every 100 flying hours (reduced to 50 hours when two hubs were found to be cracked).(15) Only with the arrival—more than six months later—of rotor hubs in which the spider arm threads were milled instead of cut (the eventual solution to the problem) was this requirement withdrawn. Consequently, for the first few months of 1953 the squadron's entire operational effort was provided by the small detachment at Kuala Lumpur, while the S-55s carried out that part of the task, mainly casualty evacuation, which the Dragonflys could not meet. The Sycamore at Kuala Lumpur, still undergoing trials, was also a considerable help in fulfilling operational tasks.

No 303 Wing at Sembawang therefore was fully stretched in providing enough serviceable Dragonflys to maintain both the detachment at Kuala Lumpur and the pilot training programme. Its difficulties were made worse by an organisational structure which was untidy in the extreme. Much of the Dragonfly second line servicing was carried out at Changi; the squadron headquarters was located at RNAS Sembawang; administrative services were provided by Tengah; tasking was in the hands of the Advanced Air Headquarters at Kuala Lumpur. To remedy this, No 303 Wing proposed that all these functions should be centred on Kuala Lumpur, although the technical, office and domestic accommodation required there was not yet ready. Accordingly, both the Wing and No 194 Squadron moved their headquarters to Kuala Lumpur on 1 May 1953, and the squadron's second line servicing followed two months later.

With RAF Kuala Lumpur, until then little more than a forward operating base under a Wing Commander, now in the process of becoming a full RAF station, it was natural and automatic for No 303 Wing to become the station flying wing, and for the second line servicing, along with the squadron engineering officer, to become part of the Technical Wing.*(16) A further organisational change was made in

---

*In view of later arguments about the respective merits of centralised as opposed to autonomous squadron-controlled servicing for helicopter units, it is important to note this early decision to centralise second line servicing and to observe that it

(continued on foot of next page)

64

February 1954 when No 303 Wing was disbanded as a separate unit and Air Headquarters Malaya moved from Singapore to Kuala Lumpur.

By the end of 1953 the Malayan Emergency was moving into its decisive phase. With the terrorists driven back into the jungle and away from the populated areas, the helicopter and its qualities of mobility and flexibility could be exploited to counter the enemy's natural advantage of inaccessibility and security from surprise. This was done in three ways: troop deployment and redeployment in the course of offensive patrol operations in selected areas; siting and supplying the jungle forts until airstrips had been built to take the Austers and Pioneers; and, following the experiments made at the end of 1952, locating the clearings which the terrorists were cultivating and destroying their crops with defoliant spray.

These crop spraying operations by helicopter began in August 1953 using the spray rig developed two years previously to spray the Singapore dairy herd grasslands. The chemical eventually chosen was a mixture of trioxine and diesolene—anything with a high toxic effect on human or animal life was avoided—carried, in the case of the Dragonfly, in a 40-gallon Hastings engine oil tank fitted with an electric pump which fed the mixture into the spray boom, mounted athwartships, through which it was discharged at the rate of ten gallons a minute by means of metered nozzles.(17) A similar arrangement was devised for the S-55.

The location of the clearings to be sprayed was plotted by the AOP Austers and when a suitable group was found a spraying operation was mounted, the Auster pilot identifying the target and directing the helicopter accordingly. The technique was for the latter to fly at about treetop height (200–350 feet) at between 0 and 30 knots, according to terrain and altitude, and to traverse the clearing as often as necessary to cover it, with the crewmen directing the pilot and at the same time controlling the electric pump which delivered the fluid. As the helicopters were operating over territory with no friendly troops below and sometimes obviously occupied by the enemy, these highly vulnerable spray runs were preceded by strafing air strikes which were normally carried out by a pair of Hornets. Their effectiveness could be measured by the fact that no helicopter was known to have been subjected to enemy fire while spraying. The effect of the chemical spray was to kill all vegetation and make the ground unusable for cultivation for some weeks.

---

was accepted without challenge; it made little difference at a time when No 194 Squadron was the only operational squadron fully based on the station (Naval second line servicing remained at Sembawang). The transfer of first line servicing to the technical wing was regarded as quite inappropriate and was never seriously considered.

Most of these spray operations took place in late 1953 and early 1954; they were codenamed Cyclone and numbered 1 to 5.(18) The AOP Austers filled the dual role of reconnaissance and providing smoke marking for the locations where the Hornet rocket and bomb strikes were required, and on at least one occasion this procedure was specially called for by a Dragonfly pilot who had seen four figures in the clearing he was about to spray. A Hornet strike was provided two minutes later. These spray operations lasted for three or four days and up to 20 clearings could be dealt with each day.

The Dragonfly proved to be quite a satisfactory vehicle for these tasks and after the first operation the S-55s were reserved for the trooping role which had a higher priority.(19) The shortage of helicopters in early 1954 put an end to crop spraying for a time and apart from a few Whirlwind sorties later that year, the technique was abandoned as the requirement diminished. The value of spraying operations had been proved, but by early 1955 the tide had irrevocably turned in Malaya. The establishment of the jungle forts had ended the inaccessibility of the remote jungle areas and at the same time provided the jungle dwelling Sakai with very welcome protection from terrorist demands. It was still vital, however, both to maintain the advances so far achieved and to keep up the pressure on the terrorists by mounting jungle sweeps by the military to make their position ultimately untenable. In both these aspects of the anti-terrorist campaign the helicopter had an essential role to play.

TYPES OF RAF HELICOPTER USED IN THE MALAYAN EMERGENCY

The further development of the helicopter role in Malaya in the 1950s depended on the introduction of the Sycamore to replace the Dragonfly and of the Whirlwind Mk 4 to replace the S-55 from which it was derived.

Introduction of the Sycamore Mk 14 in Malaya

What follows is an account of the Sycamore's first appearance in Malaya, the experiences which dictated its final Service form and its relationship to the Dragonfly for which it was the proposed replacement.

A comparison of the Sycamore with the Dragonfly in 1949 when it was first proposed to set up a Casualty Evacuation Flight showed little to choose between the two aircraft. The Sycamore was ruled out at the time for two reasons: it was not yet available and the low sweep of its main rotor was thought to be a disadvantage in jungle clearings. In addition the medical authorities were at that time dissatisfied with the athwartships stowage for casualties. In late 1952 when much more was known about the Sycamore and plans were being made to introduce it in the SAR role, the Vice Chief of the Air Staff came to the conclusion that the Sycamore was likely to be a great improvement on the Dragonfly and that if tropical trials confirmed current opinion, FEAF's doubts would disappear.(20) It was therefore arranged that as soon as the Sycamore Mk 10 at AAEE Boscombe Down had completed its trials there it would go to the Far East for tropical trials, still under the aegis of Boscombe Down, after which it would be handed over to FEAF for operational assessment.

The Sycamore was delivered to Singapore in a Bristol Freighter belonging to the Bristol Aeroplane Company in early 1953 and the Boscombe Down team then got down to work. Servicing was carried out by a small team advised by one of the manufacturers' representatives, David Vicary, who was accompanied by an enthusiastic member of their sales department, Alex Langfield. The helicopter pilots from the Casualty Evacuation Flight, who now formed the nucleus of No 194 Squadron and were acutely conscious of the marked difference in aircraft performance between flight into jungle clearings and over open airfields, watched the conduct of these trials with considerable surprise. Vertical climbs without airspeed were measured in light wind conditions by climbing to 2000 feet while formating on a Land Rover driving down wind along the runway at the same speed as the wind under the direction of an observer with a hand held anemometer. The squadron pilots knew well that the dramatic effects on the rotor of the lightest wind, when at the limits of power, could be clearly seen against a background of trees but would scarcely register on the instruments normally available for this kind of test flying. As the days went by surprise became tinged with impatience as the squadron pilots awaited their chance to fly this new aircraft and discover what it could really do: how many passengers could it lift from a clearing and at what height?(21) After a week or so the Boscombe Down team became dissatisfied with the irregularity of their results and transferred the trials to Kuala Lumpur in case more representative conditions could be found there. Consistent readings, however, were still not obtained and after another two or three weeks it was found that the wooden rotor blades, already far from new when the aircraft arrived, had suffered severe deterioration owing to the climatic conditions. Such defects as the swelling of the wooden members, the failure of glue joints and, perhaps most damaging to morale, dry rot had appeared and could be remedied only at Bristol.(22) Any further delay to the Boscombe Down team, however, was unacceptable both to them and to FEAF, and they returned home in mid March.

Fortunately the blade deterioration had not occurred before the squadron pilot who was to carry out the operational trials (Flight Lieutenant J R Dowling) had been converted to type. In this instance, conversion to type consisted of two hours' dual to first solo, one and a half hours' running landings and engine-off landings, and half an hour's night flying. In retrospect this allowance would seem hardly enough but in these particular circumstances it had to suffice.

The set of replacement blades arrived a month later and operational trials began at once. The new blades were in fine condition at the outset and this was thought to be the reason why no noticeable deterioration had occurred by the time the trials ended three months later in June 1953.(23) The original blade problem was thus submerged and no recognisable indication was present of the trouble which was to follow much later. In the light of subsequent events it would seem almost certain that the declining performance of the aircraft during the operational trials and noted in the trials report was due to blade distortion not identifiable by visual inspection rather than to engine deterioration as was suspected at the time.

The aircraft remained based at Kuala Lumpur but operated throughout Malaya, on occasions undertaking detached operations lasting several days accommpanied by the permanent servicing team (Sergeant Feeley, LAC Williams and Mr Vicary of the Bristol Aeroplane Company).

The progress of these operational trials was of the greatest consequence in the development of the helicopter role for many years to come and the manner in which they were conducted was unusual in many respects. The Sycamore, for example, though part of No 194 Squadron, was operated exclusively by the pilot detailed for the task.

The all important superiority of the Sycamore's vertical climb performance in still air over that of the Dragonfly was immediately apparent (although it deteriorated noticeably during the trial period). Further advantages were the relatively comfortable seating position (with pilot and observer side by side); the feeling of positive control which had been noticeably lacking in the Dragonfly; and the provision of a centre of gravity adjustment under the pilot's control, achieved by the electrical pumping of fluid between two tanks sited in the front and rear of the aircraft. What really established the aircraft in pilots' eyes, however, was the determination of the manufacturers to make whatever changes were needed as the result of operational experience on the direct advice of their service representative in the field, who, it was discovered later, was in almost daily communication with his Company to which he reported everything that occurred and most of what was said, including crewroom comment. When normal RAF supply channels produced no positive results, he would obtain any special spares he needed direct from his company via the BOAC Comet service then newly operating into Singapore. The serviceability rate of the Sycamore therefore was always highly satisfactory.(24)

The trials lasted for just under three months, with some 100 hours flying in all the roles undertaken by the Dragonfly, and including some special communications flights for the High Commissioner. Because of its high serviceability rate the Sycamore was a very valuable operational asset to No 194 Squadron, then in a particularly difficult phase of its initial growth and suffering at the same time from severe technical problems with the Dragonfly rotor heads. It was hardly surprising, therefore, that the Sycamore began its operational life rather sooner than had been intended. On 10 April 1953, only three days after operational practice flights had begun, a casualty occurred in a clearing being cut for practice and training purposes by troops of 22 SAS, the position being only fifteen minutes flying time from Kuala Lumpur in an area known as Ulu Langat.* The Sycamore, as the only serviceable helicopter available at Kuala Lumpur at the time, was used for the task and successfully lifted the casualty into the nearby British Military Hospital.

The final report on the Sycamore operational trials contained no surprises for the manufacturers because they had been kept so well informed throughout. Indeed the flow of information they had received from their technical representative in the Far East had been put to good use in modifying their Sycamore Mk 4, and consequently when the Air Ministry and the Ministry of Supply approached them to discuss the matter, practical solutions to the problems raised were, for the most part, already in existence. The initiative shown by the manufacturers, and the expense to which it had put them, had much to do with the substantial orders for production aircraft (Mk 14) which swiftly followed, and first deliveries to Malaya to replace the Dragonfly were being made within the year. A total of 178 Mk 14 Sycamores were eventually manufactured, of which the RAF and the Ministry of Supply received 115. Fifty went to the German Air Force, three to the Belgians, nine to the Royal Australian Navy and one to the Royal Australian Air Force.(25)

The Sycamore had certain handling peculiarities, the most prominent being direct manual cyclic control and powerful spring trimmers to balance stick forces. It was also necessary to displace the stick in opposition to these trimmers before take-off in order to avoid moving forward or rolling to the left during take-off. See Appendix 1. The lowness of the rotor blades, originally thought to be a disqualifying disability, was always a matter of concern when passengers were entering or leaving the aircraft and when there was foliage in and around landing sites, as there invariably was, but handling techniques and careful stick positioning were usually able to reduce these risks satisfactorily.(26)

The Sycamore might therefore seem an especially awkward aircraft, but apart from the problems of dual control, caused by the provision in the Sycamore Mk 14 of a single central collective lever, something of the same impression might be obtained when comparing the handling qualities of an advanced sports car with those of an old fashioned family saloon of equal power. In fact the analogy would be particularly apt; the initial discomfort of feeling the stick forces in contrast to the neutral feel

---

*The Ulu Langat clearing, considerably enlarged and thoroughly cleared, was used over the next four years as a pilot training clearing for crews at Kuala Lumpur and was regarded as a good example of what a standard clearing should be.

Operational trials with the Sycamore Mk 10 in Ulu Langat clearing near Kuala Lumpur in 1953.

The Mk 14 sycamore could carry 2 stretchers athwartships (but rarely used the upper stowage). A stretcher was sometimes not available and had to be manufactured 'on the spot'. The passenger doors enlarged in the Mk 14 to facilitate stretcher carriage are clearly shown.

of the hydraulic controls in the Dragonfly and Whirlwind was swiftly overcome by the Sycamore's rapid and precise response to its controls. The feeling of positive and direct contact with the main rotor through the stick gave a feeling of confidence and provided an immediate warning of the need to make adjustments to the flexible tabs on the blade trailing edges, by which the vibration caused by tracking and aerodynamic balancing errors had to be corrected with annoying frequency. Apart from these frequent rotor blade adjustment requirements, the Sycamore had a very satisfactory serviceability rate compared with both the Dragonfly and the Whirlwind Mk 4.

The Sycamore was regarded with enthusiasm from the start in Malaya because of its advantages over the Dragonfly in cabin size and performance, its positive handling characteristics and larger control margins, and its high serviceability rate. It was a stimulating aircraft to fly and, with its positive stick feel and apparent stability, it came as a great relief after the Dragonfly. For the first half of its 20 years in RAF service it shared with the Whirlwind Mks 2 and 4 all the helicopter tasks undertaken by the RAF. As a result it was usually compared with the Whirlwind and often to its disadvantage because of its smaller cabin space. But in some circumstances, particularly at heights of 3000 feet and above and at high temperatures as in Cyprus or Kenya, it proved superior to the Whirlwind Mk 2 in performance. Nevertheless the Sycamore was originally adopted as a light helicopter to replace the Dragonfly while the Whirlwind was described as a medium helicopter and thought of as a troop carrier. That the Sycamore was frequently a satisfactory, and sometimes even a better alternative in some theatres to the newer Whirlwind Mk 2 was a tribute to its advanced design, which dated from the mid 1940s. It became very popular with the pilots and when the last Dragonfly was replaced by the Sycamore in July 1956 there were few regrets and many long sighs of relief.

Introduction of the Whirlwind Mk 2/4 in Malaya

The Whirlwind, unlike the Sycamore, was not a new design, but a British copy of the American Sikorsky S-55 built under licence by Westland. It had the standard twist grip throttle and hydraulically assisted controls for cyclic stick and collective lever only, as in the Dragonfly. With its rotor head and blades derived from the S-51 it had obvious similarities in handling, but nevertheless represented a considerable step forward from the Dragonfly.

The Whirlwind was the first in a line of Sikorsky helicopters using the configuration in which the engine was housed in the nose with the pilot above and behind it, an arrangement which allowed a relatively capacious cabin directly beneath the rotor head and, combined with a larger offset of the flapping hinges, permitted loading and unloading without the very awkward centre of gravity compensatory adjustments necessary in the Dragonfly where the whole cabin was forward of the rotor head. In addition the Whirlwind had the advantage of a large cabin seating ten passengers.

Malay troops deplaning by rope from a Whirlwind Mk 4 of No 155 Squadron in Malaya in 1957.

Deplaning from a landed Mk 4 Whirlwind.

Disappointment however was to follow because the aircraft turned out to be decidedly unsatisfactory in performance. It had been assumed, reasonably, that the British version of an American aircraft already in service would be broadly similar to its forbear in this respect and although the Whirlwind had undergone Ministry of Supply trials it had not been possible for any of these to take place in Malaya. Demonstrations too could be misleading: for example, in 1951 an S-55 belonging to Westland Aircraft Ltd took part in an Army exercise on Salisbury Plain and with judiciously arranged refuelling on a cool day and a brisk wind flew several times with ten passengers on board. It was also claimed that the aircraft could carry six stretcher cases and an attendant,(27) whereas in severe conditions in Malaya, when the S-55 would be limited to four passengers the Whirlwind would be struggling to lift two.(28)

Worse, an anomaly in the redesigned fuel system resulted in some 40 gallons in the rear tanks being unusable in flight and in consequence the actual payload would be reduced to one soldier.(29) Even when this anomaly had been removed together with various safety features (including the fire extinguishing system and self sealing fuel tanks) the aircraft was still substantially heavier than the S-55 because certain parts were constructed from standard gauge materials and when the British standard varied from the American the thicker had to be used. Further, in these early days of helicopter operations it was not yet widely understood that a five per cent increase in the basic weight of the aircraft (which was approximately the increase in the weight of the Whirlwind over that of the S-55) was not a simple matter of a small reduction in range, but required a compensatory reduction in cabin payload (which could itself be as little as 11 per cent of the total weight). In limit conditions a variation in weight of less than one per cent could make the difference between a successful 200 feet a minute vertical climb and failure to rise from the ground cushion—and in Malaya that was often the same as being unable to take off at all.

The Whirlwind Mk 4 was derived from the Mk 2 by altering the supercharger ratio from 10.1 to 12.1. The purpose of this modification was twofold: to improve performance at heights of 3000 feet and above,* and provide an emergency reserve of power below that height by permitting overboosting of the engine when vitally necessary. It was left to the pilot not to misuse this facility, which could be employed by merely turning the throttle twist grip. No mechanical obstruction existed to prevent this being done and in consequence there was a considerable

---

*The need for improved performance at higher altitudes was brought about by the changing character of anti-terrorist operations in 1954 and the need for the security forces to penetrate the more remote and mountainous jungle areas. The supercharger ratio change conferred the minimum improvement necessary to permit operations at higher altitudes.

risk of engine damage—leading to an engine change or at best a period of unservice-ability while a special inspection was carried out—if overboosting had to be used. Additionally, it was easy enough for overboosting to occur accidentally either through mishandling or as an instinctive reaction to a dangerous situation. As a result, pilots' reports of such occurrences would on occasion take on some of the character of a confession and it says much for their self-discipline that there was never any evidence to suggest that these mishaps were being concealed.

The driving force behind the accelerated introduction of the Whirlwind into service in Malaya was the urgent need to relieve and then replace the hard worked Naval S-55s. High level discussions about the supply of additional S-55s from the United States were proving inconclusive and throughout 1954 the overriding preoccupation was the rate at which Whirlwinds could be obtained as an alternative. Further, as the S-55s were dependent on American spares the arrival of the Whirlwinds—after intense pressure—came as a considerable relief politically.(30)

However, even when a grossly inadequate performance had been improved by the measures described above, a further disappointment was to follow. Weighing and reweighing the aircraft as various items of equipment were removed revealed unexpected anomalies and, belatedly, the fact that if the aircraft was weighed with the blades on, the recorded centre of gavity position varied with the position of the blades.(31) More disturbing was the discovery that continuous flight with the centre of gravity position near either end of its permissible range—a state of affairs which the pilot would hardly notice because of the greatly improved control range as compared with the Dragonfly—caused a drastic reduction in the expected life of the main rotor drive shaft.(32)

The engine installation in the Whirlwinds, both Mk 2 and Mk 4, was the Pratt and Whitney Wasp which was also used in the Harvard, and of which large surplus stocks were available—some 300 in 1955. These engines were overhauled by BOAC under contract and subsequently modified for helicopter use by Alvis with dollar purchased conversion kits.(33) At times throughout their service in Malaya—where helicopter engines would spend a much higher proportion of their time at full power than would a fixed wing installation—the Wasp engines suffered from a number of faults. These included unexplained power deficiencies, very frequent magneto defects, oil starvation and consequent mechanical collapse, as well as incorrect assembly clearances, in the tappets for example. Starter troubles were also com-mon.(34) That the Whirlwind Mk 4 was eventually employed with success in Malaya was therefore a triumph for the RAF engineering staffs and to some extent for the pilots as well.

For the latter the Whirlwind Mk 4, when serviceable, was pleasanter and easier to fly than the Dragonfly except for its awkward power limitations. Although it had full hydraulic assistance in cyclic and collective controls it could be flown successfully for short periods in manual control in the event of hydraulic failure. Accurate flying in manual control however was an art which had to be acquired; the main difficulty lay in resisting the somewhat heavy lateral stick force which increased in proportion to the forward speed.*

The Whirlwind was provided with duplicate hydraulic systems to guard against total failure, but such failures could and occasionally did occur. Duplication however did not extend to the operating jacks at the rotor head, and there was also a condition in which failure in one part of the system could cause all the hydraulic fluid—including that in the serviceable part of the system—to be exhausted. Regular practice flights in full manual control were therefore introduced at the outset, pilots being required to fly for about ten minutes before completing an airfield landing in full manual control.

At first this exercise had to be carried out monthly by every pilot and it was considered adequate if a pilot reverting to manual control in a genuine emergency could under Malayan conditions reach an open space or even an Auster strip in up to 30 minutes' flying at 45 knots—which was normally possible. Pilots with greater physical strength might manage a slightly higher speed or a slightly longer period.(35)

In October 1955, however, practice flights in manual control were forbidden in Malaya pending the installation of an emergency servo control modification.(36) The emergency servo system consisted of supplying engine oil pressure to assist the pilot with the lateral stick forces encountered when the hydraulic servo systems failed; it by no means balanced the heavy forces encountered, but merely reduced the side loading on the stick to some extent.

In February 1956 the restriction on practice flights in manual control was lifted, but mandatory monthly practices were not reintroduced, probably because flying hours were too valuable. It was also an uncomfortable and therefore unpopular exercise. Thereafter manual control came to be regarded as a great misfortune and one pilot who experienced it in May 1958, in spite of the assistance provided by the emergency servo system, was so alarmed that although there was an Auster strip only a mile or so behind him, he did not dare to attempt the turn necessary to reach it. Instead, he laboured on for about 20 minutes in the approximate direction in which he was facing until he came to a small padang (village green) where he made a running landing under only partial control and had to brake the aircraft so fiercely that the tail cone jerked up into the main rotor disc causing

---

*The reactions of pilots to this feature provided a very revealing insight into their attitudes and opinions.

considerable damage. He was warmly congratulated on his survival and on avoiding the trees at the end of the padang.(37) Such was the shift in the official attitude to flight in manual control in the course of the first four years of operations.

POLICY DEVELOPMENTS TO MEET THE DEMAND FOR HELICOPTER SUPPORT IN MALAYA

By 1954 the problem of providing enough helicopters to meet the commitment in Malaya was causing the greatest concern at the highest political and military levels and a surge of activity in the policy-making and engineering fields. Time had always been short: with no tactical helicopter force previously envisaged, the task had been to assemble within a few months of Sir Gerald Templer's arrival as Director of Operations in late 1952 a fleet of suitable helicopters and the facilities for keeping them serviceable. Hence the use of the Naval S-55s as a stopgap and the plan to replace them with RAF Whirlwinds after a year, at the beginning of 1954.(38)

The commitment to the Director of Operations was plain: to provide a helicopter force to meet his clearly defined requirements. It should consist, according to his calculations, of enough medium helicopters to lift two infantry companies in different parts of the Federation on any one day, and periodically to lift the Federal Reserve Battalion of four infantry companies.(39) Further, by the beginning of 1955 medium helicopter support (Whirlwinds or S-55s) would be required to start one deep jungle operation every month and complete any previous operation; provide reliefs for two operations in progress; carry out 21 area domination operations and provide six airlifts of 90 men each against opportunity targets. In addition, up to five jungle forts required regular relief every six months and eight required monthly visits by teams of administrators.

For the light helicopters (Dragonflys or Sycamores) the task was estimated at two casualty evacuations, three communications and two tactical reconnaissance sorties every day.

For these tasks a minimum of ten medium and ten light helicopters would be required at any one time, or an establishment of 18 in each case.(40) To meet this requirement it was planned to provide 17 Whirlwinds plus three in reserve and 14 Sycamores with a gradual build up of Single Pioneers to undertake part of the communications task. As a precaution against delay in delivery, arrangements were also made to retain the Naval squadron of S-55s in Malaya at least until April 1955.(41)

It was a precaution which was soon to be justified: by mid 1954 the delays in the manufacture and clearance of the Whirlwind were causing considerable concern and the Ministry of Supply 'Controller of Aircraft release' (CA release) for the Sycamore

Mk 14 which was due to replace the Dragonfly in the latter part of 1954 was also taking longer than expected. As a result the Air Ministry, mindful of General Templer's warning that the rapid build up of the helicopter force to its planned size was essential to success in the anti-terrorist campaign,(42) applied heavy pressure to the Ministry of Supply but was eventually forced to circumvent all normal procedures (including financial) (43) to arrange despatch by sea in May 1954 of both Whirlwinds and Sycamores before the pending CA releases were obtained.(44)

As the Sycamore had already undergone a brief operational trial period the haste with which it was despatched to the Far East did no harm. It performed well from the outset and progressively replaced the Dragonfly between October 1954 and July 1956.(45)

The Whirlwind however was in dire trouble immediately. The change in the super-charger ratio which produced the Mk 4 had been no more than a last minute attempt to improve performance for Malayan conditions (46)—the first supercharger modification being carried out at Seletar when the aircraft arrived there in mid 1954. It failed however to disguise the Whirlwind's gross inadequacy in other respects, and the fact that the Whirlwind's payload did not match even that of the Sycamore and was only marginally better than that of the Dragonfly (47) caused consternation among the RAF and Army authorities in Malaya, as did the revelation that some 40 gallons of fuel in the rear tanks—often the maximum fuel load in Malaya—was unusable in flight as already explained.(48)

The consequences of this setback could have been of the utmost seriousness as the success of forthcoming operations depended on the availability of the 10 S-55s a day (or their equivalent) as had been promised. 'I regret to tell you,' wrote the AOC Malaya to the Director of Operational Requirements (Air), 'that your wretched Whirlwind is a complete washout, mainly because of its average increase in weight of 374 pounds above the S-55 and its fantastic fuel system ... Apart from this the workmanship and inspection of the aircraft has been appalling ... However, the significant feature is that it cannot do the job for which we have it ...'(49) And by now the problem had reached ministerial level.(50)

The solution proposed by the new Director of Operations, General Bourne, in a report to the Chiefs of Staff (30 November 1954) was to retain No 848 Squadron beyond April 1955 and until further notice against his reiterated demand for 10 S-55s (or their equivalent) a day.(51) The eight S-55s which remained in No 848 Squadron were expected to be reduced by wastage to six by December 1954; of these three or four could be available each day and by then there would also be four or five Whirlwind Mk 4s. If each of these carried between half and two thirds of the payload of the S-55, the daily availability would still be no more than the equivalent of six S-55s.(52) General Bourne did not describe this as merely inad-

A Whirlwind Mk 4 of No 155 Squadron in a training clearing in Malaya.

Troops deplaning by rope from a Sycamore Mk 14 of No 194 Squadron in Malaya in 1956.

equate; it would quite definitely place very severe restrictions on prospective operations, a statement which indicated the status which the helicopter had achieved after three years of activity. His recommendation therefore was for a further application to the United States to obtain more S-55s.(53)

The RAF was not alone in the Whirlwind fiasco. Five Naval Whirlwind Mk 1s (similar to the RAF Mk 2s) had been sent out to support the S-55s in No 848 Squadron when it had become known that it was to be retained in Malaya beyond the middle of 1954 and would therefore become a wasting force. With the same 10.1 supercharger ratio as the Mk 2, the Mk 1 was even more unsuitable than the Mk 4 for service in Malaya (54) and suffered from all its other defects. It could not be said however that the Mk 1 had been forced into service with undue haste, although it might be argued that the intention had never been to operate it inside Malaya but merely to use it as a replacement for the S-55 in the anti-submarine and SAR roles. The Mk 1s were therefore rejected even as support for the Sycamores, which were already being described as highly satisfactory and were normally carrying a useful load of three men in the communications role.(55)

A detailed examination of the situation by the Air Ministry and the Admiralty then followed at the end of which two conclusions were reached; first, that the five Mk 1s should be returned to the SAR role for which they had been intended, and second that there was no prospect of re-engining the RAF Whirlwinds before 1957, by which time the twin engined twin rotor Bristol 173 on order for SAR duties and as the Whirlwind replacement should be in service.(56) It was also agreed that an approach to the United States for more S-55s would be unwise as the original one year only diversion of No 848 Squadron from the NATO area had required the authority of the President himself (57) and the question of the squadron's with-drawal from Malaya might therefore be raised—the United States being generally unenthusiastic about giving assistance in colonial problems.

The solution therefore was to reduce aircraft weight by clearing the Mk 4 to fly without fire equipment, replacing self-sealing tanks with bag tanks and obtaining from the Ministry of Supply a list of all the equipment and structural members (cabin doors, cowlings etc) which could be removed for special operations.(58) Urgent action was also to be taken to modify the fuel system and remove the anomaly of the unusable fuel. By these means it was hoped to reduce the performance gap between the Whirlwind Mk 4 and the S-55 from three troops carried to one, and, by retaining No 848 Squadron indefinitely, to meet the trooplift requirement of 10 S-55s a day with a mixture of S-55s and Whirlwind Mk 4s by the end of March 1955.(59)

Meanwhile, the Air Ministry suggested, the Sycamore could be used to some extent for trooplifts. The objection raised by FEAF had been that its low ground clearance made it unsuitable, but in fact the fuselage ground clearance of the Sycamore

Mk 14 was greater than that of the Whirlwind and its smaller rotor ground clearance could often be offset by pilot handling technique (60)—a view which was fully justified when in later operations in Malaya the Sycamores carried out all helicopter tasks required, including troop deployment.

Technical and Supply Problems in the Whirlwinds and Sycamores in Malaya

Both Whirlwinds and Sycamores suffered severely during the main period of their employment in Malaya (1954–60) from chronic shortages of various classes of spares, and from incorrectly assembled or badly manufactured components sent out from the United Kingdom. The Whirlwinds, for example, were plagued from the outset by bad electrical connections and soldering, and by the inadequate weatherproofing of components.(61)

By February 1955 the modifications to the Whirlwind fuel system had been incorporated, but in May a long saga of servicing problems began when the first signs of trouble appeared in the wooden rotor blades of the Sycamore, a fault which remained uncured for the next four years.(62) The Whirlwind rotor also was not immune to blade problems as in August FEAF Headquarters reported that the Whirlwind rotor blades headed the list of unserviceability problems with servo control jacks in second place.(63)

In addition to the difficulties already mentioned (starter motor troubles in both aircraft types, a modification to the emergency servo system in the Whirlwind, and a succession of faults in its Wasp engines)* there were other problems, notably a periodic slipping of the torque limiting clutch in the Sycamore transmission,† often caused by inadequate degreasing of the units before despatch to Malaya (an aircraft crashed in 1956 in consequence) and tail cone attachment difficulties in the Whirlwind which led to a fatal accident and the consequent grounding of the fleet.

One of the most constant sources of trouble, however, was the unexplained variations in performance which afflicted the Sycamore rotor blades (see p 68). A modification consisting of a new coating for the blades only added to the trouble as it did not achieve the constant blade performance improvement required and its abandonment was followed by a critical shortage of unmodified blades.(64) That radical changes of this kind could be carried out only at Filton, where the rotor blades could be subsequently whirled and balanced on a special test tower, added to the problem.

---

*See p 74.

†A device to protect the main rotor and transmission from shock loading in the event (frequently experienced) of an accidental engagement of the centrifugal main clutch due to a burst of power during engine starting.

A quite separate joint service decision in London to colour all helicopter rotor blades medium sea grey on top aggravated the difficulty because the result in Malaya was an increase in internal blade temperature of 25 degrees Fahrenheit compared with white painted blades.(65) Meanwhile although the manufacturers were making strenuous efforts to solve the Sycamore blade problems, they were proving very difficult to identify. One line of experiment was an attempt to devise a finish which would exclude the damp Malayan atmosphere. Eventually a modification involving an adjustment to the cordwise C of G was made and shortly afterwards, in February 1959, a Sycamore suffered the first complete blade failure in flight with fatal consequences for all on board. Two months later an exactly similar incident led to the grounding of the whole Sycamore force for a complete re-examination of the rotor blade problem.(66) Almost exactly a year later a new standard of rotor blade was ready for testing at Seletar and between March and July 1960 the Sycamore progressively resumed its original role in Malaya.

However much helicopter operations in Malaya might be coloured for individuals by such traumatic occurrences as the Whirlwind tail cone failure and the two complete Sycamore rotor blade failures, the fact remained that the helicopter force had been created in response to an urgent operational requirement and without the opportunity for adequate planning. The assembling of the required number of aircraft was only one aspect of the problem; the absence of organised pilot training at the start was largely offset by the experience and flying background of the pilots selected for the task (nearly all were over 35). The lack of technicians with helicopter experience was partly overcome by the expertise of the RAF engineering branch, assisted from time to time by representatives from the aircraft and engine manufacturers; hydraulic controls and metal blades, for example, were fitted to Mk 2 Dragonflys to convert them into Mk 4s by airmen who had never previously worked on helicopters.(67)

The technical problems in the Whirlwind would have had less impact had there been an adequate spares backing; in November 1955, for example, seven out of 17 Whirlwinds were unserviceable awaiting spares from the United Kingdom.(68) There had been no data however from which to construct a satisfactory spares supply system and no time to establish one; nor were the manufacturers geared to meet the demand or experienced enough to foresee the problems which might arise. The Sycamores were not plagued by the same general technical unreliability and their spares supply was not placed under the same degree of strain. What made the defects in their main rotor blades so much more serious was that the remedy could be applied only at Filton and as the wooden blades were largely hand made no rapid increase in production was possible to meet changes in standard of finish.

In sum, in terms of the all important factor of regular availability, the Whirlwind in one of its best years, 1956, achieved a serviceability rate no higher than 41 per cent and the entire Whirlwind force was out of the line on four occasions in 1957 for technical reasons.(69) Before its long grounding in 1959 the Sycamore had a decidedly better record: in 1957, an average year, its overall serviceability rate, was 63 per cent.(70)

ADDITIONAL HELICOPTER ROLES IN THE MALAYAN CAMPAIGN

Once the helicopter force in Malaya had reached the minimum size needed to meet the requirements of the Director of Operations—that is, broadly speaking by late 1954—its task was to maintain the roles already developed for as long as the war went on. The Sycamores progressively replaced the Dragonflys of No 194 Squadron between October 1954 and August 1956 and by late 1955 No 155 Squadron was in operation at full strength with Whirlwind Mk 4s. The roles of tactical trooping, casualty evacuation and communications were successfully fulfilled, and—characteristically with helicopters—further roles were added from time to time.

Apart from crop spraying, which had already proved its strategic value in the anti-terrorist war, by far the most important new role was the use of helicopters in urban areas when disorder or rioting was occurring or threatened. The Dragonfly had shown the importance of aerial patrolling during the Maria Hertogh Muslim riots of 1950 (see p 44) and during the much more serious political riots in Singapore in October 1956 three Whirlwinds of No 155 Squadron played a very important part in giving aid to the civil power in collaboration with the police and the Army, flying 136 sorties for a total of 90 flying hours.

After eight years of emergency regulations in Singapore including the death penalty for carrying arms, helicopters could operate without fear of opposition. The weapons they used were of three kinds: tear gas to disperse crowds, indelible dye to make participants identifiable later and propaganda leaflets. In addition, helicopters could often disperse crowds, and prevent them from reforming later, entirely by their own action and without summoning the ground forces; a crowd of 200 students, for example, stoning vehicles on the Bukit Timah road was dispersed by the use of tear gas and indelible dye.

The helicopter's greatest advantage was its ability to monitor the situation continuously from a platform immune from retaliation and to direct police and Army patrols rapidly to wherever they were needed, so generating an awed respect for the security forces and their capacity for rapid response. The part which the helicopter played in Singapore in 1956 was therefore of considerable significance, and the results were to have far reaching consequences. 'The successful suppression of these political riots,' wrote the officer in charge of the Singapore Government's Information Service, Mr G G Tompson, 'enabled the leaders to be removed and Lee Kuan Yew to meet the political challenge as prime minister in 1961–62;

otherwise the story would have been quite different.' The riots were thus 'a critical point in the history of Singapore'.(71)

Before the riots of 1956 helicopters had not been written formally into Singapore's internal security contingency plans and there was the seemingly inevitable problem of radio incompatibility. But from then on helicopters were invariably called upon to assist the police whenever the situation demanded,(72) and in September 1957 two Sycamores were detached to Hong Kong in readiness for the October elections; there was no trouble however. In the same year a modification was developed which permitted the safe launching from the Whirlwind of tear gas grenades in clusters of eight in a three second period with a 10 yard accuracy from heights of between 100 and 200 feet.(73)

One local modification found necessary was a type of stretcher cage fitted beneath the Dragonfly in which to carry dead terrorists back for identification. It was no longer necessary to decapitate them and send only their heads back, as had once been done (see p 34), but with the security forces beginning to gain the upper hand after 1953 there were enough of the terrorists to be transported to make their carriage outside the aircraft eminently desirable in a tropical climate. A special body carrier was therefore constructed to be fixed beneath the fuselage, making loading and unloading simple and expeditious.(74)

Among the many communications flights carried out by the helicopters those for the Director of Operations were of special interest. In Malaya the terrain offered infinite opportunities for ambush and for General Templer to travel by road was a difficult and dangerous procedure involving large troop deployments to secure the route and the use of a heavily armoured convoy, in all an operation which was expensive in manpower, uncomfortable and, not least, bad for the morale of those being visited. Additionally, the High Commissioner's taste for arriving at remote places by helicopter, usually unannounced for security reasons, resulted in a degree of alertness and purposeful activity whenever a passing helicopter landed unexpectedly, perhaps through fuel shortage, unserviceability or crew fatigue.(75)

The Paratrooping and Search and Rescue Roles

Paratrooping had been foreseen as a helicopter role at an early stage of operations and successful experiments had been carried out in the S-55s of No 848 Squadron during their initial performance trials in Malaya in 1953.(76) In fact, however, at the same time as the helicopter demonstrated its value as a paratrooping aircraft, it also virtually eliminated the parachute as a method of delivering troops in strength—it was obviously better to land them by helicopter wherever possible.

Since the first use in Malaya of paratroops from fixed wing aircraft during Operation Helsby in February 1952 (see p 47) considerable thought and training had been devoted to developing and improving the techniques of parachuting into jungle and a very satisfactory method had been discovered of using abseil gear to reach the ground once the parachute canopy had been lodged in the tree tops.(77)

Few opportunities, however, occurred for major paratrooping operations against the terrorists after 1954 because an expanding helicopter force was proving itself capable of landing a greater number of specialist troops in the jungle more quickly and with less risk of personal injury than could be parachuted from the fixed wing transport aircraft previously used.

When paratroops were used on combined operations they were usually the precursors of troop carrying helicopters, but if it was necessary to achieve an extremely accurate drop into a very small target area, the helicopter could be used to great effect, particularly when the objective was rescue and no clearing existed for the helicopter to land. Thus the technique for parachuting into trees became a specialised element of casualty evacuation and rescue operations, and proved to be of the greatest value on a number of occasions.

Drops were made from Whirlwinds at a height of 1000 feet with a forward airspeed of about 20 knots heading into wind and using static line parachute deployment. Ground speed was thus insignificant, the dropping zone was in full view of the paratroops and the drops could be made with full parachute deployment in the vertical position without swing or oscillation. Great accuracy could therefore be achieved with the minimum of practice by aircrews or ground troops. The beam fitted to the cabin roof beneath the gearbox for static line attachment was not used except by the despatcher because of the risk of the static line being fouled during the drop. Instead, an additional attachment point was fitted on the main fuselage member at the forward port side of the cabin. A felt cover was fitted to the cabin floor, the sliding door removed and the starboard undercarriage members covered with masking tape; no other preparation was required. On operational drops no more than three paratroops and a despatcher could be carried because each paratrooper had up to 80 lb of arms and equipment with him including the abseil gear for lowering himself to the ground after his canopy had lodged in the tree tops.(78)

It was the troops of 22 Special Air Service Regiment who developed and became the main exponents of jungle paratrooping. They supplied jungle clearing parties for the construction of helicopter landing zones and parachute trained doctors for the emergency treatment of casualties where no helicopter landing zone existed. In June 1956, however, a Far East Air Force Jungle Rescue Team was formed at the Far East Parachute School at Changi from volunteers and trained in parachuting into the jungle.(79) It corresponded to the Desert Rescue Teams in the Middle East and the Mountain Rescue Teams which were formed much later in the United Kingdom.

One example of their work may be recorded as it shows something of the conditions under which the rescue helicopters were operating.(80) In August 1957 a Valetta crashed at 4000 feet up a jungle covered ridge in central Malaya after completing a leaflet drop. The wreck was found by an AOP Flight Auster and it seemed scarcely possible that there could be any survivors. The FEAF Jungle Rescue Team, however, was flown to Kuala Lumpur to join the Special Air Service rescue team. A combined party of 12, including a doctor, were then flown by Whirlwind to near the site of the crash and parachuted into the trees. All completed the drop without injury and reached the wreck only two hours later.

So severe had been the impact of the crash that no part of the aircraft was immediately recognisable but closer inspection revealed the badly burned front portion beneath the twisted and wholly collapsed fuselage. Of the three aircrew and four RASC despatchers there was no sign until a roughly built shelter was discovered 30 yards from the wreck and then another 300 yards away with two of the RASC men inside. The other two had also survived but were attempting to walk out of the jungle. They were found by helicopter, supplied and told to rejoin the others. The three aircrew had all been killed but the four despatchers in the back of the aircraft had survived because they had received an emergency warning from the captain and were strapped into their rearward facing seats. All were burned to some extent as the aircraft exploded shortly after they left it. They then moved away from the crash, contrary to normal survival training, because they were afraid that there were terrorists in the area, and had been unable to find their way back although the second shelter they built was only 300 yards away.

The distance to the nearest road was some 10000 yards, two days' travel for a patrol and seven to ten days' with casualties. Eight members of the rescue team began preparing a helicopter landing zone using plastic explosives and mechanical saws supplied by helicopter parachute drop, and at the end of the second day six more men were parachuted in to help. By noon on the third day the landing zone was ready to receive a helicopter, and a Sycamore, operating from a nearby detachment specially set up for the occasion, began a shuttle service bringing in members of the Court of Inquiry and taking the casualties out one at a time (the altitude was 4000 feet).

On the fourth day the helicopter continued the shuttle intermittently, as the cloud base varied, lifting out the Court of Inquiry members and some of the rescue party while awaiting the return of the two survivors who had attempted to walk out (the helicopter could not afford to stop its engine to wait on the landing zone). At noon on the fourth day the two arrived back at the crash site and in the late afternoon the helicopter was able to get in and out of the landing zone twice more to lift them out.

The remaining members of the rescue team had to walk out because at that point the helicopter pilots declined, once the operational urgency had been removed, to attempt the very difficult landing zone approach again. In this they were acting wholly in accordance with established principle in the theatre, but it was also a decision of peculiar significance: acting on their own initiative, they had decided that once all the survivors had been taken out further risk to the aircraft was no longer justified. The need to conserve the aircraft, and its appreciation by all concerned, is therefore one of the insights which this rescue operation provides; it also illustrates the problems caused by the terrain and the use of underpowered helicopters, and not least the skill of the pilots and the degree of stress under which they worked.

For those operating helicopters in Malaya, paratrooping from them was important mainly in the rescue role as an extension of the casualty evacuation task and became indistinguishable from what was known elsewhere as 'search and rescue' over land. In December 1957 serious flooding in Ceylon led to a request for international assistance. Three Sycamores of No 194 Squadron were embarked on the American aircraft carrier Princeton and taken to Ceylon where they flew 105 hours in seven days on supply and evacuation duties, subsequently returning to Singapore by the same means.(81)

As the Malayan emergency drew to its close, the helicopter force was reduced in numbers and moved from Kuala Lumpur to Butterworth in August 1959. Trooplifting operations continued at a declining rate, but casualty evacuation remained a responsibility with, as an added task, a sea rescue standby for the Australian fighter squadron then stationed at Butterworth. The Sycamores could undertake winch operations over the sea and in February 1960 those at Butterworth were fitted with SARAH (Search and Rescue Aerial Homing) radar equipment which permitted search and rescue aircraft to home on a survivor.(82)

Thus the role of search and rescue was naturally assumed by the tactical helicopter force, having been its second (but not necessarily secondary) role throughout its life in Malaya from the time when it grew out of the Casualty Evacuation Flight, itself specifically established in 1950 for that role alone. This sequence of events, the quick transition from an identifiable search and rescue role to a much larger—but unquantifiable—tactical army support requirement was repeated in other overseas theatres, notably Cyprus.

SQUADRON FORMATIONS AND DEPLOYMENTS IN FEAF

The RAF Whirlwind squadron, No 155, was formed at Kuala Lumpur in September 1954 with most of its personnel, including the squadron commander, Sqn Ldr N H Jackson-Smith, drawn from No 194 Squadron which was already in residence there.

In formal terms the new squadron's roles were identical with those of No 194 Squadron although the intention was to use it mainly for trooplifting. However, the various technical problems already described prevented it from taking its full part in trooping until the second quarter of 1955. In June 1955 the Naval Mk 1 Whirlwinds which had been attached to the squadron in the forlorn hope of helping it through its early difficulties returned to Naval SAR duties in Europe (83) and the Mk 4 Whirlwinds, now under Sqn Ldr L L Harland, began to make their main contribution to the trooping task alongside No 848 Squadron.

By the end of 1955 the 20 Whirlwinds of No 155 Squadron with the 10 Sycamores and four Dragonflys of No 194, and the remaining S-55s of No 848, were just able to meet all reasonable demands for helicopter support. The improvement in availability also permitted a degree of decentralisation with the result that more permanent detachments could be located near the major scenes of operation, able to respond to opportunity demands—a far better practice than that of allocating temporary detachments for the duration of individual pre-planned operations. In May 1955, for example, three Whirlwinds and one Sycamore were deployed at Kluang in Johore in support of the 17th Gurkha Infantry Division, and one Sycamore was detailed to Ipoh in Perak in support of the 1st Federal Infantry Brigade. Operations in south, central and north Malaya were thus covered;(84) all the helicopters involved however remained under the direct tasking control of the Joint Operations Centre established in February 1954 at Kuala Lumpur.

In March 1956 the Whirlwind/S-55 force was redeployed to facilitate second line servicing: the Whirlwinds of No 155 Squadron were withdrawn from Kluang to Kuala Lumpur and No 848 Squadron was moved back from Kuala Lumpur to the Naval servicing base which was still at Sembawang whence it continued to provide the Kluang detachment in the south until December 1956. By then the S-55s had reached the end of their useful life and a series of accidents compelled the withdrawal of No 848 Squadron after an exacting tour of nearly four years in Malaya.(85)

The disestablishment of the S-55 squadron at the end of 1956 left 17 Whirlwinds of No 155 Squadron and 14 Sycamores of No 194 Squadron to meet all demands for helicopter support in Malaya, a target which they just succeeded in achieving. The demand for helicopter support began to fall away in 1957 as the situation in Malaya improved, a decline which—as fortune would have it—coincided with the growing technical problems with the Whirlwind.

Concurrent pressures to supply helicopters to the Middle East and to build up SAR units at home led the Air Ministry to carry out a worldwide survey of new requirements, which showed that there was a net shortage of Whirlwinds. Priorities had therefore to be adjusted. No 224 Group (which had replaced Air Headquarters Malaya on 31 August 1957 following Malayan independence) responded by offering in October 1957 to reduce their Whirlwind establishment by five, and after a further

Whirlwinds Mk 4 of No 155 Squadron near Kuala Lumpur in 1956.

A Sycamore Mk 14 of No 110 Squadron paying a regular visit to a jungle fort in North Malaya in the closing days of the 'Emergency'. (Pilot Flt Lt B Cann).

plea from the Air Ministry in November agreed to a total reduction of nine, leaving eight Whirlwinds and 14 Sycamores.(86) Shortly afterwards the Air Ministry decided that since the Whirlwind was limited by inadequate performance in Malaya and the Sycamore by cabin space for SAR work at home, it would be better to withdraw the Whirlwinds from Malaya and use them to replace the Sycamores in the SAR units at home, leaving the Malayan tasks to be carried out by Sycamores alone.

The latter had by this time acquired an excellent reputation in Malaya. In spite of continuing problems with rotor blade distortion, evidently caused by the high-temperature, high humidity atmosphere, the Sycamore's general serviceability rate was high—while that of the Whirlwind was very unsatisfactory and getting worse. Earlier fears about the low ground clearance of the Sycamore rotor had been dispelled by experience and the operational payload was scarcely less than that of the Whirlwind.

FEAF Headquarters readily agreed to the changeover and the Whirlwind rundown was due to be completed by early 1959.(87) By March 1959 No 224 Group was able to advise FEAF Headquarters that when RAF Kuala Lumpur was transferred to the Royal Malayan Air Force later in the year and RAF helicopters moved to the RAAF base at Butterworth to support residual operations near the Thai border, the whole helicopter support task, including tactical troop deployment, could be carried out with an establishment of 12 Sycamores.(88)

In the following month, however, the second of the two fatal Sycamore crashes caused by main rotor blade disintegration and the consequent grounding of the whole Sycamore force for a radical reappraisal of the rotor blade problem put a temporary stop to these plans.(89) As operations in Malaya still depended on the helicopter for troop deployment and casualty evacuation there could be no question of withdrawing the Whirlwinds from the Far East whatever the pressures in Europe or the Middle East. The five remaining Whirlwinds had therefore to stay in Malaya and even be reinforced by three from the United Kingdom. Nos 194 and 155 Squadrons were disbanded at Kuala Lumpur in June 1959 and together reformed as No 110 Suadron with five Whirlwinds. In August 1959 the squadron moved to RAAF Butterworth with an establishment of eight Whirlwinds, the remaining 13 Sycamores being stored at Seletar awaiting a solution of the rotor blade problem.(90)

The arrival of No 110 Squadron marked the beginning of the last chapter in the story of helicopter operations in Malaya and also formed a link with the second great occasion on which helicopters provided essential support to the ground forces in the Far East—the operations in Borneo.

One Whirlwind remained at Kuala Lumpur in support of mopping up operations in eastern central Malaya until the end of 1959, while the squadron's remaining seven

Whirlwinds, based at Butterworth, carried on with the main trooplifting and casualty evacuation task near the Thai border.* By the beginning of 1960 operations were concentrated in the north and the troops employed were mainly Malay, Australian and New Zealand. The helicopter crews, although still faced with the same difficult terrain, were no longer under the unremitting pressure of earlier years. The war had been won and although trooplifts and aeromeds continued in some degree until early 1963 the emergency ended formally in August 1960 when the atmosphere became more relaxed. Seaside Butterworth was much more congenial than the humid claustrophobic atmosphere of Kuala Lumpur and the flat open paddy fields were a welcome relief from the sinister jungle. Most families lived on Penang Island, then and until after the Borneo campaign a most popular leave centre.

In February 1960 the Sycamores began to emerge from their enforced retirement, trials being held at Kuala Lumpur with a new batch of rotor blades. The tests were satisfactory (91) and in the course of the next four months the Sycamores began once more to replace the Whirlwinds a year later than originally planned, the last of the Whirlwinds leaving in June 1960 and the thirteenth and final Sycamore arriving on the squadron in the following September. The modified Sycamore blades, combined with a new clearance to use an extra 2″ engine boost, were now giving a very satisfactory performance.(92)

Of special interest among Sycamore operations between the summer of 1960 and the end of 1962 were: the rescue in July 1960 (in conjunction with the FEAF Jungle Rescue Team) of two Australian pilots who had ejected into the jungle after a collision; and the lifting three months later of 200 men of the East Anglian Regiment by shuttle with four aircraft. In July 1962 a record lift of 582 troops and 9300 lb of freight was carried out by nine Sycamores. By the end of 1962 however operations had been reduced to the basic tasks of aeromed (a total of 822 had been carried out since the unit moved to Butterworth) and the regular communications flights round the jungle forts, a task known as Fort Express. Additionally, every six months or so two Sycamores were required to take part in internal security exercises in Singapore, helicopters having been included in these since the 1956 riots.(93)

From 1958 to 1960 as Sycamores replaced Whirlwinds (1958), Whirlwinds replaced Sycamores (1959) and Sycamores replaced Whirlwinds again (1960), aircraft type conversions for new pilots were included in the normal squadron operational training responsibilities. In addition, No 110 Squadron attempted some experimental night flying training in June 1961—the first helicopter night flying for those pilots who had undergone basic training at CFS before it became part of the syllabus. As for

---

*Casualty evacuations were now called aeromeds.

a formal CFS categorisation scheme, none was applied to No 110 Squadron until July 1962 (when crews found little difficulty in reaching a very satisfactory standard), although there had been periodic standardisation visits by a CFS helicopter team since 1955.(94)

There was a short hiatus in September 1962 when a fatal accident was found to have been caused by tail rotor blade disintegration.(95) All Sycamores tail rotor blades had then to be replaced by sets with a different blade finish—final proof, if any was still needed, that the use of wooden components in Malayan atmospheric conditions was a recipe for trouble.

In October 1962 one Sycamore was detached to Gan in support of the RAF Regiment which had been sent to the Maldives in response to civil unrest there (Operation Flair). The aircraft returned to Butterworth in February 1963. A Sycamore was again sent to Gan in September 1963 for SAR duties where it remained until June of the following year to be activated if required, although the crews were withdrawn in the previous October; the aircraft was never called upon to function in the SAR role.(96)

For the helicopters in Malaya 1963 was a period of transition between the end of Malayan operations and the start of the Borneo campaign, and throughout that year No 110 Squadron had concurrent responsibilities in both areas. The operations in Borneo began in December 1962 with the Brunei revolt and on Christmas Eve two Sycamores were flown to Seletar and taken to Brunei by Beverley to support the ground troops there.(97) The build up of helicopters in Borneo was to come mainly from the United Kingdom but the initial two Sycamores from No 110 Squadron—itself the resident helicopter garrison—were reinforced by a third in January and developed gradually into a permanent detachment continuing throughout the year. In addition, in July a long term detachment of six Whirlwinds Mk 10 from No 110 Squadron began operations at Kuching in Sarawak.

The second generation of RAF operational helicopters was now beginning to appear in the form of Belvederes and Whirlwind Mk 10s, turbine engined helicopters to replace their piston engined predecessors (Phase 3). The Mk 10 Whirlwinds began to arrive on No 110 Squadron in July 1963 and replaced the Sycamores on the Brunei detachment in September, moving to Labuan in February 1964.(98)

As Seletar was the new main helicopter base in the Far East No 110 Squadron found itself operating the Brunei and Kuching detachments through Seletar, while continuing to meet the Malayan support commitment from Butterworth.

Trooplifts were still continuing in the north of Malaya and in April 1963 a detachment of Sycamores was sent to Kroh in support of joint Malayan/Thai troop operations over the Thailand border; by July the cumulative total of aeromeds had reached 1221.(99)

From July 1963 Whirlwind Mk 10s gradually replaced the Sycamores, although the latter continued to support Malayan operations until September 1964 when they were finally withdrawn from the Far East with the exception of two retained at Seletar until May 1967 for VIP communications duties.

In January 1964 Seletar became the squadron base and Butterworth the detachment for the disappearing Malayan commitment, reduced by the latter part of 1964 to a search and rescue standby—with Whirlwind Mk 10s—on behalf of the Australian fighter squadron at Butterworth. Support for the jungle forts came to be provided by the new Royal Malaysian Air Force using Alouette helicopters and Pioneers, and RAAF Iroquois helicopters also began to carry out some of the tasks. The RAF Butterworth detachment was finally withdrawn to Seletar in October 1964 except for one Whirlwind Mk 10 left behind for SAR duties. All effort was now directed to Borneo.(100)

Helicopter Crewmen

From 1950 to 1965 helicopter crewmen were found from among servicing personnel. The need for them had been officially recognised at the time of the Casualty Evacuation Flight (1950-52) and they were formally included in the establishments of Nos 194 and 155 Squadrons at corporal or junior technician level. The shortage of helicopter ground crews, however, meant that this part of the establishment was rarely filled. As late as November 1954 No 194 Squadron still had no crewmen posted to it to fill its eight vacancies, and was selecting and training technicians as crewmen from among its own servicing personnel.(101) With the arrival of the Whirlwind with its passenger compartment separated from the pilot the need for crewmen became all the more urgent, but power limitations still prevented them from being carried on the final stages of operational sorties, and with the aircraft away from base the technician function of the crewman was still regarded as of first importance—a situation which still continued even with the growing frequency of maritime SAR tasks after 1960 when No 110 Squadron was based at Butterworth. The technical personnel chosen were trained to a perfectly acceptable standard on the squadron—winch operations were included in the training—and it was not until the end of 1965 that they were replaced in the Far East by senior NCO aircrew in the form of retrained flight engineers.(102)

Summary

Between 1952 and 1960, the formal end of the Malayan emergency, the total number of troops lifted by helicopter exceeded 110000. In the communications role 19000 passengers and two and a half million pounds of freight were carried. Between

1950 and 1960 almost exactly 5000 casualties were evacuated by helicopter in Malaya, numerous lives being saved in the process.(103) In addition, helicopters had been largely responsible for carrying the offensive to the terrorists' jungle hideouts, a major factor in their ultimate defeat.

So ended an era not merely for Malaya, but also for the helicopter which had begun its service as a very doubtful proposition and at best a useful adjunct to ground operations, and finally became established as an essential element in fighting the guerrilla kind of war.

THE INFLUENCE OF THE MALAYAN EXPERIENCE ON THE CHOICE OF THE NEXT GENERATION OF HELICOPTERS

From 1953 until the end of the Malayan emergency the normal helicopter roles in Malaya remained on the one hand casualty evacuation, communications (passengers and light freight mainly for the jungle forts), VIP transport and special tasks; and on the other tactical troop movements, logistic re-supply and heavy freight lifting (eg earth moving and construction gear to build light aircraft strips and the jungle forts). In both cases the choice of helicopter was natural and inevitable: the Dragonfly and its successor, the Sycamore, for the lighter tasks, the S-55 and its successor, the Whirlwind, for the heavier lifts.

There was however little chance at that stage of influencing the numerical balance between the larger and smaller types of helicopter because at no time was there enough of either to meet all demands. By the time that success was in sight in Malaya mounting demands for helicopters elsewhere led to a shift in priorities. In consequence, the choice of helicopters for Malaya continued to be dictated by the shortage of resources. Nevertheless, the theories generated by the Malayan experience as to the kind of helicopters needed were to have a profound influence on the next major stage in helicopter development.

The surprisingly disappointing performance of the Whirlwind Mk 4 in Malaya was one of the factors influencing the timely decision to abandon the larger and more powerful (but heavier) Leonides Major piston engined version and obtain instead the Gnome turbine engined Mk 10 which was to give many years of excellent service in the RAF. The need for a medium sized helicopter able to carry 15 fully armed troops or 5000 lb of freight was confirmed and provided much of the impetus which finally brought the Belvedere into existence. The Whirlwind Mk 10 and the Belvedere made up the RAF helicopter contribution to the Borneo campaign, in the course of which the helicopter was once again seen to be a crucial factor in operational success.

Argument tended to centre on the size of the helicopter in relation to the number for which financial resources were available; very little attention was paid to cruising speed in the 1950s. Unlike the American experience in Korea where little or no vertical performance was needed in a largely treeless terrain and where operations were normally conducted at or above the officially permitted aircraft all-up-weight, VTOL performance was what mattered in Malaya and ranges were generally very short. It was seemingly irrelevant, therefore, that an aircraft which could climb 200 feet vertically out of the jungle could then fly at only 60 knots.

Thus the British military requirement was for VTOL performance, payload and cabin space, and it was left to civil operators with their concern with flying time (ie expense) per pound weight or per passenger to demand higher cruising speeds. The relationship between cruising speed and the weight lifted in a given time by a given number of helicopters came to be recognised by the military only some years later when the shuttle type of operation became standard. Until then larger and more powerful helicopters were seen as the whole solution.

It was this attitude which explains, at least in part, why no steps were taken officially to propose the redevelopment of the autogiro with VTOL capability. It also explains by contrast the enormous civilian effort to build and demonstrate the Rotodyne. Meanwhile, in the early 1950s, RAF and Naval hopes were centred on the development of the twin engined, twin rotor Bristol 173 which seemed to be the aircraft most likely to provide the lift capacity required for both the trooplifting task and the anti-submarine role, and from which the Belvedere eventually emerged. Both the Gnome engined Whirlwind and the Belvedere appeared in 1960 and it was on these that the development of helicopter operations in Phase 3 were mainly to depend.

References to Chapter 3

1   No 194 Sqn ORB.

2   No 303 Wing ORB.

3   Pilots' log books.

4   Land/Air Warfare, No 7, Jan/Jun 1953, app A. AHB IIJ50/141/1/1.

5   No 303 Wing ORB.

6   Ibid.

7   Eyewitness report (Wg Cdr J R Dowling).

8   No 303 Wing ORB.

9   Land/Air Warfare, No 9, AHB IIJ50/141/1/1.

10   No 303 Wing ORB.

11   Ibid.

12   Ibid.

13   Ibid.

14   Ibid.

15   Ibid.

16   Ibid.

17   Air Clues, May 1955.

18   FEAF/MIS, Nov 1954, Pt II.

19   No 303 Wing ORB.

20   ACAS(OR), 15 Aug and 6 Oct 1952 in AHB ID6/463/Pt 2.

21   Eyewitness report (Wg Cdr J R Dowling).

22   FEAF ORB, 1953.

23   No 303 Wing ORB.

24   Eyewitness report (Wg Cdr J R Dowling).

25   C H Barnes, Bristol Aircraft since 1910, 1964.

26   Eyewitness report (Wg Cdr J R Dowling).

27   No 657 Sqn ORB.

28   COS(54) 376, 7 Dec 1954 in AHB ID6/463/Pt 4.

29   COS(55) 1, 3 Jan 1955 in AHB ID6/463/Pt 4.

30   AHB ID9/621/12/Pt 2.

31   AHQ Malaya ORB, Mar 1957.

32   No 224 Gp ORB, Dec 1957.

33   CEE to AMSO, 1 June 1955 in AHB ID9/621/12/Pt 4.

34   FEAF ORB.

35   Eyewitness report (Wg Cdr J R Dowling).

36   FEAF ORB.

37   DFS records.

38   COS(54) 102, 5 Apr 1954 in AHB ID6/463/Pt 4.

39   COS(52) 544 in AHB ID9/621/12/Pt 2.

40   COS(54) 238, 20 Jul 1954 in AHB ID6/463/Pt 3.

41   Air Ministry/Admiralty report to COS, 17 Jul 1954 in AHB ID6/463/Pt 3.

42   VCAS to CA, 11 Aug 1954 in AHB ID6/463/Pt3.

43   D Pol(AS) to F6, 17 Jun 1954 in AHB ID6/463/Pt 3.

44   DGAP to CA, 31 Aug 1954 in AHB ID6/463/Pt 3.

45   FEAF ORB, Feb 1955.

46   AHB ID6/463/Pt 3.

47   COS(54) 376, 7 Dec 1954 in AHB ID6/463/Pt 4.

48   COS(55) 1, 3 Jan 1955 in AHB ID6/463/Pt 4.

49   AHB ID/53/1/60.

50   VCAS to CAS, 23 Dec 1954 in AHB ID6/463/Pt 4.

51   COS(55), 20 Jan 1955 in AHB ID6/463/Pt 4.

52   COS(54) 376, 7 Dec 1954 in AHB ID6/463/Pt 4; report by Director of Operations (Malaya) in AHB ID9/621/12/Pt 2.

53   Ibid.

54   Ibid.

55   Ibid.

56   D Pol(AS), 9 Mar 1954 in AHB ID9/621/12/Pt 2.

57   Notes on mtg at MAAG UK, 8 Mar 1954 in AHB ID9/621/12/Pt 2.

58   COS(55) 5th Mtg, 20 Jan 1955 in AHB ID6/463/Pt 2.

59   Ibid.

60 Ibid.

61 FEAF ORB, Oct 1954.

62 Ibid, May 1955.

63 Ibid, Aug 1955.

64 Ibid, 1956-58; No 224 Gp ORB, Nov 1958.

65 FEAF ORB, Sept 1958.

66 No 224 Gp ORB, Apr 1959.

67 No 194 Sqn ORB.

68 FEAF ORB.

69 ACC (No 224 Gp), 9th Report, Jan–Dec 1957 in AHB IIJ53/16/2/1.

70 Ibid.

71 R Clutterbuck, Riot and Revolution in Singapore and Malaya 1945-63, 1973, ch 7.

72 No 110 Sqn ORB.

73 AHQ Malaya ORB.

74 OC No 194 Sqn in Air Clues, May 1955.

75 Eyewitness report (Wg Cdr J R Dowling).

76 No 303 Wing ORB.

77 OC No 155 Sqn in Air Clues, Mar 1958.

78 Ibid.

79 AHQ Malaya ORB.

80 OC No 155 Sqn in Air Clues, Mar 1958.

81 No 194 Sqn ORB.

82 No 110 Sqn ORB; No 224 Gp ORB.

83 No 155 Sqn ORB.

84 CIC(FE) 55 (2), Joint Army/Air Operational Instruction No 3, 19 May 1955 in AHB ID9/621/1/Pt3.

85 COS(55) 86, 20 Oct 1955, COS(55) 89, 21 Oct 1955 in AHB ID9/621/12/Pt 2; COS(56) 434, 10 Dec 1956 in AHB ID9/621/1/Pt 3; FEAF ORB (Admin) Dec 1956, COM 60/56.

86 No 224 Gp ORB.

87 FEAF ORB.

88 No 224 Gp ORB.

89 Ibid.

90 FEAF ORB.

91 Ibid.

92 No 110 Sqn ORB.

93 Ibid.

94 Ibid.

95 Ibid.

96 Ibid.

97 Ibid.

98 Ibid.

99 Ibid.

100 Ibid.

101 No 194 Sqn ORB.

102 No 110 Sqn ORB.

103 Periodic reports of AOC Malaya and No 224 Gp; FEAF/MIS; SF/WIS in AHB IIJ53/19; FEAF monthly summaries of RAF contribution to Operation Firedog in Form Stats 122; and monthly Command training summaries.

CHAPTER 4
POLICY DECISIONS IN PHASE 2

So far, helicopter policy decisions have been considered only in relation to the urgent requirement for helicopters generated by the Malayan emergency. Admittedly, the demonstration of the helicopter's potential by the Casualty Evacuation Flight and the pressure exerted by the Director of Operations in Kuala Lumpur did produce a great upsurge in helicopter production and an increase in general interest, and in due course similar demands for helicopters were put forward in Cyprus and—on a smaller scale—elsewhere.

It would be wrong, however, to conclude that RAF activity in this field was inspired solely by operational pressures. Rather do these pressures seem to have been a justification for the very considerable effort, frustrated mainly by lack of money, already being made by the Air Ministry to introduce the helicopter in a wide variety of roles. The sudden expansion of the helicopter force which occurred in 1953 and 1954 justified earlier hopes, thwarted by the inadequacies of the R-4 and R-6, but it still fell far short of what the Air Ministry intended. That the helicopter was only reluctantly adopted by the Air Ministry was therefore a gross oversimplification of a complex problem, one aspect of which was the conflict of priorities which the RAF had still to resolve.

Air Ministry policy at the start of the second phase of military helicopter development can therefore be understood only against the background of its earlier efforts to develop the helicopter before the Malayan emergency introduced a note of urgency. In October 1945 the War Office could do no more than ask quite simply for two types of helicopter, one light, one load carrying; development in Britain had not yet reached the stage where the requirement could be stated with greater precision.(1) The Air Ministry accordingly asked the Ministry of Supply to put three types of helicopter in the 1946–47 research and development programme: a two seater AOP helicopter, an eight to ten seater, and a flying crane with a ten ton lift capability.(2)

In January 1947 an operational requirement was issued (OR 232) for an AOP helicopter based on projects in hand at the Bristol Aeroplane Company and at Fairey Aviation Ltd (the Sycamore and the Gyrodyne), but there was no project then in being which might meet the other two requirements.(3) The Land/Air Warfare Committee was therefore asked by the Air Ministry to define its needs more precisely. However, in December 1947 Service interest in the Bristol and Fairey projects was withdrawn as a result of the economy measures being recommended by the Defence Research Policy Committee (DRPC).(4) The War Office concurred in this decision and it was agreed to wait until a suitable helicopter had been produced to meet civil needs and buy it 'off the shelf' if necessary.(5) It was therefore financial stringency which produced the situation in which the RAF found itself at the beginning of the Malayan emergency when it had no suitable helicopters available.

Early in 1948 the Ministry of Supply offered to allot one of the three Sycamores, then on order, for evaluation. The offer was gratefully accepted.(6) By mid 1951 the Hoverflys at Middle Wallop, with which No 657 AOP Squadron had been endeavouring to keep alive the use of helicopters for AOP work, had been grounded for over six months because of old age and the total absence of spares.(7) In replacement the Air Ministry offered three Sycamores in late 1951, enabling No 1906 Flight to continue—ostensibly in the AOP role, although in practice these essentially civilian passenger aircraft (with the military designation Mk II) were used, until the appearance of the Skeeter in 1957, mainly for carrying VIPs and for light liaison tasks during Army exercises. For the earlier part of this six year period (1951–57) they were almost the only military helicopters in the United Kingdom apart from the embryonic SAR squadrons which were building up slowly through 1953 and 1954 and the CFS helicopter unit which also dated from 1954. They did much to stimulate enthusiasm among senior officers, successive Chiefs of the Imperial General Staff being regular passengers as well as the AOCs-in-C of Fighter Command and the AOCs of No 81 Group in whose formation they were established.(8)

The Army's policy for helicopters was defined in successive Land/Air Warfare Policy Statements. No 9, issued in 1949, laid down a requirement for a general purpose helicopter with casualty evacuation, communications and the carriage of light freight as its main roles (9) and this requirement eventually formed the basis for the order for three Dragonflys for the Casualty Evacuation Flight in Malaya. This order however was the result of force of circumstances and the Dragonfly came nowhere near to meeting the requirements laid down by the Air Ministry (OR 280 issued in 1950 in response to Land/Air Warfare Policy Statement No 9) which called for a very advanced performance particularly under tropical conditions.(10) The Sycamore and Whirlwind were likewise makeshift attempts to meet an urgent military commitment and the Air Ministry was well aware that neither could ever meet the requirements of OR 280 even if the Whirlwind was re-equipped with the Leonides Major engine (a development which in consequence was temporarily abandoned in September 1953).(11)

The General Purpose Helicopter

By this time, however, experience had shown that OR 280, as it stood, was not the best or most economical way of meeting the full requirement for a general purpose helicopter, and it was decided that the needs of both the Army and the RAF could best be met by two types: one able to perform small scale casualty evacuation and light liaison tasks for the Army, and a second and larger twin engined helicopter for the more rigorous casualty and troop transport requirements. The Sycamore Mk 14 was accepted for the lighter roles, and OR 325 was issued in April 1954 for a general purpose version of the twin engined twin rotor Bristol 173.(12) There were therefore two further types still to be found: the two seater AOP aircraft and the 10 ton crane lift.

The AOP/Light Liaison Helicopter

As early as July 1948 the Air Ministry had asked the Ministry of Supply to keep it informed on the development of the Cierva Skeeter which seemed to be a possible contender in the AOP role.(13) The prototype which flew in 1948 was not a success and the Mk 2 version which followed was rather larger and considerably modified. The Air Ministry was understandably anxious not to commit itself to a production order without convincing evidence that the aircraft would be successful—a reluctance which no doubt contributed to the feelings of frustration evident at the War Office, where the slowness of helicopter development was the target of some criticism.

Development of the Skeeter, however, turned out to be a very slow and sad story mainly owing to severe ground resonance problems which led to the loss of two of the three prototypes. In November 1952 the War Office revised its 'outline user requirements' for an AOP helicopter and reissued them in a paper entitled 'Military Characteristics of an Ultra Light Helicopter',(14) which called for a small, simple and robust helicopter with an advanced performance for the AOP, reconnaissance and communications roles. The resulting OR 319 (Ultra Light Reconnaissance Helicopter) was sent by the Air Ministry to the Ministry of Supply for action in July 1953. Seven aircraft firms produced design tenders, the winner being Fairey Aviation whose design was selected because the Ministry of Supply considered that it was the only one which could be produced in time to meet the target date of June 1957. The order, however, was cancelled, partly on economy grounds, and attention returned to the Skeeter which by 1954, although still in prototype, had been equipped with the Gipsy 10 engine and at last showed signs of having reached an acceptance stage of development at AAEE, Boscombe Down. It was, however, January 1957 before the first delivery could be made to No 1906 Flight of No 657 Squadron for AOP work.(15)

The Heavy/Medium Lift Helicopter

When proposals for a 10 ton crane helicopter and a 10 passenger transport helicopter were shelved in 1947—in the hope that both might be developed by civilian enterprise—the two projects were referred back to the Land/Air Warfare Committee for a more detailed definition of the requirements.(16) At the same time the Air

101

Ministry maintained its interest in the development of the single engined three rotor Cierva Air Horse as a possible future contender for the Army's heavy lift requirement. It seemed however to be too small for the purpose and the Ministry of Supply was told by the Air Ministry that although the Army had referred to it hopefully in Land/Air Warfare Policy Statement No 7 a much larger capacity would be needed.(17) In 1948 the Air Ministry's interest in the Air Horse was reaffirmed and the Ministry of Supply was asked to continue reporting on its development and particularly on the results of its initial flight trials.(18) The first prototype flew in December 1948 but crashed in March 1950; as a result there was a serious setback to development and after considerable redesign and ground running work the project was abandoned in 1953.

From the experience gained with the Air Horse, it was evident that the development of a helicopter to meet the heavy lift requirement was a long way off—it proved in fact to be even further away than was thought at the time. Meanwhile, the War Office had produced a more detailed requirement calling for a lift of 10000 lb over a 75–100 nautical mile radius of action; this was put before the Land/Air Warfare Transport Sub-committee in August 1951.(19) At about the same time British European Airways (BEA) announced their intention to issue a requirement for a large passenger helicopter and, as their requirement seemed to match that of the Army, the Air Ministry agreed to enter into consultation with BEA in the hope of producing a joint requirement.(20)

A considerable amount of work was done along these lines in 1952 and although a draft operational requirement was produced no action could be taken to issue it until a paper stating the helicopter requirement for the Services had received the approval of the DRPC. At a meeting in October 1952, however, the DRPC decided that in view of the research and development costs it could not approve the development of a helicopter to meet the heavy lift requirement.(21) So ended the Air Ministry's first attempt to hasten the development of a helicopter in this class.

In the years after 1945, therefore, the financial restrictions to which the Air Ministry was subject had twice been the cause of severe cutbacks in the research and development programme, in 1947 and again in 1950. The production of offensive aircraft inevitably took precedence over helicopter development and there could be no question of risking funds on helicopter projects before they had been proved successful by industry. This policy was fully justified in the case of the Air Horse, and the Fairey Gyrodyne, into which the Air Ministry might have sunk considerable funds before finding that both were failures in their existing form.(22)

All this activity was quite separate from—though coincidental with—the urgent steps taken to provide helicopter support for Malaya. The Air Ministry's reluctance to be stampeded into committing itself to unsatisfactory helicopters was thus based on practical experience rather than on what might appear to the recent convert to be a distaste for a radical new development.

To sum up: the Air Ministry had not wanted the unsatisfactory Dragonfly, but had been compelled to accept it, replacing it with the Sycamore as soon as possible. Even before the Whirlwind Mk 4 had arrived in Malaya and seemed likely to prove a fiasco, OR 325 had been issued (April 1954) and the Bristol 173 selected, not as a heavy lift helicopter but as a general purpose aircraft—to do the task required of the Whirlwind. The Sycamore too had been provided for the AOP task pending the fulfilment of OR 319 (the ultra light helicopter) with the Skeeter as a doubtful 'long stop'; the 10 ton heavy lift project had been abandoned on the grounds of cost. With so much accomplished the Air Ministry could turn its attention to its own pressing requirements in the helicopter field: anti-submarine, search and rescue, pilot training and communications aircraft.

The communications role was in fact the first task to be identified in practical terms, as the result of a tentative inquiry in June 1950 from the Secretary of State for Air to DCAS about VIP transport between Whitehall and Northolt.(23) The idea was quickly discouraged on the grounds of expense. The SAR role, however, was an obvious need, but there was still no firmly established military requirement on which to base a positive demand.(24) The Air/Sea Warfare Development Unit (ASWDU) was another clear contender and the SAR function was expected to emerge in conjunction with it.

Two years later the picture was little clearer, but official attitudes had changed considerably: it was now recognised that there was an immediate need to put an adequate number of helicopters into service not only to gain wide operating experience but also to stimulate industry to undertake the design and production of more advanced types.(25)

At an Air Council meeting in June 1952 the whole field was surveyed again and a number of tentative conclusions were reached which give some indication of official intentions at the time. The Sycamore would be found a suitable role at home although its rotors were thought to be too low for Malayan operations.

That there was now a definite requirement for helicopters in various parts of the world was accepted. Indeed, VCAS said that the RAF must experiment in the helicopter field and help in encouraging the aircraft industry to develop new types, adding that if more helicopters were ordered than were actually needed, there would be no difficulty in disposing of them to other countries where there was already a market for them.

Plainly the restraining factor in helicopter development was the difficulty in formulating a precise enough justification for their use in advance of practical experience.

However, it was decided that in addition to the Malayan requirement which seemed to justify a general transport squadron (18 S-51s and 6 S-55s), the order of priority was the Air/Sea Warfare Development Unit (already formed with three Sycamores), a Search and Rescue Flight each for Fighter and Coastal Commands and, somewhat doubtfully, No 1906 AOP Flight with Sycamores.(26) A transport squadron in Transport Command was accepted as a reasonable proposition, but the establishment of a full squadron in Malaya was held to cover that need, at least for the time being. In addition, VCAS proposed an evaluation of the Bristol 173 in the maritime and army support roles, in conjunction with the BEA study for a 30/40 seater civil helicopter, with the Army bid for a 20000 lb lift helicopter in mind. There was still some hope that the Fairey Rotodyne, then in an early stage of development, might show the way in this respect.(27)

Such was the state of official opinion when, in 1953, events began to race ahead of policy, starting with the rapid build up in Malaya already described. At this point, however, the reliability of the helicopter was challenged at a high political level. The Prime Minister (Winston Churchill) asked for accident figures for the year ending April 1953 (28) and a list was submitted showing two Dragonflys destroyed in Malaya and four Sycamores at home. The RAF rate was 18.75 major accidents per 10000 hours (6 in 3200 hours). Three of these accidents involved fatalities; in one case a soldier walked into a Sycamore tail rotor during relief operations in Holland in February 1953 when all available helicopters were sent there to help in the aftermath of disastrous floods. On 15 July 1953 the Prime Minister followed up his original inquiry with a request to the Secretary of State for Air for a report (in not more than 1000 words) on the feasibility of using large parachutes stowed in the rotor pylon to protect helicopters from the consequences of engine failure below 300 feet. It was further suggested that the engine itself might be jettisoned by an emergency lever, so slowing the helicopter down, a 'good bump' being preferable to a fatal crash.(29) These inquiries, however, had two salutary effects: they reminded large sections of the staff that helicopters could no longer be ignored, and they led many to brief themselves rapidly on the auto rotative characteristics of the helicopter at various heights and speeds in order to refute such absurd suggestions.

Two further events in mid 1953 contributed to the atmosphere of urgency which was beginning to pervade more and more departments. Lord Dowding announced his intention of raising in the House of Lords the question of establishing SAR helicopters in the Suez Canal Zone,(30) and he was advised by the Air Staff that the C-in-C Middle East had asked for one helicopter each to be provided for the Canal Zone/Sinai, Aden and Jordan/Iraq.*(31) A few days later the Minister of

---

*AOC No 205 Group in the Canal Zone had asked for SAR helicopters in the previous year, but had been told that there were not enough available.

Supply wrote to all departments concerned with helicopters asking for a meeting to discuss probable future requirements; development at home, he said, had suffered because too few helicopters had been ordered.(32) In particular, the design studies for the 40/50 seater helicopter submitted by the five leading helicopter manufacturers (Bristol, Fairey, Saunders Roe, Percival and Westland) to meet a BEA requirement should be co-ordinated with the needs of other potential users.

The reply from the Minister of Defence (Earl Alexander) was distinctly unenthusiastic; he pointed out that neither the Royal Navy nor the RAF would require in the foreseeable future a helicopter larger than what would be termed 'medium' and that the only possible military requirement for a helicopter of the size proposed was 'a not very clear one for a heavy helicopter for the Army'.(33) Lord Alexander pointed out that the Chiefs of Staff had not given a very high priority to helicopter development and hinted that if the radical review of defence expenditure then being carried out led to cuts, helicopters would be among the first to suffer.

Nevertheless, the meeting which the Minister of Supply had proposed did take place on 30 June 1953 and the three Service ministries as well as those of Defence, Supply and Civil Aviation were obliged to state their current attitudes. The Ministry of Supply felt that the Americans were forging ahead in helicopter development mainly because substantial orders were being placed for helicopters, while the United Kingdom had nothing more than a few hopeful projects and some unco-ordinated aspirations on the part of the Services and civil aviation.

The Admiralty restated its firm requirement for SAR and anti-submarine helicopters, the former need being met by the S-51 and S-55 and the latter by either the projected Bristol 173 or, if that was too large and expensive, the S-55. The possibility of a 40/50 seater troop transport was envisaged, but not as an Admiralty responsibility.

The Army reiterated its ultra light helicopter requirement, mentioned the slightly larger casualty evacuation helicopter (confirming that this was an Air Force responsibility) and reported that a working part was expected to confirm within three months a War Office requirement for a heavy lift helicopter for tactical use.

BEA considered the Rotodyne too noisy and the RAF said that its take-off performance would not meet the military requirement. The Bristol 173, in BEA's view, was too small for economic operation; the RAF said that discussions with BEA had revealed a difference in their technical requirements, the military need being for powerful vertical lift while BEA required speed (see above p 94).

Mr Profumo for the Ministry of Civil Aviation, however, professed to have detected a certain community of interest between the Services and suggested that the Bristol 173 should be ordered for the good of the export market; BEA might be able to order 10, financial problems notwithstanding, in order to get the aircraft into service. Mr Nigel Birch for the Ministry of Defence warned of impending cuts in defence expenditure which would leave little room for helicopters. Mr Low for the Ministry of Supply reiterated that helicopter development could be undertaken only if there was more than one user, and that if the Services did not share in the costs it would be uneconomic to develop a large helicopter for civil purposes.

The course taken by the discussion tended to encourage a suspicion already existing in RAF circles that the real purpose of the meeting was to persuade the Services to support research and development on behalf of civil aviation as well as themselves,(34) whereas Air Staff policy was to await the successful development of a civil aircraft and then buy it for the Services.

At the end of this important and revealing meeting the surprising conclusion was agreed that while technical experts from all parties concerned would continue to explore the possibility of moulding the various requirements for a large helicopter into one development project, an order would be placed for the Bristol 173 and the various departments involved would co-ordinate their production demands.(35)

So, the heavy lift helicopter, stifled in 1952 by the DRPC, was thrown back into the melting pot at the very point where a joint agreement was all that was needed to obtain full backing for its production. The opportunity was not to recur within the time scale of this history and by the time that BEA had begun to buy its own larger passenger helicopters from the USA in the 1960s, the financial restrictions on the RAF were so severe that an intention to purchase, reformulated annually, was withdrawn at the moment of decision (also annual) and some 24 years later there was still no heavy or even medium lift helicopter in service.

However, the political decision taken at the time to go ahead with the Bristol 173 (neither a medium nor a heavy lift helicopter), apparently on purely commercial grounds, had a most significant consequence: after many vicissitudes it resulted in the eventual appearance in 1961 of the Bristol 192 or Belvedere, just in time to play a major part in the Borneo campaign and in operations in the Aden area.

By 1953 tension between the Army and the RAF was considerable and tending to increase. A formal bid by the Army early in that year for the more rapid development of experimental transport helicopters had received an equally formal reply from the Air Council: The Army's desire to obtain wider experience of the helicopter in all theatres was well understood, but the restrictions imposed by the defence budget coupled with the inadequacies of technical development in the helicopter field made it premature to proceed with the formation of helicopter transport units at the inevitable expense of combat units.(36) Within the ministry, the Air Staff was making the point that although the helicopter front line was small, the RAF was far from indifferent to the possibilities which the helicopter opened up, and it was therefore of prime importance to spend money on research and development rather than on large numbers of current aircraft for which there was no essential task.(37) The cause of the tension between the Army and the Air Force was thus clearly revealed.

In mid 1953 therefore the known operational commitments, apart from Malaya, consisted of the development of the newly established SAR unit in Fighter Command based at Linton-on-Ouse, the Air/Sea Warfare Development Unit at St Mawgan (from which was to be formed a SAR unit in Coastal Command), the provision of three SAR helicopters for the Middle East Air Force as a result of prodding from Lord Dowding, and the maintenance of No 1906 AOP Flight at Middle Wallop, which the Army was clearly prepared to defend, come what may (even if it was used mainly for VIP transport).

Almost at once two further commitments appeared. Some action had to be taken to put training on a better footing than that provided by the ad hoc civil contracts or the unsupervised unit type pilot conversions which had been organised in the absence of formal Service arrangements. Secondly, the question of VIP transport was brought suddenly to the fore at the end of May 1953 when the Duke of Edinburgh expressed a wish to the Captain of The Queen's Flight (Sir Edward Fielden) to fly by helicopter from Buckingham Palace to Pirbright and Woolwich. The Chief of the Air Staff, when consulted, replied that if a formal request was made he would advise the Secretary of State that while there were only single engine helicopters available, flights by VVIPs such as the Duke of Edinburgh over central London involved dangers which, although slight in terms of risk, would nevertheless not be justifiable, especially just before the Coronation.(38)

The Duke of Edinburgh, however, obtained a helicopter from the Admiralty and flew to Pirbright, to the embarrassment of the Secretary of State for Air who had not been consulted by the Admiralty.(39) Urgent arrangements were therefore made to ensure that a helicopter would always be available in future, since it was obvious that the request would be repeated, and a few months later in early 1954 a RAF helicopter appeared in The Queen's Flight, borrowed from the Central Flying School.

In the previous December agreement had been obtained from the London County Council for the former Festival site on the south bank of the Thames to be used by Service VIP helicopters, while it remained available and subject to permission being sought on each occasion.(40) VIP helicopter transport was thus established on an official basis.

All the same, it remained official policy that since helicopters were 'the most expensive form of mechanical transport in existence' they were to be employed only on tasks which could be shown to be essential and not merely desirable.(41)

The Air Staff was informed that the cost of providing the general purpose transport squadron desired by the Army, so increasing the existing force of 34 helicopters by 50 per cent, was equivalent to that of half a squadron of Swifts (at 22 UE).(42) In retrospect the equation might seem an excellent reason for providing helicopters, but in 1953 it justified an automatic, immediate and total rejection of the proposal. However, the opportunity was taken to emphasise once again the Air Ministry's keen interest in research and development and the Air Staff's confident expectation that the results would lead to a soundly based expansion of the helicopter element in due course.(43) In the meantime, a strong bid for helicopters to be established for civil defence purposes was not unexpectedly thrown out by the Chiefs of Staff Committee.(44)

As far back as February 1952 Flying Training Command had put in a bid for a helicopter establishment at the Central Flying School (CFS) and the Royal Flying College at Manby for the study of instructional techniques and procedures.(45) The Malayan situation, however, had led to so severe a shortage of helicopters that there was no way of satisfying the requirement at the time, though note was taken of it as a future commitment. In late 1953 it was decided that with Sycamores replacing Dragonflys in Malaya, a unit could be set up in CFS, equipped initially with three Dragonflys, to develop a training plan and the instructional techniques for pilot training; the CFS helicopter unit accordingly came into existence in April 1954.

Between mid 1953 and mid 1954 the Air Ministry was engaged in a hectic round of consultations as they juggled with conflicting priorities—on the one hand the overriding needs of the Malayan emergency, and on the other the replacement of the Air/Sea Warfare Development Unit's Sycamores with S-55s or Bristol 173s (the latter were nowhere near ready). At the same time the conflict between the build up of the MEAF, Fighter and Coastal Command SAR units, the priorities of CFS helicopters and pilot training facilities, and the demands of VIP transport and The Queen's Flight continued against the background of a chronic shortage of aircraft and the continual failure to meet promised delivery dates. In May 1954 the Vice Chief of the Air Staff found himself having to explain to an angry Secretary of State for Air that the promise of helicopters for the Middle East made to Lord Dowding in the previous year had still not been honoured because of the need in the light of Malayan trials experience to modify the Mk 11 and 13 Sycamores to produce the Mk 14.(46) Delivery was promised for September.

Army/RAF Helicopter Responsibilities

In December 1953 the Air Council made a series of major policy decisions which defined the place of helicopters in the Royal Air Force, and at the same time took the fundamental step of passing responsibility for the operation of light helicopters to the Army.(47) The intention was to counter the false impression felt to be current that the RAF was unduly backward in the helicopter field and not sensitive enough to the demands of the Army. After due discussion the dramatic proposal put forward by the Deputy Chief of the Air Staff was accepted: that 90 ultra light helicopters should be provided to replace the 112 AOP Austers in the AOP and light liaison roles and that they should be flown and controlled entirely by Army personnel. In addition, the existing No 1906 AOP Flight should continue with its three Sycamores until they had to be withdrawn.

The reduction in aircraft numbers (from 112 to 90) was to be balanced by giving the Army access to RAF Pioneers or Beavers and to communications helicopters, the latter being established at the rate of two Sycamores at each RAF command headquarters, eight in Germany and two at Hendon for Air Ministry use. (Of these communications helicopters only the two at Hendon received financial approval and even they did not become available until helicopters were added to the Metropolitan Communications Squadron at Northolt seven years later.)

It was also agreed that positive action should be taken over the Army's desire to study the use of tactical troop/cargo helicopters in forward areas by creating a new unit in Transport Command, initially with four Whirlwinds which would be replaced in due course by Bristol 173s. The unit was to be available for exercises on the continent as required and would study freighting techniques with the Army. It would also act as an emergency pool, so releasing the RAF from its dependence on the Admiralty and the United States in such circumstances.

On the RAF side continued support was affirmed for the four categories of research and development: ultra light, basic training, general purpose and anti-submarine. Considerable increases in the front line establishment were also agreed: the number of SAR Sycamores in No 275 Squadron, Fighter Command was to be increased from eight to 16; the eight SAR Whirlwinds planned for No 22 Squadron in Coastal Command were to be replaced by Bristol 173s, as were the three Whirlwinds planned for the Air/Sea Warfare Development Unit.(48) Two Sycamores were to be established in the SAR role at the Armament Practice Camp at Sylt, and in anticipation of future training requirements 10 ultra light helicopters were included in the total package whose cost—£4½ millions—would have to be found at the expense of some other project. The Air Council hoped that its action in placing AOP and light liason helicopters under Army control and in creating a tactical helicopter unit in Transport Command would remove a long standing source of friction between the War Office and the Air Ministry.(49) It did not.

On 24 May 1954 War Office frustration at the continued absence of battlefield helicopters boiled over into a frontal attack on the Air Ministry launched by the Secretary of State for War (Mr Anthony Head).(50) On this occasion the requirement put forward was for helicopters to replace road vehicles against the background of a nuclear war, the Army arguing that as it was not fair to expect the Air Ministry to give up other aircraft to provide helicopters for another Service, that other Service (the Army) should have full authority to buy (and control) its own. Head discounted the Air Minister's claim that aircraft were his sole responsibility on the grounds that the helicopter was only 'a very distant cousin of the aeroplane' and would be used 'exclusively for functions which are the close and domestic affairs of the Army'. The echoes of 1912–17 and of the Fleet Air Arm controversy of 1937 were not lost on the Air Minister and the attack was repulsed.(51) Further evidence of the Army's intention to gain complete control was provided by an article in the Manchester Guardian of 8 May 1954—in itself proof that there was no intention on the Army side of confining the discussion to an 'in-house' debate.*

History was now repeating itself with the Army in the role played by the Navy after the First World War. Within three years (in 1957) the establishment of the Army helicopter force (officially for AOP and light liaison duties), accompanied by a further Air Ministry initiative which passed the responsibility for operating the Beavers to the Army, was to justify following in the footsteps of the Fleet Air Arm in 1937 and lead to the formation of the Army Air Corps.

Another example of the delicate state of Army/Air Force relations at this time was the question of obtaining landing sites in London for VIP helicopters. In addition to the clearance given to the South Bank site for civilian use (see p 107) Buckingham Palace had been cleared for royal flights under pressure from the Duke of Edinburgh. However, No 657 AOP Squadron, established with Sycamores and Army pilots, was in the habit of flying Army VIPs into Burton Court, Chelsea, a site which after official examination was declared to be definitely unsuitable. The Secretary of State for Air, being responsible for these RAF aircraft, felt it necessary to bring Army pilots into line with generally accepted safety standards, but thinking that a ban would be resented in view of the Army's mistaken belief that the RAF was lukewarm about the provision of helicopters for Army purposes, invited the Minister of Transport and Civil Aviation to originate the letter which he would otherwise have sent himself.(54) The Army, however, continue to fly VIPs into Burton Court until the Westland heliport at Battersea opened on 23 April 1959.

---

*An insight into the situation in the Air Ministry at the time is provided by the use to which the Air Staff put a detailed requirement from SACEUR for the provision of helicopter borne radar aids to navigation for the NATO bomber force, to be available for instant deployment throughout the AIRCENT tactical area in Europe by day and night, and in all weathers, in large, low flying helicopters.(52) There was scarcely any need to comment on the absolute impracticability of meeting this requirement in the foreseeable future, and the request was forwarded by the Chief of the Air Staff to the Air Minister as ammunition in the controversy over RAF control of helicopters in forward areas.(53)

A further source of conflict was the projected heavy lift helicopter. In 1954 there were high hopes of the Fairey Rotodyne which many confidently expected would go into service with the civil airlines. The RAF, however, was sceptical about its usefulness to the Service, mainly because it did not believe that the Rotodyne's hovering performance and vertical lift would meet the Army's requirements.(55) Moreover, at night with tip jets in action it would resemble a huge Catherine wheel and make an unprecedented amount of noise; it could hardly therefore be described as tactically discreet. In addition, the RAF was very concerned about using such a technically complicated machine in forward areas.(56)

However, on 25 September the War Office informed the Ministry of Supply directly of their staff requirement for a heavy cargo helicopter, pointing out that the characteristics sought were close to those of the proposed Rotodyne.(57) The Air Minister then circulated his copy of the Army statement to the heads of the Air Staff branches in the Air Ministry with the comment that it appeared to be the Army statement of requirement promised 'within three months' time' at the meeting held on 30 June 1953.(58) In the event the Rotodyne was not purchased and the second prototype was never built.

The RAF still pinned its hopes firmly on the Bristol 173 while waiting for the heavy lift requirement to be formulated adequately and practical evidence to be produced that a suitable helicopter was likely to be available.(59) As the Bristol 173 meanwhile seemed likely to fulfil a variety of existing roles there was considerable anxiety in the Air Ministry (well justified as events were to prove) that the Navy would again go to the head of the production line, as it had done with the Dragonfly and Whirlwind, by placing firm orders for large numbers of the 173 before the RAF could obtain Treasury approval to buy it for the various purposes it had in mind (the Air/Sea Warfare Development Unit, the SAR role, Malaya and the projected transport unit in Transport Command).(60)

In April 1954, therefore, the Air Staff issued its operational requirement for the Bristol 173 (OR 325) without waiting for a meeting of the Operational Requirements Committee (ORC), using as its excuse the plea that a Naval order for 65 aircraft was probably on its way to the Ministry of Supply.(61) Two months later a further operational requirement (OR 326) was issued for the turbine engine version of the 173, which was expected to be available in 1958/59, the grounds being that the piston engined version would have neither the range required by Coastal Command, nor the single engine performance required for long unescorted sea crossings.*(62) With BEA also interested in the turbine engined version, Bristol Aircraft suggested dropping the piston engined version in order to concentrate on the turbine engined aircraft, but the Air Ministry was not prepared to agree at that stage.(63)

---

*This was the beginning of the Belvedere story.

By late 1954 Sycamores were in use with the Air/Sea Development Unit and No 275 SAR Syadron, Fighter Command, Whirlwinds Mk 2 in No 22 SAR Squadron, Coastal Command, and Dragonflys in the Central Flying School (Instructional) Development Flight (one being detached to The Queen's Flight). By early 1955 three further major deployments had been initiated: in the Middle East (Cyprus and Jordan, in the Arabian Peninsula and Aden, and in Kenya at Eastleigh). At the same time the Joint Experimental Helicopter Unit (JEHU) came into being.

The Joint Experimental Helicopter Unit

The formation of the Joint Experimental Helicopter unit with the task of developing troop and cargo carrying techniques in tactical situations was a matter of considerable delicacy. The Air Council had agreed in 1953 to the formation of a RAF unit in Transport Command for this purpose when allotting helicopters to replace Austers in the AOP squadrons (see p 109). Throughout 1954 as the Army attempted to take over responsibility for the whole tactical helicopter field, the RAF argued cautiously against any division of supply and, especially, servicing facilities, and most vigorously against any attack on the principal of Air Force control of aircraft (including helicopters).(64)

The immediate problem however was how to equip all the new helicopter units being formed at the very moment that the operational demands of the Malayan emergency were taking first priority and the Treasury was exercising a rigid control over all orders for helicopters.(65) Every priority in fact seemed to be overriding. Building up the SAR units at home, already delayed, was a constant battle for aircraft allocations; the Middle East Air Force was demanding not only the SAR helicopters promised to Lord Dowding for Cyprus in 1953 but additional aircraft for casualty evacuation in the Mau Mau operations in Kenya; and there were further demands still for SAR helicopters for Aden and Sylt.

In addition, the Treasury's refusal to allow the RAF communications helicopters to be ordered,(66) as planned in the Air Council decisions of March 1954, meant that the CFS (Instructional) Development Flight was spending much of its time attending to high priority bids for VIP transport. Consequently, in July 1954 the Deputy Chief of the Air Staff was compelled to say that at the end of a long argument lasting many months the alternatives were—short of stopping all development and instructional work on helicopters in the RAF—either to establish two helicopters in The Queen's Flight or to be prepared to tell the Royal Family that the RAF could not meet their requirements.(67)

In the event, two Whirlwinds were established in The Queen's flight, the flow of helicopters to Malaya was maintained, and the projected Transport Command Evaluation Unit (Army troop/cargo development) was given equal priority with the home based SAR units.(68) Even so, it seemed improbable that its first two Whirlwinds would be available before the last quarter of 1955.

The Army's attitude at this time was revealed in a report on the Chief of the Imperial General Staff's conference in 1954 on heavy lift helicopters.(69) The Deputy Chief said that heavy helicopters should be very simple to control—'he envisaged a man standing in the corner of the field with a flag' and he thought it would be unnecessary to have anything on the lines of 'wireless like they have in Fighter Command'. Navigation should be restricted to map reading.

Air Force comment was broadly to the effect that if, as was envisaged, helicopters were to replace lorries, all weather capability would be needed, ie full instrumentation, radio and navigation aids. Elaborate maintenance base facilities would also be needed and the running cost of the 450 helicopters proposed would be very high. Privately, the RAF conclusion was that the impossibility of imitating in the United Kingdom the American practice of operating large fleets of helicopters in clear day weather was not understood and that to drive this lesson home the proposed RAF helicopter transport development unit should be set up as soon as possible. If necessary, the Army should be allowed to set up its own development unit, the RAF retaining control of all air traffic and navigation aids in forward areas.(70) By November 1954, therefore, the Joint Chiefs of Staff had agreed to the formation of an inter-Service unit to be known as the Joint Helicopter Evaluation Unit,(71) later renamed the Joint Experimental Helicopter Unit (JEHU). Although this action removed the need for a Transport Command Evaluation Unit in the RAF, it was still hoped that Transport Command might be able to justify helicopters as a logical extension of the medium range transport force and for spares delivery at home.(72) This line of argument did not prevail.

The Army now had authority to order aircraft for the joint unit, although it was to be manned by equal numbers of Army and RAF pilots, with a colonel in charge and a squadron leader as second in command. Servicing would be undertaken by the RAF. Formation was to take place in two phases, the first in early 1955 and the second in 1956. The two sections were initially (and predictably) called platoons, but in due course as co-operation developed, the more easily understood and appropriate title of flight was adopted. With competition for Whirlwinds intense at this stage of the Malayan build up, the only helicopters which could be obtained were Sycamores, and the first flight duly formed on 1 April 1955 with six; the second formed a year later with six Whirlwind Mk 2s.

In 1957 the decision was taken to transfer from the Air Ministry to the War Office full responsibility for AOP and light liaison aircraft, the dividing line being drawn at an aircraft all-up-weight of 4000 lb. It was this decision which opened the way for the formation of the Army Air Corps. In the same year, as the result of the findings of a government committee—the Bingley report—the role of air transport in support of the Army worldwide received acceptance and in consequence the RAF was made responsible for, inter alia, helicopter tactical troop and cargo lift in forward areas, a task which was assessed as requiring 12 Bristol 192s. This assessment was in itself a step forward of the greatest significance as it was the first occasion on which a helicopter task had received the formal definition on which the RAF could base its aircraft demands.

The JEHU's position in the light of these two developments clearly required redefinition and in July 1957 the Secretary of State for War proposed modifications in its charter.(73) His proposals would have had the effect of altering the JEHU's current task of determining whether helicopters might solve the Army's (and perhaps the RAF's) problem of mobility, organisation and administration in the field, to one of defining the optimum methods of operating a force of VTOL and STOL aircraft for logistic support in the field. The JEHU would also have had to take account of a possible Army requirement for a 4/5 seater utility aircraft, both VTOL and STOL, for use in the tactical role.

The Air Ministry was markedly unenthusiastic about these proposals, as they were seen as a manoeuvre to circumvent the 4000 lb weight limitation imposed on Army controlled aircraft, with the JEHU being used as 'a stalking horse' to cover the Army's approach to its final target (control of all tactical helicopters).(74) There was also a danger that the way was being prepared for the possible addition of fixed wing (STOL) aircraft to the JEHU establishment.

Additionally, in the Air Ministry view, nothing of value seemed to have been demonstrated by the JEHU in the course of two years' work on the tactical employment of helicopters which the RAF had not already learned from operations in Malaya and Cyprus, and to make advances in such techniques as instrument flying and night operations specialist facilities would be needed which the unit did not possess.(75) Field trials, it was felt, could be carried out, when required, by existing RAF tactical helicopter units or, where appropriate, by the Army's own new light liasion units at the Army Air Corps Centre. The acceptance of the Bingley report and the setting up of the Army Air Corps was seen by the Air Ministry not as a reason for strenghtening the JEHU but for disbanding it and using other units to carry out the investigations required, after due consultation with the Land/Air Warfare Committee.(76)

In the event a compromise was reached. The JEHU was kept in being for a further two years, its Sycamores being replaced by more Whirlwinds as the supply position permitted, and it gradually assumed the character of a tactical helicopter support squadron, which was what it in fact became at the end of 1959, but in the shape of No 225 Squadron RAF, to the disappointment of the Army Air Corps.(77)

Implementation and Development

Between 1955 and 1960 the main problem was to resolve the conflict of priorities which arose in the course of implementing the plans already made for the creation of new helicopter units, some of which needed far more support than had been expected—a notable example being Cyprus where the planned SAR flight suddenly developed into a full tactical helicopter squadron. Meanwhile the Malayan commitment continued and a new task appeared in the form of helicopter support for the units involved in the British atomic weapons tests on Christmas Island and in Australia. This requirement had to be met from the United Kingdom as FEAF had no spare capacity. At the same time far reaching decisions on replacement engines and helicopter types were being taken which were to set the scene for the third phase of RAF helicopter development.

The year 1955 was a period of unprecedented growth in helicopter units, with the Air Staff seemingly the target of intense pressures from every direction and often from a very high political level.

The situation was still far from satisfactory. With Malaya remaining the first priority, the JEHU had to be content with Sycamores instead of Whirlwinds,(78) although the SAR Sycamores promised for the Middle East in 1953 were at long last being delivered. In the same area there were new SAR commitments in Aden and Nairobi,*(79) which delayed the build up of the Fighter Command SAR squadron (No 275) begun with two Mk 13 Sycamores. The squadron was thus forced to borrow two Hiller 360 helicopters from the Naval training squadron to keep its pilots in flying practice. Meanwhile, the shortage of Whirlwinds was also delaying the build up of the Coastal Command SAR squadron (No 22) and two Sycamores had to be borrowed from the Air/Sea Warfare Development Unit (ASWDU) to save it from disbandment.(80)

The shortage of Mk 2 Whirlwinds was due in part to the Malayan emergency and the need to convert Mk 2s to Mk 4s for that theatre, and in part to a chronic shortage of Whirlwind engines, itself partly caused by the unexpectedly short life in Malaya of the reconditioned Wasp engines (only 100 hours at one stage).(81) Another cause was the hope—in the event unfulfilled—of obtaining more S-55s from the United States for service in Malaya (see p 79), which had the effect of delaying orders for the Coastal Command and JEHU Whirlwinds as well as for those needed in Malaya.

---

*With the withdrawal from the Suez Canal Zone the SAR Sycamores intended for Abyad (Sudan) and Fayid were reassigned to Nicosia and Amman.

A further complication appeared when the Foreign Secretary (Harold Macmillan) informed the Air Minister that France had asked for 20 Whirlwinds for use in Algeria and strongly urged that Britain should accede to this request.(82) The Air Ministry replied that there seemed to be no way of doing so in the light of the Malayan situation, especially as the United States would surely refuse the British bid for 30 more S-55s when it was discovered—to everyone's surprise—that Westland apparently had spare export capacity.(83) The discussions were complex and involved the Prime Minister, but it was eventually agreed that as the United States had raised no objection,(84) eight Whirlwind Mk 2s should be delivered to the French in the last quarter of 1955.(85)

Apart from the problem of Whirlwind supply, however, there were many other difficulties for the Air Ministry to resolve, always against the background of a highly critical situation in Malaya: the Whirlwind's performance defects and chronic spares shortage, Sycamore deliveries to replace the Dragonflys in No 194 Squadron and build up the Middle East Sycamore units, and the need to prepare a full case in the hope of reversing the Treasury's refusal to sanction communications helicopters in the Commands.

After a detailed survey of this last problem the Air Ministry Aircraft Establishments Committee concluded that there was a case for 34 communications helicopters divided between 2nd TAF, No 90 Group and the following Commands: Bomber, Fighter, Coastal, Transport, Home, Maintenance, Flying Training and Technical Training. Some of the helicopters were to be available for sharing with the Army, in particular the eight allotted to 2nd TAF in Germany.

In an attempt to make the case more acceptable, it was suggested that a lower figure than 34 might be put forward initially to allow experience to define the requirement more accurately.(86) In the event financial approval was not given for the purchase of any communications helicopters, but the course of events does at least indicate that the Air Ministry can hardly be accused of lack of interest in helicopters.

Meanwhile, the CFS helicopter unit formed in April 1954 to develop instructional and handling techniques, and train flying instructors and, eventually, helicopter pilots had lost one of its three Dragonflys to The Queen's Flight and was spending much of its time flying VIPs in the other two, when they were serviceable.*

---

*The unit was due to receive two Sycamores at the end of 1955 and might need three if it was to undertake all pilot training.(87)

Relations with the Royal Navy

No sooner, however, had relations with the Army been stabilised—for the time being at least—by the formation of the JEHU than the Air Ministry discovered in April 1955 (a particularly hectic year) that the Navy appeared to be taking steps which would have the effect of altering the agreement on the control of shore based squadrons with a maritime role, a responsibility which had belonged to the RAF since its formation.* The occasion was a paper by Admiral Creasy, Commander-in-Chief, Home Station (designate) on 'The Tactical Employment of Helicopters', which stated that Home and Channel Commands would require helicopters for 'minesweeping, anti-submarine, communications, and control of merchant shipping'.(88)

The Commander-in-Chief, Coastal Command (Air Chief Marshal Boothman) pointed out to the Air Ministry that the Sea/Air Warfare Committee had agreed that carrier aircraft when temporarily shore based should be operated and controlled by the appropriate RAF command, and that in any case the units proposed in Admiral Creasy's paper would have to be established specifically for employment in the Home and Channel Command areas where carriers would be most unlikely to operate. The inference was that responsibility for these minesweeping and anti-submarine operations, when of necessity shore based, belonged to the RAF, and Air Chief Marshal Boothman added that in any case operational control of aircraft so employed would reside in Coastal Command. He also drew attention to the implications of allowing established principles to be overturned in respect of helicopters merely because they were considered 'unconventional', as the same argument could later be applied to fixed wing aircraft which 'may eventually acquire devices for partial or complete vertical take off'.(89)

There seemed however to be no hard evidence of Naval intentions which would justify a direct approach to the Admiralty to resolve the issue, and in view of the obvious similarity between possible Naval intentions and the Army's recent efforts to gain control of helicopters, it was felt unwise to reopen the argument so soon after the agreement to form the JEHU.

On the other hand, to do nothing might well allow a Naval order for large helicopters to create a fait accompli, while at the same time leaving the RAF in its usual position of second place in the production line behind the Navy.(90) It was decided therefore to prepare an Air Ministry paper on the subject.(91)

---

*Relations between the Navy and the Air Force had been the subject of a special investigation by a sub-committee of the Salisbury Committee in 1923. Its conclusions were accepted by the government (see Hansard, 2 August 1923). RAF responsibility in this area was confirmed by the Inskip Committee which separated the Fleet Air Arm from the RAF in 1937.

A month later RAF fears were confirmed by an article on 'Mine-sweeping Helicopters' by the Naval correspondent of The Times published on 25 May, and although the Chief of the Air Staff confirmed to the Secretary of State for Air that a RAF paper on the subject was in course of preparation,(92) subsequent events were as predicted. By June the Air Ministry was explaining to Coastal Command that the four Bristol 191s (formerly 173s) for the Air/Sea Warfare Development Unit could not be delivered before the end of 1957 and that if the Navy did not cancel their order for 65 191s the four for the RAF trials would be delayed until the first quarter of 1958.(93) The 22 general purpose versions of the aircraft (B 192s) planned for the RAF would be similarly delayed, as the Naval version had gained design priority.(94)

In May 1956 the First Sea Lord (Lord Mountbatten) wrote personally to the Minister of Defence (Sir Walter Monckton) saying with unmistakable irony that the helicopter minesweeping trials had been a complete success but because of the government approved Inskip award, which he said forbad the Navy to use aircraft for operational purposes from shore bases, the trials had been necessarily conducted from the deck of an LST. Pointing out that the Chief of the Air Staff had no power to alter a government decision even if he wished to, he agreed that 'economical and sensible' progress was being frustrated because the correct procedure would involve an infringement of the Inskip award. What therefore did the Minister think should be the Admiralty's next step?(95) No more was heard about RAF responsibility for minesweeping by helicopter.

Development of the Bristol 192 (Belvedere)

Development of the Bristol 173 had come a long way since the Air Ministry had identified it in 1953 as the project most likely in principle to fulfil the Army's requirements for a general purpose helicopter and had issued OR 325 in early 1954 as the target which it should meet. The inadequacy of the two Leonides engines had long been apparent and their replacement by the Leonides Major was known to be no more than a short term expedient to enable trials to commence. Accordingly, four of the Leonides Major piston engined types were ordered against OR 326 (the land based maritime helicopter); they were however to be restricted to development work with the ASWDU because of their lack of single engine safety performance.

Hopes for the future fulfilment of OR 325 and OR 326 rested with the Gazelle turbine engine version (96) and an order for 65 of this type (considered the most likely helicopter to have fully adequate performance in all roles) was given design priority and led the Bristol Aeroplane Company to defer to Naval specifications in respect of fuselage shape, undercarriage type and size, etc.

The result was rather grotesque. The original 173, built for passenger use with a low undercarriage and a level fuselage with windows along both sides, was replaced

Prototype of the Bristol 113 (1954)—developed from the Sycamore and with Sycamore rotor blades (front rotor blades reversed) and powered by two Leonides piston engines, it was the forerunner of the Bristol 191 and 192 (the Belvedere).

The Bristol 192 pre-production version of the Belvedere with two Napier Gazelle turbine engines and four bladed rotors, but still with wooden Sycamore blades and fully manual controls: used for service trials. (In the background: Ampleforth Abbey.)

by an aircraft with a short fuselage (to fit an aircraft carrier lift), insufficient headroom for standing (the new version would not be required to carry passengers), a sharp nose up cant (to permit torpedo loading from the front) and an enormous undercarriage designed to allow the aircraft to be dropped at 12 feet a second on to a carrier deck rolling at 10 degrees.

Such was substantially the shape which the RAF inherited for the B 192 when the Naval order was cancelled in 1956. The two three bladed Sycamore rotors used on the 173 had each had a fourth blade added and the transmission had undergone considerable development to accommodate the increased gas turbine engine power now planned.

Problems however had been encountered with the interim Leonides Major engine (mainly oil cooling difficulties) and the latest performance estimates for what was now a heavier aircraft but still with piston engines were beginning to look less and less attractive, particularly its lack of single engine safety.

Predictably the Navy was rapidly losing interest in an aircraft which, with its weapon load, was thought to be too heavy for the carrier lift and too large unless the rotor blades were removed. When the usual transmission development problems were added to engine overheating difficulties after hovering trials in November 1956, the Navy took the opportunity to cancel their 65 aircraft altogether, a decision which was swiftly followed by the cancellation of the three B 191s destined for the Royal Canadian Navy.(97)

On the RAF side there were, in July 1955, firm orders for 21 Bristol 192s (half to replace Sycamores in Malaya and half for Coastal Command SAR) and for four Bristol 191s for the ASWDU.(98) There was no intention then to reduce these orders and it was argued that an increase might be needed if the proposals for the long term defence of Malaya after the Emergency were to be implemented—in the event they were not.(99)

Every effort was therefore made to hasten the incorporation of the Gazelle turbine engine in the B 191 and B 192 so that as few as possible of the piston engine version would have to be accepted (and later fitted with turbine engines). At the same time a number of suggestions were put forward which would have led to more B 192s being ordered: 10 aircraft were proposed for the anti-submarine and minesweeping duties then in dispute with the Navy;(100) twin engine reliability made the B 192 a candidate for The Queen's Flight; and it could also be used to re-equip the JEHU and for a freighting unit in Transport Command.(101) None of these suggestions received financial approval, but the attitude of the Air Staff was once again clearly revealed and similar proposals were revived when the cancellation of the Naval order for B 191s threatened production of B 191s and B 192s for the RAF unless a further 16 aircraft could be ordered.(102)

Meanwhile, however, the Navy had decided to buy a turbine engined version of the American S-58 (later known as the Wessex) which Westland were proposing to build under licence from Sikorsky. It was also intended at that time to use the Rolls-Royce Dart engine and Westland suggested that any problem over lack of research and development funds could be circumvented by spreading the cost over the production aircraft, thus transferring it to the Naval vote and overcoming Ministry of Supply objections on the grounds of research and development expenditure.(103)

The RAF, however, was dismayed by the Navy's unilateral cancellation of the B 191, which had been a joint project, and at finding itself under pressure to follow the Navy in backing the single engined Wessex and itself abandoning the B 191 and B 192.(104) The Air Staff argued strongly against doing so, pointing out that it was about to bring into service the first helicopter in the RAF to have completely adequate performance in all roles and theatres, together with twin engine reliability, and an aircraft which was the most advanced helicopter in the world in its class.

The Air Staff also questioned the propriety of the Navy's action, especially as the first reason given for cancelling the B 191 had been its inadequate performance in the piston engined version, but when the Gazelle engine promised more than the required performance the argument shifted to the S-58's better deck handling characteristics. The Air Staff therefore argued that the RAF's order for B 191s and B 192s should be increased by 16 if that was the only way of keeping the project going,(105) and pointed out that as the turbine engined S-58 had a less adequate performance than even the piston engined B 192 the RAF would still prefer the latter, even if research and development support for the Gazelle engine was withdrawn.(106)

This new threat had come about because of a recommendation by the DRPC that expenditure on helicopter development should be cut by £2m as part of the current attempt to reduce defence costs.*(107)

---

*The rise in government expenditure on helicopter engine and airframe development by industry over the years 1946–57 is shown below:(108)

Year	£000	Year	£000
1946–47	115	1952–53	573
1947–48	180	1953–54	1164
1948–49	127	1954–55	2916
1949–50	280	1955–56	4000
1950–51	192	1956–57	4100
1951–52	189		

Research and development expenditure thus approximately doubled each year for the first five years of Phase 2 of helicopter development, (1952–56).

The RAF, however, was successful in its campaign to keep the B 192 programme in being, and was also able to save the Gazelle engine. This the DRPC then recommended for the Naval S-58s, so creating the Wessex Mk 1.(109)

In March 1956 the planned distribution of B 192s was eight each for No 22 Squadron SAR and for FEAF, five for training and nine for the JEHU, a total of 30. The ASWDU allotment was cancelled and with it the B 191. Twelve of the 30 B 192s which the RAF was hoping to order were to be fitted with Leonides Major piston engines initially, because to wait for the Gazelle turbine engine would mean a delay of 12 months.(110) In the event only 25 B 192s were ordered for the RAF (including substitution for the bid for four B 191s), with one more for the Ministry of Supply, but the Air Staff considered that any attempt to justify more would not be successful in the prevailing economic climate.(111) No requests were therefore made for the training and JEHU tasks,(112) and by mid 1956 the Air Staff had resigned itself to a long, hard battle to obtain even the 25 B 192s asked for—the minimum number which would allow production to go ahead and the maximum which would have any chance of winning financial approval. The struggle was longer and harder than most had expected and over the ensuing four years the B 192 was almost constantly in danger of cancellation.

Apart from more general considerations of national prestige and the development of industrial expertise in helicopter design, the justification for continuing the work necessary to bring the Belvedere into being rested mainly on the recommendations of the 1956 joint service Bingley committee, set up to consider future transport requirements in cold and limited (non nuclear) war. Its recommendations endorsed by the Chiefs of Staff, included a force equivalent to 12 Belvederes for deployment to the theatre involved as part of the tactical transport force,(113) the Belvedere being now seen exclusively as a tactical transport helicopter.

In June 1956 the Air Council agreed in principle that provision should ultimately be made for a mixed force of twin engined helicopters and Pioneer type aircraft in Transport Command,(114) but within months of that decision the Air Staff was involved in a complex debate over the rival merits of the Belvedere and Wessex.(115) On the one hand, it was argued that the Wessex performance was not far short of that of the piston engine Belvedere, while on the other hand it was estimated that 12 Belvederes with Gazelle engines would equal 20 Wessex and that up to 45 Wessex would be needed to lift the same payload in tropical conditions.(116) Equipping the whole Belvedere force, however, with Gazelles would be more expensive than equipping the 14/11 mix at first intended. But against the Wessex was the fact that it would be at least a year, and possibly two years later than the Belvedere in coming into service.(117)

The battle raged to and fro in early 1957 across the whole spectrum of policy considerations, from air transportability to tactical suitability and political expediency. The Ministry of Supply joined in with a recommendation that the Belvedere should be retained and that all those ordered should be equipped with the Gazelle engine, and added that certain technical problems had arisen with the Leonides Major engine.(118) Among the many financial estimates prepared was one which concluded that it would be more expensive to the Air vote to cancel the Belvedere in favour of the Wessex and more difficult to justify publicly.(119)

Performance comparisons between the Gazelle and Leonides Major versions of the Belvedere were made in every conceivable combination of circumstances, an example being the payload which each could carry in tropical conditions at 5000 feet over a range of 100 miles, the conclusion being 5500 lb in the case of the Gazelle and 850 lb in the case of the Leonides Major. Even in standard temperature conditions at sea level with one engine failed the Gazelle version was expected to carry 3200 lb over 250 miles and the Leonides Major version only 440 lb over 50 miles.(120)

In April 1957 the Air Council finally decided to ask for 25 Belvederes, all with Gazelle engines.(121) The financial arguments continued, however, and in November 1957 the case for 25 aircraft had to be defended against a detailed calculation that 22 might be enough.(122) In reply, training requirements and wastage rates (assessed at one a year for seven or eight years), together with the unforeseen commitments, which experience had shown to be the normal lot of successful helicopters, were used to justify the order for 25 aircraft to produce the 12 UE for the overseas deployment specified in the Bingley report.

In early 1958 a new problem was put to the Air Staff: how could the Belvedere task be carried out if the order for these aircraft was cancelled to save research and development costs?(123) The question was made no easier to answer by the fact that the War Office was understood to have thrown over the whole tactical force plan agreed by the Bingley committee, on which the requirement for the 12 Belvederes was based.*(124) The Air Force answer was that there was no alternative way of meeting the task laid down (or any similar task) which did not involve a much larger expenditure on new helicopters, and that it would be very difficult to explain to the Public Accounts Committee why the Belvedere project was being abandoned at such a late stage.(125) Alternative ways, however, had still to be explored, including such absurdities as the provision of 72–108 Whirlwinds with Leonides Major engines,(126) but without War Office adherence to the Bingley

---

*The Air Staff suspected that the Army, knowing that there would be no Belvederes allotted to the JEHU, saw the RAF's purchase of that aircraft as a threat to its control of tactical Whirlwinds, and perhaps S-58s, which in 1957 it was still hopeful of gaining.

report any references to the Belvedere were necessarily somewhat vague.* To clarify the position DCAS had written in the previous month to DCIGS asking the Army to confirm that it still required the Belvederes and in the numbers ordered,(128) but DCIGS replied with no more than a short statement of confirmation but with no explanation.(129)

It was, therefore, only with the greatest difficulty that the order for 25 Belvederes for the RAF (and one for the Ministry of Supply) was kept in being until three pre-production versions of the aircraft became available in late 1960. Even then financial restrictions continued to play a part as development money was cut off before the final work was finished.

As a result, this 'ugly duckling' entered the RAF with not only the topographical peculiarities inherited from its earlier association with the Navy but also several uncorrected design faults as well. Nevertheless, it represented a historic milestone as it was the first helicopter in the RAF to be free of the problems which had plagued its predecessors: the severe restrictions placed on payload and operating profiles, especially in the tropics, by the performance limitations of their piston engines. The power/weight ratios of its turbine engines enabled the Belvedere to operate with such a huge reserve of power that in temperate conditions it rarely needed to use more than half the power available with both engines running. The limiting factor now was no longer engine power but the design strength of the transmission. Even at high altitudes in full tropical conditions, therefore, it suffered no limitation of payload or deterioration in performance, but merely a loss of single engine safety at the critical moments of take off and landing at maximum all-up-weight in the most severe conditions.

The Belvedere was also the first helicopter to equal and even exceed in service the most optimistic advance estimates of its performance, a fact which went a very long way to compensate for its lack of refinement in other respects, eg manual throttle RPM control, awkward fuselage shape, sundry maintenance problems and, in particular, its unreliable engine starting system.

The foresight and determination which the Air Ministry showed in bringing the Belvedere into service was therefore ultimately justified, and in the event its arrival was most happily timed as the availability of 12 Belvederes for overseas deployment enabled it to play a very significant and exclusive role in Aden and to contribute most notably to the Borneo operations of 1962–66.

---

*For example, the Belvedere had, it was merely said, the ability to put down 'comparatively large bodies of men in inaccessible areas, eg the Arabian Peninsula and the Horn of Africa' and a 'reasonably good ferry range', and would be of 'great value in internal security and other small operations'.(127)

Development of the Whirlwind

It was in Malaya that the Whirlwind's inadequate performance acquired critical importance, a problem which was only partially alleviated by the drastic steps taken in 1954 to enable the aircraft to fly at all (see pp 73–74). Consequently, it was in Malaya that the demands for the re-engining of the Whirlwind originated once the initial difficulties had been overcome in 1955. There was, however, no engine available in adequate numbers or with the necessary spares backing to meet the demand. A few Wright Cyclone piston engines had been obtained for the Navy to produce the Whirlwind Mk 3, but this expedient was of no help to the RAF in the time scale required and the spares shortage was acute. At that time, too, enough Bristol 192s were expected to be available by 1957 to meet the Malayan problem,(130) and it was also thought that they would replace the Whirlwinds in Coastal Command.

By 1957, however, the B 192 was being thought of as a tactical transport helicopter and it was therefore necessary to deal with the inadequacies of the Whirlwind Mk 2 in the SAR role, the best hope seeming to be the Leonides Major engine. The problem was now considerable because the Whirlwind had become firmly established in No 22 SAR Squadron in the south of England and was due to be withdrawn from Malaya to replace the Sycamores (with their smaller cabins) in No 275 Squadron in the north of England (see p 115). The need to provide eight Whirlwinds to support the atomic weapons trials in Christmas Island led to the formation of No 217 Squadron and confirmed the fact that the Whirlwind was here to stay and needed to be improved. A trial of the Whirlwind Mk 2 in Cyprus, where the Governor (Sir John Harding) was asking for a tactical troop lift helicopter, showed that even there the temperature and height factors made the Whirlwind virtually useless, and gave added impulse to the demands for re-engining.*(131)

In response to a plea from Coastal Command the Air Ministry reported in June 1957 that a detailed case would be prepared for re-engining the Whirlwinds with Leonides Major engines as soon as the results were known of the intensive flying trials being conducted by the Navy with the Naval Whirlwind Mk 7 which had been fitted with that engine.(132) At the time there seemed to be a fair prospect of success, as the Whirlwind gearbox could absorb an output of only 700 hp and the 850 hp Leonides Major engine would therefore have the additional reliability of a derated engine and still provide more power than the existing Pratt and Whitney engine of only 600 hp. The fact that the new engine was substantially heavier seemed of little importance in the context of the problems which had arisen from the Whirlwind's significant lack of power. The surplus power from the Leonides Major engine could also be an advantage in the 'hot and high' conditions of Malaya, but its greatest attraction was that its use in the Whirlwind would reduce the

---

*The Cyprus requirement was eventually dealt with successfully by the Sycamore.

compensation payable to the manufacturer following the decision to use the Gazelle engine in the B 192 and not the Leonides Major for which materials had already been purchased.(133)

With hindsight it is easy to see that it would have been an expensive mistake to have re-engined the RAF Whirlwinds with the Leonides Major engine and that serious consequences would have followed from attempting to meet the demands of the Borneo campaign with aircraft so equipped. At the time, however, most of the available evidence seemed to show that the Leonides Major engine was the appropriate choice and there was considerable pressure from all those operating Whirlwinds to give priority to the re-engining programme.

In the Navy the decision was taken early and Leonides Major Whirlwinds went into service in place of aircraft with Pratt and Whitney engines. The experience, however, was unhappy, and not only was the improvement in performance too small to justify the upheaval and expense, but the engine was also technically troublesome and, as a result, there were long delays in the re-engining programme and several aircraft were eventually lost in the sea.

The RAF, on the other hand, mindful that both the Whirlwind and the Sycamore would soon have to be replaced, and that its original operational requirement for a small tactical troop carrying helicopter had not yet been met, was considering the possibility that a much smaller turbine engine than those currently developed might be used to power the small types of helicopter in place of the heavier piston engine then in use. In November 1957 ACAS (Training) suggested that the turbine engined version of the Sycamore then being designed by the Bristol Aeroplane Company (B 203) might be considered as a replacement for both the Whirlwind and the Sycamore, arguing that the Whirlwind with the Leonides Major engine would be too heavy for the larger tasks and too large for the smaller tasks.(134) A few months later details became available of two small private venture turbine engines which seemed suitable for the size of helicopter needed to replace the Whirlwinds and Sycamores. One of these projects was a completely new engine offered by Armstrong Siddeley and designated P 181; the other was a version manufactured by de Havilland of the American GEC T 58 which had already been developed and installed in a number of American helicopters.

The advantages of fitting either of these engines in the Whirlwind were enormous: both the full performance required for SAR and—in all significant respects—that specified in the draft operational requirement for the projected Whirlwind/Sycamore replacement due in 1963/65 would be achieved. The expense of substituting a turbine engine for the Leonides Major would therefore by fully justified as it would remove the need for a completely new helicopter.(135)

126

The comparison between the Whirlwind's capability with the Leonides Major and the de Havilland Gnome engines was dramatic. Not only was there a weight saving of 765 lb, but in temperate summer conditions the extra power (1000 lb shaft horse power) enabled the take off weight permitting vertical climb to be increased to the aircraft permissible fuselage all-up-weight, a further saving of 165 lb. In addition, the cruising speed was increased from 70 to 90 knots, the net result being a payload increase in a rescue task at 50 miles' range from 1000 lb to 1800 lb.(136) The excess of shaft horse power available in temperate conditions over transmission limitations indicated that full performance would be maintained in 'hot and high' conditions of considerable severity.

Consequently, at the end of 1958 the RAF abandoned its interest in the Leonides Major engine at the very last moment and decided to re-engine its Whirlwinds with de Havilland (later Rolls-Royce) Gnome engines.(137) Thus was born the Whirlwind Mk 10, which entered RAF service in No 225 Squadron in late 1961 (a year after the formation of the Belvedere Trials Unit), just in time to join the Belvedere at the start of operations in Borneo. With the Belevedere it formed the main element in all RAF helicopter operations in the 1960s, except those in Aden, and continued in the SAR role beyond the end of 1975. The Gnome engine installation incorporated computer controlled fuel supply maintaining constant free turbine speed for varying power demands. The Whirlwind Mk 10 was thus the first RAF helicopter in which the rotor speed was controlled automatically rather than by means of a manual twist grip throttle operated by the pilot.

1 'History of the Development and Production of Helicopters on behalf of the RAF to meet Army Requirements', June 1954, in AHB ID/53/1/60/Pt 3: 25 Oct 1945.

2 Ibid, 22 July 1946.

3 Ibid, 28 Aug 1946.

4 Ibid, 12 Sept 1947.

5 Ibid, 30 Oct 1947.

6 Ibid, 20 May 1948.

7 No 657 Sqn ORB.

8 Ibid.

9 ID/53/1/60/Pt 3: 37 July 1948.

10 Ibid, Nov 1950.

11 Ibid, 16 Sept 1953.

12 Ibid, 13 July 1953.

13 Ibid, 27 July 1948.

14 Ibid, 26 Nov 1952.

15 No 657 Sqn ORB.

16 ID/53/1/60/Pt 3: 13 Jan 1947.

17 Ibid, 4 Oct 1946.

18 Ibid, 27 July 1948.

19 Ibid, 29 Nov 1951.

20 Ibid, 6 Dec 1951.

21 Ibid, 7 Oct 1952.

22 Ibid, 1 June 1954.

23 ID/6/15/Pt 1. DCAS to SofS Air, 22 May 1950.

24 Ibid, VCAS to SofS Air, 24 Nov 1950.

25 Ibid, note by VCAS, 23 May 1952.

26 Ibid, AC 11(52), 19 June 1952.

27 Ibid; Hansard, 2 Feb 1953.

28 ID/6/15/Pt 1. PM to SofS Air, 28 May 1953.

29 Ibid, PM to SofS Air, 15 July 1953.

30 Ibid, Lord Dowding to SofS Air, 15 May 1953.

31 Ibid, SofS Air to ACAS(P), 29 Apr 1953.

32 Ibid, Minister of Supply to SofS Air, 29 May 1953.

33 Ibid, Minister of Defence to Minister of Supply, 4 June 1953.

34 Ibid, DCAS to SofS Air, 5 June 1953.

35 Ibid, minutes of House of Commons meeting to discuss development and production of helicopters in the UK, 30 June 1953.

36 Air Council to War Office, 29 Apr 1953 in AHB ID9/H54.

37 ACAS(OR) to D Pol(AS), 25 June 1953 in AHB ID/53/1/60/Pt 2.

38 ID/6/15/Pt 1. SofS Air to Admiralty, 28 May 1953.

39 Ibid.

40 Ibid, Ops Ad to SofS Air, 15 Dec 1953.

41 ID/53/1/60/Pt 2. D Pol(AS) to DCAS, 4 July 1953

42 Ibid.

43 Ibid.

44 ID/53/1/60/Pt 1. COS(52) 87th Mtg, 16 June 1952.

45 Ibid, C-in-C Flying Training Command to Air Ministry, 1 Feb 1952.

46 VCAS to SofS Air, 25 May 1954 in AHB ID9/15/Pt 1.

47 ID/53/1/60/Pt 3. AC 17(53), 21 Dec 1953.

48 Ibid, DCAS to AC, 9 Dec 1953.

49 Ibid.

50 ID9/15/Pt 1. SofS War to Minister of Defence, 24 May 1954.

51 Ibid, SofS Air to AUS(G), 9 July 1954.

52 Ibid, SACEUR TO SHAPE UK, 14 June 1954.

53 Ibid, CAS to SofS Air, 5 Aug 1954.

54 Ibid, SofS Air to Minister of Transport and Civil Aviation, 30 July 1954.

55 ID9/H54. ACAS(OR) to CA, 16 Feb 1954.

56 ID6/463/Pt 4. ACAS(OR) to ACAS(P), 18 Mar 1955.

57 ID/6/15/Pt 1. War Office to Minister of Supply, 25 Sept 1954.

58   Ibid, SofS Air to CAS etc, 27 Sept 1954.

59   ID/53/1/60/Pt 2. DO(FP) to Head/F6, 26 Sept 1953.

60   ID9/H54. VCAS to DCAS, 8 Apr 1954.

61   Ibid.

62   Ibid, ACAS(OR) to DCAS, 22 June 1954.

63   Ibid, ACAS(OR) to DCAS, 8 July 1954.

64   ID6/463/Pt 3; ID9/H54.

65   ID6/463/Pt 3. DO(FP), 11 Mar 1954.

66   Ibid.

67   ID6/463/Pt 3. DCAS to AMSO, 15 July 1954.

68   Ibid, DCAS to AMSO, 22 July 1954.

69   Ibid, ACAS(Ops) to VCAS, 23 Aug 1954.

70   Ibid.

71   Ibid, D of Ops(3) to ACAS(Ops), 9 Nov 1954.

72   Ibid.

73   ID9/94/10/Pt 1. SofS War to SofS Air, 30 July 1957.

74   Ibid, ACAS(P) to DCAS, 9 Sept 1957.

75   Ibid, ACAS(P) to VCAS, 29 Nov 1957.

76   Ibid, DCAS to SofS Air, 13 Sept 1957.

77   A History of the JEHU compiled by Lt Col Fitzgerald (JEHU ops officer).

78   ID6/463/Pt 4. ACAS(P) to VCAS, 28 Apr 1955.

79   Ibid, HQ MEAF to Air Ministry, 12 Mar 1955.

80   Ibid, note by Pol(AS) 1, 27 June 1955.

81   Ibid, HQ FEAF to Air Ministry, 24 May 1955.

82   Ibid, Foreign Secretary to SofS Air, 29 Apr 1955.

83   Ibid, SofS Air to Foreign Secretary, 2 May 1955.

84   Ibid, British Embassy, Washington to Foreign Office, 15 May 1955.

85   Ibid, Air Ministry to Foreign Office and MOS, 23 June 1955.

86   Ibid, D Pol(AS) to ACAS(P), 18 June 1955.

87   Ibid, note by D Pol(AS), 8 Feb 1955.

88   Ibid, C-in-C, Home Station (designate) to Admiralty, 11 Mar 1955.

89   Ibid, C-in-C Coastal Command to DCAS, 18 Apr 1955.

90   Ibid, ACAS(P) to VCAs, 23 Apr 1955.

91   Ibid, VCAS to C-in-C Coastal Command, 12 May 1955.

92   Ibid, CAS to SofS Air, 1 June 1955.

93   Ibid, D Pol(AS) to Coastal Command, 20 June 1955.

94   Ibid, Summary of helicopter ordrs and delivery dates, 22 Mar 1955.

95   ID9/94/10/Pt 5. First Sea Lord to Minister of Defence, 7 May 1956.

96   ID6/463/Pt 3. ACAS(OR) to DGTD(A), 23 July 1954.

97   C H Barnes, Bristol Aircraft since 1910, 1964.

98   ID6/463/Pt 5. ACAS(P) to VCAS, 25 Aug 1955.

99   ID6/463/Pt 4. CIC(FE) 55(2)(Final), 31 Jan 1955.

100 ID6/463/Pt 5. ACAS(Ops) to VCAS, 27 July 1955.

101 Ibid, ACAS(P) to VCAS and DCAS, 25 Aug 1955.

102 Ibid, ACAS(OR) to ACAS(Pol), 1 Nov 1955.

103 Ibid.

104 Ibid.

105 Ibid, ACAS(P) to AUS(A), 2 Nov 1955.

106 Ibid, ACAS(OR) to DCAS, 15 Nov 1955.

107 Ibid, DC(55) 15th Mtg, 18 Nov 1955.

108 Ibid, note by Minister of Defence for Cabinet Defence Committee, 25 Oct 1955.

109 Ibid, DOR(A) to D Pol(AS), 6 Feb 1956.

110 Ibid, Air Ministry mtg, 8 Mar 1956.

111 Ibid, ACAS(P) to DCAS, 13 June 1956.

112 Ibid, D Pol(AS) to ACAS(P), 22 June 1956.

113 Bingley Cttee, 1956.

114 AC 12(56), 7 June 1956.

115 ID6/463/Pt 6. ACAS(OR) to DCAS, 1 Feb 1957.

116 Ibid, ACAS(OR) to Pol(AS) 1, 3 Apr 1957.

117 Ibid, DO(FP) to S6, 15 Mar 1957.

118 Ibid, MOS to F6, 14 Mar 1957.

119   Ibid, F6 to S6, 18 Mar 1957.

120   Ibid, ACAS(OR) to AUS(S), 11 Apr 1957.

121   AC(57) 9th Mtg, 4 Apr 1957.

122   ID6/463/Pt 6. DCAS to SofS Air, 5 Nov 1957.

123   Ibid, SofS Air to DCAS, 6 Jan 1958.

124   Ibid, AUS(A) to DCAS, 20 Jan 1958.

125   Ibid, F6 to ACAS(P), 31 Jan 1958.

126   Ibid, ACAS(OR) to ACAS(P), 6 Feb 1958.

127   Ibid, DCAS to SofS Air, 10 Mar 1958.

128   Ibid, DCAS to DCIGS, 5 Dec 1957.

129   Ibid, DCIGS to DCAS, 9 Dec 1957.

130   ID6/463/Pt 4. DOR(A) to D Pol(AS) and DO(FP), 24 Mar 1955

131   ID6/463/Pt 5. HQ MEAF signal, 17 July 1956.

132   ID6/463/Pt 6. DCAS to C-in-C Coastal Command, 3 June 1957.

133   Ibid, ACAS(OR) to DCAS, 30 May 1957.

134   Ibid, ACAS(T) to DO(FP), 25 Nov 1957.

135   Ibid, draft notes by DCAS, 25 Aug, 26 Sept and 15 Oct 1958.

136   Note by DCAS, 31 Oct 1958 in AHB ID/6/15/Pt 1.

137   Ibid, AC(58) 23rd Mtg, 20 Nov 1958.

138   Ibid, Minister of Tranpsort and Civil Aviation to First Lord of the Admiralty, 21 Dec 1954.

139   Ibid, First Lord of the Admiralty to Minister of Transport and Civil Aviation, 13 Jan 1955.

140   ID6/463/Pt 4. D Pol(AS) to ACAS(P), 8 Feb 1955.

141   ID/53/1/60/Pt 3. TFIc, 14 Apr 1954.

CHAPTER 5

THE MIDDLE EAST:
KENYA, ADEN, CYPRUS, EL ADEM AND JORDAN

In the Middle East the era of the operational helicopter began in late 1954, at the time when the Dragonflys in the Far East were being replaced by the Sycamore Mk 14s and the first SAR Squadron (No 275) was forming in Fighter Command. From then until the arrival of the turbine-engined Whirlwind in the early 1960s the full burden of helicopter operations throughout the Middle East theatre was carried by the Sycamores. Only in Cyprus was an attempt made to introduce the Whirlwind Mk 2, but it was soon shown to be less adept than the Sycamore at trooping in high temperatures at altitudes up to 4000 feet—one of the main helicopter tasks there—and was kept on the island for low level communications work.*

The first helicopter commitment in the Middle East arose out of the search and rescue requirement proposed by Lord Dowding in 1953 on behalf of the fighter squadrons based in the Canal Zone (see Chapter 4), and the three Sycamores specified for the task by DCAS in June 1953 were expected to be of value in Jordan and Aden as well as in the Canal Zone.(1) In the event, when the problems of producing the Sycamore to operational standards had been overcome, circumstances dictated that the first of the six helicopters promised to Lord Dowding for delivery between September 1954 and March 1955 (2) went in October 1954 not to the intended SAR unit in the Canal Zone or even to Cyprus, but to Kenya.(3) Later, however, Sycamores were allotted first to Aden and Cyprus in May 1955 and then during 1956 to Amman, Mafraq and El Adem.

Thus at the very outset the exclusively SAR function envisaged for the helicopter in the Middle East was pre-empted by its tactical potential, and although the single Sycamore sent to Nairobi was used mainly for military casualty evacuation, development there and elsewhere in the Middle East followed closely the pattern of tactical use already established in the Far East.

This was not, however, a deliberate policy and there was in fact no contact in the early part of the period between the two helicopter fraternities in the Middle and Far East. The former had grown up too soon to be aware of the latter's experience, let alone make use of it, and the CFS Helicopter Unit which was eventually to

---

*The record does not show why a Mk 2 Whirlwind was selected for this task. The Mk 4 with higher supercharger gear for greater performance at higher altitudes as used in Malaya would have made a better showing.

forge a link between the two was itself still in its formative stages in the early 1950s. Even within the Middle East theatre there was no contact at operating level between the helicopter crews in places as far apart as Nairobi, Aden and Cyprus. The early pilots, nearly all new to helicopters and having received only the most rudimentary civilian contract training, were in the true sense pioneers; almost totally isolated from one another, they were expected to operate in hostile environments and undertake unprecedented operational commitments which they frequently suspected (and usually correctly) to be beyond the capabilities of their aircraft. In all, their record can be seen as highly creditable.

Kenya

The environment which was most foreign to these inexperienced crews was undoubtedly that of Kenya. At their base at Eastleigh, for example, itself more than 5000 feet above sea level, they were already operating at a greater height than they had yet achieved elsewhere and some of the military operations against the Mau Mau involved troop activity up to 9500 feet and occasionally higher. On the other hand, there were compensations in the generally favourable weather, the exceptionally good visibility and the absence of strong turbulence.* All the same, in no way could the first two pilots at Eastleigh, Fg Off F A Bernard and Flt Sgt Boucher, have been adequately prepared for the very special handling techniques needed for day-to-day operations at such altitudes.

As early as November 1952 limited performance trials conducted by A&AEE with a Sycamore Mk 3 at Nairobi had shown that at maximum all-up weight at 5000 feet the aircraft needed a wind speed of 11 to 16 knots to climb vertically; alternatively, if the 'cushioned' take-off technique was used (accelerating forward from a low hover in ground effect) 300 to 400 yards were needed to reach a height of 100 feet.(4) In spite of these limitations, the GOC East Africa was still eager to have helicopters and GHQ Middle East Land Forces confirmed their acceptance of an offer of a Sycamore (to be delivered by Bristol Freighter) and requested a pilot. The Chiefs of Staff, however, were reluctant to agree, particularly as the only source from which an aircraft could be drawn was No 1906 AOP Flight (see Chapter 6), which had recently been supplied with three.(5) Also, VCAS pointed out that one Sycamore by itself would not be enough to operate on a stand-by basis, and so two months later, in January 1953, the Chiefs of Staff decided that the problems were too great and, as the Governor of Kenya was by then less enthusiastic, the idea should be shelved for the time being.(6)

---

*In the operational trials report the pilot stated: 'The helicopter is virtually unaffected by turbulence and therefore provides a much smoother ride for casualties than conventional aircraft.' The remark was true for passengers, but pilots from Malaya, Aden or Cyprus would never have spoken in those terms.

In October 1954, however, in response to further requests from the GOC East Africa, the first operational Sycamore allocated to the Middle East arrived at Eastleigh and on 29 October began operational trials. These were deemed complete after 55 hours flying in little more than a month and on 7 December the aircraft was declared operational.*(7) As the use of helicopters in Kenya had been the subject of Parliamentary Questions, a written brief on the progress of the operational trials was given to the Under-Secretary of State for Air who was visiting Eastleigh and a précis was signalled to the Air Ministry on 13 January 1955.(8) A summary of conclusions from these Phase 1 (sic) trials contained the following:

'a.   High altitude and temperatures caused appreciable loss of performance and the latter affects load carrying capacity diurnally as well as seasonally.

'b.   Above 5000 feet sustained hovering outside ground cushion is impossible, therefore the winch has been discarded.

'c.   Above 5000 feet (this figure was later amended to 7000 feet) vertical take off and landing impossible. Alighting area required is clear space 60 yards in diameter with no obstructions above 40 feet within 300 yards of line of approach and take off.

---

*Helicopter performance trials by A&AEE under the aegis of the Ministry of Supply were geared to a standard performance requirement derived originally from Malayan conditions. The standard chosen was based on the ability to climb vertically in still air at 200 feet per minute, and the variations of altitude, temperature and weight at which this minimum performance could be obtained were recorded.

Operational trials were supposedly based on practical applications of these criteria in the theatre concerned, but in the 1950s and early 1960s this data was often not available to the operational crews or was so unreliable, owing to significant differences between the trials aircraft and the operational machine (in this case the Mk 3 and Mk 14 Sycamores) or to the difficulty experienced by the test crews (not at that time experienced helicopter pilots) in obtaining accurate performance measurements, that a mainly subjective pilot's opinion of the aircraft's performance was used during operational trials to determine the aircraft's capabilities in particular areas.

In the jungle-free conditions of the Middle East, the stringent 200 feet per minute vertical climb requirement was less significant and consequently the practical payloads offered at various altitudes after operational trials were generally considerably higher than those declared in Pilot's Notes or Operating Data Manuals issued later by the Ministry of Supply.

'd. Present experience indicates that aircraft should be able to uplift one casualty from maximum 9000 feet and two maximum 8000 feet above mean sea level.'(9)

The report concluded that although more detailed technical data might be needed and trials using prepared tracks within the Forests* remained to be carried out the feasibility of using helicopters for casualty evacuation had already been proved.**

Thus in contrast to the FEAF helicopters which were already being described in Air Ministry papers as a short range transport force, those destined for the Middle East Air Force were being designated at this stage for search and rescue, casualty evacuation being considered their primary function.(11)

While the Air Ministry still awaited the full Sycamore operational trials report from Eastleigh, Press reports were beginning to appear. One described a Sycamore taking off at a height of 8430 feet and quoted RAF sources as saying that it was the first time a helicopter had risen from the ground at such a height in tropical temperatures. Another mentioned the first helicopter casualty evacuation in Kenya when a soldier was brought from the Nyeri area to Nairobi.(12)

When the operational trials report was received in January 1955 it revealed that take-off and landing performance had been measured at maximum all-up weight of 5400 lb at three airstrips between 6100 feet and 6400 feet, and with the winch removed at 7700 feet and 8200 feet. Moreover, a final take-off and landing had been carried out on the western forest edge of the Aberdares at 8500 feet with one passenger. The pilot, Fg Off Bernard, had flown solo twice to 12000 feet, and professing to be 'happy' with the situation offered room for two casualty passengers up to 8000 feet and one at heights up to 9000 feet. Serviceability was described as 'excellent'. The Sycamore had, in fact, been declared operationally ready for casualty evacuation standby in December 1954 and GHQ East Africa had issued instructions on landing site areas and procedures at the same time.(13)

It was nine months later, in October 1955, that the CFS Helicopter Unit was able to send out the first Qualified Helicopter Instructor (QHI). Fortunately this happened before the first engine failure was experienced in flight.(14) The technique

---

*Much of the Mau Mau activity in Kenya was based in the Aberdare mountains north of Nairobi, the main afforested area of the country and known simply as the Forests.

**The casualty task forecast in Kenya was based on statistics for one year from December 1953 in which 112 injuries (18 of which were battle casualties) were sustained in the field.(10)

for dealing with such an emergency had not been taught, except perhaps for an occasional demonstration at the civilian helicopter conversion courses used by the RAF at that time, and CFS had some initial difficulty in persuading the overseas units to practise a manoeuvre that seemed to them fraught with danger to an aircraft which was both valuable and difficult to replace.

No objections, however, were raised at Eastleigh and after both pilots had been declared fully competent in general handling techniques at high altitude, a satisfactory procedure for practising engine-off landings in those conditions (equally unfamiliar to the CFS pilot) was worked out in conjunction with Fg Off Bernard. In essence, this consisted of recognising a higher than usual collective lever setting during the approach, a higher initial flare with reducing collective setting to obtain maximum permissible rotor RPM or even a three per cent overspeed for up to five seconds, followed by a sustained full pitch descent to touch down. The Sycamore behaved most satisfactorily under this procedure and when a few weeks later Flt Sgt Boucher experienced the unit's first engine failure in flight he landed without damage in a comparatively small area surrounded by tall trees.

The Sycamore in Kenya was at first not part of MEAF's SAR establishment, but was supplied to the Kenya Government at a notional cost of £750 for delivery plus £75 per hour of operational flying, with the Air Ministry providing a replacement when a major overhaul was needed.*(15) Thus in mid-1955 a second Sycamore was provided and shortly afterwards the original aircraft was withdrawn for major servicing. Apart from this brief overlap there was only one Sycamore available for the final two years of the Kenya operation. During that time it operated continuously, flying a total of 506 hours and evacuating 30 casualties.(16)

Apart from pilot training the aircraft was also used frequently in the reconnaissance and communications roles, with area searches for terrorists a regular feature. In December 1955, for example, there were ten terrorist search sorties in the wheatfields of the Rift Valley and others north of Lake Naivasha, while in February 1956 the Eastleigh Sycamore assisted in flood relief operations in Tanganyika. Later, in October 1956, the aircraft was used extensively to transport HRH Princess Margaret during her tour of Kenya, the pilot having been granted his VIP qualification just beforehand by an examiner from the CFS Helicopter Unit.

Operations against the Mau Mau had been at their height when the Sycamore arrived in Kenya, but they reduced progressively over the following two years and in February 1957 the aircraft was withdrawn to reinforce the helicopter unit in Aden.(17)

---

*It became formally established in MEAF at the end of 1955.

Aden

The arrival of the first helicopters—in May 1955—created less of a sensation in Aden than elsewhere in the Middle East.(18) Khormaksar was already a large and busy complex with numerous operational aircraft, and the scenes of active operations were many miles away to the north and east. Aden was a long way from Cyprus and even further from the UK and the Far East, and the operational potential of the helicopter against a mobile and elusive indigenous enemy was far less obvious there than it was in Cyprus and Malaya. Initially, therefore, the Aden helicopters were seen as having no more than a SAR role, for which there was no urgent demand and which was inevitably only of minor importance. Aden, in fact, seemed to see even less need for this eccentric form of aviation than FEAF had done when the Casualty Evacuation Flight first appeared in 1950.

It quickly became obvious that the ground crews were inadequate both in numbers and experience,(19) yet little effort was made to demand proper technical support, and the supply of spares too was poor. Moreover, the two pilots (Flt Lts C S Bamberger and C Clay), who had received only the standard training—50 hours on the Dragonfly at Westlands followed by 10 hours' Sycamore conversion at Bristol's Filton factory—had neither the rank nor the experience in helicopters to rectify matters.

As a result, the Aden helicopter element never became a unit in its own right with the duty of compiling its own Operations Record Book (Form 540), and its activities therefore went largely unrecorded, attracting only the occasional comment amid the record of all the other activities of its parent station. Starting as a very minor part of the Aden Communications Squadron in June 1955, the SAR helicopters were transferred briefly to No 84 Squadron in January 1957, in whose records they were mentioned even less informatively than before. Five months later they returned to the station establishment, where they remained, the only regular reporting thereafter being references to servicing, engine changes and the occasional respray.(20)

The first pilot, Flt Lt Bamberger, arrived in Khormaksar on 24 June 1955 and flew 18 hours 30 minutes in 21 sorties during the following month. The second, Flt Lt Clay, arrived in August when only 1 hour 30 minutes was flown. Between then and December the maximum monthly achievement of the one and only Sycamore was 17 hours, but in November, when a second aircraft was uncrated, a mere 5 hours 25 minutes were recorded.(21) Flt Lt Clay then returned to South Cerney for CFS instructor training, returning to Aden in February 1956. Throughout that year, in the face of persistent unserviceability, due in large measure to a shortage of spares, the average monthly flying hours with two aircraft were under 20, with a peak in August of 44 hours 15 minutes (all of them training), when the pilots—now numbering three—qualified in winching from the sea.

It was not until February 1957 that an operation took place away from Aden, when Venoms and Shackletons provided air cover for a Sycamore recovering the Army victims of an ambush and five wounded dissidents. There was now much dissident activity in the hills, as well as Yemeni firing across the border, and with Venoms and Meteors being used for strafing and Shackletons for bombing, it became normal to include a Sycamore on major operations. Operating in the casualty evacuation role it would often be deployed to forward landing strips together with Pembrokes of the Aden Communications Squadron which carried patients on the longer journey from the hills back to Aden. In March 1957, for example, when Operation Zipper was mounted to clear dissident groups from the road to Dhala using twelve Venoms, four Shackletons and two Meteors, a Sycamore was employed to recover one tribesman and the body of a Meteor pilot to Thumier.(22) In June 1958 came the first serious incident when a Sycamore carrying a casualty from Dhala to Aden was hit by ground fire twice over Dubiyat while flying at 750 feet, but arrived safely in Aden with rotor blade and fuselage damage.

The need for tactical troop-carrying helicopters for operations in the Aden Protectorate was becoming more widely recognised, although it was 1963 before a Belvedere squadron was formed there for this purpose. Meanwhile the opportunity was taken in July and August 1958 to use the Royal Navy Whirlwinds from HMS Bulwark to carry troops to garrisons in Lahej and employ them on tactical operations during their short stay there.(23) A further task arose towards the end of that year when increasing labour troubles in Aden itself led to the Sycamores being used in the Internal Security (IS) role in the main base area. As a result of their rising popularity the number of helicopters in Aden had been increased by the arrival of the Nairobi Sycamore in 1957 and two more from the El Adem flight in 1958.

For the next five years the Sycamore SAR flight continued to operate in much the same way, with four aircraft for most of the time and two separate stand-by systems, one for maritime search and rescue in the Aden area and one for IS duties. These entailed either working with troops to the north or flying reconnaissance and security patrols, with occasional leaflet drops, around the main base area of Aden itself as the local situation deteriorated. The unit, still without a formal title and known simply as the Khormaksar Station SAR Flight continued unchanged, joining in operations as required, even after the Belvederes of No 26 Squadron arrived in 1963.

Then in January 1964 came the first SAR Whirlwind Mk 10, followed by a second in March, whereupon the four Sycamores were embarked in HMS Albion for return to the UK. Even that was not quite the end of their story, because the two Whirlwinds which were to complete the complement of four in Aden did not arrive until July, and the shortage of cover was felt keenly enough to necessitate the borrowing of a further Sycamore from Cyprus for the month of June.

A small group of Sycamores had thus, after a very shaky start, successfully carried the SAR responsibility in Aden and provided IS support for eight and a half years.*

Cyprus

It was not until May 1955 that the first two Sycamores arrived in Cyprus, some two years after helicopters had been proposed for the SAR role in the Middle East.(24) Much, however had happened in the interval; FEAF and Fighter Command, for example, had put in competing bids for aircraft;(25) the Sycamore production line had fallen well behind schedule; there had been many important changes in Middle East deployments; and the first of the MEAF allocation of Sycamores, which should have reached Cyprus in January 1955, had been sent to Kenya instead.

The early days of the helicopter unit in Cyprus were remarkably similar to those of the Casualty Evacuation Unit in FEAF five years before. Not only were the pilots just as inexperienced, but the station and Air Headquarters staffs knew nothing of the tactical potential of the aircraft put at their disposal. Two months before the Sycamores arrived MEAF Headquarters asked the Air Ministry to ensure that they had dual controls so that Communications Squadron pilots could learn to fly them and Staff Officers be given familiarisation training. When the Air Ministry replied that qualified helicopter pilots would be supplied with the aircraft, the request was reduced to one helicopter with dual controls.(26) In fact, no dual instruction was possible initially as none of the pilots was qualified to fly the Sycamore Mk 14, with its centrally mounted collective lever control, from the left hand seat.

While some Staff Officers expected the Sycamores to improve their chances of personal travel,(27) there was considerable nervousness at Station level over the whole situation, the Station Commander complaining that: 'The operation of this unit is hampered by the lack of directive, a proper establishment and agreed organisation and any relevant information on the operation of helicopters.'(28) HQ MEAF had in fact issued a 'general policy' for helicopters on 27 May 1955, but naturally this envisaged that SAR would be their only role in Cyprus and Aden.(29)

It was this situation that the first unit commander, Flt Lt P Fahy, encountered when he arrived in May 1955, his helicopter experience confined to the normal Westland Dragonfly course and the Bristol Sycamore conversion course. With his equally inexperienced NCO pilot colleague (Flt Sgt Harrison) he set about learning his new role. Neither had done any winching over the sea or spent more than a few

---

*See Chapter 11 for subsequent developments in Aden.

minutes hovering over a dinghy. Nor had either of them any experience of mountain flying or operating at high ambient temperatures.(30) Nevertheless, they immediately embarked upon an ambitious programme of experiments involving communications tasks over both mountains and sea. The dropping of mail to Royal Navy sloops was their first maritime task, while the regular conveyance of the RAF C-in-C between his home near Kyrenia and MEAF Headquarters at Nicosia provided useful experience in crossing the Kyrenia mountain range at different times of the day.

Although mountain flying was not an officially recognised tactical role, the need to understand the Sycamore's limits in this respect was implicit in the pilot's background training and, encouraged by the personal interest of the RAF C-in-C as a result of flying with them, a series of trials at various altitudes was begun.(31) Landings were made at different heights up to 4800 feet, culminating in a scheduled trial at Troodos (5300 feet) on 8 July. Finding crowds of sightseers assembled on the intended landing area, which was also obstructed by tall trees, Flt Lt Fahy selected an alternative site at a height of 6000 feet and after a number of trial approaches decided that he had adequate power resources with three passengers aboard. This proved not to be the case (or perhaps his technique was imperfect), and after touching down inadvertently in an overpitched condition he attempted recovery in forward flight and ended up on his side 30 feet down the slope. Nobody was injured but a number of lessons had been learnt, and the unit had only one aircraft for the next three months.(32)

Although their brief helicopter training had covered action in the event of engine failure, there had been too little time for practice and further training was patently necessary. But Flt Lt Fahy did not find it easy to obtain permission to practise a manoeuvre which seemed to entail a high risk of damage to the aircraft. Eventually the AOC Cyprus agreed to some practice engine-off landings which he himself would observe from the co-pilot's seat. Two demonstrations, however, were enough to persuade him to forbid any further experiments. The pilot subsequently reported that both landings had been safe and had caused no damage, but admitted that his nervousness due to lack of experience was probably evident.(33)

With planned engine-off landings now forbidden, mountain flying regarded as highly dangerous and one of the two Sycamores written off, those opposed to helicopters seemed to be riding high. Then in October two things happened. Field Marshal Sir John Harding became the new Governor of Cyprus and the CFS Helicopter Unit sent a QHI to visit the unit and offer advice. While CIGS, Harding had taken full advantage of the Sycamores belonging to No 1906 AOP Flight (see Chapter 6) for communications flights and had used helicopters during a visit to Cyprus in July 1955.(34) He was therefore fully aware of their tactical potential; he became a regular passenger on trips to all parts of the island and insisted on exploring the helicopter's troop carrying possibilities in all their aspects. Mountain flying trials with three passengers (or their equivalent in ballast) now received a new and urgent impetus, and with the arrival of a third Sycamore and more pilots, one well experienced, satisfactory techniques began to be established. In this as in many other ways Harding's arrival had a major impact on the security forces in Cyprus, similar to that achieved by Sir Gerald Templer in Malaya in 1952, and in several broadcasts he let it be known that 'while he was prepared to meet the Cypriots half way, he would brook no nonsense.'(35)

The visiting examiner from the CFS Helicopter Unit (Sqn Ldr J R Dowling) confirmed that operational development training was being properly conducted, but said that unless engine-off landings were regularly practised there was every likelihood of a catastrophic accident. At Station level there was still reluctance, but the point was pressed, demonstrations were given and the practice instituted.(36) Only three weeks later Flt Lt Fahy was flying from Government House carrying Field Marshal Templer, who was on a visit to Cyprus, when he experienced a total engine failure at a height of about 200 feet at an airspeed of 80 knots in the vicinity of the airfield. Thanks to his recent practice, he was able to 'avoid all the buildings and wires and landed without damage just outside the airfield.(37) This was one of three actual engine failures in flight that he experienced during his time in Cyprus, in none of which was there any consequent damage.(38) Nevertheless, practising engine-off landings in single-engined helicopters continued to arouse opposition because of the risks, and it was several more years before it became accepted as a standard requirement through the RAF.

By the end of 1955 the internal security situation in Cyprus was steadily deteriorating and Service personnel and their families, many of whom were living out in civilian hirings in Nicosia and elsewhere, were increasingly exposed to murder or abduction. AHQ Cyprus, which co-ordinated security services in the island, therefore instituted a system of 'families wardens' in the main towns and provided armed RAF patrols in the living-out areas on a roster basis.(39) There was also growing pressure for helicopter support for internal security operations and its potential for this purpose was first demonstrated in November 1955 when a Commando unit was engaged in arms searches in the Black Forest area of the Kyrenia mountains.(40)

With the withdrawal of AHQ Levant from Habbaniya in January 1956 and its reformation in Cyprus, absorbing AHQ Cyprus, the helicopter unit—the Nicosia Station Flight—became part of the Levant Communications Flight.(41) AHQ Levant itself could see no prospect of increasing the number of helicopters on the island,(42) but Harding was sufficiently convinced of their value to make representations at the very highest level in Whitehall in much the same way as Templer had done shortly after arriving in Malaya in 1952 (see Chapter 2). As a result, two more Sycamores arrived in March, making three for IS duties, followed by three more in June.(43) By the end of 1956 another four had been added making a total UE of

13 with one Command reserve. Three were fitted with SARAH for the SAR task and one was allocated for the Governor's personal use.

With the increasing size of the helicopter force crew training and the development of operational techniques necessarily proceeded with considerable urgency. Little was known in Cyprus of what had been happening in FEAF and certainly there was no first-hand knowledge. The technique, for example, of deploying troops by means of a knotted rope from a 20–30 feet hover (roping) had been used occasionally in Malaya, but had to be virtually reinvented in Cyprus, where it was much more often needed, the cost of the experiments being a series of minor and sometimes major casualties among the troops.(44)

In Cyprus, unlike Malaya, troop deployments were almost always to precipitous landing sites on mountain slopes or extremely narrow razor-backed ridges, precluding any chance of landing the helicopter. Thus, roping from Sycamores, which was not the main trooping helicopter in FEAF, became a specialised art in Cyprus. The aircraft was flown without doors, to save weight and permit rapid deployment from both sides when landed or from one side when roping; the rope itself was secured over a tripod on the starboard side using the mounts which carried the winch on SAR sorties. The upper end of the rope was secured near the collective lever by a special toggle with which the pilot could release it, so jettisoning the rope when his three passengers had departed—there was of course no crewman to pull it in. Teaching the troops roping procedures was of prime importance and became a significant element in the monthly training task throughout the remaining three years of the emergency and until the primary helicopter role in Cyprus reverted to SAR in 1963.(45)

Tactical support operations were usually arranged at very short notice, often in the middle of the night following analysis of the day's intelligence reports. As there was no planning staff with appropriate training in AHQ in early 1956, Army units had to plan these dawn operations directly with the Flight Commander. Flt Lt Fahy, who did not have enough points in the system to rate a married quarter inside the bounds of the RAF station, would have to be contacted in his flat in Nicosia and then, in defiance of the regulation that servicemen not travelling by RAF bus should be accompanied by an armed member of the security forces,(46) would load his revolver and drive cautiously to where the conference was taking place. The trooplift would then be planned in very great detail with the Army Commander concerned and a pre-dawn briefing prepared for the aircrew.(47) In spite of the seemingly ad hoc nature of these early helicopter IS operations, they were on the whole very successful.

The ranges for helicopter operations in Cyprus were short compared with those in Malaya, and with most troop movements on the ground being carried out in full view of the enemy, the speed with which the helicopter could move security forces between vantage points, and without laborious jungle clearing being required, made the small Sycamore force in Cyprus all the more effective. What was clearly needed, however, was a larger troop-carrying helicopter and in July 1956, following the FEAF precedent, a Whirlwind was requested. As the Mk 7 version with the Alvis Leonides Major engine was not expected to be available until 1957,(48) a Whirlwind MK 2 was sent for trials in Cyprus. It arrived in June and such was the interest that the C-in-C directed that the trials should proceed as rapidly as possible.(49) The results were even more disappointing than those in Malaya in 1953 (see Chapter 3). As Cyprus summer temperatures are only slightly lower than those in Malaya, the Whirlwind Mk 2 with half an hour's fuel could carry only four passengers and then only up to 3000 feet.(50) Most Cyprus trooping operations had to be carried out at higher altitudes with the additional requirement of hovering without ground effect and here the Whirlwind Mk 2 had a lower payload than the Sycamore.* Its task was therefore confined to shuttling the mail between Episkopi and Akrotiri.(52)

Concurrently with these first trooping operations in 1956, and the onerous task of providing full operational training for new pilots, most of whom were as inexperienced as the flight commander when he had first arrived, there was much to be done to develop the SAR role, for which the unit had been established initially. Sea hovering, dry and wet winching exercises, and an SAR standby had to be organised, and the fixed wing aircrews briefed and exercised in procedures. SAR development received the enthusiastic support of the air staff, and in March 1956 twenty GD Staff Officers at AHQ Levant were given wet winch training off the coast near Kyrenia, a fortunate precaution as on 13 July two of them—one being AOC Levant, AVM C D C Boyce, and the other his co-pilot—had to eject from a Vampire T 11 over Morphou Bay. Both were quickly winched into a Sycamore, so becoming the first jet aircrew to be rescued from the sea by a helicopter.

---

*Specifically, the requirement was for the roping of four soldiers at 4500 feet.(51) It seems likely that this Whirlwind was restricted to operating under the officially declared limits in which reserve power had to be available at all times to enable a vertical climb at 200 feet per minute to be made outside ground effect, whereas the Sycamores were using the less stringent criterion of what had been found after two years' experience to be an adequate power margin in Cyprus. If that was the case, the Whirlwind need not have appeared quite so inferior to the Sycamore, although it still could not meet the roping requirements for four soldiers at 4500 feet. When the official reserve power requirements to permit 200 feet per minute vertical climb were applied to the Sycamores, but not until 1959 as described below, the result was an immediate reduction of the passenger load from three to two in hot high conditions, regardless of the fact that they had been carrying three passengers for some four years.

Sycamore in transit in North West Cyprus.

Sycamore troop lift from Nicosia—Cyprus. Baggage and cabin doors have been removed. Note extra passenger carried by rotating the co-pilot's seat to face aft.

144-A

Troop training in Cyprus—deployment by knotted rope which is jettisoned by the pilot in the absence of a crewman.

Cyprus rescue of the crew of the trawler Suyeznik near Famegusta in January 1960.

144–B

Sycamore in typical troop deployment position—Cyprus.

As above.

Another problem affecting the Cyprus helicopters in early 1956 was low service-ability, and in view of the importance of the IS role the search for a solution was given the highest priority.(53) The Air Ministry sent out a Sycamore Servicing Demonstration Party and the Bristol Aeroplane Company a pilot and engineer to advise on servicing and operating techniques, the latter reporting a serious shortage of skilled servicing personnel. By late 1956, however, the serviceability rate had reached a satisfactory level, especially at Nicosia where regular helicopter trooplifts could now be planned, and by the end of the year the helicopter flight was carrying out between thirty and forty operational sorties a month.(54)

Some of these were pre-planned trooplifts and some were individual anti-terrorist actions. There was in fact more to contend with than armed gangs operating mainly in the hills; the civilian population contained many with nationalist sympathies willing to resort to violence, including children who were sometimes actively encouraged to engage in terrorist activities.(55)

By this time—late 1956—mountain flying techniques had been well developed, roping procedures were established and troop training was a regular feature. Moreover, Army Type WS 62 radio sets had been fitted to the Sycamores for contact with ground troops,(56) and a Bren gun mounting had been developed for side-firing from the aircraft.(57) On the other hand, an attempt to operate a powerful loudspeaker (Sky Shout) from the Sycamore was not successful.(58)

In September 1956 the Air Ministry decided to form the Nicosia Helicopter Flight, then part of the Levant Communications Flight, into a helicopter squadron, purely as a temporary measure as the IS task in Cyprus was expected to disappear in the following year.(59) Thus No 284 Squadron—last seen in 1945 flying Warwicks and Walruses on SAR duties in the western Mediterranean—was reformed in Cyprus in October 1956 comprising both the IS and SAR elements of the Sycamore unit. By November all the crews were fully qualified in mountain flying, winching, roping and night flying, the latter being needed for the casualty evacuation standby.*

At the end of 1956, however, with the achievement of 80% serviceability, staff shortages were beginning to appear. A strength of 15 pilots (16 established) was found barely sufficient, as was the crewman establishment of three navigators for the SAR role. Ground crew were still being used as crewmen for refuelling,

---

*No 284 Squadron's main IS operations were scarcely affected by Operation Mus-keteer, the Suez assault, in October/November. Much communications flying was generated and an additional SAR standby was mounted daily at Akrotiri where a temporary Rescue Coordination Centre (RCC) was established;(60) otherwise the main effect was a suspension of engine-off landing practices while the Nicosia runway was in heavy demand for fixed wing traffic.(61)

marshalling and directing troops in IS operations, all tasks later undertaken by specialist Mobile Air Operations and Field Refuelling units. In addition, another task was added in December when a Sycamore was detached to El Adem to mount an SAR standby for aircraft using the ranges near by, with one crew detached on rotation from Nicosia.(62) The detachment became a permanently detached flight in 1959.

The anti-EOKA* campaign peaked in early 1957 and the Sycamores were used extensively in a series of major troop operations. A typical procedure was to select a number of observation posts (OPs) and deliver to each at first light troops with kit and enough water for 48 hours; a shuttle lift of a main force would follow if required. In Operation Black Mac in January 1957, for example, eight Sycamores left Nicosia 20 minutes before dawn and four were positioned at Kakopetria (2000 feet), two at Prodrhomos (4600 feet) and two at Platres (3600 feet). These were the forward starting points for a dawn three-pronged trooplift close to the scene of operations. Each Sycamore delivered twelve troops and 1000 lb of kit in six lifts, taking between one and two hours; one of the landing sites used was at a height of 5300 feet. Aircraft were refuelled to a total of 20 gallons (40 gallons in winter temperatures) from jerrycans, while the rotors were turning and troops or loads being emplaned. After completing the first phase of the operation, four helicopters remained under the control of the army commander for the first day. Thereafter, two were provided each day for resupply, redeployment and casualty evacuation.(63)

Later, a new style of operation was developed, called 'cordon and search'. In this, helicopters were used individually to drop firing parties at each of several locations around a village or small area to prevent any movement while the ground forces approached by road. The town of Kallaki at 2800 feet on the northern slope of a steep ridge ten miles north of Limassol was dealt with in this way, with seven Sycamores positioning 21 troops around the town in about two minutes. The ground forces were then clear to enter the town from their position two or three miles down the mountain road.(64) In February 1957 in Operation Nomad five aircraft were used to make four drops each, delivering a total of 60 troops to the Kambos area at first light. Twenty more aircraft sorties placed 43 troops on the high Mathari ridge and two further aircraft positioned 21 troops overlooking the Amiandos and Khandria valleys.(65) Also in February, the village of Ayios Theodores was taken by surprise during the lunch hour when five Sycamores landed troops on the roof tops, in backyards and elsewhere. Two troop drops were made on the north ridge of Mount Olympus at 4900 feet and 4600 feet respectively, and roping was carried out in four feet of snow.

---

*EOKA: the military organisation seeking the union of Cyprus with Greece, a development which was unacceptable to Britain.

By March 1957 it seemed possible that final success in the EOKA struggle was imminent,(66) and the following month Archbishop Makarios, the Greek Cypriot political leader, returned to Athens from detention in the Seychelles and EOKA declared a truce. Nevertheless, intensive security operations continued in order to find Grivas, the EOKA commander, his armed bands and weapon stores, and while Makarios persisted with his political demands, EOKA forces were organising memorial services and issuing slogans, banners and leaflets in an effort to make an impact.(67) Systematic cordon and search operations employing helicopters, therefore, became regular occurrences throughout the island. For example, in June 1957, described as a quiet month in the No 284 Squadron ORB, five Sycamores, each with three troops, put an airborne cordon around the village of Kharch in the Kyrenia mountain range. One aircraft dropped three troops in the village to announce a curfew while the others surrounded the village. A bus and several people attempting to leave were then turned back by the helicopters, and the cordon was maintained for 45 minutes while the search was completed. Similar actions took place elsewhere throughout the following eighteen months.

Altogether between April 1956 and May 1957 the Sycamores flew 2561 operational hours delivering 3463 troops and 215000 lb of equipment; 4080 troops were trained in helicopter operational roles. A typical month's effort involved 70 reconnaissance flights, 214 trooping sorties (449 troops), 407 supply drops (78000 lb) and 697 communications sorties (961 passengers), 12 casualty evacuations and two sorties for the governor, a total of 338 hours flying.(68) Operations continued at a similar rate throughout 1957 and the early part of 1958.

In November 1957 Sir John Harding left Cyprus, handing over to Major General K T Darling as Director of Operations, while Sir Hugh Foot became governor. Harding had played a major part in bringing the helicopter force into existence, and before leaving he showed his interest and gratitude by paying a personal visit to the unit, speaking individually to the air and ground crews and having a photograph taken of the unit personnel with himself at the centre.(69)

By this time the demand for Sycamores in FEAF (see Chapter 3) was such that the Air Ministry made an urgent request to MEAF to reduce their holdings, only to be told that the IS situation in Cyprus was more dangerous than for many months and large scale operations might be needed.(70) This expected increase in sabotage was confirmed by MEAF in the following April,(71) by which time tension was also rising between the Greek and Turkish communities.

Six months later, the introduction on 1 October 1958 of the British Partnership Plan for Cyprus in the face of non-co-operation from the Greek Cypriots led to a renewal of EOKA violence. Seven British civilians were killed, one of them a woman deliberately shot. The monthly helicopter casualty evacuation record was immediately broken with 34 casualties, 32 of whom were victims of gunshots and bombs.(72) Then, in November all Greek Cypriot workers in military establishments were dismissed as a security measure.(73) With the situation growing increasingly dangerous a JEHU detachment of six Whirlwinds arrived in December, together with six Pioneers of No 230 Squadron, to provide reinforcements for the next two months.

By then, happily, conferences in London and Zurich had achieved a solution of the crisis and the stage was set for the return of Archbishop Makarios. His arrival was not followed by an immediate reduction in helicopter operations. Indeed, on 1 March, the day of his return, no less than 17 hours' reconnaissance flying was recorded and in the following month 475 IS sorties were mounted involving 165 flying hours.(74) There was, however, a change of emphasis, as most of these sorties were communications flights and the drop in actual operational flying was sharp enough for No 284 Squadron to request more exercise tasks.(75)

With military operations over, the squadron began to settle down into a regular pattern of activity, less spectacular than before perhaps, but still substantial and important: co-operation with the army generated a steady demand for helicopter support, some 40 hours a month on average but considerably less than the 130 or so hours a month devoted to crew training, including the development of night and instrument flying capabilities, and the provision of an ambulance, VIP and SAR standby service.

This pattern of activity continued with little variation until July 1963. The years between, however, were not without incident. Two Sycamores left in June 1959 to form a permanent SAR flight at El Adem, and the aircraft remaining in Nicosia were divided into two flights, one for SAR duties and the other for IS support. In August the squadron was retitled No 103 Squadron. Its aircraft establishment, however, remained unchanged until January 1961 when it was reduced by two, an acknowledgment of the very gradual tailing off in overall tasking; there was, in fact, little pressure to reduce the Sycamore strength in Cyprus significantly as the Malayan Emergency was over and the UK SAR squadron had been re-equipped with Whirlwinds.

Serviceability, however, did cause some problems. An average rate of between 61 and 77% had been recorded throughout 1958;(76) thereafter there was a fall to between 36 and 46%, coinciding with serious shortages of airframe mechanics (50%), engine mechanics (30%) and aircraft assistants (60%), shortages which were said officially to cause administrative rather than operational difficulties.(77) In addition, the Sycamores were grounded temporarily owing to the rotor blade problems which had come to light in Malaya (see Chapter 3); happily the grounding occurred when military operations in Cyprus were already over.

With the arrival of a new Squadron Commander in February 1959, special attention was given to training, safety and, in particular, the question of overloading.* Bathroom scales were used to weigh each passenger and it was discovered that the maximum weight allowance would probably be exceeded when more than two soldiers were carried. In November, however, it was conceded that three could be carried in winter temperatures at low level.(78) Yet none of the accidents which had occurred between 1955 and 1959—ground resonance, blade sailing, rolling on take-off, dropped stores hitting rotor blades, cable strikes, over-pitching and engine failure—had been attributed to overloading, although the official weight limits must surely have been frequently exceeded in the earlier days.(79)

In June 1963, however, squadron life changed abruptly. Helicopters were in urgent demand in Borneo and No 103 Squadron immediately disbanded in Cyprus to re-form in Singapore, leaving two SAR flights, No 1563 in Cyprus and No 1564 in El Adem, as the only helicopter units in the Mediterranean.

No 1563 Flight was in a sense no more than a continuation of the helicopter unit which had been established there for SAR duties in May 1955, but with four Sycamores instead of two, and six two-man crews instead of two single pilots. The lessons of the intervening years had, however, been learnt and although SAR was considered the primary role, the communications task remained of considerable importance. The Greek and Turkish community leaders were, for example, among the passengers carried by the flight in the first month of its existence.(80)

The SAR task in Cyprus was similar to that in the UK with the unit geared to the rescue of ejected or ditched aircrews, but spending much of its actual SAR effort on training and dealing with incidents of a non-Service kind such as those arising out of small boat sailing, mainly by off-duty British servicemen, and the occasional merchant ship in distress. In 1963 the proportion of operational flying (communications and SAR) to training was of the order of one to three in a monthly flying achievement of 120 hours.(81)

In December 1963 and January 1964, however, violence between the two communities increased and the ratio between operational and training flying was reversed again: a tripartite peace team was flown to a number of villages, and the RAF C-in-C relied on the Sycamores to move him rapidly between his base at Episkopi and the Joint Force Headquarters in the Carnero Hotel in Nicosia.(82)

---

*The term 'overloading' does not refer to exceeding the maximum all-up-weight design limits, but to the weight at which, at a specific altitude and temperature, the standard performance minimum of 200 feet per minute vertical climb in still air could be obtained. See footnotes on pages 135 and 144 above.

Then in February 1964 a United Nations force was introduced into the island to attempt to keep the peace between the warring communities, and a new IS communications task was therefore generated. This was taken over by a detachment of No 230 Squadron from Gutersloh, equipped with Whirlwind Mk 10s. These amalgamated briefly with No 1563 Flight to form a Nicosia helicopter squadron, in which the Sycamores retained the SAR responsibility.(83) But in the following month the pattern was established which was to endure for the next 16 years or more. The Whirlwind flight in Nicosia became part of the United Nations organisation, and No 1563 with its SAR task moved to the recently constructed airfield at Akrotiri and re-equipped with Whirlwind Mk 10s.* Strictly, its establishment was for only two aircraft, but to meet the RAF's demand for communications flying, as distinct from that for the United Nations force, it was allowed to retain for a year the two Whirlwinds which had been earmarked for the SAR flight at El Adem.(84)

El Adem

The need for a SAR flight of two Sycamores at El Adem to support the Armament Practice Camp (APC) due to be established there in late 1956 or early 1957 was foreseen by AHQ Levant in May 1956.(85) The main Air Firing and Bombing Range in the Middle East was near by, and in addition several army units were operating along the Libyan coast. Only a few minutes' flying time away was Tobruk harbour where a Marine Craft unit was located. El Adem was also a Transport Command staging post and in due course became a base for major Army and air support exercises.

In December 1956, with helicopter operations in Cyprus at their height, No 284 Squadron, newly formed there, had met the initial SAR requirement at El Adem by detaching one Sycamore from Nicosia with a small servicing party and exchanging the pilot every month.(86) The SAR cover so established was to continue with two breaks until the RAF finally left El Adem at the end of 1969.

In June 1957 the Station Flight at El Adem had two Sycamores established for SAR duties, flying between 30 and 70 hours per month between them in spite of an initial shortage of spares which caused one or other aircraft to be unserviceable on occasion for periods of a month or more.(87) In May 1958 mounting pressure from Aden resulted in the El Adem Sycamores and one of the pilots being reallocated there, in spite of the fact that the bombing range was being used by Canberras and Venoms from Malta and Cyprus, and by aircraft from the American 6th Fleet

---

*The Whirlwind Mk 10 was now replacing the obsolescent Sycamores and Whirlwind Mk 2s and 4s throughout the RAF.

in the Mediterranean; Army exercises in the area were also generating casualty evacuation sorties, which sometimes necessitated flying to the British Military Hospital at Benghazi. For the next year Royal Navy Whirlwinds provided occasional cover until two Sycamores were again established at El Adem in June 1959.(88)

The two aircraft and their crews became C Flight of No 103 Squadron* based at Nicosia in December,(89) and so came at last under the control and standardisation procedures of a fully operational helicopter squadron with a CFS-categorised QHI. When No 103 Squadron re-formed in the Far East in August 1963 leaving No 1563 Flight at Nicosia, the El Adem unit became No 1564 Flight, although QHI standardisation was still provided from the Nicosia unit.(90)

Unlike other Sycamore units in the Middle East, the El Adem flight had no wars or even local riots to contend with; nor did it suffer from terrain or altitude problems, its difficulties being confined to high temperatures in summer and occasional strong winds. Nor did its tasks vary significantly, as its main purpose was to provide SAR cover. Most of the monthly flying, therefore, consisted of continuation training, SAR with the Marine Craft unit at Tobruk, support for Army exercises, reconnaissance for desert survival courses, and the normal ad hoc communications tasks which the very presence of helicopters tends to generate. One special task was to maintain fuel dumps at Mechili, Derna, Giarabub and Capuzzo, which took the Sycamores over the whole of northern Libya, and there were also the inevitable SAR standby alerts when aircraft with technical problems were due to land: the Vulcan, Valiant, Lightning, Canberra, Heron, Javelin, Argosy and Hunter were all involved at one time or another.(91)

Although turbine-engined helicopters, the Whirlwind Mk 10 and Belvedere, were being introduced elsewhere in 1960–61, the Sycamores in El Adem and Aden went on until the mid 1960s before being replaced by the Whirlwind Mk 10 and Wessex respectively. In October 1963, however, the more modern type of helicopter appeared at El Adem during the largest joint exercise since the war, Triplex West.(92) Ten Whirlwinds Mk 10 of No 225 Squadron and two Belvederes from No 26 Squadron, all from Odiham, were flown out from the UK to Bomba, a coastal airstrip west of Tobruk. Two other Belvederes of No 26 Squadron had already passed through El Adem in February (Exercise Sandflight) on delivery flights from the UK to Aden. In March No 1564 Flight had been used for reconnaissance for the forthcoming exercise and although it was not directly involved in Triplex West itself, some communications flying was generated, notably when one of the Belvederes crashed.

The exercise came to an unexpected climax in November when the ten Whirlwinds and remaining Belvedere, together with two more Belvederes hastily despatched

---

*Formerly No 284 Squadron.

from the UK, were ordered to embark in HMS Albion and proceed to the Far East (Operation Spine) for duties in Borneo. No 1564 Flight assisted the embarkation by flying nine sorties to bring the Whirlwind crews from Albion to El Adem, before realising that the Sycamore had not been cleared for carrier deck landings because of its low rotor blades.(93)

The exercise over, No 1564 Flight settled back into its regular pattern of training and communications flights with an occasional casualty evacuation, until in May 1965 two Whirlwind Mk 10s were delivered by Beverley in exchange for its Sycamores. After crew conversion in Nicosia, the flight carried on as before until it disbanded in December 1966. Re-formed briefly in May 1969, it finally disappeared when RAF El Adem closed at the end of the year.

Jordan

In 1955, before the urgent need arose to expand the SAR helicopter flight in Cyprus, Amman had been selected as the base for a helicopter rescue unit to support the fighters based in Jordan. The first Sycamore was delivered by sea to Aqaba, where it was erected and flown on 14 January 1956 to Amman, where No 249 Venom Squadron was stationed. The one and only pilot was Flt Lt J E McCrea.(94) The Jordan flight had a short and only moderately successful life. The country was already in the turmoil which was to lead to the dismissal of General Glubb in March, but it was April before two more pilots arrived and the second aircraft did not appear until May.* The flight was used in the IS role on an ad hoc basis, typical of its tasks being the delivery on 3 March of arms, food and ammunition to a convoy stranded between Amman and Aqaba. Sadly, however it never succeeded in building up a proper technical backing and rarely achieved more than 12 hours' flying a month, the highest total, 18 hours 15 minutes, coming, perhaps significantly, in the month following a visit by the touring Sycamore technical expert from the Bristol Aeroplane Company, Mr Vicary.

In October 1956, at the time of the Suez operation, political pressures and the presence in Amman of elements of the Egyptian Air Force compelled the RAF to leave there and withdraw to new buildings at Mafraq. The Sycamores continued to operate, but only for two or three hours a month, until the British forces finally withdrew from Jordan following the termination of the Anglo-Jordanian Treaty in May 1957. The Sycamores themselves left by sea from Aqaba.(96)

---

*One of the two Sycamores was later taken out of service as no pilot was available.(95)

1   ID3/943/2/Pt1.

2   Ibid.

3   ID/53/1/133/Pt1.

4   ID/53/1/10/Pt2.

5   Ibid.

6   Ibid.

7   ID/53/1/10/Pt3.

8   ID/53/1/133/Pt2.

9   Ibid.

10   Ibid.

11   ID/53/1/133/Pt1.

12   Ibid.

13   Ibid.

14   Pilot's log book.

15   ID/53/1/133/Pt1.

16   Eastleigh ORB.

17   MEAF ORB

18   Khormaksar ORB.

19   Ibid.

20   Khormaksar ORB.

21   Aden Comm. Sqdn ORB; Khormaksar ORB.

22   Ibid.

23   Ibid.

24   ID/53/1/133/Pt1.

25   Ibid.

26   Ibid.

27   IIJ2/33/1

28   Nicosia ORB.

29 MEAF ORB.

30 IIJ2/33/1.

31 Ibid.

32 Ibid.

33 Ibid.

34 Nicosia ORB.

35 AHQ Cyprus ORB.

36 Flt Cdr's report.

37 Ibid.

38 Ibid.

39 AHQ Cyprus ORB.

40 MEAF ORB; Nicosia ORB.

41 MEAF ORB.

42 IIJ2/33/1.

43 MEAF ORB.

44 Ibid.

45 No 284 Sqn ORB.

46 AHQ Levant ORB.

47 CFS Examiner's report.

48 ID6/463/Pt.

49 MEAF ORB.

50 ID6/463/Pt5.

51 Ibid.

52 Nicosia ORB.

53 MEAF ORB.

54 Nicosia ORB.

55 AHQ Levant ORB.

56 Nicosia ORB.

57 AHQ Levant ORB.

58 MEAF ORB.

59 ID6/463/Pt5.

60   AHQ Levant ORB.

61   Nicosia ORB.

62   No 284 Sqn ORB.

63   IIJ2/33/1.

64   Ibid.

65   No 284 Sqn ORB.

66   Ibid.

67   Ibid.

68   No 284 Sqn report.

69   IIJ2/33/1.

70   ID6/463/Pt6.

71   MEAF ORB.

72   No 284 Sqn ORB.

73   MEAF ORB.

74   No 284 Sqn ORB.

75   Ibid.

76   MEAF ORB.

77   No 284 Sqn ORB; MEAF ORB.

78   No 103 Sqn ORB.

79   Nicosia ORB.

80   No 1563 Flt ORB.

81   Ibid.

82   Ibid.

83   Ibid.

84   Ibid.

85   AHQ Levant ORB.

86   No 284 Sqn ORB.

87   El Adem ORB.

88   Ibid.

89   No 103 Sqn ORB.

90   No 1564 Flt ORB.

91 Ibid.

92 Ibid.

93 Ibid.

94 Amman ORB.

95 Ibid.

96 Ibid.

CHAPTER 6

TRANSPORT, COMMUNICATION AND TRAINING UNITS IN THE UNITED KINGDOM IN PHASES 1 AND 2 (1945–62)

Introduction

We have now seen how tactical support helicopter flying developed in the 1950s in the main overseas theatres, and it is time to examine what was happening concurrently in the United Kingdom where the rapid expansion during Phase 2 was no less intense. This chapter will deal with the Joint Experimental Helicopter Unit (JEHU) which set the scene for the growth of the European-based tactical helicopter squadrons in the 1960s, and with the establishment of helicopters in the Queen's Flight, the Metropolitan Communications Squadron and the Central Flying School. First, however, we must consider their predecessor in the communications/transport field—No 1906 Air Observation Post Flight.

No 1906 Air Observation Post Flight (1)

The origins of No 1906 AOP Flight have already been briefly mentioned in the Prologue. Its precursor, No 1901 AOP Flight, flew R4 and R6 helicopters under the Ministry of Supply at Beaulieu in 1946 from whence it was relocated with its Squadron Headquarters (No 657 AOP) at Andover in 1947 with five R6 (Hoverfly Mk 2) helicopters. The Squadron moved to Middle Wallop in January 1948 and No 1901 Flight became attached to the Transport Command Development Unit at Brize Norton. As its three remaining ageing aircraft ran out of spares, the Flight became steadily less effective. The small handful of pilots dwindled to one, mainly by voluntary retirement to civilian helicopter test pilot posts. Major Gow, shortly before retiring himself, trained two more Army pilots—Major Repton and Captain Spittal—to fly helicopters and they accompanied the Transport Command Development Unit when it moved to Abingdon in June 1949. A year later the Hoverfly Flight returned once more to its Squadron Headquarters at Middle Wallop and was retitled No 1906 AOP Flight.

While this early Hoverfly unit had little effective operational capability, it had experimented with a great variety of tactical roles in addition to AOP gun direction. These had included field concealment, aerial photography, air/ground telephony, motor transport convoy shepherding, radar trials, camouflage, night flying, W/T tests, fighter evasion (with Meteors and Spitfires), comparative climb trials with the Auster MK 6 (which proved to be better than the Hoverfly) as well as participation in various roles in Army exercises. By 1949 it was becoming impossible to continue all these activities but the Flight was tenaciously maintained to keep the principle alive, to demonstrate the potential of the helicopter and to avoid losing altogether

157

Mk 11 Sycamore of 1906 Air Observation Post Flight on exercise in Germany
(1952/4)—Major B Repton and Captain J Spittal—the only two pilots.

Mk 11 Sycamore of 1906 Air Observation Post flight landing on HMS
Implacable for transit to Guyana—October 1953.

whatever pilot expertise had been acquired in Army support roles, pending the availability of more useful aircraft.

By the end of 1950, the only two reasonably complete Hoverflys remaining were grounded because of corrosion and fretting of the main rotor blade spars. Nevertheless, such was the determination of the last two pilots that they somehow obtained permission to continue flying, accepting a restriction requiring them to remain below 20 feet in the doubtful belief that they were thereby reducing the risks in the event of a major component failure. The losing battle came to an end in April 1951 but it was a further six months before the long promised and eagerly awaited Mk 11 Sycamores came to replace them.

The arrival of the Sycamore in September 1951 thus marked a second start for RAF helicopters in the Army AOP and Light Liaison roles. The case for furnishing No 1906 Flight with new helicopters had been persistently argued and there can be no doubt that the success of the first year of operations of the Casualty Evacuation Flight in Malaya and the simultaneous dramatic events in Korea eventually silenced the sceptics. Nevertheless, the modest provision of three Sycamores could hardly be expected to satisfy the demand. They were larger and heavier than was required and such a small number would be hard pressed to demonstrate the practicability of the various operational roles it might be hoped they could fill. There was however no other option since the hoped for Skeeter was still a long way from satisfactory development. In fact, light liaison was the only role these few Sycamores could properly fill. That role, however, had not acquired the status which it later achieved, and throughout the early 1950s No 1906 Flight was under periodic critical review as the RAF struggled to meet the pressing demands for new operational helicopter units both in the United Kingdom and abroad. The AOP role was nevertheless stoutly defended by the Army, and No 1906 Flight survived largely on the reputation of its earlier Hoverfly years although its Sycamores spent most of their time merely carrying VIPs on visits and appearing at demonstrations, while providing reconnaissance and mobility facilities for Commanders at Army exercises both in the UK and Germany.

The two Hoverfly pilots, Major Repton and Captain Spittal, were converted on to the Sycamore in August 1951 at BAC Filton, collected their first aircraft in the following month and took part in Exercise 'Surprise Packet' on Salisbury Plain in October. (This was the occasion when Mr Ken Reid of Westlands demonstrated the S-55 with 11 troops on board as mentioned in Chapter 3). The Sycamore was still in its proving phase and many of its component 'lives' were still very short (185 hours in some cases). By May 1952 two of the three aircraft delivered were expected to be component life-expired within two months, and the third had only 25 hours to go, while the communications and demonstration commitments were increasing. (One aircraft had to be provided for the CIGS in Buckeburg that month). In August

Whirlwind Mk 2, Sycamore Mk 14, Dragonfly Mk 4 of the CFS Helicopter Unit at South Cerney—late 1950s.

a component life increase to 250 hours alleviated the problem somewhat, but it will be seen that the unit operated very much on an ad hoc basis.

During the remainder of 1952 many Army and RAF VIPs were flown; the Minister of Defence was flown to the SBAC show; there was participation in an exercise with 2nd TAF in Germany; the AOC No 12 Group, Air Vice Marshal Atcherley, (in whose Group the unit was established) and the OC of the CFS Examining Wing, Wg Cdr Lyster, were trained to first solo stage (8 hours 20 mins and 6 hours respectively); night flying experiments were carried out, and during December 1952 and January 1953 the aircraft were prepared for a possible casualty evacuation in Kenya. During February 1953 the projected task in Kenya was dropped and No 1906 Flight was involved in the emergency helicopter rescue maximum effort generated by the disastrous floods in Holland that year. In March three Sycamores were provided as escort for HRH The Duke of Edinburgh who was touring Germany in a civilian S-51 helicopter—the first Royal flight by helicopter.

There was still no properly organised helicopter pilot training organisation in the RAF, and semi-official conversion to type tended to be done on an ad hoc basis by those who could arrange it. The AOC No 81 Group, Air Cdre Hogan, having been sent solo in a No 1906 Flight Sycamore in April 1953, experienced ground resonance while attempting to land, tried to take off again, and was fortunate to escape without any injury in the resultant disintegration.

In October 1953 a detachment of No 1906 Flight with one Sycamore was embarked on HMS Implaccable for support operations in British Guiana. It was characteristic of the state of affairs at the time that when the aircraft became unserviceable at Exmouth en route for embarkation, a step ladder had to be borrowed from a local bus company and spanners from a passing motorist to effect repairs. On arrival at the scene of operations in Guiana, or as close as Implaccable was able to go, the flight ranges required were so far beyond the capabilities of the Sycamore that nothing could be done. The detachment got home to Middle Wallop a few days before Christmas. In March 1954 a No 1906 Flight Sycamore was used in conjunction with Police voice radio for crowd control at Aintree during the Grand National.

These are examples of the general nature of the tasks which came the way of No 1906 Flight while the Sycamores were in use, but the main continuous role throughout the years 1952–56 was really VIP transport. In the later stages particularly, these aircraft were used mainly for the CIGS and GOC Southern Command, with frequent visits to Germany and Holland to carry out similar tasks. In October 1955, No 657 Squadron became No 651 Squadron. No 1906 Flight continued as before. In January 1956 a Skeeter (Mk 6) at last became available for a two-week trial with No 1906 Flight and generated considerable enthusiasm, although the first delivery of a Skeeter for unit use did not occur until January 1957 (Skeeter Mk 10).

The formation of the JEHU at Middle Wallop in 1955 did not, as might have been expected, result in the absorption of No 1906 Flight. The JEHU became the natural source of helicopters for special tasks, but No 1906 Flight continued to exist although, apart from annual training exercises in Germany, almost exclusively in the VIP and communications role. In April 1957 No 651 Squadron with its AOP Austers moved to Feltwell, leaving No 1906 Flight with its Sycamores and new Skeeters independently at Middle Wallop. The formation of the Army Air Corps in September with the all-up-weight limitation of 4000 lbs for Army aircraft, seemed to remove the last possible objection to allowing the RAF to redeploy the No 1906 Flight Sycamores to help to relieve severe shortages elsewhere. Nevertheless, the DCIGS wrote a strong plea to DCAS on 16 September (Lieutenant General Sir Richard Hull to Air Marshal Sir Geoffrey Tuttle) for the three remaining No 1906 Flight Sycamores to be retained, until a substitute could be found, for use by Members of the Army Council including the Secretary of State for War who was described as an interested and frequent user. There was no longer any pretence of tactical operational capability, nor was mention made of AOP or other specialist roles.(2) DCAS replied on 24 September by pointing out that the Royal Air Force could not afford to allow Members of the Air Council to use helicopters and neither could other senior RAF officers use them for communications. It would be difficult to retain helicopters to enable the Army to do something which a similar body of people in the RAF could not.(3) Both sides must have been well aware that, while the Treasury continued to deny funds for communications helicopters to be established (see Chapter 4), for really urgent VIP tasks the Army could mis-employ the JEHU and the RAF could continue to mis-employ the the CFS helicopter unit which by then had existed for three years. So No 1906 Flight lost its Sycamores which were redeployed by the RAF and the unit, now with Skeeters, was absorbed by the new Army Air Corps in September 1957.

TRANSPORT HELICOPTERS IN THE UK

The 1953 decision of the Air Council to establish communication helicopters at each RAF Command, eight in Germany, two at Hendon for Air Ministry use and one or more in The Queen's Flight and the Treasury refusal to agree (except for the two at Hendon) was dealt with in Chapter 4. At the same time it was intended to create a Tactical Transport Helicopter Unit in Transport Command—four Whirlwinds to be replaced by four Bristol 173s in due course—but again Treasury agreement was not forthcoming. Three years later the JEHU was formed.

160

Skeeter on trial at CFS—1955.

Sycamore Mk 13 showing the duplicated collective
lever which was replaced by a single central collective
lever in the Mk 14 production aircraft.

160–A

Jehu

The background to the 1954 decision to set up the Joint Experimental Helicopter Unit was described in Chapter 4. It is important to understand the motives and hopes of the Air Ministry at that time in order to explain the frustration and disappointment felt by the unit at the end of its $4\frac{1}{2}$ year life when it was erroneously believed to be a proving ground to justify Army purchase and control of tactical support helicopters. The Air Ministry was already fully aware of the need for tactical support helicopters and in December 1953 expected the Bristol 173 and, later, the Wessex, to meet it. Until the Bingley Report in 1957 made the RAF formally responsible for this role they could order no aircraft against the requirement, but were aware of the need for development in two areas ie the integration, control and tasking, to include cargo handling, of a force of support helicopters with the Army in a forward area; and the development of aircraft navigation, night flying and instrument flying techniques and equipment for a tactical environment. It was to examine these two areas that a helicopter unit was first proposed in Transport Command in 1954, and the acceptance of the JEHU which could undertake the first but not the second task was seen as of limited value. Thus it was that the publication of the Bingley Report was seen by the Air Ministry as an opportunity, at the end of JEHU's projected two year life, to start specialised development of this role, new in the European Theatre, while the JEHU saw it as a chance to enlarge their charter to include all VTOL and STOL aircraft in the tactical logistic role, and, in particular, to develop the 'Utility' helicopter for Army Support.(4)

The Air Ministry recommended disbandment of the JEHU in 1957, pointing out that they already had two squadrons of 'Utility' helicopters in FEAF and one in Cyprus,(5) and the compromise reached to keep the Unit in being for a further two years, as described in Chapter 4, was simply a holding action whilst the RAF was not itself in a position to find the aircraft and resources to form a tactical unit in the UK. That the RAF would eventually take over the unit, all of whose aircraft exceeded the 4000 lb weight limit for Army aviation, was inevitable.(6) In the JEHU itself, however, flushed with the success of the Suez operation and aware of its unique position in the UK while all the RAF effort was devoted to the Far and Middle East, the spirit was one of enthusiatic pioneers, with prestige and publicity scarcely less important.(7) The announcement of the Unit's disbandment in late 1959 therefore came as an unexpected shock to the Army members, including the Commanding Officer, since they quite unjustifiably considered that they were achieving their own aims with marked success in support of various major exercises. 'Stunned amazement' was described as a polite understatement of the reaction by the Commanding Officer, Lt Col D W Coyle, MBE DFC RA.(8)

Although in 1957 the RAF considered that from its own specialised point of view the JEHU had developed nothing of value not already discovered in Malaya and

Cyprus, lacking as it did the capability (in RAF terms) to develop night, instrument, navigation and underslung load techniques,(9) nevertheless very considerable progress had in fact been made in the organisation and management of a force of helicopters in close support of ground and sea operations; and in introducing some of the new facts of life to a variety of Army organisations with little or no previous understanding of helicopter capabilities and limitations. This is not to deny that valiant efforts were made by the JEHU, particularly in its last two years, to develop night techniques and to take part in radio and navigation equipment trials, but these activities were regarded as amateur insofar as they were generated and conducted within the unit. Where they became integrated with official R & D bodies—Ministry of Supply, BEA and equipment manufacturers—as they often did in the last two years, these trials were seen as not specific to the JEHU as such but natural to the RAF Short Range Transport Squadron which the unit eventually became.

In summarising the work of the JEHU it is both natural and convenient to start with the Suez operation—more accurately to the assault on Port Said (Operation Musketeer)—since not only was that the 'launching pad' from which the unit really took off, but nothing much had happened before then. But first it is necessary to explain the intended functions of the unit.

The JEHU came into existence on 1 April 1955, but for nearly a year had only six Sycamores, a number of organisational and initial administrative problems and a very broadly worded jointly agreed directive—'To collect information by practical trials to enable the two Services to determine whether helicopters or such other aircraft as may be allotted to the Unit, are likely to be a practical, efficient and economical means of solving the Army's problem of mobility, organisation and administration in the field in a future war. This may include problems which are shared with other Services in forward areas.' More specifically, the tasks laid down by the War Office were:—

'a.   To determine the limitations of helicopters, operating as a unit under all weather conditions.

b.   To determine the problems of operating a helicopter by day and night.

c.   To report on the practicability of high intensity flying by the unit in all weathers. This requires trials of:—

(i)   Aspects of ground control such as those involved in reducing turn round times.

(ii)   Flying control at landing areas.

(iii) Control and guidance of aircraft in the air.

d.   To study the tactical problems within the unit such as evasion in the air and concealment on the ground.

e.   To determine the ground organisation required for a helicopter unit at loading and unloading points.

f.   To determine the flying task a logistic helicopter unit could accomplish.

g.   To study the integration of this method of supply with the existing system of supply by air to both Army and Air Force units in the forward areas ie the Army/Air Transport Organisation, Rear Airfield Supply Organisation, Forward Airfield Supply Organisation.

h.   To determine the best means of maintenance of tactical transport aircraft in the field.'(10)

It is hardly surprising that in December 1957 VCAS commented that the JEHU had not completed any one of the tasks allotted to it by the War Office when it first came into being in 1955, partly because of slow delivery of aircraft, partly because of Suez, but chiefly because the tasks were beyond its technical capability.(11) In retrospect, it can be seen that, more than any other factor, the Suez experience was the impetus which enabled the JEHU to make whatever progress it did in later participation in various Army exercises.

It was not until March 1956, one year after formation, that it was possible to supply the JEHU with its six Whirlwind Mk 2 aircraft, thus enabling the two Flights to be formed—Sycamores for development of flying techniques and Whirlwinds for trooping and logistic roles. An Army pilot commanded one Flight and an RAF pilot the other. Equal numbers of Army and RAF pilots were distributed in each Flight and as many as possible cross-trained on both aircraft types.

Only four months later, in July 1956, the impending Suez crisis put a stop to a planned unit move to BAOR for the autumn exercises. On 1 October JEHU was embarked in the Light Fleet Carrier HMS Theseus for flying training at sea when the procedures for handling this helicopter force on the carrier deck and hangars were rehearsed.

As the unit was to be employed as a close support transport squadron under RAF control, the word 'Experimental' was temporarily dropped from the title and the JHU embarked on HMS Ocean (sister ship to HMS Theseus) in late October. Both ships (HMS Theseus with No 845 Squadron RN having 10 Whirlwind Mk 22 (American S 55) helicopters met at Malta on 31 October and had a brief practice session in which JHU from HMS Ocean and No 845 Squadron from HMS Theseus rehearsed lifting 45

Commando RM from ship to shore. The JHU aircraft were stripped of 2nd pilot seats, passenger seats and doors, enabling the Whirlwinds Mk 22 and 2 to carry seven and five men respectively and the Sycamore three. 45 Commando was to be used as a mobile reserve force for the assault and was to be lifted ashore by the JHU and No 845 Squadron from HMS Ocean and Theseus respectively. Thereafter, the helicopters were to be available for casualty evacuation and reconnaissance.(12)

Both Carriers sailed from Malta on 3 November 1956 and anchored nine miles offshore at Port Said before dawn on 6 November. The complete helicopter force from both ships flew in formation initially in four 'waves' at 70 knots low level because the LZ, near the De Lesseps statue, could only accommodate six helicopters at once. After the initial landing at 0610 hours a shuttle ferry was maintained until the whole of 45 Commando and its equipment was landed which took 1 hour 25 minutes for troops, weapons and ammunition and a further one hour for other equipment. The JHU completed seven waves of aircraft totalling 178 marines and $12\frac{1}{2}$ tons of equipment. The two helicopter squadrons together lifted 415 men and 25 tons of freight in the $2\frac{1}{2}$ hour period. The operation was described as 'the first occasion in military history in which helicopters had been used in a full-scale assault', although the procedure had been in use in Malaya, albeit on a small scale, since Operation Wellington II in 1953 (see Chapter 3, pages 61–63).

Following the assault and the casualty evacuations during and after it (96 including some Egyptians on the first day) the JHU was employed in the numerous communications, freight lifting and reconnaissance tasks in support of the continuing operation, being based ashore at El Gamil airfield from 8–23 November (451 sorties), after which the Unit was withdrawn. The Sycamores returned via HMS Eagle to Malta, thence by HMS Ocean to the UK. The Whirlwinds, however, had been grounded on 19 November suffering badly from airframe salt corrosion, and after being transported by HMS Eagle to Cyprus for inspection by the Maintenance Unit at Akrotiri, were dismantled and flown in Beverleys to the UK where they underwent extensive repair at Westland. The Outline History of the JEHU records that the cost of these repairs caused the Army Council to consider seriously whether the JEHU should be kept in existence, but that 'wisdom fortunately prevailed and shortsighted opposition to the Unit was once again defeated' there being 'little doubt that this was entirely due to the success achieved by the JEHU at Suez, demonstrating indisputably on active service that the load carrying helicopter could play a vital part in modern mobile warfare.' As has been shown there were quite different reasons for questioning the continuance of the JEHU at that time.

The first quarter of 1957 was given over to reorganising, recovering the aircraft and refitting trials equipment. The JEHU was now in a unique position. It not only possessed a dramatic and even dashing operational campaign history, but it was the only helicopter unit of any size in the UK with no dedicated operational or training task to inhibit its participation in any exercise or demonstration which might serve to prove the importance of its tactical role to any remaining military sceptics. Public recognition was also eagerly sought. Most of the RAF pilots were already highly experienced from RAF overseas operations and the whole unit had been welded into a well integrated squadron (in RAF terms) by the demands of the Suez operation, so the JEHU was well poised for the second phase of its life—post Suez. It exploited the situation with energy and enthusiasm.

This was the middle of the period of major helicopter expansion which started in the mid-1950s and several firms were working on equipment to enhance the helicopter's capability—airborne TV, Decca navigation equipment, portable glide path indicators for night approaches, Schermuly flares for emergency night landings etc. The RAF helicopter units were either overseas or fully committed to training or SAR tasks in the UK. The JEHU was available and eager to provide aircraft and crews for practically any sort of development flying these manufacturers required, although much of this experimentation was not carried out in accordance with the formal trials procedures which the RAF would have demanded through A & AEE at Boscombe Down.(13)

During the second part of 1957 and throughout 1958 and 1959, the JEHU figured as prominently as possible in as many major Army exercises as it could, with both regular units and the Territorial Army and in both the UK and BAOR. It twice embarked aircraft in HMS Ocean and once in HMS Centaur for refresher training cruises with the Royal Marines 'to keep alive the operating techniques learnt at Port Said' and on three occasions provided the 'Utility Helicopter' (a phrase by then frequently used in the JEHU) element for the annual Marines ship-to-shore lift in the Joint Services Amphibious Demonstration 'Runaground' at Eastney. This was the basis for the claim that the JEHU liaison with the RN and RM was responsible for the development of the Commando Carrier concept.

Part of the JEHU was used operationally on one other occasion after Suez. In December 1958 the Whirlwinds were dismantled and flown by Beverley to Cyprus where they were based at Nicosia to reinforce the tactical troop movements and resupply operations being conducted with the Sycamores of No 284 Squadron. After a number of mainly successful operations, and as a result of the three-Power negotiations to end the EOKA fighting held early in 1959, that activity ceased. Before the Whirlwind Flight of JEHU returned to the UK, however, use was made of the situation in which No 284 Squadron had on occasion found it necessary to provide air-to-ground Light Machine Gun (LMG) fire from the helicopter cabin. There was no policy at home to arm Support Helicopters and the JEHU had no authority to investigate the possibilities. The situation in Cyprus, however, offered the opportunity to circumvent this ban, and experimental mountings for light and medium machine guns in the open doorways of helicopters were designed and tested at home in preliminary firing trials with the School of Infantry. Subsequently, test firings were carried out on the Larnaca range in Cyprus, but no further work could be done in this direction after the JEHU Whirlwind Flight returned home in March 1959.

During the last nine months of its existence, the JEHU plunged once more into Army exercises and demonstrations but now more in the spirit of a crusade than of experimental development. The attachment of four American piston-engined H-34 (later Wessex) helicopters for Exercise Red Banner in September 1959 was not just to provide increased lift but 'to drive home the difference between our own obsolescent aircraft and the type with which it was felt a British Utility Helicopter Squadron should be equipped'. This was the period in which, as described in Chapter 4, the Air Ministry was negotiating with considerable difficulty to introduce the Belvedere for Army support, and considering (and rejecting at that stage) the possibility of the twin-turbine Wessex in lieu. To have the JEHU, which according to the Air Ministry should have been disbanded in 1957, now suggesting they should have the piston-engined Wessex to replace their Whirlwinds, could scarcely be taken seriously. In any case, the Secretary of State for War, Sir John Hare, had in 1957 reiterated his agreement to the 4000 lb weight limit for Army air-craft.(14) But the attitude of the JEHU is revealed in the Outline History of the JEHU, which quotes its Commanding Officer's assessment of priorities shortly after the return from Cyprus in 1959, followed by what were adjudged to be the 'really important tasks'. This distinction is significant:

Tasks in 1959

On the return of the Whirlwinds to the UK in March 1959 the Commanding Officer assessed priorities as follows for the remainder of the year:

1.   Completion of the trials programme, particularly on the technical side, and the following up of earlier Unit recommendations to higher authority.

2.   Training with Units of the Strategic Reserve by day and night.

3.   Maximum co-operation with all Arms Schools, to 'sell' the helicopter to the widest possible Service audiences.

'Minor commitments' were therefore firmly cut out of the programme and the Unit was thus able to concentrate on producing a 100% availability of aircraft for the 'really important occasions'. These were:

Demonstration Runaground at Eastney, in which this year JEHU supplied all the Utility helicopters taking part.

166

Annual Demonstrations of the School of Infantry, School of Military Engineering and School of Artillery as well as those of the Director-General of the Army Medical Services and the Signals Officer-in-Chief.

Demonstrations at the School of Land/Air Warfare, Old Sarum for the Staff Colleges and for various NATO and Senior Officers' Courses.

RAF Transport Command's contribution to the SBAC at Farnborough.

Annual Demonstration, School of Military Intelligence.

Regimental Day of the Parachute Brigade at Aldershot, including lifting in Bailey bridge sections for a demonstration of rapid bridge building.

In addition, because of their publicity value, aircraft were provided for:

The SSAFA Searchlight Tattoo at the White City Stadium.

The Scots Guards Tattoo in the Tidworth Arena.

Battle of Britain Displays.

The JEHU was not really a joint unit at all. Half the pilots and all the engineering support was RAF, but in all other respects it was an Army unit and the RAF took no part in its direction or tasking because it conformed in no way to the RAF concept of a Trials Unit with A & AEE direction. To the RAF therefore it did not succeed even in meeting the development tasks laid on it by the Army since it lacked the equipment and facilities which the RAF regarded as necessary for such functions. The Unit came to see itself, however, as the innovator of a new era of Army aviation in tactical support, and the experimental function implied by the title consisted in finding out how to perform that task and then demonstrating to as many significant people as possible that it could be done. The unit succeeded in its aim and felt baffled and betrayed by its own Army authorities when it was disbanded. The RAF knew it could not succeed as a Trials Unit, so was not surprised when the time came to end it. The RAF bought the aircraft and used the Whirlwind Flight to form No 225 Squadron as part of the Short Range Transport Force.

The Queen's Flight

The Queen's Flight helicopter problem was temporarily solved by borrowing a Dragonfly from CFS in October 1954, to be supported some months later with a Naval S-55 (designated Whirlwind Mk 22). The provisional intention was to establish two Whirlwind Mk 6 (VIP version of the Mk 7 Whirlwind with the Alvia Leonides Major engine)(15) because they were expected to have a superior performance and would have fully duplicated servo controls.(16) This intention was endorsed by a Working Party on the Royal Use of Helicopters in 1957 with the caveat (fortunately, as events proved) that no order should be placed until there was some experience of the behaviour of the Leonides Major engine in helicopters. In the meantime use of the borrowed Naval Mk 22 should continue. The use of Buckingham Palace as a helicopter LZ for single-engined helicopters was somewhat cautiously approved, and flotation gear for emergency landings in the river was to be investigated, it being understood that there was no intention at that stage of HM The Queen flying in a helicopter, and certainly not in a single-engined one.

The decision to cancel the Leonides Major engined Whirlwind as a replacement for the Mk 2 and 4 Whirlwind and to await the Gnome engined version (Chapter 4) had the effect of leaving The Queen's Flight with its borrowed Dragonfly and Naval Whirlwind Mk 22 for as long as they lasted, which was until mid-1957. There followed a three-year hiatus which, until two turbine-engined Whirlwinds (designated Mk 8 for The Queen's Flight version) appeared in February 1960, was partly filled by a Whirlwind Mk 2 which was obtained in mid-1958 and although not cleared for Royalty was suitable for use by VIPs. The turbine-engined Mk 8's, when they appeared, were equipped with dinghies.

A fuller account of helicopter progress in The Queen's Flight in both Phases 2 and 3 is contained in Chapter 13.

Metropolitan Communications Squadron

At the very end of the queue for helicopters came the communications task for VIP and senior Staff Officers in Whitehall, for which financial approval in principle was given in 1953. However this was submerged in the later proposal to establish 20 Sycamores for communications in the UK and Germany and was eventually shelved by the Air Council in June 1956 because of cuts in the front-line units.(17) So helicopter communications flying by VIPs in the UK continued on an ad hoc basis, using the Dragonfly on loan to The Queen's Flight for those of sufficient rank and by misemploying the CFS Helicopter Unit for other RAF officers; No 1906 AOP Flight and the JEHU for Army officers; and Navy operational or training helicopters for RN officers. SAR helicopters were also sometimes misused for urgent ambulance tasks.

In 1958 there was considerable pressure to make some proper provision for helicopter communications tasks from the London area. It was pointed out that Treasury refusal to approve expenditure on what seemed to them no more than an expensive luxury did not prevent the flights—senior RN and Army officers and civil servants always seemed able to find one of their own helicopters to carry out urgent or prestige tasks which the RAF declined because of training or operational commitments—so merely had the effect of making the RAF appear unco-operative and backward. Apart from use of the single Dragonfly in The Queen's Flight the RAF had to meet unavoidable demands under the guise of training sorties.(18)

The Queen Mother alighting from the CFS Dragonfly borrowed later
and absorbed into the Queen's flight—1956/7.

The entire CFS Helicopter Wing in transit from
South Cerney to its new home at Ternhill in 1962.
9 Sycamores, 1 Skeeter, 3 Whirlwinds, one
Dragonfly.

Three proposals were considered: to establish a Squadron of communication helicopters in the Metropolitan area; to add a further helicopter to the two Whirlwind Mk 8 which The Queen's Flight was expecting to receive shortly; and to establish extra helicopters at CFS for communications tasks. The last proposal was rejected on grounds of principle in terms of the CFS role, and the second did not offer adequate scope for the task envisaged. It was therefore decided that it would be best to begin by establishing a Helicopter Communications Squadron, albeit, because of existing deficiencies in helicopter front line units, this could not be at full squadron strength. A Helicopter Flight was therefore to be added to the Metropolitan Communications Squadron at Northolt.(19) Two Sycamores Mk 11 arrived in December 1959 and training commenced on the last day of the year,(20) almost seven years after the need for the unit had been identified and agreed. The effective life of this unit therefore does not really start until Phase 3 of the history. (See Chapter 13).

THE CENTRAL FLYING SCHOOL HELICOPTER UNIT

Ever since February 1952, Flying Training Command had been trying to establish helicopter technique study at either CFS or the Flying College at Manby, or both, as recorded in Chapter 4. In 1953 approval in principle was achieved in respect of CFS but it was decided to await the return from the Far East of one of the original Casualty Evacuation Flight pilots to command the unit. In the event, two were obtained: Flt Lt J R Dowling and Flt Lt A J Lee. The latter had been an R-4 (Hoverfly 1) pilot on The King's Flight in the late 1940s and was destined to operate one of the three CFS Dragonflys on attachment to The Queen's Flight at Benson where it became permanently resident. Flt Lt Dowling, who joined Flt Lt C Bartlett, a fixed wing qualified flying instructor (QFI) of CFS who had been waiting some weeks for the unit to be formed, first had to be turned into a QFI in order to maintain the orthodoxy of the CFS instructors' category. This was accomplished on a Piston Provost—a pattern which was to be repeated for all the early Qualified Helicopter Instructors (QHIs) who were not already QFIs.

Established for three Dragonflys, the CFS Helicopter Development Unit formed at Middle Wallop in May 1954 and immediately undertook its first task which consisted of a nine day trip around Germany—a proving flight for a forthcoming tour of British Army Units in Germany by HRH Princess Margaret. Shortly after return at the beginning of June, the unit moved to South Cerney where it was to reside until 1962 alongside the CFS Fixed Wing Basic School flying Piston Provosts, and later the aircrew Initial Training School. Thereafter the CFS Helicopter Unit, now a Wing, was to continue operations from Ternhill until moved to Shawbury in 1976.

There was just time in the last few days of June 1954 to start initial experiments with dual control before setting off for Germany once more for the actual visit by

HRH Princess Margaret. All three aircraft had to go, that for use by HRH being sumptuously furnished in blue leather for the occasion and ultimately reserved almost exclusively for The Queen's Flight, although not formally established in that role until much later. This occupied most of July so it was not until the end of that month that proper CFS work could start in earnest. The absence of established RAF helicopters in the communications role was a continual nuisance to CFS for the first few years of the helicopter unit's life but good progress was made in the first three years in contructing a sound training syllabus, preparing the basis of an Instructor's handbook, and writing a helicopter section for AP 129 (Pilot's Handbook). Several pilots were trained in the process.

The initial procedure was to 'borrow' Provost QFIs from the CFS Basic School, and experiment with different ways of teaching basic pilot helicopter skills. The experience of these CFS instructor trainees in the fixed-wing field was invaluable in obtaining critical assessment of alternative methods of introducing helicopter initial training for fixed-wing pilots, so progress was rapid. By August the training sequence to first solo was ready for demonstration and what might be called the first initial pilots' course was nominated. It consisted of the CFS Commandant—Air Cdre G J C Paul, his PA—Flt Lt K V Panter, Station Commander South Cerney—Gp Capt O I Gibson, and the Officer Commanding the CFS Examining Wing—Sqn Ldr R S Radley. Flt Lt Panter, together with the first three QFIs 'borrowed' for experimental instruction (Flt Lts C Evans, A Sharples, and J Liversidge) became so enthusiastic as a result of their contact with the helicopter that they all elected to continue in that field and went on to achieve successful careers as helicopter specialists.

By the end of 1954, the training pattern was sufficiently well developed to enable the CFS helicopter unit to invite a controlled supply of pilots who would otherwise have been processed through the 50-hour contract course at Westland Aircraft Ltd. In November 1954, Flt Lt A Shafe was the first of these and he received a 50-hour basic course on the Dragonfly followed by a 10-hour Sycamore conversion before proceeding to Sylt in early 1955 to form the 2nd TAF SAR Flight which was to remain there for seven years.

The CFS Unit was established at this time only with Dragonfly Mk 2 aircraft. A convenient arrangement was however made so that both Sycamores and later Whirlwinds could be used as required for study of instructional techniques as well as pilot and QHI conversion. The build-up of Sycamores for No 194 Squadron in the Far East, and No 175 (SAR) Squadron at Linton-on-Ouse, and Whirlwinds for both No 155 Squadron in the Far East and No 22 (SAR) Squadron at Thorney Island, produced a flow of new aircraft from Filton (later Weston-super-Mare) and Yeovil to the Maintenance Units (MUs) for distribution. There were at first no qualified helicopter pilots in Maintenance Command and so the CFS Unit was able to offer delivery of these helicopters to the MUs, thus providing useful instructor flying experience on both types. Short loans of these aircraft to CFS on delivery were negotiated as required for Sycamore of Whirlwind student pilots or QFIs to suit both CFS technique development requirements, and pilot and QHI needs for the operational units. This admirable arrangement continued throughout 1955 and 1956, CFS gradually training an increasing proportion of the operational pilots as a by-product of their development of instructional and standardisation techniques, until in early 1957 the civilian training contracts ceased altogether. The CFS helicopter unit became a squadron responsible for RAF and Army pilot and QHI training as well as QHI and helicopter unit standardisation world-wide for all three Services in accordance with the CFS charter.

In August 1955, a Skeeter was made available to CFS for a 12-day trial and evaluation period. It received a moderately enthusiastic assessment, a particular point in its favour being its suitability as basic trainer common for pilots destined for either Sycamores or Whirlwind helicopters. The Sycamore and the Whirlwind Mk 2 were markedly dissimilar mainly, but not only, because the Sycamore controls were fully manual while those of the Whirlwinds were hydraulically powered. The Skeeter succeeded in imitating the main features of both, at least in the matter of basic instructional technique. Unfortunately, an unrealistic standard of throttle/ collective lever harmonisation was demanded later by a test pilot at A & AEE Boscombe Down who was inexperienced in helicopters, and in an attempt to meet it, the then conventional relationship between throttle and lever became randomly reversed in production Skeeters, and a valuable part of their training value was lost.

One of the major flying technique developments in helicopter training accomplished by CFS in the early 1950s was a thorough practical study of engine-off landings. The requirement to be able to land successfully with no engine power available had been evident since the first helicopters were developed, and the procedure would have been fairly obvious to the earliest helicopter pilots who had flown autogyros. The helicopter had the additional advantage of a collective pitch control with which to employ rotor momentum to cushion the touch-down. While auto-rotation could be practiced by keeping the engine idling and thus disengaged from the rotors, the linking of the throttle to the collective lever meant that the lever could not be pulled up for cushioning the touch-down without serious risk of violent engine re-engagement with catastrophic results, so the engine had to be stopped completely for the full practice to be carried out. Thus, as soon as hovering take-off and landing became possible in the first helicopters, voluntarily dispensing with the engine for practice landing purposes seemed wantonly dangerous especially in view of the limited numbers of purely experimental helicopters available. Except perhaps for test pilots, the ability to land helicopters successfully with no engine power was a matter of theoretical knowledge only to most of the pre-1950 helicopters pilots, and this was also true of the Casualty Evacuation Flight pilots in Malaya who were fortunate not to experience any total engine failures during the life of that unit. By the end of 1954, CFS could demonstrate engine-off landings as an integral part of the training course, and by April 1955 was able to teach QHIs the whole sequence from any combination of practical heights and airspeeds including vertical approaches from 700 feet with no initial airspeed. (Not appropriate to the Dragonfly or Whirlwind but safe enough in the Sycamore and Skeeter). However the introduction of these practices on the operational units even in their simplest form was to take somewhat longer to accomplish, the inhertent risk of damage to the helicopter being extremely difficult to quantify and having different degrees of apparent importance in various theatres.

1955 and 1956 were crucial years for the CFS Helicopter Unit. During that period the CFS succeeded in establishing itself as the central authority for training and pure flying techniques on the helicopter as it already was for fixed wing flying. This was not simply a matter of Air Ministry decree. A great deal of helicopter expertise was being rapidly accumulated in the Far East and Middle East, and to function adequately in the standardisation role the CFS unit had to establish its credibility amongst a comparatively hard-bitten group of experienced pilots operating under considerable pressure with underpowered aircraft in very difficult flying areas and in tropical conditions. The status of the highly respected CFS Examining Wing, to which a member of the CFS Helicopter Unit was attached for overseas visits, undoubtedly helped in this respect, but care was taken to see that suitable QFIs with helicopter pilot experience in Malaya were earmarked for QHI training especially for CFS. Thus in early 1955 when Flt Lt Bartlett left CFS for Staff College, he was replaced by Flt Lt W Pinner—short-toured from Malaya for the purpose.

In January 1955 the first two fully CFS-trained helicoper pilots, Flt Lts Shafe and Clark, were qualified and sent to Sylt to start the 2nd TAF SAR unit. Both were trained on a borrowed Sycamore on delivery from Filton to the MU for despatch overseas. This was the first CFS experience of the Mk 14 Sycamore which had only one centrally mounted collective lever instead of a separate lever on the left-hand side of each seat. The nature and consequences of this awkward system, which the CFS was unable to persuade the Air Ministry would have serious effects from a training point of view, are described more fully in the detailed description of the Sycamore at Appendix 1. Two of the three QHIs then on the unit carried out the necessary training they both needed to fly the aircraft from the left-hand seat (about 10 hours each) and somewhat nervously commenced dual instruction for Shafe and Clark.

In May 1955 a QHI accompanied the CFS Examining Wing on liaison visits to Canada and the USA, during which the American experience with the central collective lever in the Hiller 360, as described in Appendix 1, was recounted by a member of the US Navy Institute of Aviation Medicine at Pensacola.

The Skeeter trials already mentioned took place in the last part of August 1955. In September, the first categorisation visit to overseas units was made in conjunction with the CFS Examining Wing who at that time had their own Valetta which they had used to visit as far afield as Cyprus, Aden and the Far East. The purpose of this first visit by the CFS Helicopter Unit was to observe the standards of the wholly civil contract trained pilots, to advise on appropriate flying techniques in relation to current theatre requirements, and to 'sell' the idea of practising engine-off landings as a regular monthly exercise. Little could be done in Aden because nobody seemed to know how to maintain their two Sycamores. The pilots refused to fly one of them which had distorted engine cooling fan blades although the technicians assured them it was serviceable. The CFS visitor was able to assure the technicians that the pilots were quite right—such was the state of affairs in late 1955. (A curiously similar situation with the Belvedere developed in Aden in 1964/65). In Nairobi, experiments had to be done by the CFS pilot to establish on the spot appropriate technique for engine-off landings at an airfield altitude of about 6000 feet. (A few weeks later a Sycamore experienced engine failure near Nairobi and the pilot landed without damage in a space almost too small to permit a safe take-off after repairs). Demonstration engine-off landings were done at Kuala Lumpur, but the risk to the aircraft was considered by the FEAF authorities to be too high at that stage to permit the procedure to be practised there as a regular exercise. In Cyprus, however, the Station Commander, Gp Capt Ivers, was convinced by the demonstration he was given and accepted CFS advice that engine-off landings should be practised. Flt Lt P Fahy, the Officer in Charge of the helicopter flight at Nicosia, reported afterwards that without this practice he doubted whether he would have survived the three actual engine failures he experienced while in Cyprus (one with General Templer on board) all of which resulted in landings without damage. (See Chapter 5). In this and in similar ways, the CFS Helicopter Unit was able to develop its reputation in the helicopter world and thus provide a generally welcome central authority for dissemination of sound doctrine.

In October 1955 CFS 'hosted' the first Helicopter Instructional Technique Conference, attended not only by HQ No 23 Group and Flying Training Command, but also representatives for the Army, Navy and civilian helicopter firms. This was to be repeated in various forms on a regular basis thereafter.

VIP flights still intruded from time to time, a notable one in 1955 being when on 6 September the Prime Minister (Sir Anthony Eden) was flown from Chequers to Farnborough for the SBAC show, and back.

It was impossible to devise a system for simulating instrument flight in the 'greenhouse' style of cockpit of the Dragonfly, but some initial experiments were

173

done with fabric curtains in the Sycamore in 1955. There was, however, no pressure whatever from the operational units for this development, and a similar lack of enthusiasm for night flying existed since neither techniques were required in Malaya or initially in Cyprus and were in any case regarded as too dangerous in the Far East for reasons of weather. The CFS Helicopter Unit had perforce to relegate both procedures to a low priority in their range of activities but nevertheless continued to experiment when possible with two stage amber, hessian screens and head-mounted visors for the Sycamore. For night flying lighting patterns the unit went no further in the mid-1950s than to suggest that a horizontal 'bar' bisected by a 'tail' in line with the approach path and thus forming a 'T' pointing into wind, would probably be a good starting point for investigative trials. The foundation was thus laid for a dispute which was to last well into the 1970s, frequently rising to quite extraordinary levels of acrimony. All the CFS Helicopter Unit could do at this early stage was to affirm that there was no reason why night flying in clear weather should not be perfectly feasible, but that no opportunity had yet occurred to enable the best lighting system to be decided.

During 1956, much progress was made in liaison work with the Royal Navy, the Army and civilian helicopter firms. Examining visits were made—really standardisation investigation—on the training provided by Westland aircraft at Yeovil and the Bristol Aeroplane Company at Filton. This was the first time the RAF had an opportunity to make any kind of critical examination of the flying training which had been given to the bulk of helicopter pilots then flying. In the absence of any formal syllabus and any kind of standard system corresponding to the principles of flying training as understood by the RAF, the results were predictably variable. Inevitably, the consequence was a progressive increase in the number of pilots being channelled through the CFS Unit until in 1957 it was accepted that all helicopter pilot training should be undertaken by CFS. The pattern was thus established whereby the CFS Helicopter Unit became responsible for running both instructor courses (the normal CFS task) and pilot training courses which would normally be done at a separate Flying Training School. The comparatively small numbers involved coupled with economic factors and the shortage of helicopters dictated this course, and these considerations remaining, the pattern became permanently established.

Also in 1956 the first standardisation visit was paid to the Royal Navy, No 705 Squadron at Lee-on-Solent acting as hosts in April. Lt Cdr E C Spreadbury, their senior pilot, spent ten days in October studying the CFS standardisation procedures at South Cerney so that the RAF and RN systems should be properly aligned. General agreement was reached. A visit was also paid to the civil pilots' training school at Hamble where about 10 hours flying on the Hiller 360 was provided for each of the two CFS QHIs. The Hiller was assessed as inferior to the Skeeter in the CFS training role since it did not provide such a good imitation of the characteristics of the RAF operational aircraft. A further examining visit to the

174

Middle East was made in June to see the four Sycamore pilots at Amman and to qualify Flt Sgt Bousher at Eastleigh as a VIP Sycamore pilot for a forthcoming visit to Kenya by HRH Princess Margaret. He was taught to do engine-off landings.

A final event of some significance in 1956 was the appearance of a CFS Sycamore at the Woolwich Tattoo in September. The helicopter was required to perform after dark and both Army and RN helicopter units had declined the offer. The organisers turned to CFS and a most interesting session of Sycamore night flying was then done each night for a week in the Woolwich stadium. The helicopter was parked each night, after the performance, outside the Royal Artillery Officers' Mess, the 'T' pattern of lights previously described being used on the cricket field as a landing position indicator. By 1957 the 50-hour pilot training syllabus was well established, together with a ground school syllabus. The instructors' training syllabus, still exclusively for existing fixed-wing QFIs, was well proven and the instructors' handbook existed in draft form. The appropriate chapter for AP 129 (Pilots' Handbook) had been issued and regular pilot and QHI training was in progress. Until November 1957 courses still consisted of only two or three pilots and two trainee QHIs but then No 9 Instructors' Course had an intake of four. The 19th Pilots' Course started in December 1957. CFS by then had two Dragonflys and had acquired a Sycamore of its own, but still relied on borrowing Whirlwinds and additional Sycamores from delivery flights as the situation required. One Skeeter T11 arrived in February 1957. The Skeeter pilot training syllabus, used initially mainly for Army pilots and instructor training, consisted of a compression of the 50-hour Dragonfly syllabus into 30 hours, followed by type conversion of 20 hours on Whirlwind or Sycamore as appropriate. A copy of the Skeeter pilot training syllabus is included in Appendix 2.

During 1957 liaison visits were made to the British European Airways helicopter training unit at Gatwick, and to Shorts in Belfast where a helicopter simulator was being designed. This never came to fruition since it was cheaper and easier to use a real helicopter. The Army AOP Helicopter Flight (No 1906) received a standardisation visit in April. A further examining visit was made to the Far East in April, and on this occasion the AOC No 224 Group (AVM Kyle) was persuaded to institute engine-off landing practice at Kuala Lumpur by Squadron QHIs after a personal demonstration session with the visiting CFS QHI. This was the first time practice engine-off landings were carried out in FEAF. Also on this trip a visit was paid to the Royal Ceylon Air Force*. In May 1957 the basic (Provost)

---

*One of the two pilots presented for standardisation test (Pilot Officer Situnayake) was found to have a natural ability far in excess of what could be expected from the very rudimentary and unsatisfactory Dragonfly training he had previously received. He subesquently made his own way to England, obtained entrance to Cranwell, and by the early 1960s was one of only two RAF Belvedere QHI and test pilots in support of the Belvedere forces then deployed in Aden and Singapore.

part of CFS was withdrawn to the main CFS base at Little Rissington, leaving the airfield at South Cerney to the helicopter unit which by now had become a CFS squadron. During the previous month, an assessment in the training role had been made at CFS of the Widgeon, a modified Dragonfly having side by side pilot seats and a Whirlwind rotor head and blades. It was not regarded favourably since it was much easier to use a Whirlwind for Whirlwind pilots and the aircraft had little relevance to the Sycamore training.

At the end of 1957 the CFS Examining Wing was disbanded, but by then the helicopter unit was sufficiently well known and experienced to stand on its own feet in the examining role. Ultimately, in 1961, the CFS Helicopter Squadron was to become a Wing having its own Examining Squadron. There was still no regular night flying and the role did not officially exist. However, an opportunity to encourage it occurred when the C-in-C Flying Training Command (AM Sir Richard Atcherley) used a CFS Sycamore to pay a formal visit to a function at his old school at Oundle on 5 July 1957. The proceedings went on until well after 10 pm and when the Air Marshal was ready to leave, the CFS helicopter pilot pointed out that he could still perfectly well do so in the Sycamore, which required only his authority for the night sortie involved. The AM accepted the advice, authorised the flight and was duly delivered at Blackbushe shortly before midnight. This one event helped considerably in encouraging development of night and instrument flying but in fact the small CFS squadron was by then fully committed to the task of coping with the flow of pilot and instructor courses and had little time or opportunity for the development work needed. It was not until 1959 that formal training in night and instrument flying could be instituted on a regular basis.

The solitary Skeeter T 11 spent most of 1958 unserviceable having broken its nose wheel doing a running landing in April. During the same year the CFS Squadron acquired its first Whirlwind and for the next three years a third category of course intake was added to the Pilot and QHI courses—that in which Sycamore operational pilots were converted to Whirlwind pilots or QHIs. (In the Far East these pilot conversions had perforce to be carried out 'in situ' as the Sycamore/Whirlwind/ Sycamore changes were made in response to technical problems—see Chapter 3).

The introduction of a separate Army Aviation organisation precipitated, at the end of 1957, high level discussions on joint Service helicopter pilot training as described in Chapter 4. It was clear that unless some special arrangement was made, the separate RN/RAF helicopter training would become a three element system because the Army intended to carry out its own pilot training. In Apil 1958 the annual helicopter training requirement was assessed as follows:

RAF —28 pilots, 8 QHIs (mixed Whirlwind and Sycamore).

RN —50 pilots, 5 QHIs (all Whirlwind). (The Navy required a further 10 QHIs but only put one third of their QHIs through CFS).

Army—26 pilots, 4 QHIs (all Skeeter).

The Army, although preferring Middle Wallop, reluctantly agreed with the RAF that if there were to be a joint Service establishment for helicopter training, it would be best to have it at South Cerney where the CFS unit was operating, and which was close to the Army Air Corps Centre. The Air Ministry was supplied with expert advice which the CFS Heliopter Unit was now competent to provide. What the RAF recommended, as a result of specialised detailed study of various alternatives, was a combined basic and advanced tri-Service helicopter pilot training school co-located with the CFS helicopter element, and acting also as a helicopter ground crew training centre. RAF SAR operational training could well be co-located with Naval operational training. Retrospectively it can be seen that the CFS Helicopter Unit had achieved a thoroughly well-founded understanding of current and future problems. However, as reported in Chapter 4, the scheme foundered in the Joint Committee of Helicopter Pilot Training because of the RN claim to superior helicopter knowledge and experience, and the determination that the establishment of a single school elsewhere than Culdrose would be unacceptable for the training of Naval pilots. Culdrose was not acceptable to the Air Ministry because the CFS experience in developing training techniques showed that the weather conditions at Culdrose were too often unrepresentative of the circumstances for which the majority of RAF and Army pilots had to be trained. There were many other subsidiary disadvantages also, but the RAF view was based on the solid progress made by the CFS Helicopter Squadron in formulating standard instructional techniques and ground school syllabi in accordance with established RAF training principles while, in contrast to the claims made for it, the Naval training squadron with its rapidly changing personnel (average tour length 18 months) had made no such progress. Contact between CFS and the Naval training squadron (No 705) had been hard to achieve and the consequence was that not more than one or two instructors on No 705 Squadron could meet RAF instructional standards. The inevitable consequence was that the three Services went their own way, although CFS did succeed in maintaining its centralised instructor categorisation and standardisation role. (Ten years later, the divergence had become even more pronounced and a similar amalgamation attempt foundered much more quickly).

During 1958, 1959 and 1960, the CFS Helicopter Squadron continued its main task of training pilots, instructors and providing Whirlwind type conversions, reaching Course Nos 31, 32 and 10 respectively, while paying examining visits to all Service helicopter units at home and overseas, aiming at a frequency of once every one or two years, as appropriate, for each. VIP and special demonstration flights still intruded from time to time, although the Air Ministry did its best to restrict them as far as possible—the Metropolitan Communications Squadron did not come into existence until the beginning of 1960—but apart from special passenger flights there were other tasks of overriding importance which still had to be done. The two major diversions during 1959 were the Daily Mail Air Race in July and the provision of a 30-minute frequency shuttle service for three days between Chequers and London for the White House Press Corps, headed by Mr Hagerty, on the occasion of the visit of the US President, General Eisenhower to the Prime Minister, Sir Harold Macmillan in August 1959. The Westland Heliport at Battersea was considered far too inconvenient for this operation and, in the planning stages, the Air Ministry had suggested that a possible solution would be to construct a floating platform made from Storey Uni-flote sections, to be moored on the Thames near the RAF Memorial and connected to the Embankment wall by a pivoted Bailey Bridge. This was considered too radical a solution by the Foreign Office and the operation seemed likely to be shelved until the American Ambassador offered the grounds of his residence in Regents Park (Winfield House) as a temporary helicopter terminal. This proved very satisfactory from a helicopter point of view and CFS set up the necessary local control there and at Chequers and operated the shuttle for the required three days to the satisfaction of all concerned.

For the Daily Mail Air Race in July 1959 the requirement was to transport a passenger between Marble Arch and the Arc de Triomphe. The RAF entry was carried by motor cycle between the starting and finishing points and Chelsea Bridge and Issy les Molineaux respectively, by helicopter between Chelsea Bridge and Biggin Hill and between Villacoublay and Issy, a dual Hunter flashing at low level between Biggin Hill and Villacoublay. CFS provided the helicopters using the bed of the Thames exposed at low tide near Chelsea Bridge for the London end of the operation. A round trip was flown at low tide each day for four days, the RAF finally winning the race by a matter of seconds. A very advanced form of helicopter handling was required to achieve the necessary advantage.

By the end of the 1960s the CFS Helicopter Squadron had completed just over 30 pilot training courses and about the same number of instructor training courses. Eleven Whirlwind conversion courses had been conducted and many senior Staff Officers had received helicopter familiarisation courses. This latter course was necessarily an informal type of training, being arranged both in time and content to suit the circumstances of the usually very senior officer concerned. It had originally been found necessary in 1954/55 to devise some policy in response to the repeated demand for helicopter experience for senior Staff Officers in various posts, since such experience was totally lacking. The CFS Helicopter Unit was acutely aware of the possible consequences of continued ignorance at these levels, with the central collective lever arrangement in the Sycamore as a constant reminder and example of the errors likely to be made in this field. It was also clear that with helicopters still, in the early 1950s, regarded with either grave suspicion or casual indifference, it was important to strike the right balance between generating enthusiasm and demonstrating the pilot's problems without appearing to invest the art with mystery. It was observed at an early stage that experienced fixed-wing pilots were generally greatly dismayed (usually secretly) at their initial inability to learn by conscious effort how to hover and carry out transitions to the hover. They usually showed symptoms of loss of confidence in themselves and unless this condition was relieved, were quite unable to appreciate the finer points of more advanced exercises designed to demonstrate the special qualities and limitations of the helicopter. (None of these helicopters had stability augmentation systems, all had manual throttle control and the Sycamore and Skeeter manual cyclic as well). The older fixed-wing pilot had to be sent solo at the earliest possible moment, otherwise continued instruction or demonstrations of manoeuvre proved counter-productive. Those having difficulty were therefore taught to fly a circuit as in a fixed-wing basic trainer, arrangements being made to ensure the entire airfield was available for the aircraft to be landed safely wherever the student was able to bring it almost to a stop. Futher instruction could then be assimilated. The nearest thing to a syllabus for this course was designed in 1955, and aimed at a two-week period. In the first week normal rate of detailed instruction to first solo was given. In the second week, the entire remaining instructional syllabus was packed into about 10 or 15 sorties. Suitably adjusted for personal idiosyncrasies, this procedure could be made to produce the right balance of enthusiasm for the helicopter and appreciation of the problems. The expectation that this Staff Officers' Familiaris-ation Course would gradually cease to be necessary after four or five years as helicopter pilots were promoted into Staff appointments was never realised. In one form or another, a corresponding procedure was still in use at CFS 20 years later, although the pyschological problems were scarcely of the same order; ubiquity and respectability of the helicopter had been achieved, refinements and automation of its most awkward controls developed and virtually unlimited power made available to recover gross errors.

In January 1961 the Skeeter T 12 was added to the aircraft inventory which consisted otherwise of Sycamores, Whirlwind Mk 2, Skeeter T 11 and one remaining Dragonfly which was still used as a back up for the Whirlwind. It could be profitably used for the early instructional technique exercises for student QHIs destined for the Whirlwind (but not the Sycamore or Skeeter), and also for Staff Officers' familiarisation. The relative utilisation of these types may be adduced from the monthly flying totals for July 1961: Sycamore 272 hours; Whirlwind 45 hours; Dragonfly 35 hours; Skeeter Mk 11 4 hours; Skeeter Mk 12 16 hours. At this stage the Skeeter was used exclusively for Army Student QHIs.

On 10 August 1961 the CFS Helicopter Wing moved to Ternhill, flying in formation all 14 of the aircraft it then possessed. Training continued unbroken after the weekend on 14 August. The newly formed 'Wing' was commanded by Wg Cdr J Corbishley appointed as Chief Instructor CFS(H). No 1 Squadron was responsible for all pilot and QHI courses, and No 2 Squadron carried out all aircraft type conversions and whatever operational training (tactical and SAR) would have been provided by an Operational Conversion Unit had one existed. No 3 Squadron was the Helicopter Examining Unit with QHI categorisation and pilot standardisation responsibilities for all Service helicopter units worldwide (including by invitation such units as the Hong Kong Auxiliary Air Force and the Royal Ceylon Air Force Helicopter Flight).

In November 1961 the first turbine-engined helicopter (Whirlwind Mk 10) was issued and delivered to CFS(H) at Ternhill. This marks the end of Phase 2 of this history in respect of the Central Flying School.

1   Nos 657 and 651 Squadron ORBs.

2   ID9/94/10 Pt 6.

3   Ibid.

4   ID3/903/19 Pt 1.

5   Ibid.

6   Ibid.

7   Outline History of the JEHU (1955–59).

8   Ibid.

9   ID9/94/10 Pt 1.

11 Ibid.

12 ID/57/1.

13 ID3/903/19/Pt 1.

14 Ibid.

15 AC Conclusions 25(26).

16 ID9/E12–30.

17 ID9/E13–40.

18 Ibid.

19 Ibid.

20 Metropolitan Communications Squadron ORB.

CHAPTER 7

MARITIME HELICOPTER UNITS IN PHASES 1 AND 2 (1945–1962)

Introduction

The Air/Sea Warfare Development Unit had the first RAF maritime helicopters in the period described in the Prologue—that is preceding Phase 1. An outline of its development activities leads on to an account of the formation of the two Search and Rescue squadrons which superseded it and became a permanently established SAR service.

Air/Sea Warfare Development Unit

When the first helicopters appeared in the late 1940s, and even when the first Sycamores became available to Coastal Command in early 1952, the Command was much concerned with anti-submarine aspects of the helicopter role, and the first RAF maritime helicopters were examined in both the anti-submarine and SAR roles, insofar as that could be done with helicopters not having specialised equipment for either role.

The Air/Sea Warfare Development Unit (ASWDU) shared with No 657 AOP Squadron the experience of experimenting with the Hoverfly helicopter in the late 1940s in the period described in the Prologue. The ASWDU actually toyed with the early R-4 (Hoverfly 1) shortly before the R-6 (Hoverfly 2) was made available to the Army pilots of No 657 Squadron, and was the first fully RAF aircrew manned unit to do so. It also discarded them before No 657 Squadron when it became apparent that they had no useful function in operational terms, that is in maritime rescue or anti-submarine operations.

Helicopters in the ASWDU reappeared in a more practical form with the advent of the early Sycamores (Mks 11, 12 and 13) in early 1952; four were established at about the same time as the three provided for No 1906 Flight of No 657 Squadron in late 1951, although it was February 1952 before the first one was available for the ASWDU. The first three pilots* were posted in December 1951—the month when the headquarters of the ASWDU moved from Calshot to St Mawgan—and in January they were given Sycamore conversion training by the Bristol Aeroplane Co Helicopter Division at Filton. Evaluation in the visual search role by the ASWDU started immediately afterwards in February 1952, with the arrival of their first aircraft.

---

*Flight Lt J I G Minifie, Fg Off F A Bernard and Fg Off J I Williamson

Navigation trials were commenced in April 1952. This particular aspect of helicopter flight was to remain as the one constant development task throughout the life of the helicopter unit in the ASWDU, SAR and anti-submarine trials being attempted fitfully as equipment, aircraft serviceability and opportunity varied. There was considerable suspicion that the helicopter, being capable of sideways flight in the hover, could not be relied upon to travel in the direction in which it was pointing when in the cruise, and this made the prospect of successful DR navigation over the sea a subject of continuous concern. There was no navigational equipment apart from a compass. Winches were not initially available, and for the first few months there was little to be done except navigation trials and aircraft handling exercises, and of course the inevitable demonstration flights, including one for HRH The Duke of Edinburgh in May. Night and instrument flying trials were recorded as occurring in June, but no description exists of their nature. Both Sycamores then on the unit took part in a Seaward Defence exercise with the Shackletons at RNAS Donibristle (Exercise Castanets) during which shadowing of sumberged submarines was described as 'successful'. Generator spares were delivered to a ship cruising at 20 knots.

Other maritime tasks were tried in the ensuing few months such as sighting 'snorkelling' submarines (3–6 miles achieved) and hovering with a hydrophone on the end of 140 ft of cable—even with the hydrophone submerged 40 feet and 100 yards from the submarine, the cavitation noise from the submarine's propellors was completely drowned by the noise from the helicopter rotor. In between, VIP sorties and demonstration flights proliferated—CAS (Sir John Slesslor) was flown to Rugby School—but in September 1952 a disastrous crash occurred during a public demonstration after dark in the Speedway Stadium at St. Austell. The aircraft is thought to have over-pitched on take-off. It crashed in the coach park killing one civilian and seriously injuring another. Seven others were less seriously injured by rotor blade fragments and the pilot (Flt Lt Minifie) died a few hours later. Over-confidence and lack of experience are obvious conclusions retrospectively, but the fact that such a demonstration was attempted after dark in a confined space in the presence of the public and with such limited performance aircraft, gives a clear indication of the boundless enthusiasm but ignorance of realities which existed at that stage.

SAR equipment at the end of 1952 consisted of a rope ladder and safety line, these being fitted at the cost of the dual controls and the second pilot's seat. It is hardly surprising that during Exerise Ardent, when a Sycamore was based at Linton-on-Ouse for daily SAR standby at Patrington, the conclusion was reached that a winch would be essential for sea rescue operations. There were, however, no winches yet available and when the first one did appear in early 1953, the aircraft was immediately diverted to A&AEE Boscombe Down for MOS clearance. On its return in June 1953, it was immediately allocated to the newly forming No 275 Squadron and sent to Odiham to lead the formation flypast for the Royal Review of the RAF—the only helicopter to take part.

Meanwhile, concentration on the problem of navigation over the sea was relentlessly maintained, a determined effort to produce some data having been made in December 1952 when a series of reciprocal track flights was made between Plymouth and Newquay (33 miles) accompanied by an Anson with a drift sight to calculate the wind in order to eliminate a variable which would otherwise have disguised the deeply held suspicion that the helicopter might be flying sideways. In a further attempt to find out which way the helicopter was going, a 10-inch length of cord was attached to the outside of the centre lower nose perspex, and its trail angle compared with a line drawn on the perspex parallel to the aircraft's longitudinal axis. It was recorded that it worked satisfactorily above 55 knots, but the conclusion that the helicopter did in fact go the way it was pointing above these speeds (in balanced flight) was evidently not made, and navigation flight trials remained as a constant task thereafter. Indeed, in January 1953, after a tail rotor drive shaft failure, it was decided that no more maritime reconnaissance role evaluation would be possible, and future trials would concentrate exclusively on navigation. It seems not to have been noticed that pilots in Malaya at this time frequently relied absolutely on the helicopter behaving exactly like a fixed-wing aircraft in respect of compass headings when crossing areas of featureless jungle or when doing timed runs to a clearing.

Throughout the remainder of 1953 and 1954 activities such as those described continued at low frequency, aircraft availability being a continuing problem with the Sycamore still in the teething trouble stage, while the formation of No 275 SAR Squadron with Sycamores at Linton-on-Ouse in early 1953 lost the ASWDU its preferential position in the queue for Sycamore winches. In June 1953, for instance, of the three ASWDU Sycamores, the one with the broken tail rotor drive shaft was still at the contractor's factory at Weston-super-Mare, the winch-fitted aircraft from A&AEE had been returned but had gone immediately to Odiham for the Royal Review as already mentioned, and A&AEE had now got the third one. Nevertheless in August a sea search for a Sabre pilot was carried out (he was picked up by ASR launch) and in September two Sycamores recorded 51 hours 'uneventful operations' at RNAS Abbotsinch including several VIP flights and dropping of sandbags to simulate mines. In September 1953 the unit was declared ready for 'live' winching operations when aircraft were available.

Little flying was achieved in 1954—one Sycamore carried out exercises with the Royal Navy at Eglinton and Roborough and in November a Meteor pilot was located by an ASWDU Sycamore and rescued in co-operation with a Royal Naval helicopter. SAR and navigation trials continued.

In 1955 a navigation aid was at last provided. GEE was installed in one aircraft, and an in-shore anti-submarine role was added to the trials programme. In February the ASWDU joined in the emergency helicopter food lift (Operation Haylift) dropping hay for moorland ponies and supplies of animal foods to farms cut off by widespread snow. In March 1955, the ASWDU had to lend two of its three Sycamores to the newly formed No 22 (SAR) Squadron at Thorney Island because the delay in supplying that Squadron with Whirlwind SAR helicopters threatened disbandment of the unit before it had been able to start flying.

It was clear by then that the ASWDU anti-submarine roles for helicopters could scarcely advance until much better helicopters were available, and it was decided that SAR tasks as well as future development of this role would henceforth be done by the recently formed Nos 275 and 22 SAR Squadrons. In June 1955 the ASWDU Sycamore establishment was reduced to two, and they started to be used for light liaison tasks—both went to Wildenrath that month to help in an Army Excercise, Carte Blanche. Nevertheless, the rising need for helicopter SAR for civilians was already being felt, and in July an attempt was made to rescue two holiday makers cut off by the tide. Fitting of winches to the ASWDU Sycamores had already been abandoned and the rescue failed because 'the woman would not climb the rope ladder'. The police were summoned to deal with the problem. In November 1955, the last of many co-operative ventures with the Royal Navy is recorded for the ASWDU helicopters when in-shore anti-submarine trials were conducted together with No 845 (RN) Squadron at RNAS Lee-on-Solent. In December 1955, helicopter operations with the ASWDU finally ceased, pending the arrival of the Bristol 192 expected in 1958. Trials still listed for the ASWDU helicopters in their last month included SAR, in-shore anti-submarine and, inevitably, navigation. However, by the time the B.192 had become the Belvedere (1960) it had also become exclusively a tactical transport helicopter as explained in Chapter 4. The two SAR squadrons were doing all the rescue work, of which there was a great deal (mainly for civilians), and the need for a special development unit for RAF maritime helicopters had disappeared along with the anti-submarine role which, for helicopters, passed wholly to the Royal Navy.

The helicopter unit in the ASWDU had lasted just under four years and apart from the dramatic accident in the first year (1952), had acquitted itself remarkably well. It was the first RAF unit to be equipped with Sycamores (apart from No 1906 Flight of No 657 AOP Squadron which had a mainly passenger-carrying role) and these early Sycamores were particularly unsuitable for the ASWDU tasks. They were designed as passenger vehicles and the cabin was more like that of a five seater motor car, a non-removable bench seat for three occupying the space behind the side-by-side pilot and co-pilot seats. There were depressions in the floor to accommodate the passengers' feet. The pilot training was rudimentary—50 hours on the Dragonfly at Westland's in Yeovil, followed by a 10-hour type conversion at Filton. There was no CFS unit to advise or control techniques until the unit was about to disband. For most of the time they could not obtain winches, and when they did they had to devise their own techniques. In spite of this they not only succeeded in laying the foundations of the SAR Squadrons which formed in 1953 (No 275) and 1955 (No 22), but attempted night flying trials and even devised their own two stage amber screens with which to try instrument flying. If they failed to make significant progress in their assigned tasks, it was certainly not for want of enthusiasm and imaginitive effort.

Helicopter Search and Rescue

Although prior to 1957 all the RAF operational helicopters (as distinct from 'trials' aircraft) for which financial approval was given by the Treasury were ostensibly for rescue duties (tactical uses in Malaya and elsewhere being regarded as special cases from a financial point of view) as explained in Chapter 4, the SAR task in the UK was never seriously interrupted by military tactical demands (except in Northern Ireland and briefly in Christmas Island) and was therefore never relegated to second priority. In contrast to overseas theatres, the UK-based SAR force grew up with total dedication to rescue as an exclusive role while for obvious reasons activity was almost from the beginning mainly directed towards the maritime environment. The UK-based SAR helicopter force was thus a basically different type from that which developed in overseas theatres and, later, for Army support in the UK. It has remained quite separate ever since, having its own operational training, standardisation and categorisation authority, originally under Fighter and Coastal Commands and later No 18 Group in Strike Command.

Policy Decisions Accompanying the Formation of the SAR Squadrons

In October 1952 the global strategy envisaged two SAR squadrons of 16 helicopters each, one in Coastal Command with S-55s (Whirlwinds) and one in Fighter Command with S-51s (Dragonflys). Almost immediately, a 12% cut in expenditure caused these figures to be halved while the Sycamore was to be substituted for the Dragonfly in Fighter Command.(1)

In February 1953 the Treasury at first declined to authorise the purchase of the S-55s on the grounds that Sycamores were already being obtained.(2) The Air Ministry had to explain that the Sycamore was suitable for fighter crews, but the increased range, payload and cabin size of the S-55 was needed for the heavy aircraft crews (five men at 100 nm range) and added that the RN was already planning to use the S-55 for SAR tasks. At this stage the failure of the Westland Whirlwind to match the performance of the American S-55 was still not recognised. However, by May 1953 the firm plan was for eight Whirlwinds and eight Sycamores for Coastal Command and Fighter Command respectively; and a month later, three Sycamores were approved for SAR duties for the Middle East Air Force in response to a demand by Lord Dowding. (The modification of the Sycamore to produce the Mk 14, and the overriding priority for the Malayan Theatre were to delay their arrival for over a year as mentioned in Chapter 4).

During the latter part of 1953, having achieved the setting up of No 275 SAR Squadron in Fighter Command and agreement for No 22 Squadron in Coastal Command, the Air Ministry continued attempts to enhance their capability, briefly considering a scheme to re-engine the Whirlwind with two Leonides engines,(3) but concluding that the twin rotor B-173 would be a better alternative to meet the operational requirement which had been defined (OR 280). By the end of the year the Air Council was considering plans to increase the eight Sycamores for No 275 Squadron to 16, changing the eight Whirlwinds of No 22 Squadron to eight B-173s during 1956 and providing three B-173s for the ASWDU in the same year.(4) No 22 Squadron remained scheduled to receive eight Whirlwinds.

As described in Chapter 4, the period from 1954–1960 was one of considerable turmoil in the helicopter world due mainly to pressure of expanding operational needs in FEAF and MEAF. But this was also the period when the UK helicopter SAR force was coming into existence. The CFS Helicopter Unit was trying to expand to take over helicopter training from the less than satisfactory civilian contract training, BFAP required SAR helicopters in Aden and Kenya, helicopter SAR was wanted for the Fighter Armament Practice Camps at Sylt, a SAR/IS presence was wanted in Northern Ireland, the JEHU had to be built up, and a helicopter SAR/Communications Unit had to be provided to accompany the nuclear testing programme in Christmas Island. The Queen's Flight and Metropolitan Communications Squadron were both waiting for their own helicopters. No advance provision existed for all these essential commitments and, to make matters worse, the entire Whirlwind force had to be re-engined in the latter part of this period by means of a comparatively radical and therefore time consuming operation to install turbine engines.

It was hardly surprising therefore that when, in September 1960, the recently formed Army Air Corps experienced technical problems which threatened to ground all their Skeeters for a considerable time, and RAF help was requested on behalf of No 1 British Corps in Germany, all that could be offered was three Dragonflys— to the chagrin of CFS who were using the remaining Dragonflys for the Staff Officer Familiarisation Course.(5) (In the event the Skeeter problem was not as protracted as feared and only two Dragonflys had to go, but three RAF pilots had to be re-converted on to the Dragonfly to go with them).

Throughout all the negotiations to resolve these conflicting priorities, policy for SAR operations in the UK remained consistent with the principle conceived in 1945 when the first R-4 Hoverflys came to England, and specifically defined in 1952. Nevertheless it took about three years (1953–1956) to build up the force to the point where the nine planned deployed Flights were able to offer standby cover over the whole of the East and South Coasts, Wales and part of the Irish Sea. (The Whirlwind 2s and Sycamores had an effective maximum radius of action in the SAR role of 50 nm). During the first two years the embryonic No 275 Squadron spent much of its time dashing to and fro with a mere handful of Sycamores in an attempt to provide cover where fighter exercises were taking place. But by the end of 1956 the pattern of nine deployed Flights of two aircraft each shared by Nos 275 and 22 Squadrons was in being and has scarcely altered since.

RAF Responsibility for Civilian SAR

The RAF Search and Rescue organisation, consisting of maritime patrol fixed-wing aircraft and Marine Craft Unit launches, which had expanded so notably during the 1939–45 war years, provided cover for civilian rescue operations as an 'act of grace'.(6) In February 1947 the Ministry of Civil Aviation had proposed that the Air Ministry should assume responsibility for operation and administration of all SAR arrangements for both civil and military aviation. The Air Ministry and MCA had agreed as follows:

'(a) The Air Ministry will assume responsibility for the operation and administration of all seach and rescue arrangements for military and civil aviation in the United Kingdom and in those areas overseas in which the Royal Air Force maintain facilities.

(b) The Air Ministry will make available to civil aviation the facilities of the search and rescue organisations at present in being.

(c) The Air Ministry will not be pressed to make any increase in establishments of personnel, aircraft or other equipment on account of the requirements of civil aviation for search and rescue. If it becomes necessary to provide increased facilities for civil aviation, the Ministry of Civil Aviation will provide them, or (if for example facilities are called for overseas which the Ministry of Civil Aviation cannot provide) will report the position to the International Civil Aviation Organisation (ICAO). Operational control of any facilities provided in the United Kingdom by the Ministry of Civil Aviation will rest with the Air Ministry.

(d) The Air Ministry will make available for publication by ICAO all information about arrangements for search and rescue which is not secret.

(e) The Ministry of Civil Aviation will be responsible for international negotiations about search and rescue, but will be advised by the Air Ministry. At conferences an Air Ministry Adviser will be attached to the Ministry of Civil

Aviation for the conference and will be regarded as a representative of the Ministry of Civil Aviation during that period.

(f)   The Ministry of Civil Aviation will reimburse to the Royal Air Force the extra cost incurred in operating for civil needs RAF search and rescue aircraft and other RAF facilities. This reimbursement will take the form of the annual provision in Estimates of a sum based on the average extra expenditure actually incurred over a period. The Ministry of Civil Aviation will decide in what cases charges should be made against aircraft owners for search and rescue operations, and will collect and keep the sums in question, consulting the Air Ministry about the amount of the charges.(7)

This agreement was in force when the SAR helicopters first appeared. Consequently, in November 1959, when a critical shortage of Whirlwinds (caused mainly by corrosion problems)(8) made it necessary temporarily to close one of the SAR detachments, and Thorney Island was selected as having the least urgent operational task in relation to RAF operational fighter activity, the Air Ministry was not prepared for the outcry which resulted. It was easy to silence the request from Flying Training Command for a special helicopter detachment at Thorney Island for Cowes Week, but not so simple to refuse the request from the Chief Constable of Sussex that the detachment should re-open 'for the coming summer months', especially in the presence of several letters from the Mayors of South Coast towns to the Secretary of State, and two Parliamentary enquiries.(9) The possibility of providing occasional detachments to Thorney island from other Flights was examined, but there was no way of doing this without losing RAF operational standby cover elsewhere. Of more long term importance, it was recognised that as a matter of principle RAF helicopters had to be deployed strictly in accordance with Service requirements, so the 1947 Agreement had to be invoked.(10) Nevertheless, from this time onwards it became progressively more difficult for the RAF to withdraw a SAR Flight for purely military reasons, the public (including coastguards and police) having become accustomed to having a rescue facility available locally, especially in heavily populated holiday areas.

Although in this case the RAF's position was maintained, action was taken to replace the missing SAR cover on the South Coast as soon as the aircraft supply position eased by deploying the Felixstowe Flight to Tangmere in June 1961, Tangmere being chosen at least partly 'because it is nearer to those South Coast towns where most incidents can be expected in the summer'.(11) (The Felixstowe detachment was replaced by one at Manston which itself became the subject of a similar controversy when the RAF later withdrew it for purely RAF reasons and then wished to re-open it in the 1970s).

By March 1961, the Air Staff was able to promise that when the Tangmere and Manston detachments were operational (the latter in August), continuous helicopter cover would again be available from Montrose in the North East to Weymouth. Practically the whole of Devon and Cornwall as well as South Wales was to continue being covered from Chivenor with the Valley detachment covering North Wales and the Liverpool Bay area. No mention was made of the helicopters then in Northern Ireland (see below) as they were no longer regarded as primarily for SAR purposes.

Although the build-up of the UK SAR force faced conflicting aircraft supply priorities and seemed frustratingly slow to those involved, it can be seen retrospectively in a different light. Apart from rescue technique to be developed, and the major difficulty of establishing workable communications with the various sources of demand for assistance, both in summoning helicopter attendance and then in dealing with it when it arrived, the record shows that each time a SAR Flight was established it seemed to be almost immediately operationally involved to the limits of its capability.(12) Neither the size nor nature of the commitment to civilian rescue had been foreseen, and although the cautious provisos of the 1947 Agreement could not be denied, it became from the beginning progressively more difficult politically to operate or deploy the SAR Flights exclusively in respect of purely Service interests. Fortunately conflict of interests was rare, being confined to those occasions when a SAR Flight had to be closed down (eg Thorney Island in 1959). Nobody (apart from the Treasury) ever objected to one being opened. The Thorney Island detachment had to be closed temporarily because there was no way of providing enough aircraft for all Flights then in being, but apart from Manston in the early 1970s (Phase 4) it was generally found possible to align Service and civilian requirements in all the areas, even where the purely Service needs in respect of SAR standby seemed to be diminishing.

Communications equipment posed other problems. Whilst the radios provided for the helicopters were compatible with those used by other Service aircrews for whom the SAR service was provided, they were not compatible with any of the differing types used by the Police and Fire Services, the Coastguards and the Royal National Lifeboat Institution. Since uniformity of equipment was not, for financial and other reasons, a feasible proposition, the problem from an official viewpoint continued unsolved for over 20 years by which time another dimension in the form of civilian Mountain Rescue Teams had been added to it.

It was, however, dealt with unofficially to the benefit of all concerned. Initially the main users of the SAR helicopter service, and virtually the only civilian contacts, were the Coastguards and the RNLI. As the personnel of the deployed Flights became acquainted personally with these local civilian authorities, it became very obvious that it was essential in their mutual interests to provide radio communications. Accordingly, the practice grew of borrowing radio sets from the organisation concerned, and carrying them (without formal authority) in order to achieve the desired result. Later, when land rescues became more frequent and the Police were involved, a new difficulty arose because of a Home Office regulation of considerable antiquity which forbade any radio set to be operated on a Home Office frequency unless by a policeman or fireman. This difficulty had still not been officially overcome in the early 1970s but most Chief Constables readily authorised the loan of radios to the SAR Flights when the occasion demanded.

In these and many other ways the SAR Flights became integrated with the local rescue services, and this process was officially endorsed in November 1955 when No 275 Squadron was authorised to undertake direct liaison with the Coastguard and RNLI in their various areas.(13) A limited degree of autonomy was thus passed to the Flights at an early stage, it being recognised that where immediate response to an urgent rescue call was vital to success, higher authority to react could not necessarily be obtained in time.

Command and Control

Initially the first SAR helicopters, being in Fighter Command, were operated under the Figher Sector Controls. When the two UK Rescue Co-ordination Centres were set up in November 1969 at Pitreavie Castle near Edinburgh and Mountbatten near Plymouth, permanent operational control of the SAR Flights was passed to the appropriate RCC. Although from time to time the Coastguards, having official responsibility for action in respect of all marine incidents offshore, voiced the opinion that they should have executive control of helicopters allotted to deal with such incidents, the RAF could never consider passing operational command of its helicopters to a civilian authority. From the very beginning however the sensible and necessary delegation of authority for immediate response to individual Flight Commanders, and their personal liaison with local Coastguards, allowed a good practical working relationship to develop, and no significant disputes occurred at any time in the following 20 years. The SAR Units were initially established with Squadron Leaders in command of Squadrons and Flight Lieutenants in charge of Flights—a situation which became unique in RAF aircraft operational units and still continues.

Nos 118 and 217 Squadrons

Apart from the difficulties of priority encountered in building the UK SAR helicopter force, two diversions infringed directly on the SAR squadrons themselves. In July 1957 No 275 Squadron opened a SAR Flight at Aldergrove in Northern Ireland, while in late 1956 No 22 Squadron formed 'GRAPPLE' Flight at St Mawgan and despatched it to Christmas Island in February 1957 to provide SAR and communications services for the British nuclear test programme. The Northern Ireland Flight behaved like the overseas helicopter units and acquired a tactical role which gave it a permanence not originally expected. In January 1958,

GRAPPLE Flight, now expected to operate eight Whirlwinds until beyond 1970,(14) became No 217 Squadron and in April 1959 the Aldergrove SAR Flight, already involved in internal security operations, became No 118 Squadron equipped with three Sycamores. In the event No 217 Squadron reduced from eight to five Whirlwinds in February 1958,(15) ceased operations in October 1959 and was disbanded with the withdrawal of the nuclear task force. No 118 Squadron, on the other hand, although regarded as of a temporary nature, became the subject of repeated pleas for its continued existence by various authorities in Northern Ireland when the general shortage of Whirlwinds elsewhere tempted the RAF to withdraw it. In February 1960 the Squadron Commander (Sqn Ldr David Toon) argued that the unit would be needed indefinitely and that it should be deployed forward from Aldergrove (ie nearer the border).(16) The Air Ministry did not foresee it continuing beyond September 1960. (The Helicopter Short Range Transport Force was by then building up and it was assumed that the Army support being provided by No 118 Squadron would become the responsibility of Transport Command and possibly met by a detachment from the new (ex-JEHU) No 225 Squadron).(17) In August 1960 the RUC joined in the demand for the retention of No 118 Squadron and in September the Air Ministry agreed to a further unspecified period of existence for the unit.(18)

By March 1961 the question of retention of No 118 Squadron had become the subject of correspondence between the Secretary of State for Air (Julian Amery) and the Home Secretary (R A Butler). The Prime Minister of Northern Ireland (Lord Brookeborough) had intervened at the last minute to prevent the disbandment of No 118 Squadron and in April 1961, Mr Amery granted a further indefinite stay of execution.(19) The unit in fact continued until the second half of 1962.

End of Phase 2 for SAR

As far as the main UK SAR force was concerned, the exchange of Sycamores for Whirlwinds with FEAF in 1959, following the transfer of No 275 Squadron to Coastal Command in the previous year, ended the 'ad hoc' experimental initial period for UK helicopter SAR by creating a homogeneous Whirlwind SAR force in Coastal Command which practically coincided with the decision to re-engine the Whirlwinds with the Gnome gas turbine, thus setting the scene for the whole of Phase 3.

THE SAR SQUADRONS

No 275 Squadron (later No 228 Squadron)

No 275 (Search and Rescue) Squadron was re-formed in No 13 Group of Fighter Command at RAF Linton-on-Ouse on 13 April 1953 with three pilots (including the

Squadron Commander—Flt Lt D C Kearns) and three crewmen/navigators. The second of the two Sycamores Mk 13—the original complement—arrived on 16 April, and SAR standby commenced on 20 April—10 minutes readiness during normal working hours and one hour otherwise, daylight operations only. An abortive search for a reported ditching was the first operational sortie and was carried out on 18 April.

Throughout 1953 and 1954, the acquisition of Sycamores to fill the establishment was agonisingly slow, No 275 Squadron being in competition with the New No 194 Squadron in Malaya for the Mk 14 Sycamores. Nevertheless, with its two Mk 13 Sycamores the squadron immediately started to respond to a series of demands for operational SAR standby tasks at various places on the East Coast, simulating the later pattern of fixed detachments by appearing for a few hours or days at a time, for example at Patrington, Strubby, Sutton-on-Hull, North Weald, Coltishall, Boulmer, Acklington, Leuchars, Bridlington Bay, Manston, Marham, Thornaby, Horsham St Faith and Bampton.

In June 1953 the Squadron rushed the TV films of the Coronation from Alexandra Palace to Heathrow and Blackbushe for onward travel by Canberra to Canada, and in the following month, after leading the Royal Review flypast at Odiham (when the RAF Ensign was flown from the Sycamore's weighted winch cable), the TV film of that event was flown by No 275 Squadron helicopter from Biggin Hill to Alexandra Palace.

Apart from these dramatic diversions there was little scope for misuse of the two Sycamores on non-SAR tasks and the crews were occupied in whatever time remained after positioning flights with providing SAR standby at a very large number of places, with educative demonstrations and teaching themselves how to carry out winching operations with a crew consisting only of pilot and navigator.

In the early and mid-1950s the proportion of incidents involving aircraft crashes on land for which helicopters were alerted in eastern England was much higher than was the case later. A large number of Venoms, Vampires and Meteors were flying at that time and crashes and bale-outs were comparatively frequent. The first actual rescue carried out by No 275 Squadron was of a Venom pilot recovered from Boulmer (disused at the time) to Acklington in August 1953.

Early in 1954, at the end of the first nine months of operations after a brief grounding of the Sycamores (torque limiting clutch slipping), it was found necessary to augment the Auster Mk V which had been acquired to keep the crews in what was described as 'flying practice', with two Hiller 360 helicopters borrowed from the RN Helicopter Training Unit at Gosport. These were much appreciated and in March 1954, when they arrived, no less than 148 sorties were flown. In the following month both the AOC and the SASO of No 13 Group were trained to first solo standard on these little two/three seater helicopters.

Throughout 1954 meetings and planning continued for the eagerly awaited Mk 14 Sycamores but Cyprus and Aden now joined FEAF in competing for Sycamores and it was not until February 1955 that a third Sycamore arrived. The first permanent No 275 Squadron detachment was promptly formed at North Coates. In the meantime, the trickle of crews arriving on the Squadron all required not only Sycamore conversion but general flying practice and No 275 Squadron developed its technique for acquiring alternative aircraft. In August 1954 only three sorties were flown by Sycamores against 21 by Hillers, 13 by Anson, 15 by Auster, nine by Chipmunk and three by Oxford. The Mk 13 Sycamores were now used only in the training role for the new crews (four of the seven crews being held in readiness for overseas duty in MEAF or FEAF), the Hillers were used for land rescue and the Anson for sea searches. The Squadron HQ and basic standby moved from Linton-on-Ouse to Thornaby in November but no sea rescue was possible for most of the last part of 1954 although some sort of standby was maintained as it had been since the Squadron came into existence, perhaps prematurely, in April 1953.

1955 was the year when the renaissance of the helicopter became effective in all theatres, not least in the UK SAR world. No 22 Squadron was formed at Thorney Island with Whirlwinds (although its beginning was almost as frustrating as that of No 275 Squadron as described later). No 275 Squadron started a steady build-up of operationally capable helicopters (Mk 14 Sycamores) and by May both Hillers had been returned to the RN. The Squadron managed somehow to hang on to its two Chipmunks for a further year, and the two Ansons became permanently established for communication duties, but the Squadron started to assume the operational helicopter posture which was to last for many years. As aircraft and crews arrived, permanent Flight detachments of two aircraft were rapidly set up to provide practical emergency cover—North Coates in February, Leuchars in June and Horsham St Faith in September, with the Squadron Headquarters co-located with the Flight at Thornaby.

Until June 1953, the pilots were all trained on the Dragonfly, having received a 50-hour course at Westland. The CFS helicopter unit then started to supply crews more appropriately trained and fully Sycamore converted. This was fortunate in the case of No 275 Squadron because by then they only had one Mk 13 Sycamore left—that is, with fully duplicated flying controls for training purposes—and that was crashed in November. The Mk 14 Sycamore had only one collective lever, centrally mounted, which meant that the instructor, sitting on the left, had to use opposite hands for cyclic and collective controls from the standard right and left conditions to which everyone was trained. (This problem affected CFS as reported in Chapter 6). Only after a special course could pilots successfully accomplish this change, and even then not always satisfactorily. The consequence was that no further dual instruction on the Sycamore was possible on the Squadron, at least until the first ambidextrously trained instructor could be provided by CFS, and that was not until April 1956.

As already mentioned RAF CFS-trained pilots only began to be provided in mid-1955. It was not until April 1956 that CFS was able to produce a Sycamore QHI for the Squadron training officer post. Prior to that, the pilots were generally ignorant of many aspects of helicopter flight, and none were qualified to carry out practice engine-off landings.

There was an illuminating example of this lack of background knowledge in March 1956. It was the practice to simulate instrument flying conditions by means of a locally made vision restricting visor, the navigator sitting in the left hand seat (without controls) as a look-out. On this occasion the pilot was simulating an instrument approach to land, using 3000 feet as notional ground level. Having accidentally lost all airspeed in the later stages of this simulated approach, the aircraft suddenly built up an alarmingly increasing rate of descent. As it passed 800 feet at 3–400 feet per minute descent, the navigator reached over and removed the pilot's restrictive visor, and both were equally surprised that after applying full power the pilot was unable to reduce the descent sufficiently to prevent the aircraft crashing although it was checked sufficiently to allow them both to survive unhurt. The pilot was on the point of receiving full blame for this incident. When at a later date, it was reported to CFS the event was immediately recognised as due to Vortex Ring (see Chapter 2), a condition in which the pilots had clearly received inadequate instruction; nobody on the Squadron seemed aware of this obvious conclusion, still less of the avoidance and recovery procedures.

From September 1955 and through 1956, No 275 Squadron developed steadily in the pattern which was in future to become typical for the helicopter SAR units. In January the use of the aircraft as an all-round rescue vehicle became appreciated in snow rescues and emergency supply deliveries, and proper liaison with HM Coastguards and the RNLI was authorised on a formal basis. In February 1956 the first ship rescue was carried out when 11 seamen were ferried from the stranded Norwegian vessel Dovrefjell in four sorties from the Pentland Skerries. There was at that stage however little discrimination in the choice of tasks accepted—at the behest of the RSPCA food supplies were carried to a group of swans distressed by the freezing over of Hickling Broad. In April, the first RAF pilot was lifted direct to a civilian hospital and the Neil Robertson stretcher (see under Techniques below) was used for the first time in lifting a patient from a boat. Also in April, the first CFS-trained QHI arrived to fill the training officer post, dual training again became possible on the Squadron and, most importantly, training in the technique of carrying out engine-off landings could at least become general. This was just in

Winch fitted to Sycamore Mk 14.

Double lift development.

time for the first engine failure over the sea in June which occurred without injury to the crew.

In the absence of any Operational Training Unit it was inevitable that No 275 Squadron would have to fill this role. In fact, it not only had to perform that function for its own build-up of detached Flights, but also for the Sycamore units being formed in Sylt, Aden and especially Cyprus.

For No 275 Squadron the second half of 1956 was bedevilled by the unexpected build-up of Sycamores (and pilots) in Cyprus. By September the strength was down to seven Sycamores against an establishment of 16 but by the end of the year the situation was improving again. In June and July 1957, two new detachments were opened—Chivenor and Aldergrove—the latter being the first helicopter SAR unit to be based in Northern Ireland. The North Coates Flight was moved to Leconfield to where the Squadron HQ also moved from Thornaby in September. In October the Flight at Thornaby moved to Acklington and by the end of the year, the full complement of six Flights was established with a total strength of 15 Sycamores at Leuchars, Acklington, Leconfield, Chivenor, Coltishall and Aldergrove, thus providing cover over much of the east and west coasts. Night flying exercises were started in earnest.

By April 1958 all No 275 Squadron crews were fully trained for night and instrument flying and practiced in engine-off landings, and in May were officially cleared for night transit flying and rescue sorties over land. There was a comparatively large number of land rescues during this period as the RAF still had many fighter aircraft exercising in the northern and eastern areas of the country. In July, for example, aircraft incidents necessitating the call-out of No 275 Squadron involved an Auster, a Provost, a USAF B66 bale-out, a Sea Venom short of fuel, and a parachute sighting, as well as a submarine search, a range accident, several medevacs and numerous bathers in difficulty—in all 24 operations. In August, one of the busiest months of the year, 21 operations of this nature were carried out. In May 1958, Coastal Command assumed responsibility for all Search and Rescue, and No 275 Squadron was transferred to No 18 Group. In the following November the Chivenor Flight handed over to a No 22 Squadron Flight. In April 1959 the Aldergrove SAR Flight was withdrawn, but by then the tactical capabilities of the helicopter in the internal security role were being realised and it was replaced by a new Sycamore Squadron—No 118. By then, the No 275 Squadron Sycamores were being replaced by Whirlwinds as the exchange with FEAF started to occur, but almost immediately the transfer of aircraft stopped following the prolonged grounding of the Sycamores in Malaya. From May 1959 the Squadron operated a mixture of Whirlwinds and Sycamores until in December the Whirlwind conversion could be resumed with the Whirlwind Mk 4s starting to arrive from FEAF as the Sycamores there revived with new blades.

In September 1959, No 275 Squadron was renamed No 228 Squadron. In May 1960 the last Sycamore SAR operation was carried out, consisting of a medevac from Colonsay to Oban and, with 11 Whirlwinds established, SAR operations continued unabated with Flights at Leuchars, Acklington, Leconfield (Squadron HQ) and Coltishall.

Techniques

The initial intention that a survivor would be presented with a strop on the end of the winch cable to which he would attach himself was clearly unsatisfactory since many survivors did not know what to do, and many of those who did were physically incapacitated. Almost since the Squadron formed experiments had been going on with a net designed by Lt Cdr Sproule RN with which a survivor could be scooped out of the water without taking any active part in the rescue himself. The Sproule net had been designed for use with the Dragonfly and although some satisfactory results had been obtained with the Sycamore, there was a problem with the position of the engine exhaust which tended to burn the net, and sometimes the survivor as well.

By July 1955 the awkward conclusion had to be faced that the only really satisfactory solution was for the navigator/crewman to go down on the winch cable, the winch being operated by the pilot in response to crewman directions via an extremely long inter-com cable. This produced technical and handling problems of its own, and experiments with the net as an alternative were continued throughout the following years and into 1958. However, in December 1955 during a practice lift a Sycamore struck the Bell Rock Lighthouse and both pilot and crewman were killed. Recovery of the bodies by helicopter turned out to be impossible because the net could not be used on land, and there were problems with the long inter-com cable which prevented a 'double lift' (ie with the crewman going down on the bottom of the winch cable).

The only satisfactory solution was now seen to consist of adding a third crew member to operate the winch with the crewman on the end of the winch cable, notwithstanding the loss of range and cabin space that this entailed. By January 1956 this conclusion was starting to be reluctantly accepted for the Sycamore squadron—it having been adopted at the outset for the Whirlwinds of No 22 Squadron with their much larger cabin space. Nevertheless, the carriage of a third crew member was still regarded as such a disadvantage that experiments in the Sycamore continued for a further year with the long inter-com cable and mirrors through which it was hoped the pilot could see enough of what was happening to operate the winch satisfactorily. It was not until August 1957, however, that crewmen started to be trained purely as winch operators for No 275 Squadron to be added to the previously standard basic crew of pilot and navigator; meanwhile

Double lift training.

'Sproule' Net.

Trawling for survivors with 'Sproule' net.

Helicopter crewman preparing casualty for
helicopter lift while the rescue helicopter stands off
out of danger from pitching superstructure.

development of the Sproule net still continued, until in June 1958 a satisfactory version was able to be put into production—only nine months before all the SAR Sycamores were to be exchanged for Whirlwinds ex Malaya.*

Towards the end of this period, therefore, pilot operation of the winch was going out of favour, largely because of unreliable communication with the crewman on the end of the cable, and where the rescue net could not be used, it was recognised as essential that a third crew member had to be employed.**

Until the fitting of Decca, which was still under consideration for the Sycamores in 1958, the only navigation aid was the VHF fixer service provided by the Sector Control operated primarily for the fighter force. For homing on survivors, the Squadron Anson was equipped with SARAH in June 1954, and the Sycamores shortly afterwards. In September 1955, SARAH Mk 2 was standard fit in SAR helicopters and it and its successor (SARBE) remained so for more than 25 years.

The standard stretcher used for lifting casualties by helicopter was the 'Neil Roberston'—a rigid board with enveloping wrap-around sides stiffened with wooden slats. The subject is thus cocooned in a stiffened body length 'straight jacket' and the stretcher can be safety suspended from the winch cable and generally manhandled as required. The Neil Robertson stretcher became standard equipment in helicopters from 1956 onwards.

End of Phase 2

In October 1962 Whirlwind 10s started to replace their piston-engined predecessors (Mks 2 and 4) in No 228 Squadron; in November some were on SAR standby and by December the changeover was complete, thus ending Phase 2 for this unit.

No 22 Squadron

Coastal Command had to wait until 1955 before being able to set up its helicopter SAR squadron using Whirlwinds, pending expected substitution of the Bristol 173 at a later date. Even then, the shortage of Whirlwinds because of the Malayan demands very nearly ruined the unit at the outset. No 22 Squadron re-formed as a

---

*It will be appreciated that much of the pressure to exchange the SAR Sycamores for the Malayan Whirlwinds was generated in 1957 by these cabin space/performance considerations, and not only because of the reduced confidence in the Whirlwind and the popularity of the Sycamore in Malaya. See Chapter 3.

**20 years later, with winch cables in excess of 200 ft in use, the requirement for the crewmen to have voice communication with the aircraft had again become vital and was being dealt with by use of small radio sets.

helicopter SAR squadron at Thorney Island in No 19 Group in February 1955, its tasks being sea rescue and search and rescue over land and adjacent waters to a range of 60 nm. It had an initial establishment of eight Whirlwinds Mk 2 and was planned to operate four detached Flights to provide SAR cover over the South and South East coast and Wales, one being located at Thorney island together with the Squadron HQ, operational training facilities and second line servicing. The Whirlwind crew was to consist of pilot, navigator and crewman, pilots initially being transferred from the ASWDU.

The very next month there were well-founded rumours of imminent disbandment as no aircraft had arrived, and all postings to the Squadron were suspended. However, two Sycamores were allotted from the ASWDU to enable the Squadron to continue forming and by May 1955 the unit had two Sycamores and an Anson, and was looking and functioning very much like a Flight of its predecessor, No 275 Squadron, in its early days.

The critical shortage of aircraft was not of long duration and when in the following month four Whirlwinds arrived, the first two Flights were immediately set up, one at Thorney Island and the other at Martlesham Heath. The inexperience of the crews did not prevent them from carrying out a successful public demonstration of the Sproule Rescue Net on the Welsh Harp in the same month.

With the main cabin below and behind the Flight Deck the need for a third crew member in the Whirlwind was more immediately obvious than had been the case when No 275 Squadron had started with Sycamores, and provision had been made in the Unit Establishment for them. A specific crewman trade did not, however, exist, and while in Malaya the deficiency had been made up by using technical ground tradesmen, the servicing problem away from base was not so pressing for No 22 Squadron and in July 1955 three administrative orderlies were allotted for crewman duties, receiving an extra one shilling and sixpence per day for the privilege.

The 'double lift' technique (crewman descending on the bottom of the winch cable) later found to be necessary in many cases in No 275 Squadron was adopted at the outset and in August 1955 the first live rescue by No 22 Squadron was carried out successfully, two double lifts being made to lift two people stranded under overhanging rocks near Beachy Head. These involved the crewman wading ashore under the cliffs to reach the survivors.

In September 1955 the third Flight of No 22 Squadron was established at Valley to provide West Coast SAR cover and became operational the following month— nine months after the Squadron was formed. It was the first SAR Flight to have a navigator as Flight Commander.

Bringing a casualty aboard in the Neil Robertson stretcher.

SAR training by the CFS Flight at Valley.

SAR cliff rescue training by the CFS Flight at Valley.

SAR training with Mk 10 Whirlwind with crew of three.

There followed a further brief period when aircraft were in very short supply—one Whirlwind was taken away to be sent to FEAF and another was found to be suffering from the corrosion which was to be the bugbear, particularly of the magnesium alloy Sikorsky Helicopter used in a maritime environment, for many years to come. A Sycamore had to be borrowed again from the ASWDU to maintain the SAR standby on the South Coast.

By April 1956, just over one year since formation, No 22 Squadron was operational with all four Flights, the last one being at St Mawgan where the Squadron HQ also moved in June of that year. The Flight at Martlesham Heath moved to Felixstowe in April.

The Flights at Thorney Island, St Mawgan and Felixstowe were controlled by the Southern Rescue Co-ordination Centre (SRCC) at Plymouth, that at Valley being in the geographical area covered by the Northern RCC at Pitreavie Castle. Operations only differed from those of No 275 Squadron in that there were more holiday boating accidents to deal with on the South Coast than in eastern England and the area was not so heavily involved with military air traffic as in the east and north east. Decca replaced GEE as a navigation aid in 1958, the latter having been inherited from the ASWDU, and SARAH was in general use for locating military survivors by 1955.

No 22 Squadron gave birth to a further SAR Squadron in the Far East in 1958—No 217 Squadron—through a detached Flight of No 22 Squadron sent to Christmas Island in February 1957 to provide SAR and communications flying for the task force concerned with the British nuclear tests (Operation GRAPPLE) in the Far East. 'Grapple Flight', as it was called, formed at St Mawgan in October 1956 with four crews and two aircraft of No 22 Squadron. The Flight embarked on HMS Warrior on 30 January 1957, and after SARAH and winching practice in the Azores, some continuation flying training in Haiti, two days in Jamaica and occasional turns at 'Plane Guard' for the RN fixed-wing aircraft, arrived in Christmas Island on 4 March 1957 and commenced SAR standby on 6 March. Characteristically the helicopter facility became indispensable and consequently grew so that after nine months of mainly communications flying but with continuous SAR standby, No 217 Squadron was formed to carry on the task, and residual GRAPPLE Flight personnel returned to be once more absorbed in the main element of No 22 Squadron. A lecture on SARAH was given by request to the US Coastguards as the party passed through Hickham Air Force Base (Honolulu) on the way back to Lyneham in January 1958.

The pattern of operations established in the UK as soon as the deployed Flights were operational remained substantially unchanged for many years. The aircraft were tasked at 30 hours flying per month each and thus a total of about 240 hours was flown annually. This figure remained substantially constant while the operational call-outs fluctuated seasonably with weather and holiday patterns, averaging about 200 per year from mid-1957 onwards. A typical figure for land as opposed to sea rescue call-outs would be 10%.

In November 1958 the No 22 Squadron Flight at St Mawgan moved to Chivenor to replace the No 275 Squadron Flight which was withdrawn as part of a geographical rationalisation of responsibility, and a Headquarters Flight formed at St Mawgan mainly for training new crews but also having a SAR standby facility. This training Flight acquired the status of an OTU in July 1959 and continued to maintain a limited operational capability while providing SAR operational training for the new pilots arriving from the CFS Helicopter Training School and Navigators/Signallers arriving direct.

In December 1959 the Flight at Thorney Island had to be temporarily withdrawn, leaving SAR cover on the South Coast on an 'ad hoc' basis by the Royal Navy until in May 1961 the Felixstowe Flight was moved to Tangmere and was replaced on the South East Coast in July by the fourth Flight at Manston. The OTU was then in a position to provide standardisation checks for No 275 Squadron, the whole SAR helicopter force by then being equipped with Whirlwind Mk 2. Conversion to the turbine engined Mk 10 Whirlwind started in May 1962 and was complete by September of that year, thus concluding Phase 2 for No 22 Squadron.

SUMMARY OF THE SITUATION IN 1960

In the first phase of its development the helicopter had shown that, in theory at least, it had the capacity to improve substantially the flexibility and capability of any unit engaged in tactical situations unsuited to motor transport. In the second phase this capacity had been generally recognised as an essential element in nearly all forms of military activity. In the RAF, however, the helicopter had come to maturity in a period of the greatest difficulty. The development of the nuclear deterrent and the emphasis placed on the bomber, fighter and maritime roles, combined with ever present financial stringency, produced a very unfavourable climate for the development of what some still saw as an aeronautical aberration.

Inter-Service Relations

The arrival of the demonstrably practical helicopter had produced a reaction on the part of the other two Services reminiscent of what had taken place between 1912 and 1918. On that occasion the situation had been resolved by the formation of the Royal Air Force, a step taken with the full backing of government. No such support was given now and, left to itself and beset by many other problems, the RAF was by no means certain that it wished to embrace the whole helicopter element. The Fleet Air Arm, in one sense, had not been its concern since 1937; nor did there seem to be any sound reason for re-establishing a new version of the old Army Co-operation squadrons to undertake with ultra light helicopters the AOP and light liaison tasks. On the other hand, this was clearly a line of thought which could not be allowed to go too far, and the dividing line between Army and RAF responsibility was therefore arbitrarily drawn to exclude anything much larger than the Skeeter or Fairey ultra light helicopter, ie at 4000 lb weight. The problem was thus shelved for the time being, but not solved, as an artificial limit of this kind would inevitably be eroded as helicopter technology developed. The seeds of trouble sown in the 1950s germinated in due course: the developed Skeeter became the Scout and Wasp, which turned into anti-tank and anti-submarine weapons carriers; the Scout replacement became the cargo/troop carrying Lynx and so the dividing line between Army and RAF responsibility became progressively more difficult to distinguish—a situation which promised conflict at some future date.

Operational Achievements

Within the area of activity which seemed proper to the RAF there were grounds for satisfaction, in that all urgent operational demands had been met, although only just. The Malayan operations had been satisfactorily concluded and helicopter support maintained throughout by one means or another. The nuclear weapons trials in the Pacific had been supported by a Whirlwind squadron and in Cyprus the struggle against terrorism had been transformed by the arrival of tactical helicopters. A limited casualty evacuation service had been provided in Kenya; SAR detachments had been set up in Malaya, Cyprus, El Adem, Jordan and Sylt, and a squadron of Sycamores had been sent to Northern Ireland in 1959. In England a basic SAR service with somewhat limited performance was provided by two permanent Whirlwind squadrons deployed along the east and south coasts; in addition, The Queen's Flight had two Whirlwinds and the Metropolitan Communications Squadron was on the point of opening a VIP and staff helicopter service from Northolt.

The Development of Roles

At the end of the 1950s the JEHU had been transformed into a tactical helicopter support squadron. Thus the tactical helicopter role was officially accepted as an RAF task, whereas previously SAR, casualty evacuation and, exceptionally, communications had been the only roles which the RAF could specify in its applications to the Treasury for new helicopters, except when the Army was already committed to a conflict and the application was therefore too late.

All helicopter deployments in the 1950s—in the Far East, the Middle East, Aden and Northern Ireland—began as casualty evacuation or SAR and went on to play an essential part in tactical operations, living up to their reputation in that role. The lesson was obvious and gave added impetus to helicopter development in both the technical and philosophical spheres. What was not appreciated so readily was that tactical demands overseas, being more urgent than the SAR standby role and therefore usually taking precedence, soon ceased to be regarded as a diversion of effort from the primary task. All the overseas units became 'de facto' tactical units and the SAR task was carried out as a secondary role when circumstances allowed.

Only in the United Kingdom (excluding Northern Ireland) did this reversal of role not take place, the obvious reason being the absence of any operations requiring tactical helicopters. Communications flights were therefore the only diversion which the SAR standby helicopters had to resist and such resistance was not difficult. Thus the SAR units in the United Kingdom, originally established for Coastal and Fighter Commands, retained their exclusive SAR status when those Commands disappeared and their role continued to be regarded as completely distinct from that of the tactical helicopter units of which the first to be established was No 225 Squadron at the end of this second phase of helicopter development.

In the overall picture, however, these SAR units had been relegated to second place and in the 1950s their formation and build up were substantially delayed by the shortage of helicopters caused by the proliferation of tactical tasks overseas carrying a higher priority. With hindsight it can be seen that it was the exclusive nature of its SAR role, as developed in the United Kingdom in the 1950s, and maintained automatically in subsequent years, which eventually enabled the United Kingdom SAR force to generate its own operational requirement for a new type of helicopter—the Sea King—without reference to the needs of the tactical helicopter force, rather than having to content itself with a modified version of an aircraft suited to tactical operations.

Some confusion, in fact, arose from the differing attitudes of the SAR organisations maintained by the RAF and the Navy, the latter being operated more in the manner of the RAF units overseas. In 1954, for example, the Minister of Transport and Civil Aviation asked the First Lord of the Admiralty why Naval SAR helicopter services were not available on Sundays and public holidays, and for periods of about two weeks at Christmas, Easter and in August, while the RAF's SAR service was continuous.(138) The First Lord replied that Naval SAR services were provided on an ad hoc basis by helicopters disembarked from ships and, as such, were part of a training and not an operational command.(139) In other words the SAR service so provided was a peacetime bonus rather than a formally established commitment and the manpower and technical backing was provided accordingly. This difference in approach to SAR in the United Kingdom was to reappear from time to time in later years.

Training

By the end of the second phase of helicopter development the Central Flying School helicopter unit had been in existence for six years. Originally established in 1954 to develop helicopter instructional and handling techniques and train a nucleus of flying instructors,(140) it had compiled the official air publication dealing with training helicopter pilots and instructors including a categorisation scheme, and was currently training and testing helicopter instructors for all the Services in accordance with the CFS charter.

It was also responsible for training RAF helicopter pilots. The original conception in 1954 had been that when Service pilots were trained by the Services themselves, and no longer by the aircraft manufacturers on an ad hoc basis, a joint Service organisation was obviously desirable. With the small numbers involved the acceptance of this idea seemed to be guaranteed by the economies it would produce.(141) But in the event it appeared that the intensity of Naval feelings on the matter had been sadly underestimated.

Later, in 1957, when the Army Air Corps came into being, a further formal attempt was made to arrange joint Service pilot training and a joint Service committee was formed to agree basic principles. However, no agreement could be reached even on the location of a joint unit, the Army and the RAF being prepared to defer to each other if necessary and accept either South Cerney (CFS) or Middle Wallop (AAC). But neither was willing to accept Culdrose where the Navy was determined to remain (and with a Naval captain in charge). Helicopter pilot training therefore remained irredeemably single service.

Aircraft Type Development

Through all the pressures, and occasional dramas, of this second phase the Air Ministry had succeeded in avoiding the temptations of committing itself to ill founded, if initially attractive, courses of action over the many helicopter projects being urged on it from various quarters. Although there were very few staff officers in the Air Ministry with helicopter experience, the Air Staff emerged from this hectic period with no costly millstones round its neck. On the contrary, the RAF was entering the 1960s with two splendid examples of helicopter technology: the Belvedere with its remarkable lifting capacity and the economic and efficient Whirlwind Mk 10, backed by the cheap and reliable Sycamore which maintained essential operations during the changeover period and thereafter remained available for the less onerous training and communications tasks well into the 1970s.

1   ID/53/1/60 Pt 2.

2   Ibid.

3   Ibid.

4   Ibid.

5   IIA/11/2/30 Pt 3.

6   ID9/G4-1.

7   Ibid.

8   IIA/11/2/30 Pt 3.

9   ID9/G4-1.

10   Ibid.

11   Ibid.

12   ORB.

13   ORB.

14   IIA/11/2/31 Pt 2.

15   Ibid.

16   IIK/128/2/197.

17   Ibid.

18   Ibid.

19   ID3/943/2 Pt 1.

PHASE 3—1960–1971

INTRODUCTION

The third phase of helicopter development in the RAF belongs to the years 1960–71, a period in which the helicopter force built upon the achievements of earlier types of rotary wing aircraft in both tactical operations overseas and search and rescue duties at home. Further, the more advanced helicopters now coming into service, with turbine engines, metal blades and improved controls, were able to offer a far better level of performance in all the established helicopter roles.

Fortuitously, the growing sophistication in helicopter design and performance coincided with increased operational demands: the Malayan Emergency was followed by Confrontation in Borneo, and turmoil in Cyprus by a rising tide of unrest in Aden and neighbouring territories, the main helicopter burden now falling on the Belvedere and Whirlwind Mk 10, to be joined a little later by the Wessex Mk 2.

Nearer home, the main change was the formation of tactical support helicopter (SH) squadrons in Germany and the United Kingdom, and the establishment of operational training and technical support elements at Odiham for the Belvedere, Whirlwind and Wessex units overseas. Deployment of the SAR squadrons remained much as before, except that one detachment at a time was temporarily withdrawn while it exchanged its Mk 2 Whirlwinds for Mk 10s.

Meanwhile, although the turbine-engined helicopter was now predominant, the stalwart Sycamore continued in service throughout the 1960s in the transport role from Northolt; it was also to be found in the short range transport (SRT) force now forming in the United Kingdom, and at the Central Flying School for training duties; and it continued—for a time—in the support role overseas, in El Adem, Cyprus and the Far East, Aden, and briefly in Kenya.

Minor taskings for the 1960s included a two-year limited scale support operation in British Guiana, mounted by Whirlwinds; the continuing SAR deployment in Cyprus carried out by a flight (No 1563) of Whirlwind 10s at Akrotiri; and from 1964 the provision of a communications flight in Nicosia tasked to support the United Nations Force in Cyprus (UNFICYP) and made up of a series of rotating detachments from the helicopter squadrons based in the United Kingdom and Germany (Nos 230, 18 and 72).

The three wooden-bladed pre-production Belvederes leaving Weston-super-Mare on delivery to Odiham by the Belvedere Trials Unit—October 1960.

Pre-production Belvedere of the BTU near Odiham. Note the small wheels and large tail stabilisers—both modified in the later production aircraft.

CHAPTER 8

INTRODUCTION INTO SERVICE OF THE BELVEDERE

The era of the turbine-engined helicopter began with the arrival of the Belvedere at its trials unit in 1960. With it, however, came another radical change: no longer was maximum engine power the sole criterion determining all-up-weight limitations and performance capabilities. The crucial factor now was transmission design strength which limited the amount of power to be tolerated from the new turbine engines.

The Belvedere was the first multi-engined helicopter in the RAF (its forerunner, the Bristol 173, having been the first twin-engined helicopter in the world); it was also the first RAF twin main rotor helicopter and the last purely British-designed and built large helicopter. Consequently, the history of its introduction into service and deployment overseas in the Middle and Far East is of particular interest.

The Belvedere Trials Unit

Something has already been said about early problems with the Belvedere: arguments over the tactical use of helicopters and the financial consequences of developing a new twin-engined rotary wing aircraft (see Chapter 4). During 1958 and early 1959 major technical development problems were encountered and it was found necessary to redesign the main gear box and tail plane, and introduce metal rotor blades and power assisted controls. In July 1959, with the estimated CA release date put at December 1960, it was decided to form a RAF Trials Unit of three pre-production aircraft, which were expected to become available in July 1960, although still with wooden blades and manual controls. Formation of a Trials Unit would enable valuable experience to be gained on the Belvedere before its introduction into service in the Far East.(1) Training of five pilots with Sycamore experience began at the contractors' airfield at Weston-super-Mare in July 1960, although it was not until three months later that the three pre-production aircraft were formally handed over to the unit, which then moved to Odiham to start work.

In theory the Belvedere was still competing with the Wessex Mk 2 for a place in the future SRT force (although the latter was not yet built); and in fact an investigation in early 1960 (2) had led to the decision <u>not</u> to place a further order for the Belvedere in preference to the Wessex on the grounds of relative costs and the number of problems with the Belvedere still to be resolved. Costs were indeed mounting: since, to save time and money, no prototype had been ordered, every change in design had to be incorporated into each production aircraft during construction and at very considerable expense. By July 1959 expenditure already amounted to £370000 per aircraft, a figure which had risen to £390000 by October;

in contrast, the estimated cost of the Wessex at that time, with a projected CA release date of 1962, was £185000.(3) Consequently, no further Belvedere order was expected.

At that time the proposal was for a force of turbine-engined Whirlwind Mk 10s and twin Gnome-engined Wessex Mk 2s, with the addition of twelve Rotodynes to provide the crane lift which the Army insisted was necessary and for which Treasury approval had already been given in spite of RAF doubts about the capability of the Rotodyne to meet the requirement.* Later, in the face of declining estimates of performance and escalating costs, the decision was taken to cancel the aircraft.

Meanwhile, although the Belvedere had been put—prematurely—into production, the radically new design of this tandem rotor, twin-engined aircraft was giving rise, predictably, to problems in two areas where bold new experiments were being carried out: power-operated controls and, particularly, transmission gearboxes. In essence, the 5000 lb or so all-up-weight Sycamore with one three-bladed main rotor had become a 20000 lb all-up-weight Belvedere with two four Sycamore-bladed main rotors and still (in 1960) with full manual controls. Further, it was to be ready for squadron service by 1961 equipped with metal and therefore completely redesigned rotor blades and fully duplicated power controls—although only one development aircraft had been ordered on which to prove these 'modifications', with a further two for A&AEE trials. To compound the problem, as a duplicated power system was still only in the development stage, flight testing was to go ahead on a development aircraft with only single channel power operated controls. One result of this was that as all test manoeuvres had to be demonstrated under safe control in full 'manual' before test measurements for clearance could be recorded under 'servo' control, each section of the flight envelope had first to be tried out in full manual control, something which could not be repeated in the production aircraft as these had no provision for voluntary manual reversion.

In fact, the 20000 lb all-up-weight metal-bladed Belvedere was much easier to fly in full manual than the Whirlwind, with its single three-bladed rotor and 8000 lb all-up-weight, which was manageable only for short periods, at restricted speeds and with special lateral bias assistance in the cyclic control.(5) That this should be so seems to be a point in support of Raoul Haffner's argument that a manual

---

*ACAS(OR) summed up the position in October 1960: 'This aircraft will meet the War Office requirements (three tons internally over 200 nm radius or six tons externally over 20 nm radius). However, it is a complex and expensive aircraft which will require an enormous amount of development before it is introduced into service . . . It is unlikely to be available before 1965 and because of its complexity I have grave doubts about its suitability for use in the tactical transport role.'(4)

capability should be demonstrated before power assistance was applied, a theory discounted as either impractical or irrelevant by the Sikorsky school of development, which concentrated on making a single main rotor large enough in relation to the weight to be lifted and on dealing with whatever control forces were encountered by introducing more powerful control assistance. Indeed, even by the time the Wessex came on the scene power to the controls was no longer referred to as 'assistance'; the pilot was contributing nothing whatsoever to control power and no provision was made for him to do so.*

The lateral stick forces proportional to speed felt in the single main rotor helicopters in manual control were translated in the Belvedere into a load on the rudder pedals as each counter rotating rotor experienced a lateral force in the opposite direction and opposite lateral tilt of the rotors was used in yaw control. In the development Belvedere bias assistance to oppose this force was provided by a single piece of 'bungee' or elastic cord. On the one occasion when this broke, the pilot was surprised and even momentarily disconcerted, but nothing more.(6) None of the production Belvederes ever suffered a total power control failure and consequently flight in full manual control was never experienced in the metal-bladed Belvederes, apart from the development aircraft. There is, however, no reason to believe that the result would have been more than uncomfortable, as the whole manual linkage remained and was used for control, driven by power operated jacks in parallel with the linkage.

The three pre-production aircraft used by the Belvedere Trials Unit operated in full manual control throughout the life of the unit and having the well tried Sycamore blades and tie-bar attachments produced generally acceptable stick forces. The only occasion on which manual control forces interfered with the successful completion of a manoeuvre occurred on the very last flight of the trials aircraft during a rehearsal for the Farnborough SBAC show in August 1961, when with 25 troops on board a moderately steep 'flare' position of about 20 degrees was used for deceleration to the hover. What was later described as aerodynamic interference between front and rear rotors produced a heavy lateral leftward load on the stick coupled with a steep tail down pitching movement which forced the pilot to release the collective lever in order to apply both hands to the cyclic stick and so prevent

---

*A further effect of the trend to increased weight was a growth in the size of tail rotors as engine power increased, and quite soon sideways facing tail rotors were using as much power as the main rotors of small helicopters. It is a matter for speculation whether this configuration would have become so universally accepted but for the untimely demise of the Air Staff's first choice for an operational helicopter: the Gyrodyne with its forward facing offset propeller to counter torque (see Chapter 2).

the aircraft rolling to the left. The aircraft sank towards a landing in a marked nose up attitude and the rear rotor struck the ground. The final landing, however, was soft enough to cause no injuries, although both the rear rotor and the front undercarriage disintegrated, the latter shearing off because of the forward motion.

As this was the last flight planned for the pre-production manual aircraft and it was clear that the metal-bladed power controlled machines would not suffer similar control problems, a detailed analysis of the causes of the accident was not considered worth while and the SBAC display went ahead successfully with the newly delivered production Belvederes.

The crash of August 1961 was the second of the only two serious accidents suffered by the Trials Unit, the first having occurred at the outset on 22 November 1960. A Belvedere with an underslung land rover and trailer experienced what seemed to be a double engine failure at about 150 feet shortly after lift-off at Odiham. One engine stopped and the pilot waited expecting the other to go to double the power selected, as it was supposed to do. As this did not happen, the load was jettisoned and an emergency landing made straight ahead. The aircraft landed softly, but ran forward slowly, the very small wheels (replaced by larger ones on the production aircraft) penetrating the soft surface and the front undercarriage shearing off. Little other damage was suffered however. It was not possible to discover exactly what had happened as the very experienced pilot had instinctively prepared for an engine-off landing at the first sign of trouble and carried out the appropriate procedure within seconds. All the same, there was a possibility that when the failure occurred he had operated the dump valve switches for the wrong engine by mistake, since the likelihood of this happening was already recognised because of the lateral disposition of switches relating to engines longitudinally disposed in the fuselage. On investigation the second engine was found to be serviceable, although it did fail a bench test to establish whether it automatically selected emergency (ie double) power when it should do; and eighteen months later fears about a possible mistake with the switches were tragically confirmed.

The Belvedere Trials Unit was tasked for intensive flying trials, but had no specific brief for flying patterns and merely proceeded to insert its three Belvederes into the current programme of Army exercises for which No 38 Group provided helicopter support. The principal squadron involved was No 225, formed from the now disbanded Joint Experimental Helicopter Unit (see Chapter 6) and still operating Sycamores and Whirlwinds 2s. The contrast, therefore, even with the trials unit Belvederes, was dramatic. With their external load lift capability of 5000 lb (soon to be raised to 6000 lb) and a capacity for 28 troops (without seats), it was immediately obvious that a new era in helicopter support had arrived and many demonstrations were arranged. Jeeps with trailers or Wombat anti-tank weapons, 105 mm guns and crews, a crashed Meteor, 80 foot sections of prefabricated bridging, a group of three assault boats, and a mobile operating theatre are examples of

Last flight of the wooden-bladed full manual controlled pre-production Belvedere, just prior to the crash while rehearsing for the 1961 SBAC show at Farnborough. The Sycamore type rotor blades are clearly shown.

The result of loss of a nut retaining part of the Belvedere control linkage—Aden.

the many loads carried, the last mentioned at a NATO field medical demonstration near Paris.*

The Belvedere inevitably dominated every exercise it attended, generating an enthusiasm among its prospective users comparable with that produced by the Casualty Evacuation Flight Dragonflys in the Far East in 1950. Not only was it the first of a new generation of truly powerful helicopters, it was also the most powerful of them all. Consequently, the trials unit crews were not likely to be unduly dismayed by the defects recorded in the fortnightly (and later monthly) reports which they prepared.(8) They were aware, for example, of the gearbox troubles described below, because they interfered from time to time with their flying programmes, but they were in no position to appreciate how close the project would come to cancellation because of these problems, particularly as support for it in Whitehall was still somewhat mixed. Requirements for a wide range of modifications, from the design of the pilot's seat cushion to major changes to the engine controls, were regularly produced in complete confidence that they would be dealt with satisfactorily as a matter of routine. What mattered to trials unit personnel were the demonstration lifts of Army vehicles and weapons, and the provision of living proof to all concerned that 28 troops could be lifted merely by removing the seats (a practice later forbidden when the numbers carried were limited to eighteen seated passengers), and that the aircraft even at the hover could remain unaffected, and needing no corrective action when one engine was voluntarily stopped, since the remaining engine immediately doubled its power output, although no rotor RPM governor was provided.**

Consequently the Trials Unit expected a solution to be found when it pointed out that the front tank could not be refuelled with the engine running (and therefore

---

*During the life of the Trials Unit, on 30 June 1961, one of the production Belvederes, XG 461, was flown by the test pilot from Battersea heliport to Paris, returning on 2 July, and established a record for the inter-city crossing of 1 hour 41 minutes, which was not broken until 1980 when a Sikorsky S-76 (Spirit) made the same flight in 1 hour 20 minutes. The Belvedere cruised at an airspeed of 120 knots increasing to 140 knots at very low level.

**This was accomplished by a change in the mechanical gearing between the throttle twist grip in the cockpit and the fuel metering unit for the engine which was still running, the change being initiated electrically by the loss of torque in the engine being stopped. This sequence was designed to prevent either engine operating in emergency power when the other was still running, with serious risk of overloading the transmission, while at the same time maintaining the proper relationship between the pilot's twist grip throttle control and the collective lever when one of the engines had stopped.

the rotors turning), because with the operator standing on a ladder, and uncomfortably close to the jet efflux and hot jet pipe, the four-foot long dip stick would project through the front rotor disc. No solution however was forthcoming. Again, the unit did not expect to find that the electric winch with 200 feet of cable being developed for the Belvedere would never materialise and that no alternative would be found. Another problem was one which the unit considered too well known to need further airing: as the yaw control by differential lateral tilt was part of the cyclic control system, failure here could well be catastrophic. It was known that the yaw cables which operated part of the system were being renewed more frequently than planned and that the chief designer considered that they should be replaced by rods. It was therefore assumed that a remedy would be found, but a crash in Borneo in May 1963, killing six senior Army and police passengers, followed by another yaw cable failure in Aden in October 1964, showed otherwise.

By far the most serious defect from the operators' point of view was the Cartridge/Avpin engine starting system, and the need to replace it was the most important of the major modifications sought by the Trials Unit, and one which, it knew, would take all its powers of persuasion if it was ever to be achieved.* What the Unit did not know, however, was that the fate of the Belvedere already hung in the balance and that any modification not essential to actually getting the aircraft to fly was very unlikely to be approved. A modification which involved so time consuming and costly a change in engineering policy as a new starting system would almost certainly kill the whole project for both financial and practical reasons.

The question of the Cartridge/Avpin starting system is important because the decision to retain it not only affected the whole operating pattern of the production aircraft—to say nothing of their reliability at critical moments—but also led to a number of explosions, followed by fire, causing damage varying from slight to the total loss of two aircraft.** The defect was therefore very public and the aircraft's reputation suffered accordingly. Injury to personnel was fortunately limited to

---

*Avpin was the service name for Iso Propyl Nitrate, a high energy fuel which burns in an oxygen free environment. In the Cartridge/Avpin starter system a cordite cartridge was fired delivering under pressure a measured quantity of Avpin into a combustion chamber and simultaneously igniting it. The resultant pressure was used to spin a starter turbine linked, during the starting cycle, to the main engine compressor turbine.

**About half way through the life of the Belvedere, in the mid 1960s, the need to provide additional protection for the pilot was accepted. However, although slight damage had already been caused by enemy ground fire in both Aden and Borneo, the only armour plating ever fitted was behind the pilot's seat, which was felt to be uncomfortably close to the obviously explosive starter turbine of the front engine.

Avpin starter explosion—Aden.

Avpin starter explosion and fire—Singapore.

occasional sprains, and a broken ankle and wrist caused by the pilot evacuating the aircraft without waiting for the ladder.

What the Trials Unit appreciated—even before taking delivery of its aircraft—was that it was inappropriate for a helicopter intended for field operations in the Far East to rely on a cordite cartridge sensitive to damp, and on a flammable and highly toxic fluid, producing a poisonous vapour, as well as being explosive under pressure and capable of burning in an oxygen-free environment (and therefore virtually inextinguishable). Additionally, as it was a substance which was likely to be available only at major bases and airfields, extra supplies would have to be carried in the aircraft at some risk. Without these two relatively exotic chemicals there was no way of starting the engines.

With hindsight the problem of the Belvedere starting system can be seen as an example of the consequences which arose from relating fixed wing practice too readily to helicopters. The engineering planning staffs had no obvious means of knowing why a starting system already standard on a number of fixed wing aircraft (the Javelin, Hunter and Canberra, for example) should not be used with similar engines on the helicopter. It may be argued that the number of starts required in the case of a tactical helicopter compared with, say, a Hunter or Canberra, was not taken fully into account with the result that the burden on the starter mechanism was more serious than was appreciated. But such an argument says little for the level of experience and technical control provided by the Ministry of Supply over the contractors concerned.*

Unfortunately this error in principle was made worse in practice by a second problem noted by the Trials Unit: even when Avpin and cartridges were available and the latter fired successfully, the number of starting failures was depressingly high. In December 1960, for example, out of 266 attempts to start, 107 were unsuccessful. Over a longer period, and in spite of the best efforts and constant attention on the part of the contractors' experts, out of 789 attempts 197 were unsuccessful, including 73 occasions on which the starting system failed to produce a high enough compressor speed.(9) It seemed patently obvious that a different starter system should be developed.

That the problem had not emerged earlier was due to the fact that the manufacturer's Belvedere was equipped with relatively heavy electric motors for starting the engines. These had to be supplied with power from an external starter vehicle incorporating a generator which provided a very heavy electric load for the 25 second starting cycle. As a result the development aircraft could not be restarted away from base unless that particular type of starting generator was available.

*The Ministry of Supply, which had been formed from the Ministry of Aircraft Production and Supply in 1946, became the Ministry of Aviation in 1959.

The Cartridge/Avpin system was the choice made to replace this electric system, but there were alternatives under development for the Napier Gazelle engines, including a particularly attractive high pressure air starter, the requirement being to spin the main compressor turbine up to 8000 RPM. The air at 3000 lb/sq in was stored in a 13-inch diameter fibre glass sphere and simply discharged into a starter turbine linked to the main engine compressor turbine. There was no risk of fire or explosion and very little mechanical complication.

This was the system demanded by the Royal Australian Navy for the Wessex Mk 1s which Westland was building for it and equipping with a single Napier Gazelle engine as used in the Belvedere. The Royal Navy Wessex Mk 1 was equipped with the Cartridge/Avpin starter, but the Mk 3 was given the high pressure air starter system.

The compressed air starter was particularly well suited to the helicopter because, in theory, the aircraft could be made to recharge the air bottles once the rotors were turning without recourse to external supplies or equipment. There was, therefore, in principle an alternative and clearly preferable starting system available, but it was too late to incorporate it in the Belvedere, where the choice was stark: to make the best of the existing system or face cancellation. That the air starting system could not be fitted in the Belvedere, although the aircraft was still very much in the development stage, is a measure of the constraints operating at the time.

Other causes of starting failures were malfunctions of the starter turbine, which suffered from heavy pollution from the starter cartridges themselves, and a tendency for all three cartridges in the starter breech to fire simultaneously, so leaving a dead cartridge in position for the next attempt to start. A further difficulty was that each time the starter breech was reloaded, after an interval of ten minutes to allow the system to cool down, it was essential to refuel with Avpin—a time-consuming and messy procedure—in order to ensure that enough was available for another three starting attempts. If a cartridge was fired with too little Avpin available, an area of Avpin vapour—referred to by the manufacturers as the 'critical bubble size'—would appear in the Avpin system and almost certainly explode during the next starting attempt. These technical problems have been described in some detail because in the particular circumstances surrounding the Belvedere—questions of time scale and cost—decisions were taken which were to have important consequences.

With the Belvedere the starting problem was made worse during the trials phase by a tendency for one or other engine to stop of its own accord owing to an elaborate safety mechanism of very doubtful value incorporated by the engine manufacturers. They were concerned that if a failure occurred in the transmission (ie in a part of the system for which they were not responsible), the free turbine, for which they were responsible, would at normal throttle settings reach a speed at which it would disintegrate in a matter of a second or so. To overcome this danger—and discounting the fact that most transmission failures in a Belvedere would be the equivalent of a main spar failure in the wing of a fixed-wing aircraft—they incorporated a torque sensor in the output side of the free turbine which, if it detected a loss of torque while the throttle was open beyond what was called 'turbine bursting fuel flow', would cut off the fuel and extinguish the engine. To ensure that the device was inoperative when the engine was started (zero torque) and run at 'ground idle speed', it was set or 'armed' only as the throttle was opened slightly. Unfortunately, 'turbine bursting fuel flow' still occurred at the low throttle settings frequently used in a lightly loaded Belvedere while decelerating to the hover, when random variations in disc loading (and therefore torque) were experienced for aerodynamic reasons, and small fluctuations in the rotor synchronising shaft reduced the torque momentarily in one or other engine past the critical figure, with the result that the engine promptly shut down.

Until a better setting could be found for the arming position for the throttle—one which had more regard for operational needs than for 'turbine bursting fuel flow'—the Belvedere needed even more frequent engine restarts, a process which could be carried out only while landed in order that the throttle for the engine to be started could be fully closed. An extract from the trials unit report describing a demonstration for the Royal Engineers at Chatham illustrates the problem. Part of the task was to lift a 74 foot section of prefabricated bridge weighing 3500 lb to a prepared position and then tow two assembled piers into place to complete a heavy pontoon bridge:

'The carriage of the MEXE bridge on the first two days was unsuccessful for reasons which will be of especial interest, the sequence of events being as follows:

a.   The aircraft lifted the bridge satisfactorily and carried it to the demonstration site, but the timing arrangements had become confused on the ground and a 15 minute delay was requested. The aircraft returned the load to the pick up point and prepared to land alongside to wait.

b.   While reducing power, No 2 engine stopped itself on the low torque trip (Mod 541 not embodied) . . .

c.   While attempting to land fully so that No 2 engine could be restarted, the small wheels dug into the ground causing onset of padding . . . The aircraft was then flown on No 1 engine to the parade ground so that the throttles could be fully closed to permit restarting of No 2 engine.

217

d.   On attempting to start No 2 engine, it was found that all three cartridges had already fired on the previous start, and so re-cartridging and Avpin refuelling was carried out . . .

It was then too late to lift the bridge for the demonstration.

On the second day the timing was again confused, so that the order to start was late, but only slightly so. However, engine surging was experienced so shut down was necessary. Once again restarting was found to be impossible as all three cartridges had fired on one engine, and by the time the re-cartridging had been done, the audience, who were sitting in the rain, had lost interest and gone to lunch. This consequence was merely degrading and slightly absurd, but it is not difficult to imagine operational conditions in which it would have been quite serious.

The remainder of the demonstration on these days and the whole of it on the last two days was completely successful, particularly the towing sequence once the correct technique had been established. This item attracted considerable interest, and further requests perhaps with larger loads may be expected.'

A less obvious, but in the longer term more damaging, consequence of these starting problems was to reduce the Belvedere's load carrying capability. The unreliability of the starter system made it risky to shut down the engines at distant or isolated locations and in consequence refuelling was impossible because, as described above, the long dip stick would pass through the front rotor disc and with either engine running the rotors could not be stopped. As a result the Belvedere almost always carried enough fuel for its return journey to base, a procedure which added on average some 1000 lb in weight for half the total operational flying time, equal in fact to the average total payload offered by the Whirlwind Mk 10 in similar conditions. Thus the decision to choose the Cartridge/Avpin starter system, and adhere to it, had very damaging consequences not only for the aircraft itself, but also for its efficiency as a load carrier throughout its service life.

However, it may be assumed that when the Trials Unit's recommendations were turned down, the full consequences could not have been foreseen. Indeed, even without hindsight, rejection of the Unit's recommendations must have seemed justified if, as appeared likely, the alternative was to risk cancellation of the aircraft altogether, which would have been the almost inevitable result of two major problems coming to light simultaneously—over the starter system, for example, and the gearbox malfunctions which were causing widespread consternation. With hindsight, ample justification is provided by the many important tasks which the Belvedere carried out successfully, and the highly satisfactory level of performance and reliability in all other respects which the aircraft eventually achieved.

The Belvedere Trials Unit, although due to last only six months, continued for another four until the end of August 1961, when No 66 Squadron was formed with the first production Belvederes just in time for them to appear at the Farnborough SBAC show at the beginning of September. Throughout its chequered and sometimes turbulent eight-year existence the Squadron experienced no operational problems with its aircraft which the Trials Unit had not foreseen either as possible or even in some cases as likely, and the failure to take action on most of its recommendations was a constant source of bewilderment to the crews, as was what often seemed to them to be an ambivalent attitude to the Belvedere adopted by higher authority.

Meanwhile, much had been happening at staff level while the Trials Unit had been at work and during the months leading up to the formation of the three Belvedere squadrons. On 19 July 1960, before the three pre-production aircraft were formally handed over, VCAS was informed that the revised date for the first Belvedere squadron to reach the Far East was March 1961, with July as the earliest date for it to become operational. The return of the Far East Air Force Sycamores, destined for CFS, would therefore have to be delayed. The blame was put on development difficulties with the duplicated power controls. A week later the arrival date was put back still further to August 1961.(10) A&AEE tropical trials at Idris in Libya (with single power control jacks) had reported fuel metering and control difficulties at the upper end of the flight envelope (above 17000 feet).

On 17 November the delays were discussed at ministerial level and a fire at the Weston-super-Mare factory was advanced as a further reason for postponement. The CA release was now to be put back from December 1960 to March 1961 and the Trials Unit would work with a restricted flight envelope release.(11)

The possible double engine failure at Odiham already described, occurring only a month after the Trials Unit was formed, was particularly embarrassing, but in April 1961 a further very serious defect appeared when the main gears in both front and rear gearboxes failed on the test rig at Weston-super-Mare. It seemed likely that they would need redesigning and in the meantime the Trials Unit gearboxes were restricted to a life of 100 hours. With no established spares back up available at this stage there was an obvious danger of the aircraft being grounded.

A month later the whole future of the Belvedere was again in serious jeopardy. The Ministry of Aviation advised that the aircraft was unacceptable and the drafting of Trials Unit crews to the Far East Air Force was suspended. Air Plans put forward three alternatives: accept the aircraft with gearboxes limited to a life of 100 hours (the Army, however, would object on the grounds that these would soon be used up); modify the gearboxes to achieve a life of 250 hours (a palliative inspiring little confidence); or refuse to accept the aircraft, which was the Air Plan's recommendation on the grounds that it would force the whole issue. It was argued that gearbox failure in the air would be catastrophic (and one had occurred in test after only 41 hours): depending on where the failure occurred, all power could be lost to one rotor or, at best, the linkage which kept both rotors turning at the same speed would be lost and, as the rotors overlapped, they could be expected to destroy each other. With only enough gearboxes to supply the Trials Unit for one more month, it was proposed to disband the Belvedere squadron now forming and replace the whole force of 25 Belvederes with 57 Whirlwind Mk 10s.*

There were now two schools of thought within the Air Staff, one headed by VCAS which accepted the proposal to cancel the Belvedere, and the other by DCAS, but made up of only the Operational Requirements cell (DDOR 7), which recommended that the search for a solution should continue. The latter, however, was in a somewhat difficult position as it had argued in May 1960 that the Belvedere, although previously suspect, was now showing great promise. This view had been dismissed by the aircraft's detractors with the contemptuous comment that DDOR 7's hobby horse had now 'broken into a gallop'.(13)

Fortunately, a few days later in May 1961, DCAS was able to announce a two-stage modification plan for the gearboxes with a solution promised by September or October.(14) The result would be a gearbox life of 250 hours rising by stages to 1000 hours. By July the rig testing of these modifications had been carried out satisfactorily and during the following month the transmission trials were completed. The fourteenth production Belvedere had now flown and the first two aircraft were cleared for delivery to the RAF at the end of August, allowing the Trials Unit to re-form as No 66 Squadron and preparations for the move to the Far East to be resumed.

It was now eight years since the Air Ministry had turned to the Bristol 173 as the type of helicopter best suited to its needs (see Chapter 4) and yet the aircraft had only just been brought to a difficult birth as the Bristol 192 after a very troubled gestation period, during which it had been extensively redesigned to meet the special requirements of the Royal Navy. Solutions for most of the technical problems remaining after the many complicated policy issues had been dealt with had had to be found with the aircraft already on the production line, a situation made worse by the fact that the Belvedere represented a very significant jump in three areas

---

*The relative payloads then expected over a 50 nm radius of action in the tropics were: 4200 lbs for the Belvedere and 1850 lbs for the Whirlwind at sea level, and 3700 lbs and 1500 lbs respectively at an altitude of 2000 feet (12)—somewhat ambitious figures for the Whirlwind which apparently took no account of crewmen or survival equipment.

of helicopter technology simultaneously: the use of turbine engines in rotary wing aircraft, the coupling of two engines to the transmission system, and the tandem rotor configuration. In many respects the Belvedere was then well in advance of its nearest rival, the Vertol 107 which later became the Boeing Vertol Chinook.

A final moment of crisis was still to come, however. In January 1962, with eight production Belvederes already delivered to No 66 Squadron at Odiham, a new fault was revealed when several sets of roller races in the transmission system were found to have collapsed. The engineering staffs predicted gloomily that rectification and testing could not be completed in less than eight months. No 66 Squadron's deployment to the Far East was postponed and all the Belvederes were grounded.(15) However, the cause of the trouble was soon identified as cold weather which had the effect during the starting process of delaying the circulation of thickened oil to the three gearboxes from the single pump employed. The aircraft clearance was accordingly amended to forbid start up in ambient temperatures of less than plus five degrees centigrade (awkward at Odiham, but hardly a problem in the Far East) and by 9 February the deployment plan was once more in train.

The Formation of the Belvedere Squadrons

No 66 Squadron re-formed officially at Odiham from the Trials Unit on 15 September 1961, equipped with six Belvederes and two more allocated for training, as part of the light cargo force which had been established to support the Far East Land Forces (FARELF). Its personnel moved to the Far East Air Force (FEAF) in the spring of 1962 to take over its six Belvederes which had been sent there by sea. No 72 Squadron, which was to stay in the United Kingdom, formed at the end of 1961 with the Belvederes remaining at Odiham, and No 26 Squadron, destined for Aden and Air Forces Middle East (AFME) forming from it in June 1962, building up slowly and moving overseas piecemeal between January and October 1963. No 72 Squadron stayed at Odiham, acting as a training unit for No 66 Squadron and as a base for No 26 Squadron, while also providing to some extent the facilities needed to carry out and test the many airframe and engine modifications still required on the Belvedere even after it had entered operational service. No 72 Squadron was thus functioning almost as a Belvedere training and modification depot, while at the same time making an occasional contribution to Army exercises and demonstrations. One of its first tasks was to lift the spire on to the roof of the new Coventry cathedral and surmount it with a piece of impressionist sculpture (see Chapter 10).

In October 1963 three more Belvederes were sent to the Far East as part of the plan to strengthen the helicopter force there during the period of confrontation with Indonesia over Borneo. Their departure signalled the end of No 72 as a working Belvedere squadron and after two last aircraft had been despatched to Aden in

March 1964, what remained of it at Odiham was reduced to the status of a conversion unit to supply replacement aircrew to No 66 and 26 Squadrons, while No 72 Squadron itself re-formed immediately at Odiham as the second Wessex squadron.

No 26 Squadron disbanded in Aden in November 1965, having virtually collapsed at the end of 1964 after three of its aircraft had been written off in the previous six months following major technical failures, and after attempts to restore service-ability in the remaining four had met with an evident lack of success. The four were transferred to FEAF where, by contrast, No 66 Squadron was going from strength to strength, as indeed it continued to do until its disbandment in March 1969.

References to Chapter 8

1   IIA/11/2/30/Pt 3.

2   Ibid.

3   Ibid.

4   Ibid.

5   Author's experience.

6   Chief test pilot.

7   ID9/F1-101.

8   Belvedere Trials Unit reports.

9   Ibid.

10 ID9/F1-101

11 Ibid.

12 Ibid.

13 IIA/11/2/4/Pt 4

14 ID9/F1-101.

15 Ibid.

CHAPTER 9

POLICY CONSIDERATIONS IN THE FIRST PART
OF PHASE 3 AND THE FORMATION OF THE SRT FORCE

In a paper written in May 1959 VCAS argued that the campaigns in Malaya and Cyprus had proved conclusively that helicopters had an essential role to play in British defence policy, that they would continue to be needed through the 1960s in the Arabian Peninsula and in Africa, and that the RAF would be open to severe censure if it failed to respond. A case could therefore be made, he believed, for ordering 32 Whirlwind Mk 10s immediately in order to provide a global establishment of 21 over five years. He emphasised that these helicopters would be additional to purely Army requirements for short range transport, as the term was then defined.(1)

VCAS's paper represented the RAF's last attempt to put forward a tactical helicopter requirement of its own, basing its argument on the need to avoid a repetition of the situation which arose in the 1950s when there were too few helicopters available to deal with the Malayan and Cyprus emergencies. The RAF, however, was no more in a position in 1959 to put forward a requirement of its own than it had been in 1948, particularly as the Bingley Committee on transport requirements had only recently made it clear that the RAF's responsibility in respect of tactical helicopters should be limited to meeting Army needs—which had still to be identified. But, as a decision on them was soon to be taken, the Air Council decided to defer action until the detailed requirements for the new short range transport force had been announced.

What happened in the policy sphere at this time is of particular importance as it was to lay the foundations of the RAF's tactical helicopter force in the 1970s. In the meantime the helicopter operations in Aden and Borneo in the 1960s were another ad hoc response to sudden emergencies and the helicopters employed in those territories on counter-insurgency and anti-guerrilla duties were those scheduled to form the new short range transport and light cargo forces. Consequently, although the views which VCAS expressed in May 1959 proved justified, part at least of the proposed new helicopter force was available in time.

At the end of 1959, following a recommendation to the Chiefs of Staff by the Bingley Committee, it was decided in a Long Term Defence Review that, inter alia, the air transport force for Army support should contain an element described as a 'light cargo force' and made up of 38 Twin Pioneers and 12 B 192s, later known as Belvederes. In the case of the helicopters this ruling was interpreted to mean 25 Belvederes to support a unit establishment of 12 with a service life of 10 years.(2)

By early 1960, however, the practice of assessing tactical lift requirements in terms of 'company lifts' in the various theatres had become generally accepted. So, the short range transport (SRT) requirement for late 1961 was put at a simultaneous two-company lift (250 men) in each of five theatres: the United Kingdom, Germany, Cyprus, Aden and the Far East. It was agreed at the outset that of this total one two-company lift would be supplied by the Royal Navy, and in all subsequent discussions about the size of the SRT force, this Naval contribution was assumed to remain unchanged. Consequently, references to that discussion here take into account only the RAF contribution and assume the addition of a Naval two-company lift. To these two-company lifts was added an airborne logistic support element, referred to as the light cargo force and consisting entirely of helicopters (including the Rotodyne), with the capability of lifting a total of 100 tons a day worldwide with a 200 nm radius of action. A further element was to consist of a tactical transport force to lift two battalion groups, a task for which 30 Beverleys and 24 Hastings would be needed together with 50 Armstrong Whitworth 660s, which were described as having a STOL capability.(3)

Some time later all tactical transport helicopters came to be referred to as 'support helicopters', including those in both the short range transport force and the light cargo force, but in the early 1960s the two elements were discussed and planned quite separately. The Belvedere was thought of then as part of the light cargo force and quite distinct from the SRT force which was to progress from Sycamores and Mk 2 and 4 Whirlwinds to Whirlwind Mk 10s and Wessex Mk 2s. With only small-scale operations in Aden and none as yet in Borneo the SRT force could be whittled down in 1960 and 1961, and the Belvedere could still be regarded as a candidate for the light cargo force, and not as the heavy element of the SRT force which it inevitably became.

The process of whittling down began in December 1959 when the Land/Air Warfare Committee argued a need for only a six company lift, three being located in Germany; the requirement would then be 16 Whirlwind or Wessex squadrons and 18 Rotodynes. The Treasury promptly stepped into the arena with a strong protest against buying the Wessex, at least in the numbers proposed. They argued that the only reason for having them in addition to, or instead of, Whirlwinds appeared to be their capability to carry Jeeps underslung, and that the order should be limited to the number needed to meet that particular requirement. In reply, the War Office explained why it was preferable to have 10 men in one Wessex helicopter rather than five each in two whirlwinds. The RAF supported the Army in seeking to have the main part of the SRT force equipped with Wessex, but was not directly involved in the detailed examination carried out by the Treasury in January 1960, during which the balance of the argument tilted against the Army. At the same time, the proposed light cargo force was to consist of eight Rotodynes in Germany and 22 Belvederes divided between Aden and the Far East, with a total lift capability of one hundred tons a day.(4)

In February 1960 the Air Ministry obtained War Office agreement to putting forward a proposal for a five-company lift, a figure which, it was hoped, might prove more acceptable. It then explained to the Treasury in detail why one Wessex did not equate with two Whirlwinds and why therefore it was requesting authority to order 30 Wessex in addition to the 40 Whirlwinds already authorised. Meanwhile the Ministry of Aviation, concerned that the Rotodyne would prove too noisy for the civil market, had asked whether the RAF would accept six of them, if they were ordered for BEA and then not given clearance. The RAF, still convinced that the Rotodyne would not prove acceptable for military use, replied that it had no authority to place an order, but was then faced with a rapid change in the situation when the Chiefs of Staff, determined to press ahead with initial orders for the SRT force, invited it to obtain enough aircraft for a six company lift.(5) With the 40 Whirlwinds already authorised constituting half the requirement, what was now needed was 35 Wessex and nine Rotodynes, with a further build-up in prospect. The RAF parried with the comment that Faireys, the Rotodyne manufacturers, would need a minimum order for 12, only to find a month later that the Treasury had in fact agreed, albeit reluctantly, to the purchase of all 12 aircraft.(6)

The Belvedere, being part of the light cargo force, was not involved directly in these negotiations, as was the Rotodyne which seemed for the moment immune from any risk of cancellation because of its specialised role in the SRT force of providing the crane lift held to be essential in the battlefield area or close to it. All the same, in May 1960 the RAF carried out a high level enquiry into the possibility of replacing some of the Wessex in the proposed SRT force with Belvederes, since a heavier lift than could be provided by the Wessex—now described as an assault troop lift helicopter—would be needed if, as the RAF expected, the Rotodynes did not materialise.(7)

The situation was made more complex during these first six months of 1960 by the presence of a number of cross-currents: the future of the Belvedere itself was still in doubt (see Chapter 7), and pressure to buy the Rotodyne was intensifying,(8) although this was now being countered by a RAF proposal to replace it with the fixed-wing twin-engined Caribou. VCAS indeed wrote to the C-in-C Far East Air Force to explain that the Rotodyne would be ordered only if the government insisted and that the Caribou would be a much better proposition, an idea which the C-in-C was invited to put to the Army in the Far East as part of the campaign in London 'to help stamp out the Rotodyne'.

It will have been noted that if the Caribou could be regarded as a potential replacement for the Rotodyne, the latter must now be seen in the light cargo role rather than as the crane lift for the SRT force. That this was how the RAF had begun to look upon the Rotodyne is confirmed by a further variation in the company lift costings: in June 1960 Air Plans proposed a five-company lift, two in the United

Kingdom/Germany (21 Whirlwinds), one half in Cyprus, one and a half in Aden and Kenya (22 Wessex), and one in the Far East (27 Whirlwinds to be replaced later by 14 Wessex). The Chiefs of Staff approved these proposals, but added four Rotodynes for cargo lift in each of the three overseas theatres.(9) Clearly the argument that the presence of the Rotodyne in the SRT force was justified by a supposed crane lift requirement had been abandoned, while for its part the RAF was now convinced that the light cargo force task could be met by 14 Belvederes and 18 Caribous.(10)

In the second half of 1960, after the Belvedere Trials Unit had been formed, opinion hardened against the Rotodyne. Air Plans proposed deleting it from the Order of Battle on the grounds that it was too expensive, too late (it was not now due until 1966) and unnecessary, because its crane lift had not been shown to be essential and should a small-scale lift be needed it could probably be provided by the Belvedere up to two or even three tons.(11)

The debate was then complicated by the Army putting forward a firm requirement for 40% of the cargo lift (54 tons a day for 30 days) to be carried by VTOL aircraft over a 200 nm radius. The Rotodyne itself was not mentioned specifically, although the new Westland Westminister was suggested as a possible choice. In reply, the RAF contended that it was completely inappropriate to carry cargo over 200 nm by helicopter. What was needed was a judicious mix of fixed-wing STOL aircraft and helicopters, the latter operating over only the last 25–50 miles. Consequently, the task of lifting 136 tons a day should be carried out by a force of 14 Belevederes and 26 Caribous (an increase on the 18 originally proposed).* These were in addition to the SRT requirement, which the RAF currently put at 27 Whirlwinds and 57 Wessex, both types incidentally being now referred to as 'utility helicopters', a term not used before and seeming to indicate a growing preference for a standard, simple and rugged machine as the battlefield helicopter of the future.(12)

In October 1960 the respective Army and Air Force positions on the shape of the future light cargo force were restated by the Land/Air Warfare Committee. The Army continued to put forward a short-term demand for a mix of Belvederes with either Chinooks or Westminsters, with full supply support by VTOL aircraft as the long-term objective. The RAF however argued that a mix of STOL aircraft and Belvederes was, in all respects, the much better interim solution, but to make their proposal more palatable they offered to raise the establishment of the Belvedere element in the light cargo force to 18, so committing the entire fleet apart from

---

*The Army demand for the Rotodyne and later the Westminister (which the RAF also considered unsatisfactory) bore a strong resemblance to the campaign mounted in the early 1950s to buy the Air Horse (see Chapter 4).

two aircraft retained for training purposes. By November 1960 a compromise had been reached: the light cargo force was to consist of 32 Caribous delivering 172 tons a day over 165 nm, and 18 Belvederes lifting 100 tons a day over 35 nm. Meanwhile, the SRT force was still geared to a five company lift, three rising to four by Wessex, and two reducing to one by Whirlwind.(13)

These decisions, however, left the Minister of Defence in a very difficult position as he was personally committed to supporting the Rotodyne and would be faced with a soaring burden on the defence budget if civil orders too did not materialise. 'The decision already announced,' he wrote, 'about military support for the project could only be reconsidered if there was an identifiable change in the technical situation or military requirement since it had been taken . . .'(14) By now, however, matters had gone too far and there were no alternatives remaining. The Rotodyne order was cancelled and in due course the Caribou project too was dropped. In all, it was a most unfavourable moment for the Belvedere Trials Unit to draw attention to major faults in their pre-production aircraft (see Chapter 8).

As has already been seen, the Belevdere entered squadron service with some technical faults still to be remedied and in consequence the compromise reached in November 1960 was not fully implemented.(15) Instead of receiving the promised nine aircraft each the two squadrons which were to operate overseas, No 66 in the Far East and No 26 in Aden, were allotted only six each for the moment, while a third squadron, No 72, was formed with the remaining six aircraft to provide training and technical support for the overseas squadrons.(16)

Happily, there was no urgent need as yet for the Belvederes either in the Far East or in Aden; the Brunei revolt had not yet begun and in Aden the military threat was less of a concern than were the accommodation shortage and the difficulty of providing the new helicopters with hangar space and technical facilities; these were not expected to become available until March 1963.(17) By then, however, both theatres would be in deep crisis with an inevitable rise in the demand for helicopter support. This would be met, as it happened, in Aden by the Belvederes originally intended for the light cargo force and used there for gun and troop lifts until overtaken by technical problems, and in Borneo by a mix of Belvederes and SRT force Whirlwind Mk 10s, which were to fill the gap while the Wessex Mk 2s went through the seemingly normal development cycle of promises, delays, cancellation threats, reassessments and late deliveries.

The Introduction of the Wessex

In February 1961, in an unprecedented reversal of roles, the Royal Navy requested access to the Wessex Mk 2s ordered for the RAF. With previous Westland aircraft—

the Dragonfly, Whirlwind and initially the Belvedere—the Navy had been given priority, one result being the great difficulty the RAF had had in obtaining Dragonflys for the Malayan campaign (see Chapter 2). Since then naval and air force policies had diverged and when the two Services began to replace their earlier marks of Whirlwind the Navy ordered the Mk 7 (the Leonides Major piston-engined version),(18) while the RAF chose the Mk 10 with its Gnome turbine engine. The Mk 7 was not a success in terms of performance or reliability and the Navy soon ordered the Wessex to replace it, choosing however the Mk 1 with its single Napier Gazelle engine. The failure of this version to carry out the commando lift role led the Navy to ask for early access to the Mk 2 which was on order for the RAF, offering the Mk 1 in its place. The RAF's Director of Operational Requirements responded with the comment that the RAF should not be expected to suffer because of a mistake, whose consequences were entirely predictable, and that if the Mk 1 could not carry out the trooping role for the Navy, neither could it for the RAF. He suggested, however, that the Navy could be offered a number of Whirlwind Mk 10s,(19) which over a 50 nm radius of action could carry a payload of 1500 lb, compared with 550 lb for the Mk 1 Wessex and 3000 lb for the Mk 2 version. Thus the Whirlwind Mk 10s being obtained for the RAF could carry almost three times the payload offered by the Wessex Mk 1, which was the Navy's chosen replacement for its own failing Whirlwinds. The RAF's suggestion was not taken up.

By September 1961, with the future of the Belvederes virtually settled, it was the Wessex Mk 2 which became the centre of attention as the potential backbone of the new SRT force. Two factors, however, were working against the new aircraft. First, a CA release date for the order placed in 1961 had been expected by the end of 1962, but a postponement to 1963 now seemed inevitable. Second, DCAS had raised further doubts by suggesting to CAS that the decision to buy the Wessex might have been wrongly based: the War Office requirement was for a payload of 3650 lb at 7000 feet in ISA+30 degrees centigrade with a radius of action of 50 nm, whereas in those conditions the new aircraft would have a radius of action of only 30 nm. The Chinook, he added, could be available in the same timescale, with a rear loading ramp, lower initial costs and considerable development potential. He made no firm recommendation, however, to scrap the Wessex in favour of the Chinook, suggesting only that the latter should be kept in mind should the Wessex situation deteriorate further.*(20)

By May 1962 the inevitable slippage had taken place and with the Wessex not expected to enter squadron service until 1964, VCAS formally recommended that

---

*The Wessex Mk 2 was, in fact, a twin turbine-engined version of an old Sikorsky design which first appeared as the S-58 and was itself a development from the piston-engined Whirlwind.

it should be replaced by the Chinook.* The SRT force had now been scaled down to a four company lift worldwide—one each in Aden and the Far East, and two in the United Kingdom and Germany—and could be met by one squadron of six Chinooks in each theatre.** The total cost for the Chinooks was put at £14492000 compared with £17460000 for a further delivery of Belvederes, which would need a redesigned fuselage to enable them to carry troops. How reliable these figures were was a matter of some doubt and CAS was advised to hold an Air Council meeting and be on his guard against Ministry of Aviation opposition.(21) DCAS's submission to the Air Council meeting suggested that there were four choices open: 29 Chinooks, or 21 Chinooks and 30 Wessex, or 42 Belvederes, or 60 Wessex. The cost was put at £19 million, plus or minus £2 million, for each option, but with cheaper running costs for the Chinook. The Belvederes and Wessex, he concluded, would both need replacing by 1970, but the Chinook might run on until 1975 with only six needed to supplement the original 29 and ensure that the fleet stayed the course.(22) The effect on British industry of cancelling the Wessex would be unfortunate, he agreed, but the blame would be theirs, because they had persistently failed to meet promised delivery dates.

In the event, it was decided that the Wessex could not be cancelled, and after lengthy discussions, which included such aspects as the desirability of buying British, it was proposed to continue with it but with minimum backing only, pending possible replacement by the Chinook, which might be built in the United Kingdom.(23) At this stage the future of the Wessex looked as bleak as had that of the Belvedere at the height of its misfortunes. In mid-1962, therefore, buying the Chinook seemed a distinct possibility, a course which would have radically altered the whole subsequent development of the SRT force. In fact, the failure to follow up a number of possible developments in the case of the Belvedere, together with a reluctance to accept the Chinook, ensured the survival of the Wessex, even though it continued to suffer design and development delays, especially over the gearbox coupling for the twin engine installation. Indeed, in September 1962 the Ministry of Aviation warned that because of problems in that area CA release for the Wessex would be delayed until the end of the year. The contractor's delivery date was now March 1963, but according to confidential advice from the Ministry

---

*This recommendation might seem a remarkable volte face on the part of the Air Staff which had fought hard for the Wessex as the Whirlwind replacement. It was, however, the result of a very detailed study of the data then available, supported by what later proved to be a highly professional assessment of the Chinook's development potential. Although the recommendation to buy the Chinook was rejected in 1962, it stood the test of time and was put forward repeatedly in the following years until finally accepted 18 years later.

**The reduction from five company lifts to four was achieved by deleting the half company lifts intended for Cyprus and Kenya.

of Aviation more realistic dates would be September for temperate climates and some time later for tropical clearance.(24) The SRT force was further scaled down, reducing the four company lift to three, by deleting Aden from the list of locations to be served.

It might perhaps have been thought that in view of the helicopter's operational achievements and its firm place in the RAF's future plans it would have been fully accepted at last as an aspect of air power—in spite of production difficulties and reservations over delivery dates. But there were some who remained unconvinced of its lasting relevance and were awaiting the moment when fixed-wing technology would catch up, as it were, and restore aviation to its rightful path of development. In September 1962, for example, the Secretary of State for Air had reviewed the Wessex situation along with past and present problems with the Belvedere. He concluded that there seemed to be a large number of different types in service, with British helicopters prone to extraordinary difficulties, both during development and in the course of subsequent service. Capital and running costs were very high and it seemed possible—in his view—that the helicopter had only a limited future, as other VTOL developments (ie fixed-wing) might soon come to light. He could see no significant inroads being made by rotary aircraft in the field of civil aviation, and he suggested that it might be wise to discourage exclusive concentration on helicopters by civilian manufacturers such as Westlands, even if it meant company closures.*(25)

There was no radical change in the situation during 1963: the Wessex continued to survive, but with its backing limited to an order for six additional aircraft with which to prolong the service life of the Wessex fleet until 1968. The Army, meanwhile, had used the shortage of RAF helicopters in Aden and the Far East to back its own claim for more Scout helicopters and an interim purchase of Alouettes.(26) In March 1964, with the Wessex delays continuing, still due in the main to the coupling gearbox, AMSO vented his frustration on the Ministry of Aviation. He rejected any attempt to put the blame on the contractors, arguing that the present delay was due to an agreement made by the Controller of Aircraft in the Aviation Ministry to divert eight engines and four gearboxes to Iraq, an arrangement which it was promised would delay RAF deliveries by no more than a month, although it now seemed that they would not be completed until well into 1965.(27) As on a very similar occasion in 1952 when during a dire shortage of Dragonflys in Malaya export orders to Iraq and elsewhere were found to have had Foreign Office support (see Chapter 2), high level pressure had to be brought to bear. As a result the Air Council was confident that deliveries would be speeded up and that the two new Wessex squadrons would become operational by the end of 1964.(28)

---

*Two years earlier the then Minister of Aviation, Mr Duncan Sandys, had encouraged Westlands to absorb both Fairey Aviation helicopters and the helicopter division of the Bristol Aeroplane Company.

The Formation of the Wessex Squadrons

The Wessex Trials Unit was formed at Odiham in mid-1963 and reconstituted as No 18 Squadron at the beginning of 1964. A few months later a second Wessex squadron was formed, taking over the number plate of the home-based Belvedere squadron, No 72, now reduced in status to that of a Belvedere Conversion Unit. Both squadrons continued to operate Wessex helicopters until the beginning of the 1980s, No 72 based in the United Kingdom and No 18 mainly in Germany.

In mid-1965 a third Wessex squadron, No 78, was formed and sent to Aden to replace the ailing Belvedere squadron there, No 26. After the withdrawal from Aden in 1967 it moved to Sharjah and remained there until 1971, when British forces left the Gulf. In the last four years of its existence (1968–71) it gave rise to an independently operating SAR flight in Bahrein to which a communications task was added in 1969 (acknowledged by a change in title to Comsar Bahrein). After 1971 the aircraft along with the other assets of the two units were used to re-equip the two remaining Whirlwind squadrons in the Far East, No 28 in Hong Kong and No 103 in Tengah, and were the first Wessex to operate in that theatre.(29)

The Introduction of the Whirlwind Mk 10

The introduction of the Whirlwind Mk 10 was comparatively smooth, production delays being measured in months rather than years, as was the case with the Belvedere and Wessex. Apart from the addition of fully duplicated power controls, the only other basic change from the Mk 2 and Mk 4 was to substitute the de Havilland Gnome gas turbine for the Pratt and Whitney piston engine and make the consequent changes in the shape of the nose cowlings. The original transmission and rotors were retained, and the only significant technical problems to cause delay and continue into the operational life of the aircraft were connected with the automatic computer-controlled fuel flow device.(30)

The Whirlwind Mk 10 was the first RAF helicopter to appear with automatically governed constant rotor speed control, and an ability to revert to manual pilot control in the event of computer malfunction, not uncommon in the first few years, was a necessary provision. Computer-controlled fuel flow was incorporated as much to protect the engines as to assist the pilot, since mishandling of the manual throttle, particularly during start up, was all too easy and the resultant surge could ruin the engine in seconds. Computer failures normally had only two consequences: 'frozen fuel flow', a self-explanatory term, or, more often, engine shut down. Pilots, therefore, had to stay in practice both in reverting to manual throttle control and, especially, in making engine-off landings, an easy manoeuvre with the Whirlwind in the right terrain.

These were all mainly teething troubles, which could be overcome satisfactorily, given a little time. Consequently, the formation of Whirlwind Mk 10 squadrons went ahead without much difficulty. The use of the original Whirlwind transmission with a limiting power acceptance of 700 lb shaft horsepower (which could not be obtained with the piston engine), but now driven by a Gnome engine which was not only lighter than its predecessor but was also able to supply 1100 lb shaft horsepower, resulted in a near trebling of the payload at sea level in temperate climates, with a reduction of only three per cent in tropical conditions. A further reduction of only twenty per cent would be experienced at 7000 feet in the tropics. With the additional advantage of an increase in cruising speed of almost fifty per cent the Whirlwind Mk 10 represented as remarkable a step forward in light helicopter performance as did the Belvedere in its own heavier class.

The Formation of the Whirlwind Mk 10 Squadrons and the Short Range Transport Force

The plan formulated in 1961 included the deployment of one Whirlwind Mk 10 squadron in the United Kingdom, a second in Germany, and two more in the Far East. The United Kingdom squadron was already in existence: No 225, the first official tactical helicopter squadron, formed from the disbanded JEHU (see Chapter 6) and equipped originally with a mixture of Whirlwind Mk 2s and Sycamores; these were replaced by Whirlwind Mk 10s in mid 1962. At almost the same time a second Whirlwind Mk 10 squadron was formed by re-equipping a former Pioneer squadron, No 230; this was then despatched to RAF Germany. The two Whirlwind Mk 10 squadrons intended for overseas already existed as Sycamore squadrons, Nos 103 in Cyprus and 110 at Butterworth; both were re-equipped early in 1963 and were deployed to support operations in Borneo.*

Thus by 1963, with the Borneo campaign underway and the pace of operations quickening in Aden, the long term plans for the five company lift, reduced to four in 1961 and then to three a year later, had happily resulted in the right number of squadrons being available to meet the demands of the Borneo campaign, albeit with Whirlwinds instead of Wessex, but including No 66 Belvedere Squadron.** In Aden No 26 Belvedere Squadron, having been committed to that theatre under the 1961 plan, and being unaffected by its subsequent removal from the list of planned

---

*Whirlwind Mk 10s were also used to re-equip the two UK SAR squadrons, Nos 228 and 22, in late 1962; others were planned for the SAR role in Cyprus and Aden, but not for SRT duties in either theatre.

**Under the 1961 plan the Mk 10 Whirlwinds in the Far East were to be replaced by Wessex in 1964, but at the height of the Borneo operations FEAF refused to accept a third helicopter type and elected to continue with a larger number of Whirlwinds.

SRT locations, was available in time to provide SRT support for the Radfan operations.

By now it was clear that the neat and tidy concept of a separate light cargo force supporting a short range transport force was not going to materialise. The almost simultaneous appearance of the Belvedere and the Mk 10 Whirlwind, ideally complementing each other's capabilities, inevitably led to their working closely together during the Army exercises then being mounted with the support of No 38 Group. As a result it soon became apparent that there were numerous SRT tasks which only the Belvedere could perform; and so in the course of training there developed a level of co-operation between the Belvedere and Whirlwind Mk 10 elements which was to prove of considerable value during the Borneo campaign.

The Choice of helicopter for the SRT Force in the 1970s

With plans for the SRT force in the 1960s settled, the Air Ministry was able to look ahead and choose the ideal helicopter for the 1970s. But once again, as with the Dragonfly, the Sycamore, the early marks of Whirlwind, and the Wessex Mk 2, the RAF was to find itself committed to a helicopter which, although conscientiously chosen as the best available in the circumstances, fell short of what was really needed. However, the Air Ministry, aware of the Navy's errors of judgement over the Whirlwind Mk 7 and the Wessex Mk 1, and aware too of the need to find a replacement for the Belvedere in due course, entered into consultations with the Navy and raised a Joint Naval/Air Staff Target (JNAST 358) for a general purpose helicopter to be available by 1970 and combine the RAF's SRT role with the Navy's anti-submarine and commando carrier roles.(32) This target was, in fact, the latest version of the heavy lift project which originated in RAF proposals of the early 1950s and had given rise to the Rotodyne and Belvedere. It was now classified as a medium lift helicopter (MLH) to distinguish it from the heavy lift projects (over five tons payload underslung), which were then in an early stage of design in the United States.

For the RAF, JNAST 358 laid down a payload of 8000 lb over a 50 nm radius of action, or 5600 lb over 100 nm; and a crane lift capability of 10000 lb. For the Navy it was to carry 2000 lb of sonar equipment and to have a three hour loiter capability at a range of 30 nm from the carrier.(33) One possibility in this context, once the Westminister and the Rotodyne had been eliminated, was the WG-1, a Westland project inherited from Raoul Hafner's team in the helicopter division of the Bristol Aeroplane Company before it was absorbed by Westlands in 1960. The WG-1 was a development of the Belvedere and previously known to Bristols as the B-194; it had a tandem six-bladed rotor configuration and a small fixed wing as fitted to the original B-173, but was powered by four Gnome engines. Other theoretical candidates were a variant of the Chinook, also powered by four Gnome engines,(34) and the single main rotor helicopter (CH-53) which Sikorsky was known to be planning and which was believed to have comparable performance.

The Air Ministry, however, although not wholly disinterested in these possibilities, was much more concerned in 1964 with finding a smaller and highly tactical support helicopter, since it now saw that JNAST 358 would result in an aircraft of relatively enormous size and cost. In March of that year DCAS made it clear that the main need was for a tactical helicopter and that if the crane lift requirement were shelved, JNAST 358 should be cancelled.*(35) Accordingly, four months later a new target was produced (JNAST 365) which added air portability to the other characteristics required of the tactical helicopter. The new target resulted in the eventual emergence of the twin-engined Puma, derived from the Sud Aviation 330 but with a marked resemblance to the Bristol 214, which had generated little interest when Bristols had first shown a mock-up in London in 1959.

The Expansion of the SRT Force in Borneo

The discussions just referred to took place against a background of events which had a close resemblance to the circumstance of 1952–53 when there was an unexpected surge in the demand for helicopters to take part in the Malayan campaign (see Chapter 2). By 1964 operations in Borneo were being conducted on a scale which demanded more helicopters than were available in FEAF, even after the addition of No 103 Squadron from Cyprus, all but four of No 225 Squadron's Whirlwinds from Odiham, and three more Belvederes from No 26 Squadron, which were diverted to the Far East after a No 38 Group exercise in North Africa (see Chapter 9).**

Once these reinforcements had been despatched, however, the RAF had little more room for maneoeuvre. No 225 Squadron's four remaining Whirlwinds were one obvious possibility, but to send them would mean denuding No 38 Group of its last Whirlwinds and the only ones equipped to fire the SS-11 wire guided missile (see below under the Arming of Helicopters). An assessment of the other possibilities(36) showed that these amounted to the newly formed Wessex squadron, No 18; the Whirlwind squadron, No 230, based in Germany and earmarked to NATO for Saceur; the remaining Belvederes of No 26 Squadron; and the aircraft of the SAR and flying training establishments based in the United Kingdom.

As FEAF was reluctant to accept the engineering and supply complications involved in the addition of a third helicopter type to the force of Belvederes and Whirlwinds

---

*It was to take years of effort before the RAF obtained the MLH in the shape of the Chinook. The Navy meanwhile had found that, as with the Belvedere, it could not join in a project for a helicopter as large as that proposed in JNAST 358.

**These reinforcements from No 38 Group were known as Spine Force.

already operating in the theatre,* (the only practical possibility was No 230 Squadron in Germany. But as it was evidently not yet thought necessary to maintain continuous radio control of low flying helicopters in the European theatre, No 230's Whirlwinds were not equipped with H/F radio. In the event it was decided not to redeploy No 230 Squadron for the moment, and an offer from the Navy to provide the radios was not taken up.(37) In the following year, however, No 230 did go to Borneo, the NATO task being assumed by the Wessex of No 18 Squadron.

Meanwhile, the Royal Navy had disembarked seven of their Whirlwind Mk 7s from the Commando Carrier Albion for operations in the central and eastern brigade areas of Borneo, and there seemed little prospect of their being released to resume their seaborne role. The Navy offered them to the RAF, an idea which did not appeal to the Air Staff which had discarded all thoughts of a Whirlwind with a Leonides Major engine in 1958 (see Chapter 4). AMP replied, therefore, that he could find neither pilots nor technicians to man them, and the Navy agreed to continue operating the Mk 7s until the end of 1964 and keep six more in reserve.

However, when the question arose of providing more naval Wessex for Borneo, the Navy's Flag Officer Middle East firmly resisted any suggestion that he should send any more helicopters to the Far East. The Commando Carrier Bulwark, he argued, was already supplying Wessex to Borneo and those aboard the Carrier Centaur in the Middle East were essential for anti-submarine protection and training, and to support the Radfan operations in Aden. To this, however, the Commander-in-Chief Far East, Admiral Sir Varyl Begg, replied that the Commando Carrier's Wessex had been allocated to Borneo when only five Army battalions were deployed there; now that there were ten, more helicopter support was needed. Consequently, it was decided to form an 'ad hoc' squadron of six naval Wessex to serve in Borneo, and accept the reduction in anti-submarine capability.(38)

For the Army, the search for helicopters to serve in Borneo came at a fortunate moment, as it was currently proposing a very substantial increase in the Army Air Corps. In the circumstances the RAF was ready to support the Army bid, at least in principle, on the grounds that any further contribution to the onerous reconnaissance and communications tasks would release more of the RAF's tactical helicopters to the trooping and resupply roles. The scale of the increase proposed by the Army, however, caused considerable surprise, no less than 285 new helicopters for reconnaissance, liaison and communications duties. In the face of so wholly unrealistic a demand, and with all three Services wanting more helicopters, some coordination of the various bids was clearly essential. A RAF brief for the Minister

---

*Such problems did not affect the Royal Navy which could provide full second line servicing and crew rotation for their Wessex from the commando carrier in the area.

of Defence pointed out that an Army Air Corps helicopter force of 500 was obviously absurd when seen alongside a total RAF strength of 700 aircraft of which no more than 200 were fighting vehicles. The RAF, however, was prepared to support an increase in the strength of the Army Air Corps of 50 light helicopters pending a detailed study of what was required. In the short term 12 Army Scout helicopters were allocated to Borneo and after three had been detached to HQ 3 Divison near Colchester on the grounds that it was 'at notice' for operations, the remaining nine joined No 225 Squadron's last four Whirlwinds in Bulwark at Portsmouth for passage to Borneo.(39)

In parallel to the steps taken to increase the size of the helicopter force in Borneo, a very determined effort was made to remedy a number of technical deficiencies in the aircraft already there. The Admiralty and Air Ministry sent a joint note to the Minister of Defence pointing out that the supply of Gazelle engines for the Belvederes and of Gnome engines for the Whirlwinds and Wessex was far from satisfactory. The shortage of engines for the Wessex, in fact, meant that the Royal Navy was having to meet the Borneo requirement by restricting flying hours in other theatres. In addition, an extensive development programme was urgently needed for the Belvedere in no less than five areas: the engine starter system (there had been three serious fires already); vibration (which could not be cured without blade tracking equipment for rotor blade adjustments); yaw control (one fatal crash had already occurred due to yaw cable failure); the automatic provision of emergency power when one engine failed (this did not always occur); and the fuel system (a crash in North Africa had been caused primarily by a failure of a fuel supply line—see Chapter 10).

But as in the early 1950s constant complaints to the manufacturers at Air Ministry level produced little result and it became clear that what was needed once again was Ministerial pressure, and indeed by May 1964 there had been some positive reaction to the energetic representations made by the Minister of Defence, Mr Peter Thorneycroft. With Rolls Royce and Bristol Siddeley representatives joining others from Westlands in the Far East the technical and supply problems began to improve.

Meanwhile the Joint Staff response to the need for a larger helicopter force in the Far East had been to look again at the calculations which determined the number of simultaneous company lifts worldwide. Earlier calculations had resulted in 1960 in five-company lifts by the RAF and two by the Royal Navy's commando carriers; in 1961 in the deletion of one company lift by the RAF (half in Cyprus and half in Kenya); and in 1962 in the deletion of a further company lift by the RAF (in Aden).(41) What remained was a combined total of five-company lifts, three by the RAF (one each in the United Kingdom, Germany and the Far East) and two by the Royal Navy (split between Albion and Bulwark).(42) The level of combined

RAF and RN capability in early 1964, however, was only three-and-a-half company lifts,* and the target of five-company lifts would not be reached until 1965 when the build-up of the Wessex Mk 2 force for the RAF and Mk 3 for the Navy would be complete.**

After taking new calculations into consideration the Chiefs of Staff decided that a combined seven-company lift would be too expensive at £21 millions in relation to the other projects which would have to be forgone, and recommended a combined six company lift at £11 millions, a price which included the purchase of twenty additional Wessex at the cost of £5 millions. It was noted, however, that the Wessex was an old design and that the increase to four RAF company lifts could not be effective until 1966.***

The reaction of the Minister of Defence to these proposals for an enlarged helicopter force was notably enthusiastic, more so in some ways even than that of the Chiefs of Staff, an in marked contrast to the reactions common in the 1950s when RAF attempts to obtain more helicopters foundered in the face of continued scepticism about the helicopter itself and fear of the expense involved—at least until General Templer forced the issue in Malaya (see Chapter 2). Thorneycroft, for his part, having had some success in pressing the manufacturers to take active steps to remedy the many technical and spares problems as yet unresolved, told the Minister of Defence for the RAF on 28 May 1964 that in his opinion not enough was being done in the field of helicopters. He had always found that they ranked high in the list of demands presented to him wherever he went overseas and he was therefore giving serious consideration to a 50% increase over the next few years in the size of the helicopter force, present and planned.

To the Chiefs of Staff he added that purely theoretical calculations based on a requirement to lift a stated number of units were clearly out of tune with all the information pouring in from every operational theatre overseas, where the constant and growing demand was for more helicopters of almost every type.(45) Shortly

---

*The helicopter force in Aden was excluded from this calculation, having been deleted from the long term plan.

**The convention was that successive marks of the same type of aircraft should bear even numbers for the RAF and odd numbers for the RN. Thus the naval Mk 3 Wessex was the twin Gnome engined version following the single Gazelle engined Mk 1 and was similar to the RAF Mk 2.

***A longer term study of future SRT requirements referred to the SA 330 (which entered RAF service as the Puma) with its better ferry range and better airportability as 'more suited to the age of the Belfast'.(44) So, in its origins JNAST 365, mentioned above and leading to the Puma, had links, however indirect, with the pressures brought about by the Borneo campaign.

afterwards, however, he left office following a general election, priorities changed and calculations continued to be made on the basis of the number of simultaneous company lifts which the current administration considered was necessary and could be afforded.

At about the same time an improvement was made in the Borneo situation when VCAS recommended an official establishment of 30 Whirlwinds for FEAF, instead of 14 Wessex, representing an overall increase of two-thirds of a company lift. The change from Wessex to Whirlwinds had the advantage not only of meeting FEAF's reluctance to accept Wessex at that time, but also of avoiding any modification of the tactical replacement plans which looked upon the Puma as a replacement for the Wessex.(46)

The decision was then taken to absorb the No 38 Group element of the helicopter reinforcements provided for Borneo, ie Spine Force, into the FEAF establishment. The establishments of the two FEAF Whirlwind squadrons, Nos 103 and 110, were raised from 10 to 15 aircraft each, and the separately established SAR element was absorbed between them.* No 230 Squadron, with its Whirlwinds at last equipped with H/F radio, was transferred by the Aircraft Carrier <u>Triumph</u> to Singapore, and thence by <u>Bulwark</u> to Labuan in January 1965, to replace No 225 Squadron which was disbanded later the same year. Two of the three Spine Force Belvederes were retained in Singapore, while the third was despatched to its original destination in Aden. All Belvedere personnel in Spine Force who belonged officially to No 26 Squadron were absorbed into No 66, into which they had in practice been fully integrated since their arrival in Singapore.**(47)

The Selection of Helicopter Pilots

In the mid-1960s a dramatic change took place in the official attitude to helicopter flying as part of a normal career in the RAF. Since the early days in the 1950s pilots had been selected on an ad hoc basis and inevitably from among those who were unlikely to progress to flying fast jet aircraft. Indeed, 35 was the minimum age limit in force in the years immediately following the formation of the Casualty Evacuation Flight in FEAF, a policy which had necessarily to be revised in the

---

*It was quite usual in overseas theatres for the SAR task to be seen as just one of the specialist tasks within the helicopter role, with allowance made for it in an appropriate squadron establishment, rather than as a full-time wholly SAR dedicated task as in the UK-based SAR squadrons.

**The Belvedere sent to Aden was the one later provided for display in the RAF Museum. It had returned to operations in Borneo when No 26 Squadron disbanded in Aden in 1965 and was transported to the museum when No 66 disbanded at Seletar in March 1969.

later 1950s during the first phase of rapid expansion in the helicopter force. But selection of helicopter pilots was still very much a matter of taking those who were thought to be unsuited, or less well suited, to flying other types of aircraft.

Attention was first drawn to the resulting imbalance by the Commander-in-Chief Transport Command, Air Marshal Sir Kenneth Cross, whose command included No 38 Group. He pointed out in February 1964 that under current policy all Cranwell and university trained pilots were sent to fixed-wing units, and that as a result there were no general list officers in helicopter units under the age of twenty-five. Helicopter squadrons, therefore, were denied a fair share of the best junior officers, and what was more, Helicopter Squadron and Flight Commander posts, and those for Test Pilots and Instructors, along with staff appointments, were filled either by less than the best material or by those with greater potential but lacking in helicopter background or experience.(48)

The seemingly radical suggestion that some Cranwell graduates should proceed to a first flying tour on helicopters was not received with much enthusiasm by the Air Ministry. Their reply included the revealing comment that new pilots needed fixed-wing experience to fit them for promotion, the implication being exactly what Sir Kenneth Cross was complaining about. It was also suggested that the Commander-in-Chief had taken too little account of the situation overseas where the proportion of general list officers in helicopter units was one to six. In returning to the attack Cross pointed out that it had become evident to all that a helicopter posting was far from a promising start to a general list career, and that it was fundamentally wrong to differentiate for career purposes between helicopter and fixed-wing flying. He also expanded on a point he had made briefly in his previous submission: the SRT force was very much in the front line, frequently required to operate independently and in difficult conditions from unprepared bases, and without doubt offered a variety of experience while calling for a considerable breadth of vision. Helicopter crews were in constant and close contact with the Army and Royal Navy while on active service, and more so than in most other roles. In all, he judged it to be important to have a fair proportion of Cranwell and university-trained pilots posted to helicopter units for their first flying tour. Replying, the Air Member for Personnel promised to discuss the matter further with the Vice Chief of the Air Staff.(49)

The subject was raised again a year or so later in July 1965 by FEAF's air Commander, Air Marshal Sir Peter Wykeham, who pointed out that while the Borneo campaign had accelerated the training of helicopter pilots, its conclusion would not negate the lessons learned during it, particularly that it was vital to maintain a vigorous helicopter force and that experience of handling it effectively would form a valuable part of any future commander's Service experience. The average age of officers in FEAF's helicopter squadrons, however, was 35; there were few general list officers, and only the Squadron Commanders showed promise of moving into higher command. Exemplary though its performance was in Borneo, the helicopter force there lacked full career officers with leadership potential in the numbers needed to ensure that they could move freely to and from the fixed-wing roles.

Wykeham therefore suggested a selective increase in the number of permanent commission (general list) officers to perhaps one third of the total instead of the present one fifth, and an increase also in the number of high calibre flight and squadron commanders. Further, with enough helicopter pilots trained to the level which would enable them to transfer to and from the fixed-wing roles, there should be no objection to allowing some pilots to go direct from Cranwell to helicopter units.(50)

The Air Ministry's reaction was now entirely favourable and in September 1965 the Deputy Chief of the Air Staff was able to tell Wykeham that the policy of barring Cranwell graduates from a first tour in helicopters had been abandoned, and that the Air Ministry had already been at work on proposals of the kind suggested. It was now intended that from December 1965 some five cadets a year initially would be chosen at Cranwell to do their first operational tour in helicopters, returning afterwards to fixed-wing flying. These officers, together with the Squadron Commanders who would enter or re-enter the helicopter force as Squadron Leaders, would in time raise the General List proportion to nearly 30%. To achieve a lowering of the average age level of the force, half of all future intakes would be first tour pilots who would be retained on helicopters for at least five years; as a result the average age would be reduced to 26 or 27. Wykeham professed himself to be entirely satisfied with these proposals.(51)

So, by the mid 1960s the helicopter force had finally come of age: not only was its existence as a permanently operational entity now universally accepted, but it had also achieved a position of undeniable respectability in the career structure of the Royal Air Force—some 15 years after the first helicopter unit had been formed in 1950.

The Arming of Helicopters

To accept the helicopter as a standard tactical transport vehicle was one thing; to see it as a fighting aircraft equipped with fire power was a very different matter. A complex but intermittent discussion on the arming of helicopters had been in progress since the then Air Vice Marshal Wykeham had submitted a report to the Chiefs of Staff on his visit to the French Air Force in Algeria in October 1960. Partly as a result of that report the Air Council agreed in principle in September 1961 that some helicopters should be armed,(52) and in the following year proposals were made for equipping Whirlwinds and Wessex with SS 11 wire guided missiles,* 20 mm cannon and 2-in rockets. The plan was that a number of SRT helicopters should be fully armed to the exclusion of payload and used in company with unarmed helicopters to provide protective and offensive fire in the event of ground fire being encountered. There was little support, however, for these proposals, which also raised a number of technical difficulties, and they were allowed to founder on the grounds of cost.

It was the general belief that a helicopter was far too vulnerable to be committed in the face of enemy fire, and that it could therefore never be used in an offensive role. An Air Ministry staff meeting in 1962, attended also by Admiralty, War Office and Joint Warfare staff representatives, accepted this contention in the main, and added that before a decision was taken to arm helicopters for an offensive or armed escort role, the need for such aircraft must first be established by joint service tactical trials. In any case it was also generally accepted that the SRT force was too small to allow a proportion of its aircraft to be permanently committed to the escort and armed reconnaissance roles as the Army wanted, and that there seemed to be no prospect of obtaining helicopters allocated specifically for these purposes.(53)

At the purely practical level it was left to the Assistant Chief of the Air Staff (Operations) to point out in June 1963 that SRT helicopters were not suitable for offensive roles, that the size of the helicopter force precluded the designation of specialised escort helicopters, and that consequently there would be no joint service trials. On the other hand, however, free gun mountings would be provided in SRT helicopter cabins for purely suppressive fire, two pilots would be carried when a threat existed, and the aircraft would be equipped with armour protection for the first pilot and self-sealing tanks to safeguard the minimum fuel needed to escape from an engagement. A month later the Vice Chief of the Air Staff endorsed these proposals, but declined to issue a formal statement of Air Staff policy on the question of arming helicopters. This had now become a matter of contention with the Army Air Corps, which could not intervene directly because of the weight limitation imposed on its own helicopters (see Chapter 4). VCAS directed, however, that experiments with the SS11 should continue using the four Whirlwinds of No 225 Squadron which it was planned to equip with the necessary fixed fittings.(54)

By early 1963 the Naval Staff was able to inform their Vice Chief that RAF policy was coming into line with their own: to have fixed fittings for machine guns on all tactical helicopters, with provision for a few to be fitted with guns for suppressive fire as required. A few days later, however, on 18 December, it was reported that at Pensiangan in Borneo two out of three RAF Whirlwinds had been hit by bullets,

*The SS-11 was a French rocket missile, wire guided visually by a 'joystick' in the cockpit. It weighed 63 lb including a 13 lb warhead; it had a range of 1640 to 11500 feet and was normally to be used at distances of 1000 to 3000 yards.

some of which had penetrated the fuel tanks, while at Biawak an Army Auster had force landed as a result of ground fire and the passenger, an RAF chaplain, had been killed.(55)

The policy on suppressive fire was then urgently reappraised and at a high level Air Ministry meeting it was decided that all SRT helicopters should be fitted with Bren gun mountings, immediately in FEAF and as soon as possible thereafter in Germany. As additional measures, the despatch began of armoured vests for FEAF helicopter aircrews, while Westlands set to work on the design of a more sophisticated mounting for the FN rifle, and No 38 Group on a fitting for removable guns, including the 7.62 general purpose machine gun which eventually became standard.(56)

This was far from being the end of the matter and the progressively more vexed question of how much armour the helicopter should carry and for what purpose acquired its own momentum in the late 1960s. The role of the Army Air Corps vis-à-vis the RAF in this context opened up a whole new field of operational capability, as described in outline in Chapter 14.

References to Chapter 9

1   ID3/943/2/Pt 1.

2   IIA/11/2/4/Pt 4.

3   Ibid.

4   Ibid.

5   COS(60) 8th Meeting.

6   IIA/11/2/4/Pt 4.

7   Ibid.

8   Ibid.

9   Ibid.

10   Ibid.

11   IIA/11/4/Pt 5.

12   Ibid.

13   Ibid.

14   Ibid.

15   AC SC(61) 16/24.

16   ID3/943/2/Pt 1.

17   ID9/F1-101.

18   IIA/11/2/31/Pt 2.

19   Ibid.

20   ID3/943/2/Pt 2.

21   Ibid.

22   Ibid.

23   AC(62) 18; AC(62) 10.

24   ID3/943/2/Pt 2.

25   Ibid.

26   Ibid.

27   Ibid.

28   Ibid.

29   Ibid.

30 ID9/F2–30.

31 ID3/943/2/Pt 2.

32 Ibid.

33 Ibid.

34 Ibid.

35 Ibid.

36 ID/94/10

37 Ibid.

38 Ibid.

39 Ibid.

40 Ibid.

41 COS(62) 1.

42 COS(402) 63.

43 COS(25) 64.

44 Ibid.

45 ID/94/10.

46 Ibid.

47 Ibid.

48 Ibid.

49 Ibid.

50 ID9/Q4–28.

51 Ibid.

52 AC 16 (61).

53 ID/94/10.

54 Ibid.

55 C-in-C FE signal.

56 ID/94/10.

CHAPTER 10

THE GROWTH OF THE SRT FORCE IN EUROPE

The SRT Helicopter Force, although planned on a world wide basis, in reality only functioned in the originally envisaged mobile close support role with Army units in the European Theatre, with occasional exercise excursions in North Africa using the Libyan desert as trouble-free real estate. Actual overseas operations in the Arabian Peninsula, Malaya and Borneo were very different, being dictated by local political and topographical circumstances but essentially with comparatively permanent fixed bases and centralised control of operations and resources. In Europe the practice of committing small self-supporting groups of helicopters for specific local Army operations lasting hours or days rather than months dictated the pattern of development for tactical helicopters. Interspersed with these small operations were major Army exercises in which the larger part or even the whole of the SRT Helicopter Force was committed for a few days for exercises based on temporary 'field' bases in the operational area, these being essentially larger scale versions of the smaller exercises which occurred several times each month.

This pattern of small short-term deployments had started in the last two years of the JEHU (see Chapter 6) and was thus to some extent a continuation of an existing, rather than a totally new, procedure with No 225 Squadron being formed out of the disbanding JEHU in January 1960. Although the overseas helicopter squadrons were engaged in direct tactical assistance to Army operations, these were in the main mounted from fixed or semi-permanent bases as part of a long term policy. The close support of mobile Army formations in Europe gave rise to a form of tactical self-supported detachment activity which developed naturally into the Support Helicopter Force of the 1970s. No 225 Squadron can therefore be properly described as the first Tactical Support Helicopter Squadron in this line of development, and the first helicopter element of the new No 38 Group SRT Force. (A fixed wing element already existed in the form of No 230 Squadron equipped with single and twin Pioneer aircraft).

This Squadron of piston-engined Whirlwinds Mk 2 and Sycamores belongs in one sense to Phase 2 of this History, but it more logically finds its place here in Phase 3 since it led the way into the turbine-engined era of tactical helicopter operations with the Army without changing its character or mode of operation. The fact that it was joined at Odiham by the turbine-engined Belvederes a few months before it received its own turbine-engined Whirlwinds Mk 10 does not alter its prime position in the formation of the RAF SRT Helicopter Force.

There was to be a period of nearly four years (1960–63) during which the new helicopter force of Belvederes and Whirlwinds based at Odiham was to grow and develop its tactical role before suddenly disappearing to the more dramatic operational theatres of Aden and Borneo, handing over the European exercise tasks (mainly UK and Germany) to the Wessex Mk 2 which appeared in 1964 just in time to assume the role for which it had originally been chosen. These four years were to be most stimulating for all concerned. In spite of the departure of No 66 (Belvedere) Squadron to FEAF in 1961, there was for the first time a sizeable force of helicopters in England which could be called upon to perform the numerous tasks, both military and civilian, only possible by helicopter, without encroaching with great difficulty on the otherwise committed specialist SAR or CFS training aircraft. The Belvedere was a considerable revelation even to those already accustomed to working with helicopters in the overseas theatres, and the Whirlwind Mk 10 which appeared in 1962 was, in its own way, equally surprising in its new capability.

The formation of the Tactical Air Support Group Headquarters and Squadron organisation was dramatically sudden. At Christmas 1959 there existed only No 230 (Pioneer) Squadron operating with Southern Command (Army) and, operating more or less independently, the JEHU at Middle Wallop. On New Year's Day, 1960, No 38 Group in Transport Command came into existence at Upavon (in two huts moved there from the Isle of Wight in 1919 for use as Married Quarters) having control of No 230 (Pioneer) Squadron now also at Upavon, and No 225 Helicopter Squadron formed on the same day at Andover. This constituted the SRT Force. The other element of Tactical Air Transport Support never appeared in the guise of the Light Cargo Force that had been discussed at staff level. What did exist was given the title Medium Range Transport (MRT) and consisted of Hastings, Beverleys and later Argosys of No 46 Group in Transport Command. These were allocated for use by No 38 Group in exercises as required, Hunters from Strike Command being similarly allocated for offensive support.

There was no gradual build-up initially. The new No 38 Group plunged immediately into detailed planning for the most ambitious joint Service exercise which could possibly be mounted since it committed the entire SRT Helicopter Force and much of No 230 Squadron (as well as offensive support by both Strike Command and the Royal Navy) to support of a No 3 Division Army exercise in Libya—'Starlight I'— and as much of the MRT Force as was required to transport it and operate in the exercise area. There was just time in January for a short rehearsal (Exercise Black Pearl) at Upavon of the 'Air Maintenance System' between HQ 3 Division and No 38 Group, and the organisation and control of the 'Airhead' which was to be set up in Libya at Tmimi. The main base was to be at El Adem and the exercise took place in March.(1)

Much of the development of the SRT Helicopter Force in the following 10 years was to consist of modifications of the organisation at the various levels of control needed to enable the helicopters to be properly tasked and to respond to the requirements of troop movement, logistic re-supply, casualty evacuation, reconnaissance and communications in the numerous exercises which were generated in that period. It is not intended to trace in detail the development of these agencies in the tasking chain beyond outlining the four levels of control initially created for Exercise 'Starlight' and continuing in more or less similar form thereafter. At the top was the Joint Headquarters shared by HQ 3 Division (Army) and HQ No 38 Group (RAF). On Exercise 'Starlight' this was called the Joint Control Operations Centre—later to be simply JOC. Included in this organisation was the ATMCC (Air Transport Movement Control Centre) which also contained the link with Transport Command. This was later to be known as ASOC or ATOC (Air Support Operations Centre for Offensive Support, and Air Transport Operations Centre for MRT and SRT Support). Further forward was the BASOC (Battlefield Air Support Operations Control) divided into BASOC (OS) and BASOC (AT) for offensive and transport support respectively. This level was responsible for translating Army bids into detailed aircraft tasking and giving advice to the Army on practical air matters. Later this agency developed into a person with similar initials—BASO (Brigade Air Support Officer) permanently attached to Brigade Headquarters. Operational control of aircraft at the point of action was provided by a Squadron Air Control team or MOT (Mobile Operations Team)—later Mobile Air Operations Team (MAOT). Initially, the SRT force was based at the Airhead—the furthest forward point reached by MRT—and the Airhead had its own Operations Control, Air Maintenance Operations, corresponding to Station Operations at a permanent base. Later, this practice was used only rarely and for large-scale major exercises, helicopters being tasked through a MAOT or directly by BASO or by a 'Forward Air Transport Operations Centre' (FATOC). For Exercise 'Starlight', the SRT Force suffered considerably from being based at the Airhead and having to tolerate the very considerable dust clouds thrown up by the Beverleys, but the main problem throughout the early years was the lack of suitable radio communications without which proper tactical deployment of the SRT helicopters was not practical.

Within the limits of being the first large scale helicopter participation in a major Army exercise, Starlight was a success. The helicopters (12 Whirlwinds) had all been airlifted to El Adem by Beverleys of the MRT Force and flew 458 hours, including 63 at night using vehicle headlights for landing areas. 242 passengers were carried and there were 99 casualty evacuations. A Forward Maintenance Area (FMA) was created and operated, troop assaults were mounted and numerous VIP and other observers carried. It was however a very leisurely deployment by later standards. Arrival at El Adem took place in February for an exercise which did not commence until mid March, and the active assault phase of which lasted only three days. Before the exercise began the helicopter squadron personnel were able to undertake two desert expeditions of 12 persons using four vehicles and lasting two or three days. After return home, virtually the whole of April was devoted to cleaning and rebuilding the aircraft after their transhipment by Beverleys of the MRT Force. The extra six Whirlwinds added for 'Starlight' were removed and the Squadron reverted to its establishment of six Whirlwinds and six Sycamores.(2)

During May 1960, No 38 Group Headquarters, No 230 (Pioneer) Squadron and No 225 (Helicopter) Squadron moved to Odiham, and the pattern of SRT support for Army exercises from that base became firmly established. Odiham thus became the permanent UK base for all the RAF helicopters operating in support of the Army.

In the same month, responsibility for No 118 (Sycamore) Squadron in Northern Ireland was assumed by Transport Command vice Coastal Command (see Chapter 7) and it became a No 38 Group SRT Unit, although remaining exclusively for operations in Northern Ireland. As such, it fell to No 225 Squadron, which initially had responsibility for providing Operational Conversion Unit services for the SRT Force, to arrange Sycamore training as a SRT Unit and standardisation services for No 118 Squadron for the remaining two years of its life. In February 1962, the IRA announced cessation of its violent campaign, and in August No 118 Squadron (three Sycamores and five pilots) was disbanded.(3)

The demand for helicopter support for Army field operations had obviously been growing for some time. From the moment when the new No 38 Group/No 225 Squadron Whirlwinds and Sycamores were available for monthly tasking, that is in May 1960 when they had recovered from Exercise 'Starlight', bids for helicopter participation in various Army unit training exercises started flooding into No 38 Group. The RAF found itself fighting hard to retain the essential flying hours for Monthly Continuation Training (MCT) for the helicopter crews. The problem, basic and therefore permanent, was the divergent requirements of the soldiers and the airmen. For the helicopter crews there was the need to practise regularly the skills inherent in aircraft handling precision manoeuvres, emergency procedures, bad weather and instrument flying and night flying with all that that implied. For the soldiers the task consisted of marshalling the troops and equipment at appropriate places, and emplaning and deplaning them efficiently and safely. The control and communcations required were a common problem.

In practice, exercises designed by the Army for the Army had little relevance to the specialist training needs of the RAF, whose problem was mainly to arrive at the right place at the right time with sufficient backing to maintain whatever troop or cargo lift requirements were presented. The exercises in pure flying techniques which the RAF, with its Central Flying School purist approach, considered essential in the longer term for efficient operations, were rarely exercised in the course of the very numerous Army exercises or training sessions demanding helicopter participation. Indeed, so important for the Army was the successful performance of the helicopters that in larger scale exercises the scenario was frequently instantly re-cast to permit them to participate when real circumstances, eg weather or fuel supply problems, would have excluded them. The result was a constant tension between the pressure from the Army for more helicopter hours than could be made available, and the RAF need to reserve an adequate proportion of the hours available to practise the skills which were rarely employed in the exercise scenarios.

In general the helicopters were tasked at about 30 hours per month per established aircraft and the pilots, established at a pilot/aircraft ration of 1.25:1 or 1.5:1 were required to fly a minimum of 15 hours per month (they usually flew considerably more) for which about $3\frac{1}{2}$ were needed for pure flying training, that is, mainly night and instrument flying and emergency procedures (MCT).(4)

That the exercise scenario failed to provide realistic operational training for the helicopter crews is shown by the fact that a monthly allowance of two hours per pilot had also to be reserved for Transport Support (TS) practices, that is, training in the operational procedures associated with their specific role, although these were rarely experienced in the numerous exercises and demonstrations carried out for the Army. A further allowance of between 10 and 20 hours had to be made for operational training for each new pilot arriving on the Squadrons. For example, in April 1961, a fairly typical month containing no major exercises, Sycamores and Whirlwinds were deployed in ones and twos for two to six days at various locations on behalf of eight Army units. With a total of 222 hours each theoretically available for Whirlwinds and Sycamores, MCT plus TS plus conversion training required 54 and 80 hours respectively, while 144 and 84 respectively were expended on exercise tasks. The shortfall of 24 and 56 from the total hours theoretically available would be mainly due to exercises cancelled for weather or operational reasons, or because of aircraft unserviceability.(5)

About six times a year there were larger scale commitments requiring perhaps six or more helicopters for a Unit major exercise lasting for a week or so, and once or twice a year, major exercises involving the deployment of the whole SRT Force for up to three weeks in the UK, Germany or North Africa would be required. Except in the latter case, monthly tasking in response to numerous bids from individual units continued up to the limit of flying hours available. Allocation of the bids accepted was made by No 38 Group at a monthly meeting that invariably took the form of inviting the Army representative to allocate priorities and agree to the rejection of a large number for which flying hours were not available after the RAF had reserved its own portion for MCT, TS and pilot conversion training.

In a sense this was a healthy situation in that there was no danger of under-utilisation and consequent stagnation, but there were disadvantages. The pace of these operations left little time for constructive appraisal of what was being achieved. The fact that such a large number of Army units was involved at different places required the preparation of numerous comprehensive Operation Orders although only one or two helicopters might be involved and there was rarely any comment afterwards. The helicopters nearly always arrived, carried out the demonstration required, loaded and unloaded the soldiers presented for the event, carried their equipment inside or underslung from point A to point B or dropped the parachutists provided, all in totally unrepresentative operational conditions, and returned to Odiham to prepare for the next demonstration. It seemed to the RAF that to train the whole British Army to operate with helicopters was an impossible task since when major exercises were mounted, and regardless of the continuous monthly troop training already carried out, none of the troops present in large numbers seemed to have seen a helicopter, and a day or two usually had to be set aside before the exercise started purely for emplaning and deplaning procedures to be practised. The need for this training was scarcely debatable— there were very few who could remember the decision taken in respect of the S-55s in Malaya in 1953 when shortage of available flying hours had encouraged the conclusion that such training for military passengers was not essential, even where no crewmen were carried and the troops had never flown at all and frequently spoke no English—see Chapter 3. But this was the UK in 1960 and the Whirlwinds Mk 2 and Sycamores still had no crewmen. The risks to the soldiers from rotor blades (both main and tail rotors in the case of the Sycamore) and to the inside of the aircraft from weapons and equipment, coupled with the need for speed and efficiency in rapid troop shuttle operations, made such practice seem almost essential.

After major exercises a variety of detailed reports were prepared covering virtually all aspects of the exercise, but as these usually took some months to complete as a composite document and then circulate, planning for the next exercise was often well under way before the report on the last was received. In any case the main message for the RAF was already well known as far as the SRT Force was concerned—there was not enough helicopter lift, it was not fast enough, it was limited severely by darkness and bad weather, and above all, it was invariably adversely affected by inadequate communications.

As the frequencies used for Air Traffic Control had risen steadily since the 1940s, the VHF sets fitted to the early helicopters were already beginning to be replaced by UHF following the fixed wing practice where the need for very low level communications over more than a few miles had virtually ceased to exist. Apart from the sets provided for long-range fixed-wing aircraft, there were no lightweight HF sets being manufactured suitable for the short-range low-level work character-istic of helicopter operations. Consequently for almost the whole of this first period when the new SRT Force was operating from Odiham, control was exclusively by VHF which meant that the helicopters were beyond radio contact when more than a few miles from their controller. Flexibility was thus seriously impaired. The Army was having its own problems in this field and the consequence was that communications difficulties figured largely in the conduct of all these exercises. It was not until operations expanded in the Far East later in the 1960s, and the consequences of losing contact with helicopters shortly after take off posed an entirely different sort of consideration in that sort of terrain, that the pressure to obtain and fit HF communications became imperative. Thus HF radios were initially supplied only to helicopters in FEAF.

During the remainder of 1960 and for most of 1961, No 225 Squadron laboured on with the never ending task of troop training sorties interspersed with occasional 'set piece' exercises. Typical payloads were four or five soldiers in the Whirlwind and three in the Sycamore, or underslung loads of about 500 pounds. When deployed in 'field' locations on exercise, all the support equipment, including tentage and cooking facilities, plus all the ground crews, had to be transported in a convoy of vehicles, thus adding a further unrealistic element to the operational picture. Inevitably, this convoy got progressively larger as experience generated an ever-increasing demand for improved facilities at forward locations, piston-engined Whirlwinds Mk 2 and Sycamores being able to carry little of this material and support personnel when deploying over significant distances. On the other hand, the RAF aircrews were learning to live under simulated combat conditions, wearing Army combat clothing, tactically dispersed in the mud and general filth of 'field' locations, and subject to simulated commando style raids by the SAS in the middle of the night.

Into this picture of earnest tactical endeavour was inserted, in October 1960, the Belvederes Trials Unit in the form of three comparatively enormous uncamouflaged pre-production type Belvederes—the first turbine-engined helicopters in the RAF. Within a month they had demonstrated their ability, in trials to lift underslung loads of 3000 lbs and then 5000 lbs, recovered a crashed Meteor near Yeovil and carried underslung a Land Rover and trailer; the startling effect of these feats was only partly diminished by jettisoning the latter at Odiham from 150 feet, as a result of engine failure as reported in Chapter 8.

The Belvederes, in addition to their various trials, mainly with external loads but including carriage of 28 troops (settling on 25 as a realistic maximum),(6) joined in several of the Whirlwind/Sycamore Army exercise tasks carried out by No 225 Squadron, offsetting to some degree their obvious non-tactical size and appearance by their ability to carry with them all the ground crew and camping gear required for living for short periods in 'field' conditions.

Following the formation of the BTU into No 66 Squadron, Belvederes fitted with metal-blades and hydraulic-powered controls participated fully in these exercises, three of them first appearing at the SBAC Farnborough Show in September 1961, for which No 225 Squadron provided six Whirlwinds.

In October 1961, the first major exercise which involved operational Belvederes—'Spearpoint'—was mounted in Germany, seven Whirlwinds and three Sycamores of No 225 Squadron and three production type Belvederes of the newly re-formed No 66 Squadron being deployed to Gutersloh for the period. On this occasion the opportunity presented itself of making a significant new development in the pattern of tactical helicopter procedures. The three Belveders were in the colours appropriate to their tropical destinations—Aden and FEAF—that is, aluminium finish with white top surfaces.* Not only were they unable to nestle under the trees like the Whirlwinds and Sycamores which were disposed tactically around the periphery of a small wood which sheltered the SRT base camp, but their presence alongside provided a startling obvious eye-catching feature of very large dimensions. The Belvedere Squadron Commander offered to resolve the difficulty by utilising the capacity of the aircraft to house their own three-man crews allowing them to deploy individually either to small Army units in the vicinity, or to remote sites where the chances of their being found were slight and the consequence less troublesome for the rest of the SRT Force. Both types of deployment were tried during the exercises, the lack of radio communication with the SRT tasking authority while the aircraft was on the ground (no HF radio was fitted) being the main disadvantage. In fact the No 38 Group tasking agency (FATOC) at the SRT base found the lack of communication so unsatisfactory that the idea of tactical discreet deployment of the SRT was not supported in principle, and thus almost the only significant and radical development of SRT doctrine during this period (1960–63) failed on that account.**

A suggestion had been made by the Belvedere Trials Unit that the Belvedere might be used with minimal modification to provide a refuelling service in the field for Whirlwinds which were being employed in shuttling troops and equipment between two points in the forward area, and then having to return up to 30 miles to the SRT Base for fuel.(8) The fuel for this return journey represented a payload penalty for each of the shuttle sorties undertaken; thus the number of shuttle sorties was increased, and each flight contained a non-productive period. For these reasons it also prolonged significantly the time taken to complete a troop redeployment. The Bristol Aeroplane Company, who in 1959 were still the Belvedere manufacturers, produced a brochure showing a Belvedere refuelling a helicopter and a tank directly from its internal overload tanks, and supplying fresh water to a patrol. It was calculated that one Belvedere could refuel six Whirlwinds with one hour's fuel at a

---

*Camouflage finish was only later decided upon (1964) and then only for the FEAF Belvederes.(7)

**The principle of making small groups of up to four helicopters self-supporting in tactical locations away from a main SRT base was revived later with the arrival of Wessex and Puma helicopters.

range of 50 miles from its own refuelling point, the choice of place for the transfer being practically without limit.*

The proposal to use the Belvedere as a refuelling vehicle for Whirlwinds in a European tactical environment was not enthusiastically received at a time when the Belvedere was a contentious subject at Ministry level (see Chapter 9) and was officially destined as part of the Light Cargo Force for Aden and FEAF exclusively.**

These arguments against new roles for the Belvedere still applied in July 1962 when the Belvedere, during Exercise 'Blind Mouse 4' in Germany, demonstrated, at the request of the Army, its ability to carry (and therefore deploy in time of war) the nuclear warhead of the 'Honest John' tactical missile. A case for the retention of the Belvedere in Germany for this purpose was prepared but not agreed.

An unexpected role which the Belvedere did acquire, and one which it retained throughout its life, was the recovery of crashed aircraft or helicopters unserviceable in inaccessible places. Altogether, between 1960 and 1968, Belvederes recovered 31 crashed aircraft or parts of wreckage including 23 complete helicopters, two Austers, two Chipmunks and a hovercraft. Twenty of the helicopters lifted were in FEAF, one in Aden, one in Germany and one in England.(9)

No 72 Squadron started to re-form at Odiham in November 1961, as a Belvedere training cell, the Squadron Commander of No 66 Squadron and three crews being transferred for the purpose, and became established in December with 15 pilots, 97 groundcrew, one navigator and one adjutant.(10)

---

*In 1962, when the possibility of buying the Chinook had been raised and the Wessex was seen as the future SRT vehicle, it was pointed out that the Belvedere/Whirlwind relationship was comparable with the Chinook/Wessex one, but the Chinook was not to be purchased.

**The problem was later mitigated (Phase 4) by the use of air portable 500 gallon flexible cylinders (Seal Drums) and 20000 gallon bags (Pillow Tanks) to be positioned at forward refuelling points, although this less flexible arrangement also added further to the unreality of exercise conditions, especially when gaily painted civilian fuel bowsers had to be employed to fill the Pillow Tanks, as in Exercise Sky Warrior at Otterburn in 1971. The subject would not be raised again until 1981 when the Chinook eventually appeared.

Belvedere recovering a forced landed Whirlwind Mk 10 in
Germany during a 38 Group Exercise—1962.

Refuelling a Sycamore of 225 Squadron detached to Kenya from Odiham for flood relief
duties—November 1961.

255-A

Diversions from the SRT Exercise Task

Apart from the various demonstrations, VIP communication flights, and occasional ambulance sorties (MEDEVAC) which formed part of the continuing secondary activity of the SRT Force during the first three years of its life at Odiham, there were three major diversions of note, one for the Sycamores and one for the Whirlwinds of No 225 Squadron, and one for the Belvederes of No 72 Squadron.

In November 1961, the month when the first four brand new Whirlwinds Mk 10 arrived for intensive flying trials with No 225 Squadron, severe flooding in Kenya threatened disaster for several populated areas. On 18 November No 225 Squadron was given six hours notice to prepare and despatch to Nairobi by Beverley, four Sycamores with six pilots and ground crews. The Beverleys left on time for Eastleigh via El Adem. The Royal Navy was assisting with Whirlwinds Mk 7, but these lacked the performance to offer a reasonable payload at 5000 feet in the Nairobi area so they were confined to the coastal area and Somalia while the Sycamores flew from Eastleigh. Doctors, engineers, food and medical supplies were delivered to the stricken areas where isolated settlements were cut off by the floods. Beverley and Dakota supply drops were concurrent. On 24 November, two of the Sycamores with three pilots moved to Mogadishu and continued food delivery, medical supplies and casualty evacuation operations, responding to tasking by the District Commissioners. In early December the Sycamores moved their base first to Kisimayu and then Gelib, withdrawing to Mogadishu between 20 and 22 December. Assistance in these deployments was provided by RAF Valettas and helped by an American H-19 helicopter and an Ethiopian C-47. On 22 December the detachment was withdrawn to the UK by Beverley, having flown 97 hours on rescue and supply sorties.(11) The success of this unexpected detachment and its efficient operation in limiting conditions of altitude and temperature with piston engined helicopters says a great deal about the expertise of the pilots and the wisdom of the RAF insistence on MCT and the maintenance of pure flying standards.

Meanwhile, the first four Whirlwinds Mk 10 were undergoing intensive flying trials with No 225 Squadron, each one completing 100 hours between 4 November and 11 December 1961—a feat which attracted praise in both 'Flight' and 'Aeroplane'. On 27 December CA release was given to permit up to 1500 lbs to be carried underslung, and in April 1962 a Whirlwind Mk 10 was used to position an extremely awkwardly shaped HF aerial on an 80 foot tower. It was not very heavy—only about 200 lbs—but it consisted of a dipole with 8 reflectors varying in length from 28 to 40 feet, and a very high degree of precision was needed for its emplacement. The ability to perform feats of this nature was still in the nature of a startling revelation at that time, although this particular success was almost eclipsed by the massive national publicity surrounding the placing by a Belvedere of the spire on Coventry Cathedral which was taking place at the same time.

Rehearsals at Odiham for Coventry Cathedral operation using a mock up of the flèche.

Coventry Cathedral operation rehearsal using a mock up of the sculpture.

256–B

The possibility of lifting the spire (in the form of a flèche) and its surmounting sculpture on to the roof of the newly built Coventry Cathedral by helicopter was first mentioned by No 38 Group to No 72 Squadron at Odiham in November 1961. After a reconnaissance of the Cathedral site and discussion with the builders about the requirements and restraints associated with the task, a possible method of tackling it was worked out. The task seemed at first sight to bear little relationship to the role for which the Belvedere was intended, but the techniques which had to be developed to meet a number of highly specialised requirements had several applications in later operational tasks in the Far East. Some of the details therefore have relevance in this account.

When consultations began in November 1961 with the Consulting Engineers (Ove Arup and Partners) and the builders (John Laing & Sons Ltd) neither the flèche nor its surmounting sculpture had actually been constructed. The flèche was to be a pylon 80 feet high with a base area of three feet square made of welded manganese bronze rods diminishing in thickness towards the top. The surmounting ornament was described as 'an abstract cruciform sculpture in aluminium which will pivot and serve as a weather vane'.(12) At a planning meeting on 14 December 1961 the combined weight of the flèche and sculpture was assessed at 3700 lbs plus or minus 100 lbs. Weight of the complete assembly had previously been assessed at 4500 lbs and the figures were regarded with some scepticism by the RAF, who preferred to lift each element separately in order to be sure of preserving the ability, with the load suspended, to maintain hover outside ground effect with one engine failed. The Consulting Engineers were nervous about side loads being accidentally applied to the top of the flèche while attempting to put the sculpture in place by helicopter. By 1 March the weight calculation was as follows: flèche 3188 lbs, sculpture 1310 lbs, strop 100 lbs, aerodynamic loading 100 lbs—total 4698 lbs. To this the weight of a protective frame for the sculpture, made necessary by what was described as its abstract nature and numerous protrusions, had to be added. In all, this load exceeded by about 600 lbs the weight with which the Belvedere could have maintained a hover outside ground effect with adequate reserve power for the manoeuvring likely to be required. Fortunately the RAF plan to lift each element separately was agreed since the flèche itself could not be physically weighed in advance, could not be returned to its stowage once lifted out, and was calculated by reference to the Belvedere's torquemeters when the lift was made, to be well in excess of 3500 lbs weight. It was within the Belvedere's ability to carry this weight with one engine failed at an air temperature of $+8\,°C$, but would have been exceeded by the sculpture being carried at the same time.

The structure of the Cathedral itself complicated the task considerably the roof consisting of a concrete shell supported only by the outer walls being very delicate. The inner roof, a mesh of concrete beams carried on pillars down either side of the

Nave, contributes nothing to the support of the outer roof which was said to be only a few inches thick at the centre where the flèche was to be placed.*

The experts were also concerned about the danger of the roof being punctured; not only would it crack along the entire length, but if one or more of the concrete beams of the inner roof were broken, the geometric integrity would be lost and the structure might collapse along the whole length of the Nave. There was also a risk that significant vibration of the roof near the point at which the suspension cables carrying the engraved glass panelled window forming the entire West Wall were pegged, (only some 15 feet from where the flèche was to be placed) would cause some or all of the glass panels to fall out. The Cathedral was due to be inaugurated by Her Majesty The Queen in May.

Special techniques had to be designed for controlling the aircraft as a result of these strictures, two main considerations arising from the fact that the aircraft would be required to hover with great accuracy at a height of about 200 feet above ground for placing the flèche, and up to 300 feet when inserting the sculpture. Firstly, use of the collective lever to guarantee the very small rates of descent demanded would clearly be impractical, so it was decided to achieve a state of equilibrium with the loads about six feet above their intended places, and accomplish the descent by human muscle power applied to the loads themselves, (four men for the flèche and eight men for the sculpture). This in turn demanded an absence of turbulence and therefore restricted the operation to wind speeds of 5 knots or less. Secondly, because the Belvedere rotor speed was at all times manually controlled via the twist grip on the collective lever, very frequent reference to the RPM gauge was essential. The accuracy of hover required, so far distant from points of visual reference, practically prevented frequent reference to cockpit instruments. For these reasons, a second pilot was employed to handle the collective lever and throttle, thus performing the automatic rotor RPM governing feature provided mechanically in all later turbine-engined helicopters. (He handled the collective lever only because it incorporated the throttle.) This procedure was particularly suitable for the twin rotor helicopter since, there being no fuselage torque variations with power changes,

---

*This was the main reason for requesting helicopter assitance in the first place. The flèche with its sculpture was expected to be too delicate to be lifted from its horizontal assembly position to the vertical without support at several points, and this would have required several winches to be positioned on the roof which was not stressed to carry them. The largest crane in the country (in a Scottish shipyard) could not be erected close enough to the Nave for its 'reach' to be sufficient, while a scaffold bridge would have needed to be some 300 feet high to cross the roof diagonally and would probably have involved the removal of some ancient 'listed' buildings nearby.

Carrying the flèche along the Coventry Cathedral roof.

Securing the flèche on Coventry Cathedral.

the first pilot could be left with control of both cyclic stick and rudder pedals. The technique was described as 'Split Control' and used effectively in FEAF on a number of occasions, for example, when positioning ground radar equipment on hill top sites and for certain night flying developments.

A third major requirement was that the loads had at all times to be prevented from developing a swing, since there was no way in which the aircraft could have acted to dampen it. Accordingly, four ropes were attached to both loads, each handled by two airmen, purely to control any tendency for a swing to develop. These parties had to be duplicated in the car park from where the loads were lifted, as well as on the Cathedral roof, as the loads had to traverse the whole length of the Nave. Altogether, 24 airmen were directly involved in handling and placing the loads, with another translating into visual signals the orders coming by radio from the aircraft crewman via the control officer on the roof. The entire party was found from No 72 Squadron and RAF Odiham, the airmen being Squadron servicing crews.

Throughout March, 1962, these techniques were thoroughly tested at Odiham and the handling parties familiarised with their tasks. Models of the size and weight calculated by the experts were made of both the flèche and the sculpture plus a duplicate of the 70 feet scaffold tower in which the flèche was to be mounted prior to lifting. Both models and the strops and slings to carry both them and the real loads, were designed by Mr Wilding of Westlands Aircraft Ltd, Bristol Helicopter Division, who personally advised on all dynamic and aerodynamic considerations throughout the operation and its planning. The first model of the flèche was built by the Army, a more rigid and robust one, found to be required by the demands of the rehearsals, being constructed out of scaffold tubing by John Laings under the direction of Mr Wilding. The practice model of the sculpture was built in station workshops as directed by the Squadron Engineering Officer—Fg Off R Bates. The essential part played by Mr Wilding, by kind permission of Westland Aircraft Ltd, was the only outside assistance given to No 72 Squadron and RAF Odiham in carrying out the task. The flèche was successfully placed in position shortly after dawn on 26 April 1962 and was followed by a trial run with a dummy load representing the sculpture, partly to exercise the handling parties but mainly to identify appropriate hover reference. The sculpture was carried on an 80 feet strop in order to minimise side loads on the flèche in case of aircraft lateral movement while the three foot spike on which the sculpture was mounted was entering the tube at the top of the flèche. The clearance between the spike and the tube was about an eighth of an inch. The hover reference selected was an industrial building about two miles distant. After waiting for the wind to subside, an attempt to place the sculpture was made in late evening, but failed when the attachment of the lead rope to the end of the spike was broken as the point of the spike struck the edge of the tube. The lead rope was useful to guide the spike, but essential for pulling the load (and the aircraft) down to put the sculpture in place. It was attached to the spike by a short length of cargo lashing chain welded to the tip of the spike. The sculpture was successfully returned to its cradle in the car park, and after rewelding the chain to the spike and rethreading the rope through the flèche, a successful attempt was made to place the sculpture in the flèche shortly after dawn on 28 April, 1962.

Quite apart from the very favourable publicity resulting from the Coventry Cathedral operation, much was learnt about the technique for handling unusual loads by helicopters with a high degree of precision; this was to be of considerable value later in certain operations.*

Although trials and rehearsals for the Coventry Cathedral operation had proceeded throughout March and April 1962, the flying time involved, including transit to and from Coventry, and the two lifts which together required only 45 minutes airborne time, totalled only 16 hours.

Helicopter Crewmen

In both the Coventry Cathedral operation and simultaneous HF aerial lift carried out by a Whirlwind of No 225 Squadron, the helicopter crew consisted of three pilots.

In 1962 there was still no establishment of helicopter crewmen except for the SAR units, NCO technicians normally being used in the role, following the procedure established in the first operational helicopters in Malaya in 1950 (see Chapter 2). For special tasks however, such as those involving valuable loads or those likely to prove hazardous to the aircraft, other people or property, the practice was to use a pilot to perform the crewman's task since instructions to the pilot flying the aircraft were likely to be mandatory and in certain circumstances could have dramatic consequences. In the case of Coventry Cathedral, the pilot acting as crewman needed to have the ability for instantaneous release of the cargo hook to obviate risk of damaging the flèche by introducing side loads after the base of the

---

*The identical technique was used for a similar task when, towards the end of 1966, a problem arose in the mounting of a 30 foot high metal cross in the top of a tall slender tower of the Hakka Methodist Church in Newton Road, Singapore. The problem had been mentioned conversationally to the Air Commander Far East, Air Marshal Sir Peter Wykeham who, having been AOC No 38 Group at the time of the Coventry operation, was able to pass the task to the same pilot, Wg Cdr Dowling, then comanding the Helicopter Wing at Seletar. The success of the operation is commemorated by a metal plaque near the base of the tower ascribing the task to No 66 (Belvedere) Squadron.

Preparing to insert the sculpture into the flèche.

Completion of the Coventry Cathedral operation.

flèche was secured, or after the sculpture had been placed in the flèche. There was objection in principle to allowing such a facility to be provided for other than the pilot flying the aircraft. The pilot had to insist on a cargo hook release button being provided at the crewman's station which was in fact used, but was removed as soon as the operation was complete. Eighteen years later, the Sea King crewman was to be given the facility to manoeuvre the helicopter itself.

There was no room for a crewman in the SRT Sycamores and inadequate performance in the Mks 2 or 4 SRT Whirlwinds to warrant one. Consequently, the early Whirlwind SRT Squadrons had become accustomed to operating without a crewman, and the advent of the Mk 10 Whirlwind did not change this situation. It was the Belvedere, with its rear undercarriage and cargo hook so far behind the pilot, and the absence of any easy access between the cockpit and passenger compartment which highlighted the need for a crewman. Even so, no formal Belvedere crewman establishment was provided, the selection and training of volunteer servicing NCOs to perform the role being left to the units concerned.

Operationally this proved quite satisfactory as it had been and still was in FEAF, the airmen concerned becoming fully proficient in the role, and providing advisory assistance to the pilot in low level navigation. This 'ad hoc' arrangement however eventually came up against the administrative problem of status and remuneration. These technicians were not technically aircrew, and could not be rewarded with the sum allotted for 'crewman pay'—a phrase invented long before helicopters came into the picture—amounting to two shillings and threepence (12p) per day.

It was the Belvedere units therefore which led the way in 1961 and 1962 in proposing a new aircrew category of 'helicopter crewmen' for all helicopters, recognising that there was no existing aircrew category properly suited to the role. There was strong opposition to this proposal but two fatal accidents in which the crewmen were killed, one in Germany in 1962 and one in Borneo in 1963, highlighted the anomaly of permanently carrying crew members who had no aircrew status. In 1963, Headquarters Transport Command sponsored a FEAF suggestion that the anomaly should be removed and at a meeting held at the Ministry of Defence on 7 August 1963, it was decided that in view of the servicing requirements of the helicopter, Air Engineers should be used in the role of Belvedere helicopter crewman. Subsequently a similar case was made and approved for Wessex and Whirlwind helicopters also.(13)

By March, 1965, the distortions thus generated in the Air Engineer trade, coupled with the distaste of the Air Engineers for this new role, (the old ones found it too rough and strenous and the young ones felt it inappropriate to their engineering status) caused a new appraisal to be made. The Director of Flying Training, making a strong case against continuing to use Air Engineers in the helicopter crewman role, and a less strong one against using Air Signallers and Air Quartermasters because of their lack of engineering qualifications, said their continued use could only be justified if surpluses existed in those trades. He firmly recommended a return to Squadron servicing personnel volunteers, to be allowed for in engineering establishments, and granted appropriate status and flying pay.(14)

There were however still strong objections to creating a new aircrew trade and in any case there existed a surplus of Air Signallers. Air Engineers as crewmen had first reached No 66 Squadron in FEAF, in 1965. Air Signallers arrived as helicopter crewmen in No 110 (Sycamore/Whirlwind) Squadron in Butterworth in the same year. When those sources were no longer available, Air Quartermasters started to appear in the crewman role, reaching No 66 Squadron in 1968.

Second Two Years SRT Development at Odiham—1962/63

1962 and 1963 saw the first fruits of the policy decisions described in Chapter 9. It also saw the end of the first era of SRT development as most of the original squadrons at Odiham disappeared overseas never to return. The No 72 Squadron number plate was however transferred to the newly forming Wessex Squadron in 1964, and No 230 Squadron re-appeared briefly in 1967/68 before re-forming with Pumas in 1972 (Phase 4).

No 230 Squadron was a busy Single and Twin Pioneer SRT unit incorporating a Conversion Flight which amounted to an Operational Conversion Unit (OCU) in early 1962. It performed the unique feat of converting gradually to a helicopter unit over a period of eight months while operating all three types of aircraft with OCU services for both Pioneers and Whirlwinds Mk 10. In May 1962 the Operation Record Book records the arrival of the first two Whirlwinds on this Pioneer Squadron and 'looks forward to receiving pilots trained on helicopters (by the CFS Helicopter Training Wing) to fly them'. A QHI from No 225 Squadron started work on operational conversion for the new helicopter pilots in June. For the next five months, Pioneer operations continued but reduced as helicopters increased although the Pioneer OCU activities continued unabated. In October the Squadron received its Standard from the HRH The Duke of Gloucester, and in December a helicopter-trained Squadron Commander (Sqn Ldr Thomas) took over from Sqn Ldr West. In December 1962, Pioneer operations ceased for No 230 Squadron and the Pioneer Conversion Flight became a separate unit at Odiham. The helicopter training continued in preparation for a planned move to Gutersloh Germany which took place in January 1963.

For the next two years, No 230 Squadron operated from Gutersloh in support of the Army in exactly the same way as No 225 Squadron had done at Odiham. Major exercises in the field were interspersed with numerous short detachments with three or four aircraft and the usual activities of casualty evacuations, VIP communication flights and occasional diversions on behalf of the local population. For example in June 1963 considerable kudos was acquired when a farmer's cow was rescued from a peat bog as an underslung load.(15) There were no major technical difficulties, the Squadron achieving between 200 and 350 hours monthly and generally providing a reliable service.

The No 225 Squadron habit of operating without crewmen was automatically adopted by No 230 Squadron but early in 1964 the latter Squadron voiced the opinion that the absence of communication between the pilot and his passengers should be resolved. This echoed the conclusion of No 848 RN Squadron in Malaya after their first troop carrying operation in 1953—see Chapter 3—but nothing was done about it.

When the need to provide helicopter transport for the United Nation Forces in Cyprus (UNFICYP) arose in February 1964, the task inevitably fell to No 230 Squadron since No 225 Squadron together with the Belvedere Squadrons (except the training rump of No 72 Squadron) had departed to Aden and Borneo. Four Whirlwinds of No 230 Squadron, together with air and ground crews, were detached to Cyprus to join 1563 Flight, (see Chapter 8), briefly called 'Nicosia Helicopter Squadron', but settling down a month later as the 'UNFICYP Flight'. This detachment, rotated by No 230 Squadron every four weeks, formed the first of a series of Squadron detachments for the UNFICYP task which continued well beyond the end of Phase 4 of this account. It temporarily came to an end for No 230 Squadron when the whole unit was withdrawn to UK at the end of 1964 immediately prior to its departure to the Far East for the Borneo operations in January 1965. The UNFICYP task was carried on by the SAR helicopters of Coastal Command until the newly formed No 18 Squadron Wessex were in position in February 1965. (No 230 Squadron was destined for two further UNFICYP detachments after its withdrawal from FEAF, one in 1968 the other in 1970/71).

Back at Odiham, No 225 Squadron, re-equipped with Whirlwinds Mk 10 in the first quarter of 1962, and in conjunction with the Belvederes, continued throughout 1962 and 1963 to carry out the repetitive task of participating in numerous small scale Army exercises with occasional full scale major training operations. In June 1962, No 66 (Belvedere) Squadron departed for Singapore, only a little later than planned, and was immediately replaced by No 26 Squadron which started as a composite unit with No 72 Squadron which had existed since November 1961. No 66 Squadron aircraft had already been shipped direct to the Far East so the effect at Odiham was no more than a change of titles and personnel. No 72 Squadron functioned during this period mainly as a Belvedere OCU, using the Army exercises as part of their own training scenario, whilst giving birth to No 26 Squadron. Comments on some of the salient features of five major exercises will serve to describe the most noticeable events in this period.

The conversion of No 225 Squadron crews on the turbine-engined Mk 10 Whirlwind took place in January and February 1962, although due to delays in production the full complement of 14 aircraft was not achieved until June. So important were the Army Support exercises considered that for part of this time numbers were made up by temporary diversion of six Mk 10 Whirlwinds destined for No 22 (SAR) Squadron. The pilot conversion presented no problem since the Mk 10 Whirlwind was basically the same aircraft as the Mk 2 with its two major difficulties—manual control of rotor speed and a critical shortage of power—removed. From this moment, the ability of helicopter pilots to control rotor speed manually started to decline. By November of that year, owing to an engine computer failure which required investigation, Whirlwinds were temporarily restricted to operating without using the engine-governing computer, and as a result only previously experienced pilots could be used on Exercise 'Winged Coachman' in Northern Ireland, and even they were limited to lifting supplies of fuel and food essential to allow the exercise to proceed on the ground.

Offensive Armament. In accordance with the policy to allow limited offensive armour to be fitted to SRT Helicopters (see Chapter 9), it was announced in January 1962 that the Nord SS-11 wire guided missile (optically guided from the cockpit) was to be available for optional fitting to the Mk 10 Whirlwind. Four pilots attended a course on the weapon in Paris in January.

Exercise Blind Mouse 4. Exercise Blind Mouse 4 in July 1962 was the first major exercise in Germany in which the Whirlwinds of No 225 Squadron were joined by fully operational Belvederes. The whole of No 225 Squadron was involved, together with five Belvederes provided by a mix of Nos 26 and 72 Squadrons' crews. The exercise itself was a great success from the SRT Force point of view although it ended tragically. The Whirlwinds as usual acquitted themselves admirably, as did the Belvederes which not only demonstrated the deployment of the Honest John Tactical Rocket nuclear warhead, but recovered a Whirlwind, slightly damaged in an engine failure forced landing, minus only its fuel and main rotor blades, 25 miles to Gutersloh as an underslung load. By a cruel irony the pilot of this Whirlwind, who had suffered but survived a wire strike by a power cable over the Dortmund Ems Canal during the deployment phase of the exercise, and later carried out this successful engine-off landing without injury to himself, navigator and six troops, was returning to England on 30 July as a passenger in one of the Belvederes, having been delayed at Gutersloh for the consequent Board of Inquiry. This aircraft crashed a few minutes after take off killing all on board, including Squadron leader Watson, the CO designate of the new No 26 Squadron, who was one of the pilots. The rotor transmission was immediately suspect and all Belvederes were grounded including the three remaining at Gutersloh and one en route to the UK which had landed to refuel at Coxyde. The grounding also halted No 66 Squadron, now in Singapore and engaged in assembling and air testing their newly arrived aircraft.

This catastrophe so early in the life of this controversial aircraft caused considerable concern in Whitehall, especially as it seemed to throw doubt on the basic integrity of the twin rotor transmission. The rotors had evidently either hit each other or the fuselage, and the wreckage had burnt on impact. It was soon discovered however that the sequence had been a loss of rotor speed (from 250 to an estimated 140 RPM) allowing the rear rotor to strike the fuselage, and that the front engine was serviceable but had already stopped at the time of the crash. The conclusion was that the rear engine had failed, that the pilot had mistakenly shut down the front engine and had then failed to enter auto-rotation, presumably in the confident expectation that double power from the supposedly remaining engine would be comfortably sufficient to continue the flight. The fears expressed by the BTU after their engine failure and forced landing in 1960, that confusion was likely due to the laterally disposed switches for the longitudinally disposed engines, were now tragically justified. It was too late to re-design the cockpit, so the unsatisfactory palliative consisted of painting prominent white lines round each group of engine controls, marking them boldy No 1 and No 2 and warning the pilots to be careful. After so many years with only single engined helicopters, it is significant that it was also found prudent to issue a general instruction reminding pilots of the primary and overriding concern which should be applied to the maintenance of adequate rotor speed in all circumstances.(16) The Belvederes were ungrounded at the end of September 1962. Fifteen months after this accident, in October 1963, a similar mistake was made with happier consequences during Exercise 'Triplex West' in Libya.

In this case, the pilot was a very experienced QHI. He was flying at 300 feet with 13 RAF Regiment passengers when a mulfunction of the rear engine caused him to order the co-pilot to stop that engine. At the same time he instinctively entered a steep turn into wind and lowered the collective lever in preparation for a possible forced landing, although the remaining engine should easily have permitted the flight to continue. The co-pilot, mindful of the accident in Germany just described, delayed taking any action while trying to determine whether the first pilot had correctly identified the engine to be stopped. However he was overridden by the first pilot who himself stopped No 2 engine and was then astonished to find himself with no engine power at all. However, due to his previous precautionary steps he was then able to carry out a fully controlled engine-off landing straight ahead with only slight forward motion. There were no injuries. The ground was soft and the front undercarriage collapsed in shear when the wheels sank through the surface. The deceleration was sufficient to operate the crash switches thus isolating the electrics and enabling the subsequent investigation to prove positively that the front engine (No 1) had been switched off in flight. Thus, the first pilot had correctly stopped the No 2 engine and the co-pilot although incredulous afterwards, was shown to have simultaneously stopped the No 1 engine in error. This confusion under stress, exacerbated by the fact that in the Belvedere the pilots flew alternately from the left and right seats, was due in part to the cockpit design so that even when pilots were fully alert to the possibility of error, the wrong engine switches were likely to be selected. All that could be done was once more to warn the pilots to be careful.

As a footnote to this accident it is interesting to record that unknown to the pilots the rear end of the aircraft was on fire, as a result of a fuel leak which had caused the initial malfunction. Had the No 1 engine not been stopped in error, the pilot would have climbed to 1000 feet and set course for base and there would have been a catastrophic failure in which all the evidence would probably have been destroyed.

It was the practice during this learning phase of the Belvedere to fly with two pilots, although the aircraft specification required it to be operable by only one. It was after Exercise Blind Mouse 4 that No 72 Squadron made the recommendation that two-pilot operation should be normal (split control as used in the Coventry Cathedral operation was used for accurate emplacement of the Honest John nuclear warhead). The death of the crewman in the Belvedere accident in Germany previously mentioned revived the case for establishing an aircrew trade of 'helicopter crewman'.(17)

Exercise Falltrap. Falltrap was the name given to an exercise involving paratroops in Greece in September 1962. Whirlwinds were used to provide casualty evacuation services for the paratroops. Although only three Whirlwinds were involved, the exercise is mentioned because it shows the rate of effort which was sometimes demanded. The whole of No 225 Squadron had been deployed in Germany for Exercise Blind Mouse 4 in July. In the following September No 225 Squadron again deployed six Whirlwinds to Germany for training for 1 BR Corps and a further six for the October exercises (Desert Rat and Canada Cup) as well as three for Falltrap. This amounted to one more than the total Unit Establishment (UE). Some aircraft were borrowed from the newly forming No 230 Squadron, and two pilots (previously with No 225 Squadron) from the recently formed No 26 (Belvedere) Squadron. There were three major parachute drops during 'Falltrap' and several minor ones. The Whirlwinds lifted 110 casualties, (including some carried more than once). The three aircraft and personnel (four pilots, ten technicians, two RAF Regiment gunners and one cook) were carried to and from Greece by Beverleys of the MRT Force— once again a highly successful form of deployment.(18)

Exercise Winged Coachman. From an exercise point of view, 'Winged Coachman' was a failure but it highlighted several deficiencies in the SRT Force which were normally concealed by unrepresentative circumstances, natural or contrived, in the interests of giving the Army what it wanted. The scene was Northern Ireland in November 1962 and was to have involved six Belvederes and eight Whirlwinds. Only five of the Whirlwinds arrived, three becoming unserviceable during transit through Valley. The Belvederes were delayed for two days at Odiham by the 5°C temperature limitation for start up described in Chapter 8. When they did set off they encountered such fierce headwinds and low cloud that they were forced to divert to Tern Hill. They reached Valley to find that gales up to 58 knots prevented start up (maximum wind speed for starting rotors was 50 knots). An attempt to reach Aldergrove made two days later on 17 November was frustrated by low cloud (lack of instrument flying clearance and navigation equipment) and the Belvederes were recalled to Odiham on 20 November. The five Whirlwinds, as previously mentioned, were restricted to use of manual throttle owing to a computer defect investigation and so could only be flown deliberately in manual by experienced pilots for vital food and fuel supply sorties.(19)

Exercise Cross Channel. Exercise 'Cross Channel' was an ambitious and highly successful British/French operation in which the British troops were delivered to Toulouse in Britannias of the Long Range Transport Force, and deployed from there by Belvedere into the exercise area near Caylus, about 50 miles North East of Toulouse. Seven Belvederes drawn from Nos 72 and 26 Squadrons were used, and demonstrated convincingly what was to become a noticable feature of the aircraft—its ability to deploy successfully over much greater distances than had previously been possible. The Belvederes flew tactically at low level the whole length of France. The operation was controlled by a No 38 Group FATOC at Caylus and the landing sites by MAOT from Odiham, the latter being found by using the Belvedere's only on-board navigation aid apart from the compass—a VHF homer. The aircraft was still quite new, and apart from the now usual first aid measures to persuade the engine starters to keep functioning, there were no major unserviceabilities and all seven aircraft returned in good order.(20)

Deployment to Aden. In Janaury 1963, the time had come for No 26 Squadron to start deploying to Aden. The bold decision was taken to fly two Belvederes to El Adem to take part in an Army exercise ('Sandstorm') and then to continue to Aden round the South West corner of Egypt since flight across that country was politically inappropriate. The two aircraft flew by easy stages from Odiham on 17 January 1963 via Manston, Reims, Dijon, Orange, Nice, Pisa, Naples, Brindisi, Araxos, and Souda Bay, and reached Al Adem on 25 January. The exercise was carried out successfully and, apart from the inevitable starter motor change, without trouble.

On 22 February 1963, the Squadron Commander (Sqn Ldr Hart) arrived with three pilots to take the two Belvederes to Aden where they were due on 1 March. Accompanied by a Beverley carrying spares and servicing personnel they left El Adem on 26 February via S3 (an oilfield airstrip) to Djebel Uwainat, proceeded to Wadi Halfa on 27 February, and to Port Sudan and Massua on 28 February, arriving on schedule at Aden on 1 March 1963. Both Belvederes were serviceable on arrival and immediately commenced demonstrations and trials. The aircraft performance was found to be even better than expected, and first operations commenced in May.(21) The remainder of No 26 Squadron at Odiham was merged with No 72 Squadron pending piecemeal deployment to Aden.

Exercise Triplex West. 'Triplex West'—a full scale tri-Service exercise in Libya—was in a sense a 'good finale' for the SRT Force as first constituted and it was fitting that it should be mounted in the same area as the first one in which the Force participated in 'Starlight' in 1960. Once again El Adem was the mounting base, the forward Airhead on this occasion being Bomba, an airstrip on the coast about 50 miles west. The exercise took place during the first week of October 1963, and was to require nine Whirlwinds and two Belvederes.

The Belvederes deployed themselves to El Adem without trouble, and four of the Whirlwinds were delivered by Beverley. The decision to fly the remaining five Whirlwinds to El Adem turned out to be an unfortunate one due to a combination of bad weather and unserviceability. The route was Manston-Chaumont-Orange-Genoa-Rome-Naples-Brindisi-Andravadi-Souda Bay-El Adem, the journey starting on 21 September. The first unserviceability delayed the whole party for three days at an unscheduled stop at Nice, and by the end of the month four out of the five were unserviceable. It was clear they would not arrive in time for the start of the exercise. From 1 to 3 March the party was held up at Naples, and with more unserviceability remained at Brindisi until 6 March. They arrived at Bomba on 7 March, one day before the end of the exercise, the brunt of the work having been borne by the Whirlwinds delivered by Beverley. There were other vicissitudes; the Whirlwind detachment Commander at Bomba broke his ankle on 3 October and his replacement had to be evacuated as a casualty on the 7 October; and one of the Belvederes had crashed. It was against this less than happy background that the news was received on the 10 October that, instead of returning to Odiham, the whole force would be increased by the addition of one Whirlwind and two Belvederes and would continue eastwards to Singapore for deployment to Sarawak in Borneo.

The aircraft carrier HMS Albion was to be used to convey this group to Singapore, inaugurating a method of transferring SRT helicopters between theatres of operation which was to be used with increasing frequency in the Far East. The opportunity was taken to add two further Belvederes from No 26 Squadron Odiham for delivery to Aden en route, and these were also flown to join HMS Albion at Tobruk. The extra Whirlwind was delivered by Beverley to El Adem for embarkation with the rest of the No 225 Squadron aircraft. The resident Flight at El Adem, No 1564 (Sycamore), assisted with the embarkation as reported in Chapter 5.

Odiham had thus dispersed to the Far East all but four of the No 225 Squadron Whirlwinds, and they, fitted with Nord SS-11 missiles, followed two months later in December 1963. This marked the end of the first period of the SRT Force at Odiham. Six Belvederes had been sent to El Adem, none of which would return, and only three were left at Odiham. Three remained to be delivered from the contractors. In March, the last two Belvederes for Aden were flown to the aircraft carrier HMS Bulwark at Portsmouth for transit to Aden and regular tasking at Odiham then ceased. No 72 Squadron activity reduced to Belvedere conversion courses only, and this residue was retitled the 'Belvedere Conversion Unit' in August 1964.

In January 1964, only weeks after the departure of No 225 Squadron to the Far East, the Wessex Trials Unit, which had worked at Odiham since the middle of 1963, formed into No 18 Squadron to be joined in August 1964 by No 72 Squadron as the second Wessex Squadron. No 18 Squadron took up residence in Gutersloh at the end of that year, in order to release No 230 Squadron which was now urgently needed as further reinforcement of the FEAF helicopter forces in Borneo.

Nine of the No 230 Squadron Whirlwinds were embarked on the aircraft carrier HMS Triumph on 29 January 1965, collecting in passing their four remaining aircraft from the UNFICYP in Cyprus and replacing them with three Wessex of No 18 Squadron, also making use of the carrier transit. The Squadron air and ground crews were flown to Singapore on the 19 February ready to meet the carrier and fly their aircraft to Seletar on the 22 February. After only a few days local training, the entire unit embarked on the aircraft carrier HMS Bulwark, arrived at Labuan on 10 March and commenced operations immediately. Like the personnel of No 225 Squadron their predecessors in FEAF reinforcement the No 230 Squadron personnel were not posted for a full tour in the Far East, but for a one year period unaccompanied by families. Odiham carried a heavy administrative load on behalf of the families left behind from 1964 to 1966.

No 1310 Flight

Not quite all of Odiham's Whirlwinds went Eastward to Borneo. In 1964 the Army was dealing with an internal security problem in British Guiana during preparations for a General Election leading to Independence in 1966. Army Air Corps Alouettes were being used in support, but, as in Malaya in 1950–52 and in not dissimilar topography and climate, some troop and passenger carrying capability was needed. Two Royal Navy Wessex from HMS Devonshire had been co-opted to help but they needed replacing to allow them to return to their naval duties.

No 1310 Flight, consisting of three Whirlwinds Mk 10, three pilots, one Warrant Officer, six Senior NCOs and 32 airmen was formed at Odiham on 23 July 1964. After a brief period of training and trials with a cluster grenade discharger to launch grenades from 200 feet at 35 knots and intended to deliver tear gas or smoke to break up illegal demonstrations, the Flight deployed to British Guiana in the latter part of August. The only other special equipment consisted of arrangements for mounting a Bren Gun in the cabin doorway. SARBE was by now a standard fit in all Whirlwinds for search and rescue homings.

Two of the three Whirlwinds arrived by sea in crates at Georgetown on 24 August and had to be assembled in the harbour area so that they could be flown to their base—Atkinson Field—some 25 miles away. This task was accomplished by great effort on the part of the ground crews, most of whom were new to helicopters and unaccustomed to the tropical climate, so that the first aircraft was able to take part in a planned operation—'White horse'—on 29 August. This was a typical internal security military operation to capture known criminals with illegal arms and ammunition in the relatively inaccessible jungle hinterland. The second aircraft was ready by the following day and the third arrived in October.(22)

The Flight quickly settled down to a pattern of operations practically indistinguishable, except in scale, from that in Malaya—troop lifts to deal with dissident factions in remote jungle areas, cordon and search operations similar to those carried out in Cyprus in the 1950s, reconnaissance, communications and supply tasks and the inevitable flow of both Service and civilian casualty evacuations.

British Guiana was not excessively violent and No 1310 Flight never had to use its grenade launchers or Bren Guns. As in Malaya, crewmen were trained from amongst the ground crew NCOs and carried as a matter of course. The personnel were rotated by Odiham every six months and, as was becoming typical of the small relatively independent helicopter detachment, were extremely efficient and reliable, flying between about 60 and 90 hours each month depending on the demands made upon them. There were no major accidents and morale was consistently high.

The General Election in December 1964 went off quietly, No 1310 Flight assisting in transporting ballot boxes. Towards the end of 1965, exercises were being carried out with the new Guyana Defence Force and internal security operations were dwindling. HM The Queen was able to pay a visit in February 1966 and for this event, No 1310 Flight had to be issued with special radio sets so they could contact the Guyana Police Force (part of the internal Security Forces). The state of SRT Communications capability has been mentioned previously.

26 May 1966 was Independence Day for the newly named Guyana and No 1310 Flight took part in the ceremonial fly past, and also flew the Duke and Duchess of Kent to visit Fort Wellington, New Amsterdam, Springlands and brought them back to Georgetown. The Army Air Corps helicopters withdrew in July and in September the three aircraft of No 130 Flight appeared at a ceremonial Beating of the Retreat. The Flight was disbanded two years after its formation, the Whirlwinds being returned to the UK by a Belfast of the Long Range Transport Force.(23)

Summary of Progress for the SRT Force, 1960–1964

The SRT Force of Whirlwinds and Belvederes grew rapidly at Odiham from the beginning of 1960, and disappeared equally quickly from Odiham to Aden and the Far East in 1963, preceded by No 66 (Belvedere) Squadron in 1961 and followed by No 230 (Whirlwind) Squadron from Germany in 1964. There was scarcely any measurable development in SRT techniques during that period, the method of operating being substantially the same throughout. HF radios were being fitted to the Belvederes previously scheduled for the Far East, an addition later made to the Whirlwinds, but this was more for RAF control reasons than for direct Army assistance. Communications with the Army in the field remained substantially undeveloped. The only navigation aid which was added was Decca fitted in the Whirlwinds, but there was no other technical improvement in ability to operate at night or in bad weather. Tasking of the inevitably inadequate SRT Force in the field remained a potential cause of dispute and there was no formal approved written 'Concept of Operation' for the whole Force, neither was there opportunity to construct one in the continuous hectic preparation and execution of an unending stream of so-called training exercises.

From a purely RAF point of view the efficiency of the aircrews was eminently satisfactory and the reliability of their performance, especially when required to carry out unusually difficult tasks or to take part in unexpected overseas operations in severe conditions, fully justified the efforts to maintain expertise in pure flying techniques within the full capabilities of the aircraft. In this, the influence of the CFS Helicopter Squadron and its control of individual pilot categories inevitably played an important part, as it undoubtedly did through QHI training in the numerous aircraft type conversions carried out at Odiham. Between 1960 and 1964, all operational training for both Whirlwind and Belvedere pilots during this period of maximum rate of growth of the SRT Force was carried out on the Squadrons at Odiham; as was the aircraft type conversion for Belvedere pilots.*

On two occasions during temporary grounding of the Belvederes, in September 1962 and April 1963, the ubiquitous Sycamore was recalled from retirement in the Maintenance Unit at Wroughton to provide continuation flying practice for the Belvedere pilots, and was relinquished afterwards 'with the regret of those who had had the pleasure of flying it'.(24)

---

*The Belvedere Conversion Flight which remained after No 72 Squadron re-formed with Wessex, was eventually merged with the Wessex Conversion Flight forming the 'Short Range Conversion Unit' in 1966, becoming the 'Helicoper Operational Conversion Flight' in 1967 and, with the arrival of Pumas in 1972, achieving Operational Conversion Unit status as No 240 OCU.

References to Chapter 10

1   No 38 Group ORB.

2   No 225 Group ORB.

3   ID9/94/10.

4   No 38 Group ORB.

5   Ibid.

6   BTU Trials Report.

7   ID9/94/10.

8   ID9/W2-60.

9   No 26, 72 & 66 Squadron ORBs.

10 No 72 Squadron ORB.

11 No 225 Squadron ORB.

12 Westland Report.

13 ID9/D4-35.

14 Ibid.

15 No 230 Squadron ORB.

16 ID9/94/10.

17 Nos 26 & 72 Squadron ORBS.

18 No 225 Squadron ORB.

19 Nos 225 & 26 Squadron ORBs.

20 Nos 72 & 26 Squadron ORBs.

21 No 26 Squadron ORB.

22 No 1310 Flight ORB.

23 Ibid.

24 No 26 Squadron ORB.

CHAPTER 11

THE ARABIAN PENINSULA IN PHASE 3
(1961–1971)

Background Summary

Helicopter operations in the Arabian Peninsula had been confined to the Sycamore SAR Flight at Khormaksar from 1955 (Phase 2) until the arrival of No 26 Squadron Belvederes in 1963, marking the start of Phase 3 in that Theatre.

The period between the end of the Kuwait crisis in August 1961 and the start of the large scale operations in the Radfan area of the Western Aden Protectorate two and a half years later (January 1964) is described by Sir David Lee in 'Flight from the Middle East' as a breathing space in the sense only that it constituted a brief interlude of relative calm between serious episodes which required the participation of all the forces available.

Apart from the SAR Flight in Aden and the single Sycamore in Nairobi described in Phase 2, there had been no helicopter support in the formal tactical support role in the Theatre during the activities preceding this breathing space. Helicopter tactical involvement in the final upsurge of activity in the Radfan and in Aden itself was to be crucial to the military operations eventually conducted, although the rising clamour for independence in South Arabia, coupled with the political pressures in the United Kingdom which foreshadowed the end of Middle East Command, was finally to frustrate the strategic aims of all these operations regardless of their temporary local success.

The six Belvederes of No 26 Squadron arrived in pairs over a period of more than a year starting in March 1963, a seventh being added from FEAF in mid-1964. It was not until December 1963 that the rising tide of trouble in the recently formed Federation of South Arabia, which then incorporated the Colony of Aden as Aden State, brought political and military matters to a head with a hand grenade attack on the British High Commissioner and his party whilst they were waiting to board an aircraft on that part of the tarmac used for civil aircraft at Khormaksar. Reaction was immediate, a state of emergency was declared throughout South Arabia, the frontier with the Yemen was closed, and offensive military operations by land and air on a considerable scale were decided upon. The dissident elements among the Radfan tribes, being the greatest trouble-makers and receiving most encouragement from their masters across the Yemen Frontier, were selected as the main targets for a three battalion operation planned for January 1964. This operation, titled 'Nutcracker', relied for transport and logistic support on two

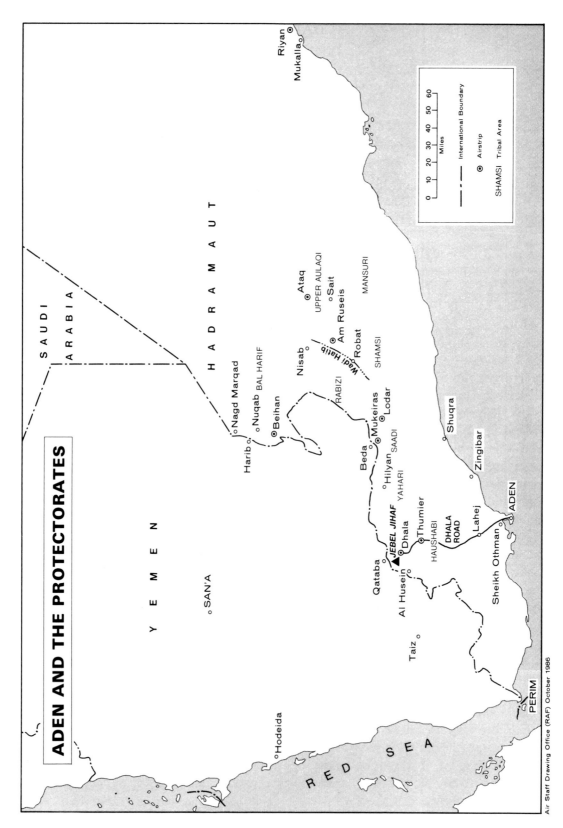

ADEN AND THE PROTECTORATES

Riyan
Mukalla

H A D R A M A U T

S A U D I

A R A B I A

Ataq
UPPER AULAQI
Sait
Am Ruseis
MANSURI

Nagd Marqad
Nuqab BAL HARIF
Beihan
Harib
RABIZI
Nisab
Wadi Hatib
Robat
SHAMSI

Mukeiras
Lodar
Beda
SAADI
Hilyan
YAHARI
JEBEL JIHAF
Dhala
Thumier
HAUSHABI
Qataba
Al Husein
DHALA ROAD
Lahej
Shuqra
Zingibar

ADEN

Sheikh Othman

Y E M E N

SAN'A

Taiz

PERIM

Hodeida

R E D   S E A

Miles

International Boundary
Airstrip
SHAMSI Tribal Area

273–A

Air Staff Drawing Office (RAF) October 1986

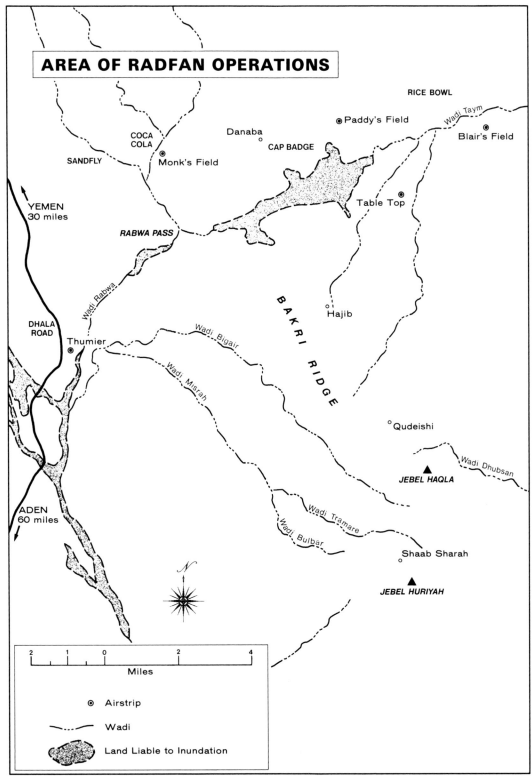

AREA OF RADFAN OPERATIONS

RICE BOWL

Wadi Taym

Paddy's Field

COCA COLA

Danaba

CAP BADGE

Blair's Field

SANDFLY

Monk's Field

Table Top

YEMEN
30 miles

RABWA PASS

Wadi Rabwa

Hajib

DHALA
ROAD

Thumier

Wadi Bigair

B A K R I   R I D G E

Wadi Misrah

Qudeishi

Wadi Dhubsan

JEBEL HAQLA

ADEN
60 miles

Wadi Tramare

Wadi Bulbar

Shaab Sharah

JEBEL HURIYAH

N

2   1   0   2   4
Miles

⊙   Airstrip

———   Wadi

Land Liable to Inundation

Air Staff Drawing Office (RAF) October 1986

273-B

26 Squadron detachment on HMS Albion during
the Mombasa/Tanganyika operation in January
1964.

26 Sqn Belvederes on HMS Centaur bound for
Dar-es-Salaam during the Mombasa/Tanganyika
operation in January 1964.

Casualty Evacuation to Thumier by Sycamore of Khormaksar SAR Flight.

Sycamore of Khormaksar SAR Flt training with RAF Marine Craft near
Steamer Point—Aden.

Belvederes and two Sycamores of the Khormaksar SAR Flight and four Royal Navy Wessex Mk 1 from HMS Centaur which happened to be available at the time. The operation lasted about three weeks.

By March 1964 it was evident that the FRA (Federal Regular Army—previously Aden Protectorate Levies) was strained beyond its resources in trying to garrison the newly controlled areas of the Radfan while manning the frontier against Yemeni incursions. It was decided to withdraw these units in the Radfan to a base at the edge of the area (Thumier), whereupon the dissidents reoccupied the area vacated and a victory was declared by Egypt and Yemen. Incursions over the border then increased as did attacks on the convoys on the Dahla Road, while the resident tribesmen joined the dissidents in increasing numbers. It was decided that still further military action involving British troops would be essential to quell the insurgency before it got out of hand. Thus in May 1964 the second and main operation commenced in the Radfan—'Operation Flamingo'.

Before this happened, however, there was a temporary diversion in the form of unrest in the newly independent East African States, and a Marine Commando force was despatched from Aden in February 1964 to deal with the military mutiny of Dar-es-Salaam. The aircraft carrier HMS Centaur, whose Wessex Mk 1 helicopters had so recently helped the Belvederes in Operation Nutcracker, were this time helped in return by two Belvederes which were embarked on HMS Centaur at Aden and used first in the seaborne troop assault and heavy lift of equipment and vehicles at Dar-es-Salaam, and subsequently on patrolling between Mombasa and Zanzibar.

The first plan for Operation Flamingo in the Radfan involved flying the whole of 45 Commando by helicopter to seize high ground and, by controlling the Danaba Basin and Wadi Taym, cut off retreats to the Yemen. No 26 Squadron then had four Belvederes, increasing to six in May. These, together with the Kormaksar SAR Flight—which had at last exchanged its Sycamores for four Whirlwinds Mk 10—and two Army Air Corps Scouts, constituted the entire helicopter force available, there being no Royal Navy aircraft carrier present at the time. This force was insufficient for the helicopter-borne troop assault required and recourse had to be made to an advance on foot with the helicopters in the support and supply role. The dominating feature named Cap Badge was eventually captured after much difficulty, and the Wadi Taym satisfactorily controlled. This experience showed that settling the Radfan was going to be a long and arduous business in which the availability of an adequate helicopter force was a major consideration.

Aggressive patrolling by the ground troops with helicopter support and re-supply continued while the return of HMS Centaur which was due later in May was awaited. Extra helicopter support including a further Belvedere and pilot from

FEAF would then be available for the next phase, the primary objective of which was the capture of Bakri Ridge. This culminated victoriously in the occupation of the formidable Jebel Huriyah, a 5500 foot peak which dominated the whole of the Radfan. This was the decisive climax of the campaign although it did not signal the end of operations in the Radfan as Government Forces, and consequently the helicopters, continued to be active at varying degrees of intensity for the whole two and a half years remaining before the final British withdrawal from Aden in 1967.

The gradual reduction of operational tempo towards the end of 1964 provided a much needed respite for Khormaksar where the Belvederes were beginning to succumb to technical problems. Yemen and Egyptian pressure was switched to the urban areas and a mounting wave of subversion and terrorism swept through Aden State itself leading directly to the withdrawal of all British Forces in 1967. Assistance was provided from time to time by Royal Navy Wessex helicopters temporarily detached from passing aircraft carriers, but the main helicopter task of maintaining the FRA and British troops in the Radfan during this period fell on the Wessex Mk II of No 78 Squadron which arrived in mid-1965 just as the Belvederes were finally collapsing and they, together with the Whirlwinds and later the Wessex of the Kormaksar SAR Flight, became progressively more involved with internal security tasks arising from the increasing subversion and terrorist activities in Aden itself in the final days before withdrawal. No 78 Squadron was the last RAF unit to leave Aden, flying a final sortie with freight and passengers from Khormaksar to HMS <u>Intrepid</u> at 1345 hours on Independence Day—29 November 1967.

Khormaksar SAR Flight

By 1963 the Sycamores of the SAR Flight had been an established feature at Khormaksar for over seven years. After a slow start, initially having been regarded with some suspicion, they had become practically indispensable both in providing a rescue capability for the fighter pilots operating in areas dramatically inhospitable in terms of topography as well as population, and in enabling VIPs and various political personages to appear at places otherwise difficult or impossible for them to reach. Such was the eventual operational reliance on this SAR Flight that there were occasions when Hunter strike operations were postponed, pending the return to standby of a SAR helicopter temporarily converted to the VIP role. This Flight was 'Khormaksar's own' and although the No 26 Squadron Belvederes and later the Wessex of No 78 Squadron borrowed crews at times it was not, despite proposals to the contrary,(1) allowed to be absorbed into the tactical helicopter squadrons until just before the final withdrawal in 1967. By contrast, in both Cyprus and FEAF the SAR function became a secondary task for the Tactical Helicopter Force. This is not to say that the Aden SAR Flight was excluded from the tactical role,

Kohrmaksar SAR Flt Sycamore over Aden.

Khormaksar SAR Flt Whirlwinds over Aden.

Gulf SAR Flt Whirlwind Casualty Evacuation to Bahrein (1967—shortly before replacement by Wessex in Comsar Bahrein).

especially when the Whirlwinds with their enhanced cabin space replaced the Sycamores. Even the Sycamores were called in to help, for example, in the first Radfan operations of January 1964,(2) while a Whirlwind, 'misemployed' for an operational reconnaissance in June 1964 was hit four times by ground fire in the Wadi Misrah two miles from Thumier.(3)

In fact the Sycamores, which had originally arrived in June 1955, had been closely associated with transport support during air operations by Shackletons and Venoms from late 1956 onwards when there was much dissident tribal activity and gunfire especially on the Yemen border,(4) but their restricted cabin size, small numbers and limited power automatically prevented them from being used in a main tactical helicopter role until the arrival of the Belvederes in 1963 made such operations possible. Nevertheless, even the SAR role throughout consisted almost exclusively of dealing with the results of ground or air activity inland from Aden and in these circumstances there was for the helicopter pilots little difference between SAR and a more formal tactical role. Frequently the Sycamores on rescue missions would themselves be supported by Venom and even Shackleton escorts to provide defence from hostile ground forces. The sea SAR role, however, was still regularly practised and full standby maintained. In May 1963, for example, the pilot of a Royal Navy Scimitar from the aircraft carrier HMS Ark Royal ejected and was rescued by Sycamore ten minutes later.(5)

Except for No 1564 Flight at El Adem, the Khormaksar SAR Flight was the last operational unit to have its Sycamores replaced by Whirlwind Mk 10s. The change took place slowly, the first two Whirlwinds arriving in January and February 1964, but requiring some role modification on arrival. The four Sycamores were flown to the aircraft carrier HMS Albion for return to the UK on 28 March but delays in modification and in the arrival of a second pair of Whirlwinds (intended ultimately to form a new SAR Flight at Muharraq) until July created a problem in Aden which was felt sufficiently keenly to cause temporary detachment in June of a Sycamore from Cyprus from where the El Adem Flight was supported.(6)

In November 1966 the SAR Flight received its first two Wessex Mk 2s, painted yellow and equipped for SAR work. The Whirlwinds, however, were retained as the internal security situation in Aden deteriorated and did not leave until May 1967. One of the Wessex was used to relieve No 78 Squadron from the increasing task of VIP transport as the internal security situation worsened (7), but once the SAR Flight had aircraft identical to the tactical force and crew borrowing between the two units became a regular and automatic procedure, the 'de facto' absorption of the SAR Flight into No 78 Squadron became inevitable, although it did not happen officially until the last few months before withdrawal when the rest of the Khormaksar establishment was being drastically reduced.

Belvederes in Aden

The arrival on 1 March 1963 of the two Belvederes constituting the first element of No 26 Squadron in Aden, as described in Chapter 10, which had flown all the way from Odiham and taken part in an Army exercise at El Adem en route (Operation Sandflight), should have been seen as a milestone in helicopter capability. The 2200 mile journey from El Adem was accomplished easily in four days, requiring 25 flying hours per aircraft (see Chapter 10). It passed almost unnoticed, in spite of the fact that Transport Command tried to generate some publicity, both to counteract general disbelief in the Belvedere itself, and to recognise that both aircraft duly arrived fully serviceable on the predicted date.

The authorities in Aden may also have had mixed feelings on the subject. Belvederes were not arriving, as it might seem in retrospect, specifically to fill a long felt need for powerful helicopter assistance in the fight against dissident tribesmen which, after several years, had become a way of life a comfortable distance away from Aden iteslf. Rather they were deployed in accordance with the previously planned worldwide five company lift capability of the new Short Range Transport Force as described in Chapter 9. Indeed redeployment had been delayed at the request of Headquarters, Air Forces Middle East the year before because of the shortage of accommodation, hangar space and technical facilities at Khormaksar (8)—hardly the response of a Command feeling dire need of tactical helicopter support.

For the Army, however, there can have been no such cautious ambivalence. During March and April 1963 the Belvederes carried out trials and training, and demonstrated beyond doubt that their performance capabilities were at least as good, and in many respects better, than predicted. All at once the ability to insert, resupply and recover whole patrols by air in places in the Jebel and Wadis north of Aden otherwise appallingly difficult to reach had become a reality, where previously the somewhat doubtful recovery of single casualties by the SAR Sycamores had been the only regular facility. Of at least equal importance was the capability to deploy and supply the 105 mm artillery guns to advantageous positions which could never have been reached otherwise.

In May 1963, three months after their arrival, the Belvederes were committed to their first formal operation (Operation Pennant) which involved four nights away from base. The engine starter troubles which became progressively worse soon forced the decision to avoid overnight stops away from Khormaksar. Anxiety on the Squadron to receive more aircraft from Odiham to build up the unit to its full size became intense, but there was no plan to repeat the self-delivery from the United Kingdom by air used for Operation Sandflight, and it is doubtful whether Khormaksar itself was enthusiastic to add to its accommodation problems. No 26 Squadron was operating from four non-air conditioned offices and two aircraft

105 mm gun having been positioned by Belvedere, being re-supplied with ammunition by a Whirlwind of the Khormaksar SAR Flight in the Gebel North of Aden.

Troops being deployed by knotted rope to defensive position near Thumier.

Beverley and Belvederes on the Strip at Thumier.

Machine gun mounting in rear hatch of Belvedere in Aden.

packing cases.(9) It was November before the aircraft carrier HMS <u>Albion</u> came past with two more of No 26 Squadron's Belvederes on board.

Khormaksar, having housed only No 8 Fighter Squadron, possessed less than 100 married quarters when the Sycamores arrived in 1955, but by 1962 had acquired its 1000th married quarter and a strength exceeding 3000 officers and airmen. At the end of 1963 it housed nine squadrons and two independent flights with a total establishment of 84 aircraft, so that although a vast building programme had been in progress for some time, accommodation needs of all kinds still presented a considerable problem.

In the meantime Belvedere operations continued on an opportunity basis—two Austers were recovered as underslung loads in June, but by July the behaviour of the starter motors which had caused prohibition of night stops away from Khormaksar were the cause of a further limitation restricting the Belvederes to an 80 nm radius of action from Aden. The Squadron Commander sought, but failed to obtain, permission to visit FEAF to see how they dealt, apparently successfully, with this and other Belvedere problems; and he also failed in an attempt to obtain field camping equipment to enable aircraft and crews to night stop away from base—already a well established No 38 Group practice at Odiham where No 26 Squadron had spent the formative months of its re-birth as a helicopter unit. To add to his frustration he was unsuccessful in his attempts to secure more suitable Squadron accommodation. All these factors doubtless enhanced the feeling on the unit that the No 26 Squadron Belvederes seemed to be regarded almost as much of a nuisance as an operational asset on the very busy and overcrowded multi-role fixed-wing operational airfield of Khormaksar,(10) described by the Commander-in-Chief in March 1964 as the largest and most complex station in the RAF.(11)

This attitude on the part of the Squadron may in retrospect seem to be somewhat paranoid, but it must be remembered that a very similar feeling of local scepticism initially prevailed in FEAF in 1950, Cyprus in 1956 and Khormaksar itself during the first years of the SAR Sycamores in 1955/56. Khormaksar in 1963 came late into the full scale tactical helicopter business, and No 26 Squadron, having grown in the enthusiastic highly mobile tactical helicopter environment of No 38 Group, was yet to make its way in what seemed by contrast to be an excessively cautious atmosphere. This factor helped to cause the sharp contrast between the development of the large tactical helicopter in Aden and that in FEAF.

In the first nine months of the Belvedere's presence in Aden—March to December 1963—not much had happened. Operational trials and training of pilots, Corporal crewmen volunteers from amongst the ground crew, and soldiers of the Federal Regular Army (FRA) in roping techniques proceeded. Operation Pennant in May served mainly to convince the authorities that the Belvedere was too difficult to maintain away from Khormaksar, especially in respect of engine starters, and by July the infant No 26 Squadron with only two aircraft was actually feeling frustrated by lack of tasking, the 80-mile radius limitation placed on their operations and the long delay in receiving more of their aircraft from Odiham. In 1963 operations in Borneo had priority and Odiham was more concerned with providing aircraft and trained Belvedere crews for that theatre. In October two pilots went back from Aden to Odiham to collect the next two Belvederes and ferry them to El Adem for embarkation on the aircraft carrier HMS Albion from which they were delivered in Aden in November. During this period the Squadron, thus reduced to three pilots, felt some dismay when another was removed for his turn in the full-time administrative post of Sergeants' Mess Treasurer, leaving only the Squadron Commander, Flight Commander and the single Squadron Navigator as the operational element. This seemed to confirm their impression that they were scarcely regarded as a vital operational asset to the Station.

The arrival of the second two Belvederes from Odiham in November 1963 occurred just as the severe conditions of the theatre were beginning to show their serious impact on the first two. Rotor blade erosion due to abrasive dust had grounded one aircraft and the second was developing a similar condition. There were insufficient rotor blade replacements. In the following month a troop deployment to a 6200 foot ridge had to be abandoned due to excessive turbulence, a most unusual but nevertheless revealing incident. Elsewhere a few successful placings of 105 mm artillery guns and crews were carried out. The following year was to be very different.

1964 was to be the year of the Belvedere in Aden, seeing both its valuable contribution to the Radfan operations as well as the beginning of its demise in this theatre.

Method of Operating in the Radfan

The pattern of bases was very close to the ideal taught by the Joint Warfare Establishment. Khormaksar was the MRT Air Head into which the long range Comets and Britannias could operate without restriction. About 40 miles north across desert at the edge of the Jebel lay the SRT Air Head at Thumier (later known as Habilayn). It consisted simply of a dusty airstrip originally 350 yards long, well suited to operations by the Twin Pioneer aircraft of No 78 Squadron. Later in the operation it was lengthened to permit use by Beverley transport aircraft. The distances from Thumier to the scenes of operation were very satisfactorily short, being only about 15 miles from the semi-permanent landing and delivery sites eventually established for the helicopters in the forward areas, and in some instances considerably less. Sortie lengths varied from five to twenty-five minutes. Indeed, from a security point of view Thumier was uncomfortably close

Belvedere positioning 105 mm guns North of Aden.

'One ton containers' ready for re-supply in forward area. Dust problem very evident in the prolonged hover required.

Belvedere landing near a Beverley at Beihan.

Belvedere at Thumier attempting to land ahead of its dust cloud.

to the enemy in the mountains and was frequently subject to rocket and rifle fire especially at night. For this reason, as well as because of total absence of servicing facilities of any sort, every effort was made to get helicopters back to Khormaksar at or soon after last light. This ferry flight was sometimes done after dark but night landings at Thumier were not practicable because airfield lighting was almost certain to attract enemy fire. This was the only operational night flying required of the Belvederes and occasionally it would have to be made on one engine when the second one defied all attempts in the field to start it. During Radfan operations, engines were never stopped away from Thumier. Refuelling there was for some time carried out by the time-consuming and exhausting use of hand pumps from 44 gallon drums; much later a bowser was provided, but it seems that initially there was little expectation of the comparatively long term continuous use of Thumier which was to become the pattern. It was over a year after the first Radfan operation before any serious attempt was made to provide restful conditions (tents and chairs) for the air and ground crews doing their daily stint in the heat and choking dust of Thumier.

Such toleration by the crews was not matched by the aircraft engines. The Belvedere with its downward pointing air intakes suffered a good deal of compressor blade erosion resulting from the self-generated sandstorm in which, in addition to take-offs and landings, it was obliged for the majority of its tasks to hover while hooking on the external loads. Adhesion of fine grit to the engine compressor blades and inlet guide vanes exacerbated the already difficult starting problems by causing engine surging. Engines with an intended life of 400 hours at that stage were on average achieving only 110 hours. At the end of May 1964 an oil and PSP landing site had been constructed at Thumier by No 5000 Airfield Construction Squadron and this helped considerably. Nevertheless, by 15 July 1964 15 'out of phase' engine changes had been carried out.

Later it was found that a further great improvement could be achieved by sealing off the whole wire cage covering the engine intake for a surprisingly small loss of only 5% of engine power of which the Belvedere had a comfortable surplus.

The further effect of this pattern of operating was that amongst the equipment which the Belvedere had to carry on leaving Khormaksar was its own spare supply of the noxious avpin starter fluid—highly toxic, explosive and virtually unextinguishable if ignited. It would not be found at Thumier or anywhere else away from Khormaksar.

Command and Control

Thumier housed the Brigade Headquarters conducting the Radfan operations and exercised operational control over the helicopters allotted daily for the task by

Headquarters AFME in Aden. Tasking was by the Brigade Air Support Officer (BASO) who lived at the Brigade Headquarters. In the later stages there was a small Air Traffic Control Organisation and an indispensable Mobile Air Movement team for assembling the freight loads in the correct size and order.

Operation Nutcracker

To return to the beginning of the Radfan operations, 'Nutcracker' in January 1964 was an assault by the 3rd Battalion of the FRA with helicopter support consisting of two Belvederes, four Naval Wessex Mk 1 of No 815 Squadron and the Sycamores of the Khormaksar SAR Flight. It was a demonstration of power aimed at the tribal stronghold in the Wadi Misrah, and aimed to convert the track in the Wadi Rabwa to one usable by jeep in order to gain access to the Wadi Taym for future use.

The four carrier borne Naval Wessex of No 815 Squadron were used to reinforce the troop and supply movements, the Sycamores of the Khormaksar SAR Flight being used mainly in the casualty evacuation role.

Between 3 and 15 January the Belvederes carried out numerous troop and resupply sorties and 105 mm gun deployments. Hunter cover was provided but right at the outset a Belvedere received 5 hits from ground fire, and the wearing of protective flak vests and carriage of light machine guns for suppressive fire was authorised. The aircraft was plagued throughout by engine starting problems, so introducing a disturbing element of unreliability into planned operations.

Shipborne Assault in East Africa

On 20 January, only five days after the Belvederes completed their task in Operation Nutcracker, two Belvederes with five pilots and six technical crewmen were embarked on the commando carrier HMS Centaur to join the Wessex of No 815 Squadron for operations with the Royal Marine Commandos in East Africa following a mutiny by the 1st Battalion of the Tanganyika Rifles. A dawn assault on Colito Barracks, Dar-es-Salaam, was carried out successfully using four Wessex and both Belvederes. The first Belvedere took 20 minutes to get started, the second one hour and 25 minutes.(12) Fortunately there was only light opposition on shore, and that was quickly suppressed. The Belvederes carried troops, Land Rovers and other heavy equipment. Later the same morning, a similar helicopter-borne commando assault was made on Dar-es-Salaam Airport where no opposition was encountered. This was also followed by much ship to shore shuttling of troops and equipment, the Belvedere engine starters continuing to cause a good deal of trouble. Although this was the second time a ship-mounted helicopter assault was made on land, the first being on the Suez Canal area in 1956, it was the first time that helicopters

Belvedere refuelling at Thumier using 44 gallon drums and a mechanical pump. Note the proximity of the front engine jet pipers.

Belvedere re-supply at Obad—6000 ft above sea level and 15 miles West of Beihan. The tail stabiliser constituted a considerable problem amongst the rocks.

Re-supply in the Radfan 2 miles East of Thumier. Note the front wheels 'castored' to prevent movement down the slope.

Belvedere in the Radfan 4 miles East of Thumier.

had led the landing and were the sole aircraft involved. Vehicles and heavy equipment were included in the helicopter lift.

Although the Dar-es-Salaam operation had been successfully completed there was still unrest in the area and the Belvederes were transferred to HMS Victorious when it arrived on 29 January to replace HMS Centaur. The original detachment starting on 20 January had been expected to last seven days, but on 10 February another ship change took place and the Belvederes appeared on HMS Albion which continued to cruise between Dar-es-Salaam, Mombasa and Zanzibar. Several exercises with the Marine Commando and the RN helicopters were arranged and were inevitably characterised by the usual struggle with the Belvedere engine starters. Much help was given by the RN helicopter technicians who were accustomed to the same starter arrangement for their Mk 1 Wessex, but for some reason the Belvederes seemed even more troublesome. Some conclusions about both the appropriateness of the rectification procedures and the nature of the problem itself may be drawn from the fact that when operational pressure was high the Royal Navy's first remedy for a failure to start often consisted of hitting the Avpin Injector a smart blow with a hide faced hammer, and this sometimes worked.(13)

On 19 February preparations were made against the possibility of having to evacuate British nationals from Zanzibar and next day HMS Albion appeared off-shore with three escort vessels. Night flying briefing was carried out for the helicopter crews, but operations were not required. HMS Albion disembarked the Belvederes at Aden on 26 February, five weeks after they had started on a seven-day detachment. Starter troubles were the only technical problems recorded by No 26 Squadron during that period but they were described as endemic. They were hardly likely to improve the Belvedere's reputations with the Royal Navy and Royal Marines. Such technical support as could be provided at long range was supplied from Khormaksar throughout the period.

Appendix No 10 to the Middle East Command ORB described the AFME operations in East Africa, mainly concerned with troop movements by Hastings and Beverley aircraft in Kenya and Somalia, without mentioning the Belvedere maritime operation at all.

Aden Operations Continued

Back in Aden, Operation Nutcracker had been described as a success in that the road through the Jebel Radfan was completed, although a further limited operation (Rustum) was arranged to maintain law and order on the doubtful assumption that such had been established. FRA patrols were, however, still being attacked and in February a Belvedere was used to ferry a Forward Air Control Post to a suitable position to control further air strikes. It returned with a dead Company Commander and two wounded FRA soldiers.

Elsewhere across-border enemy activity also continued and in March a remote Federal Guard post north of the fertile area around Beihan was attacked by an enemy helicopter escorted by two MIG fighters. The response was an attack by eight Hunters using cannons and rockets, which destroyed an enemy fort over the Yemen border. The Belvederes, still carrying only VHF radio were unable to speak to the Hunters, and this lent urgency to the belated fitting of UHF radios and homers.

The Belvederes had demonstrated some of their capability and were being regarded with new respect on the station. In April 1964, 14 months after their arrival, they acquired a single office, 15 feet × 9 feet, for use by the complement which now consisted of six pilots, including the Squadron Commander and Flight Commander, one navigator and three crewmen. There was no air conditioning. March and April represented a breathing space after Operation Nutcracker and the East African operations which was useful for new pilot training and catching up on continuation training including night and simulated instrument flying which, although not likely to be needed in this theatre, was maintained as far as possible in accordance with standard RAF practice. Even so, ad hoc tasking, eg for Army exercises, visiting the scene of a Hunter crash at 7000 feet altitude, carriage of No 13 (RE) Field Survey Team and practise firing of bren guns by crewmen in the new mountings provided in the doorways, resulted in the monthly task hours actually being exceeded.

Main Radfan Operation—Flamingo

The main Radfan operation lasted from 1 May to mid-June 1964. During the first five days the chief objective was capturing the precipitous 'Cap Badge' feature which dominated both the Danaba Basin and the Wadi Taym into which the troops were then able to penetrate in the face of considerable opposition.

Cap Badge, only 15 miles North East of Thumier, was such a dominant feature in the Wadi Taym area that it was to be permanently held by the Army throughout the whole period from its capture in May 1964 until final cessation of operations in 1967. Being a steep sided rocky outcrop rising abruptly from a flat desert area and usually surrounded by enemy, it relied heavily on helicopter support and maintenance. The usable space at the top was so small that explosives had to be used to create even a minimum sized landing site for the helicopters. Belvederes delivering under-slung loads on the only area available would often have insufficient room remaining to land in order to recover the lifting strop which was dropped with the load, and would have to recover it by means of a rope previously attached and hauled into the door by the crewman. These restrictions often applied at other landing sites where the length of the aircraft could be an embarrassment, often placing the pilot over the edge of a precipice and the cargo hook over the landing site, while the rear end of the Belvedere was projecting over another valley.(14) A constant problem was a tendency to suffer minor damage to the low slung and downward sloping tail stabilizers amongst the rocks.

The second part of the two-phase operation was delayed a few days to await the arrival from Singapore of the aircraft carrier HMS Centaur with the Royal Navy Wessex helicopters, an extra Belvedere on loan from FEAF bringing the Squadron strength up to seven, and two 5.5 inch guns from Singapore which would greatly extend the range of the available artillery. It was aimed south of the Wadi Taym at the Wadi Misrah and the Bakri Ridge and started on 24 May, culminating in occupation of the Jebel Huriyah which was successfully achieved on 11 June. For the helicopters, however, the rate of operation throughout Operation Flamingo was more or less constant, the daily supply of food, water and ammunition being a never-ending task interspersed with troop redeployment, casualty evacuation and the re-siting of artillery in commanding positions as the troops moved towards their objectives.

The following extract from the No 26 Squadron Operations Record Book for May 1964 gives a good idea of the character of the Belvedere operations during Operation Flamingo, which was also the high point of Belvedere activity in the theatre:

26 SQUADRON—MAY 1964		The entire Squadron effort this month has been devoted to Operation Flamingo in the Radfan area, Western Aden, in co-operation with the Army and Royal Marines. During this period 613 operational sorties were flown in 225 hours. The loads totalled 1083974 lbs freight, 1254 troops and passengers and 47 casualties.
Radfan	1 May	The opening moves of the operation required the support of 3 of the squadron's Belvederes; XG 467 (Sqn Ldr Hart), XG 458 (Flt Lt Woodcock) and XG 468 (Flt Lt Martin). Supplies of water, food and ammunition were carried to 3 sites on the tops of 2 ridges east of the Thumair—Dhala road and 3 miles north of the airstrip.
	2 May	Further sorties were made to the same sites as yesterday: 2 aircraft were used. The greatest problems were caused by turbulence on the ridges at midday and early afternoon. Flying

was suspended during this period and re-started at 1700 hours. This is an unsatisfactory state of affairs as the crews have a 14 hour working day.

3 May — 36000 lbs of freight and 25 passengers were carried to the ridges by 3 aircraft during the day. We are getting used to these 3 landing sites now; the beads of perspiration on the captain's brow are much smaller than they used to be. Our loading operations at Thumier are running quite smoothly as the Mobile Air Movements Section (Fg Off Bannister) now have the preparation of loads down to a fine art.

4 May — Belvederes XG 467 (Sqn Ldr Hart) and XG 468 (Flt Lt Smith) were able to complete all Operation Flamingo tasks by 12.30 hours today, by which time they had lifted 21430 lbs freight and 58 passengers and troops.

5 May — By making a 'first light' take-off from Khormaksar, 4 aircraft (XG 467, Sqn Ldr Hart, XG 463, Flt Lt Woodcock, XG 458, M Plt Bousher, XG 461, Flt Lt Smith) were able, in 18.20 hrs flying to carry 31000 lbs freight, and 179 passengers, troops and casualties. At the urgent request of the Army, Flt Lt Smith landed in the Wadi Taym under fire, with the armed escort of Sqn Ldr Hart in XG 467, to collect 9 wounded soldiers, 8 of whom were stretcher cases. Only 3 stretchers could be carried in the proper racks, the remainder being put on the floor. With 8 stretchers, 1 sitting patient, doctor, gunner and crewman on board 'standing room only' was the order of the day.

The Squadron strength was increased to-day by the arrival of Flight Sergeant Wheatley, attached from the Khormaksar Search and Rescue Flight.

6 May   In 12 hrs, 55 mins flying time, 3 aircraft carried 42300 lbs of freight and 40 people. All of our doings at Thumier recently seem to have been recorded by the various press representatives who have come in ever increasing numbers to spend a day 'up country'. Alas! As far as the accuracy of the published reports go, most of them could have stayed at home. To-day's 'Daily Telegraph', for example, paid a glowing tribute to the work being done by the 'Beverley helicopters'.

Thumair   7 May   3 aircraft (XG 468, Flt Lt Smith; XG 458, M Plt Nisbet; XG 458 later in the day M Plt Bousher) operated from Thumier to-day. Almost all of the freight carried went to 2 mountain peak landing sites known to us as November One (Cap Badge) and November Two. These vantage points overlook the Wadi Taym. The business of releasing the external load, landing alongside it to recover the strop, taking off and clearing back to Thumier for a further load now goes quickly and involves being on the ground at the site for only a little over a minute. The Army Scout helicopters are gradually learning that we become embarrassed, to say the least, if they land in the middle of the only available landing site and switch off their engines just as we start our approach—a situation which has occurred a number of times.

8 May   Amongst the passengers carried to-day was a prisoner of war, from November One to Thumier. He appeared to enjoy every minute of his flight, in marked contrast to his Marine guard! Our operations were marred by the necessity of flying XG 458 (Sqn Ldr Hart) back to Khormaksar on one engine, due to a starter failure on the other engine. Thumier airstrip is not considered secure and night stops there are avoided whenever possible. The coffins containing the bodies of 2 soldiers killed at Al

286

Nagnil were flown from the village to Thumier by Sqn Ldr Hart (XG 468).

9 May   Pilot fatigue is becoming a very real problem to us as the long working days in an unfavourable climate take their toll. Similarly our aircraft are beginning to suffer. The 'Hours to Minor Inspection' figure for several of our Belvederes is reducing at an alarming rate. Todays figures for work done were 56100 lbs freight, and 82 passengers in 11.20 hours flying time.

10 May   In a day of intensive flying, a record amount was to-day carried by Belvedere XG 458 (Sqn Ldr Hart). In 6 hours 50 mins operational flying time, no less than 45190 lbs of freight and 64 passengers, troops and casualties were flown from Thumier to the surrounding landing sites. Included in the freight were 6 Land Rovers and 2 105 mm Howitzers flown to Al Naquil: the road into the Wadi Taym is still under construction and helicopter lift was the only feasible method of getting them to the Army unit in the village.

11 May   XG 458 (Flt Lt Martin) was the only aircraft required to fly in the Radfan operation to-day. Fg Off Bannister, Mobile Air Movements Officer at Thumier, who has done much to ensure the smooth movement of loads from Thumier, was to-day relieved by Flt Lt Clelland.

12 May   Mr Duncan Sandys, Commonwealth Secretary, to-day visited the Radfan. The Squadron carried members of the South Arabian Federal Government and the Press to various Army units, including the village of Al Naquil, scene of our casualty evacuation sortie of the 5th May. Our serviceablility problems eased to-day by the extending of the Belvedere servicing cycle from 100 to 150 hours between Minor

inspections. This measure has given a new lease of life to 2 of our aircraft, XG 467 and XG 458.

13 May   Flt Lt Smith (XG 458) brought back to Khormaksar from Thumier the bodies of two members of the Special Air Service who were killed on the night of the 30th April. The Command Medical Officer (Flying) flew to-day in one of our aircraft on operations. An immediate result was the imposition of an upper limit of 3 hours operational flying per pilot per day.

14 May   To cope with the amount of urgent supplies needed by troops at places which could not be supplied by means other than helicopter, yesterday's limit of 3 hours was raised to 4. This enabled Flt Lt Martin (XG 468) and Flt Lt Woodcock (XG 467) to move a total of 48070 lbs freight and 25 passengers.

15 May   The situation in the Radfan improved sufficiently for us to send only one aircraft (XG 468—Sqn Ldr Hart). The number of landing sites in use has increased, but we are now able to fly direct to most of them, avoiding the long detours which were needed in the early days of the operation. The immediate result was more freight uplifted per hour, with a consequent saving of pilot and aircraft hours.

16 May   Mr Hugh Fraser, Under Secretary of State for Air, to-day visited the Radfan and his party and members of the press flew by Belvedere to meet the troops.

17 May   One aircraft (XG 468) flew in the Radfan operations to-day delivering a total of 20000 lbs of freight and 9 passengers.

18 May   XG 467 (Flt Lt Woodcock) was the only aircraft tasked to-day. After navigational difficulties caused by low cloud and poor visibility

the aircraft landed at Thumier, to be promptly enveloped in fog! When this cleared, one engine refused to start and it was necessary to return to Khormaksar without lifting any loads.

19 May   The movements team at Thumier changed to-day, with unfortunate results. Due doubtless to inexperience in this theatre, there were a number of delays which, with an upper limit placed on the amount of operational flying which can be done, we could ill aford.

20 May   Flt Lt Woodcock (XG 467) to-day moved 14000 lbs freight and 22 passengers in the Radfan operation.

21 May   More infuriating delays caused by not having loads ready for the aircraft were experienced to-day. Notwithstanding this, 25840 lbs freight and 6 passengers were carried in 6 hrs 30 mins flying time, but this effort required the use of 3 aircraft.

22 May   Flt Lt Martin (XG 467) carried out a casualty evacuation from the Wadi Behab, some 30 miles North East of Mukeiras, where men of 2 villages had been keeping alive their age old tradition of fighting one another. The Brigadier of the Federal National Guard and 2 Arab representatives were taken as intermediaries. Our reception was cordial, and 4 stretcher cases and 4 sitting patients were brought back to Khormaksar.
            In the Radfan Sqn Ldr Hart (XG 461) moved 20300 lbs of freight in 2 hrs 45 minutes flying time.

23 May   The entire helicopter effort in the Radfan to-day was the movement to and from the November One and Two positions. The Army have now moved across the Wadi Taym into the mountains on the south side of the Wadi, but supply of these older positions is still entirely dependent on the helicopter force.

| 24 May | The new Army positions to the South of the Wadi Taym presented some problems to-day. They are approached by a considerable detour and are situated about 5000 feet above Sea Level. Landing at the new sites is not feasible with a Belvedere because of the steep slopes and the length of the fuselage. It is advisable for the Army Scout helicopter to land to pick up our cargo strops after we have released our external loads. The alternative is to wait at the hover and use the second rope to pull the strop up. This makes us a tempting target. |

As evidence that opposition still exists close to Thumier, Belvedere XG 463 (Sqn Ldr Hart) was fired on by 2 Arabs who hid in a cave before their fire could be returned. The aircraft was undamaged. The crew were fuming with rage at not being quick enough to fire back.

| 25 May | Flight Sergeant Wheatley, who was loaned to the Squadron from the Search and Rescue Flight at a time when we were hard pressed was to-day replaced permanently by Master Pilot Watts, also from Search and Rescue. |

To-days operations in the Radfan area with 2 aircraft resulted in the unlifting of 37600 lbs freight and 7 passengers.

| 26 May | XG 461 flown by Flt Lt Woodcock was to-day hit by fire from Arab dissidents near the Echo Four landing site at Hajib in the Radfan. The rear gunner, Flt Lt Chittenden (who is attached to the unit from No 37 Squadron) returned the fire, but his Bren gun suffered a stoppage after firing 4 rounds. His comments on this situation may safely be left to the imagination. |

The Belvedere was hit 6 times and suffered damage to the rear fuelage.

| 27 May | Master Pilot Bousher (XG 457) lifted 16700 lbs freight and 25 passengers to-day. He later ferried back to Khormaksar XG 461. |

| Thumier/Khormaksar | 28 May | The squadron maintained a 1 hour standby with one aircraft which was not, however required. |

| | 29 May | Once again a standby aircraft was available but was not used. The squadron stood down after duty to-day for the remainder of the month. |

Part II   Training

Our commitments in 'Operation Flamingo' resulted in the virtual suspension of continuation training during May. The operations in the Radfan, however, provided an excess of practice in external load carrying, mountain flying and, on occasion, night and single engine flying!

Flying Times

Operational Day	222.05
Operational Night	3.35
Training Day	3.40
Training Night	Nil
Other Flying Day	6.30
Other Flying Night	Nil

Part III   Administration

The Squadron received its seventh aircraft on 22nd May, 1964. This aircraft arrived from Far East on Board HMS Centaur. (XG 474) Flt Lt Spreadbury—GD Pilot together with three airmen groundcrew arrived with the aircraft and are attached for duty with the Squadron for 2 months.

Seven Belevedere H C Mk 1 on strength of the squadron as at the end of the month.

Personnel

525752 F S Duffield, L—Aircraft fitter was promoted to the rank of Warrant Officer and posted to RAF Khormaksar.

574814 F S Ireland, E H—Airframe fitter was posted in to fill this post.

1600430 M Plt Watts, G F was posted to the Squadron from SAR Flight.

Part IV   Honours and Awards
Nil

General

Squadron Commander's Remarks A good flying month indeed. The pilots flew between 60 and 68 hours exceeding the task by more than 50 hours. But, this effort, with only $3\frac{1}{2}$ crews at the start of the operation was too much to sustain. The arrival of Flt Lt Spreadbury from FEAF eased the situation and the two new pilots from the UK will give us 5 crews when they are trained. The posting in of M Pilot Watts needing Belvedere conversion does not help as the training load is already high.

The groundcrew have done an excellent job. During the preparation for the operation very long hours were worked, which combined with the start of the Aden 'Hot Season' caused a lot of concern, but it enabled the Squadron to meet the tasks. The written congratulations of the C-in-C and GOC have been passed on to the airmen with pleasure.

All aircraft have been fired at, usually the only indication is a Radio message. The damage to XG 461, by six bullets was an unfortunate combination of cloud, which governed the approach with the external load; ground activity which had not been reported and the airspeed being low as the final run in had been commenced. It is a coincidence that the same aircraft received 5 bullets in Radfan during January, this year.

(P F HART)
Squadron Leader
Officer Commanding
No 26 Squadron

At the beginning of June 1964 No 26 Squadron felt sufficiently enthusiastic and confident to demonstrate in the time honoured way with a Squadron mass fly-past. A formation of five Belvederes was flown over Aden. Meanwhile Radfan operations continued, another rotor blade was damaged by a bullet and a Royal Navy Wessex which had toppled over into a Wadi after suffering ground resonance due to an over-loaded condition was recovered as an under-slung load by the Belvedere.

Between 30 April and 30 June the Belvederes had flown over 1000 sorties, carried nearly 1800 passengers, 48 casualties and 1111 thousand pounds of freight. In the same period the SAR Whirlwinds in 57 sorties carried 95 passengers, 26 casualties and 41.1 thousand pounds of freight. The four Royal Navy Wessex which operated in the Radfan between 24 May and 26 June only, flew 409 sorties carrying 2096 passengers and 192.7 thousand pounds of freight.

The first events presaging the collapse of the Aden Belvederes also occurred in June, starting with two Avpin fires. The first one was actually an explosion, causing the pilot to exit precipitately through the starboard hatch, breaking a wrist and ankle in his fall. It was the practice to remove the access ladder before starting engines because otherwise the rocking motions sometimes felt during rotor acceleration were liable to crumple the ladder. The front of the aircraft was severely damaged by fire. The second Avpin fire did not cause that amount of damage, being a small one occurring due to self-ignition of a small quantity of Avpin in one of the discharge tubes. It was noticed about two hours after the aircraft landed. (The Belvedere had the awkward habit of discharging Avpin unused after the starting cycle directly on to the ground, as well as Avtur fuel from the Fuel Metering Unit when the engines were shut down—both being the subject of adverse comment by the Belvedere Trials Unit, but for which no remedial action had been taken. (See Chapter 9).

The pace of operations in Operation Flamingo had also taken its toll and by 24 June all the Belvederes were unserviceable. Engine surging was being experienced both on starting and shutting down, radios were causing problems and uncured vibration in flight was getting worse.

Until July 1964 the method of correcting rotor blade tracking errors in Aden consisted of the crude system of striking the blades on a spring tension flag. It could only compare the blade flight paths while at minimum pitch when standing on the ground. There was no way of identifying errors occurring in individual blades at high lift angles, especially those required at high level landing sites. Transit cruising height in excess of 8000 feet exacerbated the problem. An optical system which permitted offending blades to be identified in flight marked a great improvement although it was a far from perfect solution. It was difficult to use when the sun was low and produced unreliable results in turbulence. This 'In Flight Tracker' was not available in Aden until July 1964 and even then the only set available was found to be unserviceable on arrival and had to be returned to the United Kingdom. The consequences was that the crews had become accustomed to accepting progressively higher levels of vibration as the rotors aged, while the errors caused by sand erosion of the long, largely unprotected, control runs were to some extent masked by the excessive rotor-generated vibrations. It was also in July 1964 that the blanking off of the wire cage over the engine intakes previously mentioned took place, but nothing could be done to protect the transmission and control run bearings. Nevertheless, in July 1964, 526 sorties were flown carrying 700 passengers and 407 thousand pounds of freight. In August 745 sorties, 2827 passengers, 24 casualties and 386 thousand pounds of freight were lifted.

The successful completion of the assault phase of Operation Flamingo made little difference to the helicopters except to reduce the rate of resupply of ammunition and casualty evacuation flights, and especially the likelihood of damage by small arms fire. Hunter attacks by day and Shackleton bombing by night finally forced the last tribes still defying the Government to surrender. Official offensive action ended on 18 November 1964. The task of resupply by helicopter remained, however, as the FRA, strengthened by British troops, continued to hold the key positions in the Radfan to counter the active subversion by Egypt and infiltration from the Yemen which continued unabated until final British withdrawal. The really critical period, however, had been during the assault phases from 1 May to mid-June 1964.

In September, two Belvederes were flown to Riyan in preparation for an expected rebellion at Mukulla, which the mere appearance of the aircraft may have done much to prevent occurring.(15) In other words, for this brief period the Belvedere was being used successfully in the numerous roles and in the manner which had become usual for helicopters in other theatres.

By October 1964 the support for Operation Flamingo was becoming more sporadic, which was fortunate because it was then that the Belvedere suffered the blows which were to finish it eventually in Aden. On 5 October, Flt Lt W S Smith, flying between Khormaksar and Thumier, experienced a yaw cable control failure—a similar defect to that which had caused the fatal crash in Borneo in May 1963 described in the next chapter. On this occasion, however, there was no crash, much to the later astonishment of the chief designer and others at the manufacturers at Weston-super-Mare. Smith was fortunately in a flight condition in which the total loss of yaw control and a large part of lateral cyclic control did not prove immediately fatal. Wallowing almost out of control, he managed to flop the aircraft on to the ground at Monks Field (an airstrip used by the Twin Pioneers) with no further damage—a feat for which he received an immediate AFC.

A little over three weeks later, on 30 October, while on a night cross-country flight, the same pilot, undergoing a check by the Squadron QHI, Flt Lt K W Woodcock, and with crewman Sgt G A Whitehead, was killed, together with the others, when the aircraft crashed near Lahej, some few miles north of Aden. The wreckage was destroyed by fire after a violent impact and, apart from finding the front engine to have been almost stopped and the rear one running at high power at the time of the crash, no conclusion could be drawn as to the original cause of the accident.(16) The aircraft had been approaching Aden at 1500 feet when there was a high pitched and heavily broken 'May-Day' call from the aircraft on UHF radio as though the operator was being violently shaken. It lasted six seconds. There were other visual reports suggesting a fire had occurred in the air. A second Belvedere in the vicinity, although not hearing the original May-Day call as he was using VHF radio, was informed by Khormaksar and then saw what he thought was a flare or small fire on the ground. He landed 100 yds away to investigate and found the remains of the crashed Belvedere burning. The cockpit was not found until the next day. The event seems to have been consistent with an explosion or fire or both in or near the front engine or its Avpin tank, but this could not be determined with certainty.

The Belvederes, grounded since the fatal crash at the end of October, started flying again on 17 November, and were at once employed in collecting the litter consisting of parachutes, containers, jerricans etc scattered over the Army posts in the Radfan following the resupply activities of the Twin Pioneers, Beverleys and Argosys of Nos 78, 84 and 105 Squadrons respectively which had been forced to carry out this essential part of the helicopter's role during the Belvedere's absence. Morale, however, had been badly shaken and there was some fear of the aircraft.(17) Added to the two deaths and one pilot with a broken wrist and ankle following the starter explosion in June, four pilots had been lost to the Squadron and only five remained including the Commanding Officer. Then on the last day of December 1964 a Belvedere carrying out underslung load training at Khormaksar had a control failure due to a servicing error, crashed on the airfield and was a total loss although without crew injury. Three Belvederes had now been lost since June leaving four remaining. All were grounded.

In December 1964 the Squadron Commander, due to be replaced at the end of his tour in March 1965, summed up the year as an excellent operational one in which the Belvedere was well proved as a work horse and in which the crews had matched all operational demands.(18) Ever hopeful, he looked forward to a new starter system and appropriate modification for the Yaw cable problem, but this was not to be. What did appear was a Command modification to introduce an armoured bulkhead to protect the first pilot from the starter turbine. Ungrounded on 8 January 1965 for air tests and training only, achieving seven hours ten minutes total for the month, complaints were made about poor spares backing. There were no spare engine starters or Avpin injectors.

At this point it is useful to compare the situation with that in FEAF where corresponding difficulties were being steadily overcome, as will be described in the next chapter. The reasons for this difference are arguable and difficult to apportion in relative importance. Certainly the morale of No 26 Squadron was at a very low ebb and the official AFME view seemed to be that the solution would consist of replacing the Belvederes with the expected Mark II Wessex as soon as possible. The flow of spares certainly seemed inadequate, notably of starters and injectors; however, control of servicing practices clearly left much to be desired and does seem to have been a significant factor. Much comment has been made concerning the severe operating conditions—sand and gypsum dust etc—but the fact is that, following Ministerial pressure in early 1964 for the manufacturers of engines and airframes to provide more immediate help in the overseas theatres as described in Chapter 9, Mr Banks of Westland Aircraft Co visited Aden in February 1965 to advise on the servicing practices—mainly vibration rectification—and achieved remarkable results. The seven-hour flying achievement in January had been followed by only four-and-a-half operational hours in February although much air testing had been done with the in-flight tracking equipment. The complication of this procedure may be judged from the fact that to solve its vibration problems one aircraft carried out no less than 23 air tests in February. It was then due for a double engine change.(19) The very next month, following the ministrations of Mr Banks, the Belvederes were back in business, flying 146 hours of which 90 were operational in the Radfan. Mr Banks, who personally had much to do with training RAF ground crews on the Belvedere at the manufacturer's establishment at Weston-super-Mare, commented that he had spent much of his time in Aden instructing tradesmen inadequately prepared before arrival. It seemed to him that many of the airmen he had trained at Westlands appeared to have gone to FEAF where the priority was higher at the time when No 26 Squadron was deploying piecemeal to Aden.

This resurgence of the Belvederes coincided with the arrival of the new Squadron Commander, Squadron Leader P D M Moore, who replaced Squadron Leader P Hart in March 1965. Unhappily for him the recovery lasted only two months although they were not without interest. The Sharif of Beihan (Ruler) requested air support following enemy attacks and two Belvederes, surprisingly, were detached for two weeks to this relatively distant place but retained there indefinitely. The crews, including the new Squadron Commander, lived under canvas with the FRA on the airstrip and operated intensively in the support role throughout April and early May. It was an active operational situation, landing sites were subject to mortar fire, three shells landed near a Belvedere delivering a load, and the redoubtable XG 474 (the RAF Museum aircraft) received a further bullet through a rotor blade. There was much fine sand—no oiled patch preparation—and XG 474 required a double engine change in the field. This was carried out successfully although the rear engine change required a hole to be dug into which the engine could be lowered. There were four minor Avpin fires, vibration was getting worse again and the task was reduced to one aircraft in late April. The Brigadier commanding the FRA forces was restricted in the reaction he was allowed to make to enemy activity, being allowed only to fire two artillery shells for each one received.(20) Squadron

Engine change at Beihan (XG474 is the RAF Museum Belvedere).

Arab village used as an army defensive position with the Wadi Taym in the background.

Leader Moore formed the opinion that the Belvedere was used on occasion to draw enemy fire deliberately so as to allow reply by the FRA 105 mm guns.(21)

This was the last operational use of the Belvedere in Aden. No operational flying had been done from Khormaksar in April and in Beihan only mapping survey teams were supported in the first half of May before returning to Khormaksar. The ground crew were absorbed into a fully centralised helicopter servicing flight formed at Khormaksar and with attention now focussing enthusiastically on the newly arriving Wessex Mk II there was no longer any hope of producing a serviceable operational Belvedere. Three pilots returned to the UK and were not replaced. The remnants of No 26 Squadron struggled miserably on through June and July doing the occasional short training flight, two of which were abandoned in July due to excessive vibration. A forthcoming visit by the Inspector General of the RAF was looked forward to in anticipation of a policy decision on the future of No 26 Squadron to end the speculation, of which there was a good deal.(22) The Squadron Commander paid a visit to FEAF, spent five days at Kuching and was greatly impressed by the contrast with conditions in AFME, commenting that operations in FEAF were rarely above 1000 feet, there was little turbulence and hardly any sand. He noted with surprise that No 66 Squadron had a shed full of spares—there were virtually none at Khormaksar.(23)

August, September and October saw a final spurt of energy to make the four Belvederes at least partially serviceable, the news having been received that provided they could be made sufficiently serviceable to fly on to the Carrier in time, they were to be delivered in November by HMS Albion to FEAF where they were eagerly awaited. Two pilots had been sent to FEAF in September for refresher continuation training on the Belvederes in order to be fit to carry out this task. The opportunity for Khormaksar to get rid of these last Belvederes evidently provided the necessary impetus and they were duly landed on the Carrier on 23 and 24 November 1965, although on arrival in Singapore (described in the next chapter) they were found to be in a condition which could not by any stretch of the imagination be described as serviceable. All except one were, however, eventually recovered to full operational standard in FEAF.

So ended the year of the Belvedere in Aden, in circumstances which gave the aircraft an indelible reputation of technical unreliability in the memory of those who happened to be in that theatre at the time and who, in the normal course of overseas postings, would see nothing of its behaviour in FEAF. The Squadron Commander of some eight months tenure recorded that it was a matter of regret that No 26 Squadron was unable to offer any help in the sharply deteriorating internal security situation developing in Aden itself. No 26 Squadron's 50th anniversary passed in October 1965 without celebration and on the 28th it was announced that the squadron was to disband a month later. There was no publicity because of the redeployment of operational aircraft involved. Nevertheless the British and

297

Federal Regular Armies acknowledged that without the Squadron support, the successful Radfan campaign could never have been envisaged.(24) Its disappearance was regretted by both British and Arab troops.(25)

Wessex Mk II in Aden

The commitment to continued tactical helicopter support for ground troops now evidently permanently required in the Radfan had transformed the picture in Aden. Although offensive operations had officially ceased when the last tribes in the area sought peace in November 1964,(26) infiltration by dissidents from the Yemen was increasing and maintenance of ground forces in the Radfan was clearly to become a long term task. The operational organisation at Khormaksar, previously divided into Tactical and Transport Wings was, in December 1964, redivided into Strike Wing, Medium Range Transport Wing and Short Range Transport Wing, the latter comprising the Helicopers, Twin Pioneers and the Communications Squadron. Although not an exclusively Helicopter Wing, it was commanded by an experienced helicopter pilot—initially Wing Commander K Fry (previously Flight Commander of the original Casualty Evacuation Flight in FEAF in 1950-52). He was succeeded by Wing Commander C Symons in October 1966.

The addition of Wessex to the Belvedere force in accordance with the planned one-company lift in Aden (part of the worldwide four-company lift deployment—see Chapter 9) had been noted by AFME in October 1964 as expected to occur in mid-1965.(28) That was the month that ended with the fatal Belvedere crash already reported, which must have planted the thought in many minds that the Wessex could well be the substitute for the Belvedere in Aden, which in fact turned out to be the case.

The position of the engine air intakes of the Wessex was no improvement on the Belvedere, rather the reverse, and engine deterioration due to sand erosion was an even greater problem. Even when the aircraft were new an alarming rate of engine changes seemed to be needed, but this was traced partly to the fact that a number of loose rivet heads embedded in grease in the nose doors during manufacture were being released into the engine intakes as the grease melted.(29) Unlike the Belvedere, however, the engines when serviceable could always be started and the Wessex had a lesser, but still useful, single engine capability.

A further advantage of the Wessex in Aden, particularly noticeable in retrospect, was that whilst on several occasions the Belvedere had to cease operations at high altitudes in the middle of the day and early afternoon due to turbulence, the Wessex appears to have had little trouble in this respect.(30) There was nothing to complain about in the control response of the Belvedere compared with the Wessex; on the contrary, it was rather better. The difference must be accounted for by the auto-stabilisation and automatic rotor speed control, both of which were lacking in the Belvedere.

In terms of general shape the Wessex benefited in Aden because of the shorter fuselage length, single tail wheel and narrowness of the rear fuselage which, being completely devoid of the low slung tail surfaces which had been added to the Belvedere in a largely unsuccessful and scarcely necessary attempt to improve stability in forward flight, had caused some difficulty in positioning the aircraft without damage in the rocky terrain of most hilltop landing sites.

As far as performance was concerned, the Wessex in Aden was well suited to the very short ranges required in the Radfan resupply operations and was able to replace the Belvedere, albeit with rather more sorties per task. There was however a sufficient number of aircraft provided. Even the 105 mm Howitzer, stripped of much of its armour and without crew and ammunition, could be lifted by the Wessex over very short ranges even at high altitude, and as the full scale offensive operations had ceased in the Radfan before the Wessex arrived, such operations could be carried out at a slower tempo without embarrassment.

In the closing days, as the internal security situation in Aden itself deteriorated sharply, the Wessex turned out to be almost ideally suited to the very localised rapid response operations demanded.

No 78 Squadron

No 78 (Twin Pioneer) Squadron was disbanded and re-formed with nine Wessex Mk II on 7 June 1965, the aircraft being delivered by the LSL 'Sir Launcelot'. The aircrew arrived together—one Squadron Leader, nine of the twelve pilots established and, a new feature, eight trained crewmen including one officer crewman leader. The ground crew were posted to the Khormaksar Helicopter Servicing Flight which, although under the command of the OC SRT Wing, removed them from the direct control of the new Squadron Commander—Squadron Leader F Braybrook. He initially attributed a rather poor serviceability rate to this and the fact that the Wessex Mk II was still new; but local conditions prevented a higher rate ever being achieved. For the first six months the Wessex had an average monthly serviceability of 21.2 per cent, in 1966 30.8 per cent and in 1967, 46.6 per cent.(31) However, the establishment of nine aircraft, rising to 14 in 1967, ensured that there were enough aircraft for tasking and sufficient operational hours available for the tasks required, even though by December 1965 continuous 24 hours per day servicing work was required at Khormaksar to achieve it.(32)

The Squadron was declared operational on 18 June 1965—11 days after arrival—and in the following month exceeded the task hours of 240 with 275 hours, of which

One of the key positions overlooking the Wadi Taym—named 'Cap Badge' (also known as 'November One').

Defensive position South of Wadi Taym (Foxtrot 3) showing the typically limited space for re-supply operations.

43 were training. An indication of what was going on in the Radfan is given by the loads lifted in July which, in addition to 2591 troops, 49 Arab and 29 British soldiers casualty evacuated, included 545000 lbs of freight,(33) much of it cement, timber and nails.(34) The anxiety to acquire new helicopter lift to replace the now almost defunct Belvederes must have been keen in AFME where the resupply of the operational areas by Twin Pioneers, Beverleys, Whirlwinds (of the SAR Flight) and Army Air Corps Scouts, was described as 'a gigantic task'.(35)

Radfan support—passenger/troop lifts, casualty evacuations, food/water/ammunition supply—formed a continuous daily task amounting to 80 per cent of operational effort in 1965,(36) two Wessex being detached daily at dawn to Habilayn (previously called Thumier) and recovered to Khormaksar at or after dusk. Night flying was starting to be developed. Not only were the Wessex crews all trained for helicopter night operations at their Central Flying School Conversion Course, unlike the Belvedere crews whose aircraft were scarcely cleared for night flying before departure from the UK, but the auto-stabilised rotor-speed governed Wessex presented much less of an adventure for night flying than had the Belvedere. A night casualty evacuation in August 1965 encouraged this development and by the end of the year, bullet and blast proof bays (Sangars) were being prepared at Habilayn to permit overnight stops by Wessex for urgent casualty evacuations. Patients could be extracted from the Radfan by night, even from such small and precipitous sites as 'Cap Badge', and often within two hours find themselves on board a long range transport aircraft en route from Khormaksar to the United Kingdom.(37)

There was much co-operation with the Royal Navy in the two-and-a-half years of the Wessex operation in Aden and not only in the Radfan. In August 1965, three Wessex of No 78 Squadron were temporarily exchanged with three Royal Navy Wessex Mk Is on the Commando Carrier HMS Bulwark for Exercise 'Mixed Crop'— a helicopter assault on the Wahidi Coast in which vehicles and guns were carried ashore by the RAF Wessex and troops by the Royal Navy Wessex Mk Is, covered by Hunters operating from Khormaksar. Several joint Service operations were mounted as the Aircraft Carriers HMS Bulwark, Albion, Eagle and Hermes passed in transit to and from the Far East.

In September 1965, support for the FRA in Dhofar was provided. During this operation the only RAF aircrew injury from the several bullet strikes received by helicopters throughout the period in Aden occurred when a pilot was wounded in the thigh.(38)

Occasional operations were mounted elsewhere in the area; for example, three Wessex were deployed in support of the FRA at Amitfa, some 60 nm east of Mukeiras in December 1965, a month of high activity for No 78 Squadron which also included a four-day deployment in the eastern extremity of the Wadi Taym.(39) Since usually only three, though occasionally four, Wessex were available out of nine, complaints of spares inadequacy were being made by No 78 Squadron. Nevertheless, the Squadron was much encouraged by the interest being shown by the upper levels of the Command in what the helicopter pilots still felt was the 'Cinderella' of the Service.(40) The new AOC, Air Vice Marshal Humphrey, had made his interest plain and frequently flew in helicopters whilst the Commander-in-Chief, Admiral Le Fanu, actually chose to operate as a Wessex crewman during a two-hour ammunition resupply operation.(41)

In early 1966 the deterioration in the internal security situation in Aden was extending the helicopter working day to the point where the effect of crew shortages due to fatigue was beginning to be felt. Eighty hours flying per week was not unusual, a typical day consisted of rising at 03.30 hours, collecting weapons, ammunition and detachment gear and being briefed to be ready before dawn to fly to the Army Establishment at Little Aden to collect troops and freight for delivery at Habilayn at or before dawn; then to be available for operational tasking throughout the day for eight or nine hours. Enjoyable though such a life may have been for most pilots, to return to Khormaksar at dusk to find Squadron or formal Station duties still having prior importance and the social round continuing, made life in Aden itself seem unrealistic compared to the harsh realities so closely experienced by the helicopter crews such a short distance away.(42) By the end of 1966 that situation was to be rudely reversed.

Extra standby aircraft were being provided at Habilayn whenever the SAS were operating—mostly along the Yemen border. The Army Air Corps Scouts were the main support for the SAS but were frequently getting hit by ground fire. In March, two Wessex with three crews and a servicing party, together with two Army Air Corps Scouts, were detached to Ataq, staging through Mukeiras, for seven days' support of a party probing nearby Wadis in some strength. In the course of this operation, 50 troops and two 150 mm Howitzers were lifted to the tip of a Jebel at a height of 7200 feet.(43)

By April 1966, 24-hour detachments at Habilayn had become standard. A tenth Wessex was delivered equipped with Infra-Red Linescan equipment intended to detect from the air mines laid in the ground, in particular on the road to Dhala. The trials with this equipment were described as successful although it was never used afterwards in that theatre.(44) A modification previously made to the Wessex nose doors to reduce sand ingestion was not found to be successful. Thirteen Gnome engines had failed due to sand damage in May and a 150 hour strip inspection was instituted. A new design for the nose doors was being considered.(45) By June the internal security situation in Aden was beginning to build up towards the chaotic scenes which characterised the final debacle in 1967. Mortar fire and mine laying were starting in Aden and there were eight killed and 52 injured that month. At the end of the first year of operations, No 78 Squadron Wessex had flown 2353 operational hours carrying 5.4 million lbs of freight, 28000 troops and 424 casualty or medical evacuations.

Wessex operations in the Radfan had become almost routine by mid-1966. Two new tactical features had been added during that year. Firstly, cordon and search operations as practised originally in Operation Wellington II in Malaya in 1953 and quite extensively in Cyprus in 1957 (see Chapter 5) were becoming standard. The helicopters were used to position troops around an area thought to contain dissident insurgents, and the place thoroughly searched while escape was prevented. Secondly, and shortly after the arrival of Wing Commander C Symons as Officer Commanding the Short Range Transport Wing in October 1966, it became the practice for offensive operations of this sort to be led by up to three Army Air Corps Scout helicopters armed with machine guns, and carrying an Air Commander for the operation—usually Officer Commanding SRT Wing himself.

One such cordon and search operation was mounted in October 1966 (Operation Fate) in conjunction with the Royal Navy. Five Wessex and one Army Air Corps Scout were embarked on a small helicopter carrier—HMS Fearless—and transported some 600 miles just over the eastern edge of the Protectorate beyond the Oman border. At dawn, troops of the First Battalion Irish Guards were positioned by Wessex at the perimeter of the village of Hauf and search troops were then landed from the ship to investigate. Surprise was complete and there was no opposition. Twenty two dissidents were captured. No 78 Squadron felt that the various commando ship and assault training exercises carried out over the past year was well vindicated. In the same month there were 84 terrorist attacks in Aden itself, 61 of them with grenades. There were four killed and 66 injured.

By the end of 1966 the Wessex of No 78 Squadron had been used to recover five Sioux and two Scouts of the Army Air Corps damaged or unserviceable in forward areas. One of the Scouts had to be jettisoned (May 1966) when the Wessex suffered an engine failure, of which there were many. In December 1966, for example, there were 13, and one engine failed a compressor check on the ground. In that month the task hours were 230, and 275 were flown including 43 on training.

Last Year in Aden

The dramatic events of the last months in Aden are chronicled in detail elsewhere, notably in 'Flight from the Middle East' by Sir David Lee. For the helicopter crews, however, the Radfan resupply and other operations continued unabated as the enormously complicated rundown of the huge Aden complex proceeded.

This was a period of very rapid development of operational techniques and modifications to the aircraft to meet the challenge of providing security by day and night in and around Aden base itself, as the various Nationalist factions infiltrated from the north and mounted terrorist rifle, grenade and mortar attacks in and around the town and airfield.

The first requirement, apart from adding an additional machine gun in the portside rear window—one was already mounted in the doorway on the starboard side—was to make a satisfactory arrangement for launching illuminating flares. The Wessex was already equipped with the Schermuly flares, attached to the undercarriage as in the Whirlwinds, for emergency landing by night, but what was required was an internal fuselage-mounted dispenser able to launch a whole series of much larger flares. Some work in this direction had already been done with the intention of illuminating targets in the Radfan for Hunter strike action but the existence over the target of flares which failed to ignite but whose parachute opened correctly created something of a hazard. Nevertheless, much success was achieved with a Shackleton Flare Chute fitted in the Wessex doorway. Up to 20 flares were carried.

Starting with a mobile searchlight as used on fire engines, a succession of different types of searchlight configurations fixed to the aircraft were tried to enable the Wessex to be used for regular patrols around and within the perimeter fence built along the boundary of Aden State; this fence was known as the Scrubber Line. The effect was mainly deterrent but if there was Intelligence warning of incursion at a particular point, the aircraft could proceed to it guided by Khormaksar radar and then illuminate it. The machine guns were loaded with tracer ammunition to enhance the effect, and if vehicles or other activities were seen, the aircraft could land and disembark a patrol to deal with them.

By February 1967 the Wessex was being used regularly for day and night internal security patrols in Aden where there were 140 terrorist attacks during that month resulting in 38 killed and 144 wounded. In the following three months both flares and searchlights were being used to assist ground troops in the Radfan operations, while the use of flame floats for target marking was also investigated. In April there were 403 terrorist attacks in Aden, 165 by grenades causing 25 deaths and 97 injured.

May 1967 was a notable month in that No 78 Squadron activity in Aden reached its peak. With task hours of 420 the Squadron flew 541. A demonstration was carried out showing the following roles:—

    a.   General purpose machine gun firing in the desert edge surrounding Aden State.

    b.   Lifting troops into night ambush positions just outside the Aden State boundary.

c. Lifting SAS troops to forward bases from Habilayn.

d. Ammunition resupply to ground troops.

e. Airlift for political affairs officers visiting sensitive area.

f. Cordon and search operations.

g. Searchlight illumination of check points around Aden State boundary.

h. Flare dropping for night Hunter strikes with rockets and cannon.

As the military and political situation deteriorated, the flexible potentialities of the helicopter were being fully and enthusiastically developed. Two Wessex were deployed to Riyan where rioting and terrorism was breaking out in the eastern part of the Protectorate. They remained there for nearly four months.

From now onwards the preparations for final withdrawal and the rising tide of violence in Aden accelerated. Large scale evacuation of families and civilians started in earnest. In June, a shortage of aviation fuel occasioned by the Arab/Israeli war complicated matters further while a mutiny by National Guard armed police in Aden led to firing inside Khormaksar itself and something like open war in Crater where the crew of an Army Air Corps Sioux, shot down by the rebels, was rescued under fire by Wessex. Troop resupply and movement continued in the Radfan culminating in withdrawal of the main body of British troops at the end of June. South Arabian Army operations were mounted with the SAS—a technique now being relied upon to ensure Habilayn was kept clear of enemy infiltration up to the last minute. Cordon and search operations were also mounted on the islands near Little Aden. Of the 61 dead and 113 wounded in June in Aden, 40 per cent were British.

No 78 Squadron had, by July, been two years in the theatre, and consequently a significant amount of crew replacement had occurred. About half the crews were now in their first helicopter tour, many of the more experienced pilots with which the squadron started having become tour-expired. Their standard was considered high, operational training in Aden averaging 50 hours, most of it on operations as co-pilot. Two pilots were always carried for night flying, and by day when opposition was considered likely, which was most of the time in the last months. Nevertheless, it was found necessary in May to attach three experienced pilots from No 72 Squadron at Odiham for three months to cover a period when the No 78 Squadron operational experience level dropped sharply while training time was hard to find. The operational standard was not allowed to fall and training and full categorization of crews in all the techniques in use continued right up to October—the month before the final withdrawal.

In July, the tactical role of the SAR flight was recognized by its inclusion in the task hours for No 78 Squadron and yet another new capability was added to the Wessex when trials showed that practice grenades could be dropped from the helicopter with sufficient accuracy to make 20 lb fragmentation bombs an effective weapon. Bomb racks holding four bombs on each side of the aircraft were quickly designed and in only two months approved as a Command modification although the bombs were never used in anger. A & AEE clearance followed in September. Crew categorization actually included clearance for use of cluster searchlights, flare dropping, machine gunnery and bombing. Engine changes continued at up to 12 per month and in the continuing search for means of reducing sand damage, the practice was developed of delivering, together with assault troops, a membrane which they could spread on the ground for the helicopter to land on when recovering them. The Riyan detachment recovered a UPS1 ground radar from Lodar at an altitude of 7000 feet, the Wessex requiring to be stripped of all possible items to enable this lift to be made. Radfan operations were beginning to reduce but aircraft were still supplied for four days a week at Habilayn for tasking by the BASO. In Aden there was a daily troop deployment from Waterloo Lines to Temple Cliff overlooking Crater.

In August the two-aircraft Riyan detachment had a busy month with political officers conducting negotiations with local officials; some parachute dropping training was also carried out. These helicopters finally evacuated the remaining British officials from Mukeiras and Lodar and withdrew to Aden at the end of the month. The provision of Sangars to protect the parked aircraft at Khormaksar from rifle and mortar fire, as had been done at Habilayn earlier, was clearly well justified. An 81 mm mortar attack on Khormaksar was abruptly terminated when one of the day internal security patrol Wessex found the culprits in a rubbish dump at Sheik Othman. The aircraft suffered nine bullet hits in the following hour. Armour plate was fitted to protect the first pilot on the starboard side and flak vests were issued. Preparations to move No 78 Squadron to Sharjah were started.

Together with the SAR flight, which since July had been included with No 78 Squadron for tasking purposes, there were now 14 Wessex with a monthly serviceability rate of around 50 per cent. The average in 1966 had been 35 per cent. By September terrorist activity was dwindling as the dissidents could see the end coming and were busy dividing up into rival nationalistic parties to seize power when the time came, but day and night helicopter patrols were maintained. Up-country operations were not yet abandoned however and when an Army Air Corps Scout was shot down near Ataq, a detachment of two Wessex was mounted to support a fire power demonstration by Hunters in reply. All up-country flights by helicopter were now accorded Hunter cover.

In October 1967, the last South Arabian troops abandoned the Radfan and were withdrawn by helicopter to a position just north of Khormaksar. The last up-country helicopter flight was to ferry their Commander—Brigadier Dyce—from Dhala on 28 October. On 17 October, eight Wessex were flown to the Commando Carrier HMS Fearless for transit to Sharjah and the remaining six performed a farewell fly past for the AOC, AVM Humphrey, on 29 October. Day and night internal security patrols continued with help from the Royal Navy by day, and the searchlight and flare equipment helicopters of No 78 Squadron by night. Training flying continued, including conversion instruction for the CinC, Admiral La Fanu. As the rest of the Khormaksar establishment disappeared around them, No 78 Squadron was happy to acquire integration of their second-line ground crew and expected, wrongly as it turned out, a similar arrangement to be made after their move to Sharjah. It was January 1971 before this reintegration was to happen, and then only for a similar reason-the rundown of establishments prior to withdrawal. It lasted for a year, that is until withdrawal from the Gulf and disbandment of the Squadron, but was recorded in May of that year as beneficial to serviceability.

November 1967, the last month of British presence in Aden, was given over to ferrying men and equipment to the ships for the evacuation. Day and night helicopter internal security patrols continued as before, No 848 RN Squadron by day and No 78 Squadron by night. The No 78 Squadron base was transferred from Khormaksar to HMS Intrepid on 25 November, a formation of three Wessex escorted the High Commissioner from HMS Eagle to Khormaksar en route to the UK by air on 28 November, and the final sortie with freight and passengers was flown by No 78 Squadron from Khormaksar to HMS Intrepid at 1345 hours on Independence Day—29 November 1967—the last RAF Unit in Aden as the ship left territorial waters at 2330 hours.

After their experiences of the past two years, there was little regret at leaving for the helicopter crews, unlike their usual reaction in similar circumstances elsewhere in the world. Independence was not being gained by the up-country tribesmen who were generally much admired, but rather by a murderous rabble in Aden well mixed with dissident Eygptian and Yemeni infiltrators. For this reason, the spectators' view accorded to the helicopter crews of the carnage in Sheik Othman as the rival Nationalist parties attempted to annihilate each other, afforded a certain ironic satisfaction, and the destructive fires started in Aden by celebratory firing of mortars on Independence Day evening provided an unexpectedly cheerful spectacle for the departing ships.

Although it was a No 78 Squadron responsibility, it was probably the members of the SAR Flight who instigated the plan to paint RAF roundels on two large spherical marine marker buoys, welded to each other by a length of chain, and to hoist them by helicopter to the summit of the rocky crag in Aden known as Shamsam where the chain was securely fixed in a hole filled with concrete. The ex-Army Air Corps Sioux helicopters left behind in Aden and intended for the new State forces, lacked the power to lift them down, and they could scarcely be cut free without risking much damage to dwellings further down the mountain. The message from the RAF was unmistakeable if slightly obscene, and was felt by the Squadron to be a satisfactorily appropriate expression of their feelings. Nobody was reprimanded.

Helicopters in the Persian Gulf

Following withdrawal from Aden, No 78 Squadron was based at Sharjah for the remaining four years of British presence in the Persian Gulf. The Search and Rescue Flight originally intended for Muharraq, but diverted to the more pressing needs in Aden, was now able to be deployed as originally planned. The SAR task was hardly an operationally onerous one and the absence of a helicopter element in the Gulf Communication Flight inevitably led to frequent demands on the SAR Flight for VIP and staff communication journeys. The position was regularised at the end of 1968 by retitling the unit a Communications and Search and Rescue Flight— COMSAR Bahrein.

The withdrawal from Aden was followed by a build-up of British forces in the Persian Gulf, and although there was little operational pressure in the absence of enemy activity, No 78 Squadron was as busy as ever supporting an intensive series of training exercises, introduced partly to publicise the presence of the two British battalions at Sharjah and Bahrein, and partly to foster closer co-operation between the three Services. These Army, as well as the RAF, personnel were by this time on short unaccompanied tours from nine to thirteen months duration so the turnover was quite rapid and generated a continuous training requirement for both soldiers and helicopter crews. For the helicopters, crew training now had priority over tasked hours, and the monthly totals showed a regular excess of training over operational hours flown. This situation was directly opposite to that which had existed in Aden, and became not unlike that at Odiham where a more or less continuous stream of Army exercises required helicopter support (see Chapter 10). The nature of these Exercises and their locations varied from assault landings over beaches to parachute drops on the Jebel Akhdar in Oman and the occupation of the high altitude airstrip at Saiq. In the absence of an actual enemy, SAS troops were used to represent dissidents creating a realistic simulation of operations and providing the helicopters with a real task in support of these troops in the dramatically inhospitable mountains of Central and Eastern Oman. Real dissident activity was not entirely lacking but these frequent exercises doubtless provided an effective deterrent to any significant renewal of such activity in Central Oman and in the Trucial States.

The Wessex serviceability declined sharply after the excitement and stimulation of the last days in Aden, but there were three other factors which contributed greatly to this effect. Firstly, sand ingestion was an even bigger problem than it had been in the Radfan, leading to a higher rate of engine failure. Secondly, the ground crew

78 Squadron crew in Aden showing the 0.76 mm GP Machine Gun mounted in a Wessex. The crew are wearing Flak Vests and a 'Mae West' fitted with a Sarbe beacon.

78 Squadron Wessex operating near Sharjah in 1971.

78 Squadron Wessex operating near Sharjah in 1971.

turnover was now so rapid that the experience level lowered significantly—in July 1968 for example only the Squadron Engineer Officer and three of the 75 airmen ground crew had previous experience with helicopters, and only one of them with the Wessex. In July 1968 the first-line servicing was at 60 per cent of planned strength and the second-line at 70 per cent. In the same month, eight engine changes were required in six aircraft at the end of a single Army exercise. The pilots were reduced to an average of 9 hours 40 minutes flying each—well below the 15 hours considered the minimum monthly requirement for maintenance of standards. Lastly, the very high temperatures over the summer months were frequently referred to as the cause of poor serviceability rates, particularly in the first two years at Sharjah. In July, August and September 1968 for example, the hours flown by No 78 Squadron were 151, 159 and 159 respectively. In October and November they achieved 237 and 231 respectively, attributing the change to the cooler weather.(46) They celebrated the event with a seven-aircraft formation flight and the resumption of regular engine-off landing practise—the first exercise to be dropped when the flying hours were restricted. By 1969, May was being referred to as the end of the exercise 'season' and August the beginning of preparations for the start of the exercise 'season' in September.

The provision of HF radio for helicopters has already been mentioned (see Chapter 10) but it was not until December 1968 that this facility was provided for the Wessex in Sharjah. For the first time they had ground-to-ground communications away from base, and a safety radio network was able to be established. The very late provision of this type of radio, the need for which had been clearly demonstrated in FEAF more than ten years previously, gives some clue to the degree of priority afforded to helicopter ancillary equipment in the field of communications. The same applied to navigation equipment.

The sands of both Aden and especially Sharjah had had a serious effect on the aircraft, and not only the engines. A complete refurbishing scheme had to be arranged in the UK, the Wessex being returned by Belfast freighter in rotation, starting in November 1968. By April 1969 the aircraft strength had fallen from 14, including the two at Muharraq, to nine—that is seven at Sharjah. Nevertheless average monthly flying hours comfortably reached between 200 and 250 while 273 in July was described as 'very good for the hot season'. In this period the Squadron had two Squadron Leaders (including the Commanding Officer), two Flight Lieutenants, 12 Flying Officer pilots, one Flight Lieutenant Navigator and 12 crewmen. Record flying hours of 330 were achieved in October 1969 with only nine aircraft and the main technical problems seemed to be solved. The aircraft strength fluctuated between nine and twelve throughout 1970 due to the refurbishing programme and occasional poor serviceability was blamed on spares shortages and ground crew inexperience—circumstances which had been known to occur together in other theatres giving rise to the suspicion that the latter may sometimes cause the former.

In October 1970, No 78 Sqadron completed an exercise in desert conditions and recorded the fact that no engine changes took place as a result. This, it was thought, was due to the use of new techniques. It would seem that taking off straight into forward flight and landing at constant power running forward slowly to minimise sand ingestion had only just been disovered, or else forgotten and rediscovered in No 78 Squadron at this late date.

The nearest thing to a real operation for the helicopters in this four-year period in Sharjah occurred in December 1970 when it was decided to disrupt some dissidents in the mountains of the Musandam Peninsula in Oman. For 12 days Operation Breakfast (also known as Operation Intragon) employed all seven of the Wessex then on the strength of No 78 Squadron in support of the Trucial Oman Scouts and SAS. Aircraft and crews were armed but there was no opposition. The only navigation aid then or even in that theatre for the helicopters was the 'Violet Picture' homer in the aircraft which could be used in conjunction with the SARBE used by the SAS.

1971 was the last year of the British presence in Sharjah, as well as in the whole of the Gulf. As in Aden, whilst all other units prepared for departure, the supposedly reduced helicopter tasking in fact continued at a high level because of a flood of late short notice bids for assistance. Much to their delight, the second-line servicing was returned to the control of the Squadron and serviceability continued satisfactorily. By March the unit was down to six aircraft but flew 226 hours. Limited night flying had been carried out in the previous year, but night transits were not uncommon and the occasional night casualty evacuation was now being done. There were no special aids apart from the searchlight clusters inherited from the last days in Aden. Exercises continued almost to the last minute, one actually taking place in October. As an operational training area for helicopters in desert and mountain terrain, Sharjah could scarcely have been excelled and its loss could not be made good elsewhere.

The No 78 Squadron disbandment parade took place on 26 November 1971, although the last operational flight was flown a few days later on 1 December. Sir Geoffrey Arthur (the Political Resident) and his Personal Assistant were taken by helicopter to three locations for formal abrogation of the Treaties of the Trucial States. The Ensign was lowered at Sharjah on 14 December 1971, and at Muharraq on the following day, leaving the Staging Post at Masirah Island as the last tenuous British presence in the Gulf area.

Since June 1965 when the Squadron was re-formed in Aden, No 78 Squadron Wessex had flown 18764 hours of which 6766 were operational. They carried over 12 million lbs of freight, 128156 passengers and 1176 medical evacuations.

1   Squadron Leader Hart.

2   Middle East Command ORB.

3   No 26 Squadron ORB.

4   Khormaksar ORB.

5   Ibid.

6   Middle East Command ORB.

7   Squadron Leader Timbers.

8   Middle East Command ORB.

9   No 26 Squadron ORB.

10 Squadron Leader Hart.

11 Middle East Command ORB.

12 No 26 Squadron ORB.

13 Squadron Leader Hart.

14 No 26 Squadron ORB.

15 Squadron Leader Hart.

16 Accident Board of Inquiry.

17 Flight Lieutenant Perrott.

18 No 18 Squadron ORB.

19 No 26 Squadron ORB.

20 Air Commodore Moore.

21 Ibid.

22 No 26 Squadron ORB.

23 Air Commodore Moore.

24 No 26 Squadron ORB.

25 Khormaksar ORB.

26 Middle East Command ORB.

27 Khormaksar ORB.

28 Middle East Command ORB.

29 Squadron Leader Braybrook.

30 Wing Commander Symons and others.

31 Middle East Command ORB Appendices.

32 No 78 Squadron ORB.

33 Ibid.

34 Squadron Leader Braybrook.

35 Middle East Command ORB.

36 Squadron Leader Braybrook.

37 Ibid.

38 Middle East Command ORB.

39 No 78 Squadron.

40 Ibid.

41 Ibid.

42 Squadron Leader Braybrook.

43 No 78 Squadron ORB.

44 Middle East Command ORB.

45 Ibid.

46 No 78 Squadron ORB.

CHAPTER 12

THE FAR EAST IN PHASES 3 AND 4—1962-1972

Introduction

Phase 3 of the helicopter history started with the introduction of turbine-engined helicopters. In the Far East, Belvederes arrived in May 1962 followed by Whirlwinds Mk 10 in July 1963. Overlapping from Phase 2 and still in residence at Butterworth was No 110 Squadron with Sycamores, being the residue of the piston-engined helicopter force which operated in the Malayan Campaign of the 1950s, and which in 1962 was still busy with the remnants of the defeated, but never wholly destroyed, Communist terrorist forces lurking mainly in the vicinity of the Thai border (see Chapter 3).

The dominant feature in Phase 3 in the Far East was the Borneo Campaign, although the Belvederes had arrived in Singapore some seven months before the Brunei Revolt in accordance with the planned deployment of the Support Helicopter Force, to provide a simultaneous four-Company lift worldwide. They, together with the No 110 Squadron due to be re-equipped with Whirlwinds Mk 10, were to provide the light cargo element of the one-Company lift for the Far East (see Chapter 9). The Brunei Revolt was the start of what turned out to be four years of exciting and challenging helicopter flying in support of Army operations in the jungles of North Borneo as well as some in Malaya (West Malaysia).

The Borneo Campaign itself is fully described elsewhere, the account here being limited to a mere outline forming the background against which the helicopter operations can be seen to have relevance. Examples of the activities of individual helicopter squadrons in the Campaign serve to describe some of the less usual tasks demanded of them and the conditions they encountered.

The official ending of Indonesian hostilities in 1966, the disbandment of the Belvedere Squadron in 1969, the rundown of FEAF in 1970 and finally the replacement of the then remaining Whirlwinds by Wessex in 1972 constituted the change to Phase 4 which, with the exception of No 28 Squadron in Hong Kong, was short-lived in the Far East and is included here for the sake of continuity and later clarity, since Phase 4 belongs chiefly to the European theatre.

Period Preceding the Brunei Revolt

In Chapter 3, the ending of Phase 2 in the Far East was recorded as occurring when the Brunei Revolt of December 1962 resulted in three Sycamores of No 110 Squadron, then at Butterworth, being despatched by Beverley from Singapore to Labuan.(1) Phase 3 actually commenced seven months earlier with the arrival of the Belvederes in the Far East and that short period constitutes the continuation of the Belvedere story from the point where it was left at Odiham in Chapter 8.

In April 1962, six Belvederes were crated for transfer by cargo ship to Singapore. This was an entirely new procedure and was supervised by the manufacturer's representatives amongst whom was Mr J Banks, who subsequently had much to do with the Belvedere in both the Far East and Aden, some of whose later comments are quoted in due course. The shipment produced no problems and, surprisingly, nor did the reassembly in Singapore, which was supervised by Flt Lt Munro, the first Belvedere Squadron Engineer Officer whose later comments are also quoted since they provide informed opinion on the sharply contrasting difference between the fortunes of the aircraft in FEAF and Aden respectively. As reported in Chapter 8, this first Belvedere Squadron, No 66 was formed out of the Belvedere Trials Unit, including both air and ground crews and the Trials Unit Engineer Officer.

The aircraft were not unloaded on the Seletar slipway and re-erected under the ageis of No 390 Maintenance Unit as might have been expected. The crates were handled at the Naval Base and the aircraft were towed by road on their own wheels (without rotor blades) travelling at night the few miles to the Royal Navy Air Station Sembawang—a grass airfield between the Naval Base and Seletar. Here, some 15 miles and therefore comparatively remote from the nearest FEAF engineering complex at Seletar where the air and ground crews were posted and residing, the aircraft were rapidly made ready for flight by their own Squadron ground crew, a facility regarded as most helpful by the Squadron Engineering Officer.(2) Shipped in April, the first two aircraft were flying from Sembawang by May, and able to participate in a FEAF exercise in June.(3)

These first six months were extremely valuable in providing a working-up period for the Belvederes in view of what was to come later in Borneo. Apart from a few weeks in August and September when all Belvederes were grounded pending investigation of the fatal crash in Germany reported in Chapter 10, during which time the last two of the six Belvederes arrived in crates and were reassembled at Sembawang, trooping and resupply operations were conducted with comparatively little trouble. The engine starter systems were still new and the ex-BTU ground crew knew well how to persuade them to function, so even they produced no serious problems at this stage. Two foreseen difficulties however became immediately apparent—shortage of crewmen and the total absence of winches.(4)

There was still no formal policy for providing crewmen for helicopters and although the BTU and Belvedere Squadrons had made a strong case for an appropriate establishment in 1961 and 1962, it was not until August 1963 that the decision by the Air Ministry to establish crewmen in respect of helicopters was taken, the initial intention being to use air engineers for the role.(5) In mid-1962 therefore,

Unlike the Whirlwind, the Sycamore could be loaded into the Beverley without the need to interfere with the rotor hub and blades. This method of deployment was used as part of the immediate response to the Brunei revolt.

The first Belvederes in Malaya were shipped to the Singapore Naval Base and towed by road to Sembawang overnight for re-assembly.

because they could not function safely and effectively without them, the Belvedere Squadrons were still selecting and training their own crewmen from amongst their technical ground crew, thus following the procedure adopted by their predecessors in the Casualty Evacuation Flight of 1950. In order to obtain the maximum benefit from the engineering expertise available whilst the aircraft were deployed away from base, the tendency, as before, was to use senior NCO ground crew when possible, although Corporals and Junior Technicians were also employed. The result was a more or less chronic shortage of senior NCO technicians.(6)

The No 66 Squadron Unit Engineer Officer was himself awarded the Queen's Commendation for valuable services in the air at the end of his tour in August 1964, having flown well over 450 hours in Belvederes as a crewman and, occasionally, as co-pilot, mostly on operations in Borneo.(7) It was not until October 1963 that the first aircrew crewmen (Air Signallers because they happened to be in surplus at the time) arrived on No 66 Squadron.

The lack of winches in the Belvedere was felt almost immediately in Malaya in 1962. The electric winch designed for the aircraft, dependent for its control on variable electrical resistance, had been found during tropical trials at Idris in North Africa to be virtually uncontrollable and had simply been abandoned.(8) As an alternative, fit and practised persons could be expected to climb down reasonably short lengths of rope, but their recovery posed a more difficult problem especially in jungle sites. In December 1962 the pilot and navigator of a Javelin, having ejected and landed in the jungle (the former being suspended from a tree) had to be recovered by being hauled up manually by rope to the rescuing Belvedere. A block and tackle arrangement was rigged and very shortly afterwards the same procedure was used to rescue six survivors from a sinking launch.(9) It was a desperate remedy.

A much smaller difficulty is recorded because of the related dramatic events which followed. The control cables, known as the 'yaw cables', by which opposite lateral cyclic tilt was applied to the rotors by the pilot's foot pedals were unexpectedly reduced to a life of 100 hours in December 1962. This inevitably produced a temporary shortage of the item. Subsequently yaw cable failures in flight occurred in May 1963 in FEAF and October 1964 in AFME. In the FEAF case the result was a catastrophic crash in which the crew of three and six passengers were killed. The only possible conclusion was that the yaw cables constituted a feature requiring redesign, and the chief designer at the time, Mr McClements, confirmed this view.(10) Reducing the cable life to 100 hours was neither a satisfactory nor a reliable solution. That it had to be accepted is further evidence of the inherent disadvantages under which the Belvedere was labouring. Soon afterwards the yaw cable life was reduced to 50 hours, but a proposal by the manufacturer to replace the yaw cables by control rods was not implemented.

The Brunei Revolt of December 1962 signalled the end of anti-Communist terrorist activities in North Malaya as a main preoccupation of the FEAF helicopter force although military activity near the Thai border and communications flights for the jungle forts in North Malaya never actually ceased. The size of the task may be judged from the fact, for example, that in July 1962 the nine Sycamores at Butterworth carried 582 troops and 9300 lbs of freight, and by the end of the year had carried their thousandth aero-medical patient since arriving at Butterworth in mid-1959.(11) The No 110 Squadron Whirlwinds Mk 10 did not replace the Butterworth Sycamores except for SAR standby, but were used in September 1963 to replace those Sycamores detached for operations in Borneo. Assumption of the support helicopter role in North Malaya by Alouettes of the Royal Malaysian Air Force and Iroquois of the Royal Australian Air Force was a gradual process, and it was not until October 1964 that the Sycamores were formally withdrawn from operational tasking on the mainland of Malaya. Four then remained and were established to provide two for daily use by the Air Commander in the communications role in Singapore. Even that was not quite the end of the Sycamore in the SH role. Apart from the two brief detachments to Gan in October 1962 and August 1964 already mentioned in Chapter 3, the Sycamores, having moved to Seletar, were once more pressed into operational service in November 1964, joining the Belvederes and Whirlwinds Mk 10 in support of the ground forces opposing the Indonesian incursions then taking place in South Malaya. Two Sycamores continued in the VIP communications role for nearly four more years, and after having served for 13 years in Malaya, Borneo, Singapore and briefly in Gan and Hong Kong, their final retirement in FEAF in May 1967 was marked by a ceremonial formation flight escorted by Whirlwinds.

The SAR standby task on behalf of both the RAAF fighter units based there and also of visiting fighter and bomber exercise detachments from Tengah, required one Whirlwind Mk 10 detachment to Butterworth which continued to be met by No 110 Squadron until August 1965, and thereafter by the other Whirlwind Squadron, No 103, until March 1967. Apart from this continuing SAR task at Butterworth, major attention centred on Borneo and Singapore from the start of operations in Brunei in December 1962.

Borneo—Outline Description

The island previously known as Borneo lies about 400 miles east of Singapore and measures about 800 miles from north to south by 600 miles east to west. The southern and western three-quarters of the island, almost completely undeveloped, was ceded by the Dutch to Indonesia in 1949 and thereafter named Kalimantan. The remaining quarter consisted of Sarawak in the west (approximately 24000 square miles) and North Borneo (later Sabah) to the north east (approximately 24000 square miles), which together constituted British Borneo; and, sandwiched between them, the independent Sultanate of Brunei (a mere 2500 square miles

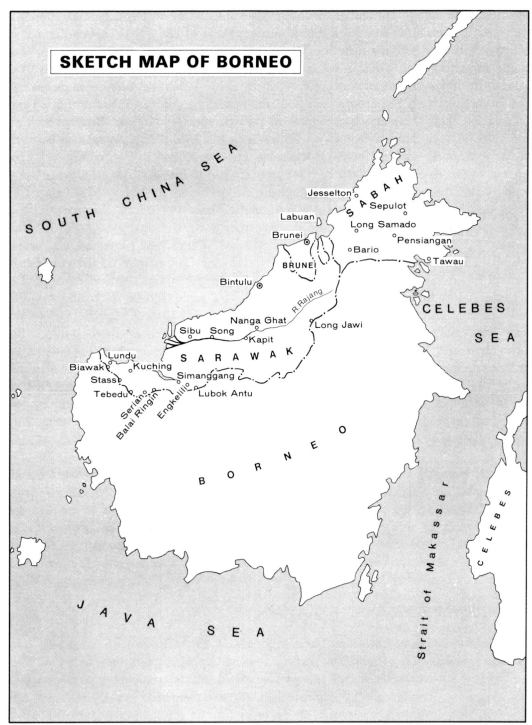

SKETCH MAP OF BORNEO

SOUTH CHINA SEA

Jesselton

S A B A H

Sepulot

Labuan

Long Samado

Brunei

Pensiangan

BRUNEI

Bario

Tawau

Bintulu

CELEBES

R Rajang

SEA

Nanga Ghat

Long Jawi

Sibu Song

Kapit

S A R A W A K

Lundu

Biawak

Kuching

Stass

Simanggang

Tebedu

Lubok Antu

Serian

Balai Ringin

Engkelili

C
E
L
E
B
E
S

B O R N E O

Strait of Makassar

J A V A   S E A

Air Staff Drawing Office (RAF) October 1986

316-A

approximately). Together they have an area comparable to that of England and Scotland, but their frontier with Kalimantan stretches for nearly 1000 miles, mostly along the top of the watershed in the east and north, with ground heights up to 8000 feet, often not easy to locate accurately in the hills but much more difficult to recognise topographically in the lower and flatter regions of Sarawak. The entire country is covered with primary jungle with extensive mangrove swamps in coastal areas. There are few roads near the coasts and none at all inland except in the vicinity of Kuching (capital of Sarawak), Sibu in the central area and in Brunei. Sarawak is delineated in 'Divisions' numbered one to five reading from west to east, thus Kuching is in the First Division and Bario in the Fifth Division. The small but pleasant island of Labuan lies 20 miles off the Brunei coast and was part of British North Borneo (Sabah).

Hazards

The climate of Malaya was briefly described in Chapter 2. That in Borneo is of a similar pattern but more intense, that is to say, the morning mist and low cloud is more frequent and more tenacious, the afternoon thunderstorms start earlier and are more widespread and the overall rainfall is even higher. In addition operations, especially in North Borneo and the fourth and fifth divisions of Sarawak, involved moderately high altitudes amongst mountainous scenery at least as difficult as the worst Malaya had to offer and which, for most of the campaign, was so poorly mapped that quite large mountains were either wrongly placed by several miles or else omitted altogether. In these circumstances radio navigation aids would have been of limited use even if they had been available which they were not. Initially, the helicopters had no HF radios and VHF or UHF contact was non-existent beyond a few miles from base. It follows that the helicopter crews had a daunting task, and that many sorties had to be flown to find and redirect Army patrols who were geographically lost—a situation which occasionally affected the helicopter pilots themselves. Pensiangan in Sabah, for example, a bowl-shaped amphitheatre in a deep valley, was notoriously difficult to find by using the only maps that were initially provided. It was also one of the more topographically difficult sites for the MRT Beverleys to locate for the frequent supply drops required.(12)

Later in the campaign, as a result of urgent survey work which was aided both by helicopter transport for Army survey teams and extensive photographic reconnaissance by FEAF Canberras, more useful maps became available but even these were woefully short of accurate detail in many areas. Also, they virtually stopped dead at the Kalimantan Border, so the helicopter crews were presented with quite useful mapping detail which ended sharply with the line of the border and gave only the most vague indications of what lay beyond this invisible barrier up to the very edge of which they had to operate. In one particularly large blank area across the Kalimantan Border near Engkelili in the third division of Sarawak, the cartographer had indicated his total inability to provide significant information by inscribing the message 'Here be dragons'. The absence of accurate maps was but one indication of the remoteness of the interior of the country from the fragmented ribbons of development near the coast. Only five months after starting operations, a Sycamore of No 110 Squadron discovered a 'new' village of about 300 people whose existence was previously unknown. A police superintendent was flown in by helicopter to establish control.(13)

There were a few unmanned airstrips suitable for light fixed wing aircraft, but no comprehensive pattern of such facilities.

Borneo—Political Background

Both North Borneo and Sarawak had originally been part of Brunei's empire until Sarawak was ceded by the Sultan to Sir James Brooke in 1841, thus founding the dynasty of the White Rajahs. It became a British colony after the Japanese occupation in 1945. Brunei became a British Protectorate in 1888, and North Borneo was ceded as a British colony in 1891. Thus, in 1962 we were dealing with a British Protectorate (Brunei) as an independent enclave between two British Crown Colonies—British North Borneo and Sarawak. The formation of the Federation of Malaysia in September 1963 incorporated North Borneo (now named Sabah and including Labuan) and Sarawak to constitute East Malaysia, an event which the Indonesians greatly resented and which was the chief reason for previous border attacks from Kalimantan escalating into what President Sukarno of Indonesia called 'Confrontation'.

The independent Sultanate of Brunei suffered an internal revolt in December 1962, shortly before the formation of Malaysia. Disaffected elements in the State objected to the plans to form Malaysia out of what used to be Brunei's empire as much as did the Indonesians, albeit for different reasons. There was in any case an element of social unrest in Brunei itself due partly to the maldistribution of the considerable wealth derived from the oil wells at Seria. At all events, it was in Brunei that the first trouble appeared but, although exacerbated by infiltrators from across the border, it broke out inside the country as well as taking the frontier incursion form of activity which was to characterise the Confrontation operations to which it was the curtain raiser.

As in Malaya in the 1950s, the native people took little or no direct part in the war, but in this case the indigenous population did not include the Malay presence— 54% in Brunei but only 7% in Sabah and about 20% in Sarawak. There were, however, an estimated 30000 Indonesians living in Sabah—two thirds of them in the Tawau region. As in Malaya, the Chinese residents were the principal fertile field for the Communist influences which were active in supporting the Indonesian-organised incursions. The Chinese represented about 20% of the population of Sabah and about 30% of that of Sarawak and in the latter the local terrorist sympathiser situation in the populated areas was not dissimilar to that in Malaya in the 1950s. The truly indigenous people are the Land Dyaks, Ibans and half a dozen other tribes—agricultural people living in Longhouse communities and generally supportive of the security forces. Borrowing a phrase from the days of General Templer in Malaya some 10 years previously, much attention was paid to obtaining the support of all types of local communities by influencing their 'hearts and minds', and in this activity the helicopters naturally played a major part.(14)

The Brunei revolt was crushed within ten days but mopping up operations continued for about four months, during which time numerous SAS patrols supported by helicopters operated in the border area engaged more in catching the escaping perpetrators than opposing further incursions.(15) Thereafter there was no further significant trouble in Brunei itself in the Confrontation period.

In April 1963, before the mopping up of the Brunei revolt had quite finished, the Confrontation war had begun with a cross border raid at Tebedu, and the build-up of British Forces in Borneo already in progress was accelerated, and with it the larger scale and long term commitment of RAF helicopters.

This period from the Brunei revolt in December 1962 leading up to the full-scale Confrontation activities following the declaration of the State of Malaysia in September 1963, constituted for the helicopter units a build-up period comparable to Phase 1 of the helicopter history (1950–52) when the Dragonflys of the Casualty Evacuation Flight in Malaya provided a very limited service in support of ground troops not yet able to conduct the full-scale effective operations which were soon to be needed. For the helicopter crews, many of whom had operated in the Malayan emergency of the 1950s, the similarity of the operating conditions at this early stage of the Borneo operations was heightened by the fact that there was often mutual personal recognition between the RAF helicopter pilots and the SAS troops who now met each other again in jungle clearings exactly like those in which they had last met in Malaya ten years before.(16)

The Start of Operations

On 8 December 1962, civil disturbance in Brunei was recognised as armed rebellion. The British response in Singapore was to implement the contingency plan prepared for this eventuality (Plan Ale), suitably updated by the addition of helicopters to the forces to be despatched by air—there was no doubt in this Theatre about the vital role of the helicopter. Troops were embarked in four Beverleys of the MRT force at Seletar for transit to Labuan and the aircraft carrier HMS Hermes was loaded to such an extent with motor transport, personnel and support equipment that there was no room for the three RAF Sycamores and Belvederes which had been added to the force. After some discussion the three Belvederes were cleared for take-off with overload fuel tanks at 19500 lbs all-up weight (1000 lbs over normal limits) and flew direct the 400 odd miles to Kuching and thence to Labuan on the 17 December—a total of eight hours flying time—with no untoward effects apart from a heavier than usual vibration during the first hour or so of flight after each take-off. The aircraft were serviceable on arrival and went to work deploying and supplying a troop of the Royal Marines with 105 mm guns and ammunition.(17) The three Sycamores were flown by Beverley to Labuan with six pilots and twelve ground crew on 28 December and were flying by the following day.(18)

An opportunity to demonstrate the 'hearts and minds' philosophy with considerable effect was provided almost at the very outset of operations in Borneo when in January 1963, with the Brunei revolt barely suppressed, military follow-up action was briefly interrupted to help the civilian population to deal with the consequences of a period of rain which was excessive even by Borneo standards. Sixteen inches of rain fell in one week in Brunei and the fourth and fifth divisions of Sarawak and much flood relief and rescue work had to be done. The effect on the attitude of the local population was most beneficial for the security forces, particularly at this early stage of the campaign. The principle of helping the local population whenever possible, particularly with helicopter lifts and medical casualty evacuations, was followed throughout the whole ensuing period of military activity.

Development of the Campaign

In the immediate aftermath of the suppression of the Brunei revolt, most helicopter tactical activity was concerned with moving the SAS patrols to and fro in the border areas. The RAF had, at this stage, only three Belvederes and three Sycamores in Borneo, based on Brunei Town airfield. The commando carrier HMS Albion was in the Far East and Royal Navy Whirlwinds Mk 7 and Wessex Mk 1 were pressed into service to assist. A naval helicopter presence was maintained thereafter in various locations from the commando carriers continually in transit between Singapore, Borneo, Hong Kong and Australia for the remainder of the Borneo campaign. In addition to their work near the border, Belvederes were used in lifting heavy machinery for airstrip construction or improvement, for example at Long Seridan and Meligan, as well as in their new role of recovering disabled helicopters. In the first two months of 1963 they lifted two RN Whirlwinds from Brunei to HMS Albion and one RN Wessex onto a barge for return to HMS Albion. Other similar operations are described later.(19)

There was no large-scale military activity immediately following the suppression of the Brunei revolt, rather a steadily mounting threat as propaganda from Jakarta was matched by the gathering of Indonesian-trained raiding parties along the whole length of the Kalimantan border, and especially in the first and second divisions of Sarawak. A corresponding build-up of British troops took place and the RN helicopters were deployed to Kuching. In early 1963, FEAF was still awaiting the delayed arrival of the Mk 10 Whirlwinds, but in the meantime had only the three

Belvederes and Sycamores to deploy. In fact, the Sycamores were withdrawn to Butterworth in March but had to be returned to Brunei in the following month, where they were used mainly in Sabah and the fourth and fifth divisions of Sarawak. In July 1963, FEAF was at last able to deploy the first six Whirlwinds Mk 10 to Kuching, and No 224 Group in Singapore assumed from the Royal Navy responsibility for helicopter operations at the airfield. Two Belvederes were added, being transported by HMS Albion.(20) The Sycamores were finally withdrawn to Butterworth in September. The pressure to provide helicopters was now severe and it will be seen why the allotment of Mk 10 Whirlwinds to replace the Mk 2s for SAR in the United Kingdom was delayed at the end of Phase 2 as mentioned in Chapter 5. The fitting of H/F radios in the helicopters had now become so urgent that No 224 Group was demanding the quickest solution regardless of whether or not it was the best. The AOC was applying urgent personal pressure on the Vice Chief of the Air Staff to obtain priority for Borneo at the expense of other commitments if necessary.(21) A hangar was to be built for the Belvederes at Kuching. By July, the Borneo helicopter deployment was one Belvedere and three Sycamores at Brunei, two Belvederes and six Whirlwinds at Kuching. On 1 August, No 103 Squadron, having disbanded in Cyprus (see Chapter 5) re-formed at Seletar with 10 Whirlwinds Mk 10 alongside No 110 Squadron. Air Ministry agreed H/F SSB radio for Borneo helicopters and the Collins 618-T3 set was approved for the purpose. The FEAF helicopter force of two Whirlwind and one Belvedere squadrons was now complete, and what may be described as the first of two phases of the Borneo operation ended in September 1963. Thereafter, there was a considerable further increase in helicopter strength and activity.

There may be a tendency to think of the Borneo campaign as the main reason for the existence of the FEAF helicopter operations, in which case the retention of the two Whirlwind and one Belvedere squadron bases in Singapore would be surprising. Similarly, there was no attempt to deploy No 224 Group HQ from Seletar to Borneo. Tasking agencies and local controller teams had to be created specifically for Borneo operations. The fact was that FEAF was a complete and virtually independent air force having front-line operational units in all the main specialisations—bomber, fighter, transport (long, medium and short range) and maritime, together with two large Maintenance Units—one engineering and one for all aspects of supply. Its primary task was to support the Commonwealth Strategic Reserve and, in the process, to provide air defence for Singapore and Malaya. The FEAF contingency plan for Borneo was but one of the many envisaging possible conflagrations throughout the Far East. The fact that it was the only one to require full implementation did not by any means exclude efforts in other directions and throughout the Borneo Confrontation period elaborate exercises with the Commonwealth Brigade in Thailand and elsewhere continued unabated, as did air defence exercises in Singapore.(22) Thus, when in September 1963 the declaration of the formation of the Federation of Malaysia resulted in Confrontation escalating to a state amounting to undeclared war, it was No 38 Group resources from the

United Kingdom which eventually had to be obtained to provide and maintain adequate helicopter support for the increased Army activity. Meanwhile the policy for the three FEAF helicopter squadrons remained as:

a. Tactical support for the Far East Strategic Reserve.

b. Support for civilian authorities including border security and Borneo territories.

c. Internal security.

d. Aero-medical evacuation.

Three Belvederes and six Whirlwinds—three from each of Nos 103 and 110 Squadrons—were retained at Singapore for training and seven days per week dawn to dusk standby for SRT support operations in West Malaysia (Malaya). No 110 Squadron had the additional task of a single aircraft standby at 15 minutes readiness for SAR at Butterworth, plus the Sycamore communications tasks for the Air Commander. The policy for the FEAF SRT helicopter squadrons therefore resulted in a deployment of 12 Whirlwinds and five Belvederes in Borneo, and six Whirlwinds, three Belvederes and two Sycamores at Seletar in Singapore (23) with one Whirlwind detached to Butterworth.

Confrontation

'Spine Force' was the name given to the No 38 Group elements added to the FEAF helicopter force in late 1963 for the second phase of the Borneo operations which consisted of ten aircraft of No 225 (Whirlwind) Squadron and three Belvederes of No 26 Squadron not yet delivered to join the first two No 26 Squadron aircraft in Aden—see Chapter 11. The personnel strength was 27 officers and 112 NCOs and airmen. The suddenness of this deployment may be deduced from the fact that Odiham had deployed to North Africa for Exercise Triplex West practically the whole of No 225 Squadron plus three of the Belvederes destined for No 26 Squadron and it was at the end of that Exercise that they were told they were to deploy to the Far East instead of returning to Odiham—see Chapter 10. The crews returned to the United Kingdom for embarkation leave, and preparation for a one-year unaccompanied tour in the Far East, all of which was to be spent in Borneo. The No 26 Squadron Flight Commander recalls that one result of this rapid preparation for a tour in an area with limited support establishment involved medical and dental checks resulting in the precautionary extraction of 146 teeth from the airmen selected.(24) A tenth Whirlwind was transported by Beverley to join the nine Exercise Triplex West aircraft at Bomba in North Africa ready to embark with the two Belvederes (one had crashed at Bomba during the exercise—See Chapter 10) plus a replacement for the crashed aircraft already embarked on HMS Albion, which then delivered the entire No 38 Group task force to Singapore on 20 November. The air and ground crews were flown from UK to Singapore arriving on 13 November. After Theatre operational training at Seletar lasting about three weeks the entire Spine Force was transported by aircraft carrier to Borneo and became operational in December.(25)

Nos 103 and 110 Squadrons had deployed in Borneo on a rotational basis about two-thirds of their aircraft strength and the addition of the whole of No 225 Squadron virtually doubled the Whirlwind force in Borneo. Similarly, the three Spine Force Belvederes (making a total of ten in FEAF) plus one from Singapore went to increase the Borneo detachment from three to seven aircraft. The result was an almost instantaneous doubling of the helicopter force available in Borneo, one effect of which was to permit a more flexible and efficient deployment pattern to a larger number of forward bases, and thus to provide better and more immediate response to the more organised and widely dispersed Indonesian incursions which now developed under Confrontation policy. The Royal Navy helicopters of No 845 Squadron were moved from Labuan to Kuching with deployments at Sibu and Nanga Gaat thus assisting in the first, second and third divisions of Sarawak.(26) In January 1964 the RAF deployments were seven Whirlwinds at Labuan, six Belvederes and eight Whirlwinds at Kuching, with one, two or three Whirlwinds deployed further at Milegan, Tawau, Long Semado and Simanggang. Bullet-proof vests were issued, Whirlwind pilot seats were fitted with armour-plate and bren gun fittings were provided in doorways. All helicopters were being fitted with H/F radios. The last four Whirlwinds of No 225 Squadron, fitted with the wire guided SS11 missile, were despatched from Odiham to Kuching. Phase 2 of the Borneo operations was now in full swing.

Army Deployments

The Army was strung out all along the Kalimantan border, having a chain of patrol bases from which about two-thirds of the occupants were out on patrol at any one time. Each battalion had a frontage of about 100 miles or more and an attempt was made to construct permanent helicopter landing points every 1000 yards or so for both tactical troop movements and casualty evacuation.(27) The troops were rotated from Singapore every four months (six months for the Gurkhas) and, in the absence of roads, relied completely on the helicopter force to accomplish the changeovers. In order to maintain constant operational readiness whole units had to be inserted and withdrawn in one day, while a similar two-way mass movement had to be conducted on the same day by the MRT force between Singapore and Labuan or Kuching, the latter having severe accommodation problems for troops in transit.(28) Whereas in Malaya during the 1950s operations had involved up to 24 battalions, not including the Police Field Force, with only limited troop lift capability by helicopter, in Borneo in 1964 there were only some six battalions plus some local auxiliaries but with helicopter support the operational usefulness of this force was reckoned to be effectively tripled.(29) By the end of 1964 there were ten battalions.

In early 1964 with the Indonesian and internal threats increasing, the forward platoon patrol bases started to become Company bases and to look like jungle forts, complete with 105 mm gun emplacements in and out of which the Belvederes moved the guns as required. The Belvederes were also heavily involved in the construction of these forts which required comparatively large quantities of barbed wire and, especially, corrugated iron panels.(30) Some were very close to the Indonesian border, for example Stass and Biawak in the first division of Sarawak, and aircraft flying much above 50 feet were liable to be fired on by heavy machine guns from across the border. In these cases the MRT food, water and ammunition resupply air drops had to be replaced by tactically flying helicopters able to keep out of sight of the enemy by literally hiding behind the trees.(31) Navigation errors by the helicopters operating so close to the border were liable to be fatal, particularly in the first and second divisions where the border was not always defined by obvious topographical features such as mountain ridges and was often invisible. In November 1956 the pilot of a Whirlwind from Kuching flying from Bau to Stass—a flight of some 10 minutes—evidently mistook a small hill across the border for a similar one near Stass itself, overflew his target by a few seconds and was promptly shot down by machine gun fire with fatal results.(32) In December 1964, Wg Cdr Ross, an RAF chaplain, was killed by enemy fire from across the border whilst travelling as a passenger in an Army Air Corps Auster carrying out a mail drop at Biawak.

The regular standard helicopter tasks required by the Army in the operational circumstances of the second main phase of the Confrontation war consisted basically of the daily maintenance supply of food, water, kerosene and ammunition to the Company and patrol bases screening the Kalimantan border. Although the whole border had to be watched it had become clear that there was a large but not unlimited number of places where the Indonesians could organise border crossings. When these occurred, rapid troop redeployments were needed in the forward areas, and to meet these demands numerous small helicopter detachments were employed, maintained and changed with complete flexibility as the local situation demanded and the overall picture permitted—an example of centralised control of tactical air power.

Forward airheads used were initially Brunei in the east and later, as the activity increased, Labuan where facilities were easier to arrange, and Kuching in the west. Such few airstrips as there were became natural bases, able to accept the single and twin Pioneers and heavy supply drops by the Beverleys, Hastings and Argosys of the MRT force. The main strips used throughout were at Lundu in the first division, Simanggang in the second division, Sibu in the third division, Long

Re-fuelling the front tank of a Belvedere at a forward base in Borneo. Note the proximity of the front engine jet pipes to the re-fuelling airman, and the fuel dipstick which passes through the rotor disc.

Belvedere re-fuelling at a typical semi permanent Army base near the Indonesian border.

Forward semi-permanent army post near the Indonesian border, with 105 mm positioned by helicopter in its emplacement centre left of the picture. Note also the extensive use of corrugated iron, all of which had to be delivered by air.

105 mm gun placed by helicopter in its firing position near the Indonesian border.

Semado and Bario in the fourth and fifth divisions and Sepulot and Tawau in Sabah. RAF helicopter detachments were maintained at all these strips and, as the situation demanded, at forward locations of Company or Platoon HQs. For example:—

From Kuching—Balai Ringin, Serian, Tebedu
From Simanggang—Engkelili, Lubok Antu, Jambu
From Sibu—Song, Kapit, Nanga Gaat (permanent detachments), Long Jawi
From Labuan—Pensiangan, Meligan, Long Pasia

The following extract from the Operations and Exercises section of No 110 Squadron Operations Record Book gives some indication of the sort of operations being undertaken in late 1964, and considered by the Squadron as worthy of comment as distinct from the more regular continuous task of troop redeployment, resupply and casualty evacuation. It starts with a reference to the Indonesian incursions in Malaya (West Malaysia) which are outlined in the subsequent narrative.

Extract from No 110 Squadron ORB—December 1964

'Seletar Operations

There was little call for operational Whirlwind flying during the early part of this month. Over the Christmas period another Indonesian landing by sea of some 30 Indonesian soldiers and Malaysians took place. The Squadron provided an aircraft on Christmas Day for this operation. Again aircraft unserviceability plagued the Squadron and training flying was restricted.

Borneo Detachment

No 110 Squadron continued to meet their commitment in the Borneo territories and two aircraft are based at Bario in support of the Army units there, 2/6th Ghurka Rifles. During the early part of December the Bario detachment was unusually busy. The Director of Operations has now given permission for forces in the border area to counter incursions and pursue the enemy up to 5000 yards beyond the border. This has increased the scope of offensive patrolling and the use of Landing Points (LP) very close to the border has become a regular occurrence.

Three incidents typical of the kind of operations in which the Squadron aircraft take part are worthy of note. One patrol from D Company 2/6th Ghurka Rifles led by Major Robinson, was landed close to the border near Long Rapung by a Whirlwind from the Squadron, Captain, Flight Lieutenant D A W Todman. Some days previously a small "hide" had been constructed and it was from this that a man using a powerful monocular could observe a track used frequently by Indonesian patrols. A successful operation followed in which Squadron aircraft resupplied the troops. The troops were subsequently lifted out by helicopter.

The second incident concerning troops from the same Company took place between the 7 and 13 December. A Platoon deployed in the Long Banga area was airlifted to an LP at 5100 feet very close to the border. The crew of the aircraft was: Captain—Flight Sergeant Spinks; Second Pilot—Flying Officer Edwards. It was the intention of the Platoon to penetrate the maximum distance across the border and set up a small base. On a subsequent resupply run the same crew, who incidentally were carrying out theatre conversion for Flying Officer Edwards, found that the LP was unmanned and therefore insecure. The small party who were to have returned from the forward base and secured the LP had run into a band of 90 Indonesians. They were unable to reach the rendezvous and one man was wounded. Two soldiers were killed in the subsequent follow-up action against the 90 Indonesians. The Platoon at the forward base now appeared to be cut off from its supplies and the LP was unmanned and therefore insecure. This was particularly significant to the helicopter crew as Indonesians were now known to be in the area in strength. However, the crew, knowing the nature of the situation and the pressing need for medical assistance flew into the LP eight Ghurkas and a Medical Orderly with supplies. This patrol had instructions to push through to the forward base and the wounded man. It was unfortunate that this rescue Platoon put in by the helicopter was unable to continue after they had lost one man on the track which had been mined. Shortly after this incident the beleaguered Platoon started to cut a new track back to the LP. Carrying the dead and wounded they reached the LP 25 hours later. Both parties were lifted out by aircraft of this Squadron and fresh troops were lifted in to replace them. Operations in this area continue.

The third incident highlights the value of Sarbe beacons, now standard equipment with each Special Air Service patrol. A small party of SAS troops became separated during a night patrol and one man failed to arrive at the rendezvous the following morning. A search was mounted and two small patrols were airlifted to the area by Squadron aircraft. The 'Violet Picture' UHF presentation was switched on by the lead aircraft and a strong signal was received emanating from a Sarbe beacon in the area. The aircraft was homed to this beacon which was found situated in a disused clearing. A grateful SAS soldier was airlifted out.

Monthly Achievements

The monthly flying achievement is as follows:

    a. Operational hours   240.35

    b. Operational sorties   782

    c. Non-operational sorties   140'

West Malaysia

In the second half of 1964, the Indonesians temporarily switched the emphasis of their incursion activity to the southern part of West Malaysia (Malaya),(34) making several landings by small boats driven by powerful outboard engines. Initial landings were at three points in South Johore, as well as one on Shell Island near Singapore. On 2 September a major parachute assault was made by night when 97 troops were dropped by C-130 transport aircraft near the town of Labis in Johore. The communal situation in Singapore was already very tense—there had been political rioting and consequent curfews during July and August—and the war seemed to be getting uncomfortably close. Preparations for the arrival of the Bloodhound Anti-Aircraft Missile Squadron (No 75) in Singapore continued, anti-aircraft guns were deployed around the main installations and local aircraft dispersal schemes on the Singapore airfields were prepared.(35) Seletar helicopters, at first given deployment positions on the Station golf course, were later directed to Sembawang for dispersal. Sandbag blast walls were erected at the entrances to important buildings, air raid shelters were constructed(36) and watchers, including personnel of the FEAF band, were deployed by helicopters to man four visual reporting points (VRP) on the nearby islands (two more VRPs were provided by the Marine Craft Unit).(37) The RAF Regiment was deployed in its primary role of airfield defence at Butterworth, Tengah and Seletar, but a Flight of No 15(F) Squadron RAF Regiment defending the airstrip and helicopter detachment at Sepulot in Borneo was not disturbed.(38)

The Indonesians who actually landed did not have much success. Insurgents in Singapore were quickly rounded up; those in the jungles of Johore took a little longer to find, but were bombed by Shackletons and vigorously harried by air strikes by Hunters and Canberras, Whirlwinds and Sycamores (the latter only recently relegated to the VIP communications role for the Air Commander) providing the aerial platform for the FACs, as well as acting with the Belvederes in their standard support role for the ground forces.

The helicopters, of critical importance in these operations, were found from the rumps of Nos 103, 110 and 66 Squadrons not deployed to Borneo, but retained in Singapore for just such an eventuality and normally employed in exercises with 28 Commonwealth Brigade in Malaya, providing operational training for new pilots and monthly continuation training for those rotated from the two or three-week detachment periods in Borneo which was the usual pattern for the Singapore-based squadrons. The many new helicopter pilots arriving during this period from the UK for the FEAF squadrons received highly realistic operational training in this period even before going to Borneo. By October, the Indonesian parachutist parties in the Labis area had all been accounted for—28 killed and 63 captured.(39)

Further small incursions by boat continued for two months or so, but met with no success whatever. The boats could not be hidden from the helicopter and Pioneer reconnaissances flown along the beaches soon after dawn, daily at first and subsequently at irregular intervals. The Indonesians were dismayed to find they were given no help or encouragement by the Malaysians in the incursion areas,(40) and in addition confessed to being confused and demoralised by the continual sound of helicopters.(41) Some were captured while still at sea. In April 1965, for example, the enemy casualties in what was now known as Operation Oak Tree were 38 killed, 39 captured, 10 drowned.(42) Between August 1964 and March 1965 there were 41 landings, attempted landings or acts of sabotage. 740 Indonesians were involved of whom 451 actually landed. 142 were killed and 309 captured.(43) The last incursion in West Malaysia was by 25 Indonesians at Penggarang in May 1965 and, like the others, was swiftly contained by helicopter-borne troops. Beach reconnaissance around the lower part of the Malay Peninsula continued with diminishing frequency for a further year. Borneo operations, by contrast, continued at a rising rate through 1965.

Borneo Operations—Second Stage

The slight reduction of activity in Borneo during the Indonesian incursions into West Malaysia (Malaya) came to an end in mid-1965. During that year British and Commonwealth troop strength doubled from approximately 10000 to 20000.(44) The political decision originally made to eschew any move which could possibly be construed as offensive action was carefully maintained. Thus, the presence of Javelins and Hunters served to deter the Indonesian Air Force from offensive action, but they never fired over the border. Cautious cross-border forays by the SAS in hot pursuit of fleeing Indonesians or in establishing ambush positions were eventually permitted in specifically authorised cases only, and for strictly limited ranges of between 1000 and 5000 yards.(45) Great care was taken to prevent general knowledge of these activities since it was of paramount importance to avoid accusations of aggression and the risk of precipitating escalation of the conflict. Even when the Whirlwind was shot down in November 1965 only a few hundred yards over the border at Stass, strong pressure from Kuching for a Hunter strike on enemy troops in the area so that a SAS rescue party could attempt a possible rescue was resisted as being 'provacative', even though Hunters were positioned at Kuching in readiness for such a sortie.(46) Cross-border fire by 105 mm guns on specific targets was permitted and enemy mortar fire was returned.(47) All military initiative was left to the enemy, the objective being solely to detect rapidly and defeat any incursion across the border, while awaiting political acceptance of the situation by Indonesia.

For the helicopters then, the second phase of the Borneo operations consisted of their becoming more active and more efficient in performing the tasks carried out in the first phase but for a much larger number of troops. It also meant more specialised development of techniques in three main fields:

a. the covert insertion and recovery of SAS troops or emergency casualty evacuation in deep jungle with helicopters having a maximum winch cable length of only 50 feet; (See Appendix 3).

b. the positioning of ground radar equipment in jungle sites;

c. development of night landing techniques in jungle sites—mainly for casualty evacuation. (See Appendix 4).

In each of these roles the Helicopter Wing formation at Seletar was able to play a major part in co-ordinating trials for new tasks as well as initiating development of new techniques and equipment.

Continuing Build-Up of the Forces

The build-up of forces in Borneo continued throughout 1965 to match the increasing Indonesian activity. In January 1965, No 230 Squadron—the last SRT Whirlwind Squadron in No 38 Group—was withdrawn from Germany to Odiham, relieved of its UNFICYP role in Cyprus by Wessex of No 18 Squadron (see Chapter 10) and strengthened by the absorption of No 1310 Flight from Guyana (see Chapter 10). Its thirteen aircraft were delivered by the aircraft carrier HMS Triumph to Singapore on 22 February 1965 and after about two weeks Theatre training were, like those of No 225 Squadron before them, delivered complete in this case by the aircraft carrier HMS Centaur to Labuan, where they arrived on 10 March and commenced operations on the Sabah/Kalimantan border on the next day.(48) At the end of 1965, No 225 Squadron, having arrived with the Spine Force in December 1963 for a one-year unaccompanied tour, was approaching its second one-year tour expiry date, but apart from the United Kingdom SAR units there was now no 'pool' of Whirlwind crews with which to replace them. No 225 Squadron was disbanded and its aircraft distributed between Nos 103 and 110 Squadrons, and a proprotion of its personnel was absorbed into FEAF on a two and a half year tour basis.(49)

No 66 Squadron, having lost one aircraft to Aden (XG 474—the RAF Museum aircraft) shortly after the Spine Force reinforcement, now benefited from the collapse of the Belvederes in Aden (see Chapter 11) and in December 1965 received from the disbanding No 26 Squadron their remaining four Belvederes (including XG 474). The aircraft were transported to Singapore on the aircraft carrier HMS Albion in December 1965, although they were in such bad condition that it took some four months of extensive servicing before they were all considered fit for operations in

Helicopters requiring redeployment between Singapore and Borneo were usually carried as deck cargo either on RN Aircraft carriers when available, or on civilian ships.

Manoeuvring a Belvedere on a supply ship deck prior to being lifted off by crane.

329-A

It was possible to fly single Belvederes directly on to the supply ship deck.

Four Belvederes and one Scout as deck cargo on the Maxwell Brander.

Twelve Whirlwinds of 230 Squadron on HMS <u>Bulwark</u> in Singapore Naval base estimate from UK to Borneo early in 1965.

Preparing to re-deploy a 105 mm gun near the Indonesian border.

FEAF. In February 1966, conversion of Belvedere pilots at Odiham ceased and local conversions in FEAF were started. No 66 Squadron looked forward to receiving the last three Belvederes from the OCU at Odiham later in the year.(50)

In the first half of 1966, British forces in Borneo, including the helicopters, had reached their peak. Army deployments in forward bases were well established, reliable maps were at last readily available, radar cover was established, airstrips and helicopter pads development was complete and the general level of experience was high. In January 1966, the RAF helicopter deployments were as follows:

a.　No 66 Squadron. Three Belvederes at Seletar. Five Belvederes at Kuching. (When the ex-No 26 Squadron Belvederes from Aden became operational in May, this was increased to five and seven respectively).

b.　No 103 Squadron. Four SH Whirlwinds plus two SAR Whirlwinds at Seletar, one SAR Whirlwind at Butterworth, twelve SH Whirlwinds at Kuching (with detachments at Lundu and Simanggang).

c.　No 110 Squadron. Four SH Whirlwinds plus two communications Sycamores at Seletar, six SH Whirlwinds at Kuching, six SH Whirlwinds at Sibu (with detachement at Nanga Gaat).(51)

d.　No 230 Squadron. Twelve SH Whirlwinds at Labaun (with detachements at Sepulot and Tawau).(52)

All were working at the maximum rate possible.

The attention paid to ensuring that the military actions and general behaviour of the Security Forces was popular with the indigenous population succeeded. The hearts and minds of the Ibans, Dyaks and the rest were generally on our side and against the Indonesians—occasionally dramatically so. In June 1966 a Whirlwind pilot—Flying Officer Ramshaw—based at Nanga Gaat (a forward permanent helicopter deployment from Sibu in the third division of Sarawak) was returning to base in the late afternoon having spent much of the day ferrying troops on the Kalimantan border near Long Jawi. When only a few miles from Nanga Gaat he found himself hemmed in a narrow river valley by violent thunderstorms. Although he had seen a Longhouse he could not find any clear area in which to land and wait for the weather to improve, and was eventually forced to shut down on a temporarily exposed shingle bank in the middle of the river.(53) Two Ibans came past in a canoe and pointed out the obvious fact that the river would shortly rise and cover the shingle bank to a depth of 'two men high'. They returned after about half an hour and announced the unlikely news that a place was now prepared for the helicopter on the bank opposite the Longhouse a short distance away. With

330

nothing to lose, Flying Officer Ramshaw took off and was surprised and relieved to find a cleared flat space which had not been there before. The inhabitants of the Longhouse, recalling that a helicopter clearing had been cut there a year or two previously, had all emerged, crossed the river and removed the secondary jungle which had covered the site. Ramshaw and his crewman plus his passenger—a Gurkha Corporal who fortunately spoke some Malay—were entertained in the Longhouse overnight and the helicopter recovered undamaged to Nanga Gaat the following morning. In August 1966 a Belvedere was landed on the dry edge of the river near the Longhouse and the headman—Ugoh Anak Belayong Teliai—was presented with a certificate signed by the FEAF Air Commander and recounting the incident in English, Malay and the appropriate Iban dialect.(54) Twenty years previously, perhaps much less, these people had been head hunters. Their antagonistic response to Indonesian incursions and approval of the Security Forces' anti-Indonesian operations was naturally a critical element in the campaign.

In early 1966 the Indonesian political scene had started to disintegrate visibly, and by March it was being described as 'in chaos'.(55) A Communist coup having failed in late 1965, Sukarno had lost power to Suharto in an anti-Communist Army coup and on 11 August 1966 a peace treaty was signed with Malaysia. Confrontation has lasted three years and eight months. Although there was a major Indonesian incursion (about 50 men) into Borneo in late August resulting in a brief but large increase in helicopter-borne troop movements, it was rapidly contained and many Indonesians were captured in the Long Semado area.(56) The war was suddenly over.

Command and Control of the Helicopter Force

The command structure in the Far East during the Borneo campaign was unusual in many respects and, on occasion, difficult to understand. This was due chiefly to the simultaneous tri-Service organisations in Singapore and Borneo, the latter being subordinate to the former in individual Service posts, but with a Joint Force Commander in Borneo having overall operational command in Borneo, and reporting direct to the C-in-C Far East—the latter post created to head the tri-Service Joint Force Headquarters organisation named 'Headquarters Far East Command', which came into being purely coincidentally with the start of Borneo operations on 1 January 1963 at Phoenix Park, Singapore. Thus the RAF had a Commander Air Forces Borneo (COMAIRBOR) in the Joint Headquarters at Brunei—later Labuan—with a BASO who became Forward Air Commander in the Joint Headquarters at Kuching, reporting either through the AOC No 224 Group or directly to the Air Commander in FEAF Headquarters in Singapore, but under the operational command of the Commander British Forces Borneo (COBRITBOR), responsible directly to the C-in-C Far East.

The height which the troops had to jump from the Belvedere was rather too high for comfort wearing full kit, but to use the ladder was even more difficult and slow.

Semi permanent Belvedere LZ in Borneo.

Semi permanent Belvedere LZ in Borneo.

Recovering a forced landed RN Whirlwind Mk 7 from Brunei to HMS Albion in January 1963.

Belvedere preparing to deploy 'Green Archer' radar near the Indonesian border.

Deploying Bloodhound anti aircraft missile to Kuching from the ship in which it was sent from Singapore.

Whirlwinds Mk 10 over Singapore.

The Whirlwind Mk 10 could deliver the 105 mm gun and ammunition, but the gun had to be stripped to allow the load to be spread over several sorties.

The Belvedere had a permanent LZ built for it on the top of Penang Hill in North Malaya, where the aircraft was used extensively to deliver components for the Ground Radars station being built there.

The permanent helicopter base at Nanga Gaat had sites for five helicopters, one large enough for a Belvedere.

This apparently alternative command structure for individual Service Chiefs was reflected in the lower echelons where the Seletar-based No 224 Group Helicopter Squadrons (Nos 66, 103 and 110) maintained permanent detachments at Labuan and Kuching and whose Station Commanders responded through COMAIRBOR and COMBRITBOR to C-in-C Far East, or COMAIRBOR and No 224 Group to FEAF, but not through Seletar. Even when reporting on administrative matters, the Commanding Officers of Seletar-based Squadrons spoke to No 224 Group through the Commanding Officer of RAF Seletar when in Singapore; through the local Commanding Officer of Labuan or Kuching when in Borneo; and even, on occasion, through the local Commanding Officer and COMAIRBOR direct to FEAF. It was not unknown for a Squadron Commander, while moving between Borneo and Singapore, to make use of more than one of these channels as seemed appropriate to him at the time, to achieve a solution of some administrative, personnel or even operational equipment problem which was proving intractable through the base organisation at Seletar.(57) Tasking of the helicopters was simple and direct through the Joint Operations Centres at Kuching for operations in the first, second and third divisions of Sarawak, and Labuan for operations in the fourth and fifth divisions of Sarawak, Brunei and Sabah.

Organisation of the Helicopter Force

The FEAF helicopter base organisation included a Helicopter Wing Headquarters, about which more will be said later, which had two main functions; to co-ordinate training, standardisation and maintain categorisation for the crews as they arrived from the UK or rotated from Borneo; and to provide Seletar with a Helicopter Flying Wing organisation paralleling the existing Flying Wing Headquarters but concerned only with the three helicopter squadrons on the station. With the exception of the Indonesian incursions in West Malaysia in late 1963 and early 1964, all the main helicopter operations took place in Borneo, so regular visits to the operation areas were necessary for the Helicopter Wing staff. The position of the Helicopter Wing Commander was at times quite delicate, for example when visiting Kuching, whose Commanding Officer was also a Wing Commander. Each regarded the helicopter crews, their performance and their welfare, as his own direct responsibility. The Station Commander of Seletar visited 'his' helicopter crews at Kuching and Labuan and on one occasion, the Station Commander of Odiham—the official home of No 225 Squadron—also paid a visit to Kuching to see how 'his' squadron was getting on.(58) A further difficulty was that while the No 38 Group Spine Force Belvederes and crews had been absorbed by No 66 Squadron within two months of arrival,(59) the separately established No 38 Group Whirlwind Squadron—No 225—had not. The No 225 Squadron aircraft, theoretically as well as practically, still belonged to No 38 Group since they had no connection with Seletar and were allotted, complete with ground crews, for exclusive use by COMAIRBOR, on a one-year unaccompanied basis. The Seletar Helicopter Wing had no formal connection with them whatever, but the reality of the situation was that they, together with the Nos 110 and 103 Squadron detachments, formed part of the total Whirlwind force in Borneo and were tasked as such.

As a final twist to the complicated administrative position, while the aircrews of the three Seletar-based helicopter squadrons were rotated on a two, three or four week cycle through Singapore and Borneo, most of the ground crews were not. For reasons of efficiency of work rates and economy in traffic of personnel between Singapore and Borneo, it was found preferable to supply the ground crews in Borneo from the UK on a one-year unaccompanied basis. This gave them a completely different lifestyle from their collegues on the same squadrons who were based in Singapore with their family lives, golf courses, boat and sailing clubs, parties, nightlife and a five-and-a half day working week. Whilst neither group was envious of the other, the one-year unaccompanied six/seven days per week work group in Borneo tended to regard themselves as more professional than their supposedly hedonist colleagues in Singapore.

Helicopter Engineering Control Organisation

The Engineering staffs who controlled the technicians paid little heed to the delicate pattern of responsibilities in the executive tapestry—merely running Seletar, Labuan and Kuching from No 224 Group and FEAF Headquarters as RAF Stations having particular engineering problems. The Command background situation described may have added stimulus to the almost universal engineering staff preference, completely victorious in Aden and much in evidence in FEAF during this period, to amalgamate the servicing for co-located squadrons or detachments and avoid having technical ground crews with exclusive allegiance to particular flying squadrons, especially ones with such a variety of executive controls. The result was that the centralisation, decentralisation and partial centralisation of the helicopter ground crews proceeded more or less continually in FEAF (and to some extent in the UK) throughout the 1960s and early 1970s.

Without exception, the Squadron Commanders resisted the centralisation trend most vehemently, being acutely aware of their reliance on the morale and motivation of the airmen to respond with selfless dedication and disregard of formal working hours, to the fluctuating operational urgency of their work. This stimulus, it seemed to them, could only be effectively applied within the squadron as a unit under pressure—a glimpse of the obvious they thought, more especially in terms of previous experience of the Royal Air Force.(60) This view was naturally shared by the GD officers further up the Command chain, albeit with the diminished vehemence more appropriate to senior staffs required to respond with reasoned argument to the barrage of statistical justification deployed by the senior engineering staffs freshly imbued with the latest concepts embodied in the then newly current term—

'Management'. In May 1966, a survey by engineering staffs of servicing in Borneo concluded that there should be visiting Management Teams consisting of a technical officer and four NCOs, convinced of the value of Management aims in improving servicing support, having no other servicing responsibilities and reporting direct to Headquarters FEAF.(61)

In July 1964 the Whirlwinds and crews at Labuan, having been contributed in roughly equal parts by Nos 103 and 110 Squadrons during the build-up period, achieved their ambition to divide the now more settled operational and servicing tasks along Squadron lines. Each provided their own first and second line servicing under their own engineering officers. Both Squadrons had rejoiced at recovery of Squadron control at Labuan and all Squadron servicing at Seletar, and in June 1965 the Commanding Officer of No 110 Squadron, having presumably heard of the latest centralization plans about to be announced, commented on the importance of having Squadron ground crew owing allegiance to the Squadron.(62) In mid-1965 a determined effort was made by Headquarters FEAF to amalgamate all helicopter servicing under Station rather than Squadron control. At a conference in FEAF, the Air Staffs reluctantly conceded that there was no arithmetical answer to the brilliantly presented graph and chart case for centralised engineering control at all levels unveiled by the FEAF Senior Engineer staffs, and described as incontrovertible in argument by the FEAF Financial Adviser.(63) Reorganisation of Station servicing was planned for Seletar, Kuching and Labuan which would be fully centralised for both first and second line servicing and even include fixed wing aircraft with the helicopters, that is giving the Station engineering organisation freedom to deploy all technicians within the Station as required, regardless of the flying units being served, and leaving the latter no airmen at all. The beleaguered Air Staffs reluctantly acceded to this plan but imposed three innocuous 'conditions':

a.   the flexibility of the Whirlwind Force was not to be impaired;

b.   the reorganisation would only be allowed to continue if substantial economy was being achieved;

c.   the decision was subject to alteration or rejection after six months.(64)

This policy was issued in September 1965. The Commanding Officer of No 110 Squadron immediately recorded his dismay and in October the Commanding Officer of No 103 Squadron described the adverse effect on general morale amongst the airmen. In November, the Commanding Officer of No 110 Squadron reported that at Seletar enthusiasm for No 110 Squadron by the airmen who had belonged to it was undiminished, and added that the case for squadron servicing was not susceptible to numerical measurement in a form which would influence the Finance and Establishment branches. To this the Station Commander, Group Captain (later Air

Chief Marshal) R W G Freer added in his own hand on the Squadron ORB the comment 'hear hear'.(65) In December 1965 No 110 Squadron was, with due ceremony, presented with its Standard. The airmen who had belonged to the Squadron were drawn from the centralised servicing pool for the occasion and participated in the parade with great enthusiasm. It was not until May 1967 that Nos 110 and 103 Squadrons, now with different Squadron Commanders, recovered control of their own first line servicing. Both had complained of abysmal serviceability in the preceding months at Seletar and No 110 Squadron reported Squadron servicing as an 'immediate success' with more serviceable aircraft than they could use at first, and the total of 396 monthly hours against a target of 400 as 'a rare achievement'.(66) In July the Commanding Officer of No 103 Squadron reported exceeding the Squadron task for the third month in succession, adding that he hoped they had 'now heard the last of centralised servicing'.(67) In September 1971, with FEAF disbanded, the move of No 103 Squadron, the last RAF Squadron in Singapore, to Tengah was used as a reason for once more separating the Squadron servicing from the unit and attempting to run it as part of the RAF Support Unit Engineering Organisation. Three months later, the Squadron Commander was complaining that this had been a 'misguided decision'. The airmen were arguing about to whom they belonged, and he affirmed that 'socially' (that is unofficially and for all practical purposes) what was called the Whirlwind Servicing Flight was part of No 103 Squadron. It was not until June 1972 that his successor was able to announce their formal return to Squadron control, by means of an official statement as follows:

'The long battle for Squadron autonomy reached a satisfactory result during the month with approval to full autonomy. Many things have changed in the Royal Air Force over the years but it is still very true that airmen are the lifeblood of a Squadron and vice versa. Whether you call it "management, leadership or esprit de corps" it is blatantly obvious that people work better in an environment that allows personal contact through all levels, a sense of involvement in the task, identification with, and pride in, a unit and its record. I am most pleased to command a "proper" unit again.(68)

Signed P R BOND
Sqn Ldr
OC No 103 Squadron
RAF Support Unit Tengah

5 July 1972'

Significantly, the large servicing centralisation reorganisation of mid-1965 did not include the Belvederes. No 66 Squadron had had a bad time in mid-1963 and 1964. Following a fatal crash (YAW cable failure) in 1963, second line servicing had been transferred from Squadron control to the Station Technical Wing. Several starter explosions, persistent vibration problems due to absence of proper rotor blade tracking equipment and various other difficulties had shaken the morale of both air and ground crews. By 1965, there was good evidence of recovery from these difficulties and there seemed no point in opening the possibility of interfering in any way with the now highly specialised Belvedere servicing teams in Seletar and Kuching. Certainly, the Officer Commanding the Engineering Wing at Seletar saw no advantage in attempting to mix them with the Whirlwind crews on the other side of the airfield. Control of their own second line servicing had been returned to No 66 Squadron in July 1964 along with Nos 103 and 110 Squadrons—the very opposite procedure to that being practised in Aden. In late 1965, as the Whirlwind serviceability declined following application of full centralisation of servicing, that of the Belvederes improved.(69)

Although in 1967 the Belvedere second line servicing at Seletar was transferred once more to the Station Engineering Wing alongside the Whirlwind second line servicing,(70) this was mainly an organisational device and did not dilute the Belvedere specialisation. Belvedere first line servicing remained under Squadron control. It must be remembered that throughout this whole period, in contrast to the later practice, for example, at Odiham in Phase 4 (the 1970s), first line servicing included by far the largest element of rectification work, and that was the key to the number of operational aircraft actually available for tasking. Second line servicing was involved almost exclusively with statutory minor and major inspections. Both the No 66 Squadron Commander and Engineer Officer later testified to the crucial value of unit pride and competitive spirit both between the Belvedere technicians and others, as well as between the one-year unaccompanied airmen at Kuching and their unknown colleagues on $2\frac{1}{2}$ year tours in Seletar.(71) The Squadron Commander summed up the attitude as essentially: 'We have got to make them fly because if we don't, nobody else will'.(72)

The Belvederes went on to achieve a very satisfactory utilisation rate until the day when the Unit was disbanded some four years later.(73)

Technique Developments and the Helicopter Wing

The Helicopter Wing Headquarters at Seletar had been formed in October 1964 at the instigation of the Station Commander—Group Captain Freer. He had been concerned that the workload generated by the three helicopter squadrons being added to the fixed wing complement (which included a Beverley Squadron and a large Twin and Single Pioneer Squadron, all having detachments in Borneo) was beyond the capabilities of a single established Officer Commanding Flying Wing, particularly one who had no helicopter experience. Unlike the previous Helicopter Wing—No 303—formed in 1952 in Malaya as a mainly administrative device (see Chapter 3) the Helicopter Wing formed at Seletar in 1964 was a Seletar Flying Wing Establishment and consequently had no individual number plate. Apart from its function in the Station organisation it also provided co-ordination of the Helicopter Squadron's monthly continuation training and categorisation requirements, gradually acquiring for the purpose a small staff of QHIs who were initially drawn from the squadrons themselves. The single QHI established on each squadron was frequently unable to meet all the on-site training requirements for squadrons split between two or three locations more than 400 miles apart, for example regular engine-off landing practice for the Whirlwind and Sycamore pilots which was not practised solo, and renewal of out-of-date pilot categories. The Squadron Commanders themselves were greatly stretched having semi-permanent detachments in both Kuching and Labuan—an equivalent deployment in Europe amounting to an Odiham-based squadron with permanent detachments in Hamburg and Oslo, another at Aberdeen (representing Butterworth) and all, including the Headquarters Base, having an immediate operational task. They also had to provide individual theatre conversion training at Seletar for the more or less continuous stream of new pilots arriving to replace those tour expired. In early 1966 the Seletar Helicopter Wing acquired the role of Belvedere OCU on the transfer of that function from Odiham to Seletar.(74)

Quite apart from these predictable tasks for the Helicopter Wing, a third role soon appeared, arising from the technique and equipment modifications characteristically generated in an active operational theatre. The small Helicopter Wing staff was, fortuitously, in a position to co-ordinate and progress the various developments demanded but, more especially, to observe, identify and devise new solutions for most of the problems arising. There was a comparatively large continuation training, theatre conversion and night flying training task at Seletar. However, except for the few months in late 1964 and early 1965 when the Indonesians were attacking South Malaya, there was usually sufficient flying capacity for experimenting with techniques and equipment modifications, and a large number of pilots (up to 70 excluding those of the No 38 Group squadrons) from whom to gather a consensus of reactions. There was no equivalent of A&AEE or any other body claiming exclusive rights to development progress; but a ready enthusiasm in Group and Command Headquarters to encourage and apply quickly, if possible, any appropriate procedures recommended at the operational level. In these respects the opportunities for rapid and positive development progress were uniquely favourable; but when active operations in Borneo ceased, the impetus for such innovations fell back to its more usual rate of scarcely discernible change. In some respects the advances made were never consolidated in the United Kingdom. Four examples are given below.

Emergency Long Lift Hoist

The solution to the problem of having a 50 foot winch cable—no longer than that found to be unsatisfactory in Malaya 10 years previously (see Chapter 3)—became known as the multi lift hoist method and was derived from an idea first formulated in No 225 Squadron in May 1964.(75) This somewhat desperate remedy consisted essentially of supplying a webbing line of the required length (normal maximum 200 feet) and raising or lowering it 50 feet by means of repeated attachments of the winch hook. The procedure is comparatively complex to describe so the Standard Operation Procedure for its use eventually issued by Headquarters FEAF and dated 8 January 1966 is attached as Appendix 3.(76) It could take up to 20 minutes for the whole procedure to be completed for one man during which time the Whirlwind was required to maintain an accurate hover at up to 200 feet with almost full left rudder, probably uncomfortably close to trees. After five complete cycles of the winch it required a 10-minute pause to cool down. Abseiling eventually replaced this system for inserting troops but the multi-lift hoist method remained the only practical way of lifting them from deep jungle. In September 1965, four months before the multi-lift hoist system was approved for use, a No 225 Squadron Whirlwind was faced with the problem of recovering a casualty from a position just beyond the reach of the winch cable, and too late in the evening to allow for enlargement of the clearing. The casualty was carried on an extended strop at 20 knots to a place where the aircraft could land and recover him.(77) Such drama gave a powerful impetus to the trials to obtain official clearance for the multi-lift hoist system.

As it was obvious there would never be a winch for the Belvedere, some thought was given to an alternative method of inserting and recovering whole patrols in deep jungle. Insertion of troops involved the use of abseiling as for the Whirlwind, but the system proposed for recovering them consisted in essence of carrying ballast of greater weight than the load to be lifted, and disposing of it in appropriate quantities as a counter weight to the loads to be raised. The system envisaged using the webbing cages known as 1-ton containers employed for freight delivery by the MRT Force—one each at front and rear of the Belvedere cabin, with a length of webbing strop running through the fuselage carried by two pulleys—one each on the roping brackets outside the front and rear hatches, and adjusted for length so that with one 1-ton container lowered to the ground, the other was level with the hatch at the opposite end of the cabin. It was calculated that up to four soldiers could enter the container on the ground, the crewman could load the upper container with ballast (about 1000 lbs) and on releasing a brake, the upper and lower containers would change places. The process would be repeated until the ballast was exhausted and the aircraft would complete the procedure at a slightly lower all-up weight at the end of the operation than at the start. A working mock-up of the system was made and demonstrated in the Belvedere at Seletar at a height of 200 feet above ground using sandbags for ballast and pay load, but the end of the war in Borneo put a stop to this development which, in the subsequent peaceful atmosphere, tended merely to excite tolerant amusement. Nevertheless it attracted a monetary inventions prize from the Air Commander. It was named the Seletar Helicopter

Winchless Elevator (SHWEL). In the post-Borneo period, there was a slow development in which the cargo winch fitted in the Beverley was adapted and mounted on the floor of the Belvedere, operating through a pulley outside the main door. In September 1968, a trial with a 400 lb load was successful,(78) but the system was never used operationally.

The SHWEL could have been developed for the Whirlwind or any other helicopter (although attention would have had to be paid to adequate spacing between the ascending and descending loads). It was not. For the following sixteen years, that is, until the last SAR Whirlwinds in the UK were exchanged for the Wessex with 300 feet of winch cable, the FEAF emergency long-lift hoist, known in the UK as the 'multi-lift hoist', was available for mountain and cliff rescue where the SAR Whirlwind could not get within 50 feet of the rescue. All subsequent helicopters fitted with winches were supplied with an adequate length of winch cable.

Ground Radar Carriage

There were two ground radar equipments which had to be deployed in jungle areas—UPS1 for air space control and Green Archer for locating the origin of enemy mortar fire. The UPS1 cabin weighing about 4000 lbs was well within the Belvedere's lifting capability and with some splitting down of components could even be carried by the RN Wessex Mk 3 (ceiling 3500 feet—maximum range 50 miles—9 sorties) (79), but being a brick shaped box 13 feet×6 feet×4 feet it was difficult to control in forward flight since it spun and consequently developed a swing. After various unsuccessful attempts to add stabilising tail surfaces or drogues, the solution consisted of adding four false sides to the box to form a regular hexagon which could then spin without swinging at speeds up to 90 knots. Thus the Belvedere was able to deploy it from Labuan to Bario.(80)

Green Archer required more frequent deployment over shorter ranges since it was part of a tactical weapon system. In the second phase of Borneo operations the company bases near the border, already described as resembling jungle fort, were tempting targets for Indonesian mortars from across the border, particularly at night when the launching point might be expected to be safe from identification. Green Archer could detect the launch and calculate its origin so fast that it was frequently possible to fire a return round with great accuracy immediately after or sometimes even before the incoming shell landed. The radar vehicle was moved with its crew and equipment, normally by two Belvederes, from site to site with gratifying success in discouraging enemy mortar fire.(81) The task of placing the Green Archer was one of considerable delicacy, and the 'split control' technique with two pilots was used, as developed three years earlier for the placing of the spire on Coventry Cathedral (82) (See Chapter 10).

339

Helicopter Refuelling

With refuelling bowsers only available at main airfields, helicopter refuelling remained a significant problem. Since the days of Phase 1 when petrol had to be poured through filters out of four-gallon tins, the appearance of the turbine helicopter at Phase 2 resulted in the change to 44-gallon drums of Avtur and a sharp increase in the work involved in transferring the larger volumes of fuel consumed. The Belvedere represented a much larger jump in the size of fuel transfer required, not only because of its larger engines and the fact that there were two of them, but also because refuelling stops were reduced to a minimum owing to the unreliability of the engine starter systems. For several years this problem had resulted in the provision of a series of more or less unsatisfactory portable petrol-driven pumps which, in the nature of things, were either unserviceable and absorbing the time and effort of the aircraft technicians attempting to repair them, or somewhere else when wanted. Although theoretically portable, they were all too heavy to be carried everywhere in each helicopter and the time-consuming and exhausting alternative of carrying and using a manually operated 'wobble pump' was often the only solution for individually operating helicopters in forward areas. It would take about 20 minutes of energetic wobble pump work to transfer fuel for one hour for a Whirlwind and up to an hour to supply a Belvedere for an hour and a half.

The solution proposed was to transfer the fuel from the 44-gallon drums by pressuring them with air from the engine compressor, and to modify the Belvedere fuel intake to permit engine running refuelling. The war in Borneo stopped in 1966 before either modification was complete, and when the pressurised drum was first used on an exercise in Malaya in July 1968 (83) the emphasis was on modifying vehicles, eg the Landrover, to provide a servicing platform with a 24-volt electrical system for Whirlwind starting. Two years previously it would not have occurred to anyone in the Helicopter Wing to propose for tactical helicopter use anything dependent on the presence of a surface vehicle. Exercise areas on the other hand, even if not actually accessible to surface vehicles, were and perhaps always will be served from bases which are, and after operations in Borneo ceased only exercises were carried out.

Helicopter Night Flying

Perhaps the most significant radical development of helicopter techniques during the Borneo campaign was, ironically, one which had only limited application at the time, but its subsequent treatment provides an insight into the contrasting attitudes in a distant operational environment as against the more formal committee procedures of the very numerous formations feeling a need to be heard in the United Kingdom. There was no tactical night flying requirement in Borneo apart from emergency casualty evacuation and, very occasionally, recovery to base after dusk or early positioning for dawn operations—the latter extremely rare because of the morning mists in jungle areas. Even for these infrequent tasks, and because it was a standard role for Support Helicopters and therefore had to be practised monthly, regular night flying training was instituted. The night flying lighting pattern had not changed since the first cautious steps taken by the new CFS Helicopter Unit in 1954 resulted in a 'T' shaped pattern which it was hoped would give pilots an indication of approach direction with lateral level as well as descent paths by observing the relative apparent length of each element of the 'T'. It did not. Nevertheless, in 1965 this pattern had already been standard for some time and was known as the NATO 'T'.

Monthly continuation training was normally carried out in Singapore rather than Borneo but night flying in such a brilliantly illuminated area was of little value. The Helicopter Wing instituted night flying training on unmanned Auster strips in South Johore, acquiring its own MAOT to provide control and tactical lighting, in conditions which were more often nearly completely dark than those normally obtainable in the United Kingdom. In these circumstances it was discovered that if the standard NATO 'T' formed the only lights of any sort visible to the pilot, with no apparent horizon and cloud obscuring the stars, a successful approach was often impossible and inherently dangerous in a confined space. This was confirmed by the visiting categorization examiner from the Transport Command Examining Unit who encountered these conditions during his six-monthly visit in March 1965.(84)

The Helicopter Wing set about designing a lighting pattern which would give the pilot the approach information he needed, that is, position vertically and horizontally in relation to the desired descent path, together with a positive indication of the safe limits of error in both respects. In accordance with the discipline of actual war conditions, a further stipulation accepted was that whatever lighting pattern was chosen, it had to be possible to construct it out of materials which it was reasonable to expect jungle patrols to carry. (This virtually eliminated sophisticated glide path/angle of approach indicators in boxes together with delicate optical systems which were, in any case, of very limited value when used singly). The pattern was to indicate also a point in space where the helicopter could hover with an external load just clear of the ground and it was to use the minimum number of lights consistent with safety. Such a pattern meeting all these criteria was found surprisingly quickly and, over the course of about three months (about 12 night flying sessions) with opinions on each development being expressed by the pilots of all three FEAF squadrons, it was finally reduced to a mere five lights, and these consisted of hand held torches. All the pilots expressed satisfaction with this new lighting pattern for use at night in confined spaces, and many of the newer pilots, having previously been privately baffled by the only other pattern they had ever seen—the enigmatic 'T'—were extremely enthusiastic.(85)

Nanga Gaat from ground level in its usual state of brisk activity.

The first operational use of the SHNAP was made at this site in a rubber estate in central Malaya when several re-supply sorties were carried out in total darkness by a Whirlwind of 103 Squadron as part of an Army/RAF exercise. The three poles for the red lights (see Appendix 4) have been enhanced on the photographic print.

It remained to write a simple set of instructions which any of the various nationalities of soldiers in Borneo could follow so that they could construct the pattern wherever they were. British, Malay and Gurkha troops were shown to be perfectly capable of setting up the patterns, it was demonstrated to and accepted by the Forward Air Commander in Kuching, was backed by both CFS and the Transport Commanding Examining Staff (TCES), was approved by Headquarters No 224 Group, and used by night in a comparatively small clearing during a 28 Brigade exercise near Malacca (Exercise Kangaroo Tail) in July 1965—some five months after development work started.(86) A permanent version was erected at the Kuching Hospital. Inter-Service agreement was then sought and in June 1966, at a tri-Service Conference in Headquarters FEAF, the Seletar Helicopter Night Approach Pattern (SHNAP) was agreed as the standard pattern in the Far East, the Royal Navy stipulating only that it was not applicable for use on board RN ships. Instructions for laying and using the pattern were then issued in a pamphlet bearing the crest of Headquarters, Far East Command, and was thus applicable to all three Services.(87) A copy of its contents, which include both a description of the pattern and the manner of its use, is included at Appendix 4. The SHNAP attracted the second L G Groves Memorial Prize for contribution to flight safety in 1966.

By October of that year, 116 pilots in the Far East (not including Army Air Corps and Royal Naval helicopter pilots) had been fully trained and categorised with the system and about 600 incident free hours had been flown. This represented some 4000 night approaches of which approximately 1500 were carried out in forward locations under tactical conditions and control.(88) The SHNAP continued in use in the Far East until July 1967 when, to the dismay of the Helicopter Wing, it was replaced on orders from MOD by the ill-fated diamond pattern generated by the Army Air Corps and described below.

In 1966 the Commander-in-Chief Far East forwarded to Whitehall and the Joint Warfare Establishment the results of all this development work and recorded the tri-Service agreement successfully achieved in the Operational Unit in the Far East. In the UK, apart from No 38 Group, CFS and the TCES, the SHNAP was ignored at first and then suppressed. The consequent arguments which took place and which lasted nine years involved Headquarters No 38 Group, Headquarters Air Support Command, Headquarters Strike Command, the Joint Warfare Establishment, the Joint Helicopter Tactical Development Unit (JHTDU) and the Joint Helicopter Tactical Development Committee (JHTDC); subsidiary roles were played by TCES and CFS. If considered relevant, a description of them would belong in Phase 4 under the title of 'Policy Considerations in the 1970s' in a continuation of this history. The file (89) constitutes a well documented example of the contrast already mentioned between development motivated by real operational conditions, and the complex motives of peacetime committee work. In summary, the SHNAP, although never criticised adversely in operational use, was suppressed in the UK in favour of a rival (Army) system which was belatedly recognised by MOD (Air) as unacceptable to the Royal Air Force and was eventually forbidden by No 38 Group as positively dangerous, but not until 1972.(90) The SHNAP was officially revived in 1973, endorsed at the final of several tri-Service practical night flying tests, officially accepted in 1974 by the JHTDC (now under the title 'Proportional Lighting System') and finally strangled in paperwork when the instructions for laying the pattern, prepared in the JHTDU, were judged to be too complex for practical use. Its origins and use by Malay, Gurkha and British troops in Borneo had evidently been completely forgotten and at the time of writing (1982) all that remains is the original NATO 'T' from the early 1950s, which proved unsatisfactory in real operational service and remains so. Even when embellished with an expensive optical AAI, as is the current practice, for reasons fully explained by Headquarters Strike Command in November 1972 regarding the use of a single AAI (91) it remains unsatisfactory for use in confined spaces in total darkness and for stream landing several helicopters; thus the progress made in Borneo was effectively lost. With the Borneo war 15 years in the past, innovation was concentrated on the sophisticated developments of night vision goggles, although ground lighting patterns were still regarded as necessary for landing. The SHNAP, with its three poles, five hand torches and ten yard length of string, did not fit this high technology image.*

A third pattern, which also used a three-dimensional display to replace the standard 'T', had been produced in Germany by a pilot of No 230 Squadron in 1964, and was known as the 'Forest T' after its inventor. It attracted the L G Groves Memorial Prize for contribution to flight safety in 1965, but was not suitable for use in FEAF, mainly because of the weight of equipment involved and the limited range (500 yards) at which it could be interpreted. It served to show, however, that dissatisfaction with the NATO 'T' was not confined to the Far East and also that

---

*Quite unknown to those responsible for developing the SHNAP, a paper entitled 'Helicopter Night Flying—Triangular Ground Lighting Pattern' dated 26 May 1954, had been prepared at A&AEE, Boscombe Down, and was not noticed until early in the 1970s. It reports trials with a pattern described as of American origin and consisting of three lights—two on the ground 25 feet apart and one at a height of five feet a short distance in front of them.(92) Except for minor dimensional differences, this pattern is almost identical to that described in the SHNAP pamphlet, Chapter 1 para 13 under the heading 'Emergency SHNAP' (see Annex 4). Although unsuitable for most jungle terrain, this version was included because it could be laid by a solitary person in comparatively open spaces and was an obviously valuable derivation for emergency use from the more comprehensive full SHNAP which required five lights, three of them at a height of 5 feet six inches. This independent double invention of the same principle for a helicopter approach lighting pattern was not known by the participants when the arguments and trials were conducted between 1965 and 1974.

a three-dimensional pattern of lights was seen by a third independent developer as an attractive solution to the problem.

It is likely that the Forest T formed the basis or at least the 'trigger' for the development of the Army Air Corps three-dimensional lighting pattern known as the 'Diamond' which emanated from Germany shortly afterwards, and appeared in opposition to the SHNAP in the arguments already mentioned which started in the UK in 1967.

Withdrawal from East Malaysia

Following the Peace Treaty in August 1966, British withdrawal from Borneo (but not Brunei) started immediately, and helicopter activity consequently increased sharply for a few weeks. No 230 Squadron, in mid-1966 based in Labuan with detachments at Sepulot and Tawau, exchanged them for Bario and joined with No 110 Squadron in the last operations to sweep up the Indonesians involved in the incursion launched in the Long Semado area of the fifth division of Sarawak in the latter part of August. In the following month, No 230 Squadron was withdrawn and returned to the UK and No 38 Group to whom they belonged, six Belfast sorties being used to accomplish the move. Since their arrival in Labuan in March 1965 with 13 Whirlwinds they had lost one, flown 8550 hours and carried 39779 troops, 414 casualties and 3.3M pounds of freight.(94)

The No 103 Squadron detachment withdrew from Kuching to Seletar in October 1966. The two remaining FEAF helicopter squadrons (Nos 66 and 110) continued assisting the withdrawal of British troops and their replacement (on a much reduced scale) by Malaysian forces, and were then left with a maintenance support role for the Malaysians who initially lacked sufficient helicopter forces for the task. This continued support, reduced to six Whirlwinds at Labuan and four Belvederes at Kuching, and including some MRT assistance and personnel to run the airfields at Kuching, Labuan and Tawau, was authorised to continue until March 1968 without any charge being raised for their services.(95) The six Whirlwinds withdrew from Labuan to join the four Belvederes at Kuching in February 1967, and on the 20th of the same month the Belvederes, after flying a farewell formation of all four aircraft, were shipped back to Singapore. Since January 1963 between three and seven Belvederes had flown in Borneo 4555 hours, carried 10M pounds of freight and 95000 troops.(96)

The No 110 Squadron Whirlwind tasking at Kuching was not heavy and, shared with No 103 Squadron (aircrew only) on a monthly rotation, continued to decline until in September 1967 the detachment reported that it was reduced to an ambulance and flying doctor service for the first division of Sarawak.(97) The last RAF unit in Borneo, No 110 Squadron, left Kuching on 6 November 1967, after a series of farewell parties culminating in a reception given by the Malaysian Infantry Brigade then in residence, and with the whole Station waving goodbye (how different from Aden!) flew via Sibu and Labuan to Kota Belud for a joint contingency exercise with No 99 Gurkha Infantry Brigade near Mount Kinabalu which lasted until 19 November.(98) This instant replacement of Borneo operational tasks with FEAF-sponsored exercises was characteristic of what was already happening with the rest of the helicopter force, now all back in Singapore. A further sign of the new patterns was a reconnaissance of Hong Kong for future detachments carried out in the same month by No 110 Squadron. Happily, all tasks were completed in time for the whole of No 110 Squadron to join together in Seletar on 29 November (the first time since 1962) to celebrate the Squadron's 50th anniversary. No 103 Squadron had celebrated a similar event two months previously. This did not prevent the Squadron Commander commenting adversely on the low serviceability state caused by persistent low frequency vibration—adding sardonically that the Belvedere was not the only one to suffer this way.(99)

After Borneo

1967 and 1968 were peaceful years in FEAF. All of the helicopter force was back in Singapore by the end of 1967. The Sycamores were at last retired from service in FEAF in May 1967, there now being ample alternative VIP lift available. Much greater helicopter participation in No 28 (Commonwealth) Brigade exercises in West Malaysia (Malaya) was now possible and was used fully. The helicopter squadrons busied themselves with developing their capability for mobility in deployment—a feature scarcely required in the static bases used in Borneo—and doing the various interesting , useful and amusing things which seem to arise when helicopters are about with no pressing operational tasks to burden them.

In December 1966, the Officer Commanding the Helicopter Wing, who had placed the spire on Coventry Cathedral in 1962 (see Chapter 10), was able to repeat the trick using the identical technique, with a 30 foot high cross which the building contractor was reluctant to install in the top of the tower of a new Hakka Methodist church in Newton Road, Singapore. The successful event was recorded on a brass plate in the base of the tower.

In a reversal of situations, the Belvedere Squadron now regarded the detachment remaining in Borneo since Confrontation ended as providing an excellent opportunity for theatre operational training for the crews which were now all being trained on the Squadron, and were accordingly being rotated every two weeks.(100) In December 1966, Belvedere first line servicing at Kuching was being done under cover for the first time but there was little time to enjoy it since, as already reported, the last four aircraft were withdrawn in February 1967. Three of them were shipped on the LST Maxwell Brander and delivered direct to Butterworth—

A Belvedere of 66 Squadron positioning the cross on the steeple of the Hakka Methodist Church in Evelyn Road Singapore in December 1966. The technique was the same as that for placing the sculpture in the flèche in the Coventry Cathedral operation. The ground handling party can be seen at the base of the steeple.

345–A

66 Squadron near the end of its life in early 1969, flying all eleven Belvederes in formations round Singapore.

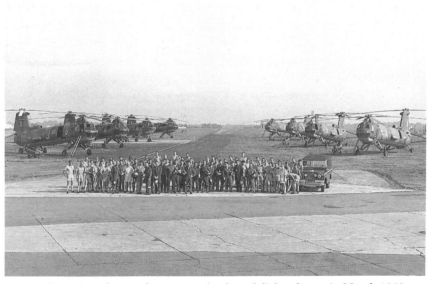

66 Squadron air and ground crews on the day of disbandment in March 1969 with the eight aircraft used for the final ceremonial demonstration at Seletar.

the Belvedere's first operational base when they arrived in FEAF in 1962. Operation 'Hill Climb'—the carriage of a large amount of radar equipment to the top of Penang Hill—had started in April 1966 with 53 Belvedere loads. In March 1967 the task was to be continued with 65000 lbs of equipment (32 sorties). Two months later, 33 steel beams weighing up to 3500 lbs each had to be taken to the same site which, being very small, was now heavily obstructed by the various radar aerials and equipment previously delivered. The 80 foot strop had to be used to keep the aircraft clear of obstructions and the resultant hover height placed the aircraft some 3000 feet above the nearest ground visible to the pilot. Once again the split control technique used on the Coventry Cathedral operation and several times subsequently, had to be employed in order to achieve the accuracy required. Operation Hill Climb continued monthly through 1967 until September, and included a successful calibration service provided by a Belvedere hovering at 7000 feet, positioned by radio instructions from a theodolite operator on the ground. This procedure produced unexpected problems in turbulent conditions when sudden height losses of up to 800 feet were experienced. The Butterworth Belvedere detachment was withdrawn to Seletar in October, bringing No 66 Squadron together for the first time since 1962. They flew a nine Belvedere formation round Singapore to celebrate and two days later demonstrated their pride and confidence by flying eleven of the twelve aircraft then on strength in the largest Belvedere formation ever assembled.(101)

No 103 Squadron, having left Borneo in October 1966, almost immediately after troop withdrawals were complete, inherited the SAR standby tasks at both Seletar and Butterworth, as well as the first tentative exercises for the RAF in January 1967, providing tactical support for the security forces in the Hong Kong border areas. These were to lead to a detachment of six Whirlwinds, shipped to Hong Kong on the aircraft carrier HMS Triumph in September 1967. This detachment, initially for three months, became permanent in the sense that it never withdrew, but after being shared on a rotational basis with No 110 Squadron through the remainder of 1967, grew into a new helicopter squadron, No 28 Squadron, on 1 March 1968, adopting the number plate of the departing Hunters.(103) This Squadron was destined to outlast all the others and eventually, in 1975, to be the sole remaining RAF helicopter squadron in the Far East, providing the link with Phase 4 of this history in much the same way that the solitary Sycamore squadron at Butterworth (No 110) had formed, in 1962, the connection between the Malayan operations of Phase 2 and the Borneo campaign in Phase 3.

HQ No 224 Group was reduced to a mobile role in February 1967, having operational control of tactical squadrons and units only when assigned by FEAF for specific operations and exercises. It had no administrative function.(103) In October 1968 it was fully absorbed into FEAF HQ as a Joint Warfare Branch.(104)

Throughout 1967 and 1968, numerous exercises with No 28 (Commonwealth) Brigade were flown in which Whirlwinds and Belvederes complemented each other in the same way as had been found so effective in the pre-overseas development days at Odiham in 1960–62 (see Chapter 10). Conditions described on occasion as 'extremely rugged' posed no problem for the Belvederes which were, nevertheless, continually plagued by starter failure, including explosions. The Belvedere modification to permit engine running refuelling (involving the fuel tank drainage points) was still proceeding at the stately post-Borneo rate when it had to be pre-empted in emergency. In August 1967, a party of VIPs was to be flown ashore from the aircraft carrier Hermes which was found to be 40 miles off station. The Belvedere had to be refuelled on the carrier deck with rotors turning and only the rear engine was stopped.(105)

In November 1968, a No 103 Squadron Whirlwind had to carry out an engine-off landing into jungle. The crew of two were rescued by another Whirlwind using the multi-lift tape method. The crewman spent an hour suspended from the aircraft amongst the trees under the jungle canopy, transferring the survivors from the tapes to the winch 50 feet above ground level—a feat for which he received the AFM.(106)

In addition to the Army-generated exercises the Helicopter Wing was, during this period, able to institute its own Squadron mobility exercises in which small groups of helicopters were detached to live independently for a few days at chosen locations in Malaya. Such exercises were both useful and popular, as were various opportunities to practise deck landings and to take part in small-scale Naval assault exercises with the Royal Navy ships which were in frequent transit. In October 1968, four Whirlwinds and crews were carried by the LSL Sir Galahad for an exercise with the Australians in North East Queensland.

The usual SAR sorties continued as a permanent backdrop to all these other activities, and represented perhaps the only role in which the climate was usually a help rather than a hindrance. Sometimes there was flood relief work, for example in North East Malaya in January 1977, and once, in September 1966, one Whirlwind was taken by Beverley to Laos where flood relief work was required near Vientiane. 71 helicopter hours were flown on this task.(107) Crews for SAR, although specially practised for the role, were exchanged regularly with the other squadron crews and there was no sharp division between the SAR and SH roles as existed in the United Kingdom. SS-11 firing was another speciality spread amongst the Whirlwind crews in this period.

The Reduction of FEAF

In most respects, 1967 and 1968 were golden years for the personnel of the FEAF helicopter force, who lived in the comparative luxury of the Singapore base, most of them with their families. Flying tasks were always interesting, usually congenial, there was no enemy and the future seemed bright in the short term. No 66 Squadron, evidently expecting their Belvederes to be replaced by Chinooks, recorded in November 1967 that this was not now going to happen, and they looked forward to prolongation of the Belvederes beyond March 1969.(108) The 1966 Defence Review made it clear that a UK-based contingency force would replace expensive overseas garrisons, and subsequent White Papers forecast large reductions in the Far East. The policy for world-wide deployments on which the original arguments for the Belvedere were based (Chapter 9) were no longer valid. The idea of a light cargo force to support a short range transport force had long since vanished, but the need for a heavy lift helicopter had been amply demonstrated. However the decision to get rid of the Belvedere in favour of the Chinook had been taken as long ago as 1965 (see Chapter 13) and it was too late to reverse it when the Chinook was cancelled in late 1967.(109)

In August 1967 FEAF expected to lose Seletar by 1969. In October the Government Defence White Paper announced withdrawal from Arabia in 1968, and from the Far East by the mid-70s. It seemed to FEAF that the SEATO obligations and Malaysian Defence Agreements were to be 'honoured only by talk'.(110) By January 1968 the plan was for total withdrawal from Singapore, Malaysia and Brunei by December 1971. After a change of government in the UK, this plan was modified by the Five Power Agreement of 1971 (Australia, New Zealand, United Kingdom, Singapore, Malaysia) and some Whirlwinds were consequently to be retained for use in this ANZUK force which would be formed when FEAF disbanded.

Against this ominous background the last large scale joint tactical exercise scheduled to be mounted by Headquarters, Far East Command, was planned for March 1969 and titled 'Crowning Glory'. It was a notable success, particularly for the Belvederes, for which it turned out to be a singularly apt title. Having broken several records in the first two months of 1969 (ten Belvederes flew 331 hours in January) Belvedere XG 474, due for inspection, was 'retired' as the most travelled Belvedere to the RAF Museum. All nine remaining aircraft were deployed in Malaya at the end of February in readiness for Exercise Crowning Glory in March. Typically, four were delayed by engine starter troubles. 315 hours were flown in the first few weeks of March, and an eight Belvedere formation flew a farewell circuit of Singapore on the day before disbandment of the Squadron—there would have been nine but, consistent to the last, one engine starter exploded at the outset.(111)

On 20 March 1969, after a parade reviewed by the Air Commander and witnessed by most of the FEAF Air Staff, a final six aircraft formation, complete with underslung 105 mm guns and gun crews on board, flew a farewell demonstration placing the guns and their crews on the flying boat slipway at Seletar, where they fired a salute. XG 474, the Museum aircraft, made the last landing on the Seletar slipway where Seletar's first aircraft came ashore in 1928.(112) The next morning, the remaining nine aircraft started to be broken up for sale as scrap, and No 66 Squadron disbanded for the fourth time since 1916.

From 1964, the year when the Spine Force build-up became effective, the Belvedere utilisation had increased annually. In the ensuing years the addition of the Aden No 26 Squadron and Odiham OCU Belvederes continued the trend. The following table shows the annual increment of hours flown, together with the average number of Belvederes available for use in FEAF from early 1964 to March 1969:

Average No of Aircraft Available	Year	Hours Flown	
8	1964	1547	
8	1965	2336	
12	1966	3243	
13	1967	3320	
12	1968	3536	
10	1969	903	(in $2\frac{1}{2}$ months)

The instantaneous demise of the Belvedere with no replacement available seemed in Singapore to be arbitrary and damaging, such was the status the aircraft had achieved in the last four years. The FEAF Chief of Staff (Air Vice Marshal Le Cheminant) had proposed to VCAS that three of the last nine aircraft could profitably be maintained for some time yet.(113) Apart from valuable support for No 28 (Commonwealth) Brigade, there was the question of recovery of the radar station on Western Hill, Penang, most of which had been positioned there by Belvedere in the previous few years. It was suggested also that there were useful roles for the aircraft in theatres other than FEAF. As will be seen in the last chapter (Policy Considerations 1965–70), the fate of the Belvedere had been sealed as early as late 1965, largely as a result of its difficulties in AFME, and for the last three and a half years the Whitehall staffs had concerned themselves with the question of how quickly they could get rid of the aircraft by replacing it with the Chinook. Such was the anxiety to eliminate this technically troublesome helicopter that even some remedial modifications (such as a new engine starter system) had been denied, not merely because the Belvedere had a short projected life beyond 1966, but for fear of having its life thereby extended still further.(114) A decision in November 1967 which meant that the Chinook would not appear for several years, if at all, resulted in the Belvedere being retained until March 1969, but late suggestions from FEAF that even three of them should be kept in service beyond that date were swiftly and firmly squashed in London on personnel, technical and, especially, financial grounds. (See Chapter 14).

On 28 March 1969, Seletar closed as a flying station. With one exception the Whirlwinds of Nos 103 and 110 Squadrons had all been flown to their new base at Changi, and at 2015 hours the last Whirlwind took off from the Officers' Mess lawn for its delivery flight to join the others. The drama of the situation was enhanced by the extinction of all the airfield lights as soon as the aircraft left.(115) As a station however RAF Seletar did not close until March 1971.

The End of FEAF

The disbandment of No 66 Belvedere Squadron in March 1969, followed a few days later by the closure of Seletar as a flying station, effectively ended the Helicopter Wing in its original form, although it helped the two remaining Whirlwind squadrons to continue to function as a helicopter force in their new base at Changi. When the incumbent of the post of Officer Commanding Helicopter Wing became tour-expired in July 1970, he was not replaced. Seven months later, in February 1971, No 110 Squadron disbanded (for the fourth time in its life) leaving No 103 Squadron as the last helicopter squadron in Singapore.

Much attention has been focussed on the technical peculiarities of the Belvedere, but it must not be imagined that the generally reliable Whirlwind was without serious design and material faults which, had the aircraft not been far more numerous than the Belvedere, would have grounded the fleet completely from time to time. In the last two or three years of FEAF, it was decided that the rather high incidence of engine rundowns was due to water ingestion and that redesign of the nose doors was required. Meanwhile, flying in heavy rain was to be restricted—this in South East Asia and after ten years in service. Gearbox troubles, partly due to corrosion, caused much trouble (all but one of No 110 Squadron aircraft were grounded for this reason immediately after arrival at Changi),(116) but perhaps the most ironical circumstance of all, remembering the Sycamore rotor troubles suffered by No 110 Squadron at Butterworth in 1961 (see Chapter 3) which had been easily explained as due to using wooden blades in tropical climates, was a spate of Whirlwind metal tail rotor blade failures. Their replacement rate overloaded the supply sources to such an extent that a shortage reported in January 1970 had grown by March to a point where No 110 Squadron had only two aircraft left with tail rotors.(117) By April, No 103 Squadron reported that few crews had even managed to complete their monthly continuation training; both squadrons were detaching crews to the Hercules and Argosy squadrons for supernumerary flying duties and the Air Commander was going to work by car.(118) There was limited participation in a major No 28 (Commonwealth) Brigade exercise 'Bersatu Padu' in June 1970, but this resulted in there being no tail rotors at all. Significantly, priority was now accorded to No 28 Squadron in Hong Kong whose unit establishment was raised from six to ten with a task, in addition to reconnaissance and internal security duties, of being able to lift a complete platoon with weapons.(119) The situation was not back to normal until December.

Operations in this period consisted of the usual SAR tasks and participation in the No 28 (Commonwealth) Brigade exercises in Malaya; several multi-tape lift rescues were carried out and the SAR detachment at Butterworth which had been maintained almost continuously since the Sycamores first went there in August 1959 (Phase 2) was finally withdrawn in May 1970, the task now being handed over to the Royal Malaysian Air Force. These Whirlwinds of No 103 Squadron, which had supplied the detachment for the last five years, were the last RAF operational aircraft to be permanently based on Malayan soil.(120)

These last two years in FEAF, with the helicopter units continuing to do what they did before but without much conviction, correspond roughly to the continuation of No 103 Squadron in Cyprus after the end of the emergency there (Chapter 7), and the four years for No 78 Squadron in Sharjah after leaving Aden (Chapter 10). Everything except SAR operations was training, but exercises with the Army were called operations.

Eventually, in 1971, FEAF started to disintegrate visibly. No 103 Squadron, due to outlast FEAF, was fighting to maintain its mobility—the accepted operational word meaning independence as far as the Squadron was concerned—but by May 1971 there was no 'mobility equipment' left to issue. By August, with all around them preparing to depart but with No 103 Squadron still receiving replacement crews from the UK, they could not even obtain jungle green clothing to equip the newcomers.(121) Women and children were leaving and general disbandment of the huge FEAF structure was well advanced. The SAR Flight in Singapore was finally disbanded on 31 August. Since its inception in No 103 Squadron as a separate Flight on 1 February 1964 (previously part of No 110 Squadron), 511 emergency calls had been answered including aircraft incidents, land/sea casualty evacuations, and searches. The multi-tape rescue procedure had been used several times. Theoretically, the SAR role was now the responsibility of No 120 Squadron of the Singapore Air Force (SAF) equipped with Alouette helicopters, but doubts about the practicality of this arrangement may be deduced from the fact that two RAF SAR Whirlwinds were specifically recorded as retained on standby until 6 September to provide cover for the Lightning pilots of No 74 Squadron.(122) In fact, the continued inability of the SAF fully to carry out the SAR role was obvious and, although not officially admitted as a formal operational responsibility, No 103 Squadron continued to maintain crews in practice and, as far as possible, to provide a modified standby alert (there was no establishment provided) for the following three years. September 1971 for No 103 Squadron consisted of farewells and departures. On the 10th twelve Whirlwinds (nine in formation) flew from Changi to what was to be their last Far East location at Tengah and on the 15th a six-aircraft formation accompanied the official handing over of Tengah to the SAF. On the 18th a two-aircraft formation joined a Bristol Freighter for the last Battle of Britain celebration at Changi and a fly past was arranged for the Commander-in-Chief's farewell parade at Sembawang on 29 October 1971.(123)

Far East Epilogue

Under the new Five Power Agreement, No 103 Squadron now became the air element of the RAF Support Unit which constituted the RAF element of the ANZUK force stationed at the SAF base, Tengah. The rest of the RAF Support Unit consisted of a small administrative staff headed by a Wing Commander, an Air Movements Section to handle the Air Support Command traffic (mainly VC10s in transit to Hong Kong and Brunei), and an Engineering Squadron into which, to the considerable annoyance of No 103 Squadron, its ground crew disappeared.(124) In July 1971, during the rundown of FEAF, the Squadron had recovered control of its first line servicing. Now it had lost it again. However, with FEAF disbanded, the RAF Support Unit became a unit in Air Support Command, and following an on-site establishment review by the Org 2 (Establishments) staff of that Head-quarters in April 1972 (headed coincidentally by the ex-Commanding Officer of the Seletar Helicopter Wing) the Squadron reverted in July 1972 to full autonomy as a mobile squadron with its own first and second line servicing as well as five RAF Regiment personnel.(125) This was the occasion for the triumphant farewell homily delivered by the outgoing No 103 Squadron Commander in July 1972 quoted earlier.

Whatever may have been the political advantages of this lingering presence of United Kingdom forces in the Far East after the general withdrawal, the effect for the RAF Helicopter Force was almost absurd. It was immediately confined to Singapore airspace except for formally arranged ANZUK exercises for which full diplomatic clearance had to be obtained from Kuala Lumpur in advance, and was supposed to include full nominal rolls of all participants. Several exercises had to be cancelled at the last moment because diplomatic clearance from Kuala Lumpur had not been granted in time. Practical training in jungle areas became almost impossible although in the course of 1972 some limited progress was made in persuading Kuala Lumpur to allow the occasional navigation exercise for one or two aircraft, but on strictly limited routes. In August, the Squadron succeeded in arranging a two-week camp exercise at Jason's Bay in South East Malaya, with its own servicing, catering and RAF Regiment personnel, but this was wholly exceptional. Some relief from this claustrophobic and frustrating situation was provided by a regular crew exchange programme with No 28 Squadron in Hong Kong.(126)

In August 1972, the first Wessex started to arrive to replace the Whirlwinds, and Phase 4 for the Far East helicopters may be said to have started. In the same month, the last nine Whirlwind formation was flown and in October the Wessex takeover was completed, crews having been detached in turn to Odiham for conversion training in the previous few months. The Whirlwinds were removed in pairs by Belfasts to the UK.

The eight Wessex aircraft, initially plagued by much corrosion, gradually recovered and by August 1973 were able to achieve a 100 per cent formation demonstration. Restrictions on training in Malaya gradually relaxed but remained irksome and the continuing crew exchange with No 28 Squadron in Hong Kong (equipped with Wessex just before No 103 Squadron) was much valued. The few ANZUK exercises were enthusiastically enjoyed—the ability to carry ten troops (twelve over shorter ranges) was a fillip to morale and the first taste of auto-stabilisation was greatly enjoyed. Operational (ie exercise) hours exceeded training hours for the first time in mid-1973.(127)

No 103 Squadron worked on for the following two years in this strange twilight of reality. While aware all the time of the token nature of their effectiveness, morale was high and in spite of severely restricted flying areas the Squadron succeeded admirably in maintaining expertise in all their operational roles, including SAR. There was no surprise when, at the end of 1974, the Defence Review presaged the final withdrawal from the Far East; the only remaining question was whether the Squadron would be withdrawn to the UK or disbanded. The latter course was taken and in July and August 1975 the No 103 Squadron Wessex were transported in pairs by Belfast to the UK. The Squadron disbandment in August was celebrated by a reception in the Officers' and NCOs' Messes, and attended by the British High Commissioner to mark the end of the British military presence in Singapore. No 103 Squadron sent a farewell signal to Hong Kong ironically acknowledging that No 28 Squadron was now the best squadron in the Far East.(128)

References to Chapter 12

1   No 224 Group ORB.

2   Squadron Leader Munro.

3   No 66 Squadron ORB.

4   Ibid.

5   ID9/D4–35.

6   No 66 Squadron ORB.

7   Squadron Leader Munro.

8   Mr J Banks.

9   No 66 Squadron ORB.

10 Wing Commander Dowling.

11 No 110 Squadron ORB.

12 Wing Commander Dowling.

13 No 110 Squadron ORB.

14 Pocock 'Fighting General'.

15 Sir David Lee.

16 P D A Austin.

17 No 66 Squadron ORB.

18 No 110 Squadron ORB.

19 No 66 Squadron ORB.

20 No 224 Group ORB.

21 Ibid.

22 FEAF ORB.

23 Ibid.

24 P D A Austin.

25 No 224 Group/No 66 Squadron/No 225 Squadron ORBs.

26 FEAF ORB.

27 Pocock.

28 Sir David Lee.

29 Pocock.

30 No 66 Squadron ORB.

31 Wing Commander Dowling.

32 Ibid.

33 No 225 Squadron ORB.

34 FEAF ORB.

35 Ibid.

36 No 110 Squadron ORB.

37 No 234 Group ORB.

38 Ibid.

39 Ibid.

40 FEAF ORB.

41 No 103 Squadron ORB.

42 No 224 Group ORB.

43 Sir David Lee.

44 Pocock.

45 Ibid.

46 Wing Commander Dowling.

47 No 66 Squadron ORB.

48 No 230 Squadron ORB.

49 No 224 Group ORB.

50 No 66 Squadron ORB.

51 FEAF ORB.

52 No 230 Squadron ORB.

53 No 110 Squadron ORB.

54 Wing Commander Dowling.

55 FEAF ORB.

56 No 230 Squadron ORB.

57 Wing Commander Dowling.

58 Ibid.

59 No 66 Squadron ORB.

60 Nos 103, 110 & 66 Squadrons ORBs.

61 No 224 Group ORB.

62 No 110 Squadron ORB.

63 Wing Commander Dowling.

64 No 224 Group ORB.

65 No 110 Sqadron ORB.

66 Ibid.

67 No 103 Squadron ORB.

68 Ibid.

69 Squadron ORBS.

70 FEAF ORB.

71 P D A Austin/Squadron Leader Munro.

72 P D A Austin.

73 No 66 Squadron ORB.

74 ID9/941/11.

75 No 225 Squadron ORB.

76 FEAF ORB.

77 No 225 Squadron ORB.

78 No 66 Squadron ORB.

79 No 224 Group ORB.

80 No 66 Squadron ORB.

81 P D A Austin.

82 No 66 Squadron ORB.

83 FEAF ORB.

84 Squadron Leader A S Clarke.

85 II/80/61/24.

86 No 103 Squadron ORB.

87 II/80/61/24.

88 Ibid.

89 Ibid.

90 Ibid.

91 Ibid.

92   Ibid.

93   Ibid.

94   No 230 Squadron ORB.

95   FEAF ORB.

96   No 66 Squadron ORB.

97   No 110 Squadron ORB.

98   Ibid.

99   Ibid.

100   No 66 Squadron ORB.

101   Ibid.

102   No 28 Squadron ORB.

103   No 224 Group ORB.

104   FEAF ORB.

105   No 66 Squadron ORB.

106   No 103 Squadron ORB.

107   Ibid.

108   No 66 Squadron ORB.

109   ID9/941/11.

110   FEAF ORB.

111   No 66 Squadron ORB.

112   Ibid.

113   ID9/941/11.

114   Ibid.

115   No 103 Squadron ORB.

116   No 110 Squadron ORB.

117   Ibid.

118   No 103 Squadron ORB.

119   FEAF ORB.

120   No 103 Squadron ORB.

121   Ibid.

122   Ibid.

123   Ibid.

124   Ibid.

125   Ibid.

126   Ibid.

127   Ibid.

128   Ibid.

CHAPTER 13

UNITS IN EUROPE IN PHASE 3—1962-1972

Introduction

The beginning of Phase 3 and overseas deployments described in Chapters 10, 11 and 12 traced the Belvedere and Whirlwind Units which went to Aden, Borneo and Guiana in the early and mid-1960s, and the Whirlwind Squadron (No 230) established in Germany in 1962 before it too, in 1965 and 1966, played its part in Borneo. Support Helicopters Units remaining in Europe consisted of two Wessex Squadrons—Nos 72 and 18, with No 230 (Whirlwind) Squadron sharing the Army exercise task in the UK and Germany before and after its one and a half year stint in Borneo.

All three squadrons shared in turn the United Nations Forces in Cyprus (UNFICYP) communications tasks from 1964, until No 84 (Whirlwind) Squadron was formed there at the beginning of 1972 (Phase 4) also incorporating the SAR task in Cyprus previously carried out by No 1563 (Whirlwind) Flight. No 1564 (Whirlwind) SAR Flight at El Adem, having received its Whirlwinds Mk 10 in 1965, was withdrawn at the end of 1966, and re-formed for a brief seven-month period in 1969 leading up to the closure of El Adem as a Royal Air Force base.

In the UK, the two SAR Whirlwind Squadrons, Nos 228 and 22 (the former being retitled No 202 Squadron in mid-1965) continued with Whirlwinds Mk 10 from late 1962 until the end of the 70s, that is, well into Phase 4.

The Central Flying School expanded its pilot and QHI training task in Phase 3, first with Dragonfly, Sycamore and Whirlwinds Mk 10, with the Skeeter added for Army Air Corps needs, and later with Sioux and Whirlwinds Mk 2/4. A comprehensive programme of standardisation visits to all Service helicopter units including liaison with some foreign air forces had been instituted by the CFS in the 1950s, and was expanded during the 1960s. Both Transport Command and Coastal Command instituted operational categorisation schemes with examining visits to all RAF helicopter units on a regular basis.

The Queen's Flight was mentioned briefly in Chapter 6. Its growth in both Phases 2 and 3 is described here in more detail.

The Metropolitan Communication Squadron (retitled No 32 Squadron early in 1969) acquired a helicopter flight at the beginning of 1960, equipped with Sycamores which were gradually replaced by Whirlwinds Mk 10 starting in 1970. The last Sycamore flight in the RAF did not occur until August 1972.

Support Helicopters in Europe in Phase 3

Following the brief lives in Europe of Nos 225 and 230 Whirlwind Squadrons, the former in the UK and the latter in Germany, before their departure to FEAF in 1962 and 1965 respectively, the Helicopter Transport Support role was sustained by No 72 Squadron in the UK and No 18 Squadron in Germany, both newly equipped with Wessex Mk 2 in the first half of 1964. While the dramatic events in AFME and FEAF were being played out in Aden, Borneo and Singapore, the SRT Helicopter Force in the UK and Germany proceeded with the continuing routine task of supporting Army exercises in the UK and Germany, with the unexpected bonus of a larger Wessex force than had been planned, due to the decision by FEAF not to replace its Whirlwinds with Wessex during the Borneo campaign (see Chapter 14). Rejoined by No 230 Whirlwind Squadron which returned from FEAF in October 1966, the UK/Germany SH Force remained substantially unchanged until the Pumas arrived in 1971, marking the start of Phase 4.

No 18 Squadron re-formed as a Wessex squadron at Odiham in February 1964, containing the Wessex Conversion Unit. Crewman training by CFS had started in 1962 but practically the whole output was still being absorbed by the overseas units which had hitherto managed with volunteers from amongst the technical personnel on the units. No 18 Squadron itself had initially to use volunteer technicians as crewmen. They were expected to do 40 hours flying each month in addition to their normal technical duties, and received two shillings per day (10p) in acknowledgement.(1)

The remaining assets of No 72 (Belvedere) Squadron formed the Belvedere Conversion Unit when the Squadron reformed as the second Wessex squadron in August 1964. The Wessex Conversion Unit was transferred from No 18 Squadron to No 72 Squadron at the end of the year in readiness for No 18 Squadron's move to Germany in January 1965, where it replaced No 230 (Whirlwind) Squadron which was going via Odiham to the Far East. At the same time No 18 Squadron inherited the UNFICYP task in Cyprus from No 230 Squadron. The No 72 Squadron build-up was accelerated so that in May 1965 it could be split to form No 78 Squadron in Aden (see Chapter 11) this being the last exodus from Odiham to east of Suez. No 230 Squadron was the only one to return, which it did in October 1966.

Prior to 1967 the SH Force was prepared for a continuing world-wide role and the exercise schedule reflected this. In addition to the more or less continuous Army exercise support tasks in the UK and Germany, deployments continued for exercises in the Middle East. In September 1965, No 72 Squadron (depleted after forming No 78 Squadron) flew its seven available aircraft with long range tanks to Bomba in North Africa via Lyons, Nice, Pisa, Naples, Malta, Idris, Benina and El Adem. Remembering the debacle for No 225 Squadron in Exercise Triplex West in 1963 (see Chapter 10) the force was accompanied by an Argosy with spares and technical support. All returned satisfactorily in October. A similar self-flown deployment of four aircraft to Malta occurred in June 1966, and in the following August two Wessex were carried to Cyprus in a Belfast—an event which was greeted with the enthusiastic comment that the Squadron was now able to deploy anywhere.(2)

Much effort was devoted in 1966 and onwards to the deployment of day and night large scale troop movements and logistic resupply, as well as the domestic and technical equipment to maintain the force in field conditions. In March 1967, Exercise Stardust involved technical and logistic support of a brigade and required ten Wessex of No 72 Squadron, eight Whirlwinds of No 230 Squadron (newly returned from FEAF) plus 16 Royal Navy Wessex of No 848 Squadron. A typical task was the lift of a battalion to a forward position by 20 Wessex. No 72 Squadron had assumed the UNFICYP task (four aircraft) from No 18 Squadron in December 1966 and was to hold it for about a year.

Both Nos 18 and 72 Squadrons built up steadily so that by February 1967, No 72 Squadron had 20 Wessex and at the end of that year No 18 Squadron had a similar strength. At this point the question was raised whether it was appropriate to have units of this size as individual squadrons. The decision was taken to raise the established level of command in the Wessex units and in early 1967 the Squadron Commander posts became established at Wing Commander level—thus creating a precedent followed thereafter in the SH world (but not by the SAR Squadrons). No 230 Whirlwind Squadron, established for ten Whirlwinds rising to 13 by mid-1968, was to remain under the command of a Squadron Leader until re-established with 13 Pumas in 1971. In both Germany and the UK in the late 1960s the transport helicopter lift available was thus of unprecedented size and generated much enthusiasm for that reason, although its quality in terms of realistic capability and reliability had hardly improved at all. Apart from basic DECCA position finding navigation equipment, there was none of the tactical navigation facilities which came in the following decade, and no specialised night flying equipment. More serious was the problem of icing. In conditions of high humidity, the original nose door configuration of the Wessex tended to encourage ice formation in the engine air intakes with consequent high risk of damage to the engines. As a result, a minimum air temperature operational limit of plus 5° centigrade had to be imposed—as had been for the Belvederes (see Chapter 8) albeit for different reasons.

For all practical purposes therefore the Wessex force, although comparatively large, had no comprehensive IFR and very little night flying capability, while for a considerable time was subject to grounding when temperatures of less than plus 5° centigrade were experienced. Operations by night or at first and last light in Europe were unlikely to be completed since daylight operations required a visibility of half a mile with a minimum cloud base of 100 feet, rising to three miles and

700 feet by night, and great caution had to be exercised with regard to humidity and air temperatures.(3) All this added up to a potentially impressive but thoroughly unreliable service, and it will be seen that Army exercises which had to be planned in such a way that they could continue in some form in the event of last minute cancellation by the helicopter force, were unlikely to be more realistic than those of the early 1960s during the transition from Phase 2 to Phase 3 (See Chapter 10) when the capabilities of the helicopters themselves were so unsatisfactory. The fact that all real operations involving the Support Helicopters during the previous 15 years had taken place in tropical or near tropical conditions and with little or no night flying requirement, must have been a significant factor leading to the inadequately equipped force of the late 1960s.

Nevertheless considerable progress was made in building upon the framework of ground/air co-operation in field operations started in 1960 with No 225 Squadron (ex JEHU) and the Belvedere squadrons before their departure overseas. The practical problems involved in field deployment and operations on a realistic scale were becoming better understood and the deployed facilities required by the Support Helicopters themselves were being demonstrated, especially in the larger scale exercises now possible. Even if at first it required especially favourable weather conditions, the techniques for mounting light assault operations by helicopter were being developed in 1966, and Standard Operating Procedures for the force designed and brought up to date. The effort in this period to achieve realism as far as possible in field exercises, coupled with the emphasis on the limitations imposed by lack of night and all-weather capability, undoubtedly enhanced the drive to remedy these defects for the SH force which was to exist at the beginning of Phase 4 when the crews from overseas had returned and the Puma was entering service. Nevertheless, it was an uphill struggle to convince all, including the budget controllers, of the essential nature of the expensive equipment needed to provide a night and all-weather capability for the SH force, and its relative impotence without it. Progress was very slow.

No 18 Squadron

Following the Defence Review of 1967 and the announcement of withdrawal from east of Suez responsibility and sharp budget cuts (see Chapter 12), a flying unit had to be withdrawn from Germany to the UK. It was hardly surprising that the choice fell on the helicopter squadron—not then regarded as a vital front-line unit. No 18 Squadron was withdrawn and redeployed to Acklington in January 1968 from where it was to help No 72 Squadron by dealing with Army exercises mainly in the northern part of the country. In the following month, however, the Squadron had to provide three aircraft and crews on permanent standby against the possibility of a German border incident, a contingency requiring helicopter assistance for which No 18 Squadron had long been prepared, but now had to mount from

Acklington. By May 1968, No 18 Squadron had six aircraft in Germany for Army training and two were permanently retained there for border incident standby. Eight were there for Army training exercises in September and October, twelve for a NATO exercise in February 1969 plus two for internal security duties in Berlin for the presidential election, and by May the continual detachments to Gutersloh were replaced by an officially permanent presence. The Squadron Headquarters moved from Acklington to Odiham in July 1969 and the Germany detachment continued on a permanent basis until in August 1970 No 18 Squadron returned officially to Germany with twelve aircraft at Gutersloh and four at Wildenrath.(4) The withdrawal of the Squadron from Germany in 1967 and its piecemeal return over the following two and a half years shows that the Support Helicopter force in that theatre had, unnoticed by some, already become indispensable.

During its last six months at Odiham, No 18 Squadron relieved No 72 Squadron of the helicopter support task in Northern Ireland and detached six aircraft there in addition to its deployments in Germany. This was the beginning of the commitment with the security forces in Northern Ireland which was to escalate and continue well into Phase 4. The task again devolved upon No 72 Squadron when No 18 Squadron went back to Germany in 1970.

No 230 Squadron

Returning from FEAF in October 1966, No 230 Squadron spent January 1967 retraining, updating categories and requalifying in engine-off landing practice, becoming available for No 38 Group exercise tasking in February. It must have seemed to the Squadron that little had changed since its departure to FEAF in early 1965. The Operational Record Book describes 'typical 38 Group tasking' with 3-5 day detachments on exercise. Even the field refuelling facilities were unchanged and complaints about the portable refuelling pumps continued as before (see Chapter 10). In June, for example, four Kelston pumps were taken on an exercise deployment and after two days' operations only one was still serviceable. Neither technical nor domestic ancillary equipment requirements of the SH force were high on the list of financial priorities.

No 230 Squadron was not large, having only ten aircraft which were expanded to thirteen early in 1968 to allow four to be detached to Cyprus to take over the UNFICYP task from No 72 Squadron. The Whirlwinds self-deployed with long range tanks via Lyons, Nice, Pisa, Rome, Brindisi, Andravida, Athens and Rhodes, returning the same way (Kerkira instead of Andravida on return) and handing the task back to No 72 Squadron in February 1969.

Back at Odiham in 1967 No 230 Squadron, like No 72 Squadron, experienced a similar reorganisation to that occurring in FEAF—centralisation of servicing and loss of Squadron ground crew (see Chapter 12). It was similarly short lived. In March 1969 No 230 Squadron was moved to Wittering where the No 38 Group Harriers were building up. The Squadron navigators, having been absorbed into Operations Plans at Odiham together with the first line ground crew, were returned to the Squadron. This reorganisation—really a return to a Squadron formation— was specifically mentioned in the ORB for April as 'working well'—especially the first line servicing'. The squadron now had ten aircraft, 24 officers and 64 first line airmen.(5)

In February 1970 No 230 Squadron again took over the UNFICYP task, and continued with it until the end of 1971 when No 84 Squadron was formed in Cyprus at the beginning of Phase 4. With only six Whirlwinds left at Wittering, No 230 Squadron spent 1971 tasked by No 38 Group, giving hovering experience to the new Harrier pilots and preparing to become a Puma squadron at Odiham.

A Puma conversion unit was set up at Odiham in late 1970 (described loosely in the ORB as a Puma OCU) and in the last quarter of 1971 there appeared at Odiham what was called 'No 230 Squadron—Puma Echelon' consisting of four pilots, three crewmen, a Ground Liaison Officer and four ground crew. The Whirlwinds left Wittering in December 1971 and No 230 (Puma) Squadron was established at Odiham on 1 January 1972. Simultaneously, the Wessex Helicopter Operational Conversion Flight amalgamated with the Puma Conversion Unit to form No 240 Operational Conversion Unit.

No 72 Squadron

In the second part of Phase 3 and well into Phase 4, No 72 Squadron could be described as 'Odiham's own'. As a Belvedere squadron it had given birth to No 26 Squadron which went to Aden. As a Wessex squadron it split to form No 78 Squadron which replaced No 26 Squadron in Aden in 1965, but it remained based at Odiham for some 20 years receiving the freedom of Basingstoke in July 1968. In the second half of the 60s it was the mainstay of the No 38 Group exercise, demonstration, technique and equipment development work and military and civilian casualty evacuations (there were very few civilian helicopters at the time). It controlled the helicopter Operational Conversion Flight and there was a small continuous Internal Security Intelligence task as well. In 1965 engine-off landings were being practised on a three-monthly basis but the records do not show when this exercise was discontinued.

Some of the larger exercises involving No 72 Squadron in the 60s have already been described. There were certain other events which have some significance. In July 1967 No 72 Squadron records the imposition of centralised servicing (see No 230 Squadron above and Chapter 12) as being 'against the wishes of the

Squadron Commanders'. (No 18 Squadron was spared because of its move from Germany to Acklington rather than Odiham). First line servicing was returned to No 72 Squadron in July 1969, coincidentally with the deployment of four aircraft to Ballykelly, at the start of the Northern Ireland disturbances which were to continue for several years. In August this detachment was increased to six and moved to Aldergrove where all subsequent deployments were to be based. No 18 Squadron took over this task briefly in early 1970 while No 72 Squadron sent ten aircraft to the Far East for Exercise Bersatu Padu (see Chapter 12), the first and last of what was vainly hoped would be regular large-scale exercises in the Far East mounted from the United Kingdom. On return, No 72 Squadron resumed responsibility for operations in Northern Ireland which were increasing in intensity. In October 1970 the new Phase 4 exercise deployment pattern was initiated with Exercise Deep Express involving four Wessex in support of the Allied Command Europe Mobile Force (Land) in Turkish Thrace.

The flexibility of the SH force was dramatically demonstrated in December 1967 when the crash of the Queen's Flight Whirlwind (see below) was followed by the grounding of all Whirlwinds, which included the entire SAR force. The order for No 72 Squadron to take over the role was received at 1100 hours on 13 December and by 1945 hours on the same day Wessex SAR standby was provided at Chivenor, Valley, Acklington, Leconfield, Leuchars and Coltishall with a further two aircraft on standby at Odiham. By the end of the following day the Nos 22 and 202 SAR Squadrons' crewmen were qualified on the Wessex. The SAR role for No 72 Squadron ended on 5 January 1968.

In September 1968 No 72 Squadron Wessex appeared in support of Harriers at the SBAC Show. A typical month's work at this period consisted of a series of four aircraft detachments and a total of about 500 flying hours; in November 1968, for example, 303 operational hours and 197 training hours were flown, although in the previous month the figures were 453 and 243 respectively. The establishment was for 20 aircraft and 30 pilots. The Northern Ireland commitment of six to eight aircraft detached was routine by 1970 and the pattern for Phase 4 was established.

The Queen's Flight

For the Queen's Flight, Phase 3 was late in starting. The explanation requires reference to events in Phase 2, and as indicated in Chapter 6, both Phases 2 and 3 for the Queen's Flight are described together for clarity and continuity.

The first RAF Helicopter Royal Flight was for HRH Princess Margaret visiting British troops in Germany in June 1954. Although planned and organised by the

Queen's Flight, it was carried out using a Dragonfly borrowed from the newly established CFS Helicopter Unit and flown by Flt Lt J R Dowling. The Royal flight was from Costedt near Buckeburg to Sennelager and had to be aborted after one hour's flight due to bad weather. The Dragonfly, sumptuously furnished for that occasion, was temporarily attached to the Queen's Flight in September 1954 together with a CFS pilot (Flt Lt A J Lee—previously one of the Hoverfly pilots in the King's Flight flying mail to Balmoral in 1947, and recently returned from Malaya). Other early Royal users of the helicopter were the Duke and Duchess of Gloucester and the Queen Mother but it was Prince Philip who became the champion of the helicopter.

Having qualified as a helicopter pilot under the auspices of the Royal Navy, Prince Philip continued to use the Naval Whirlwind Mk 22 for official visits, and this lead was followed by other members of the Royal Family until eventually Royal helicopter flying was carried out solely in the Naval Whirlwinds, although the flights continued to be planned and organised by the Queen's Flight. The Dragonfly was used for route and landing site reconnaissance, communications work and pilot continuation training, since a Queen's Flight pilot always accompanied the Naval helicopter on Royal flights.

Agreement in principle by the Air Council for two helicopters to be established in the Queen's Flight had been obtained in June 1954, but took a long time to become reality. It was December 1955 before a decision to establish a training Whirlwind in the Queen's Flight was taken, to be effective in the Spring of 1956 and followed by two VVIP versions a few months later. The training aircraft, only held for the first week in June, demonstrated the unsuitability of this underpowered Pratt and Whitney engined helicopter for the Royal Flight while it soon became clear that the modifications needed, principally duplicate power controls, would delay for an unacceptably long time the appearance of the two VVIP versions. Sycamores were offered as a temporary solution but were rejected as unsuitable in size and shape.

In November 1956, the Air Council decided that the policy of establishing Whirlwind helicopters on the Queen's Flight should be reconsidered when a firm estimate for the Mk 5 (with the Alvis Leonides Major engine) could be provided against an agreed Standard of Preparation. A draft form of the Standard of Preparation was issued in February 1957, but a whole year went by with interminable discussions and bickering on minor differences of furnishings, radio and engineering fitments, and general finish, before the draft was agreed by all the interested parties. This was not however, significant for by this time the Leonides Major had run into serious development problems and it seemed likely that delivery of the first aircraft would take at least another year after a contract had been placed. Meanwhile the Naval Whirlwind, now flown by Lt Cdr E C Spreadbury, carried out most of the Royal flights whilst the Dragonfly continued to operate from Benson; in August 1956 the Dragonfly carried out the first of what were to become annual flights, delivering Royal Mail to Her Majesty's Yacht Britannia which was cruising off the Western Isles with the Royal Family on board.

In July 1958 a contract for the VVIP Whirlwinds (now known as Mk 8s) had at last been placed with Westlands, delivery being expected the following Spring, and a Mk 4 aircraft was collected from Aston Down at the end of the month for crew training. The faithful Dragonfly, XF 261, was returned to South Cerney in August 1958 but again the change proved somewhat premature in terms of crew training, for in January 1959 the Leonides Major was still giving trouble and the first engine had not even arrived at Westlands. Despite these delays, the Queen's Flight Captain—Air Cdre Fielden—continued to press for the establishment of two helicopter crews on the Queen's Flight. In 1954, a meeting of senior RN, Army and RAF representatives had agreed that, as the Naval and Military helicopter resources were greater than those of the RAF, which might have been unduly strained by the provision of two crews for the Queen's Flight, one of the eventual crew vacancies should be filled alternately by Naval and Army officers. Air Cdre Fielden now felt that as the Naval authorities had been so helpful with previous helicopter trips, and as in any case the Army had no Whirlwind qualified pilots, the Admiralty should be invited to appoint a Naval helicopter pilot to join the Queen's Flight when the VVIP helicopters were delivered. Lt R M Kerr, who had taken over the Naval Whirlwind flying from Lt Cdr Spreadbury, was selected to fill this post—one which is incidentally, still in 1983 filled by a Naval pilot. Lt Kerr eventually joined the Flight in January 1960 and, having subsequently transferred to the RAF, remained until 1976 as Prince Philip's personal helicopter pilot.

The Leonides Major engine continued to give trouble and by June 1959 all the Naval Whirlwind Mk 7s, from which the Queen's Flight machines were derived, had been grounded for modification. A new series of trials was started at Culdrose in July 1959, the successful outcome of which resulted in the Mk 8s receiving their release to service in October 1959 by which time, however, Air Cdre Fielden was showing interest in the Gnome gas turbine powered version of the Whirlwind. The first of the new Mk 8 aircraft was collected from Boscombe Down on 1 October and the second from Yeovil on 5 November. The Mk 4 Whirlwind was soon disposed of and there followed a short period of crew training and working up before the helicopters were successfully introduced to Royal flying on 23 February 1960, with a flight from Kensington Palace to Papworth—almost four years after the originally projected date of introduction.

The cancellation by the RAF of the re-engining of Whirlwinds with the ill-fated Leonides Major engines and the substitution of Gnome gas turbines did not extend to the Queen's Flight. The VVIP Mk 8 Whirlwinds, partly perhaps because they were derived from the Naval Mk 7s but doubtless also because they had only just been obtained after such a long struggle, continued in the Queen's Flight until the

RAF changeover from the Mk 2 and 4 to the Mk 10 was practically complete. In early 1964 the change was made and the Mk 12 (VVIP version of the Mk 10) Whirlwinds arrived marking the start of Phase 3 for the Queen's Flight.

The fatal crash in December 1967 described in Chapter 14 dealt a severe blow to the Queen's Flight by killing the new Captain and Engineer Officer of the Flight as well as the crew. The party was on its way to Yeovil for a conference at Westlands concerning the standard of modification required to prepare the Wessex Mk 4 for the Queen's Flight. The subsequent grounding of the Whirlwinds, followed by another grounding a few months later, did not enhance the Whirlwind's reputation on the Queen's Flight, but in any case, the twin-engined reliability of the Wessex and the obvious advantage of its cabin size ensured that the Whirlwinds would be replaced as soon as possible. In both 1967 and 1968 No 72 Squadron at Odiham was called upon to lend a Wessex for flights by HRH Prince Philip, and when the first Wessex Mk 2 was delivered to the Queen's Flight for crew and technician training in December 1968, it was used quite extensively for Royal flights even before the first VVIP Mk 4 Wessex arrived on 25 June 1969.

The second Wessex Mk 4 was duly delivered on the appointed day—1 July 1969— and after the phasing out of the Whirlwinds and the allocation of the Mk 2 Wessex to No 72 Squadron, the helicopter part of the Queen's Flight stabilised satisfactorily with these two aircraft for several years. This constitutes the start of Phase 4 of the Queen's Flight.

Metropolitan Communications Squadron/No 32 Squadron

The Queen's Flight was late in entering Phase 3 with turbine-engined helicopters, but the Metropolitan Communications Squadron was even later. In fact, it did not have any helicopters until November 1959, and then operated Sycamores until 1972, with a gradual replacement by Whirlwinds Mk 10 starting in 1970. The Squadron did not really fit the pattern of phases which has been used to describe the progress of the rest of the helicopter force.

The reluctance to allow the RAF to spend money on helicopters purely for communications tasks was mentioned in Chapters 4 and 6, and the consequent misuse of Central Flying School and occasionally Search and Rescue helicopters for the most pressing communications tasks during the 1950s (mainly VIP trips) became progressively more disruptive of their specialised roles. The Royal Navy and the Army, by contrast, had no hesitation in finding helicopters for their own VIPs, but there was developing a much wider recognition that there was a considerable number of Staff Officers below VIP category whose effectiveness could be greatly enhanced by access on a regular basis to small transport helicopters. There could, however, be no question of purchasing aircraft specifically for that purpose.

C Flight (Helicopters) was formed in the Metropolitan Communications Squadron at Northolt in November 1959 with two Mk 11 Sycamores.* Lacking night flying or any form of navigation equipment the helicopter flight flourished only modestly but by the end of 1962 had four aircraft. The Mk 14 Sycamores were now surplus in comparatively large numbers having been withdrawn from the Far East—Phase 3 was beginning everywhere else in the helicopter world.

Initially, tasking for the helicopters was done by the Air Transport Operations staff in the Air Ministry but by 1968 the role had been assumed by No 38 Group. There were now five aircraft and the Flight was finding the longer and more difficult flights demanded by No 38 Group progressively more of a challenge; it was becoming clear that a more suitably equipped helicopter would soon be needed. A regular task was a daily shuttle between Northolt, HQ Strike Command at High Wycombe and No 11 Group Headquarters at Bentley Priory. Between 1968 and 1970 some 20–40 passengers were flown monthly on this regular run and by mid-1971 the figures were between 50 and 70.

No 32 Squadron—a Canberra Squadron of the Near East Strike Wing—was disbanded in Akrotiri in 1969 and the number plate allocated to the Metropolitan Communications Squadron. In January 1970 No 32 Squadron received its first Whirlwinds Mk 10 and by the end of the year all the Squadron helicopter pilots had been converted and categorised on both Sycamores and Whirlwinds (another Squadron type conversion). The second Whirlwind, fully VIP-equipped, came in early 1971 from the Queen's Flight which was now entering Phase 4 with its Wessex Mk 4. Spread over the following two years, the five Sycamores were replaced on a one for one basis by Whirlwinds Mk 10, ending in August 1972 when the last Sycamore in the RAF departed for the Torbay Aircraft Museum. En route, it was landed on the lawn of the Officers' Mess at Upavon where the AOC of Air Support Command presided at a luncheon attended by the Sycamore designer Mr Raoul Hafner and several of his design and engineering staff from Filton and Weston-super-Mare where the Sycamores had been built in the days of the Bristol Aeroplane Company in the late 1940s and early 1950s. After lunch, the Sycamore joined an escort of three Wessex and three Pumas from Odiham for a flypast before proceeding on its way to Torbay.

Insofar as there was a Phase 3 for the helicopters of No 32 Squadron, it consisted of the two-year long substitution of Whirlwinds for Sycamores in 1970 and 1971. Phase 4 may be said to have started following the ceremonial departure of this last Sycamore from the Phase 2 period.

---

*The Mk 11 was an early version of the Sycamore which could not be used operationally in the Short Range Transport role and, having a substantially different cockpit layout from the Mk 14 Sycamore which was in general RAF use, could not even be used in the training role. These were survivors from No 1906 AOP Flight (Chapter 6) which became surplus on the formation of the Army Air Corps in 1957.

TRAINING IN PHASE 3

The Central Flying School

Towards the end of Phase 2 in August 1961, the CFS Helicopter Squadron had moved from South Cerney to Tern Hill and become a Wing with two squadrons—one training squadron with 'basic' and 'advanced' phases for both pilot and QHI training, and one 'standards' squadron to deal with the rising pilot and QHI categorisation commitment; the expanding programme of visits to all Service helicopter units at home and overseas; and foreign Air Force liaison exercises. The CFS Helicopter Wing had by then acquired a somewhat motley collection of helicopters—two Dragonflys, two Whirlwinds Mk 2/4, eight Sycamores and two Skeeters—reflecting the 'ad hoc' character of the unit's growth over the previous eight years. The arrival of one Whirlwind Mk 10 in November 1961—the first turbine powered helicopter at CFS—marked the start of Phase 3. The piston-engined Whirlwinds were phased out in the following five months.(6)

At Tern Hill the Helicopter Wing expansion programme was completed in the first quarter of 1962 with the split of the Training Squadron into two separate squadrons, one for basic pilot/QHI training and one for advanced pilot/QHI training. The standards squadron became No 3 Squadron.(7) (Ten years later the division was made between pilot and QHI training, each squadron having basic and advanced flights). A training flight was established at Valley in March 1962 for mountain flying training in Snowdonia and SAR sea training for crews destined for that role. Formal crewman training started in May and, being for SAR crews initially, was for the most part carried out at Valley. The syllabus for pilot training, originally 50 hours on one type of helicopter but progressively increased to 80 hours (50 basic and 30 advanced) on two helicopter types, now reached 100 hours with the inclusion of night and instrument flying plus mountain and maritime exercises. There being no OTU, CFS was performing the introductory part of an operational training unit course, so reducing the diversion of operational squadrons to the training tasks for new crews. The course at Valley was adjusted to suit crews destined either for the SRT or SAR role as required.

The number of simultaneous courses had grown considerably. In September 1962, for example, there were two pilot courses in progress—one at the basic stage (Sycamore) and one at the advanced stage (Whirlwind)—one crewman course, two QHI courses, one Staff Officer familiarisation course and one pilot refresher course. The Valley detachment had become permanent.(8)

QHIs, in addition to those needed for basic pilot training, were established on the operational squadrons at a rate determined by the number of permanent detachments maintained by those squadrons. The CFS courses varied considerably in size as the demand for QHIs fluctuated and new helicopter units were formed. In February 1965, for example, No 54 Basic Pilot Course consisted of 17 students out of a student population of 44 officers and 12 airmen aircrew—the latter being crewmen. QHI courses were naturally much smaller. In June 1965, for example, there were ten courses in progress—four basic pilot training, three QHI, one refresher and two crewman courses—one (SRT) at Tern Hill and one (SAR) at Valley. In January 1966 there were no less than five QHI courses running—No 89 with three RAF, four RN and one Australian Army students, No 91 with six RAF students, No 92 with three RAF and five RN students, No 93 with one RAF, two Army and one Australian Army students, No 94 with three RAF students.(9)

The training syllabus was treated with considerable flexibility to accommodate these different requirements but remained basically similar to that shown in Appendix 2 expanded to include night and instrument flying, mountain flying and basic SAR training. The basic pilot course which had grown to 100 hours by 1962 remained substantially at that figure while various combinations of training helicopters were tried. CFS issued standard syllabi for rotary wing training in April 1972 which specified the QHI course as 68 hours in 12 weeks on either Sioux or Whirlwind, 45.45 hours basic and 59.15 advanced in 23 weeks for pilot training including two and a half weeks at Valley for mountain flying and sea winching, and for Harrier conversion pilots six hours in Whirlwinds in five days (no solo). The Skeeter, used for Army QHI courses and as a lead-in to the Sycamore or Whirlwind for pilot courses was replaced by the Sioux (Bell 47) in November 1964 but in February 1965 three basic students were trained experimentally throughout on the Whirlwind, in accordance with one theory of how to obtain the best results with economy.(10) (This system was used for training the pilots of No 230 Squadron at Odiham—see Chapter 10—and again at CFS in 1973 when the Sioux was phased out).

Standardisation visits to all operational helicopter units were a well-established regular feature by 1962, and the time was coming when CFS was to find itself advising on operational rather than only pure flying matters. In February 1962, Transport Command acquired a Squadron Leader from CFS (Sqn Ldr A J Clarke—late of Malaya) and included him in the Transport Command Examining Unit, thus allowing CFS to revert to its proper role of standardising and categorising QHIs and sampling the quality of the output from the Flying Training School (in this case CFS itself), leaving the operational standard to be measured by the Operational Commands. Coastal Command established helicopter crews in its own Categorisation Board for the same purpose in respect of SAR units. The CFS continued to visit all units in its role of observing pure flying standards and checking on the performance of recently qualified pilots from the training machine.

Between 1962 and 1972 the CFS Helicopter Wing was highly active in all its roles—pilot, QHI and crewman training; standardisation and examining; and foreign Air

Force Liaison visits. In addition, communication and demonstration tasks seem to have been accepted with some abandon. In June 1967, for instance, there were 17 'special flights' as follows:—

One Whirlwind	—Wycliffe College, for the AOC RAF Record Office.
One Whirlwind	—CFS Garden Party at Little Rissington.
One Sioux	—Tushingham Gala.
One Sioux	—Little Rissington Display.
Three Sioux	—Little Rissington Display Team.
One Whirlwind	—Radley College for the AOC No 25 Group.
One Whirlwind	—Gaydon—Solihull—AVM Robinson.
One Whirlwind	—Solihull Carnival.
One Whirlwind	—Static Display Valley—Prince Philip.
One Whirlwind	—RAeS Garden Party—Desborough House—Ripley.
One Sioux	—Colston Display.
One Whirlwind	—Principal Medical Officer, Technical Training Command to Lake Bala.
One Whirlwind	—Shrewsbury Agricultural Show.
One Whirlwind and	
Three Sioux	—Demonstration, Royal Observer Corps Day.
One Whirlwind	—Sutton Ashford Schools' Careers Convention.
One Whirlwind	—GOC West Midland District to Scarborough.
One Whirlwind	—Lake Bala.

In the same month a liaison visit was paid to the Royal Danish Air Force Helicopter Wing at Vaerloese, and a standardisation check made on No 22 (SAR) Squadron. In the following month there were 18 special flights and one of the regular visits to the French Air Force at Chambery. Flying times split between course training and 'other' flying in typical high season months of July and September were as follows:

Month	Aircraft Type	Dual and Solo Training	Other Flying
July	Whirlwind	469	264
	Sioux	314	91
September	Whirlwind	681	176
	Sioux	318	170
		1782	701(11)

By 1965 the demand for Sycamore pilots had reduced almost to zero and the Sycamores were being used rather unsatisfactorily as the basic element leading to an advanced phase in the Whirlwind. There was considerable pressure at CFS to replace the Sycamore by the Sioux in the basic phase and in February 1966 there seemed to be a good excuse for doing so. A tendency for the Sycamore to roll to port on take-off if certain precautions were not taken is described and explained in the notes on the Sycamore in Appendix 1. These precautionary techniques had evidently been allowed to fall out of prominence and in February 1966, while a Board of Inquiry was still investigating an accident at CFS, another occurred. Five new Sioux had recently been delivered. The CFS Sycamores were grounded and remained so pending a decision on their continued suitability in the training role. The result was the disposal of the CFS Sycamores in May–August 1966, and there followed a six-year period of stability in which the Sioux filled the basic role and the Whirlwind the advanced. In February 1968, with a strength of 16 Whirlwinds and ten Sioux, a formation consisting of eleven Whirlwinds and ten Sioux was flown to celebrate the 50th Anniversary of the RAF.

In October 1972 the two squadrons at Ternhill, previously carrying out both pilot and QHI training, one on Sioux (basic stage) and the other in Whirlwinds (advanced stage) were reorganised to separate pilot and QHI training, each squadron having a basic and an advanced flight. This set the pattern for the later change (Phase 4) when No 2 Flying Training School was reformed to carry out the helicopter pilot and crewman training, leaving the Central Flying School Helicopter Unit to its own special functions in line with the rest of the CFS.

Phase 3 ended for CFS in December 1973 with the completion of No 138 Basic Pilots' Course, the last to use Sioux and Whirlwind. The Sioux was phased out and 'all through' training on the Whirlwind instituted. Phase 4 began at the same time with the introduction of the Gazelle (SA 340) in the instructional role for QHI training.

Transport and Coastal Command Examining Tasks

From the formation of the CFS Helicopter Unit in 1954 until 1962 the CFS was responsible for and actively engaged in operational standardisation visits to all helicopter units. In 1960, for example, CFS visits were paid to the Army Air Corps Centre, the Metropolitan Communication Squadron, the Queen's Flight and the two Search and Rescue Squadrons in the UK; to No 110 Squadron at Butterworth, the Royal Malaysian Air Force in Kuala Lumpur and the Hong Kong Auxiliary Air Force in the Far East; and to the SAR Sycamore Flight at Khormaksar in the Middle East and No 103 Squadron at Nicosia and El Adem.

With the addition of helicopter operational examining staff to Transport and Coastal Commands (Transport Command Examining Unit and Coastal Command Categorisation Board in 1962 and 1963 respectively) the CFS visits did not greatly diminish, but they changed in character to the extent that pure flying standards and techniques were observed and categorisation of unit QHIs became the main function. Operational categories for all crews became the responsibility of the

Operational Command examiners whose visits to units were now added to those of the CFS. In the mid-1960s, for example, this included four squadrons in the Far East (three with detachments in both Singapore and Borneo), one flight at Nicosia and El Adem, one SRT squadron and one SAR flight in Aden, one flight in Guiana, two squadrons and a conversion unit at Odiham, the Metropolitan Communication Squadron at Northolt, the Queen's Flight at Benson and the two Search and Rescue squadrons at nine locations in the United Kingdom. The RMAF and Hong Kong Auxiliary Air Force were regularly included in Far East visits by invitation.

It may seem that the examining visits of the CFS, added to those of the TCEU (retitled Transport Command Examining Staff—TCES—in 1964 and Air Support Command Examining Unit—ASCEU—in 1967) created a heavy additional load on the very busy overseas operational units. But in fact the value in maintaining and enhancing standards was generally apparent and the service provided was enthusiastically welcomed by most crews and especially at all supervisory levels.

Only the Transport Command examining responsibility has been mentioned in respect of the overseas units and that is because until the late 1960s the SAR function of overseas helicopter units was secondary to the tactical role, and the helicopter examiners of the Coastal Command Categorisation Board concentrated their efforts on the exclusively SAR-dedicated UK SAR squadrons. It was not until the FEAF operations began to run down and the SAR role, still officially secondary, began to assume relatively greater importance, that the Coastal Command Helicopter examiners started regular visits to the Far East. It was not until then that the diminishing Far East authorities made a plea for co-ordination of the three types of examining visits which otherwise were tending to become a main feature of life for the reducing helicopter force. Co-ordination of visits was arranged because of the obvious inappropriateness of having two separate operational helicopter examining teams, in addition to the Central Flying School, visiting one helicopter unit in Singapore and one in Hong Kong on a six-monthly basis, simply because the SH and SAR roles were performed by separate units under different Commands in the UK. On the withdrawal of the last helicopter squadron from Singapore the SH helicopter force returned to its main role in the United Kingdom and Europe where SAR continued to be provided by a separate specialised maritime Group.

The regular standardisation and categorisation of the widely dispersed helicopter units throughout the world from the mid-1950s and through the 1960s was assiduously pursued and undoubtedly greatly enhanced the flexibility and efficiency of the developing RAF helicopter force to a degree which can scarcely be exaggerated.

The SAR Squadrons in the UK in Phase 3

The pattern of the UK SAR helicopter force was established in Phase 2 as described in Chapter 7. Phase 3 started for the SAR force at the end of 1962 by which time both Nos 228 and 22 Squadrons had exchanged their Whirlwinds Mk 2 and were fully equipped and trained on the Whirlwind Mk 10.

The drama following the closure of the central South Coast flight of No 22 Squadron at Thorney Island had continued through 1960 (see Chapter 7) and had shown that however well justified the RAF was in legal terms in spending defence funds and deploying the SAR flights solely for the benefit of RAF fixed-wing aircraft crews, the public had already learned to regard them in much the same way as they did the Royal National Lifeboat Institution, and fierce lobbying by local officials could force or at least influence modifications to the RAF deployment plans. Thus in mid-1961 the flight at Felixstowe, due to be deployed to Manston, appeared instead at Tangmere—closer than Thorney Island to the South Coast towns whose Mayors had been most pressing. A further flight then had to be established at Manston.(12) An additional motivation for this change existed because there was some Air Staff annoyance that in the holiday weeks, the Solent and South Coast generally were treated to frequent views of rescue helicopters flying to and fro bearing the words 'Royal Navy' in large letters, but since these were anti-submarine warfare equipped aircraft often not available for rescue tasks, they could not be placed on SAR standby and were operated only during standard working hours. As such, they were no more than an occasional bonus to the regular seven-days a week SAR service which the RAF was obliged to operate.(13)

In May 1964, due to closure of Tangmere, D flight of No 22 Squadron moved to Thorney Island, thus returning the South Coast helicopter flight to its former home whence its withdrawal had caused so much trouble in 1960. In March 1969, history was repeating itself when D flight of No 22 Squadron at Manston was selected for closure. There was a shortage of crews, while the RAF fighter activity, and therefore SAR requirement, was decreasing in the North and it was judged that the Manston area could be covered by Coltishall to the north and east and Thorney Island to the west and south. This upset the local authorities at Margate to such an extent that a civilian (Bristow) helicopter was hired to provide local helicopter SAR cover. The arguments which took place in the early 1970s when the RAF wished to reactivate its SAR flight at Manston belong in Phase 4 of this history, ie after the disbandment of Coastal Command in November 1969 which marked the end of Phase 3 for the SAR Force.

At the beginning of Phase 3 then (ie the end of 1962) the RAF No 228 Squadron deployments were at Acklington, Leconfield (including Squadron Headquarters and a Communications Flight consisting of one Anson), Leuchars and Horsham St Faith. The latter flight was moved to Coltishall in April 1963. No 22 Squadron deployments were at St Mawgan (including the Headquarters Flight and SAR Operational Training Flight), Chivenor, Tangmere, Valley and Manston. The SAR Operational Training Flight at St Mawgan was able to disband in 1962 as the Central Flying School took over the task with its detachment at Valley, the QHIs from St Mawgan then forming the helicopter element of the Coastal Command categorisation board.

The arrival of the Whirlwinds Mk 10 in the latter part of 1962 marked January 1963 as the beginning of Phase 3 for the SAR squadrons. They continued to operate as before but with up to 30% increase in fuel/pay load as well as speed, the aircraft had a greatly enhanced range and were able to respond more successfully to a wider range of tasks; and the public were becoming progressively more aware of and reliant upon the rescue service thus provided.

As the SAR service broadened its scope, so the method of recording SAR incidents became progressively more detailed and descriptive. Categories of incidents recorded were under only four headings in the early 1960s, but after the introduction of the Mk 10 Whirlwind and the consequent growth in use of the service, these categories had grown to seven. Direct comparisons before and after are therefore difficult to make, but based on the four categories of incidents in use in 1960 and 1961 (the last two years of the Mk 2 Whirlwind) an approximate comparison can be made with incidents grouped under the same four headings for 1965 and 1966 as follows:

Category of Incidents	User	Number of Incidents 1961/62	Number of Incidents 1965/66
Aviation emergencies	Military and Civil	61	219
Shipping		19 (16 rescued)	97
Civilians	Bathers, Yachtsmen	190 (89 rescued)	938 A total of 97 lives were saved and there were 66 false alarms
Casualty Evacuation (air ambulance)	DHSS	141	162

This demonstrates the huge jump in all SAR operations except casualty evacuation (later referred to as aero-medical evacuation in order to describe the increasing use of SAR helicopters as air ambulances for transfer of patients to or between hospitals at the request of the Department of Health and Social Security, as opposed to the direct delivery to hospital of injured rescued persons). The figures show the number of times the SAR helicopters were scrambled (that is, launched) to deal with the types of incident shown, and do not indicate whether or not the intended operation was actually carried out; for example, in 1966 No 22 Squadron records 34 aviation incidents resulting in 14 persons being rescued, 69 aero-medical patients carried of whom seven were lifted from ships (thus becoming casualty evacuation as opposed to aero-medical), 70 swimming incidents resulting in the rescue of 16 persons, 252 small boat/yacht etc incidents involving 137 rescues, 59 operations on behalf of persons marooned on cliffs resulting in 61 rescues, 56 operations and 42 rescues described as miscellaneous, and 27 false alarms. Nos 22 and 202 Squadrons had slightly different ways of categorising operations in their Operational Record Books making comparison and totalling extremely difficult.

The system of dividing operational SAR sorties into different statistical groupings continued to change into the late 1960s, and a longer view than is available in this history would be needed to assess any significance. In the meantime the following chart, deduced from the Coastal Command and Squadron ORBs shows the fairly constant rate of total effort.

No 22 SQUADRON

Year	Total Hours	Operational Hours	Operational Sorties	Persons Lifted
1964	4227	551	352	46
65	3651	536	304	45
66	4228	748	352	62
67	4085	508	340	42
68	4153	617	346	51
69	3553	457	296	38
70	3245	498	270	42

No 228/202 SQUADRON

Year	Total Hours	Operational Hours	Operational Sorties	Persons Lifted
1964	2647	268	294	30
65	3032	270	303	27
66	3332	366	333	37
67	3714	334	338	30
68	3855	404	321	34
69	4170	430	347	36

On 28 August 1964 No 228 Squadron disbanded (for the fourth time since 1918) and immediately reformed as No 202 Squadron with the same role and deployments as before, having been selected to carry that title after No 202 (Hastings) Squadron was disbanded, its meteorological reconnaissance role having come to an end.

The four flights of No 202 Squadron covering the East Coast of Britain had generally longer ranges to fly than the five flights of No 22 Squadron which, being deployed in the more highly populated South, consequently dealt with the higher rate of emergency incidents. The result was that whereas only about 14% of No 22 Squadron's flying time was classed as operational, the corresponding figure for No 202 Squadron was 10%. The remainder was classed as training. These figures varied little year by year from 1964–1970, as did the total annual flying rate which averaged 3877 hours for No 22 Squadron and 3458 for No 202 Squadron. Both squadrons flew at a similar intensity as far as monthly hours were concerned (30 hours per established aircraft) regardless of the number of emergency scrambles, this being the rate required to keep all crews in full practice—ie about 15 hours per month per pilot. Only about two hours of this was essential in non-SAR roles— for example, instrument and night flying and periodic engine-off landing practice. In other words, a much greater rate of operational flying could have been accepted, but no reduction of aircraft or crews was possible in the absence of such demands while the SAR emergency service had to be maintained.

There was no promised night flying rescue task because the Whirlwinds lacked appropriate equipment such as auto stabilisation, target illumination, radar etc for the role in complete darkness. On the other hand it was judged that there would be many occasions when, although what was required was technically night flying, nevertheless conditions of partial darkness might be such that the crew considered the task could still be carried out.

The policy therefore was to offer a fifteen minutes readiness emergency SAR helicopter standby throughout the hours of daylight, but no more than a possible capability by night, for which a one-hour standby was provided. In practice, most night operations requested were in fact successfully carried out.

The proliferation of gas/oil rigs in the North Sea greatly enhanced the effective range of the SAR helicopters of No 202 Squadron by providing the refuelling points out to sea, and from the mid-1960s onwards were in regular use as forward operating bases. In January 1967, for example, the rig Neptune was used as a night landing base for an aero-medical evacuation carried out at dawn from a trawler. Shortly afterwards the oil rigs Orion and North Star were used to double the Whirlwind radius of action out to sea for a particular aero-med lift from a ship, providing both fuel and radio communications.

Throughout the period it was the policy to provide 'top cover' (a high flying aircraft acting as a communications link) for the helicopters—a standard precaution for single-engined aircraft operating significant distances over the sea. This could usually be arranged by designating an aircraft already patrolling or exercising in the area to act as a link with the RCC. Sometimes however this was either impractical or extremely difficult to arrange at short notice, but the absence of top cover would not normally prevent the helicopter from responding to an emergency call. This problem was to remain until the single-engined Whirlwind was replaced by the twin-engined Wessex in the late 1970s (Phase 4), but the oil rigs scattered widely throughout the North Sea were particularly helpful to the limited range Whirlwind not only as refuelling points but also as communication relays, navigation aid and emergency refuges.

In the 1960s, with the bulk of the SRT/SH Force overseas in Borneo, Singapore, Aden/Bahrain, Cyprus, Guiana and Germany, and with very few civilian helicopter operators in the UK, the two SAR squadrons constituted the main RAF helicopter force for much of the time. Their use for ferrying patients between hospitals as required by the medical authorities (Aeromed) only started to diminish when, in 1969, it was decided that non-emergency cases, ie those where more than 24 hours notice could be given, would be carried by the SH force. For much of this period the SAR squadrons were the sole, but highly successful, RAF representatives in the international 'helicopter meet' which took place annually from 1967 onwards. They usually won.

By the end of the 1960s the SAR squadrons were more than ever indispensable. The expansion of their operational capability involved them in more dramatic situations which earned them an increasing number of honours and awards—a trend which was to continue through the following two decades. As already mentioned, the withdrawal of the flight at Manston in 1969 resulted in considerable uproar and caused the Department of Trade to employ a civilian Whirlwind for local rescue services. This demonstrated better than anything the status of the RAF SAR helicopter service in the public eye.

It is not possible to point to any particular moment when the demands of the civilian population for the services of the RAF SAR helicopters became strong enough to attempt to challenge RAF deployment patterns, but the events of 1960 surrounding the RAF withdrawal of SAR from Thorney Island already mentioned, came as a surprise to many. The RAF accession to local demands seems to have set a precedent, although it worked the other way round in respect of withdrawal from Manston in 1969. The fact was that by the end of the 1960s, having once had SAR helicopter services, nobody was prepared to do without them. Fortunately for both the RAF and the coastal communities, the RAF requirement for total helicopter SAR cover round the coast of England and east of Scotland satisfied both parties. Where the RAF case was from time to time temporarily slightly weak, for example, in respect of Leconfield and Chivenor in the late 1960s and early 1970s, the strong civilian local feeling already expressed elsewhere was a factor which had to be given some weight. For the crews of Nos 202 and 22 Squadrons, their civilian 'clients' provided a welcome continuous useful activity, the RAF demands for actual rescue being mercifully rare. However, they did occur from time to time, and when successfully answered, produced a powerful boost to morale. For example, No 22 Squadron commented in November 1968 that 'the Squadron's whole existence was justified by the rescue of both pilots of a Gnat 18 nm south of Valley'. Having ejected, they were rescued by two double lifts after only 20 minutes in the water.

On 27 November 1969, Coastal Command was disbanded at a stand-down ceremony at St Mawgan, and on the following day No 19 Group was retitled Southern

Maritime Air Region (SOUMAR). From then on Nos 202 and 22 Squadrons both came under No 18 Group—now of Strike Command. This concluded Phase 3 for the SAR squadrons, but a trend had been set which was to dictate the development of the SAR force in the 1970s (Phase 4). The Whirlwind Mk 10, which has been described as an enormous improvement in range, speed and lifting capacity over its predecessor, the Mk 2, was in the late 1960s already being found wanting in all these respects. What had been happening since the Sycamore started in SAR in the mid-1950s (Phase 2) was that, as the benefits of SAR by helicopter in general were being recognised, the task was growing faster than the aircraft. The first pressure—cabin space—encouraged the use of the Whirlwind Mk 2 to replace the Sycamore. Demands for more lift, range and speed made the Whirlwind Mk 10 especially attractive in the early 1960s (Phase 3). Limitations of the single-engined helicopter over the sea, and lack of auto-stabilisation for full night flying capabilities, added to the continuing pressure for more speed and lift capability, generated a demand for the twin-engined Wessex in Phase 4. All these aircraft were found as a 'spin off' from the developments taking place in the SH world, but the apparently insatiable demand for bigger, faster and especially more reliable rescue services focussed attention on a truly all-weather capability. The efficiency of the successfully developing SAR force in the 1960s (Phase 3) was thus directly responsible for the entirely new situation in Phase 4 when, quite independently from the SH force procurements, the SAR force actually generated its own 'Operational Requirement' for a new specialised SAR all-weather helicopter. The Sea King thus became a logical if unforeseen development from the SAR Sycamores of No 275 Squadron in 1953.

Helicopter Development Unit

After the disbandment of the JEHU at the end of 1959, there was pressure to replace the capability for research and development of helicopter techniques in the Army support role. In 1961, a Helicopter Development Unit (HDU) was formed at Old Sarum alongside the School of Land/Air Warfare (SLAW).

As a RAF unit it had a short and uneventful life. It was supplied initially with three Sycamores Mk 12—surplus because they were useless for anything other than passenger flying—and this at a time when the operational scene was dominated by the Belvedere and Whirlwind Mk 10. In 1964 they were replaced by three Sycamores Mk 14—also because they were now in surplus—but these were withdrawn early in 1965. Inevitably little, if any, development was achieved. Shortly afterwards it ceased to be a RAF unit and acquired joint Service status, a series of title and organisational changes bearing witness to the contrasting views, uncertainties and doubts about the appropriate formation for a transport helicopter development unit, especially one with no operational aircraft. There was no Central Helicopter Establishment to advise or control such researches, while the Joint Helicopter

Tactical Development Committee (JHTDC) in Whitehall could not fulfil such a role.*

During the 1960s much 'rationalisation' took place. The SLAW amalgamated with the Amphibious Warfare School to form the Joint Warfare Establishment (JWE). The HDU, having become the Short Range Transport Development Unit (SRTDU), emerged in 1968 as the Joint Helicopter Development Unit (JHDU) and together with the Air Transport Development Unit (ATDU)—previously the Transport Command Development Unit (TCDU)—and the Army Air Transport Development Centre (AATDC) became one of the three elements of the new Joint Air Transport Establishment (JATE). The JHDU, consisting of a Commander RN (in a rotational post), a Lt Cdr, a Major and a Sqn Ldr, had no aircraft except the elderly RN Whirlwind already mentioned. The Unit was intended to undertake joint development of techniques and equipment affecting more than one Service, but at the time continuous change in the operational units required the concentration in the front line of all the experience and practical development available. The RAF, along with the other two Services, was unwilling to allot helicopters and crews to the JHDU for development work which was already proceeding apace in their own operational units. The JHDU therefore became a forum for theoretical doctrine with a briefing function for the JWE and its courses, and thus acquired the title Joint Helicopter Tactical Development Unit (JHTDU).

An example of a major development exercise was the assessment of several rival helicopter tactical night lighting systems using torches, one of them being the SHNAP which was already in joint Service use in the Far East, but not in Europe (see Chapter 12). A tri-Service practical demonstration was arranged as a result of which the crews involved were unanimously in favour of the SHNAP which was consequently recommended for joint Service use. The JHTDU then prepared an instructional document for troops laying the pattern which was of such length and complexity compared to the slim pamphlet used in the Far East (example at Appendix 4) that the system was judged to be impractical for field use and the whole idea was dropped.

---

*The RN, having maintained a Hiller HT1 at Old Sarum in the mid-1950s for the benefit of the SLAW, supplied a Dragonfly Mk 3 in the early 1960s, replaced by a piston-engined Whirlwind Mk 3/7 which lasted into the mid-1970s. The Army Air Corps looked after its own affairs at Middle Wallop.

References to Chapter 13

1   No 18 Squadron ORB.

2   No 72 Squadron ORB.

3   Wg Cdr Smith.

4   No 18 Squadron ORB.

5   No 230 Squadron ORB.

6   CFS ORB.

7   Ternhill ORB.

8   Ibid.

9   Ibid.

10   Ibid.

11   Ibid.

12   ID9/902/5/Pt 4.

13   Ibid.

CHAPTER 14

POLICY CONSIDERATIONS IN THE SECOND HALF OF PHASE 3
1964-1971

Introduction

During the transition from Phase 3 to Phase 4 of the Helicopter History, that is from the end of large scale operations outside Europe to the concentration instead on NATO requirements in the face of the mounting threat from Russia and the Warsaw Pact countries, there were two main fields of helicopter policy development: the maintenance and replacement of the current operational helicopters: and the appearance of the offensively armed helicopter and consequent expansion of the Army Air Corps. Both were to be greatly affected by the Anglo-French helicopter package which, together with the initially frustrated Chinook, constituted the next generation of helicopters supporting ground troops in or near the battlefield. The Wessex continued to provide a significant if diminishing contribution to the Support Helicopter Force.

The use of the word 'Support' in this context requires some definition. While the Army Air Corps helicopters, whether offensively armed or not, can be properly described as acting in support of the ground forces, the expression 'Support Helicopter' was used by the RAF to designate exclusively the troop carrying and logistic resupply roles accepted for the RAF. This emanated from the original pre-helicopter identification of air support roles as Offensive Support (OS) and Transport Support (TS)—the former consisting of fixed wing fighter ground attack aircraft and the latter of tactical fixed wing aircraft. RAF helicopters were naturally incorporated into the latter group as part of the Short Range Transport (SRT) Force and when the Pioneers disappeared without replacement in the late 1960s a purely helicopter SRT Force remained. Since no offensive role was seen for helicopters by the RAF, the renaming of this group as the Support Helicopter (SH) Force seemed logical, but the expression 'SH' thus became formally recognised as referring only to the troop carrying and logistic resupply roles of the RAF. Any putative offensive support role for helicopters was argued exclusively by the Army Air Corps and rejected by the RAF on the grounds that that function was the responsibility of the RAF and the helicopter was not regarded as suitable to perform it. There was much discussion of the subject during this period concerned with the arming of helicopters for defensive or offensive purposes, resulting in the expansion of the Army Air Corps and the RAF's loss of exclusive responsibility for OS helicopter operations. It is necessary to bear in mind that the RAF, in determining the armament appropriate for SH, was concerned only with troop carrying logistic resupply helicopters. There was no ready-made phrase to describe Army Air Corps offensively armed helicopter projects—they could not be called OS helicopters without accepting their right to exist which would, in turn, have resulted in retitling the RAF SH Force as transport support helicopters, which in fact is all they were.

The replacement of the Whirlwind by the Wessex had been decided in the policy considerations of the first half of Phase 3 (Chapter 9). The disappearance of the Whirlwind from the SH Force marking the start of Phase 4 occurred in the late 1960s and early 1970s and a comment on its general aspects up to that point is included here. Of more complex significance was the demise of the Belvedere which was decreed in the first part of this period, and took effect in March 1969. The event and its timing coupled with the sharply conflicting views on the viability of that remarkable helicopter are of sufficient significance to require a critical review of its comparatively short Service life.

The Belvedere in Retrospect

Retrospective impressions of Service aircraft tend naturally to be based on a consensus of opinion formed by personal experiences and general observation and, in the case of aircraft based mainly overseas, these views are sharply limited by the fixed dates of individual overseas tours. Thus, for all who served in Aden between 1963 and 1965 the overall impression of the Belvedere was one of an unmitigated disaster despite the fact that it did useful work in early 1964. A less intensely adverse but still generally unfavourable opinion is likely to be found amongst those who served in the Far East in 1963 and 1964; thereafter, until the first quarter of 1969 when the Belvedere finished, it was seen more and more as a uniquely valuable VTOL load carrier, well liked by the pilots and marred only by a persistently unreliable engine starter system and, for the RAF servicing organisation, the fact that it required a constant struggle to keep vibration levels within bounds by frequent rotor blade tracking and drag damper adjustments.

A basic disadvantage suffered by the Belvedere in FEAF and Aden, and to a lesser extent in the United Kingdom, was an absence of detailed experience-backed servicing data from the manufacturers who, in fairness, had not had sufficient chance to acquire it themselves before the aircraft was thrust into operational service. One of the Westland representatives at the time describes the aircraft builders drawing on their own long experience in dealing with helicopter problems on an 'ad hoc' basis in the final production stages and initial flight testing as the aircraft was manufactured; and even records one case of a Belvedere with control or vibration problems so intractable that it was known at the factory as a 'rogue', and merely issued with its own individual maximum speed limit in order to meet the delivery timescale demanded.(1) The problems had eventually to be sorted out by progressive checking and replacement where necessary of the various control and rotor head components involved, in the time-honoured way of the early heli-copters.* Thus in Aden in 1965, the visiting Westland representative was able to rectify all four unserviceable Belvederes in the space of four weeks, but only a month after his departure they were all unserviceable again, apparently irremediably, until the chance came to get rid of them to FEAF on an aircraft carrier. Even then, a Westlands technician had to assist in their emergency recovery to enable them to fly to the aircraft carrier.

As will be seen below, the fate of the Belvedere was sealed in Whitehall as early as 1965, largely a result of its behaviour in AFME. Through 1964 and early 1965 energetic high level action in Whitehall had been focussed on dealing with the main Belvedere problems. It was hoped that the Plessey Olympe gas turbine starter would solve the engine starter problems by 1966; control modifications (yaw cables) and enhanced fire warning and suppression were being given high priority; and automatic rotor speed governing was being progressed. ACAS (Operations) advised VCAS in February 1965 that the AOC AFME could be assured that with all these remedies plus the In-Flight Tracker soon to be delivered, their problems should be solved. This contention, he said, was supported by the history of the Belvedere in FEAF.(2)

Following a visit to FEAF, AFME replied with a detailed apologia in June 1965 which concluded that the Belvedere, described as 'a cumbersome and temperamental piece of machinery' whose engine starting was 'a most delicate and dangerous procedure', could not be made to work satisfactorily or economically in AFME. It was claimed that operational conditions in FEAF seemed to be much more favour-able than those in AFME. In particular:

a.   The majority of sorties flown in FEAF were below 2000 feet while in AFME they flew up to 8000 feet.

---

*Some 18 years later, in spite of advances in manufacturing techniques and use of new materials, the almost intractable nature of this problem is illustrated in comments made by the Squadron Engineer Officer of No 33 (Puma) Squadron reported in the RAF News, July 30–August 12, 1983—13: 'The black art is vibration, where experience and luck are the two ingredients of successful rectification. It is a skill which can only be partly taught: the remainder is experience. Most vibration problems originate in the main rotor head, and the basic procedure is simply to try different combinations of blades until you find four that run smoothly together. Theoretically they should all be interchangeable, but in practice it doesn't work out quite like that. Changing one of the £18000 blades requires around two hours work, and a particularly elusive source of vibration can keep an aircraft on the ground for several weeks before a cure is finally effected. Out in the field, the Squadrons usually carry minor defects if they cannot be readily fixed, and then do a comprehensive rectification on return to base.'

b.   There was no dust or sand problem in FEAF.

c.   Turbulence in FEAF was relatively insignificant.

None of these statements could be accepted at their face value in FEAF since Belvederes operated satisfactorily up to 8000 feet in Sabah and frequently experienced very severe turbulence. There was certainly less sand and dust, but this only affected the rate of engine changes and was satisfactorily solved by the intake blanks designed in AFME. Insofar as the sand in Aden may have contributed to the rate of rotor blade erosion, there is no evidence or likelihood that this would have caused more vibration problems than the tropical rain which was such a particularly damaging feature in FEAF operations.

In addition to the hazards mentioned, it was claimed by AFME that the Belvederes required 74 manhours work per flying hour but were only established for 21.4 manhours; and that 25.5 manhours per flying hour were needed for rectification with an establishment allowing only 7.7 manhours. It was admitted that the FEAF establishment was similar to that in AFME—one Flt Lt and 53 NCOs and airmen for the five Belvederes at Kuching compared with one Flt Lt and 55 NCOs and airmen for the six (in reality only four) Belvederes in Aden, but the argument rested on the misconception that the sand, turbulence and high altitude operations in AFME caused the vibration troubles and thus generated a heavier rectification load. High altitude operations would certainly have exacerbated the vibrations generated by rotor imbalances, but could not be cited as their cause. The fact was that despite spending many extra hours attempting to do so they could not cure the vibration problems in the Belvedere. That the vibration was capable of being solved is shown by the success of the Westland expert, Mr Banks, whose services were described by the AFME report as invaluable but setting 'standards impossible to maintain'.(3)

Finally, the AFME report cited Belvedere XG 474 (the Museum aircraft) which had recently returned from a two-month detachment in Beihan (see Chapter 10), and was currently undergoing a major inspection. It was stated that if vibration recurred on this aircraft after the inspection (as was clearly expected), the case would be proved that the Belvedere was not an economically sound proposition in AFME. The recommendation was that the Belvederes still due for delivery to AFME should be cancelled, the remainder reallocated to FEAF and the Wessex expected soon for No 78 Squadron should be advanced to replace the Belvederes. This course was accepted in Whitehall where, by late 1965, determination to replace the troublesome Belvedere with the Chinook at the earliest possible moment had been growing for some time.

The technical condition of the four aircraft from Aden, when seen in FEAF, was described as appalling. One had a partially seized throttle mechanism; a second had a completely seized front engine; and a third had a control rigging problem and flew from the aircraft carrier to Seletar in a continuous gentle left-turn with the cyclic stick held for much of the time against the right hand stops in the fully forward position. All four aircraft were flown the few miles from the carrier to Seletar by No 66 Squadron crews soon after the ship passed Changi Point, the Royal Navy having declined in advance to allow the aircraft to fly off after the carrier arrived at the Naval Base.(4) One of the aircraft, described in Aden as a 'rogue' (ie impossible to correct in terms of power/performance/control rigging) was later found to have several hundred pounds of sand beneath the floor. Many control and rotor head components required regular greasing and the No 66 Squadron Engineer Officer suspected that they had received no attention since delivery from the Contractor.(5) Clearly, the servicing in Aden left much to be desired, but it must be remembered that these particular aircraft had been virtually abandoned by AFME some months before the opportunity came to get rid of them, partly because there seemed little chance of making them serviceable and partly because the Wessex Mk 2 was arriving to replace them (Chapter 11).

There seems to be no absolutely reliable evidence or single theory to explain the difference in outcome of the Belvedere's fortune in Aden and FEAF. The No 66 Squadron Commander, Engineer Officer and the Westland representative saw no reason to believe that the Aden climate or topography adversely affected the aircraft, and the Westland representative emphatically denied that sand and dust was a problem significantly affecting anything other than the engines, and said that in this respect the Belvedere was better off than the Wessex, Whirlwind and some fixed wing aircraft as well.(6) Engine changes were technically not a particular problem for the Belvedere.

Blade tracking problems were common to both theatres, although the In-Flight Tracker (IFT) was sometimes more difficult to use in Aden since it used an optical rotor blade sighting system and electronic timing comparison for identifying blade divergences, and the equipment did not perform well in strong sunlight, at low sun angles or in heavy turbulence.(7) Hence the 23 consecutive air tests flown by XG 474 in Aden mentioned in chapter 12. In FEAF, IFT measurements were often taken in the course of operational sorties.(8)

It is true that FEAF inherited the Belvedere Trials Unit servicing personnel in 1962, and they were better experienced than the technicians sent to Aden in 1963 who had received only a short qualifying course with Westlands at Weston-super-Mare. It is difficult, however, to accept that this difference should still exercise a noticeable effect some two years later. Of more significance perhaps, was the fact that in the totally centralised servicing organisation at Khormaksar, the Belvedere servicing personnel were not always devoted exclusively to that aircraft. On the contrary, when in 1965 the new No 26 Squadron Commander visited FEAF to compare servicing and operational practices, he commented that he had considerable difficulty in obtaining servicing personnel from the Station Engineering Wing at Khormaksar. This, he was told, was because the Belvedere was the least cost-effective aircraft on the Station in terms of servicing manhours per flying hour achieved; and since the Station was less than 100% manned against establishment (80% at the time for the trades concerned), there were times when no servicing personnel were available to work on the Belvederes.(9) This very marked contrast with the autonomous or semi-autonomous servicing control in No 66 Squadron FEAF seems likely to have been one of the major factors resulting in the grossly disparate fortunes of the Belvedere in the two theatres.

The only other feature clearly emerging as likely to have been significant in this respect is that of aircrew morale, and this seems to have been affected adversely in Aden in three ways:

a.   Headquarters FEAF was, after twelve years' experience, warmly appreciative of helicopter capabilities when the Belvederes arrived in 1962 and were ready to do whatever was necessary to encourage them to function effectively. Headquarters AFME on the other hand was not yet convinced of the true value of the military mobility conferred by the large helicopter. The attitudes at Khormaksar in 1963 to the newly arrived No 26 Squadron, as perceived by the Squadron at least, were less than enthusiastic (see Chapter 11).(10)

b.   On an early visit to AFME the Westland representative was made aware by one of the most experienced pilots, that it was suspected that the Belvedere was being treated in a cavalier way by the less experienced pilots and that there was a lack of proper supervision.(11) This pilot was killed shortly afterwards during a cross-country night flight following an unexplained structural failure in the aircraft or its control systems.

c.   That accident, together with a yaw cable failure three weeks earlier, a crash following control failure on the airfield (servicing fault) (12) and several starter explosions, combined to produce in Aden a marked reluctance both by crewmen and some pilots (13) to fly in the aircraft.

In FEAF, on the other hand, a yaw cable failure at a very early stage (1963) which resulted in the death of all on board, produced no more than normal momentary anxiety, while engine starter failures, explosions and fires were regular occurrences.

Transmission failure—generally expected to have catastrophic consequences in a twin rotor helicopter—happened only twice. Both cases occurred in FEAF and involved the same aircraft. Neither event caused damage which amounted to a reportable accident. Unlike that of the later Chinook, the rear rotor of the Belvedere, although overlapping the front rotor, did not pass through the front disc in flying manoeuvres normal to the flight envelope, and so the blades would not necessarily strike each other if the synchronous transmission failed—at least until the rotors were almost stopped after landing and the closing down of the engines, when blade droop would cause the rear rotor blade tips at the front to pass below those at the rear of the front rotor. Also unlike the Chinook, the Belvedere, having an engine beneath each rotor, would not, if the synchronising shaft failed, be left with all the power to one rotor and none to the other—merely an adjustable imbalance. In January 1968, having just completed an abseiling exercise for SAS troops at Grik in North Malaya, Belvedere XG 468 was hovering at 100 feet when the synchronising shaft connecting the two rotors broke. The aircraft landed successfully and the rotors did not touch each other until they were almost stopped.(14) Four months later, the same aircraft was hovering at 4000 feet near Mersing in South East Malaya while providing a calibration target for the Air Defence Ground Radar Station at Bukit Gombak in Singapore. A failure in the front gearbox was followed by an immediate forced landing in a sharply confined space—gaining the pilot a Green Endorsement in his log book. After a gearbox and synchronising shaft change in the field, the aircraft resumed flying six days later.(15) These two cases were classified merely as 'incidents', but would have been profoundly disturbing had there been any general lack of confidence in the aircraft.

The only questionable effect on morale noticeable in No 66 Squadron occurred early in the Borneo campaign when, in mid-1964, pilots were not required to complete their two or three week stint at Kuching if the aircraft serviceability was too low to employ them fully. There was some suspicion by the incoming Squadron Commander in 1964 that vibration levels—essentially a subjective judgement prior to the fitting of vibration meters—were held to require rectification too often, thus permitting an early return to Singapore by some pilots.(16) Whether this was so or not, a change in the system requiring the completion of fixed periods at Kuching regardless of aircraft serviceability soon coincided with a reduction in Bedvedere rectification rates in Borneo. Generally morale in No 66 Squadron was extremely high and in April 1965, for example, all five Belvederes in Kuching were flown in formation to celebrate 100 per cent serviceability, and the starter explosion which followed soon afterwards was regarded merely as part of the accepted pattern. The eleven ship formation in October 1967 speaks for itself (Chapter 12).

It appears then that there may have been inappropriate Station servicing organisation and some initial lack of understanding in the Middle East theatre at Command, Station and/or Squadron level, which may have contributed to the ultimate fate of the Belvedere there. In the presence of evidence from FEAF, however, the conclusion must be that—as for all aircraft properly supported at staff level, serviced by dedicated specialists and flown by well supervised crews—the Belvedere was eventually no different from the first version of any other successful RAF aircraft, and better than some, with the sole exception of its engine starter system which, having been denied resolution for financial and future planning reasons (see below) was still being discussed and modified by the contractors (AEI) as late as 1967.(17)

Retrospective View of the Whirlwind in FEAF

Quantitatively, the Whirlwind Mk 10 in the Far East as well as elsewhere gave the impression of being a highly reliable, comparatively cheap, rather slow but flexible aircraft whose somewhat restricted payload (between one third and one quarter of that of the Belvedere) was nevertheless such and enormous improvement over the previous Mk 2 and 4 piston-engined versions that its qualitative defects seemed relatively minor, especially when compared to the notorious Belvedere problems. At least an attempt was made to correct them by modification action. The difference, however, was mainly one of scale, since some of the technical defects of the Whirlwind Mk 10 would probably have proved quite disastrous in practical terms had they occurred in the tiny Belvedere force. Throughout the main Confrontation period there were about 45 RAF Whirlwinds available in FEAF but never more than eight Belvederes up to the end of 1965, rising to 13 in 1967 (after Confrontation).

In July 1967, one of the two Mk 12 Whirlwinds of the Queen's Flight (VIP versions of the Mk 10 Whirlwind) suffered structural failure while carrying a crew of two and the Captain of the Queen's Flight together with the Flight Engineer officer. All were killed. At first it was thought this was due to a fatigue crack found in the spar of one of the rotor blades, and all Whirlwinds were grounded except for operational flights, pending Non Destructive Testing (NDT) of the rotor blades.(18) This was followed in December 1967 by the discovery of a serious fatigue crack in the spar of a Belvedere rotor blade originating from a score mark occurring during manufacture. 50 per cent of all Belvedere blades in FEAF were then found to have scribing or other marks on the blade spars, but in the same month the more serious news was revealed that the Queen's Flight crash resulted from loss of the rotor head caused by fatigue failure of the main rotor drive shaft originating in the manufacturing process of the high tensile steel shaft which was unique to the Whirlwind. All Whirlwinds were grounded and all Whirlwind gearboxes had to be returned to Westlands. Of 104 shafts inspected (RAF and RN) 42 were initially rejected, although some of these were later recovered after remedial action.(19) Replacement became a matter of extreme urgency and the priorities were allocated as follows:

1. FEAF SAR

2. Hong Kong

3. MEAF SAR

4. UK SAR

5. Flying Training Command

6. Balance of FEAF Support Helicopters

7. No 38 Group

8. Others

A two-year modification programme also had to be instituted for all existing Whirlwind (and Wessex) rotor blades, and serious doubts were expressed about quality control at Westlands.(20)

In early 1970, the rate of failure of Whirlwind tail rotor blade bonding had reduced stocks to a point where the shuttling of individual tail rotor blades between the UK, Hong Kong and Singapore was needed to avoid grounding of the whole fleet, and this did in fact occur from time to time in Singapore at this period (see Chapter 12).

Throughout the whole period from the introduction of the Whirlwind Mk 10 in 1962 to 1971, the Whirlwinds had suffered a series of more or less unexplained engine failures in flight, mostly taking the form of compressor stalls or progressive power loss described as engine rundown. In the early days these were mostly attributed to computer or computer-throttle actuator malfunctions, but many were not satisfactorily diagnosed. Later theories included malfunctioning of Inlet Guide Vanes or Fuel System Components, dirt and/or corrosion in the compressor, aerodynamics of the intake with door design changes coupled with rain ingestion and crosswind effects. In the UK it seemed that winter temperatures made matters worse. It was not until March 1971 that Strike Command generated a full study by the Director of Flight Safety (DFS) by complaining that they had experienced ten engine rundowns in 1970 and five in the last four months, adding that the trouble had existed undiagnosed for ten years. AMSO reported to VCAS in April 1971 that there had been a tendency to assume a solution was found as each of the various troubles had been identified and modification action taken but it was difficult to reproduce the effects and inconsistent results were produced after changing from one door shape to another. The lastest mystery was stalling of the engine compressor four or five minutes after rain ingestion was stopped.

DFS produced a report in May 1971 (21) recording that Whirlwind engine rundown had been a major cause for concern since the aircraft first entered service. Of the 65 Whirlwind Mk 10 accidents which had occured since then, 35 (53.8%) had been initiated by this cause resulting in twelve aircraft being written off and 23 suffering Category 3 or 4 major damage at an estimated cost of £1¼ million. The rate had been seven rising to eight per 10000 flying hours and recent reports indicated an upward trend. 32 per cent in FEAF and 40 per cent of the total in the UK were due to 'causes unknown' and 72 per cent of these remained unknown after investigation by the manufacturer. In the Wessex, the gnome engine had reduced from an initial peak of 14 rundowns per 10000 flying hours on entry to service to six from 1965 until 1969 and thereafter to three. Statistics suggested that the Whirlwind problem was worse at low power settings in winter in the United Kingdom, and due to water ingestion in FEAF, and recommended a study of nose door shapes and the effect of low temperatures on minimum fuel flow settings.

Thus, while a statistical survey defined the situation for all to see, there was still no specific solution available. At least the Belvedere engines, once started, very rarely malfunctioned thereafter.

Policy Effects of Belvedere and Whirlwind Experiences up to 1971

In the case of the Whirlwind, no new policy stance was needed as a result of operational experience. The case for the Wessex to replace the Whirlwind was already well established and the change had begun in the UK in 1962 with Nos 228 and 22 Squadrons at Leconfield and St. Mawgan. The engine rundown problem had never been seen as a long term difficulty having for ten years been apparently on the very threshold of a solution, until Strike Command, who were going to be left with the Whirlwinds in the SAR and communications roles for the indefinite future (that is until the Wessex replaced the Whirlwinds in all other roles) drew attention to the actual situation as described above. Even then there was no undue excitement. Eight or nine unexplained engine failures per 10000 flying hours did not seem especially daunting to practical operators and although Buckingham Palace confirmed after the fatal accident to the Queen's Flight Whirlwind in July 1967 that it had not been the practice for Her Majesty The Queen to use helicopters and saw no reason to suppose that policy would change, once the main rotor drive shaft defects had been remedied Prince Philip and other members of the Royal Family resumed flying in the remaining Whirlwind Mk 12 of the Queen's Flight, pending its replacement by the Wessex.(22) The need to find a better and air portable replacement for the SH Force of the 1970s was a seperate discussion and it is described later.

For the Belvedere, however, the effect of its behaviour on policy was much more profound. The refusal by AFME in June 1965 to believe that the Belvedere could be made to work satisfactorily in Aden (23) finally ended any remaining support for the aircraft in Whitehall and, by implication, any support there might have been for a developed version as a successor (eg WG7). Even before 1960 there had been a lobby in MOD which believed that the Vertol 107 (predecessor of the Chinook) was preferable to the Belvedere which was then in the throes of early development (see Chapter 8). The fact that the Vertol 107 was in many ways, including control and stability, in an even earlier stage of development than the Belvedere, was not generally recognised. The unfortunate consequences in the early Chinook (CH-47) became clear in 1965 at about the same time as the death knell was sounded for the Belvedere. Two simultaneous arguments then took place—how to get rid of the Belvedere and how to obtain the Chinook—against the background of a policy which called for a future SH capability to provide a seven-company lift (24) which is described later.

How to Get Rid of the Belvedere

In June 1965 VCAS recorded that since 1961 the Belvedere was notorious for unserviceability and rate of wastage. The engine starters had caused two aircraft to be written off, resulted in Category 2 damage to two more and had caused 37 categorisable incidents since the beginning of 1963.(25) Even with the latest modifications the AVPIN system remained dangerous both inherently and in vulnerability to enemy ground fire. This was supported by DFS with the information that Belvedere wastage was double that of the Whirlwind and that the aircraft had the highest write-off rate of any aircraft in service—more than double the next highest. The Director of Air Engineering (D Air Eng) joined in with statistics showing that the Belvedere rectification was four times more expensive in manhours than the Whirlwind or Wessex, in scheduled servicing 12 per cent more than the Whirlwind and 50 per cent more than the Wessex, and in costs per flying hour for all servicing in the ratio of 12 : 6.5 : 9 for Belvedere/Whirlwind/Wessex respectively, but no comment was recorded on the small size of sample then available, or on the size, payload and speed of the Belvedere. From then onwards all discussions started from the premise firmly and repeatedly urged by the Assistant Chief of the Air Staff (Operational Requirements) that the Belvedere should be disposed of and replaced by the Chinook by whatever means and as soon as possible.(26)

On 4 August 1965 a meeting was convened by the Minister of Defence for the Royal Air Force attended by CAS, VCAS, DCAS, ACAS(OR) and DG Eng intended to relate the Belvedere to current general helicopter policy. The Minister agreed with the principle enunciated by ACAS(OR) that the Belvedere should be deleted as soon as possible but he was not sure about the availability of the Chinook to replace it. The question of the modification to introduce the Olympe engine starter to deal with the Belvedere starting problems had been discussed by the Air Force Board in the previous month and the point was taken that it would be difficult to justify the modification unless the aircraft was to remain in service for at least two years subsequently, ie until 1969 (which in fact it did). The resurgence of the Belvedere in FEAF, where it was at last beginning to demonstrate its longer term potential, was clearly something of an embarrassment in this atmosphere and DG Eng said that while it now appeared to be satisfactory in FEAF, it was 'not being used in real operations'. This extraordinary statement is not explained further in the records, neither is the reply to the consequent question by CAS as to how or whether the Belvedere could be kept out of the battle.(27) The feeling was clearly that the starter modification should not be incorporated because it might extend the Belvedere's life and ACAS(OR) asked DG Eng directly whether the Belvedere was now otherwise modified to a safe standard for the next two years—ie to 1967. DG Eng replied that it was, with the proviso that the engine starters could still blow up. CAS thought this was contradictory. The decision was to delay three months to November pending the forthcoming September evaluation of the Chinook.

The following month AUS(AS) repeated the warning to the Minister that if the Olympe starter was fitted the Belvedere might have to be retained in service for some years to come, and at a meeting on 24 August 1965 (28) the Air Force Board agreed to defer the engine starter modification pending a clearer picture of the future size and shape of the helicopter force with particular reference to the Chinook. No further attempt was made to replace the Belvedere engine starter system. CAS advised the COS Committee that the RAF did not wish to keep the Belvedere longer than was absolutely necessary.(29)

How To Obtain The Chinook

In February 1965 the Chiefs of Staff discussed the need for an increase in SH for a seven-company lift and recorded that the required Wessex increase would take two years but the Chinook would be available in the current year and should therefore be the preferred choice.(30) It was thought possible that two per month might be obtained starting in July. It was recognised that certain difficulties might arise—there might be political problems in buying American so soon after the purchase of Phantoms and Hercules and, it was now noticed, there were many modifications and much development work still needed on the Chinook. It was decided to send an investigating team to the United States in March to evaluate the situation. What they found was not encouraging. Following two fatalities all Chinooks were grounded and remained so throughout the visit. A failure in the stability augmentation system (none was necessary on the Belvedere) had resulted in a complete loss of control, there were technical problems with the blade droop stops, there had been fires in the aft pylon after gearbox oil starvation and also following a double engine failure, a blade root had failed resulting in blade disintegration and all of the eight major accidents recorded so far had terminated with a major airframe fire. Ease of escape from the cabin was most unsatisfactory—only three push-out windows were provided and two of these would be lost if the aircraft fell on its side. A delay of at least one year was expected with a possible in-service date at the end of 1967.

The Operational Requirements branch of MOD now demonstrated a single-minded determination not to be deflected from obtaining the Chinook similar to that which had been needed six years earlier to bring the Belvedere to life. They recommended waiting for the Chinook problems to be solved and resisted any idea to add to the Wessex force even if an increase in SH should be approved; or that the S-61 or RN Wessex 5 should be accepted in order to help the RN to obtain the S-61—evidently a proposal which had been made or was being prepared. By February 1966 they were advising Air Plans to refuse to discuss a trade-off of SA-330s (Puma) against a Chinook order and not to 'give up the ghost' because there might be financial difficulties with the Chancellor; they urged that the Chinook would have great value in logistic support and could lift the P-1127 (Harrier); and, finally, that failure would mean expensive attempts to keep the Belvedere in service—a course which had already been agreed as a most unproductive exercise.(31) As a final fall-back position, the recommendation was that the intended Chinook numbers (24 to support a UE of 18 were intended) (32) could be further reduced to 15 supporting a UE of 12 so that it became no more than a Belvedere replacement rather than the widely flexible multi-role aircraft they envisaged. The important thing was to get some into service.

At this point a red herring appeared in the form of the Sikorsky CH-53. (The French three-engined Super Frelon had also been considered but discarded because of inadequate performance). In August 1965 the Ministry of Technology was preparing a paper on the whole field of helicopters and the industrial implications having an implicit threat to the very continuance of Westlands. By December they were applying pressure in support of Westlands for the tactical version of the Sikorsky SH-3D (CH-3C—later CH-53) as a competitor for the Chinook (33), Westlands expecting to build the aircraft under licence as in the case of the previous Sikorsky designs—Wessex, Whirlwind and Dragonfly. During 1966 this option was kept alive with tentative interest shown by the German Air Force and a detailed comparison was made. The CH-53 was expected to have a similar performance to that of the Chinook but while being more modern it was not yet ready and so unproved. The favourable German reports were regarded with some caution as they were known to be biased towards a single main rotor configuration.(34) The costs would be 25 per cent higher than for the Chinook, and although there was a last minute offer by Sikorsky to reduce the price, the clinching argument and the one placed first in the brief for the Secretary of State in March 1967, was that to choose the CH-53 would delay the date for the Belvedere replacement.(35)

Treasury approval was obtained early in 1967 for the purchase of 15 Chinooks to support a UE of 12, including two for training. Belvedere unit viability experience was quoted to support the case for placing them all together and, since they were not air transportable and the active service areas of responsibility were mainly east of Suez, they were to be located in the Far East where they would directly replace the existing Belvederes.(36)

To prepare for the introduction of the CH-47 Chinook into RAF service, a combined Ministry of Technology and RAF Group consisting of a management team (Wing Commander Engineer team leader, Pilot deputy team leader, one Squadron Leader Electrical, a Secretarial officer and a representative from the appropriate Finance Branch), and a Provisioning Team (one Squadron Leader, one Flight Lieutenant and three civilian supply experts) was dispatched to the United States Army AVCOM at St Louis in April 1967. A CSDE technical servicing team consisting of one Squadron Leader and two Flight Lieutenants was set up at the manufacturer's plant in Philadelphia.(37)

All went well and arrangements were made in October 1967 for a CH-47 to carry out a demonstration at Odiham which took place in early November. However, the Defence Review of 1967 which announced (inter alia) a sharp reduction in defence spending and the intention to withdraw completely from east of Suez by December 1971, had virtually demolished the arguments chosen to support the case for the Chinook, all of which were destined for the Far East. On 22 November 1967, with the RAF Chinooks appearing on the production line, a signal from the Ministry of Technology to the United Kingdom CH-47 teams in the United States announced the cancellation of the Chinook order.(38)

Offsetting to some extent the brutal finality which seemed to be implied by this sudden shock, Air Plans took the opportunity to remind the Air Staffs that in April 1966 (39) DCAS, in setting out the SH requirements for the 1970s, made the point that the helicopter crane lift facility was not exclusively tied to military deployment plans and that aircraft recovery was a valuable role as well. The P-1127 (11000 lbs), Wessex (9000 lbs), SA-330 (8200 lbs), also bulky spares such as engines for the P-1127 (Harrier) were all legitimate loads for the crane lift helicopter, the case for which might possibly be raised again sometime in the future.(40) In fact the raising and dashing of hopes in this respect continued throughout the 1970s— that is, beyond the scope of this part of the history—finally succeeding with Chinook deliveries in 1980.

The 1965 decision to discard the Belvedere in favour of the undeveloped CH-47 rather than to solve its problems with the modifications known to be needed, had two main consequences: firstly, there was no heavy lift helicopter at all for over ten years after the Belvedere, whose life had, surprisingly to some quarters, been very successfully prolonged until 1969, when it ceased to exist; secondly, the opportunity to design and build a British-developed successor to this comparatively very advanced twin rotor helicopter was permanently lost.

Future Plans For The Support Helicopter Force

Apart from the formation of a new helicopter squadron in Hong Kong (No 28 Squadron) and support for the UNFICYP Forces in Cyprus mentioned later, basic policy discussion in the second half of the 1960s was concerned mainly with updating the plans for the Support Helicopter Force for the 1970s after the Belvedere and Whirlwind were to have been replaced. The Wessex Mk 2 although new in the early 1960s was realistically seen as basically obsolete and no more than an interim vehicle but the only one actually available on which calculations could at first be based. In any case, there was likely to be a hiatus until 1970 before the aircraft to meet NAST 365—the 'utility' battlefield helicopter (see Chapter 9) would be available and in the meantime there was a rising demand which needed to be satisfied.

In early 1965, the requirement was for a six-company lift—two by the Royal Navy and four by the RAF—and this was translated into 54 Wessex for the RAF plus 16 representing the logistic support requirements currently being supplied by the wasting Belvedere force. There was reluctance to increase the Wessex force both because of the timescale involved and the prejudicial effect this would be likely to have on the progress of NAST 365. This, together with the Army heavy lift requirement and the support likely to be needed for the forthcoming Kestrel (Harrier), was the first argument deployed in the efforts to obtain the Chinook which was optimistically described as having only financial difficulties in its way.(41)

In August 1965) the Royal Navy withdrew anti-submarine warfare as a role for NAST 365, announced that they preferred the SH3D (CH 53) and would therefore withdraw completely from NAST 358 (heavy lift helicopter). NAST 365 was then redrafted exclusively as a tactical helicopter and discussion centred on how many there should be and what mix was desirable with the Wessex and hoped for Chinook.

Shape of the Support Helicopter Force

The calculations based on the number of companies requiring helicopter lift and the types of helicopter likely to be available had always been the crucial denominators of the size and shape of the SH force. A third element was added to these considerations in the mid-1960s—that of air portability of the helicopters and their likely permanent deployment pattern. From 1965 until the end of 1967 some permanent deployment in the Far East was assumed, but by January 1966 both the Army and the RAF had concluded that in any case the main SH force should be air portable.(42) Self-ferry was too difficult, ship transport would be too slow and adequate support for the helicopters after an initial ship-mounted assault would be lacking. The Army stressed the importance of immediate helicopter support from the moment of the initial assault. Available airlift consisted of the small fleet of Belfasts (six) and the more numerous and therefore more reliable Hercules. All this added up to strong pressure to obtain the SA-330 (Puma) helicopters, ideally to replace all, but initially at the very least a significant number, of the Wessex (which would not fit in the Hercules) on which plans current in 1965 depended. Chinooks replacing the Belvederes and placed in the Far East were assumed throughout as part of the background scenery.

There had since 1964 been a Helicopter Sub-Group of an Anglo-French Aircraft Working Group which is mentioned later, exploring the possibility of formulating a joint RAF/Army/RN/French Operational Requirement and preparing for possible collaboration. In March 1966 this Group undertook a detailed examination of the SA-330 with strong encouragement from the French.

There was a momentary interruption in this enthusiastic progress when the Foreign Office suddenly inserted a bid to have the Italian Agusta 205 considered for collaborative development for diplomatic reasons. This was sharply rebuffed by the Air Force Department OR branch as a non-starter, at the same time pointing out that collaboration with the French offered the only chance of expanding British industry with original as opposed to foreign licensed activity.(43)

A note by the Defence Secretary in January 1966 foresaw with remarkable accuracy, with the exception of the Chinook, the future pattern as:

    a.   SA 330s arriving in the early 1970s.

    b.   Wessex used for the training role and replacing the SAR Whirlwinds.

    c.   24 Chinooks starting to replace the Belvederes in 1966.

    d.   Sycamores in the training role to be replaced (SA-340?) in 1967.(44)

The case for as many SA-330s as could be afforded to replace the Wessex was strengthened by the RAF calculation that while two SA-330s could be loaded in the Belfast in 13 hours, two Wessex would take 24 hours due to the need to remove the rotor heads. Four SA-330s could be loaded in 33 hours but two Wessex was the maximum load. Perhaps more realistically, two SA-330s could be loaded in a Hercules in 43 hours, but the Wessex could not be carried thus at all. In an example it was said that two days spent dismantling Far East based SA-330s in order to carry them in indigenous Hercules to an operational scene in, for example, Africa, was greatly preferable to waiting, perhaps for weeks, for Belfasts or sea lift to become available.(45)

Size of the SH Force

As recorded in Chapter 9, the SH requirement expressed in terms of company lifts had been calculated in 1964 as six companies, two of which were to be carried by the RN Commando ships and the other four by the RAF. All subsequent calculations of the number of companies to be lifted included the two by the Royal Navy—a requirement which remained unchanged.

In 1965 the total company lift required had grown from six to seven. By April 1966 the Chiefs of Staff had established a requirement for seven and a half companies disposed as follows:(46)

    a.   Two and a half companies East of Suez—one company air portable based in Singapore, one company in the Commando Ship East of Suez and a half company in the Persian Gulf.

b.   Two companies, both air portable—ie deployed by Hercules—for the strategic reserve in the UK.

c.   Two for BAOR.

d.   One in the Commando Ship normally West of Suez.(47)

Because it was assumed that financial constraints would prevent this plan being approved, the generally agreed procedure seemed to be to state this requirement and then acknowledge the overriding economic strictures by voluntarily reducing the bid for planning purposes. Thus, the five and a half company lift for the RAF (13 SA-330s, or 20 Wessex per company) was argued for three companies by SA-330 (39 Unit Establishment) and two and a half companies by Wessex (50 Unit Establishment) supported by 18 Chinooks. These figures were then reduced, in deference to the economic situation, by one company of SA-330s in BAOR (in order to maintain the all important East of Suez needs) and a reduction in the number of front-line Chinooks from 18 to 12. (15 Unit Establishment). The package could then be produced showing a reduction in costs from £214M to £176M with the SA-330 bid reducing from 68 to 48 and the Chinook purchase initially at least 15.(48) The Chief of the General Staff showed his reluctance to accept this deal by pointing out that in the 52 operations in which the Army had been involved since the Second World War there had seldom if ever been enough helicopters and that the priority given to helicopters compared to other requirements should be extremely high. The Air Force Department added in a note to the Chiefs of Staff that the strategic reserve and its helicopter force were now inseparable and that a seven and a half company lift was the true minimum requirement. Nevertheless, it was agreed that for financial reasons the bid should stand at six and a half company lift.(49)

As a result of Stage II costings produced after the July 1967 Defence Review, a further half company lift was deleted from the post-1975 requirement which therefore stood once again at six company lifts, two of which were to be provided by the Royal Navy.(50) At the same time the Finance Branch (F6) noted an improved planned wastage rate for the SA-330 and caused some consternation by recalculating the requirement as 43 instead of 48 aircraft.(51) These two setbacks were followed swiftly by the announcement in November 1967 of the intention to withdraw completely from East of Suez by December 1971 and to reorientate our strategy towards NATO and Europe. The whole helicopter exercise had to be done again.

It had already been accepted that any forced cuts in the previous plans were to be felt mainly in the heavy lift helicopter field (Chinook) rather than in the air portable support helicopter capability.(52) This latest news, coupled with the fact that the whole of the proposed Chinook force was to be located in the Far East, ensured the cancellation of that programme.

In February 1968 AUS(AS), after mentioning defence budget reductions of £110M in 1969/1970 and £210–£260M in 1972/1973, observed with surprise that attempts were being made to justify the same size of Support Helicopter Force as before the East of Suez decision was taken. He suggested 25 SA-330s might be enough. VCAS refused to accept that elements of the front line could be specifically identified with the East of Suez strategy, adding that this was not how we used air power.(53) In spite of this we had lost the Chinook and there could be no case for reducing the numbers of SA-330s. There had been a change of strategy and it was appropriate that the matter should be re-examined under a Central Staffs Chairman. Air portability was now more important; training areas were widely separated; the Allied Command Europe Mobile Force had to be supported; NATO required increased mobility and the Harrier would need considerable helicopter support. Nevertheless, the number of SA-330s he was defending had shrunk further from 43 to 40.(54)

In January 1968 the Army and Air Force Departments had agreed a position based on the following assumptions:

  a.   BAOR would remain at a strength of six Brigades of which one would be deployed in the UK.

  b.   The strategic reserve Division would be assigned to NATO in a mobile role but would retain some internal security commitments outside Europe.

  c.   The amphibious force would remain in being with a role on the flanks of NATO.

The two-company lifts to be provided by the Royal Navy would normally be embarked in the Commando ships. If as was assumed these were given a role on the flanks of NATO, the number of support helicopters available for the Army would be reduced to a four-company lift.(55)

In 1966 the Chiefs of Staff noted that HQ BAOR had stated an operational requirement for the equivalent of a ten-company lift for fighting the Corps battle in general war. In view of the low probability of war in Europe they did not consider it realistic to provide this number but they did state that a two-company lift was the absolute minimum general purpose support helicopter force for BAOR.

A study approved by the Chiefs of Staff was examining the earmarking of the Third Division (the strategic reserve) for Allied Command Europe with one Brigade in the central sector in an air mobile role, and another in North Norway requiring a three-company lift and a half company lift respectively. Relating this to the 1966 assessment the deployed commitment would be:

a. Strategic reserve—three and a half company lifts.

b. Six other BAOR Brigades—two company lifts.

To this must be added a Squadron to be provided for the Air Mobile Force (Land), half of which would be provided by the UK.(56) The incipient formation of a six aircraft squadron in Hong Kong was known about, but the prolongation of No 103 Squadron in Tengah with the ANZUK Force (see Chapter 12) until 1974 could not have been foreseen at that time. The irreducible minimum therefore stood at the six company lift already planned. The air mobility of a proportion of this force to meet internal security operations in Dependant Territories as well as its load lifting capability in the absence of the Chinook was adduced to support the bid for 40 SA-330s. As an insurance against future degradations of these figures in the event of further changes in defence policy, it was argued that any possible future surplus of helicopters would be absorbed by diverting up to one company lift worth of Wessex into the training and SAR roles so that there would have to be a reduction to below a three and a half company lift for the Army before there would be a serious risk of surplus helicopters, and as that would be below the acceptable minimum for NATO support operations, the order for 40 SA-330s was justified.(57)

The conclusion that, whether on the criteria used to establish the requirement in 1966 or on the strategy likely to result from the forthcoming Defence Review in 1968, the planned SH Force of six company lifts (two by SA-330s) was still necessary, set the scene for Phase 4 for the Support Helicopter Force in the 1970s.

Anglo French Helicopter Package

As already mentioned, the Helicopter Sub Group of the Anglo French Aircraft Working Group had been working since 1964 in preparation for future collaboration following the formulation of a joint operational requirement, and by 1966 was making a detailed study of the SA-330—the aircraft in which the RAF was primarily interested. Joint Franco/British configuration, joint production, possible use of the Gnome engine, a version for the Royal Navy and costs for various sizes of order were discussed.(58) A long study of air portability was undertaken which succeeded in establishing the need for as many SA-330s as could be afforded, rather than the Wessex, to go with our transport fleet of Hercules and the very few Belfasts.

The expression 'utility' helicopter had first been used in the early 1960s to denote the type of rugged simplicity thought to be appropriate for the front-line battlefield troop-carrying but also multi-purpose helicopter envisaged as a replacement for the Whirlwind. By the mid-1960s it was becoming clear that the trooping role could not be readily mixed with the anti-tank rocket, cannon and machine-gun-firing helicopter envisaged by the Army, and the term 'utility helicopter' came to be used to describe the latter. It was at least partly euphemistic since the role of the ground attack helicopter, which was what was really meant, was not yet fully accepted. (Policy for the armed helicopter is discussed later). The SA-330 seemed likely to meet the needs of the RAF in the trooping and resupply role, but it was by no means a simple and rugged ground attack aircraft, although it was rather too large for the Royal Navy which also had a role for the attack helicopter. The Westland WG-13 appeared to fill the attack torpedo role and, still known as the utility helicopter, became the Anglo element of the joint Anglo-French Package. The RAF interest was limited to training and possibly communication work for the WG-13.

The third part of the trio now being jointly discussed was a much smaller machine filling the existing Army role of Light Observation Helicopter (LOH) and for this the SA-340 was proposed—the RAF and Royal Naval interest being confined to training and special liaison roles.

By October 1976 the RAF had calculated its bid for SA-330s as 68, to provide three squadrons of thirteen—that is a three company lift. It was recognised, as previously explained, that the third company lift might have to await a more favourable financial climate, and so while 68 was the initial bargaining figure, 45 or 48 was seen as the realistic requirement initially.

In January 1967 the LOH (SA-340), Utility Helicopter (WG-13) and Support Helicopter (SA-330) were discussed jointly with the French as a complete package. Estimated quantities were as follows:—

    a.   LOH-UK 620 (Army 550, RN 50, RAF 20)
            France   100 (all Army)

    b.   Utility
            UK   374 (Army 250, RN 100, RAF 24)
            France   230 (Army 150, Navy 80)

    c.   Support
          Helicopter
            UK   48 (RAF)
            France   130 (Army)

Of the UK figures in this assessment, those for the Support Helicopter were by far the firmest.(59)

The Secretary of State endorsed this package deal, a Ministerial agreement was signed on 16 January 1967 to allow development planning to start and in February 1967 a Memorandum of Understanding for the Joint Anglo-French Helicopter Programme reached the final stage of ratification.(60) The RAF version of the SA-330 was to be the same as the French except for British communications and navigation equipment, instrument panel, improved air portability and a UK paint scheme. Deliveries were planned to take place between 1970 and 1973. The RAF proportion of the order was too small to justify arguments for using the British Gnome engine.

During the second half of 1967 and throughout 1968 the by now absolutely standard and apparently inevitable progression of alarms and crises were generated by the nevertheless unexpected rises in both costs and aircraft weight, the latter causing a reduction in promised performance. The RAF requirement for a load of 4000 lbs at 5000 feet altitude, ISA plus 20° temperature, and 200 feet per minute vertical climb at take-off, was for a radius of action of 75 nautical miles. 55–47 nautical miles now seemed to be the figure being offered.(61) Pressure on the French to upgrade the engines or otherwise restore the performance was demanded, but as the Deputy Director of Operational Requirements pointed out, we had tied the French to the WG-13 and the RAF was now tied to the SA-330. Eventually, the French were able to offer a radius of action in the stated conditions with a guaranteed minimum 57 nautical miles, a possibility of 69 nautical miles, with a 95 per cent probability of 63 nautical miles.(62) This was accepted.* There was a brief drama when the RAF order for 48 SA-330s was reduced to 43 as already described. The French found out about it prematurely and there was a sharp argument between the Ministry of Technology and the Air Force Department of MOD as to who had weakened our bargaining position,(63) but all in all, with its awkward supply and technical problems and the complicated financial adjustments, the whole deal went through comparatively smoothly.

At the end of 1968, the RAF reviewed its training and communications policy in respect of the SA-340 and WG-13 requirements, and concluded that the surplus Whirlwinds being thrown up by the withdrawal from FEAF were a better source of communications aircraft to replace the ageing and obsolete Sycamores still in use (five in the Metropolitan Communication Squadron and due for retirement in 1971) than the expensive and small SA-340. In the training pattern it was decided to replace the Sioux (Bell 47) in the basic phase by the SA-340, but then to progress

---

*in 1983 a calculation based on a particular but typical Puma at Odiham considered as it would have been in 1971, that is prior to the subsequent increases both in basic aircraft weight and permissible all-up weight, showed that a radius of action in these conditions would have been about 55 nautical miles. A later increase in basic weight due to modifications, coupled with a rise in permissible all-up weight would have increased the figure to 65 nautical miles, while the introduction of the more efficient plastic rotor blades in the early 1980s together with a further increase in the permissible maximum all-up weight resulted in a radius of action in these conditions of about 90 nautical miles. Any further increases in maximum permissible all-up weight could extend this range still further.

in the advanced stage to the readily available Wessex instead of the expensive WG-13 which could then be deleted from the intended RAF inventory. This left the RAF interest in the Anglo-French Package as a total number of SA-330 now reduced to 40, and a very small number of SA-340s.(64)

Names For The Anglo-French Helicopters

Choosing names for the three helicopters in the Anglo-French Package was taken quite seriously in that in January 1968 all the staffs of the Ministry of Defence Air Force Department were invited at Director level to submit proposals. The names were to be short, similar in both French and English, appropriate to the operational use of each aircraft and not already in use.(65) The Secretariat issuing the direction set the tone for what was clearly going to be a popular word game by pointing out, for example, that 'Discorde' with or without an 'e' would be a non-runner. The response was enthusiastic and two months later it was possible to issue what was described as a summary of 69 suggestions received, although since there were only very few duplicated proposals, what was offered was more in the nature of a summarily chosen list:—

For the SA-330:— Atlas, Machete, Mistral;

For the SA-340:— Vedette, Lynx, Hirondelle;

For the WG-13:— Guillemot, Cormorant, Sirocco.

The Air Force Board opted out of selecting names for the WG-13 and SA-340 because they had only a minority interest and preferred to leave it to the Army and Navy to choose, but agreed on Machete with Atlas and Mistral as alternatives for the SA-330. In July 1968 all three were opposed by the Ministry of Technology on the grounds that Machete had different pronunciations, was irrelevant to aviation and in any case was claimed by the Army to be a piece of Army equipment. In August the deputy Chief of the Air Staff then offered Normandy and Consort with Brigand, Carosse, Gauntlet and Warrior as alternatives, adding that none seemed fully appropriate and that the French suggestion of Puma was more suitable for a ground attack aircraft. In September the Air Force Board considered Normandy and Consort and in October settled on Normandy. But the French said Puma for the SA-330 and Gazelle for the SA-340, and so it was.(66) The WG-13 was later named Lynx.

The Armed Helicopter

With the support helicopters being occasionally shot at in Aden and Borneo and in the light of evidence from the Americans in Vietnam, the Senior Air Staff Officer in FEAF declared in December 1963 that operational helicopters needed two pilots, both partly protected by fixed seat armour, that all crew members should wear armoured torso protection and that at least an emergency portion of the fuel should be in self-sealing tanks (see Chapter 9). Shortage of SH lift precluded heavier equipment as well as further SS-11 guided missile fits. (The RAF had four Whirlwinds equipped for SS-11 firing—see Chapter 9. The Royal Navy had several more). On 14 January 1964 the Deputy Chief of the Air Staff issued the basic policy for armed RAF support helicopters based on the premises that helicopters would not intentionally be committed to an opposed assault unless fixed-wing ground attack aircraft were available; and that the SH lift capability would not be significantly degraded. Consequently fixed armour protection would be provided for first pilots only (although two pilots would be carried on operations), free-mounted guns would be carried for prophylactic fire and to respond to unexpected attack, crews would wear armoured vests and self-sealing tanks would protect at least emergency fly-out fuel supplies.(67)

This policy, reiterated as an order to all Commands and Groups in October 1964,(68) remained the unchanging RAF attitude during all the subsequent turmoil surrounding the steadily mounting pressure throughout the late 60s to enhance the fighting ability of the military helicopters. The first attempt to introduce change, drawing on the practice of France and the United States, sought to provide extensive armament and armoured protection to a small proportion of the SH Force which could then act as escort to the troop-carrying SHs. This was resisted on grounds of shortage of existing SH lift which, as already stated, was not to be reduced. It should be noted here that while it was not intended to launch SHs against known opposition, the possibility of meeting enemy defensive fire was, as far as the RAF was concerned, to be countered by the 'availability' of fixed-wing ground attack aircraft, and this highly orthodox if somewhat entrenched response was also maintained throughout later arguments.

What followed looked sometimes like a simple Army/RAF inter-Service chauvinistic dispute and while there may inevitably have been some elements of such a natural response on both sides, in the early stages at least the discussions and proposals were conducted against the background of real fighting in two overseas theatres with a perilously small but absolutely vital transport helicopter force. Thus, the RAF refused resolutely to accept a policy which would allow any SH to be committed where there was a high risk of encountering enemy fire, so attempts to increase offensive or defensive armour in helicopters beyond the 1964 policy were automatically opposed. At a more theoretical level was the conviction that if offensive air action was needed, firstly it was a Royal Air Force responsibility to provide it and, secondly, it should be carried out by fixed-wing aircraft or, later perhaps, by some entirely new variant, but never by helicopters as then understood.

The Army on the other hand was acutely aware, particularly in Borneo, of the impracticability of summoning fighter ground attack aircraft to deal with any type of fleeting targets including those unexpectedly encountered during SH trooping operations, and quite naturally sought to fill what they saw as a gap in the low speed short-range, quick response air capability by adding some offensive role to the aircraft already at their disposal, that is anti-personnel bombs and bomb sights in Beavers, and machine guns, 2-inch rocket launchers and anti-tank guided weapons (SS-11) in Scout helicopters. The bombing equipment for the Beavers was proposed by the Deputy Chief of the Imperial General Staff—Lieutenant General Sir John Hackett—in February 1964, saying it was purely for Beavers to use in the course of normal reconnaissance sorties or counter-insurgency operations in Borneo, while the anti-tank weapons were to be merely a mobile reserve at Unit and Brigade level. He emphasised that nobody need fear that the Army Air Corps was building up a massive ground attack capability.(69)

The response in the Air Ministry Policy Branch was one of outrage—engagement of armour from the air was a Royal Air Force or Royal Naval responsibility. What may well have been an entirely logical Army response to a real situation nevertheless appeared to the RAF to be the cynical fulfilment of a long predicted power bid. Sir Dermot Boyle, chief of the Air Staff in 1959, was quoted as warning that further encroachment by the Army Air Corps could be expected after the bid to exceed the agreed 4000 lb weight limit in order to obtain control of the Beaver. The then War Minister (Mr Soames) was quoted as saying there was no intention to use them outside the liaison role—there was no need for anxiety that they 'might hang bombs on the aircraft and turn them into a fighting platform'. Now they were asking for a bomb sight to be fitted. RAF Twin Pioneers would be fitted with bomb racks but if the requirement was for counter-insurgency operations as opposed to armed SRT operations, the RAF must be seen to be ready and willing to provide support. In this case the addition of a few armed piston Provosts into FEAF would be preferable to allowing the Army Air Corps to acquire a new role recognised by Ministers.(70)

Air Staff advice was not from one direction only. In February 1964 the Director of Air Staff Briefing, Air Commodore le Cheminant, commented that the 1956 agreement that the Army would be responsible for 'unarmed aircraft used solely in the AOP and Light Liaison roles with a maximum all-up weight of 4000 lb', had been followed by a progression through a planned front-line of 21 Beavers and 21 Scout helicopters (unarmed) to the present proposal (February 1964) for 285 light helicopters and offensive armament for the Scout/Beaver component. At each stage (on formation of the AAC—no wish to exceed 4000 lb all-up weight; on exceeding 4000 lb weight—no intention to arm the aircraft; now on proposing to arm certain aircraft, there was no intention to build up a ground attack capability) the War Office had assured the RAF that there was no intention of straying outside the AOP/light liaison role.(71) On the face of it the RAF seemed to have good reason to believe that the Army was deliberately moving step-by-step towards development of their own fighter ground attack substitute. At this stage the rockets and anti-tank guided weapons (SS-11) proposals had not been mentioned, although they were to be only two months later. Air Commodore le Cheminant felt that Army development of armament for the helicopters could not be opposed in principle and could ultimately be helpful to the RAF, but bombs on Beavers was a different matter. He suggested that if the RAF established a squadron of Beavers in FEAF, AFME and No 38 Group for offensive support work the question of Army control of the Beavers could be re-opened.(72)

In the ensuing Air Staff discussion the decision was, and remained so in subsequent crises when the demands for armed helicopters became acute, not to appear unwilling to co-operate but to pass the problem for detailed study by a Joint Service Committee, in this case charging the Assistant Chief of the Air Staff (OR) to ensure that the Assistant Chief of the Defence Staff (OR) did not proceed unilaterally but in full consultation with the Joint Warfare Committee. The Chief of the Air Staff replied to the DCIGS merely that the clearance and provision of machine guns for the Army Air Corps Scout helicopters in the Far East was being actioned and that the other requirements would be studied by the Joint Warfare School.

In April 1964 the Chiefs of Staff Committee (73) discussed a report from Headquarters FEAF which listed the three Service practices in respect of armed helicopters:

a. Royal Navy—Hiller helicopters—no armament.
Wasp (Naval version of Scout)—primary anti-submarine role only.
Wessex—side firing machine guns plus two fixed forward firing guns—50 per cent of aircraft with fixed fittings for SS-11 missile and 50 per cent with fixed fittings for launching 2-inch rocket projectiles—emergency fly-out fuel protection, seat pan armour and flak vests for crews.

b. Army—The offensive support role is not supported except for suppressive fire for success in the primary role, that is reconnaissance and light liaison. Nevertheless equipment to allow attacks on opportunity targets or engagement of tanks with SS-11 guided missiles should be provided for both Scout and Unit light helicopters. Armour for pilot seats is regarded as an unacceptable weight penalty, but armoured vests for the crews was agreed. Emergency fuel protection is being examined.

c. RAF—SRT aircraft are not hazarded in an offensive role. Any armament or armour has to be capable of being fitted in 15 minutes. Fixed forward firing machine guns have no value in this context but all helicopters should have provision for mounting operator aimed waist guns. Torso armour for crews, emergency fuel protection and armour for the first pilot seat are all required.

The Chiefs of Staff concluded bafflingly that there was nothing in the paper to require alteration of the single-Service policies for arming helicopters, but then implied a special case for Borneo operations by disagreeing in principle with the offensive role for the small number of helicopters in Borneo which might suffer high losses.

At this point a highly embarrassing mistake was made in Borneo (Operation BLUNT) when a purely offensive helicopter operation was mounted on 31 March 1964 without prior approval being sought from the Commander-in-Chief Far East. The Air Task Force Commander and Director of Operations Borneo approved a plan by the Commander Western Brigade and the Forward Air Commander to mount an assault on an enemy camp in a good defensive position on the top of a mountain ridge on the Indonesian border south of Simanggang, using artillery and SS-11 firing helicopters in support. The helicopters concerned were Royal Naval Wessex but could equally well have been RAF Whirlwinds. Six SS-11 missiles were fired and the position was taken with one of the enemy dead. During the withdrawal there was further enemy contact and the helicopters were again committed, firing two more SS-11 missiles and fixed front and cabin mounted machine guns. One more of the enemy was killed. The operation was successful and no aircraft were lost, so there was no need for public recriminations. The point was noted, however, that this was undoubtedly an offensive air action and would have been even if the helicopters had carried troops. In fact they were not used in the transport role at all. It was feared that a dangerous precedent had been set but appropriate apologies were made, the Air Task Force Commander admitted he should have sought prior approval of Commander-in-Chief Far East, and it was confirmed that FEAF was maintaining the previously agreed policy.(74) There was no significant change in this position in the remaining life of FEAF. The next moves were made in the United Kingdom about two years later—in 1966.

The SH force in the United Kingdom for most of Phase 3 consisted of 72 (Wessex) Squadron at Odiham in No 38 Group—part of Transport Command with Head-quarters at Upavon. The Squadron responded to bids for SH participaton in exercises from the Army Headquarters at Salisbury. The Army Air Corps Centre at Middle Wallop was close by. It was therefore natural that No 38 Group and Transport Command should be acutely conscious of Army thinking in respect of SH development and it was the Commander-in-Chief of Transport Command, Air Chief Marshal Sir Kenneth Cross, who warned in March 1966 that the Army was thinking in terms of Short Range Transport armed assault and promising a policy proposal soon.(75) In the following month it duly appeared and called for a change in the existing (1964) policy to allow support helicopters to take part in the assault role or to escort other helicopters in that role. He advised urgent action to provide fixed fittings for both armament and protective armour.(76) The same month VCAS discussed with CAS the Army intention to submit a paper to the Joint Warfare Committee about the arming of helicopters, and as a result the Army was persuaded to withdraw it in favour of initiating a much broader study by the JWC on the Army/RAF offensive support requirements including the P-1127 (Harrier), Jaguar and armed helicopter, thus avoiding precipitate decisions.(77) In March 1967, the new C-in-C Transport Command (soon to be re-named Air Support Command), Air Marshal Sir Thomas Prickett, complained that in spite of his predecessor's efforts there was still no advance on the 1964 policy and drew attention to a recent meeting between Flag Officer Naval Flying Training, General Officer Commanding No 3 Division and the Air Officer Commanding No 38 Group after which the latter urged provision for a forward fixed gun firing capability for the RAF support helicopters to establish compatibility with the RN practice.(78) At that operational level the RAF seemed ready to concede the Army case for moving away from the purely defensive posture for the SH.

In June 1967 the JWC spoke after a full and detailed study. The four conclusions did not seem especially contentious but the meeting(79) was momentous in that it formally initiated the role for the Army helicopters to carry and use offensive armament. The conclusions were:

    a.   The offensively armed helicopter would in no way affect the validity of other existing forces (ie the RAF need not fear that the fighter ground attack roles would be superseded by this new facility).

    b.   There was a need for helicopter-mounted point defence during transport operations as well as for prophylactic area fire to protect support helicopters.

    c.   The Army needed the facility to attack special small targets and to provide ground convoy protection, especially when there was no time to summon RAF fighter ground attack support.

    d.   The Royal Navy required to mount attacks on enemy surface ships, there being no question of RAF fighter ground attack being available for this task.

The Air Force Department accepted these conclusions with considerable misgivings(80). Their support was limited to recognizing the usefulness of helicopter-mounted light machine gun fire in internal security operations or in the later stages of airborne operations after fighter ground attack aircraft had withdrawn. They did not agree with the Army case for attacking opportunity targets and thus for armed reconnaissance sorties, nor for anti-tank guided weapons (ATGW) roles which seemed likely to lead to specialised armed attack helicopters which would not be cost-effective. The helicopter was a bad weapons platform and the result would be a loss of flexibility in other SH roles.

It seemed to the AFD that the thin edge of a dangerous wedge had been driven home although it was recognised that it was important not to appear reactionary. The Air

Staffs were concerned that a new branch of aviation seemed to be opening up without proper guidance—there would shortly be more advanced derivatives of the helicopter offering a variety of armed roles with important implications not least in command and control, and it would be wrong to allow a fixed wing/rotary wing split to develop between the Services since both would be required in future generations of aircraft; moreover, the effect on training costs and careers of having more than one flying service in a cost-limited force structure should be considered. If it was then proved that rotary wing aircraft were valid for ground attack and close support weapon systems, the initiative should be taken and an Air Staff Requirement should be drawn up. Meanwhile the Army should reappraise their policy for obtaining large numbers of helicopters for uneconomical deployment down to Unit level. AUS(AS) added that Army helicopter figures should be subject to the same strictures as were applied to the RAF order for the SA 330s, and not regarded as immune because of the device of treating helicopters as an item of unit equipment akin to three-ton lorries.(81)

In September 1967 the Air Force Department commented on the conclusions of the Joint Warfare Committee in JWC 9/67, now endorsed by the Chiefs of Staff, expressing the view that RAF SH should have button-on (ie easily and temporarily fitted) armament fit to provide suppressive fire power on those occasions when the operational situation demanded it; whether or not the armament should be fitted for a particular operation should be at the discretion of the Air Commander, for the ability of the SH to carry out its primary task remained of overriding importance. All Wessex and Whirlwind squadrons were therefore to be scaled with free-firing General Purpose Machine Guns (GPMG) using standard 7.62 mm ammunition.(82)

During the closing weeks of 1967 the Army enthusiasm for creating an instant new ground attack Air Force reached a climax, was then partially defused, and finally settled down into a more cautious rational examination of practical and cost-effective courses of action. In December the Army Department stated that they could not live with the RAF limitation of having only 'button-on' armament, as they needed a turret-mounted gun for range and accuracy and so wanted 30 WG 13s in the fully armed role as offered to the French. At an Army Board meeting on 15 December it was claimed that the agreement by the Chiefs of Staff to the recommendations in JWC 9/67 for the Army to operate armed helicopters cleared the way for obtaining a purpose-built helicopter for the offensive armed role with a turret-mounted gun. However, this turned out to be more than even the Army Board could swallow. It was pointed out that the versatility of the general purpose helicopters in Borneo was indisputable and, furthermore, the turret-mounted gun was useless against tanks—an early indication of the new thinking which was to crystalize the policy for the offensively armed helicopter as an anti-tank weapon for the next decade and beyond. At the same time the Army Aviation policy of scattering helicopters across the board down to Unit level was refined to one where centralised control could be operated over squadrons allotted at Corps, Division and Brigade levels.(83)

Meanwhile the C-in-C Air Support Command (still Air Marshal Sir Thomas Prickett), like his predecessors acutely aware of practical pressures arising from the close liaison between Army authorities in Salisbury and the AOC No 38 Group, returned to his previous argument. The requirement he now stated was for a 250 knot helicopter, providing two hours airborne Forward air Control at a radius of action of 75 nautical miles, and able to fire SNEB rockets, 30 mm cannon, 7.62 light machine guns, grenades and ATGWs. It was to carry two pilots with dual controls, be robust and air portable. He opined that if it were not proposed by the RAF, it would be demanded by the Army. He was also concerned that all air-to-air and air-to-ground support, reconnaissance, parachute assault, resupply and logistic support must be co-ordinated under one Air Commander exercising the proven principle of central theatre control for maximum flexibility and economy for all air power functions.(84)

Whitehall, however, had now moved beyond this stage in respect of the specialised armed helicopter, and the Air Force and Army Departments together were preparing to study in much greater depth the longer term developments which might be both practical and appropriate. VCAS's reply to the C-in-C in January 1968 summed up the Air Force Department view of the whole subject. He was aware that, although the quality of the RAF's close support capability would be much improved with the introduction of the Phantom and the Harrier, the Army feared that there might still be a gap in the spectrum of close support weapons. The General Staff had recently stated a firm requirement for an armed version of the WG 13 which they had intended to table in the ORC (Operational Requirements Committee), but the Army Board, approaching the problem with some caution, had invited DCGS (Deputy Chief of the General Staff) to make a more detailed study of the need for a specialised armed helicopter and to report back about mid-1968. The AFD would be keeping a careful watch on this study since a specialised armed helicopter appeared to be of little use outside the fire support role and would thus not be very cost-effective. On the other hand the use of button-on armament would leave the helicopter free for its usual range of roles when not required for fire support.

On a more positive note, VCAS continued, the Future Operational Requirements Evaluation Committee had been speculating on the basic conflict between the need for speed as a protection against ground defences and the advantages of slowness when acquiring and aiming at targets. It was necessary, they believed, to study the tactical advantages which might result from an aircraft which could fly economically, and with good manoeuvrability, throughout the speed range, from moderately high tactical speeds down to, and including, vertical or short take-off and landing. Such a performance range might be achieved in the future by high speed rotor craft but there could be several other technological possibilities including the addition of high lift devices to a fixed-wing aircraft. This might allow speed and height to be freely exchanged to suit a wide variety of levels of warfare and different tactical situations, and might be a particular advantage in hilly terrain (including jungle) and at night in bad weather. It was of course very uncertain what performance bracket could be achieved (and by what date), nor could one be sure that a wide speed range aircraft would be more cost effective than separate slow and fast aircraft, each providing V/STOL. However, the prima facie case definitely warranted further examination and technological advice was being sought from the Ministry of Technology with the aim of raising an Air Staff Target.

At the same time it was intended to conduct tactical trials in the low-slow corner of the flight envelope using both helicopters and slow-flying fixed-wing aircraft on a comparative basis. These would involve comparing results achieved by the Hunter, representing the high-speed aircraft, with those of representative current helicopters against an inconspicuous target. Both the frequency and speed of target acquisition and the exposure time to ground fire would be recorded and the results compared. Obviously there were limitations to such an investigation, but the AFD was convinced that some practical work of this kind must be undertaken urgently. The General Staff had therefore been invited to co-sponsor this trial, and Air Support Command would shortly be tasked in co-operation with Southern Command. VCAS concluded by hoping that the results would lead at least to an Air Staff Target.

It will be seen from this that the RAF was once more acting in its traditional and inevitably unpopular role in the helicopter world of mitigating fierce enthusiasm for a short term albeit highly exciting development, in favour of a realistic and widely based professional assessment of real alternatives. Just as the Air Staff had opposed enthusiasm for the Air Horse in 1947 (see Chapter 4), and the Rotodyne in 1960 (see Chapter 9), so now they urged caution in dedicating expensive and vulnerable helicopters exclusively to the ground attack role. This time, however, there were two crucial differences:

a. Something new had to be done to oppose the vast tank forces of the Warsaw Pact powers poised to sweep across Europe.

b. 'Button-on' armament might seem to preserve the flexibility of the helicopter, the implication being that it could easily be unbuttoned, but technical advances such as target acquisition, laser range finding, infra-red and low light television equipment were to specialise the armed helicopter to such a degree that it was inevitably going to become almost totally dedicated to the ground attack role.

The consequence was that while the RAF successfully 'won the game' in preventing the acceptance of the fully dedicated ground attack helicopter, they inevitably 'abandoned the match' (at least for the time being) by ensuring that only the Army Air Corps would develop the ground attack armed helicopter, while the RAF adhered primly to its purely transport role with light machine guns carried at times of danger.

The reply by VCAS to the C-in-C Air Support Command did not mention command and control aspects which were to be left for later discussions when the development possibilities were properly identified. Meanwhile, the Future Operational Requirement Evaluation Committee had already been tasked (October 1967) with considering the long term trends in the offensive support role—ie after the Phantom.(85)

The series of trials promised by VCAS took place in 1968 and 1969 to establish the viability of the helicopter in the offensive support role both in respect of target acquisition and, in particular, vulnerability—the targets by this time having become almost exclusively tanks, no doubt influenced by the late 1967 decision on withdrawal from East of Suez and the consequent increased concentration on the possible land battle in Europe. They were in four phases and were conducted under the titles HELTANK and SPARROWHAWK. Regardless of these trials, the Army Department was fully convinced that the helicopter was an essential weapon in dealing with the Russian tank threat in Europe, and in February 1968 the Chief of the General Staff proposed to the Secretary of State that there was an immediate and urgent need to equip 30 Scouts with SS11 missiles for anti-tank defence. He added that a GSR (General Staff Target) for the next generation of anti-tank helicopter weapons would follow shortly. From this time on, the Army Department conducted the argument in terms not of whether to arm helicopters with ATGW but which missile to choose.

By July 1969 the Operational Requirements Committee had provisionally approved the General Staff Requirement for Anti-Tank Guided Weapons for the WG 13 and SA 340 (Lynx and Gazelle), subject to review of further information on the vulnerability studies still in progress (HELTANK and SPARROWHAWK). Both the Army and the Royal Navy were showing signs of irritability with the Air Force Department's continuing concern about helicopter vulnerability, and were locked into highly complex discussions with the Ministry of Technology about suitability, timescale and price of various missile options.(86) VCAS declined to participate in a 'presentation' to the Minister because the Air Force Department felt that studies had not yet shown that arming of helicopters was an effective way of carrying out the tasks due to their vulnerability both from the ground and the air.

In October 1969 the Assistant Chiefs meeting recorded that recent studies (particularly SPARROWHAWK) had not yielded conclusive evidence on the kill rate for armed helicopters. Although there was not a firm case to support helicopter-borne ATGW, they nevertheless decided to accept the requirement in principle and allow development of SWINGFIRE (the current favourite missile) to proceed, while adding that further studies were needed to establish the facts.

At the end of 1969 the SPARROWHAWK and HELTANK reports were analysed in detail. As might be expected the results were largely inconclusive showing both that helicopters could hit tanks with guided missiles, and could themselves be shot down both from the ground and air. There were too many variables on which assumptions had to be made to establish firm predictions, but some especially dangerous situations could be identified. Thus, ATGW helicopters should not be committed to attack static concealed defensive positions, but in a mobile situation, committed 'with prudence', they could make a 'useful contribution to anti-tank defence'. Insofar as specific calculations could be made, it was tentatively calculated that six tanks could be destroyed per helicopter lost. The Operational Requirements Committee accepted that 'the ATGW helicopter could make a useful contribution to anti-tank defence', and endorsed the General Staff Requirement (3431) for the Lynx and Gazelle on 18 December 1969.(87)

The Air Force Board was only marginally concerned with the detailed discussions which went on during the next two years with the Ministry of Technology and Finance Branches about which ATGW missile should be ordered, how many and when, so long as they counted as button-on armament and did not lead to a specialised ground attack armed helicopter. Similarly, when in July 1970 the Royal Navy proposed a study of helicopter vulnerability in attacking gun-defended Fast Patrol Boats, the RAF replied merely that as they did not propose to use helicopters to attack FPBs, there was no need to co-sponsor that study. The final step in this phase of development concluded in September 1971 when a joint Army/RAF Working Party on the Specialised Armed Helicopter issued its report. It concluded that:

a. A purchase of specialised Armed Helicopters could not be justified at the present time.

b. The identified primary offensive task of Army helicopters—the destruction of armour—could be performed satisfactorily by Utility or light helicopters fitted with ATGW systems, and

c. The Joint Helicopter Tactical Development Committee should be invited to task the Joint Helicopter Tactical Development Unit to periodically review the requirement for Specialised Armed Helicopters and to take account of any changes that might occur in the circumstances in which they would be provided and operate.

These conclusions were duly agreed by the Air Force Board. To demonstrate their unchanging adherence to previous doctrine they added that the Director of Air Plans had made it clear to the Army Department that the Royal Air Force was interested in considering any weapon system—even with a performance less than those of its present or projected aircraft—which might be viable in a Priority 1 situation. Thus, for example, the Royal Air Force would wish to consider fixed-wing aircraft such as the NJT (New Jet Trainer—Hawk) rather than Specialised Armed Helicopters.

The Chief of the General Staff gave his support to the conclusions and recommendations of the Report.(88) And so the RAF remained exclusively with its Search and Rescue and Support Helicopters but with fittings for free-firing machine guns in the latter.

Colonel John Everatt-Heath writing in 'NATO's 15 NATIONS'—an independent review of economic, political and military power—October/November 1982, Volume 7, No 5, comments regarding the place of the helicopter on the battlefield:

> '. . . after an initial period of scepticism (the helicopter) is now appreciated and every nation that can afford them already has combat helicopters.'

and later:

> 'The NATO combat helicopter is regarded as equipment of the ground forces operating in a ground environment as part of an all arms formation . . .'

Even at the time of writing (1983) there exists a considerable divergence of views on the precise point, if there is one, where helicopter support ceases to be an RAF responsibility and belongs more properly with the Army, but it is clear that at the outset of the development of the combat helicopter, the Air Force Department saw no role for itself and deprecated the concept.

1   J Banks.

2   ID9/941/11.

3. Ibid.

4   Wing Commander Dowling.

5   Munro.

6   J Banks.

7   Ibid.

8   Munro.

9   Wing Commander Dowling.

10 No 26 Squadron ORB.

11 Banks.

12 No 26 Squadron ORB.

13 Flight Lieutenant Perratt.

14 No 66 Squadron ORB.

15 Ibid.

16 Wing Commander Austin.

17 No 66 Squadron ORB.

18 ID9/941/9.

19 Ibid.

20 Ibid.

21 Ibid.

22 Ibid.

23 ID9/941/11.

24 ID9/F5–42.

25 ID9/941/11.

26 Ibid.

27 Ibid.

28 AFB 11(65).

29   ID9/F5–41 Pt 1.

30   ID9/F5–42.

31   Ibid.

32   ID9/F5–43.

33   ID9/F5–41 Pt 1.

34   ID9/F5–46.

35   ID9/F5–43.

36   ID9/F5–42.

37   Group Captain Ramsden.

38   Ibid.

39   COS 49(66).

40   ID9/F5–42.

41   ID9/F5–41 Pt 1.

42   ID9/F5–41 Pt 2.

43   ID9/F5–70 Pt 1.

44   ID9/F5–41 Pt 2

45   Ibid.

46   ID9/F5–70 Pt 1.

47   COS 22;/66.

48   ID9/F5–41 Pt 2.

49   Ibid.

50   ID9/F5–70 Pt 1.

51   Ibid.

52   ID9/F5–41 Pt 2.

53   ID9/F5–70 Pt 1.

54   Ibid.

55   Ibid.

56   Ibid.

57   Ibid.

58   ID9/F5–70 Pt 1.

59   Ibid.

60 ID9/F5-72.

61 Ibid.

62 ID9/F5-70 Pt 2.

63 ID9/F5-70 Pt 1.

64 ID9/F5-70 Pt 2.

65 ID9/F5-73.

66 Ibid.

67 ID9/941/12.

68 AF/F4-5 Pt 3.

69 ID9/941/12.

70 Ibid.

71 Ibid.

72 Ibid.

73 COS 136/64.

74 ID9/941/12.

75 Ibid.

76 AF/F4-5 Pt 3.

77 Ibid.

78 ID9/941/12.

79 JWC 9/67.

80 AF/4-5 Pt 3.

81 Ibid.

82 ID9/941/12.

83 Ibid.

84 AF/F4-5 Pt 3.

85 ID9/941/12.

86 Ibid.

87 Ibid.

88 Ibid.

APPENDIX 1   A DETAILED DESCRIPTION OF THE CHARACTERISTICS OF THE SYCAMORE

The Sycamore played a prominent role in all theatres where helicopters were used, for practically the whole period covered in this history. Its handling characteristics were quite unique and so was its appearance. Some of the reasons for these qualities require explanation.

The Sycamore was a completely individual development by the Bristol Aeroplane Company, not derived from any previous production helicopter, and it displayed characteristics which reflected specific personal convictions of its designer— Mr Raoul Hafner. One of the most significant of these features concerned the manner in which control forces were balanced and compensated in the rotor system, thus permitting easy manual control at all weights and speeds, and eliminating totally any requirement to fit hydraulic assistance as was becoming necessary in the Sikorsky helicopters. This feature had a considerable influence later and is referred to in relation to the control system of the Sycamore's successor—the Belvedere.

It is not intended to give here a study of all the engineering innovations involved in the Sycamore beyond referring to the use of tie-bars to carry blade centrifugal forces rather than the flapping hinges. Hafner himself regarded this as the most productive and important modification to previous helicopter design. What is offered rather is a brief explanation of the unusual handling characteristics experienced by the pilots and the reasons for them. The only seriously objectionable modification was not put there by Hafner or the Bristol Aeroplane Company.

BASIC AIM: Basically, Hafner wanted a fast manually controlled helicopter which cruised and stood on the ground with the fuselage substantially level. The manual control was dealt with by rotor blade design and the tie-bars just mentioned. The fuselage was streamlined to produce a sleek, low drag shape with a short rotor pylon and an extremely compact rotor head. The determination to have a level fuselage in the cruise and when standing on the ground produced some handling problems during take off and in the hover, but these were acceptable on the grounds that the helicopter spent only a minute fraction of its time in the take off and hover, and the cruise condition should be the one on which to concentrate.

SOLUTION: It seemed reasonable to arrange for the fuselage to be level in the cruise with the cyclic stick substantially central, instead of the stick forward nose down attitude normal to other helicopters in forward flight. This was achieved by tilting the rotor head forward about 5 degrees. The inevitable consequence was that in take off to the hover, which was the normal sequence for getting airborne, the Sycamore which sat in the conventional level attitude when on the ground, had to

419

assume a nose up attitude (about 5 degrees) immediately on leaving the ground. In other words, the pilot had to hold the cyclic stick aft of the central position before leaving the ground if he wished to avoid taking straight off into forward flight.

Secondly, in pursuance of the same principle, the control system was arranged so that the lateral movement of the stick towards the advancing side of the rotor disc which was necessary in other helicopters as forward speed increased was eliminated in the Sycamore so that the disc tilted fore and aft as the stick was moved fore and aft at cruising speed rather than in the hover. The designer's aim was achieved in that the stick was thus central both fore and aft and laterally in the steady cruise condition, rather than forward and slightly to one side as was the requirement in the Sikorsky helicopters where the stick was central in the hover. The consequence was that during take off to the hover, the Sycamore pilot not only had to hold the stick back to avoid moving forward, but this action also tilted the disc to the left (because there was no airspeed) and had to be compensated by displacement of the stick to the right to achieve a vertical take off.

The stick trim controls were by comparatively powerful springs tensioned by two wheels, one for fore and aft and one for lateral forces. These wheels were set before take off to balance the stick forces in the correct position for hovering flight, but as the aircraft was level when at rest and had to assume a nose up attitude on leaving the ground, the pre positioning of the stick aft and to the right had to be done against the pressure of the springs. If the pilot failed to find the correct position, he was made immediately aware of an error in the fore and aft sense because he could see and correct any tendency for the aircraft to move forward or backwards.

Insufficient right pressure on the stick was more difficult to detect because sideways motion was resisted by the non-castering main undercarriage wheels. In this case if power was increased slowly (and the ground effect was comparatively powerful beneath the unusually low rotor disc) the aircraft could pivot in the rolling plane on its port wheel quite rapidly before achieving take off power, and if this movement was not corrected in time, the main rotor would disintegrate on contact with the ground and the aircraft would fall on its left side.

If the stick were correctly positioned before take off, or if the 'unstick' was performed reasonably smartly there was no danger. Both precautions were part of the basic technique and only if both were omitted was there any risk. All the pilots were taught these techniques and for several years there was virtually no trouble. One or two incidents gave rise to the general impression that the Sycamore had some sort of inbuilt tendency to roll to the left on take off, but it was not until February 1966, when CFS had three such accidents in one month, that it was concluded that the aircraft must be at least partially at fault and the occasion was taken after ten years service to hasten their withdrawal from the training scene in favour of the Sioux.

It can be seen clearly in retrospect that this was a case of an important technique losing significance by usage over the years. The Sycamore continued however to be used for VIP communication flying for six years afterwards.

Central Collective Lever

The control peculiarities described above were no particular problem to pilots once they had become accustomed to them. Of much more concern was the fitting of a shared central collective lever in the Mark 14 Sycamore.

The earlier Sycamores (Mark 10 and Mark 11) had been built in the days when helicopter first pilots sat on the left side of the cockpit simply because that was the side used by fixed-wing pilots. By the time the Mark 14 Sycamore appeared, the more sensible position in the right seat had become the norm. The main reason was because the pilot could not relinquish his hold on the cyclic stick even for an instant without going out of control, and the cyclic stick was normally held in the right hand. The collective lever could be released for short periods (not for long because of the manual rotor speed control) and so the left hand was partially free to operate switches, radio, trimmers and instruments as required, and these facilities had to be mounted centrally. A further benefit of moving the first pilot to the right-hand side was to remove the left-hand collective lever from the port side doorway for operations. The requirement should have been to mount a removable collective lever to the left hand side for use in training sorties but unfortunately in the Mark 14 Sycamore the opportunity was taken to mount a single collective lever between the two seats, ostensibly for use by either pilot. Thus the pilot in the left seat would have to operate the cyclic stick with his left hand and the collective and throttle lever with his right hand—ie the reverse of the usual arrangement. In addition, in order that the pilot in the left seat would be able to operate the throttle with his right hand, the twist grip had to be turned through a right angle so that it was presented athwartships on the end of the lever.

This regrettable aberration produced the most serious and only really thoroughly objectionable feature of the Sycamore. It was directly responsible for the total write off of several aircraft involving one fatality and very numerous incidents or near accidents, as well as extending the instructor's course on the aircraft by at least ten hours for each pilot (ie 30%) and often more. At the same time it made it impossible for Squadron or Flight Commanders to perform dual checks on their pilots unless they happened to have completed the CFS instructors course themselves, which was rarely the case. The fact was that only the helicopter pilots who had tried it knew how difficult it was to change hands on the controls and how

421

frequently the aircraft would very nearly crash while attempting to manoeuvre near the hover or in transitions to hover while flown from the left seat.

Confusion could occur at any stage of flight, particularly in moments of stress, but the most common effect was felt in the hover where any tendency to sink or move backwards was likely to be instinctively answered by an upward and backward movement of the left hand and a simultaneous forward pressure by the right hand. From the left hand seat of the Mark 14 Sycamore, the effect would be to accelerate the movement of the aircraft backwards and downwards. If it struck the ground before this response could be corrected, the aircraft would crash tail rotor first quite slowly but very completely, with considerable danger to bystanders. Very few realised how much practice would be needed for an experienced pilot to become fully competent (even if never at ease) in handling the aircraft in all manoeuvres from the left hand seat and the problem was not recognised in the Air Ministry where there were no helicopter pilots at that time. When this unfortunate error was recognised it was too late to reverse it. The Staff Officers who allowed it had no reason to suppose there was any greater problem involved than in changing hands to operate central throttles while flying in right or left hand seats in most fixed wing aircraft. When they were told by CFS that the problem was of a different order they did not believe it because it seemed to be an unsupported assertion. There was no comment from A & AEE.

The Sycamore was not different from other early helicopters in that control at or near the hover was almost entirely achieved by means of carefully acquired conditioned reflexes in the pilot, but not all helicopter pilots were aware of this fact. It needed a psychologist to explain that if that were so, then changing hands on the controls would produce a permanently dangerous condition. Unfortunately, the need to obtain psychological advice in this respect was not realised at the time. It was later learned that this condition had been experienced in America some years previously where a similar mistake was made (and expensively corrected) with the original Hiller 360 and before that in the Sikorsky R4. The effect on the pilot was known to the US Naval Institute of Aviation Medicine psychologists as 'retroactive inhibition'. The condition was recognised in theory by the IAM at Farnborough as 'negative transfer'. Both agreed it was a situation to be avoided, but it was too late when this evidence was discovered during a visit by the Central Flying School to the USA in 1955, for a change to be made to the Mark 14 Sycamore. The consequence was that almost the only pilots who ever flew the Mark 14 Sycamore from the left seat were those who had undergone the Instructor's course at the Central Flying School.

APPENDIX 2   CFS HELICOPTER FLYING TRAINING SYLLABI

1. Three syllabi are included—that for the Skeeter ab-initio helicopter pilot training (1957) is derived directly from the original Dragonfly and Sycamore sequences planned for 50 hours and formulated in 1956.

2. The second specimen syllabus (1959) consists of the complete ground and air sequence up to the start of operational training.

3. The third syllabus is a 1967 refinement and expansion of the 1959 syllabus to 60 hours and assumes the previous completion of a basic stage on the Sioux.

APPENDIX to CFS/C.9/40/15/Air
dated 26th June, 1957

ROYAL AIR FORCE SYLLABUS FOR AB INITIO HELICOPTER PILOT TRAINING—SKEETER

DUAL   SOLO

PART A—PRE-SOLO

Ex. 1   Familiarisation with Helicopter Type

    (a)   Explanation of aircraft
        (i)   Externally
        (ii)   Internally
    (b)   Cockpit layout
    (c)   Controls
    (d)   Aircraft systems
    (e)   Drills and desirability of systematic checks

Ex. 2   Preparation for Flight

(Before Flight)
    (a)   Clothing and flying equipment
    (b)   Aircraft acceptance and authorisation
    (c)   External Aircraft check
    (d)   Cockpit check
    (e)   Clearance for starting
    (f)   Starting and warming up
        (i)   Normal
        (ii)   High Winds
    (g)   Cockpit checks and run up
    (h)   Take off checks

(After Flight)
    (a)   Running down
        (i)   Normal
        (ii)   High Winds
    (b)   Leaving the Helicopter

Ex. 3   Air Experience

Ex. 4   Effect of Controls (translation flight)   .15

    (a) Cyclic stick
    (b) Collective pitch, throttle and rudder
    (c) Engine handling
    (d) Further effect of cyclic stick due to
       (i)   Airstream
       (ii) Disc loading
    (e) Further effect of collective pitch—throttle closing—
       autorotation

Ex. 5   Power and Speed Changes   .30

    (a) Handling of cyclic stick with reference to:—
       (i)   Stability
       (ii) Attitude and airspeed
    (b) Handling of collective lever, throttle and rudder,
       practice in:—
       (i)   Power changes with constant RPM
       (ii) Correction of RPM with constant power
    (c) Handling of all controls, practice in:—
       (i)   Straight and level flight
       (ii) Climbing and descending (with medium turns)
          at recommended power
    (d) Reference to instruments
    (e) Engine handling
    (f) Look out

Ex. 6   Autorotation   .30

    (a) Look out
    (b) Entry and development of autorotation
    (c) Control of speed and RPM
    (d) Recovery of powered flight
    (e) Verbal warnings

Ex. 7   Hovering   .30

    (a) Effect of controls in hovering flight, both separately
       and inter-related
    (b) Hovering, cyclic stick only

(c) Hovering, using collective lever, throttle and rudder only correcting for inaccuracies resulting from translation
(d) Hovering, using all controls
(e) Demonstration of ground cushion effect
(f) Effect of .variations in wind strength
(g) Slow forward, sideways and backwards flight in the ground cushion

Ex. 8 Take-off and Landing   .30
(after explanation of ground resonance)

(a) Landing, using cyclic stick only
(b) Landing using collective lever, throttle and rudders only
(c) Landing using all controls
(d) Take-off using cyclic stick only
(e) Take-off using collective lever, throttle and rudders only
(f) Take-off using all controls
(g) Conditions favourable to ground resonance
(h) Mislanding
(j) Overpitching

Ex. 9 Transitions   .15

(a) Transition from hover to forward flight and climb
(b) Transition from approach to hover
(c) Overpitching

Ex. 10 Circuits   1.00   1.00

(a) Recommended circuit pattern, with reference to proximity of fixed wing a/c
(b) Going round again
(c) Action in event of engine failure in circuit

Ex. 11 Demonstration of Engine Off Landing   .15

Ex. 12 First Solo   .15

426

PART B—POST-SOLO

Ex. 13 <u>Sideways and Backwards Flight</u>   .15   .15

    (a) Sideways flight, with particular reference to power, height and directional corrections required due to translation (Heading into wind)

    (b) Backwards flight, as above

    (c) Combination of sideways and forward and backward flight

    (d) Look out

Ex. 14 <u>Turns on the Spot</u>   .15   .30

    (a) Hovering across wind and downwind

    (b) Turns on the spot through varying degrees up to 360°

    (c) Assessment of wind strength and control during turns on the spot

Ex. 15 <u>Taxying</u>   .15   .15

    (a) Use of controls, and control of forward speed

    (b) Taxying over rough ground with reference to ground resonance

    (c) Use of brakes

    (d) Taxying out of wind

Ex. 16 <u>Engine-Off Landings</u>   3.00   1.30

    (a) Autorotation to 50 feet, re-engagement and over-shoot

    (b) Engine-off landings at low forward speed

    (c) Verbal instructions and acknowledgements

Ex. 17 <u>Vortex Ring State</u>   .15

    (a) Demonstration
        (i)   Symptoms and characteristics
        (ii) Methods of recovery
        (iii) Recommended method

    (b) From vertical descent with power

    (c) From engine re-engagement during autorotation

    (d) From powered approach downwind

Ex. 18   Forced Landing   1.00   1.30

    (a)   Autorotation at different air speeds
    (b)   Controlling angle of descent by
        (i)   Changing airspeed
        (ii)   Changing RPM
    (c)   Autorotation into fields after simulated engine failure, showing different height lost in left and right turns
    (d)   Manoeuvre margins
    (e)   Steep turns in autorotation
    (f)   'Spot' engine-off landings

Ex. 19   Low Flying   .45   1.00

    (a)   Familiarisation of low-flying training area
    (b)   Use of controls with reference to speed and height
    (c)   Effect of wind with constant ground speed fast and slow
        (i)   Into wind
        (ii)   When turning
        (iii) Downwind
        (iv)   Across wind
    (d)   Low flying in bad visibility
    (e)   Steep turns
    (f)   Slow flying in restricted areas

PART C—APPLIED FLYING

Ex. 20   Advanced Manoeuvres   2.15   2.15

    (a)   Steep turns, including max-rate
    (b)   Out of wind take-off and landing
    (c)   Downwind transitions
    (d)   Sideways and backwards flight heading out of wind
    (e)   Transitions from the hover to the hover
    (f)   Quick stops
    (g)   Turns on the spot in min. radium
    (h)   Clearing turns
    (j)   Hovering at height

(k) Vertical climb at 200′
(l) Vertical descent from 200′
(m) Approach from confined spaces
(n) Take-off and landings in confined spaces
(o) Take-off and landings in confined spaces
(p) Loading and unloading in the hover
(q) Advanced co-ordination exercises

Ex. 21   Pilot Navigation   1.00   1.00

(a) Map reading
(b) Calculating fuel requirement, with reference to load-
     ing and C of G

Ex. 22   High Altitude Simulation   .45   .30

(a) Running take-off and reduced power (Demo)
(b) Running landing from engine-assisted approach at
     reduced power
(c) Demo. Jump take-off with reduced power

Ex. 23   Flying at Loading and C of G Limits   .45   .15

(a) Take-off at max. AUW
(b) Transitions at max. AUW
(c) Circuits and landings at max. AUW
(d) Take-off and landing at max. forward C of G Limit
(e) Take-off, circuit and landing with rearward C of G

Ex. 24   Flight at High Altitude   .30   .30

(a) Effect on control in basic manoeuvres
     (i)   Cyclic
     (ii) Collective
     (iii) Throttle
(b) Autorotation
(c) Limitations

Ex. 25   Instrument Weather Procedure   2.00

Ex. 26   <u>Night Flying</u>   2.00   .30

    (a)   Cockpit checks
    (b)   Lighting of landing area
    (c)   Take-off and transition to climb
    (d)   Circuit
    (e)   Approach and hover
    (f)   Landing
    (g)   Going round again
    (h)   Use of landing lamp

TOTAL   18.45   11.15

CFS ORB
March 1959

Royal Air Force
Helicopter Pilot Conversion
Ground Training Syllabus

Foreword

Introduction

1. This syllabus covers the ground training required for student pilots who have obtained their flying badge on fixed wing aircraft and who require conversion to helicopters.

The Aim

2. The Aim of the syllabus is to accompany the flying training so as to give a basic understanding of the principles of flight pertaining particularly to helicopters, the technical knowledge required to operate the aircraft being used for flying training, and the special problems of airmanship involved.

The Syllabus

3. The syllabus is designed to parallel the flying conversion syllabus, which extends in scope up to, but not including, operational training. It is divided into three parts:—

(a) Part I   Principles of Flight.

(b) Part II   Technical Subjects.

(c) Part III Airmanship and Navigation.

Co-ordination with Flying Syllabus

4. It is recommended that the flying instructor should personally deal with Part III at least on the ground training syllabus, and should have completed sections 1 and 2 before the time for first solo has been reached. By the same time Part I section 1 to 5 inclusive should have been covered, and Part II sections 1 to 5 inclusive.

Helicopter Pilot Conversion
Ground Training Syllabus Part I

Principles of Flight

Aim

The aim is to give the student a clear, simple, but sound understanding of the principles of flight involved in rotary wing flight as compared with fixed wing flight.

Section	Subject	Hours
1.	Introduction	1

Definitions
Comparisons with Fixed Wing
Creation of Thrust
Freedom of Movement
Directional Control
Different Configurations

2.	Controls	2

Collective Pitch Lever
Linkage with Throttle control
Hand Throttle
Cyclic stick
Tail Rotor-drift, -side force-roll
Manual/Serve controls
Flapping, Feathering, Dragging
Phase lag and advance angle

3.	Hover and Transition	2

Hovering—ground effect
Transition to forward flight
Translational lift
Aerodynamic forces affecting rotor rpm and Lift
Transition to hover
Power required curve
Overpitching
Take off and landing
Effect of altitude/temperature/humidity

4.	Vortex Ring	1

Cause
Occasions in Practice
Recovery action

Section	Subject	Hours

5. <u>Forward Flight</u>   1

Dissymetry of lift
Limits of forward speed and effect of altitude
Stability—angle of attack and speed
Stick forces in manual

6. <u>Ground resonance</u>   1

Definition
Sources of resonance
Conditions causing resonance
Corrective Action

7. <u>Control on the Ground</u>   1

Taxying
Running take off and landing
Blade sailing

8. <u>Centre of Gravity and Loading</u>   1

Positioning of C of G and method of calculating
Limits of movement
C of G compensation
Use of fuel
Effect on controls
Max AUW

9. <u>Autorotation</u>   2

Method of obtaining Autorotation
Effective blade section—L/D curve
Effect of varying rotor RPM
Effect of varying airspeed
Effect of aircraft AUW
Effect of altitude
Effect of flare
Engine off landings
Speed/height range for safe engine off landings

10. <u>Range and Endurance</u>   1

Helicopter Pilot Conversion
Ground Training Syllabus Part II

Technical Subjects

Aim

The aim is to give the student a basic understanding of construction of the helicopter he is flying and the function of its main components, together with a general knowledge of the inspection cycles, and a detailed knowledge of the daily servicing.

Section	Subject	Hours
1.	General Description	2

Configuration and Construction
Landing gear
Flying Controls—layout and operation
Leading particulars and dimensions
Rotor hubs
Rotor blades

Section	Subject	Hours
2.	Power Unit	1

General description and installation
Engine starting and stopping
Engine ground checks
Limitations and engine handling

Section	Subject	Hours
3.	Transmission	1

Clutch
Gearboxes and free wheel unit
Universal couplings and drive shafts
Rotor starting and stopping

Section	Subject	Hours
4.	Fuel and Oil	1

Feul—Installation and position of components
　　　Management of fuel system
　　　Consumption and grade of fuel

Oil　—Installation and position of components
Management of system
Consumption and grade of oil

Section	Subject	Hours
5.	**Ancillary Equipment**	1

Electrical system
Vacuum system
Brakes
C of G compensation system
Rescue hoist

Section	Subject	Hours
6.	**Servicing**	2

Cycle of inspections
Daily Inspections in detail—theory and practice

Helicopter Pilot Conversion
Ground Training Syllabus Part III

Airmanship and Navigation

Aim

The aim is to enable the student to make full use of the special abilities of the helicopter as opposed to a fixed wing aircraft, whilst appreciating its limitations and the precautions to be taken.

Serial	Subject	Hours
1.	**Emergencies**	2

Action in the event of fire—in the air—on the ground
Action in the event of engine failure
Action in the event of tail rotor failure
Engine and handling for engine off landings and autorotation practice
Types of vibration and possible causes
Ditching

Serial	Subject	Hours
2.	**Air Traffic Control**	1

Circuits and approach and departure systems at base airfield
Procedures to adopt when visiting other airfields

Serial	Subject	Hours
3.	**Navigation**	2

Particular problems of pilot navigation arising from slow, low level flight

Serial	Subject	Hours
4.	General Considerations	2

Selection of cruising height for X-country flights
Bad weather procedures
Considerations when landing away from airfields
Technical kit required for operating away from base

ROYAL AIR FORCE SYLLABUS FOR HELICOPTER PILOT CONVERSION
ARRANGED IN SEQUENCE

DUAL   SOLO

PART A—PRE-SOLO

Ex. 1   Familiarisation with Helicopter Type

    (a) Explanation of aircraft
        (i)   Externally
        (ii) Internally
    (b) Cockpit layout
    (c) Controls
    (d) Aircraft systems
    (e) Drills and desirability of systematic checks
    (f) Emergencies

Ex. 2   Preparation for Flight   .15

    (Before flight)
    (a) Clothing and flying equipment
    (b) Aircraft acceptance and authorisation
    (c) External aircraft check
    (d) Cockpit check
    (e) Clearance for starting
    (f) Starting and warming up
        (i)   Normal
        (ii) High Winds
    (g) Cockpit checks and run up
    (h) Take off checks

    (After flight)
    (a) Running down
        (i)   Normal
        (ii) High winds
    (b) Leaving the helicopter

Ex. 3   Air Experience   .15

Ex. 4   Effect of Controls (translational flight)   .45

    (a) Cyclic stick
    (b) Collective pitch, throttle and rudder
    (c) Engine handling

437

(d) Further effect of cyclic stick due to:—
(i)   Airstream
(ii) Disc loading
(e) Further effect of collective pitch—throttle closing—
autorotation

Ex. 5   <u>Power and Speed Changes</u>   .45

(a) Handling of cyclic stick with reference to:—
(i)   Stability
(ii) Attitude and airspeed
(b) Handling of collective lever, throttle and rudder,
practice in:—
(i)   Power changes with constant RPM
(ii) Correction of RPM with constant power:—
(c) Handling of all controls practice in:—
(i)   Straight and level flight
(ii) Climbing and descending (with medium turns)
at recommended power
(d) Reference to instruments
(e) Engine handling
(f) Look out

Ex. 6   <u>Autorotation</u>   .45

(a) Look out
(b) Entry and development of autorotation
(c) Control of speed and RPM
(d) Recovery to powered flight
(e) Verbal warnings

Ex. 7   <u>Hovering</u>   .45

(a) Effect of controls in hovering flight, both separately
and inter-related
(b) Hovering, cyclic stick only
(c) Hovering, using collective lever, throttle and rudder
only, correcting for inaccuracies resulting from
translation
(d) Hovering, using all controls
(e) Demonstration of ground cushion effect
(f) Effect of variations in wind strength
(g) Slow forward, sideways and backwards flight in the
ground cushion.

Ex. 8   Take-off and Landing   .45

(After explanation of ground resonance)
(a) Landing, using cyclic stick only
(b) Landing using collective lever, throttle and rudders
     only
(c) Landing using all controls
(d) Take-off using cyclic stick only
(e) Take-off using collective lever, throttle and rudders
     only
(f) Take-off using all controls
(g) Conditions favourable to ground resonance
(h) Mislanding
(j) Overpitching

Ex. 9   Transitions   .30

(a) Transition from hover to forward flight and climb
(b) Transition from approach to hover
(c) Overpitching

Ex. 10 Circuits   1.00   1.30

(a) Recommended circuit pattern, with reference to
     proximity of fixed wing a/c
(b) Going round again
(c) Action in event of engine failure in circuit
(d) Circuit in manual control from downwind position

Ex. 11 Demonstration of Engine Off Landing   .15

Ex. 12 First Solo   .15

PART B—POST-SOLO

Ex. 13 Sideways and Backwards Flight   .45   1.30

(a) Sideways flight, with particular references to power,
     height and directional corrections required due to
     translation. (Heading into wind)
(b) Backwards flight, as above,
(c) Combination of sideways and forward and back-
     wards flight
(d) Look out

439

	DUAL	SOLO

Ex. 14　Turns on the Spot .... .45　1.30

    (a)　Hovering across wind and downwind
    (b)　Turns on the spot through varying degrees up to 360°
    (c)　Assessment of wind strength and control duirng turns on the spot

Ex. 15　Taxying .... .15　.15

    (a)　Use of controls, and control of forward speed
    (b)　Taxying over rough ground with reference to ground resonance
    (c)　Use of brakes
    (d)　Taxying out of wind

Ex. 16　Engine-Off Landings .... 3.00　1.30

    (a)　Autorotation to 50 feet, flare, re-engagement and overshoot
    (b)　Engine-off landings at low forward speed
    (c)　Verbal instructions and acknowledgements
    (d)　Dangers

Ex. 17　Vortex Ring State .... .15

    (a)　Demonstrations
        (i)　Symptoms and characteristics
        (ii)　Methods of recovery
        (iii)　Recommended method
    (b)　From vertical descent with power
    (c)　From engine re-engagement during vertical autorotation
    (d)　From powered approach downwind

Ex. 18　Forced Landing .... 1.30　3.00

    (a)　Autorotation at different airspeeds
    (b)　Controlling angle of descent by
        (i)　Changing airspeed
        (ii)　Changing rpm
    (c)　Autorotation into fields after simulated engine failure, showing different height lost in left and right turns

    (d) Manoeuvring margins
    (e) Steep turns in autorotation
    (f) 'Spot' engine-off landings

Ex. 19 <u>Low Flying</u>   .45   1.00

    (a) Familiarisation of low-flying training area
    (b) Use of controls with reference to speed and height
    (c) Effect of wind with constant ground speed fast and slow
       (i) Into wind
       (ii) When turning
       (iii) Downwind
       (iv) Across wind
    (d) Low flying in bad visibility
    (c) Steep turns
    (f) Slow flying in restricted areas

PART C—APPLIED FLYING

Ex. 20   5.45   13.45

<u>Advanced Manoeuvres</u>

    (a) Steep turns, including max-rate
    (b) Out of wind take-off and landing
    (c) Downwind transitions
    (d) Sideways and backwards flight heading out of wind
    (e) Transitions from the hover to the hover
    (f) Quick stops
    (g) Turns on the spot in min. radius
    (h) Clearing turns
    (j) Hovering at height
    (k) Vertical climb to 200'
    (l) Vertical descent from 200'
    (m) Approach to confined spaces
    (n) Take-off and landings in confined spaces
    (o) Take-off and landing on sloping ground
    (p) Loading and unloading in the hover
    (q) Advanced co-ordination exercises

		DUAL	SOLO
Ex. 21	Pilot Navigation	1.00	2.00

    (a) Map-reading

    (b) Calculation of fuel requirements, with reference to loading and C of G

		DUAL	SOLO
Ex. 22	High Altitude Simulation	.45	.30

    (a) Running take-off with reduced power (Demo)

    (b) Running landing from engine-assisted approach at reduced power

    (c) Demo. Jump take-off with reduced power

		DUAL	SOLO
Ex. 23	Flying at Loading and C of G Limits	.45	.15

    (a) Take-off at max. AUW

    (b) Transitions at max. AUW

    (c) Circuits and landings at max. AUW

    (d) Take-off and landing at max. forward C of G limit

    (e) Take-off, circuit and landing with rearward C of G

		DUAL	SOLO
Ex. 24	Flights at High Altitude	1.00	1.00

    (a) Effect on control in basic manoeuvres

        (i)   Cyclic

        (ii) Collective

        (iii) Throttle

    (b) Autorotation

    (c) Limitations

		DUAL	SOLO
Ex. 25	Instrument Weather Procedure	1.30	2.00
Ex. 26	Night Flying	1.00	2.00

    (a) Cockpit checks

    (b) Lighting of landing area

    (c) Take-off and transition to climb

    (d) Circuit

    (e) Approach and hover

    (f) Landing

    (g) Going round again

    (h) Use of landing lamp

HELICOPTER PILOT TRAINING SYLLABUS
WHIRLWIND STAGE—60 HOURS/12 WEEKS

Exercise	Dual	Solo	TOTAL
Conversion, GH and Revision	10.30	8.15	18.45
Instrument Flying	7.15		7.15
Approach, Landing and Take-off from Confined Areas	1.45	1.30	3.15
Night Flying	2.30	1.45	4.15
High Altitude Flight	.45	—	.45
SRT—Load carrying in formation to confined areas ⎫	1.00	1.00	2.00
S & R—Wet Winching ⎭			
Winching	3.45	3.45	7.30
Trooping	.45	.45	1.30
Tactical Low Flying	1.15	1.15	2.30
Mountain Flying	4.15	.30	4.45
Load Carrying	.45	.45	1.30
Homing Techniques	.45	.45	1.30
Exercise (SRT or S & R)	1.30	1.00	2.30
Tests	2.00	—	2.00
TOTALS:	38.45	21.15	60.00

HELICOPTER PILOT TRAINING SYLLABUS
WHIRLWIND STAGE
60 hrs/12 weeks
SEQUENCE OF FLIGHT INSTRUCTION

Sortie No	Exercises	Dual	Solo	Total	Outline of Sortie
1	3-7 16	1.00		1.00	Effect of controls, attitude and Power changes, level flight climbs, descents, turns, autos, engine off landings (2)
2	7-11 16	1.00		1.00	Autorotations, hovering, take off and landing, transitions circuits. Engine off landings (2)

Sortie No	Exercises	Dual	Solo	Total	Outline of Sortie
3	7–11 16 12	1.00	.15	1.15	As above, Engine off landing (2) First Solo
4	13–15 revise 7–11	1.00		1.00	Sideways backwards flight, spot turns, taxying circuits
5	11 13–15		1.00	1.00	As above
6	16–18	1.00		1.00	Forced landings, engine off landings
7	18		.45	.45	Forced Landings.
8	18		.45	.45	Forced Landings
9	16	.45		.45	Engine off landings (primarily full flare and constant attitude)
10	24	1.00		1.00	Marginal power operations
11	24		1.00	1.00	As above
12	22 23	1.00		1.00	Landing on sloping ground and out of wind, downwind transitions quick stops, emergency turns.
13	22 23		1.00	1.00	As above
14	16	.45		.45	Engine off landings (primarily full flare and constant attitude)
15	7–11 13–15 18 22–24		.45	.45	Revision
16	7–24 (as req)	1.00		1.00	Conversion Test
17	25	.45		.45	Instrument indications, scanning techniques, changing speed, attitude power climbs, descents, turns, autorotation
18	25	.45		.45	As Sortie 17+QGH—Comp. 'in'
19	25	.45		.45	As Sortie 17 including I/F take offs and QGH—Comp. 'cut'
20	25	.45		.45	As Sortie 19 except QGH to be speechless and including GCA—Comp. 'in'

Sortie No	Exercises	Dual	Solo	Total	Outline of Sortie
21	26	.45		.45	Approach to, landing in and take off from a confined area.
22	26		.45	.45	Approach to, landing in and take off from a confined area
23	17 28	.45		.45	High altitude to 10000′ and vortex ring
24	Underslung loads	.45		.45	Pallet and netted standard loads
25	As above		.45	.45	As above
26	27	1.00		1.00	Night circuits and landings, schermuly firing
27	27		1.00	1.00	Night circuits and landings
28	27	.45		.45	Night underslung loads
29	27	.45		.45	Night circuits and landings QGH
20	27		.45	.45	Night circuits & landing. QGH
31	Trooping	.45		.45	Hover jump, roping
32	Trooping		.45	.45	As above
33	Tact low flying	1.15		1.15	X-country to Valley
34	As above		1.15	1.15	As above
35	29	1.00		1.00	Tactical formation to a confined area
36	29		1.00	1.00	As above
37	26	1.00		1.00	Approach to, landing in and take off from a confined area
38	26		.45	.45	As above
39	25	.45		.45	IF take off, autos, Emergencies, unusual attitudes, speechless QGH Comp. 'out'
40	25	.45		.45	As above
41	25	1.00		1.00	GCA approaches Comp. 'in' and 'out'

Sortie No	Exercises	Dual	Solo	Total	Outline of Sortie
42	25	1.00		1.00	Consolidation, let downs & standby horizon
43	25	.45		.45	Instrument rating test
44	7–11 13–15 22 24 26		.45	.45	General handling
45	As above		.45	.45	As above
46	Dry winching	.45		.45	Single, double & stretcher lifts
47	As above		.45	.45	As above
48	As above	.45		.45	As above
49	As above		.45	.45	As above
50	Drum winching	.45		.45	Single lifts
51	As above		.45	.45	As above
52	Wet winching	.45		.45	Single and double lifts
53	As above		.45	.45	As above
54	Deck winching	.45		.45	Single and double lifts
55	As above		.45	.45	As above
56	Decca homing	.45		.45	Use of Decca and Sarbe equipment
57	Sarbe homing		.45	.45	As above
58	Mountain flying	1.15		1.15	Wind finding & initial approaches
59	As above	1.15		1.15	Approach to spurs and pinnacles
60	As above	1.15		1.15	Approach to ridges and bowls
61	As above	.30		.30	Revision
62	As above		.30	.30	Approaches as briefed
63	16	1.00		1.00	Engine off landings (primarily gentle flare)
64	16		.30	.30	Engine off landings (gentle flare only)

446

Sortie No	Exercises	Dual	Solo	Total	Outline of Sortie
65	7–26	1.00		1.00	General handling
66	18 22 24 26		0.45	0.45	As above
67	7–26	1.00		1.00	Final handling test
68	Tactical Exercise	1.30		1.30	Exercise in all aspects of specialisation at end of course
69	As above		1.00	1.00	As above
Total		38.45	21.15	60.00	

SAR Students do two hours extra winching instead of Sorties numbers 35 and 36.

APPENDIX 3   EMERGENCY OPERATING PROCEDURE—
MULTI-LIFT-HOIST

1. The procedure for recovering persons from a hover height of more than the 50 foot winch cable was called the Multi-Lift Hoist or Multi-Tape system.

2. The sequence is complicated to describe, so the HQ FEAF operating procedure is repeated here in full. It provides a vivid example both of the ingenuity and determination of the helicopter crews, as well as of the failure to pay adequate attention to the urgent recommendations from FEAF in the mid-1950s that helicopters in the Far East Theatre should have winch cables at least 200 feet in length.

EMERGENCY OPERATING PROCEDURES

HELICOPTER EMERGENCY MULTI-LIFT HOIST

Introduction

1. Helicopters may be required to recover live loads whilst hovering at a height greater than the length of the winch-hoist cable. This may be achieved by using a multiple tape system in conjunction with the winch-hoist.

2. This method may also be used to lower personnel into confined areas eg medical or rescue teams, however, the ABSEIL methods for lowering loads from helicopters are generally more appropriate for this purpose.

3. The multiple tape procedure requires a high degree of concentration and skill on the part of the helicopter crew for long periods at the hover. For this reason and because of the hazards associated with the jettison of loads under these conditions, the procedure is to be used only in emergency circumstances. Under normal circumstances, the clearing should be enlarged or the load positioned at an alternative pick-up point where a landing or direct winch-hoist recovery may be effected.

4. The Emergency Operating Procedure listed hereunder details the equipment to be used and the operating technique to be adopted when recovering loads by means of the Multiple-lift Hoist method.

Personnel

5. The following personnel are required:

    a.   Pilot.

    b.   Winch Operator.

    c.   Winchman. (Descends on winch cable to link up tapes).

    d.   Crewman. (Assists winch operator).

    e.   Medical/Rescue staff as required.

Equipment

6. The following equipment is required.

    a.   Helicopter with a serviceable winch and cable cutters and with a MONO RAIL fitted.

    b.   Multi lift equipment consisting of:

        (1) 4×50' tapes (LONG TAPE)

        (2) 1×5' tape (SHORT TAPE)

        (3) 2×BOSUN'S CHAIR

        (4) 1×WINCHING STROP

        (5) 1×NEIL ROBERTSON STRETCHER

        (6) 1×SHARP KNIFE TO CUT TAPE

        (7) 200' ABSEIL TAPE AND ROLLERS FOR MEDICAL OFFICER

        (8) 200' ABSEIL TAPE FOR EMERGENCY USE

Pre-Flight Checks

7. The Authorising Officer is to ensure that:

    a.   The level of emergency justifies the use of this equipment.

    b.   The Captain and crew are competent to carry out the task.

    c.   The Captain and crew understand this EOP.

    d.   The crew is properly constituted.

8. The Captain of the aircraft is to ensure that:

    a.   His crew understands this EOP

    b.   The equipment is complete and fully serviceable.

    c.   The medical officer, if carried, understands the EOP.

    d.   The medical officer understands Abseilling Drills.

    e.   The medical officer is briefed on the use of the bosuns chair.

f.   The medical officer is briefed on the Neil Robertson stretcher.

g.   The emergency procedures are understood.

9. The Captain is to ascertain:

a.   That the medical officer realises that once he is lowered he may not be recovered immediately into the aircraft at heights in excess of 100 feet.

b.   What equipment the medical officer requires to be lowered with him, eg Stretcher, bosuns chair, strop.

Operation

10. Standard winching patter is to be used throughout the operation. When the captain positions the aircraft at the hover over the selected clearing the winchman is to confirm that the ground is visible and that the secondary growth is not a hazard which may snag the tapes.

11. The hover must be established for about 30 seconds before the tape is lowered, to ensure that light foliage will not be blown over the clearing by the down-wash.

12. If a medical officer is lowered, he is to be in a bosuns chair and is to carry all his equipment with him.

13. If no man is to be lowered the tapes are to be connected and lowered one by one until they touch the ground.

14. Details of lowering and raising are contained in Paras 21 and 22.

15. One lowering or raising sequence to 250 foot extension can be expected to require a five minute hover.

Emergencies

16. General. On no account is a cable or tape, which is snagged on a tree, to be freed by raising the aircraft.

17. Empty Tape. If a tape should snag a tree with no one on the end, the following procedure is to be followed:

a.   The winch operator informs the captain.

b.   The winch operator attempts to free the tape by hand.

452

c. The Captain gives the order 'CHOP THE TAPE'.

d. The tape is cut. (By the winch operator or by the crew man when directed by the winch operator).

18. <u>Tape with Man Attached</u>. If the tape should snag a tree with a man attached, the following procedure is to be followed:

a. The winch operator informs the Captain.

b. The winch operator lowers the winchman who attempts to free the tape.

c. The winchman is lowered with 200 foot Abseil tape which he secures to a tree and lowers the remainder past the man on the end of the tape and thence to the ground.

d. The man on the tape secures himself to the Abseil tape.

e. The winchman is winched into the aircraft.

f. The Captain gives the order 'CHOP THE TAPE' three times.

g. The tape is cut. (By the winch operator or by the crew man when directed by the winch operator).

Notices

1. Personnel or casualties left in the tree after the tape is cut will become the subject of a further recovery operation which may take some considerable time to effect.

2. Because of the weight limitation on the Winch-Hoist (450 lbs) only one person at a time may be recovered at heights requiring more than one extension tape.

3. Attention is drawn to the cycling limitation on the Winch Hoist ie, 5 complete cycles followed by a 10 minute cooling period.

4. The duties of the Crewman may be undertaken by the medical officer in circumstances where he is not required to be lowered.

19. The following is a description of the procedure to be carried out and list of terms used in lowering a medical officer and raising a casualty using the Emergency Multi Lift Hoist.

20. <u>List of terms</u>.

    a.   Captain—Pilot of aircraft.

    b.   Winch Operator—Man operating the winch.

    c.   Winchman—Man on the winch cable.

    d.   Crewman—Man assisting the winch operator.

    e.   Medical officer—Man to be lowered to the ground.

    f.   Casualty—Man to be raised from the ground.

    g.   Cable—Winch cable.

    h.   Short tape—5 feet tape with ring on upper end, a hook on the lower.

    j.   Long tape—50 feet tape with ring on upper end, a hook on the lower.

    k.   First tape—First long tape to be lowered out of the aircraft.

    l.   Second Tape—Second long tape to be lowered out of the aircraft.

    m.   Third Tape—Third long tape to be lowered out of the aircraft.

    n.   Fourth Tape—Fourth long tape to be lowered out of the aircraft.

<u>Description of Method</u>

21. <u>Lowering</u> (if the medical officer cannot abseil to the ground).

    a.   The ring of the Short Tape is attached to the monorail.

    b.   The ring of the FIRST LONG TAPE is attached to the hook of the SHORT TAPE.

    c.   The Medical officer's BOSUN'S CHAIR is attached to the hook of the long tape.

    d.   The Winch Operator lowers the winchman and medical officer until the medical officer is supported by the First Long Tape.

    e.   The crewman pays out the First Long Tape.

f.   The Winchman unhooks the medical officer from the cable and is winched back in.

g.   The medical officer is now 50′ below the aircraft, supported by the First Long Tape and the Short Tape attached to the Monorail.

h.   The Winchman is winched up until he is level with the ring (TOP) of the first tape.

j.   The ring of the First Tape is attached to the cable.

k.   The Winchman is raised, releasing the load from the Short Tape.

l.   The hook of the Short Tape is unhooked from the ring of the First Tape and the Second Tape introduced.

m.   The ring of the Second Tape is attached to the hook of the Short Tape.

n.   The hook of the Second Tape is attached to the ring of the First Tape.

o.   The Winchman is lowered whilst the crewman pays out the Second Tape until the weight of the medical officer is supported by the Second Tape.

p.   The Winchman removes the cable from the ring of the First Tape and is winched up.

q.   The medical officer is now 100 feet below the aircraft, supported by the First Tape, the Second Tape and the Short Tape attached to the Monorail.

r.   The Third and Fourth Tapes are introduced in the same way until the medical officer reaches the ground.

s.   The maximum length of lowering is 250 feet made up of First, Second, Third and Fourth Tapes plus 50 feet of cable.

22. Raising. Assuming that the medical officer has been lowered on four tapes, or that four tapes have been lowered to the ground on the end of the winch cable, the following procedure is to be used:—

a.   The ring of the Short Tape is attached to the monorail.

b.   The casualty is attached to the hook (LOWER) end of the First Tape.

c.   The cable is raised until the ring (TOP) of the Fourth Tape is level with the hook of the Short Tape.

d.   The ring of the Fourth Tape is attached to the hook of the Short Tape and the cable winched out until the weight of the casualty is supported by the Short Tape. The cable is removed from the ring of the Fourth Tape.

e.   The casualty is now supported 200 feet below the aircraft by four long tapes and the Short Tape attached to the monorail.

f.   The Winchman is lowered until he is level with the ring (TOP) of the Third Tape.

g.   The Winchman attaches the cable to the ring of the Third Tape and is winched up until he is level with the hook of the Short Tape. The Crewman collects and rewinds the incoming tape.

h.   The Fourth Tape is removed from the Short Tape and the ring of the Third Tape.

j.   The ring of the Third Tape is attached to the hook of the Short Tape.

k.   The Winchman is winched out until the weight of the casualty is supported by the Short Tape.

l.   The cable is removed from the ring of the Third Tape.

m.   The casualty is now supported 150 feet below the aircraft on three tapes and the Short Tape attached to the monorail.

n.   The Winchman is winched out until level with the ring (TOP) of the Second Tape and the procedure is repeated twice more to recover the Second and First Tapes.

o.   The casualty is then level with the cabin door.

STANDARD OPERATING PROCEDURE
WINCHING INTO JUNGLE CANOPY

Introduction

1. Due to the density of the jungle canopy it may be impossible for troops to be roped, winched or abseiled to the ground.

2. This SOP lays down the procedure to be carried out when winching troops into the jungle canopy; the troops carrying equipment to enable them to make their own way to the ground.

Equipment

3. The following equipment and personnel are required:

    a.   Whirlwind with serviceable winch.

    b.   Winching strop.

    c.   Pilot and Winch Operator trained in winching.

    d.   Troops equipped with abseil equipment or lowering ropes.

Pre-flight checks

4. Before flying the Captain of the aircraft is to ensure that:

    a.   He and the crewman understand this SOP.

    b.   The winch is serviceable.

    c.   The winch cable cutter is loaded.

    d.   The troops understand the signals to be used by them.

    e.   The troops understand the emergency procedure if the cable is fouled or jammed.

f.   The troops are briefed on standard helicopter procedures.

g.   The troops are equipped with and understand the use of their own lowering equipment.

Winching

5. Having checked that sufficient power is available to manoeuvre outside ground effect the pilot is to come to the hover over the desired area. The winch operator is to select a part of a tree which, in his opinion, will bear the weight of the soldier. He is then to use standard voice marshalling to bring the aircraft overhead the selected point. The Stick Leader is then to be winched down in a strop, followed by the rest of the stick in turn.

Hand signals (troops)

6. The following hand signals are to be used by the man in the strop:

Message	Signal
Winch Down	One arm extended, Palm Down repeatedly moved downwards.
Winch Up	One arm extended, Palm Up repeatedly moved upwards.
Stop	One arm extended horizontally.
Firm Footing Obtained Give me slack cable	One arm 'Thumbs Up'
Secure to Tree	Strop removed and held at arm's length

Winching precautions

7. The following precautions are to be observed during winching:

a.   The man in the strop is to secure himself to the tree before removing the strop.

b.   The winch operator is to keep the strop in sight at all times during the operation.

c.   The Captain should not leave the area until he is satisfied that the troops can reach the ground.

Fouling of the cable

8. The following procedures are to be carried out if a cable becomes fouled and no attempt is to be made to free the cable by raising the aircraft.

    a.   Empty Strop. The winch operator is to attempt to free the strop and cable by hand but if necessary the cable is to be cut.

    b.   With a man in the strop. The man is to try and gain a firm foothold and then discard the strop, the winch operator is to attempt to free the strop and cable by hand but if necessary the cable is to be cut. If the man is unable to gain a firm foothold then he is to secure his abseil gear to the hook and abseil as rapidly as possible to the ground. When the man has reached the ground the winch operator is to attempt to free the strop, cable and tape by hand but if necessary the cable is to be cut.

    c.   If the winch operator loses sight of the man or a fouled cable he is to winch out and maintain slack for at least one minute, before attempting to free the cable.

Jamming of the winch

9. If the winch should jam with a man suspended in the strop, the procedure outlined in para 8b is to be adopted.

Note   (1) the event of a winch failure the operation may be continued by using the abseil technique.

    (2) In certain circumstances consideration may be given to fly the man out while suspended and proceed to a cleared area.

APPENDIX 4   SELETAR HELICOPTER NIGHT APPROACH PATTERN
(SHNAP)

1. Later referred to as the 'Support Helicopter Night Approach Pattern' the tri-Service agreed pamphlet authorising the use of the SHNAP in the Far East area is self-explanatory and is therefore included complete.

2. It should be noted that the four Chapter layout was only used to make the universal usage of the SHNAP easier to envisage. In practice, Chapter 1 was the only one issued to MAOTs and troops and Chapters 2, 3 and 4 were only used where permanent installations were needed. Chapters 5 and 6 were no business of the troops.

Seletar

Helicopter

Night

Approach

Pattern

SELETAR HELICOPTER NIGHT APPROACH PATTERN

FIGURE 1

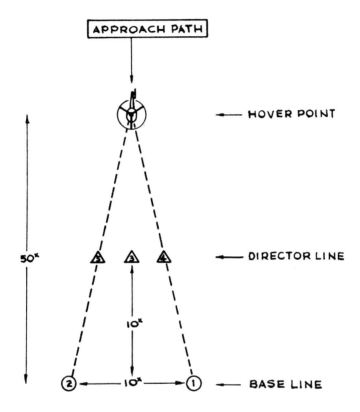

APPROACH PATH

HOVER POINT

50ˣ

DIRECTOR LINE

10ˣ

② ←—— 10ˣ ——→ ①   BASE LINE

Chapter One

CONSTRUCTION OF THE PATTERN

Requirements

Five torches

Three poles 5' 6" high

One piece of string (10 yards long)

Laying the Pattern   (Figure 1)

1.   Select the desired hover point which should be hard and flat enough to permit the helicopter to land if that is required. Mark it with a man or pole. This is the "HOVER Point".

2.   Select the widest and flattest approach path. If the area offers a large choice of open approach paths, the following criteria should be borne in mind as advantages:

a. The approach path should, ideally, be "into wind" for the aircraft. If a wind of any strength more than light is experienced from any direction behind the aircraft on the approach, it may not be safe to continue the descent.

b. If possible, an approach path should be chosen which has a take-off path in line with it, that is, approximately the same compass heading as the approach.

3.   Turn about with the back towards the approach path and move 50 paces from the hover/landing point on the same compass heading as the approach path and turn about to face up the approach. Move to right or left to bring the Hover Point marker in line with the centre of the approach path. Mark the position. This is the centre of what is called the "BASE LINE".

4.   From the centre of the Base Line, facing the Hover Point fold the 10 yard string and measure five yards right and mark position one. Place a torch on the ground pointing unobstructed up the approach path. Measure five yards left from the centre position and mark position two. Place a torch on the ground pointing up the approach path. Check that positions one and two are ten yards apart on a line at right angles to the approach path. This is the completed Base Line.

5.   Measure accurately 10 yards forward from the centre of the Base Line, towards and in line with the Hover Point. This is position three and requires a torch 5' 6" above the ground pointing back up the approach path. Mark it with a man or pole. This is also the centre of what is called the "DIRECTOR LINE", and is a key position.

FIGURE 2

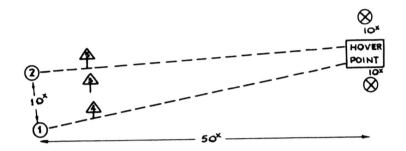

FIGURE 3

PILOTS VIEW

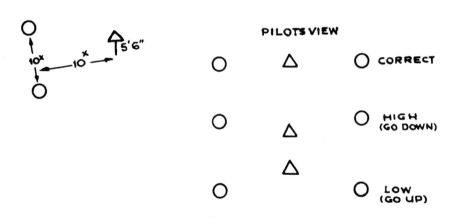

6. Using the 10 yard string, mark a line parallel to the Base Line through position three. This is the Director Line.

7. Facing up the approach path, move right along the Base Line to position one and site a man or pole on the Director Line exactly in line with the Hover Point. This is position four and requires a torch at a height of 5' 6" similar to position three.

8. Move left along the Base Line to position two and site a man or pole on the Director Line exactly in line with the Hover Point. This is position five and requires a torch at a height of 5' 6" similar to positions four and three. Check that positions four, three and five are in a straight line and the torches are at the same height. This defines the Director Line.

9. If the ground is suitable and lights are available, place a light each side of the Hover Point and 10 yards away, i.e. 20 yards apart. (This is helpful but not essential - see Figure 2).

10. Ensure that all lights are firmly secured in order to withstand the violence of the helicopter downwash.

11. Stand at the Hover Point and ensure that the lights on the Base Line at positions one and two are unobscured and clearly visible from that position.

12. The SHNAP is now ready for checking.

Emergency SHNAP

13. In emergency, with an approach path 45 degrees wide, clear to a range of approximately two miles, the SHNAP can be laid and flown with positions one, two and three only. This is called the EMERGENCY SHNAP and can be laid by one man, alone. It does not define a Hover Point and the aircraft will land a few yards in front of position three. (Figure 3).

Colour of Lights

14. There must be a clear colour contrast between the lights on the Base Line and those on the Director Line and it is desirable that all lights appear with approximately equal intensity. If there is a difference in brightness after applying the colour contrast, it is important that the Base Line should not appear less bright than the Director Line. If it cannot be avoided, it is acceptable for the Base Line to be rather brighter than the Director Line.

FIGURE 4

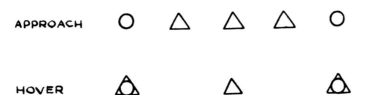

APPROACH

HOVER

FIGURE 5

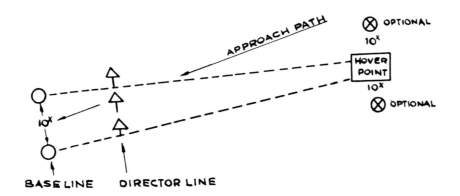

OPTIONAL

10^x

HOVER
POINT

10^x

OPTIONAL

APPROACH PATH

10^x

BASE LINE   DIRECTOR LINE

Chapter Two

LEVELLING THE PATTERN

1.   The pilot flies the SHNAP by positioning the aircraft on the approach path which he finds by adjusting his height until the Director Line appears to be level with the Base Line, thus putting the aircraft on the 10 degree slope, and then moving laterally until the Director Line appears between the two Base Line lights without overlapping them. The approach path is thus defined both vertically and laterally.

2.   As the pilot approaches the hover point, the Director Line will appear to get wider, and when the outer two Director Line lights appear coincident with the two Base Line lights, he knows he is the measured 50 paces from the SHNAP and is over the Hover Point which has been selected. (Figures 4 and 5).

3.   When the pilot has achieved a position in which all the lights appear in a straight line, the line itself provides him with a representation of the horizon, so it must be approximately level. Further, if it has proved impossible to find a level piece of ground on which to construct the SHNAP, some adjustment must be made to ensure that the approach path has not been made too steep. The method for correcting for sloping ground is now described.

   a.   The Base Line must first be levelled. In the absence of special levelling equipment, the following method is recommended :

      (1)   Take the 10 yard string and stretch it taut between the Base Line Lights.

      (2)   Hold level with the string a mess tin or similar container filled with water and observe the direction of the slope.

      (3)   Raise the lower one of the Base Line lights as necessary to make the string level.

      (4)   The new centre of the Base Line must be marked.

   b.   The slope, if any, between the Director and Base Lines must now be checked and the measurement should be made between the centres of each line. If it is downwards from the Base Line to the Director Line, the vertical angle of approach will be reduced, and provided the vertical clearance checks described later are still satisfactory, the approach will be flatter and therefore easier for the pilot, and no further adjustment need be made.

   c.   If there is a slope upwards from the centre of the Base Line to the centre of the Director Line, the approach path will be steepened and an adjustment must

be made to reduce the approach angle to the standard 10
degrees by raising both the Base Line lights until the
slope is cancelled. The position three light at the
centre of the Director Line will now be a true 5" 6"
above the Base Line and will indicate a true 10 degree
approach path.

d. The outer two Director Line lights must be adjusted
if necessary to make the Director Line horizontal using
the centre light as a height datum.

FIGURE 6

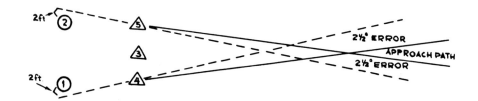

FIGURE 7

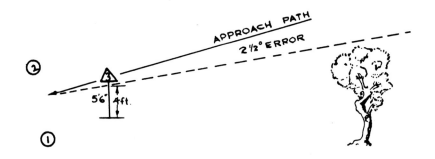

Chapter Three

CHECKING THE APPROACH AND TAKE OFF PATH DEFINED BY THE SHNAP

Checking the width of the Approach Path and Noting Obstructions (Figure 6).

1. Stand at position 2 and sight through position 5. This line define the edge of the approach path to your right.

2. Move two feet to your left (this allows the pilot a 2½ degree error outside the approach path) and note the highest obstruction which appears to the left of this line through position 5, up to a range of about two miles in an arc of about 45 degrees left.

3. Stand at position 1 and sight through position 4. This line defines the edge of the approach path to your left.

4. Move two feet to your right and note the highest obstruction which appears to the right of the line through position 4, up to a range of about two miles in an arc whose righthand limit has been defined by the previous sighting.

Checking the Approach Vertical Clearance above Obstructions (Figure 7)

5. Sight from a point level with the lights on the Base Line through a point 18 inches below the light at position 3 towards the highest obstruction noted in the previous observations from positions 1 and 2. This line defines the lowest edge of the approach path (being 2½ degrees below the 10 degree slope and must pass above the highest obstruction observed in the approach path.

6. If this line does not pass above the obstruction, the light at position 3 may be withdrawn towards the Base Line, a maximum distance, of three yards, making its distance from the Base Line a minimum of seven yards. This steepens the approach angle to 14 degrees approximately. Do not steepen the approach path unnecessarily.

7. It should be noted that if this procedure has to be followed, the lights at positions 4 and 5 should not be similarly withdrawn towards the Base Line. These positions are used for ranging by the helicopter pilot, and the amount by which they appear below positions 1, 3 and 2 (which should appear to him in a straight line), is an indication to him of how far you have been obliged to steepen the approach path to clear the obstruction. They also serve as a constant height indication at the hover point when they are aligned with positions 1 and 2.

8.   If after moving position 3 the full three yards towards the Base Line, the sighting line from a point level with the lights on the Base Line, through the point 18 inches below the light at position 3 still does not pass above the obstruction, the approach is not acceptable for use in darkness.

9.   Record the compass heading of the approach path measured from the Hover Point towards position 3.   The pilot must be informed of this.

Checking the Take Off Path

10.   Where there is a take off path available in line with the approach path so that the helicopter does not have to turn round and take off in the reverse direction up the approach, the same lateral and vertical clearances should be measured by constructing a landing pattern, for sighting purposes only, at the hover point and facing the take off path.   The take off path may be back up the approach path if necessary, but as this requires the helicopter to turn round over the hover point, more cleared space is required.   (See Chapter Four).

11.   Record the compass heading of the take off path measured from the hover point.   The pilot must be informed of this.

12.   Remove the hover point marker.   The lighting pattern is now ready for use.

FIGURE 8

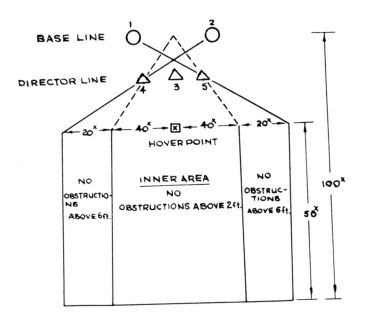

BASE LINE

DIRECTOR LINE

HOVER POINT

NO OBSTRUCTIONS ABOVE 6ft.

INNER AREA
NO
OBSTRUCTIONS ABOVE 2ft.

NO OBSTRUCTIONS ABOVE 6ft.

FIGURE 9

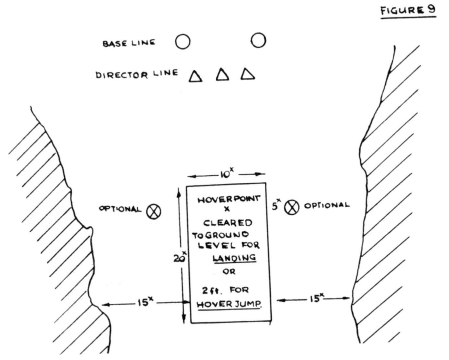

BASE LINE

DIRECTOR LINE

OPTIONAL

HOVER POINT
X
CLEARED TO GROUND LEVEL FOR LANDING
OR
2 ft. FOR HOVER JUMP.

OPTIONAL

Chapter Four

GROUND CLEARANCE CHECKS FOR HELICOPTER NIGHT OPERATIONS

Clearing the Hover Point for a Confined Area having only a

Single Approach/Take Off Path   (Figure 8).

1.   If it is required to land a helicopter at the hover point, the edges of the area which it is necessary to clear completely to ground level are defined by two lines sighted from the centre of the Base Line through positions 4 and 5 respectively to a distance of 70 yards (i.e. about level with the hover point which is 50 yards from the Base Line) thence parallel to each other a further 50 yards.   The furthest edge of the cleared area is thus 100 yards distance from the Base Line.   It is 40 yards wide from the distant edge to the hover point, thence narrowing to 0 at the centre of the Base Line.

2.   A further space outside cleared area should have no this obstructions above six feet and its edges are defined by lines sighted through positions 1 and 5, and 2 and 4, to a position level with the hover point, at which distance they are 80 yards apart.   Thence parallel to each other for a further distance of 50 yards.   This area cleared to a maximum of six feet obstructions thus extends 20 yards sideways outside the fully cleared area.

3.   If it is not necessary to land the helicopter, the area defined by these outer lines should be cleared to six feet height, and the inner area should have no obstruction higher than two feet.

Clearing the Hover Point for a Site having an Open Take Off

Path Approximately in Line with the Approach Path.   (Figure 9).

4.   In this case it is assumed that the same lateral and vertical angles of clearance provided for the approach path as defined by the lighting pattern, are available on the take off path.   That is, that the helicopter is not required to turn round over the hover point in order to face the approach path for take off.

5.   If it is required to land the helicopter, the completely cleared area needs to be 10 yards wide, and 20 yards long, in line with the approach and take off paths.   There should be no obstruction above six feet for a further 15 yards on either side of the hover point, (i.e. total width 40 yards).

6.   If it is not necessary to land the helicopter, the hover point should be an area 10 yards wide by 20 yards long, in line with the approach and take off paths, with no obstruction higher than two feet.   There should be no obstruction above six feet for a further 15 yards on either side of the hover point (i.e. total width 40 yards).

Chapter Five

OPERATION OF THE SHNAP

Information needed by the Pilot

1. The pilot needs to know the following facts before he can begin his approach; and this information must be transmitted in advance :

    a. The Grid Reference of the Landing Site and its height above sea level.

    b. The compass heading of the approach path.

    c. The compass heading of the take off path.

    d. Whether the site is suitable for landing or is only prepared to permit hovering. (See Chapter 4).

    e. Circuit direction right or left, having regard to local terrain.

2. If radio contact can be made with the aircraft, this information should be repeated by that means, together with a statement of the current wind conditions in the following form :

    a. Wind light and variable.

    b. Wind light from the North, South, East or West (or North West, South East, etc).

    c. Wind moderate from...............direction as above.

    d. Wind strong from.................direction as above.

Chapter Six

PILOT PROCEDURE

General

1.   Before joining the pattern, the following information must be checked :

    a.   The Grid Reference of the Landing Site and its height above sea level.

    b.   The compass heading of the approach path.

    c.   The compass heading of the take off path (in case an overshoot is necessary).

    d.   Whether the site is suitable for landing or is only prepared to permit hovering.   (See Chapter Four).

    e.   Direction of the circuit.

2.   The safe circuit includes an area of one mile to one side and two miles on a reciprocal of the SHNAP direction.   The standard night circuit will thus be within the limits of one mile laterally and two miles "downwind" of the SHNAP.

3.   All aircraft will approach the landing site aiming to arrive overhead at Safe Circuit Height.   Safe Circuit Height is 700 feet above the SHNAP or 300 feet above ground in the circuit, whichever is the higher.   If overhead at above the Safe Circuit Height, i.e. Transit Safety Height, standard night circuit procedure will be flown, reducing height at 400 feet per minute until the Safe Circuit Height is reached.

4.   If required, the safety of the SHNAP both vertically and laterally may be checked by observing the continuity of the presentation while crossing the Safe Approach from one side to the other on the lower edge of the indicated approach path but without descending below a chosen safe height.   If, for example, 700 feet is chosen as the lowest safe altitude for checking a particular SHNAP, it may be done by finding the Safe Approach Sector at a height of 1000 feet (i.e. at a range of 2000 yards, the slope being 10 degrees) and then descending to 750 feet and crossing the approach from side to side while seeing the pattern remains unobscured by obstructions.   For this particular case, it is necessary to ensure that there are no obstructions above 500 feet within a range of two miles in line with the approach path, but suitable heights/ranges for carrying out this check may be selected to suit the particular terrain surrounding the Landing Site concerned.

Downwind

5. On reaching the Safe Circuit Height overhead the SHNAP, a 10 second cross wind leg is flown before turning on to the downwind leg.

6. On completion of the turn, fly 1000 yards downwind at 70 knots (30 seconds approximately in nil wind) then commence a Rate One turn to the base leg.

Base Leg

7. Reduce speed on the base leg to 50 knots. Height must be maintained until the SHNAP is visible.

8. If the indication is "HIGH", height is to be reduced until the lights are in line, or to 500 feet, whichever is the higher. Height of 500 feet in the Safe Approach Sector will place the aircraft 1000 yards from the SHNAP.

9. If on reaching 500 feet, the indication is still high, the aircraft is too close and must overshoot.

10. If the indication is "LOW" at 700 feet, the aircraft is at too great a range downwind. 700 feet must be maintained and the aircraft turned towards the SHNAP until the height indication is correct. The aircraft should then resume the base leg heading unless the safe azimuth indication for the approach has already appeared, in which case the approach may be continued by turning finals.

Finals Leg

11. When the aircraft enters the Safe Approach Sector, i.e. the Director Line lights just inside the Base Line lights, the aircraft turns finals, reducing speed to 40 knots and commences a rate of descent of 400 feet per minute. Speed is reduced at about 10 knots per 100 feet of height until the hover point is reached.

NOTE. Regardless of what colour combinations are provided, the pattern is capable of interpretation by its shape alone. The Director Line is unbroken and central in the Safe Approach path and must be thought of as an obstruction over which the pilot is required to fly.

INDEX

Names

482

Flights:

1310: 269, 270, 329
1448 Rota Autogiro Flight: 2
1448 Rota Calibration Flight: 4
1563 SAR: 149–151, 207, 263, 359
1564 SAR: 149, 151, 152, 268, 276, 359
1901 AOP Flight: 6, 157, 183, 186
1903 AOP Flight: 55
1906 AOP Flight: 11, 19, 44, 52, 100, 101, 104,
    107, 108, 134, 141, 157–160, 168, 175, 369
Casualty Evacuation Flight: xi, 28, 32, 33, 36,
    43, 44, 46, 47, 51, 53, 55, 59, 66, 67, 86, 92,
    99, 138, 140, 158, 169, 172, 213, 240, 298, 315,
    319
Gulf Comms. Flight (COMSAR): 307
Khormaksar Helicopter Servicing Flight: 299
King's Flight, The: 6, 169
Levant Communications Flight: 142, 145
Nicosia Helicopter Flight: 366
Queen's Flight, The: xi, 57, 107, 108, 112, 116,
    120, 157, 160, 167, 168, 169, 170, 188, 203,
    359, 365–369, 373, 374, 390, 392

Squadrons:

1 CFS(H): 179
2 CFS(H): 179
3 (Heli. Exam Unit): 180, 370
8: 278
15 (F) (RAF Reg't): 327
18: vii, 207, 233, 236, 237, 263, 269, 329,
    359–363, 365
22 (SAR): 109, 112, 115, 122, 125, 186–189, 192,
    195, 197–202, 234, 264, 272, 359, 365, 372,
    375–380, 392
26: 139, 151, 221, 222, 229, 233, 236, 240, 263,
    264, 266–268, 273–275, 277–279, 282, 284,
    292, 293, 296, 297, 322, 329, 330, 349, 364,
    387, 388
28: 233, 313, 346, 349, 350, 352
33: 385
37: 290
66: 219–222, 229, 234, 240, 248, 253, 255, 260,
    262–264, 271, 297, 314, 315, 327, 329, 330,
    332, 335, 336, 344, 346, 348, 349, 350, 387–389
72: 207, 221, 222, 229, 255–257, 259, 262–264,
    266–269, 271, 304, 359, 360–365, 368, 408
74: 351
75 (Bloodhound SAM): 327
78: 233, 275, 276, 279, 295, 299–309, 351, 360,
    386
84: 138, 295, 359, 364
103: 148, 149, 151, 233, 234, 236, 240, 316,
    321–323, 327, 329, 330, 332–336, 344, 345,
    347, 350–353, 373, 401
105: 295
110: 89, 91, 92, 234, 240, 262, 313, 316, 318,
    321–323, 325, 327, 329, 330, 332–336,
    344–346, 350, 351, 373

118: 192, 193, 197, 250
120 (SAF): 351
155: 82, 86, 87, 89, 92, 170
175: 170
194: 51, 59, 60, 61, 64, 65, 67, 68, 82, 86, 87, 89,
    92, 116, 170, 194
202: 359, 365, 377–380
217: 125, 192, 193, 201
225: 114, 127, 151, 167, 193, 204, 212, 234, 236,
    238, 240, 243, 247, 248, 250, 253, 256, 260,
    262–264, 266, 269, 322, 323, 329, 332, 338,
    360, 362
228: 193, 198, 199, 234, 359, 375, 377, 392
230: 148, 150, 207, 234, 2, 237, 240, 247, 248,
    250, 262, 263, 266, 269, 271, 272, 329, 330,
    343, 344, 359–361, 363, 364, 371
240 (OCU): 271
249 (Venom): 152
275 (SAR): 109, 112, 115, 125, 133, 184–189,
    192–198, 200–202, 380
284: 145, 147, 148, 150, 165
529 Autogyro: 4, 5, 6
651: 159, 160
656 Air OP: 31, 41, 60
657 AOP: 6, 12, 100, 101, 110, 157, 159, 183,
    186
705 (RN): 27, 174, 177
815 (RN): 281
845 (RN): 163, 164, 186, 323
848 (RN): 59, 61, 77, 79, 83, 87, 263, 306, 361
5000 Airfield Construction Sqn: 280
Aden Communications Sqn: 138, 139, 153
British Utility Helicopter Sqn
CFS Helicopter Sqn: 176, 177, 178
Far East Communications Sqn: 28
Helicopter Communications Sqn: 169
Metropolitan Communications Sqn: xi, 57, 109,
    157, 168, 169, 177, 188, 203, 359, 368, 369,
    373, 374, 403
Middle East Communications Sqn: viii
Short Range Transport Sqn: 162, 167
Tactical Support Helicopter Sqn: 247

Wings:

303: 59, 61, 64, 65, 336
CFS Examining: 170, 172, 173, 176
CFS Helicopter Wg: 179, 370
Tactical Wg: 298
Transport Wg: 298

Groups:

11: 369
13: 193, 195
18: 187, 197, 380
19: 200, 379
23: 173

484

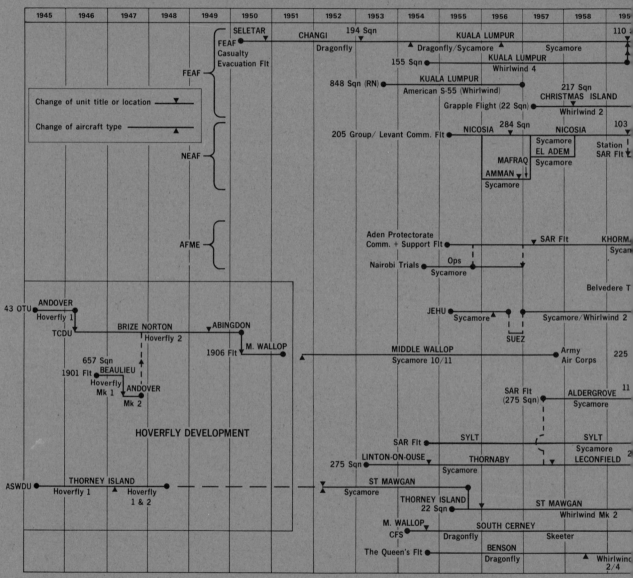

| 1945 | 1946 | 1947 | 1948 | 1949 | 1950 | 1951 | 1952 | 1953 | 1954 | 1955 | 1956 | 1957 | 1958 | 195 |

SELETAR ▼   CHANGI   194 Sqn ▼   KUALA LUMPUR   110

FEAF ●   Casualty   Evacuation Flt

FEAF

Dragonfly   ▲ Dragonfly/Sycamore ▲   Sycamore

155 Sqn ●   KUALA LUMPUR
Whirlwind 4

848 Sqn (RN) ●   KUALA LUMPUR
American S-55 (Whirlwind) ●

217 Sqn
Grapple Flight (22 Sqn) ●   CHRISTMAS ISLAND
Whirlwind 2

205 Group/ Levant Comm. Flt ●   NICOSIA   284 Sqn ▼   NICOSIA   103

NEAF

Sycamore
EL ADEM   Station
SAR Flt ▼

MAFRAQ   Sycamore
AMMAN ▼
Sycamore

AFME

Aden Protectorate
Comm. + Support Flt ●   ▼ SAR Flt   KHORM
Sycam

Nairobi Trials ●   Ops ▼
Sycamore

Belvedere T

Change of unit title or location ——— ▼

Change of aircraft type ——— ▲

43 OTU ● ANDOVER
Hoverfly 1

TCDU   BRIZE NORTON   ABINGDON
Hoverfly 2   M. WALLOP

1906 Flt ▼

JEHU ●   Sycamore ▲ ●   Sycamore/Whirlwind 2
SUEZ

MIDDLE WALLOP   Army   225
Sycamore 10/11   Air Corps ▲

657 Sqn
1901 Flt ● BEAULIEU
Hoverfly   ANDOVER
Mk 1   Mk 2

HOVERFLY DEVELOPMENT

SAR Flt
(275 Sqn) ●   ALDERGROVE   11
Sycamore

SAR Flt ●   SYLT   SYLT
Sycamore
LINTON-ON-OUSE ▼   THORNABY   LECONFIELD   2
275 Sqn ●   Sycamore ▼

ASWDU ●   THORNEY ISLAND
Hoverfly 1   ▲ Hoverfly
1 & 2

▼   ST MAWGAN
▲ Sycamore

THORNEY ISLAND   ST MAWGAN
22 Sqn ● ▼   Whirlwind Mk 2

M. WALLOP ▼
CFS ●   SOUTH CERNEY
Dragonfly   Skeeter

The Queen's Flt ●   BENSON
Dragonfly   ▲ Whirlwin
2/4